W9-BVZ-136

A Distant Soil™ II
The Ascendant

Y 741.5 DIS 2
Doran, Colleen, 1963-
A distant soil

NEWARK PUBLIC LIBRARY
NEWARK, OHIO 43055-5054

7390595

For my teachers:
George Beahm, Steve Rude, Curt Swan,
Frank Kelly Freas,
my parents
and the many others who have been my guides.

A Distant Soil II
The Ascendant

Colleen Doran
CREATOR

Anita Doran
ASSISTANT

Mary Gray
COPY EDITOR

[A DISTANT SOIL:]

Jason

Liana

Rieken

Rienrie

D'mer

Dunstan

Minetti

Kirov

Kovar

Beys

Bast

Jason and Liana are the children of Aeren, a fugitive from the planet Ovanan. Both children possess extraordinary psychic abilities, but Liana was born with the power of the Avatar, the religious leader and protector of Ovanan. The Avatar's power can only be controlled by one being at a time and as long as Liana lives, she is a threat to Ovanan which has sent its massive warship Siovansin to Earth to assassinate her.

Rieken, the leader of the Ovanan resistance movement and his bodyguard D'mer have also come to Earth in human guise to gather a brave team of human men and women to infiltrate the *Siovansin* and destroy Ovanan's evil Hierarchy.

Jason is soon captured by Ovanan agents. They drug him, and he appears to die from an overdose. In reality, a physician working for the Resistance slips Jason into a coma and delivers him safely to

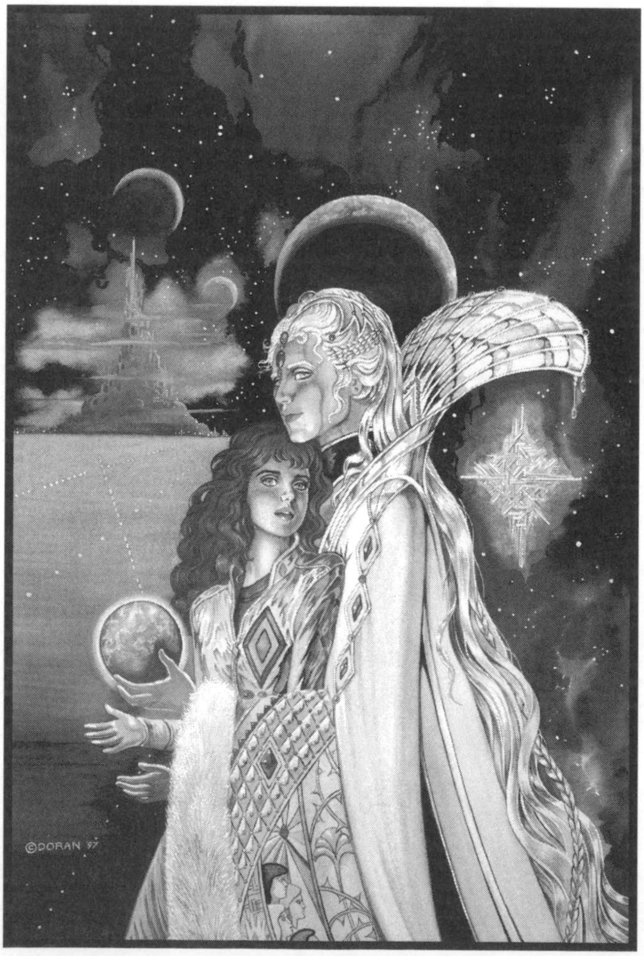
©DORAN '97

Liana

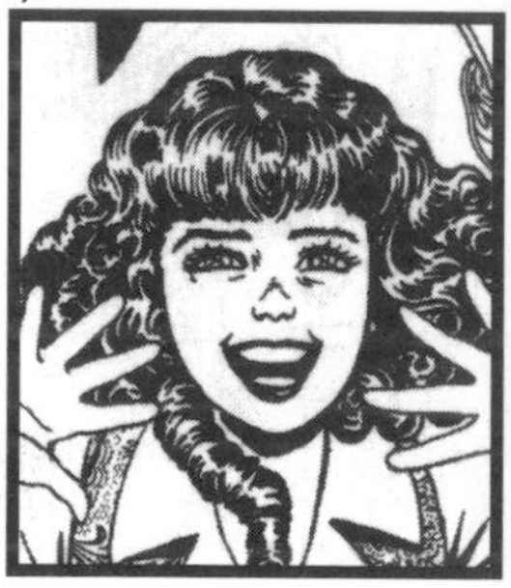

Jason

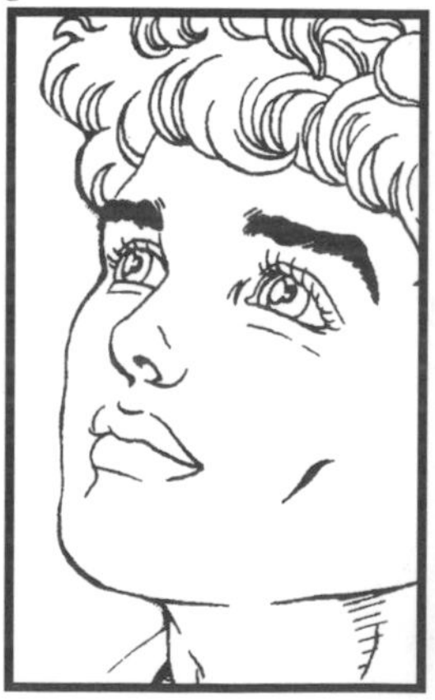

WHAT HAS GONE BEFORE

Resistance headquarters deep in the bowels of the *Siovansin*. Meanwhile, another battle is occuring in the other-dimensional world Avalon, a place where legends live and the only thing standing between Earth and the forces of the Dark are the Gates, protected by King Arthur and the Knights of the Round Table. Sir Galahad falls defending one of these Gates and stumbles through it, landing in our world where he joins Liana and her new companions Brent, Reynaldo and Chris. All agree to aid Liana and the Resistance.

Meanwhile, Rieken and D'mer have recruited Corrine and her magician sidekick Dunstan, Minetti a policeman, and Serezha Kirov, a Russian dissident, as well as the beautiful Bast, an Ovanan shapechanger in exile. She discovers Rieken's terrible secret: he is, in fact, the Avatar Seren himself, in reality a pawn of the Ovanan Hierarchy.

Galahad

D'mer

Vinyr

Rieken

Major Kovar

Bast

Dunstan

Minetti

Corrine

Niniri

Ninivir

Brent

Serezha

Chris

Merai

Sere

Vinyr

ADS [A DISTANT SOIL:]

Jason

Liana

Rieken

Rienrie

D'mer

Dunstan

Minetti

Kirov

Kovar

Beys

Bast

Rieken's champions gather at a secluded site to summon the shuttle that will take them to the *Siovansin*, but they are discovered and confronted by a Hierarchy warship. Rieken draws on the Avatar's power to destroy the warship so he and his champions can escape, but the Hierarchy senses the Avatar's touch on the power of the Collective and the Hierarchy's sadistic Sere pays a call at the Avatar's apartments to interrogate him. She slaughters most of the Avatar's staff but is stopped by Major Kovar before she can invade Seren's private chambers. Niniri, also one of the Hierarchy, arrives, theorizing that the child-Avatar Liana destroyed the ship and orders Sere to leave the Avatar in peace.

Meanwhile, Rieken's champions accustom themselves to their new surroundings and D'mer attends Rieken, who is in trance, exhausted after destroying the warship.

Sere

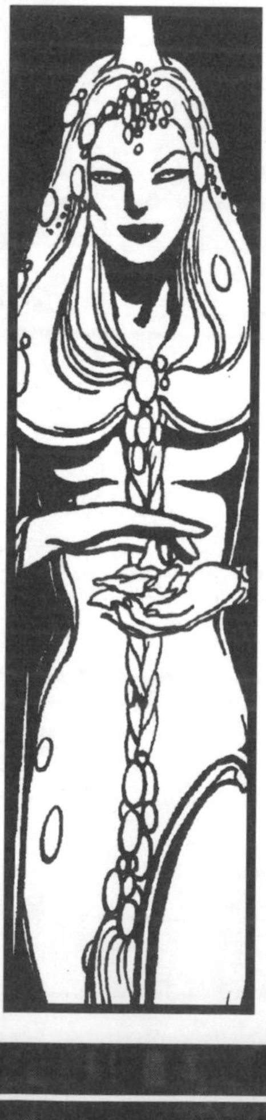

Beys

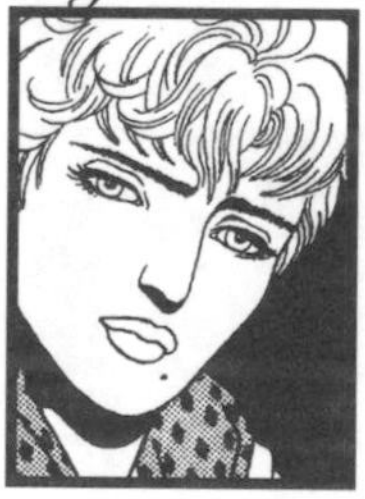

Dunstan

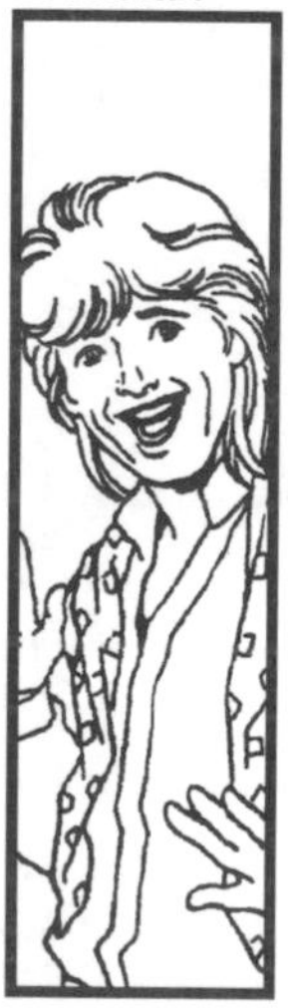

Niniri

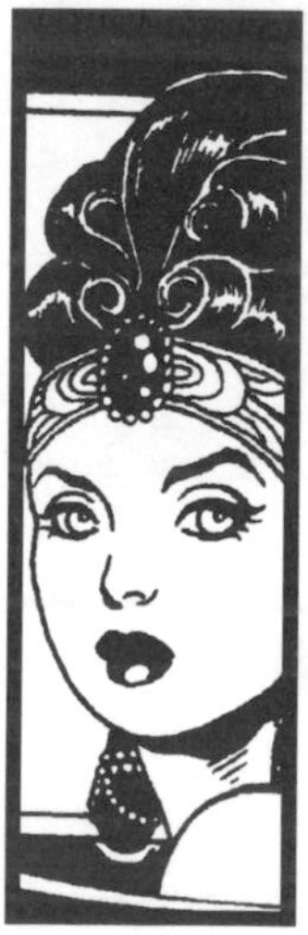

Serezha

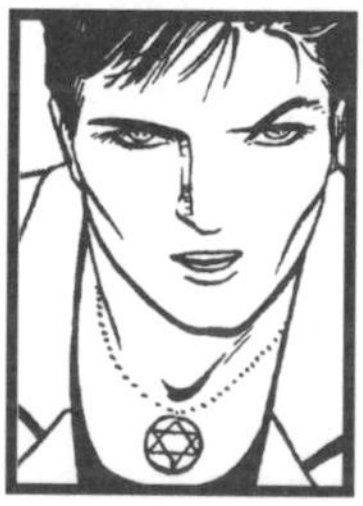

Ninivir

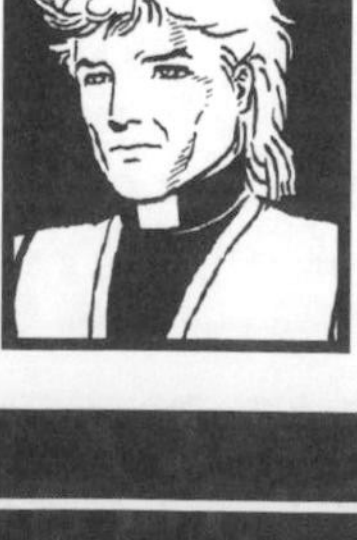

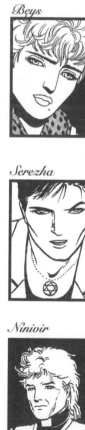

Brent

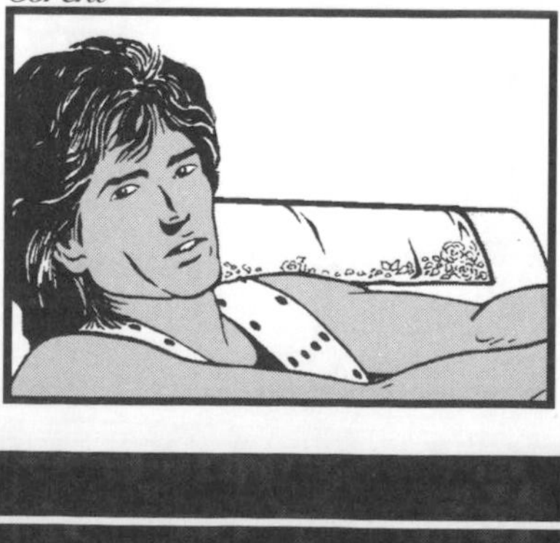

WHAT HAS GONE BEFORE

In the *Siovansin*, Jason has recovered from his overdose. The beautiful Resistance leader Beys takes Jason on a tour of the ship and tries to convince him to join their cause. She wants him to help the Resistance kill the Avatar. Jason is suspicious of their motives and is disturbed by the strange customs of Ovanan. The Resistance is equally suspicious of Jason and worries that he may be a Hierarchy spy. Jason agrees to undergo a Resistance initiation if the Resistance agrees to tell him everything they know of his father who began the Resistance movement before he fled Ovanan.

Back on the shuttle, Rieken/Seren is in deep trance and begins to dream...

Minettie

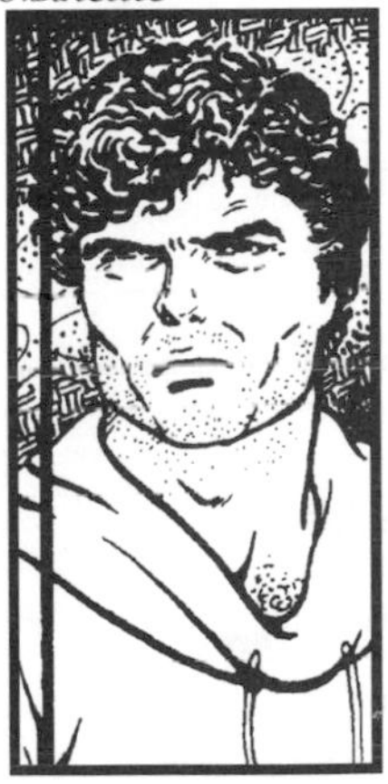

Chris

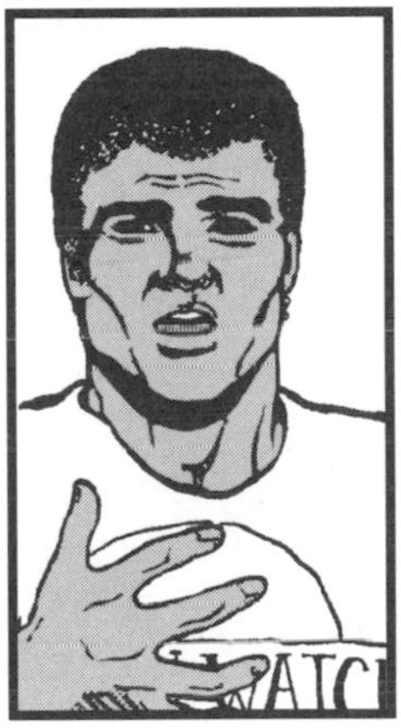

Rienrie

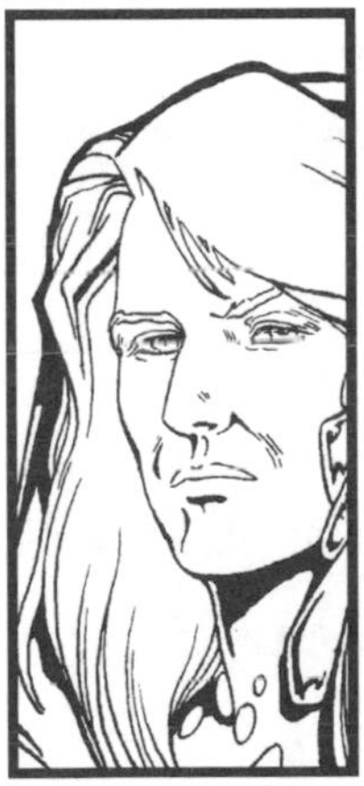

Reynaldo

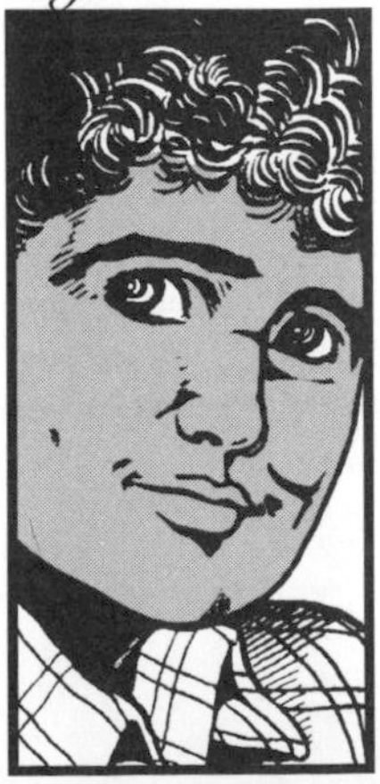

Corinne

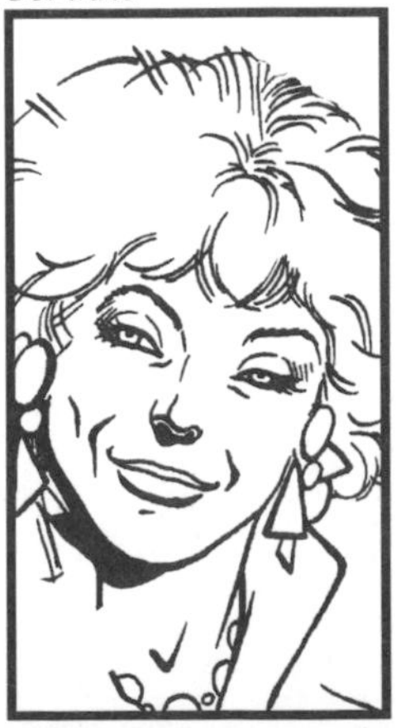

Galahad

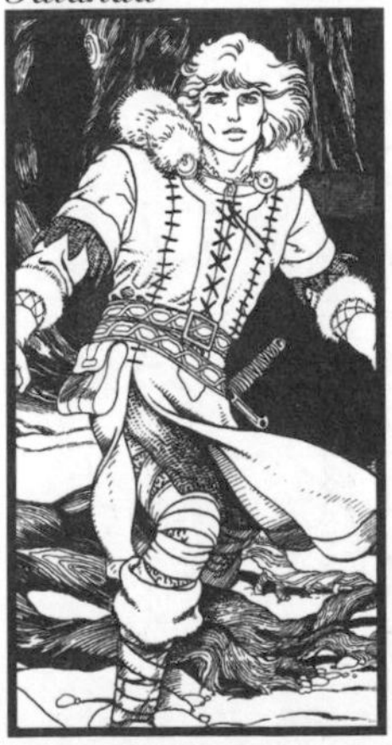

Dunstan
Minetti
Corrine
Niniri
Ninivir
Brent
Serezha
Chris
Merai
Sere
Vinyr

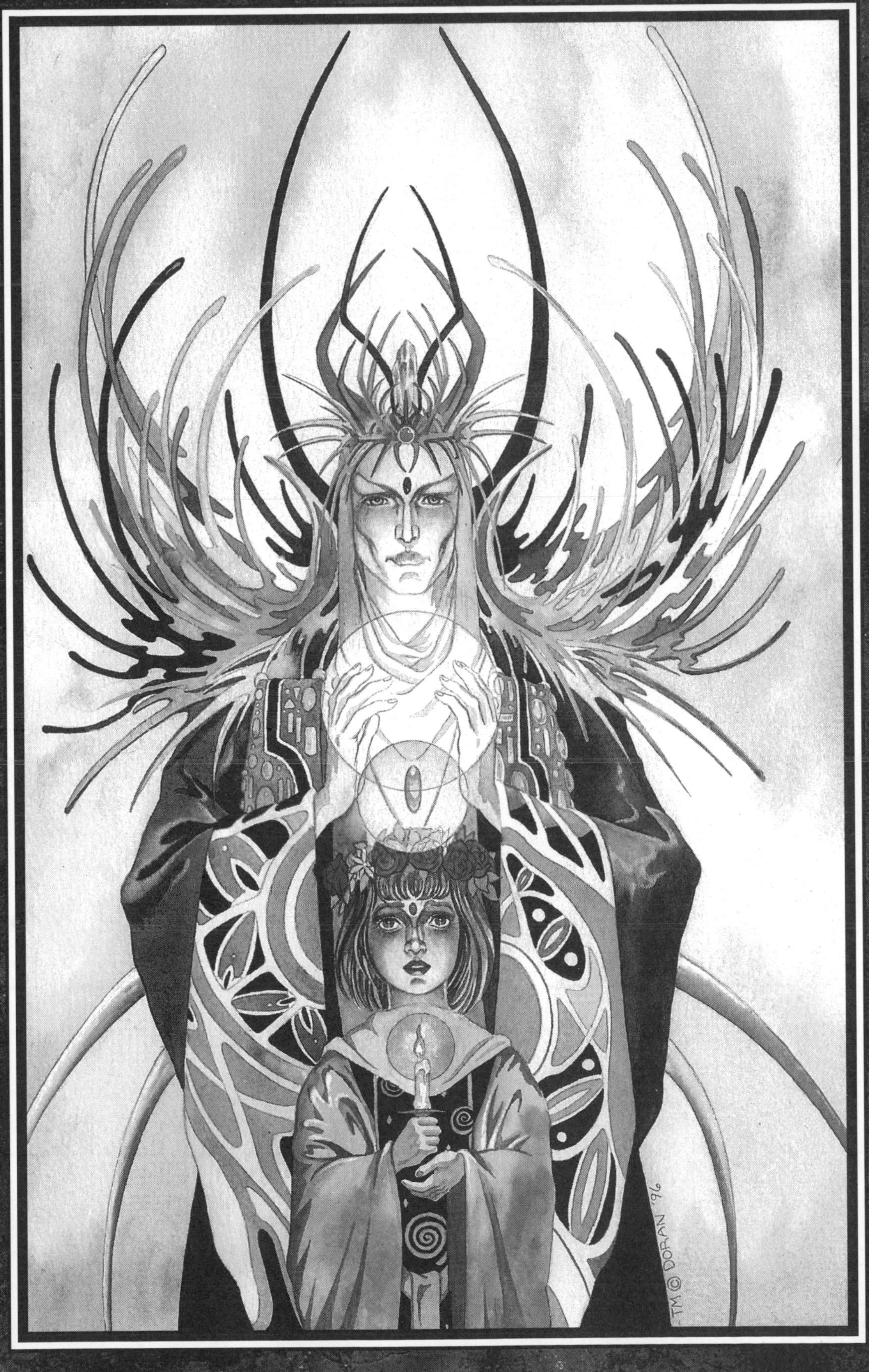
TM © DORAN '96

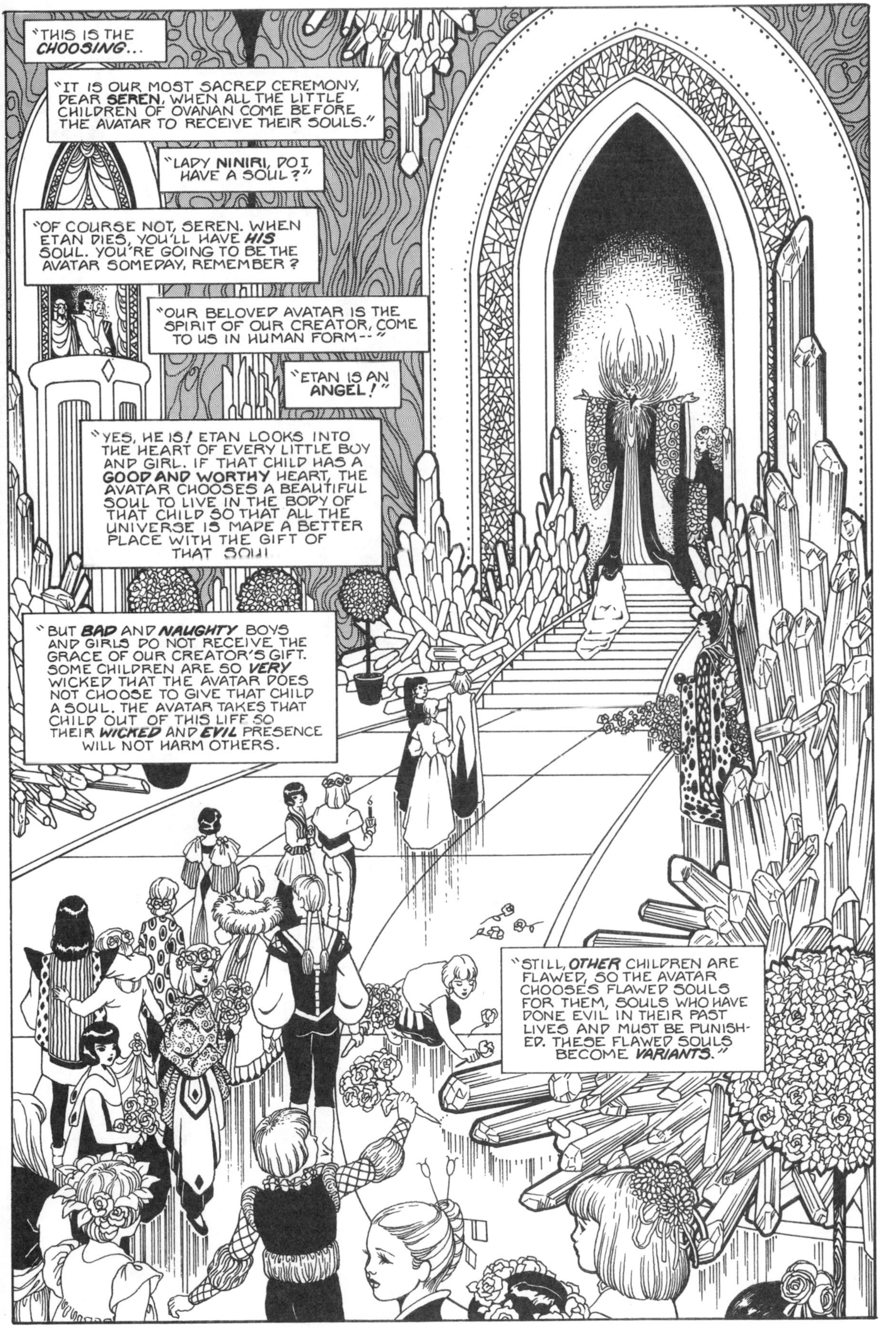
"THIS IS THE CHOOSING...
"IT IS OUR MOST SACRED CEREMONY, DEAR SEREN, WHEN ALL THE LITTLE CHILDREN OF OVANAN COME BEFORE THE AVATAR TO RECEIVE THEIR SOULS."
"LADY NINIRI, DO I HAVE A SOUL?"
"OF COURSE NOT, SEREN. WHEN ETAN DIES, YOU'LL HAVE HIS SOUL. YOU'RE GOING TO BE THE AVATAR SOMEDAY, REMEMBER?
"OUR BELOVED AVATAR IS THE SPIRIT OF OUR CREATOR, COME TO US IN HUMAN FORM--"
"ETAN IS AN ANGEL!"
"YES, HE IS! ETAN LOOKS INTO THE HEART OF EVERY LITTLE BOY AND GIRL. IF THAT CHILD HAS A GOOD AND WORTHY HEART, THE AVATAR CHOOSES A BEAUTIFUL SOUL TO LIVE IN THE BODY OF THAT CHILD SO THAT ALL THE UNIVERSE IS MADE A BETTER PLACE WITH THE GIFT OF THAT SOUL.
"BUT BAD AND NAUGHTY BOYS AND GIRLS DO NOT RECEIVE THE GRACE OF OUR CREATOR'S GIFT. SOME CHILDREN ARE SO VERY WICKED THAT THE AVATAR DOES NOT CHOOSE TO GIVE THAT CHILD A SOUL. THE AVATAR TAKES THAT CHILD OUT OF THIS LIFE SO THEIR WICKED AND EVIL PRESENCE WILL NOT HARM OTHERS.
"STILL, OTHER CHILDREN ARE FLAWED, SO THE AVATAR CHOOSES FLAWED SOULS FOR THEM, SOULS WHO HAVE DONE EVIL IN THEIR PAST LIVES AND MUST BE PUNISHED. THESE FLAWED SOULS BECOME VARIANTS."

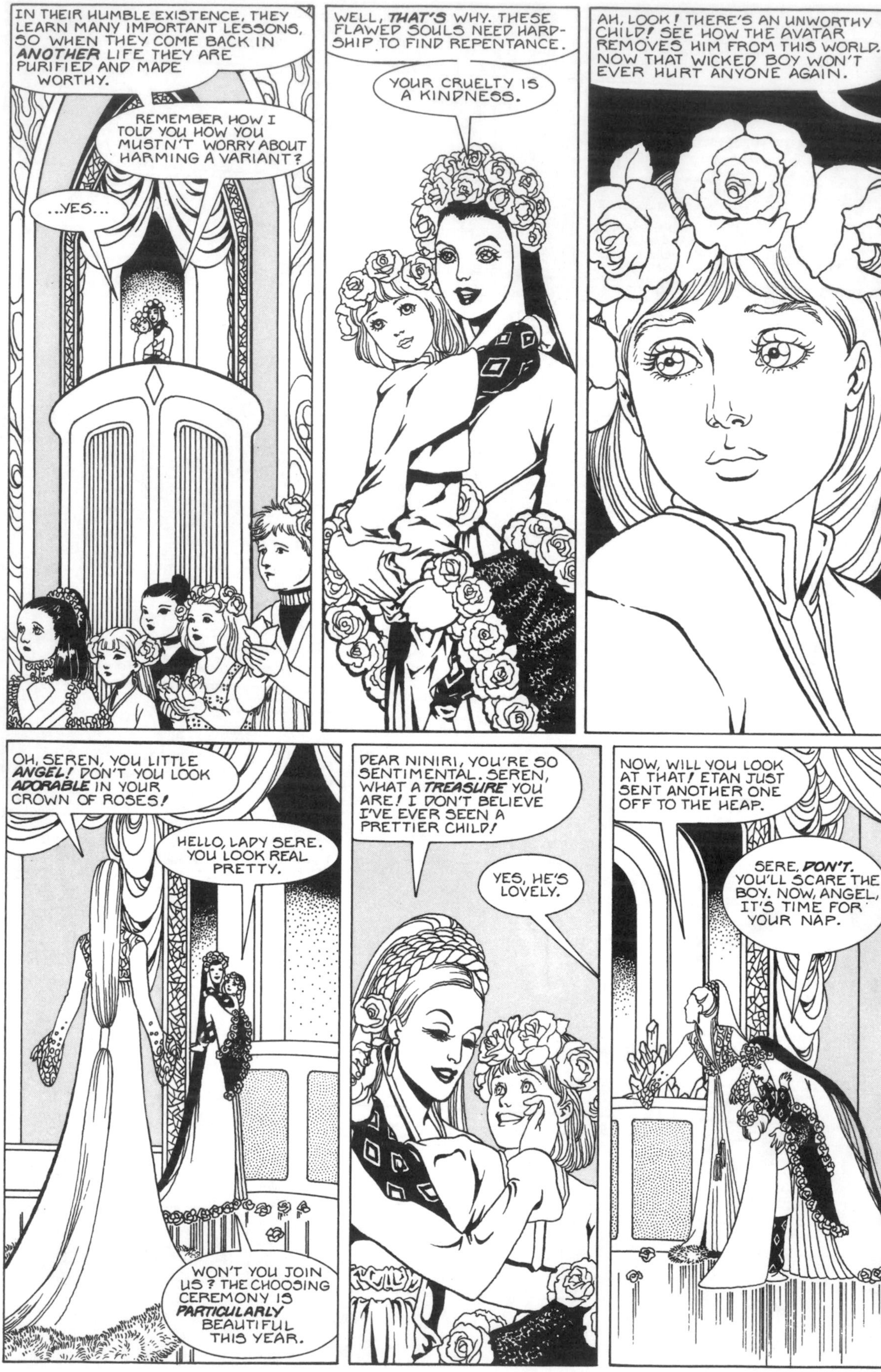
IN THEIR HUMBLE EXISTENCE, THEY LEARN MANY IMPORTANT LESSONS, SO WHEN THEY COME BACK IN ANOTHER LIFE THEY ARE PURIFIED AND MADE WORTHY.
REMEMBER HOW I TOLD YOU HOW YOU MUSTN'T WORRY ABOUT HARMING A VARIANT?
...YES...
WELL, THAT'S WHY. THESE FLAWED SOULS NEED HARDSHIP TO FIND REPENTANCE.
YOUR CRUELTY IS A KINDNESS.
AH, LOOK! THERE'S AN UNWORTHY CHILD! SEE HOW THE AVATAR REMOVES HIM FROM THIS WORLD. NOW THAT WICKED BOY WON'T EVER HURT ANYONE AGAIN.
OH, SEREN, YOU LITTLE ANGEL! DON'T YOU LOOK ADORABLE IN YOUR CROWN OF ROSES!
HELLO, LADY SERE. YOU LOOK REAL PRETTY.
WON'T YOU JOIN US? THE CHOOSING CEREMONY IS PARTICULARLY BEAUTIFUL THIS YEAR.
DEAR NINIRI, YOU'RE SO SENTIMENTAL. SEREN, WHAT A TREASURE YOU ARE! I DON'T BELIEVE I'VE EVER SEEN A PRETTIER CHILD!
YES, HE'S LOVELY.
NOW, WILL YOU LOOK AT THAT! ETAN JUST SENT ANOTHER ONE OFF TO THE HEAP.
SERE, DON'T. YOU'LL SCARE THE BOY. NOW, ANGEL, IT'S TIME FOR YOUR NAP.

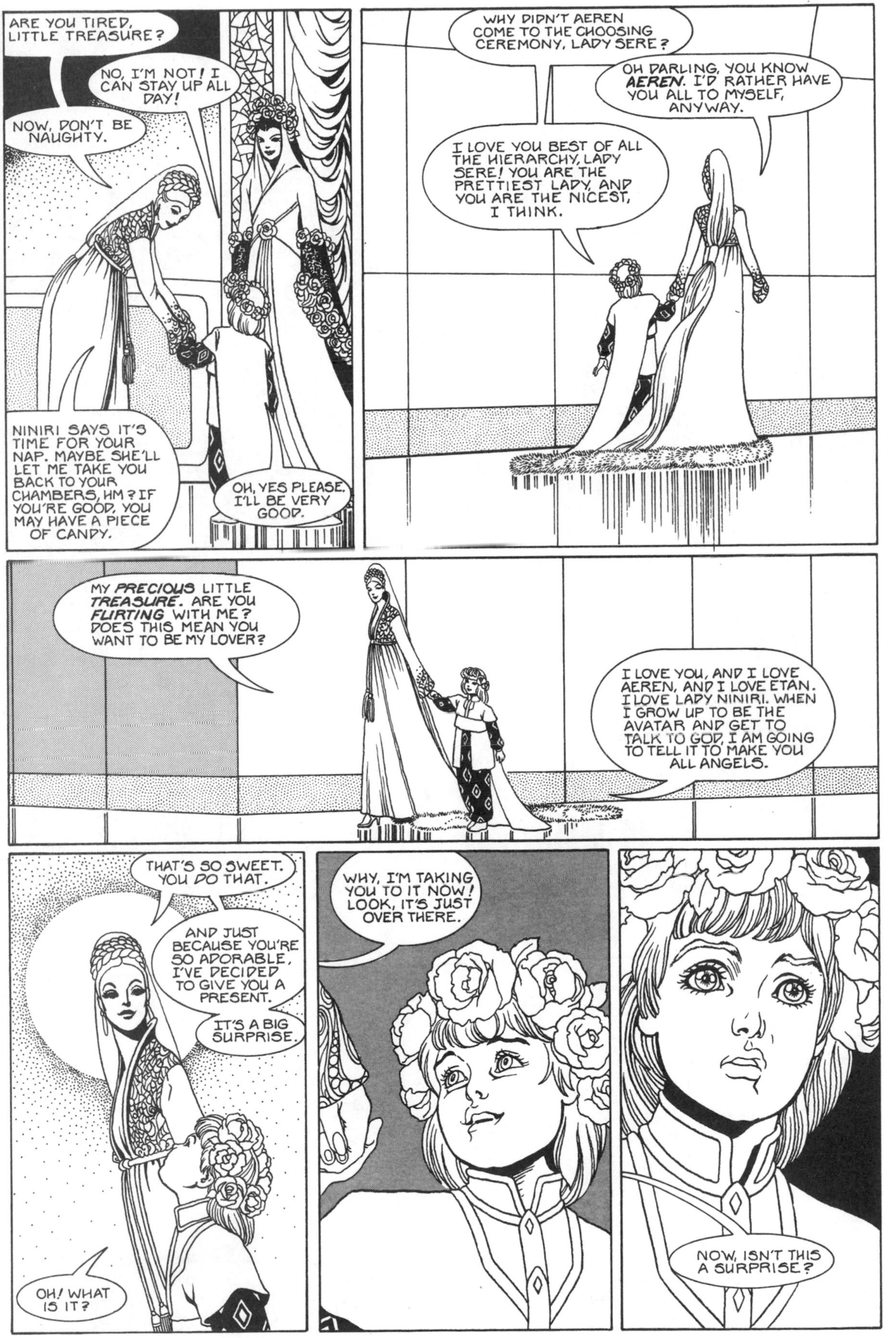
ARE YOU TIRED, LITTLE TREASURE?
NO, I'M NOT! I CAN STAY UP ALL DAY!
NOW, DON'T BE NAUGHTY.
NINIRI SAYS IT'S TIME FOR YOUR NAP. MAYBE SHE'LL LET ME TAKE YOU BACK TO YOUR CHAMBERS, HM? IF YOU'RE GOOD, YOU MAY HAVE A PIECE OF CANDY.
OH, YES PLEASE. I'LL BE VERY GOOD.
WHY DIDN'T AEREN COME TO THE CHOOSING CEREMONY, LADY SERE?
OH DARLING, YOU KNOW AEREN. I'D RATHER HAVE YOU ALL TO MYSELF, ANYWAY.
I LOVE YOU BEST OF ALL THE HIERARCHY, LADY SERE! YOU ARE THE PRETTIEST LADY, AND YOU ARE THE NICEST, I THINK.
MY PRECIOUS LITTLE TREASURE. ARE YOU FLIRTING WITH ME? DOES THIS MEAN YOU WANT TO BE MY LOVER?
I LOVE YOU, AND I LOVE AEREN, AND I LOVE ETAN. I LOVE LADY NINIRI. WHEN I GROW UP TO BE THE AVATAR AND GET TO TALK TO GOD, I AM GOING TO TELL IT TO MAKE YOU ALL ANGELS.
THAT'S SO SWEET. YOU DO THAT.
AND JUST BECAUSE YOU'RE SO ADORABLE, I'VE DECIDED TO GIVE YOU A PRESENT.
IT'S A BIG SURPRISE.
OH! WHAT IS IT?
WHY, I'M TAKING YOU TO IT NOW! LOOK, IT'S JUST OVER THERE.
NOW, ISN'T THIS A SURPRISE?

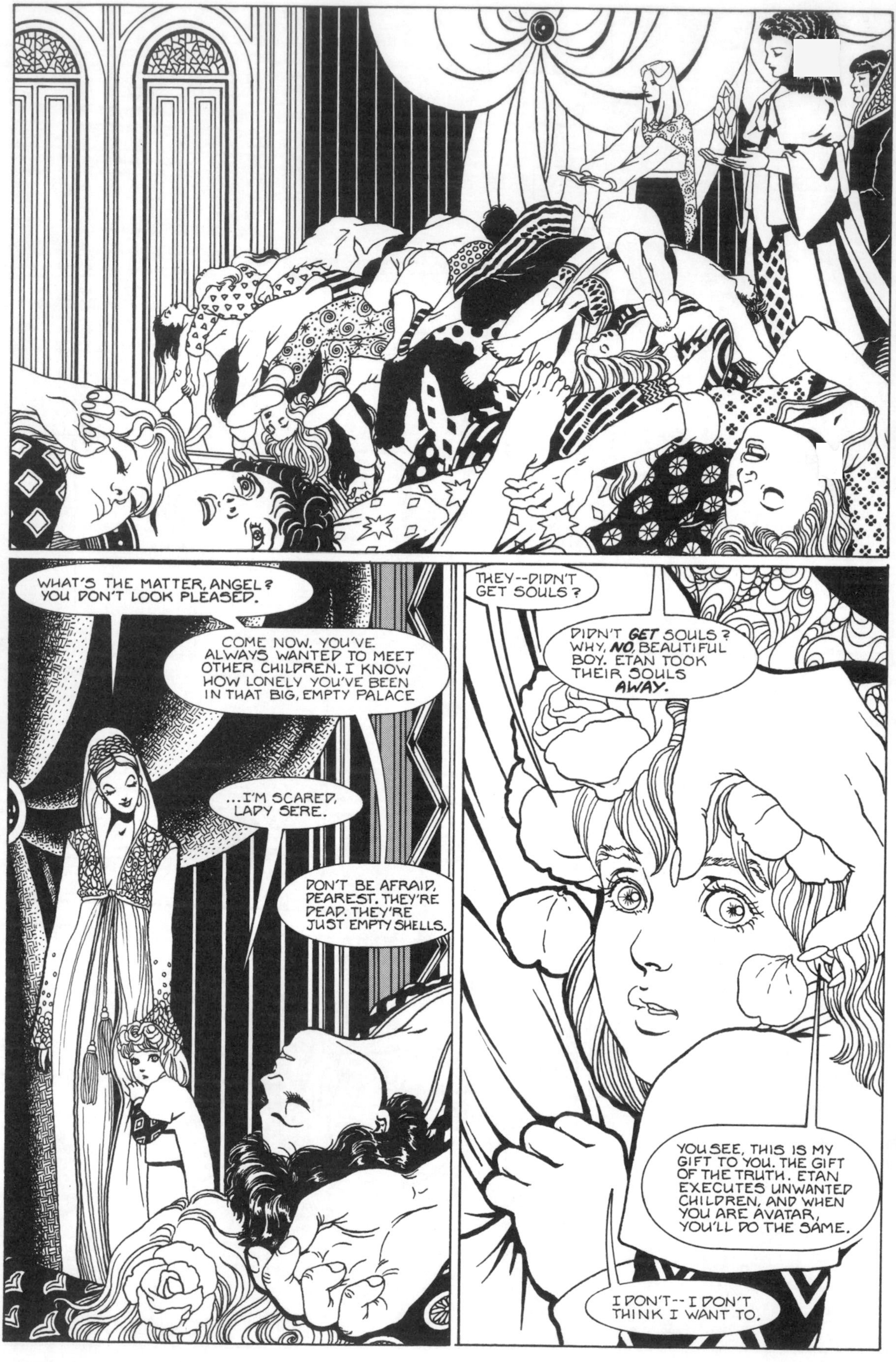
WHAT'S THE MATTER, ANGEL? YOU DON'T LOOK PLEASED.
COME NOW. YOU'VE ALWAYS WANTED TO MEET OTHER CHILDREN. I KNOW HOW LONELY YOU'VE BEEN IN THAT BIG, EMPTY PALACE
...I'M SCARED, LADY SERE.
DON'T BE AFRAID, DEAREST. THEY'RE DEAD. THEY'RE JUST EMPTY SHELLS.
THEY--DIDN'T GET SOULS?
DIDN'T GET SOULS? WHY, NO, BEAUTIFUL BOY. ETAN TOOK THEIR SOULS AWAY.
YOU SEE, THIS IS MY GIFT TO YOU. THE GIFT OF THE TRUTH. ETAN EXECUTES UNWANTED CHILDREN, AND WHEN YOU ARE AVATAR, YOU'LL DO THE SAME.
I DON'T-- I DON'T THINK I WANT TO.

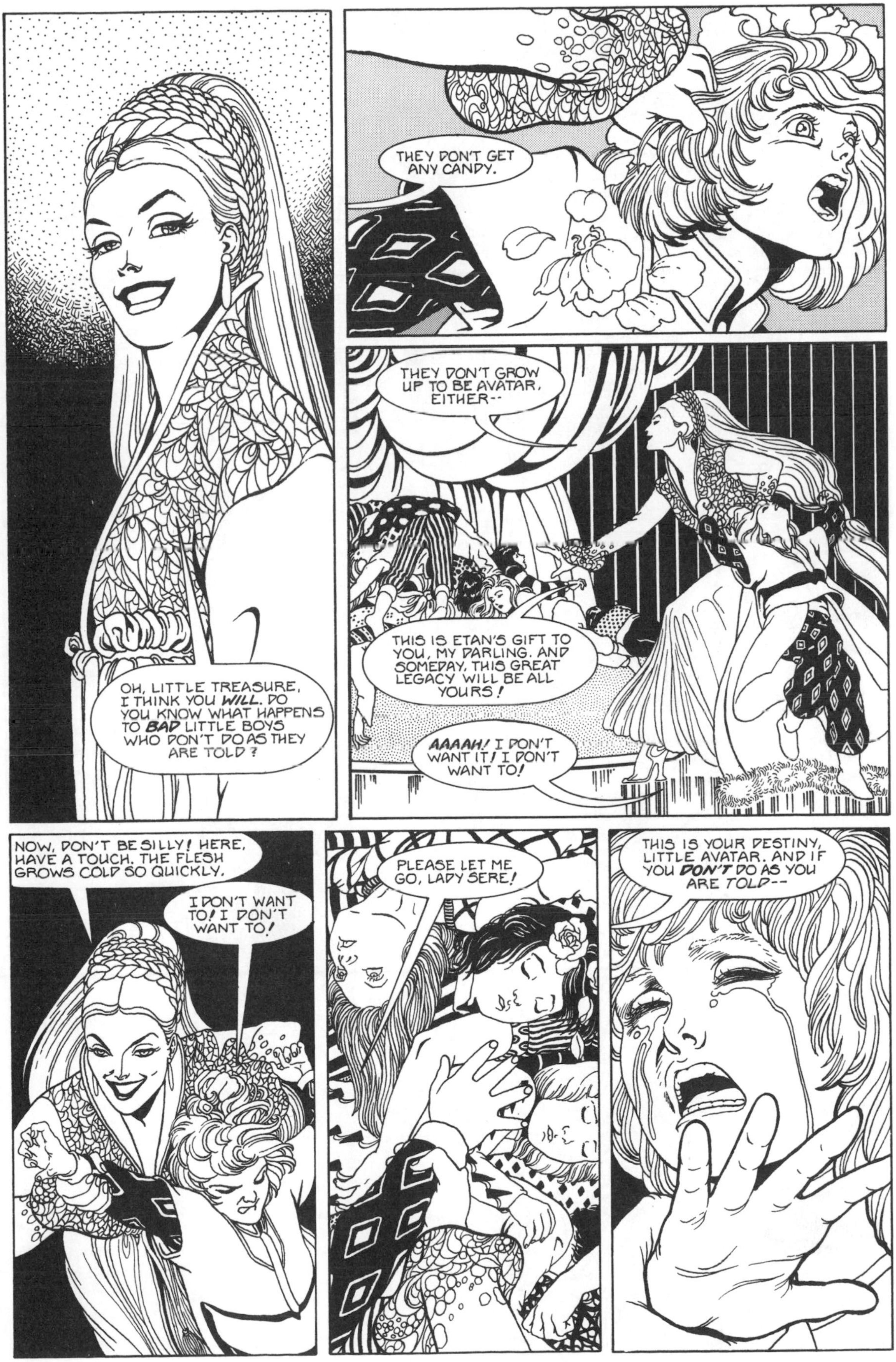

OH, LITTLE TREASURE, I THINK YOU WILL. DO YOU KNOW WHAT HAPPENS TO BAD LITTLE BOYS WHO DON'T DO AS THEY ARE TOLD?
THEY DON'T GET ANY CANDY.
THEY DON'T GROW UP TO BE AVATAR, EITHER--
THIS IS ETAN'S GIFT TO YOU, MY DARLING. AND SOMEDAY, THIS GREAT LEGACY WILL BE ALL YOURS!
AAAAH! I DON'T WANT IT! I DON'T WANT TO!
NOW, DON'T BE SILLY! HERE, HAVE A TOUCH. THE FLESH GROWS COLD SO QUICKLY.
I DON'T WANT TO! I DON'T WANT TO!
PLEASE LET ME GO, LADY SERE!
THIS IS YOUR DESTINY, LITTLE AVATAR. AND IF YOU DON'T DO AS YOU ARE TOLD--

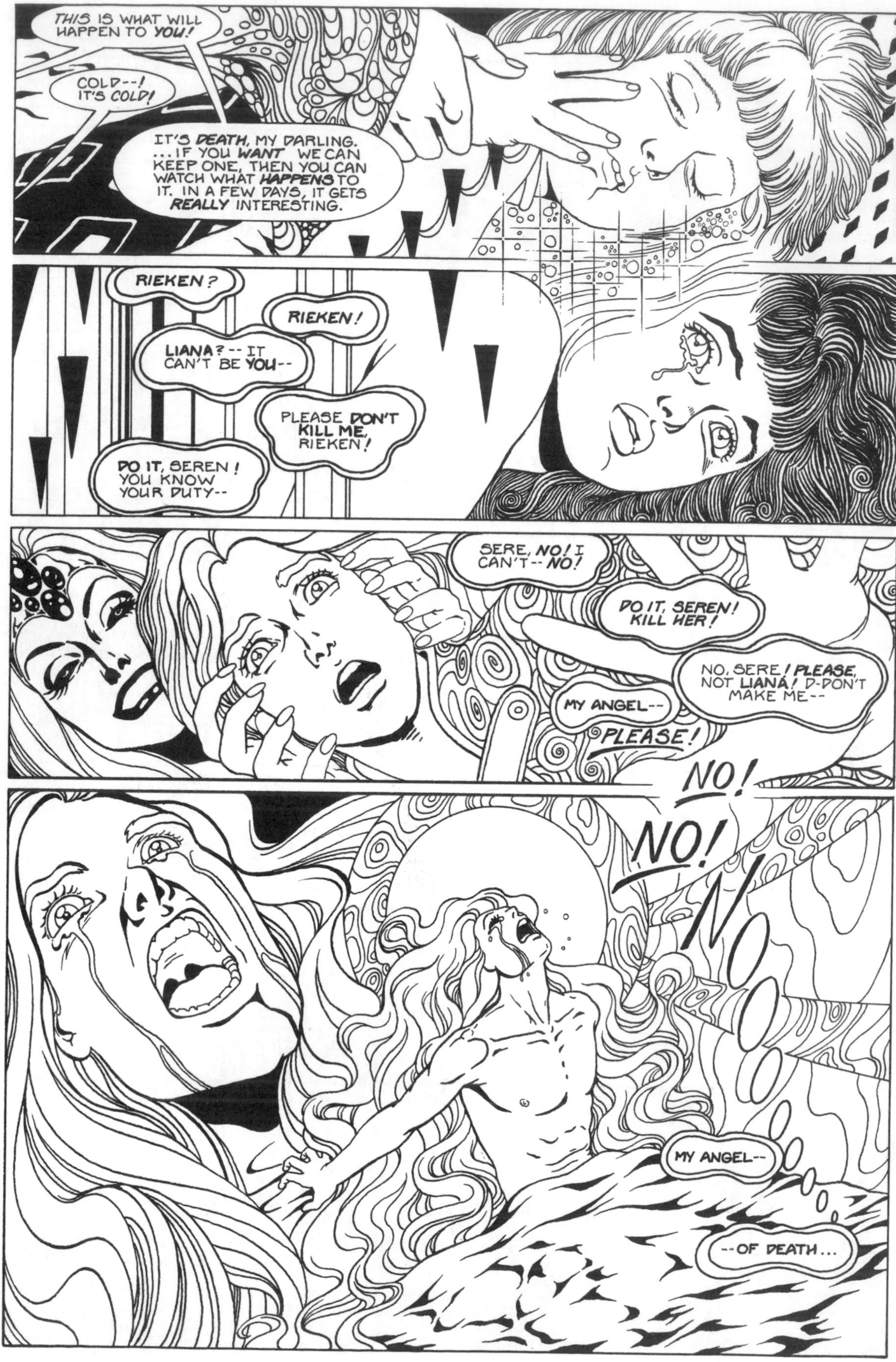
THIS IS WHAT WILL HAPPEN TO YOU!
COLD--! IT'S COLD!
IT'S DEATH, MY DARLING. ...IF YOU WANT WE CAN KEEP ONE, THEN YOU CAN WATCH WHAT HAPPENS TO IT. IN A FEW DAYS, IT GETS REALLY INTERESTING.
RIEKEN?
RIEKEN!
LIANA? -- IT CAN'T BE YOU--
PLEASE DON'T KILL ME, RIEKEN!
DO IT, SEREN! YOU KNOW YOUR DUTY--
SERE, NO! I CAN'T-- NO!
DO IT, SEREN! KILL HER!
NO, SERE! PLEASE, NOT LIANA! D-DON'T MAKE ME--
MY ANGEL--
PLEASE!
NO!
NO!
N
MY ANGEL--
--OF DEATH...

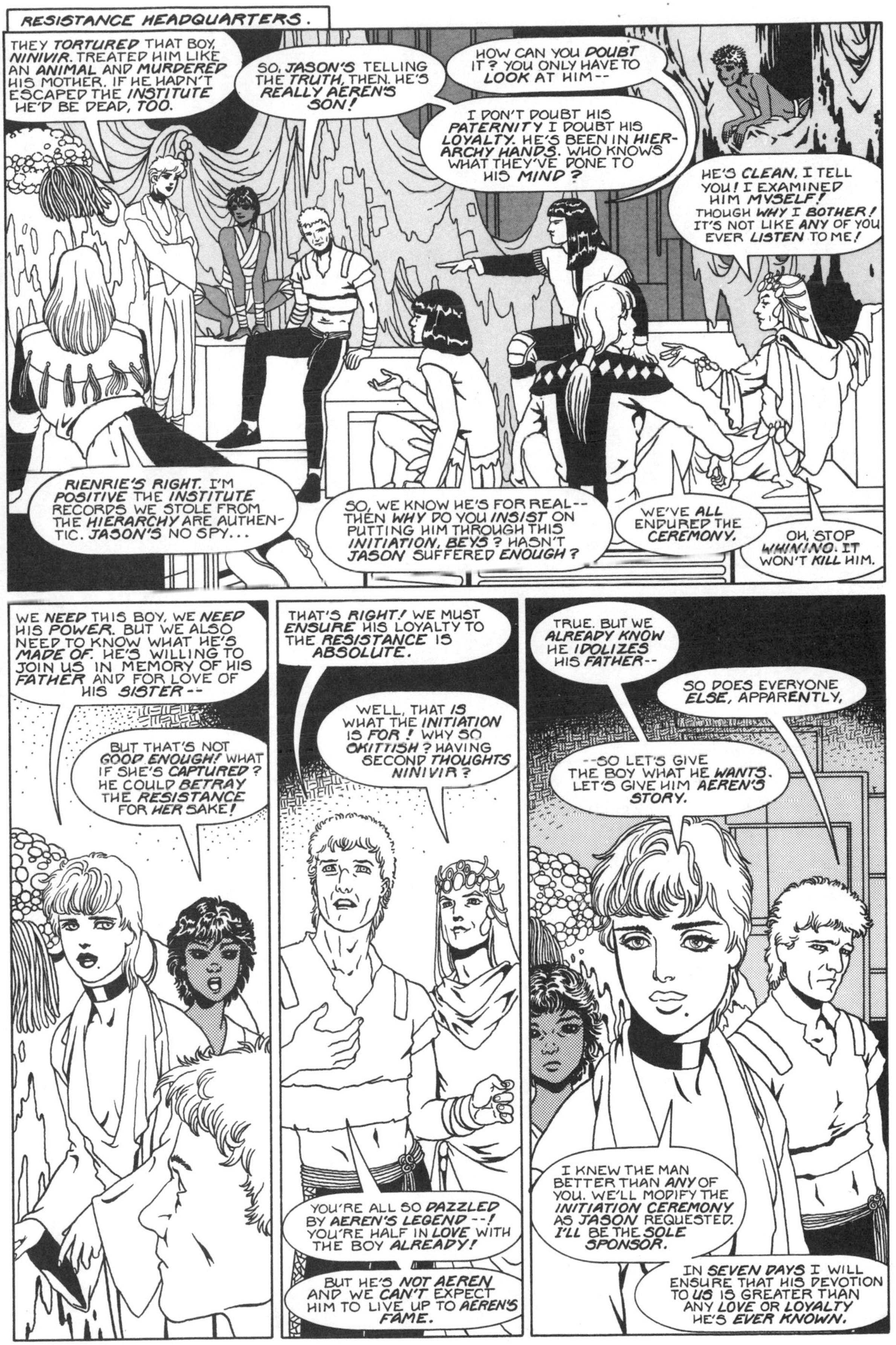
RESISTANCE HEADQUARTERS.
THEY TORTURED THAT BOY, NINIVIR. TREATED HIM LIKE AN ANIMAL AND MURDERED HIS MOTHER. IF HE HADN'T ESCAPED THE INSTITUTE HE'D BE DEAD, TOO.
SO, JASON'S TELLING THE TRUTH, THEN. HE'S REALLY AEREN'S SON!
HOW CAN YOU DOUBT IT? YOU ONLY HAVE TO LOOK AT HIM--
I DON'T DOUBT HIS PATERNITY I DOUBT HIS LOYALTY. HE'S BEEN IN HIERARCHY HANDS. WHO KNOWS WHAT THEY'VE DONE TO HIS MIND?
HE'S CLEAN, I TELL YOU! I EXAMINED HIM MYSELF! THOUGH WHY I BOTHER! IT'S NOT LIKE ANY OF YOU EVER LISTEN TO ME!
RIENRIE'S RIGHT. I'M POSITIVE THE INSTITUTE RECORDS WE STOLE FROM THE HIERARCHY ARE AUTHENTIC. JASON'S NO SPY...
SO, WE KNOW HE'S FOR REAL-- THEN WHY DO YOU INSIST ON PUTTING HIM THROUGH THIS INITIATION, BEYS? HASN'T JASON SUFFERED ENOUGH?
WE'VE ALL ENDURED THE CEREMONY.
OH, STOP WHINING. IT WON'T KILL HIM.
WE NEED THIS BOY, WE NEED HIS POWER. BUT WE ALSO NEED TO KNOW WHAT HE'S MADE OF. HE'S WILLING TO JOIN US IN MEMORY OF HIS FATHER AND FOR LOVE OF HIS SISTER--
BUT THAT'S NOT GOOD ENOUGH! WHAT IF SHE'S CAPTURED? HE COULD BETRAY THE RESISTANCE FOR HER SAKE!
THAT'S RIGHT! WE MUST ENSURE HIS LOYALTY TO THE RESISTANCE IS ABSOLUTE.
WELL, THAT IS WHAT THE INITIATION IS FOR! WHY SO SKITTISH? HAVING SECOND THOUGHTS NINIVIR?
YOU'RE ALL SO DAZZLED BY AEREN'S LEGEND--! YOU'RE HALF IN LOVE WITH THE BOY ALREADY!
BUT HE'S NOT AEREN AND WE CAN'T EXPECT HIM TO LIVE UP TO AEREN'S FAME.
TRUE. BUT WE ALREADY KNOW HE IDOLIZES HIS FATHER--
SO DOES EVERYONE ELSE, APPARENTLY.
--SO LET'S GIVE THE BOY WHAT HE WANTS. LET'S GIVE HIM AEREN'S STORY.
I KNEW THE MAN BETTER THAN ANY OF YOU. WE'LL MODIFY THE INITIATION CEREMONY AS JASON REQUESTED. I'LL BE THE SOLE SPONSOR.
IN SEVEN DAYS I WILL ENSURE THAT HIS DEVOTION TO US IS GREATER THAN ANY LOVE OR LOYALTY HE'S EVER KNOWN.

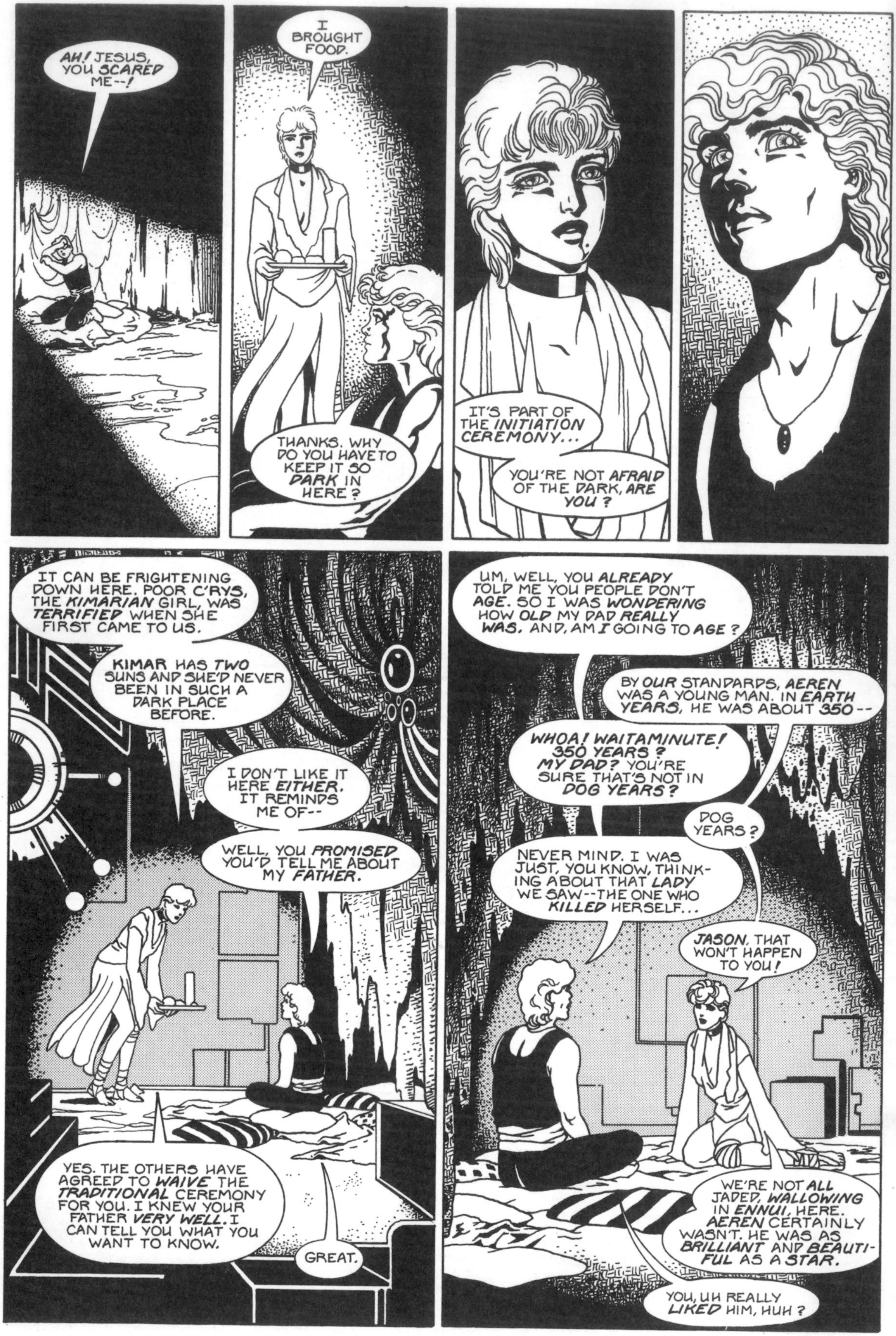
AH! JESUS, YOU SCARED ME--!
I BROUGHT FOOD.
THANKS. WHY DO YOU HAVE TO KEEP IT SO DARK IN HERE?
IT'S PART OF THE INITIATION CEREMONY...
YOU'RE NOT AFRAID OF THE DARK, ARE YOU?
IT CAN BE FRIGHTENING DOWN HERE. POOR C'RYS, THE KIMARIAN GIRL, WAS TERRIFIED WHEN SHE FIRST CAME TO US.
KIMAR HAS TWO SUNS AND SHE'D NEVER BEEN IN SUCH A DARK PLACE BEFORE.
I DON'T LIKE IT HERE EITHER. IT REMINDS ME OF--
WELL, YOU PROMISED YOU'D TELL ME ABOUT MY FATHER.
YES. THE OTHERS HAVE AGREED TO WAIVE THE TRADITIONAL CEREMONY FOR YOU. I KNEW YOUR FATHER VERY WELL. I CAN TELL YOU WHAT YOU WANT TO KNOW.
GREAT.
UM, WELL, YOU ALREADY TOLD ME YOU PEOPLE DON'T AGE. SO I WAS WONDERING HOW OLD MY DAD REALLY WAS. AND, AM I GOING TO AGE?
BY OUR STANDARDS, AEREN WAS A YOUNG MAN. IN EARTH YEARS, HE WAS ABOUT 350--
WHOA! WAITAMINUTE! 350 YEARS? MY DAD? YOU'RE SURE THAT'S NOT IN DOG YEARS?
DOG YEARS?
NEVER MIND. I WAS JUST, YOU KNOW, THINKING ABOUT THAT LADY WE SAW--THE ONE WHO KILLED HERSELF...
JASON, THAT WON'T HAPPEN TO YOU!
WE'RE NOT ALL JADED, WALLOWING IN ENNUI, HERE. AEREN CERTAINLY WASN'T. HE WAS AS BRILLIANT AND BEAUTIFUL AS A STAR.
YOU, UH REALLY LIKED HIM, HUH?

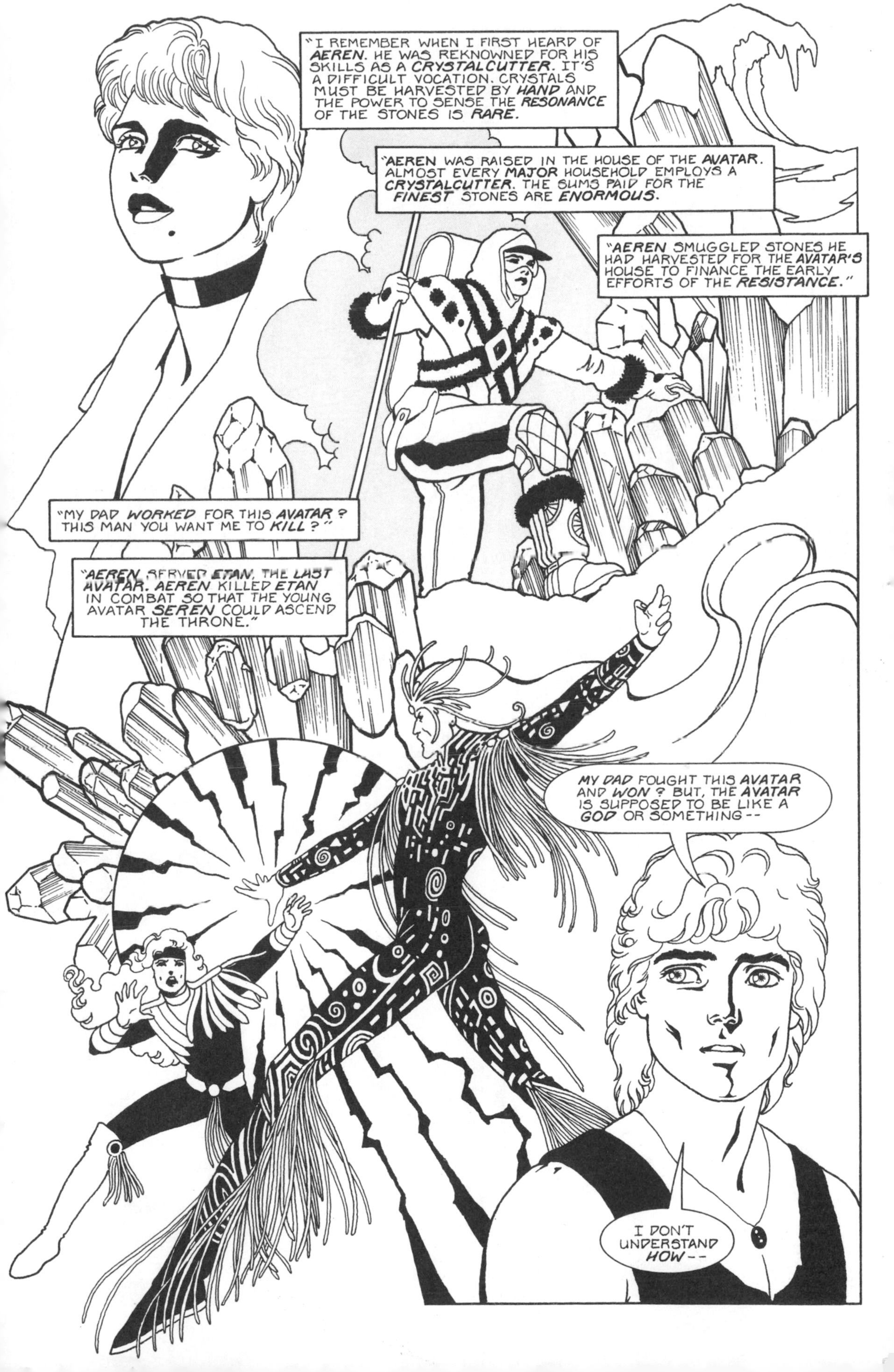
"I REMEMBER WHEN I FIRST HEARD OF AEREN. HE WAS REKNOWNED FOR HIS SKILLS AS A CRYSTALCUTTER. IT'S A DIFFICULT VOCATION. CRYSTALS MUST BE HARVESTED BY HAND AND THE POWER TO SENSE THE RESONANCE OF THE STONES IS RARE.
"AEREN WAS RAISED IN THE HOUSE OF THE AVATAR. ALMOST EVERY MAJOR HOUSEHOLD EMPLOYS A CRYSTALCUTTER. THE SUMS PAID FOR THE FINEST STONES ARE ENORMOUS.
"AEREN SMUGGLED STONES HE HAD HARVESTED FOR THE AVATAR'S HOUSE TO FINANCE THE EARLY EFFORTS OF THE RESISTANCE."
"MY DAD WORKED FOR THIS AVATAR? THIS MAN YOU WANT ME TO KILL?"
"AEREN SERVED ETAN, THE LAST AVATAR. AEREN KILLED ETAN IN COMBAT SO THAT THE YOUNG AVATAR SEREN COULD ASCEND THE THRONE."
MY DAD FOUGHT THIS AVATAR AND WON? BUT, THE AVATAR IS SUPPOSED TO BE LIKE A GOD OR SOMETHING--
I DON'T UNDERSTAND HOW--

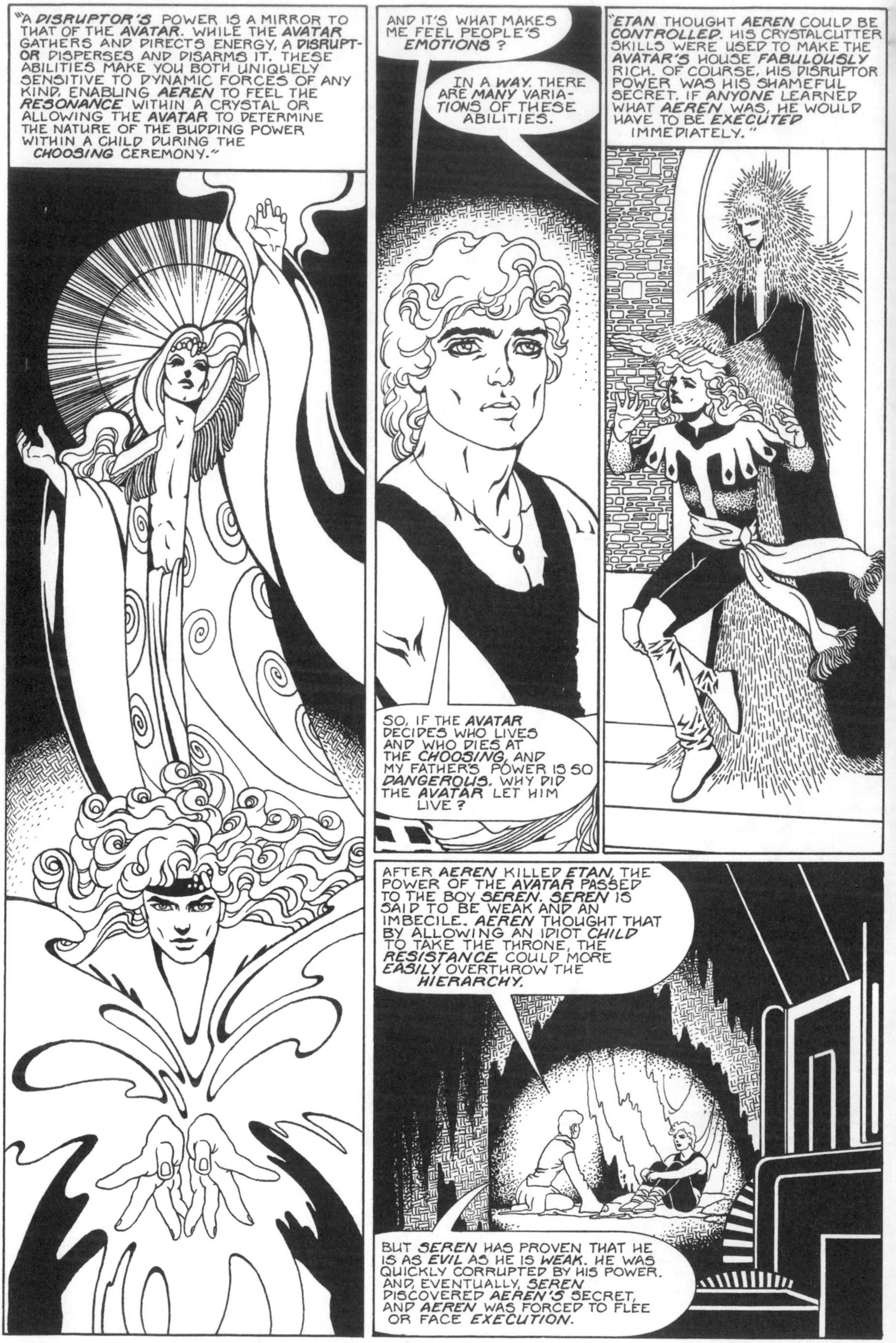
"A DISRUPTOR'S POWER IS A MIRROR TO THAT OF THE AVATAR. WHILE THE AVATAR GATHERS AND DIRECTS ENERGY, A DISRUPTOR DISPERSES AND DISARMS IT. THESE ABILITIES MAKE YOU BOTH UNIQUELY SENSITIVE TO DYNAMIC FORCES OF ANY KIND, ENABLING AEREN TO FEEL THE RESONANCE WITHIN A CRYSTAL OR ALLOWING THE AVATAR TO DETERMINE THE NATURE OF THE BUDDING POWER WITHIN A CHILD DURING THE CHOOSING CEREMONY."
AND IT'S WHAT MAKES ME FEEL PEOPLE'S EMOTIONS?
IN A WAY. THERE ARE MANY VARIATIONS OF THESE ABILITIES.
"ETAN THOUGHT AEREN COULD BE CONTROLLED. HIS CRYSTALCUTTER SKILLS WERE USED TO MAKE THE AVATAR'S HOUSE FABULOUSLY RICH. OF COURSE, HIS DISRUPTOR POWER WAS HIS SHAMEFUL SECRET. IF ANYONE LEARNED WHAT AEREN WAS, HE WOULD HAVE TO BE EXECUTED IMMEDIATELY."
SO, IF THE AVATAR DECIDES WHO LIVES AND WHO DIES AT THE CHOOSING, AND MY FATHER'S POWER IS SO DANGEROUS, WHY DID THE AVATAR LET HIM LIVE?
AFTER AEREN KILLED ETAN, THE POWER OF THE AVATAR PASSED TO THE BOY SEREN. SEREN IS SAID TO BE WEAK AND AN IMBECILE. AEREN THOUGHT THAT BY ALLOWING AN IDIOT CHILD TO TAKE THE THRONE, THE RESISTANCE COULD MORE EASILY OVERTHROW THE HIERARCHY.
BUT SEREN HAS PROVEN THAT HE IS AS EVIL AS HE IS WEAK. HE WAS QUICKLY CORRUPTED BY HIS POWER. AND, EVENTUALLY, SEREN DISCOVERED AEREN'S SECRET, AND AEREN WAS FORCED TO FLEE OR FACE EXECUTION.

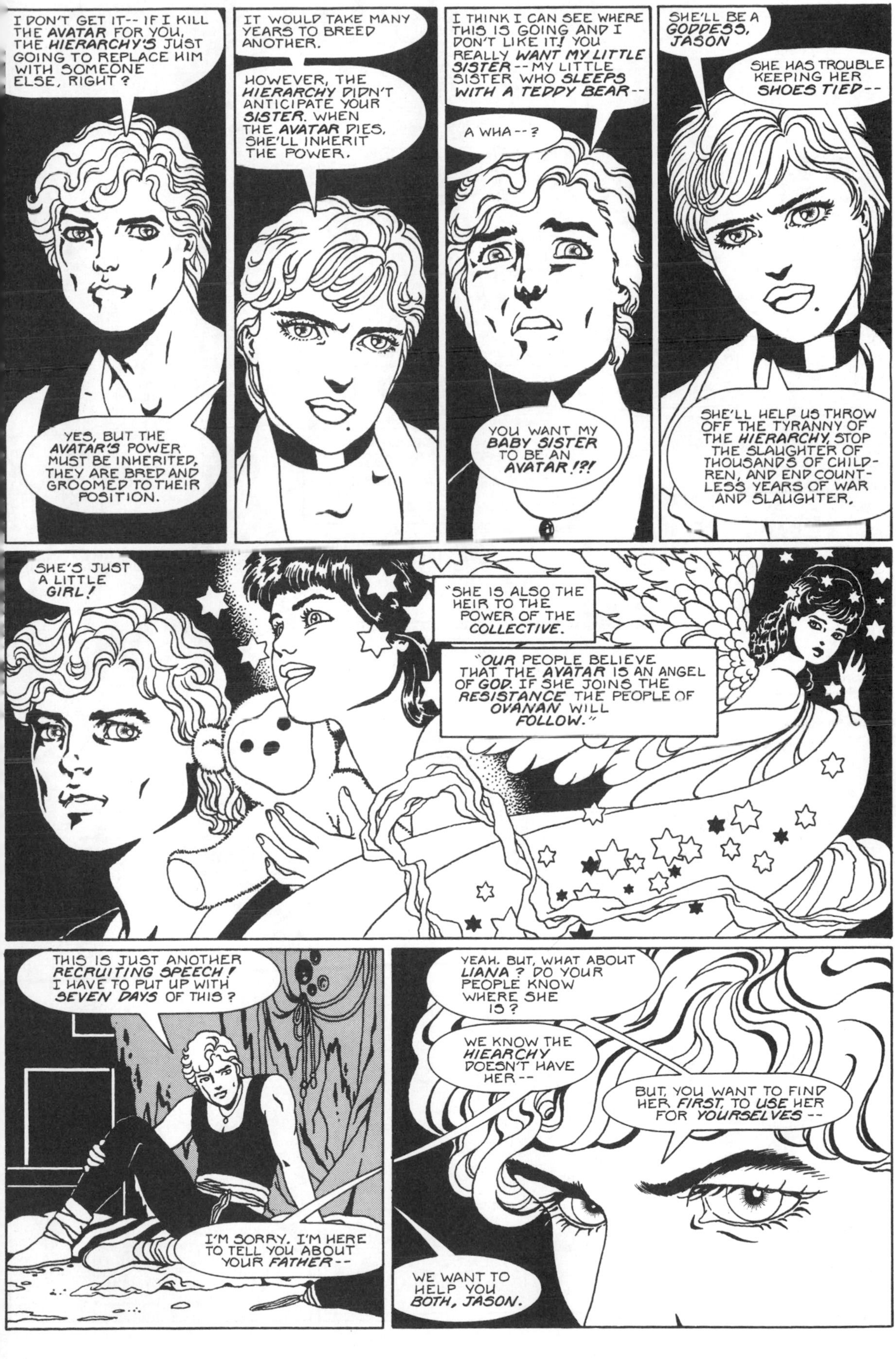
I DON'T GET IT-- IF I KILL THE AVATAR FOR YOU, THE HIERARCHY'S JUST GOING TO REPLACE HIM WITH SOMEONE ELSE, RIGHT?
YES, BUT THE AVATAR'S POWER MUST BE INHERITED, THEY ARE BRED AND GROOMED TO THEIR POSITION.
IT WOULD TAKE MANY YEARS TO BREED ANOTHER.
HOWEVER, THE HIERARCHY DIDN'T ANTICIPATE YOUR SISTER. WHEN THE AVATAR DIES, SHE'LL INHERIT THE POWER.
I THINK I CAN SEE WHERE THIS IS GOING AND I DON'T LIKE IT! YOU REALLY WANT MY LITTLE SISTER -- MY LITTLE SISTER WHO SLEEPS WITH A TEDDY BEAR --
A WHA-- ?
YOU WANT MY BABY SISTER TO BE AN AVATAR !?!
SHE'LL BE A GODDESS, JASON
SHE HAS TROUBLE KEEPING HER SHOES TIED --
SHE'LL HELP US THROW OFF THE TYRANNY OF THE HIERARCHY, STOP THE SLAUGHTER OF THOUSANDS OF CHILDREN, AND END COUNTLESS YEARS OF WAR AND SLAUGHTER.
SHE'S JUST A LITTLE GIRL!
"SHE IS ALSO THE HEIR TO THE POWER OF THE COLLECTIVE.
"OUR PEOPLE BELIEVE THAT THE AVATAR IS AN ANGEL OF GOD. IF SHE JOINS THE RESISTANCE THE PEOPLE OF OVANAN WILL FOLLOW."
THIS IS JUST ANOTHER RECRUITING SPEECH! I HAVE TO PUT UP WITH SEVEN DAYS OF THIS?
I'M SORRY. I'M HERE TO TELL YOU ABOUT YOUR FATHER --
YEAH. BUT, WHAT ABOUT LIANA? DO YOUR PEOPLE KNOW WHERE SHE IS?
WE KNOW THE HIEARCHY DOESN'T HAVE HER --
BUT, YOU WANT TO FIND HER FIRST, TO USE HER FOR YOURSELVES --
WE WANT TO HELP YOU BOTH, JASON.

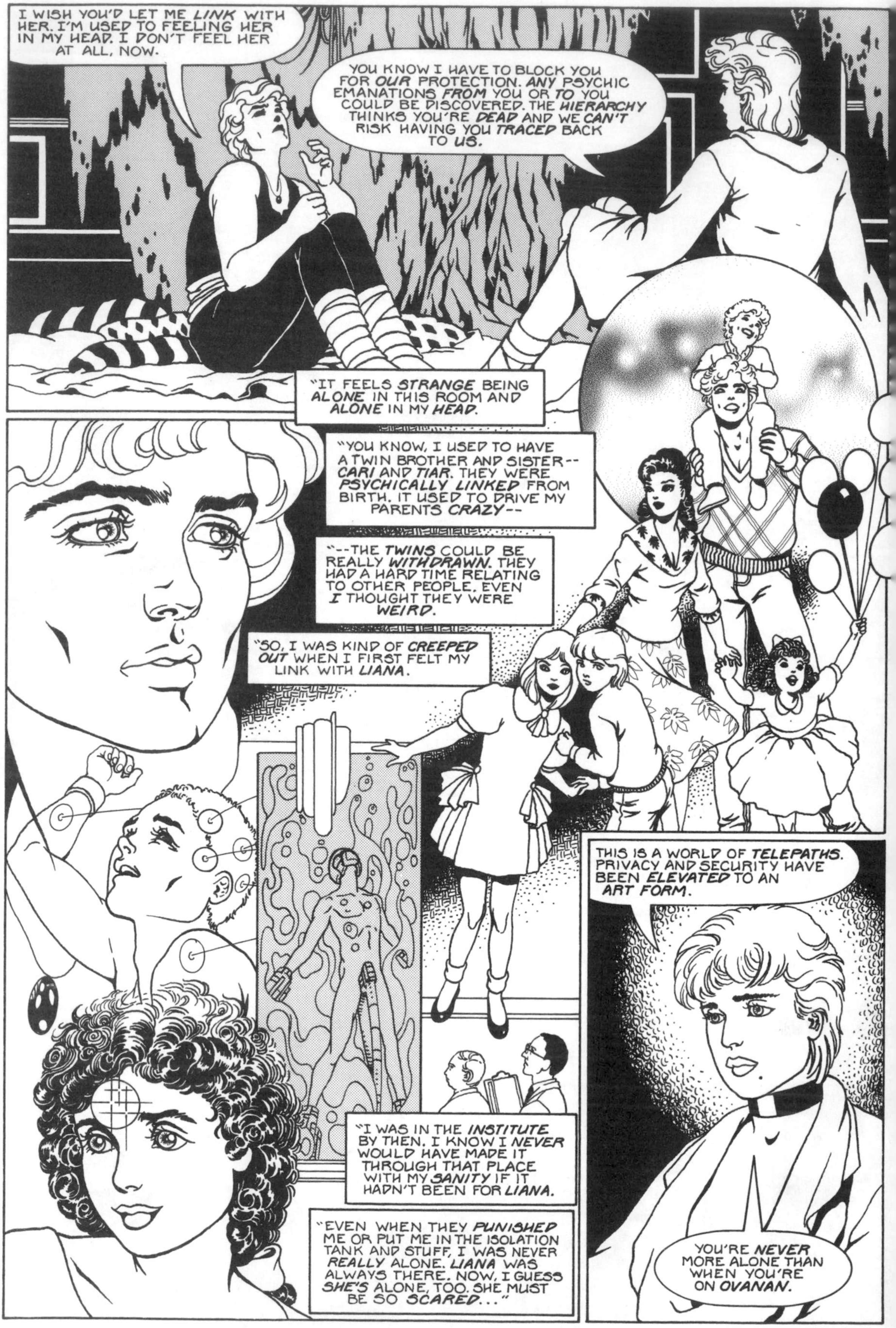

I WISH YOU'D LET ME LINK WITH HER. I'M USED TO FEELING HER IN MY HEAD. I DON'T FEEL HER AT ALL, NOW.
YOU KNOW I HAVE TO BLOCK YOU FOR OUR PROTECTION. ANY PSYCHIC EMANATIONS FROM YOU OR TO YOU COULD BE DISCOVERED. THE HIERARCHY THINKS YOU'RE DEAD AND WE CAN'T RISK HAVING YOU TRACED BACK TO US.
"IT FEELS STRANGE BEING ALONE IN THIS ROOM AND ALONE IN MY HEAD.
"YOU KNOW, I USED TO HAVE A TWIN BROTHER AND SISTER-- CARI AND TIAR. THEY WERE PSYCHICALLY LINKED FROM BIRTH. IT USED TO DRIVE MY PARENTS CRAZY--
"--THE TWINS COULD BE REALLY WITHDRAWN. THEY HAD A HARD TIME RELATING TO OTHER PEOPLE. EVEN I THOUGHT THEY WERE WEIRD.
"SO, I WAS KIND OF CREEPED OUT WHEN I FIRST FELT MY LINK WITH LIANA.
"I WAS IN THE INSTITUTE BY THEN. I KNOW I NEVER WOULD HAVE MADE IT THROUGH THAT PLACE WITH MY SANITY IF IT HADN'T BEEN FOR LIANA.
"EVEN WHEN THEY PUNISHED ME OR PUT ME IN THE ISOLATION TANK AND STUFF, I WAS NEVER REALLY ALONE. LIANA WAS ALWAYS THERE. NOW, I GUESS SHE'S ALONE, TOO. SHE MUST BE SO SCARED..."
THIS IS A WORLD OF TELEPATHS. PRIVACY AND SECURITY HAVE BEEN ELEVATED TO AN ART FORM.
YOU'RE NEVER MORE ALONE THAN WHEN YOU'RE ON OVANAN.

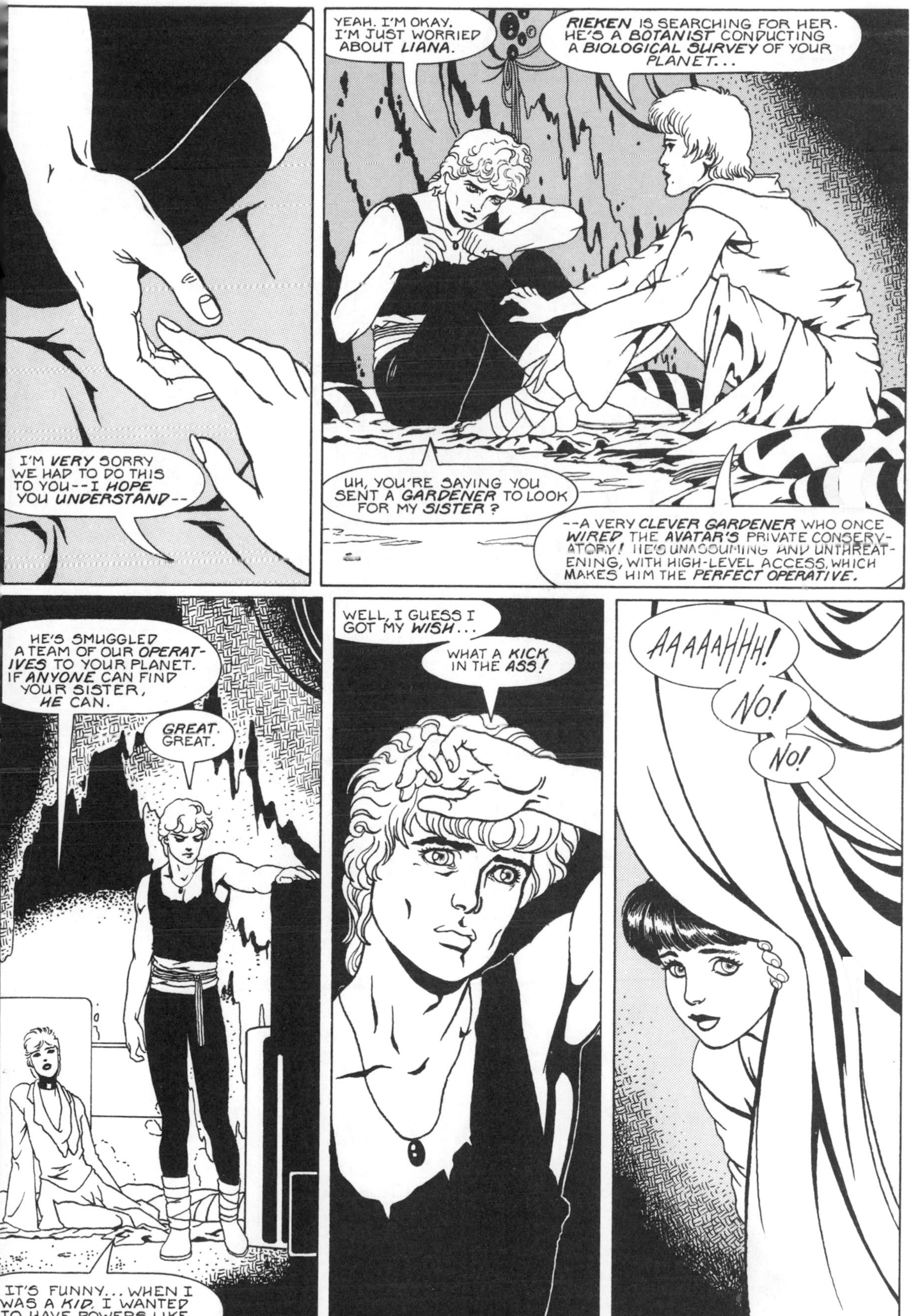
I'M VERY SORRY WE HAD TO DO THIS TO YOU--I HOPE YOU UNDERSTAND--
YEAH. I'M OKAY. I'M JUST WORRIED ABOUT LIANA.
RIEKEN IS SEARCHING FOR HER. HE'S A BOTANIST CONDUCTING A BIOLOGICAL SURVEY OF YOUR PLANET...
UH, YOU'RE SAYING YOU SENT A GARDENER TO LOOK FOR MY SISTER?
--A VERY CLEVER GARDENER WHO ONCE WIRED THE AVATAR'S PRIVATE CONSERVATORY! HE'S UNASSUMING AND UNTHREATENING, WITH HIGH-LEVEL ACCESS, WHICH MAKES HIM THE PERFECT OPERATIVE.
HE'S SMUGGLED A TEAM OF OUR OPERATIVES TO YOUR PLANET. IF ANYONE CAN FIND YOUR SISTER, HE CAN.
GREAT. GREAT.
IT'S FUNNY... WHEN I WAS A KID, I WANTED TO HAVE POWERS LIKE MY DAD MORE THAN ANYTHING!
WELL, I GUESS I GOT MY WISH...
WHAT A KICK IN THE ASS!
AAAAAHHH!
NO!
NO!

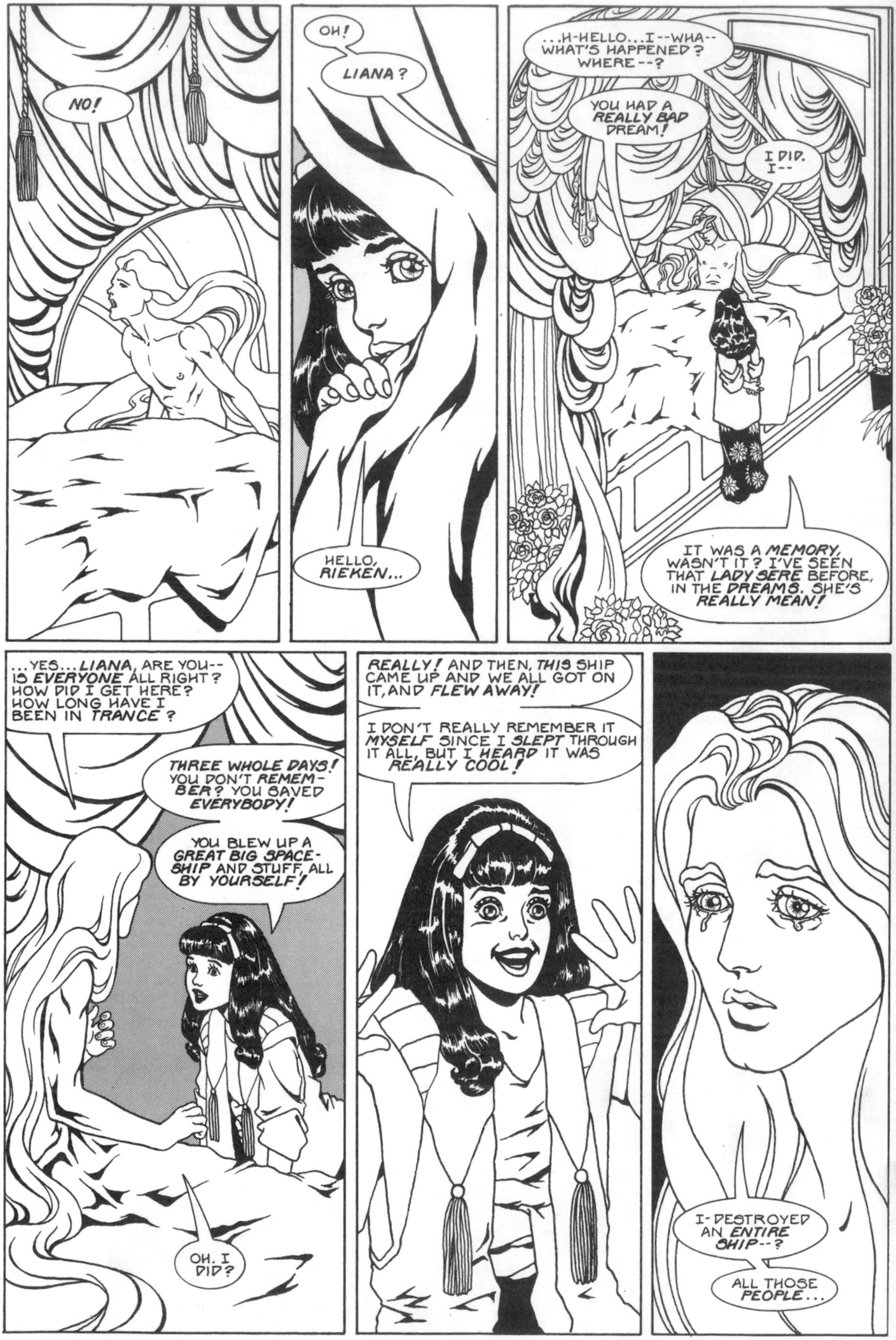
NO!
OH!
LIANA?
HELLO, RIEKEN...
...H-HELLO...I--WHA-- WHAT'S HAPPENED? WHERE--?
YOU HAD A REALLY BAD DREAM!
I DID. I--
IT WAS A MEMORY, WASN'T IT? I'VE SEEN THAT LADY SERE BEFORE, IN THE DREAMS. SHE'S REALLY MEAN!
...YES...LIANA, ARE YOU-- IS EVERYONE ALL RIGHT? HOW DID I GET HERE? HOW LONG HAVE I BEEN IN TRANCE?
THREE WHOLE DAYS! YOU DON'T REMEMBER? YOU SAVED EVERYBODY!
YOU BLEW UP A GREAT BIG SPACESHIP AND STUFF, ALL BY YOURSELF!
OH. I DID?
REALLY! AND THEN, THIS SHIP CAME UP AND WE ALL GOT ON IT, AND FLEW AWAY!
I DON'T REALLY REMEMBER IT MYSELF SINCE I SLEPT THROUGH IT ALL, BUT I HEARD IT WAS REALLY COOL!
I-DESTROYED AN ENTIRE SHIP--?
ALL THOSE PEOPLE...

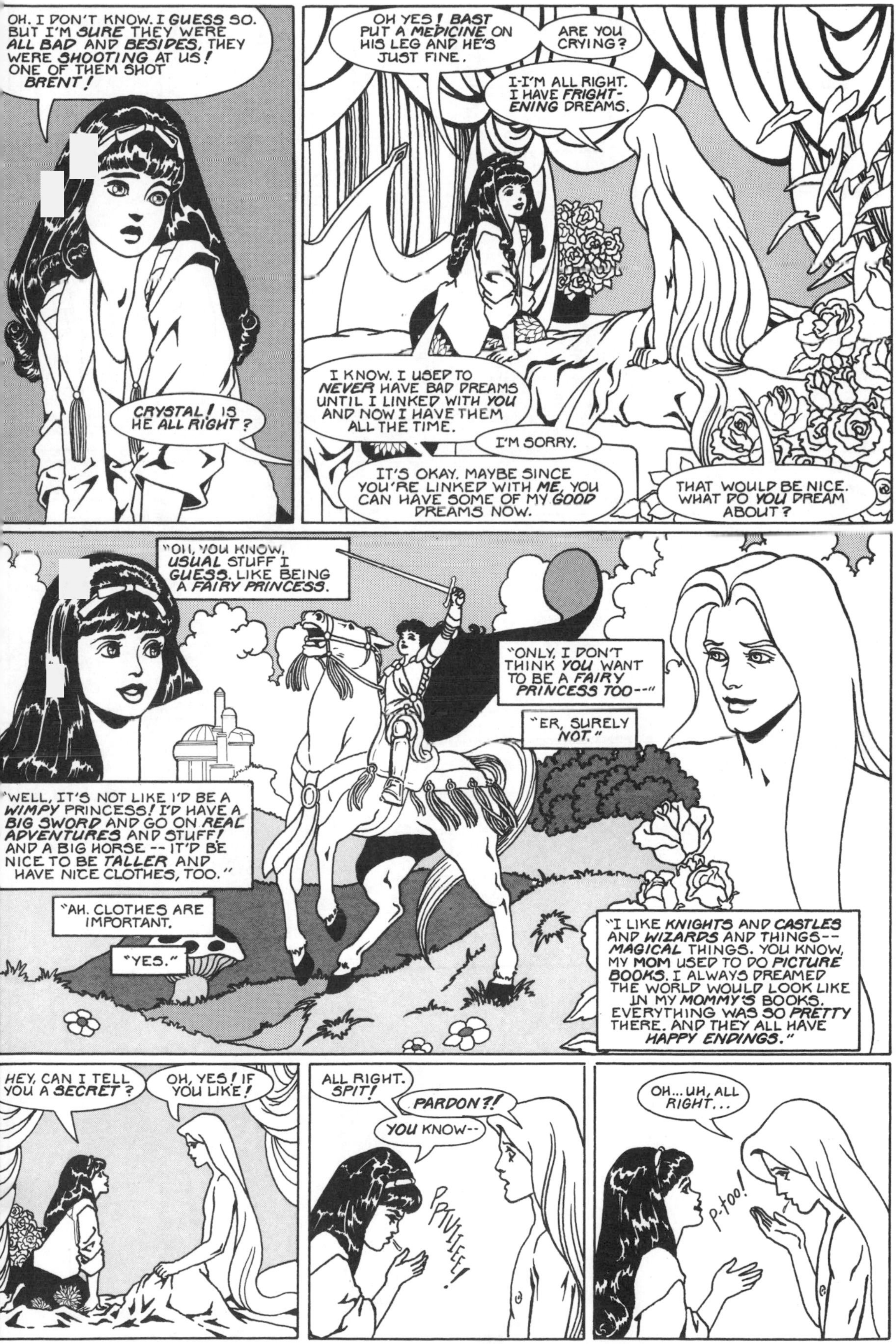
OH. I DON'T KNOW. I GUESS SO. BUT I'M SURE THEY WERE ALL BAD AND BESIDES, THEY WERE SHOOTING AT US! ONE OF THEM SHOT BRENT!
CRYSTAL! IS HE ALL RIGHT?
OH YES! BAST PUT A MEDICINE ON HIS LEG AND HE'S JUST FINE.
ARE YOU CRYING?
I-I'M ALL RIGHT. I HAVE FRIGHT-ENING DREAMS.
I KNOW. I USED TO NEVER HAVE BAD DREAMS UNTIL I LINKED WITH YOU AND NOW I HAVE THEM ALL THE TIME.
I'M SORRY.
IT'S OKAY. MAYBE SINCE YOU'RE LINKED WITH ME, YOU CAN HAVE SOME OF MY GOOD DREAMS NOW.
THAT WOULD BE NICE. WHAT DO YOU DREAM ABOUT?
"OH, YOU KNOW, USUAL STUFF I GUESS. LIKE BEING A FAIRY PRINCESS.
"ONLY, I DON'T THINK YOU WANT TO BE A FAIRY PRINCESS TOO--"
"ER, SURELY NOT."
"WELL, IT'S NOT LIKE I'D BE A WIMPY PRINCESS! I'D HAVE A BIG SWORD AND GO ON REAL ADVENTURES AND STUFF! AND A BIG HORSE -- IT'D BE NICE TO BE TALLER AND HAVE NICE CLOTHES, TOO."
"AH. CLOTHES ARE IMPORTANT.
"YES."
"I LIKE KNIGHTS AND CASTLES AND WIZARDS AND THINGS-- MAGICAL THINGS. YOU KNOW, MY MOM USED TO DO PICTURE BOOKS. I ALWAYS DREAMED THE WORLD WOULD LOOK LIKE IN MY MOMMY'S BOOKS. EVERYTHING WAS SO PRETTY THERE. AND THEY ALL HAVE HAPPY ENDINGS."
HEY, CAN I TELL YOU A SECRET?
OH, YES! IF YOU LIKE!
ALL RIGHT. SPIT!
PARDON?!
YOU KNOW--
PPTUIEEE!
OH... UH, ALL RIGHT...
p-too!

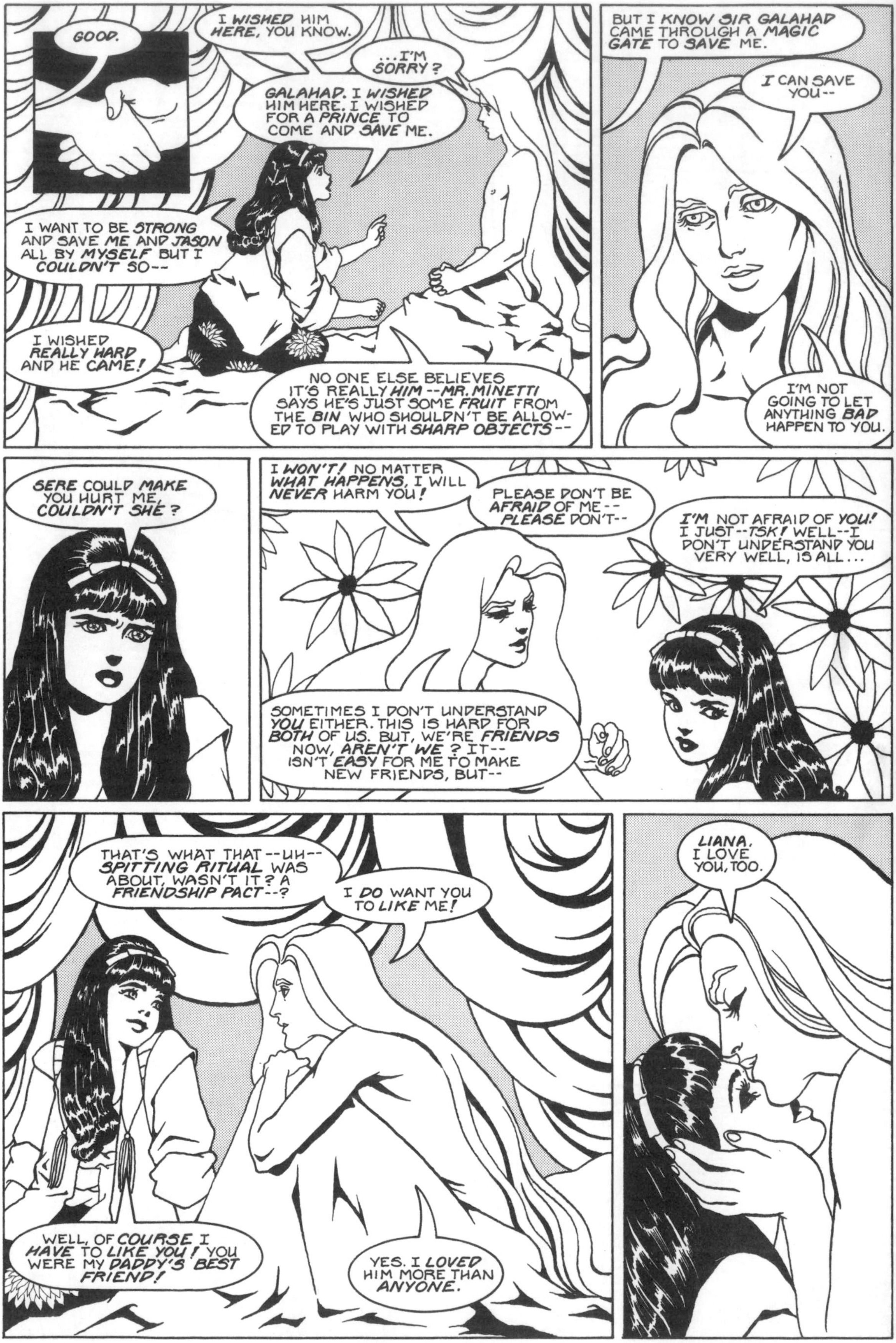
GOOD.
I WISHED HIM HERE, YOU KNOW.
...I'M SORRY?
GALAHAD. I WISHED HIM HERE. I WISHED FOR A PRINCE TO COME AND SAVE ME.
I WANT TO BE STRONG AND SAVE ME AND JASON ALL BY MYSELF BUT I COULDN'T SO--
I WISHED REALLY HARD AND HE CAME!
NO ONE ELSE BELIEVES IT'S REALLY HIM --MR. MINETTI SAYS HE'S JUST SOME FRUIT FROM THE BIN WHO SHOULDN'T BE ALLOWED TO PLAY WITH SHARP OBJECTS--
BUT I KNOW SIR GALAHAD CAME THROUGH A MAGIC GATE TO SAVE ME.
I CAN SAVE YOU--
I'M NOT GOING TO LET ANYTHING BAD HAPPEN TO YOU.
SERE COULD MAKE YOU HURT ME, COULDN'T SHE?
I WON'T! NO MATTER WHAT HAPPENS, I WILL NEVER HARM YOU!
PLEASE DON'T BE AFRAID OF ME-- PLEASE DON'T--
I'M NOT AFRAID OF YOU! I JUST--TSK! WELL--I DON'T UNDERSTAND YOU VERY WELL, IS ALL...
SOMETIMES I DON'T UNDERSTAND YOU EITHER. THIS IS HARD FOR BOTH OF US. BUT, WE'RE FRIENDS NOW, AREN'T WE? IT-- ISN'T EASY FOR ME TO MAKE NEW FRIENDS, BUT--
THAT'S WHAT THAT--UH-- SPITTING RITUAL WAS ABOUT, WASN'T IT? A FRIENDSHIP PACT--?
I DO WANT YOU TO LIKE ME!
WELL, OF COURSE I HAVE TO LIKE YOU! YOU WERE MY DADDY'S BEST FRIEND!
YES. I LOVED HIM MORE THAN ANYONE.
LIANA. I LOVE YOU, TOO.

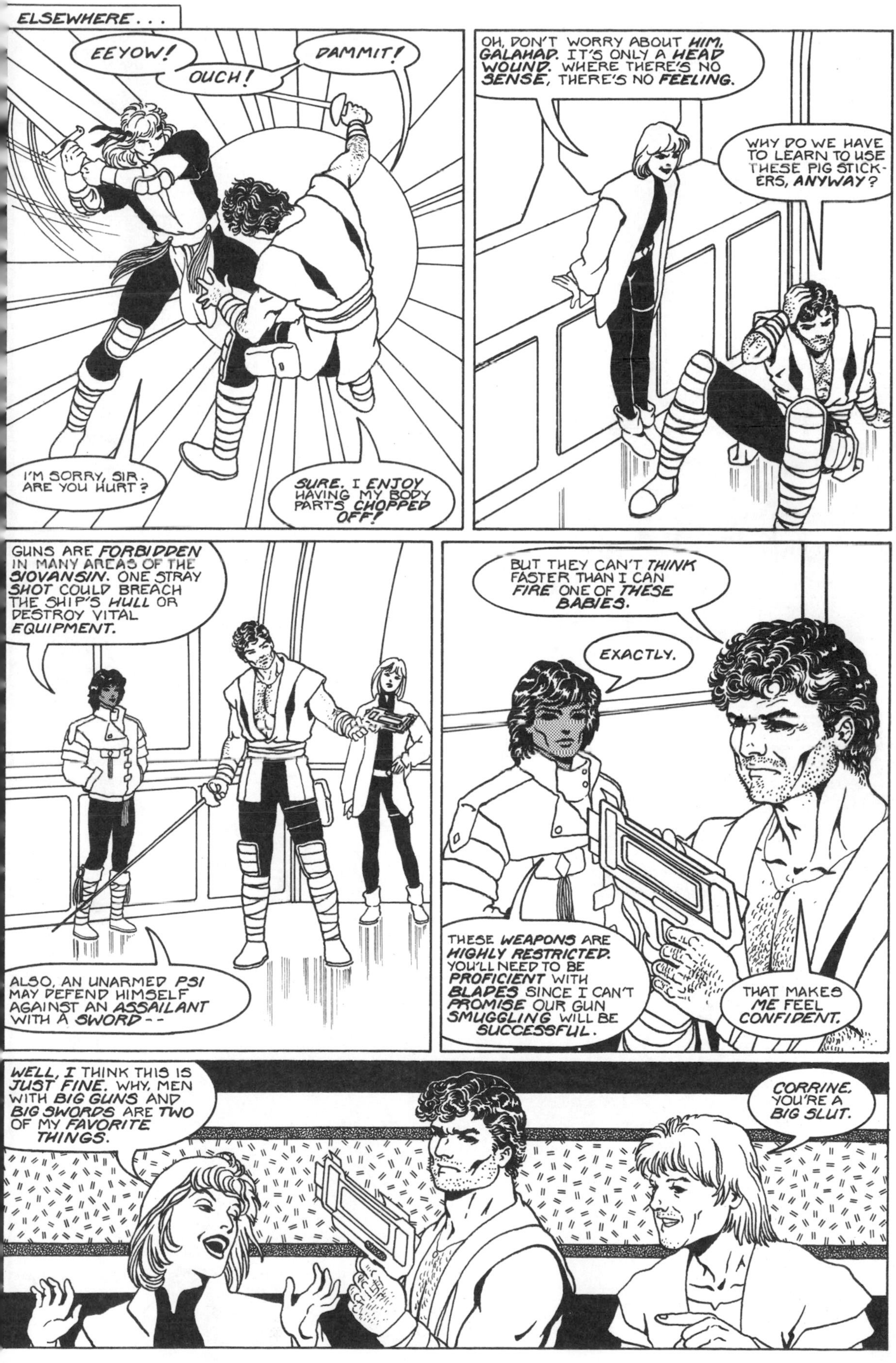
ELSEWHERE . . .
EEYOW!
OUCH!
DAMMIT!
I'M SORRY, SIR. ARE YOU HURT?
SURE. I ENJOY HAVING MY BODY PARTS CHOPPED OFF!
OH, DON'T WORRY ABOUT HIM, GALAHAD. IT'S ONLY A HEAD WOUND. WHERE THERE'S NO SENSE, THERE'S NO FEELING.
WHY DO WE HAVE TO LEARN TO USE THESE PIG STICKERS, ANYWAY?
GUNS ARE FORBIDDEN IN MANY AREAS OF THE SIOVANSIN. ONE STRAY SHOT COULD BREACH THE SHIP'S HULL OR DESTROY VITAL EQUIPMENT.
ALSO, AN UNARMED PSI MAY DEFEND HIMSELF AGAINST AN ASSAILANT WITH A SWORD--
BUT THEY CAN'T THINK FASTER THAN I CAN FIRE ONE OF THESE BABIES.
EXACTLY.
THESE WEAPONS ARE HIGHLY RESTRICTED. YOU'LL NEED TO BE PROFICIENT WITH BLADES SINCE I CAN'T PROMISE OUR GUN SMUGGLING WILL BE SUCCESSFUL.
THAT MAKES ME FEEL CONFIDENT.
WELL, I THINK THIS IS JUST FINE. WHY, MEN WITH BIG GUNS AND BIG SWORDS ARE TWO OF MY FAVORITE THINGS.
CORRINE, YOU'RE A BIG SLUT.

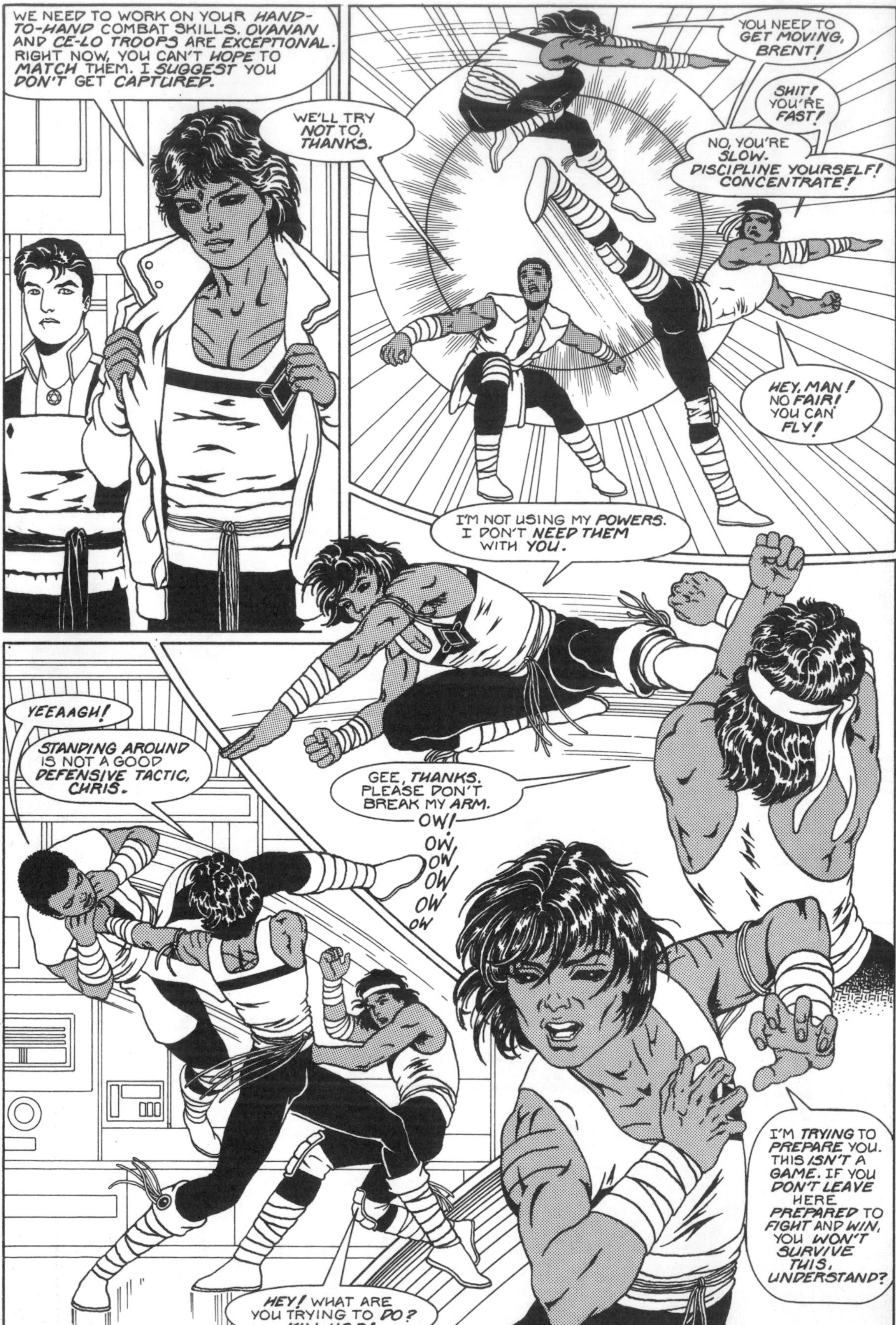
WE NEED TO WORK ON YOUR HAND-TO-HAND COMBAT SKILLS. OVANAN AND CE-LO TROOPS ARE EXCEPTIONAL. RIGHT NOW, YOU CAN'T HOPE TO MATCH THEM. I SUGGEST YOU DON'T GET CAPTURED.
WE'LL TRY NOT TO, THANKS.
YOU NEED TO GET MOVING, BRENT!
SHIT! YOU'RE FAST!
NO, YOU'RE SLOW. DISCIPLINE YOURSELF! CONCENTRATE!
HEY, MAN! NO FAIR! YOU CAN FLY!
I'M NOT USING MY POWERS. I DON'T NEED THEM WITH YOU.
YEEAAGH!
STANDING AROUND IS NOT A GOOD DEFENSIVE TACTIC, CHRIS.
GEE, THANKS. PLEASE DON'T BREAK MY ARM.
OW! OW, OW OW OW OW
HEY! WHAT ARE YOU TRYING TO DO? KILL US?!
I'M TRYING TO PREPARE YOU. THIS ISN'T A GAME. IF YOU DON'T LEAVE HERE PREPARED TO FIGHT AND WIN, YOU WON'T SURVIVE THIS, UNDERSTAND?

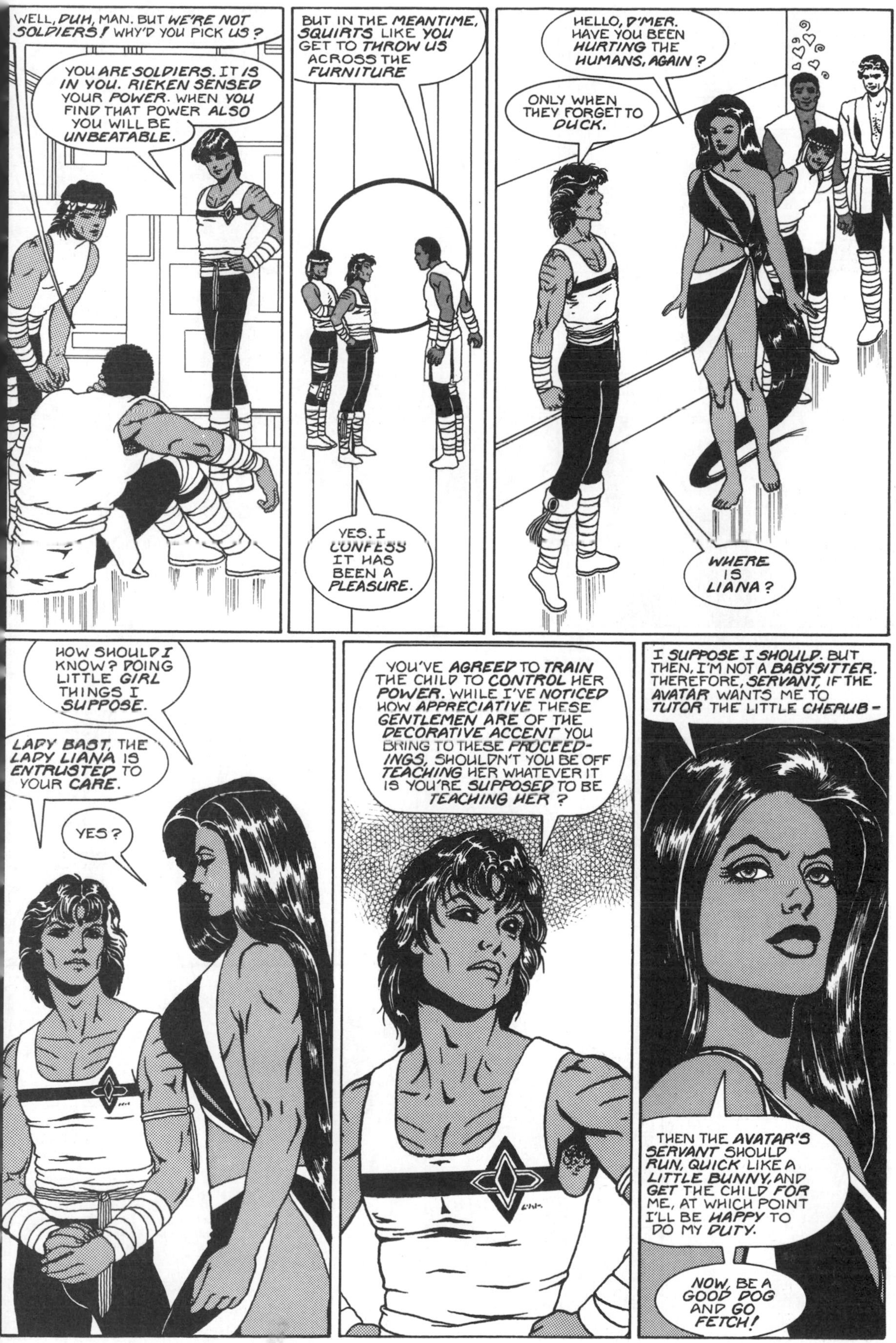
WELL, DUH, MAN. BUT WE'RE NOT SOLDIERS! WHY'D YOU PICK US?
YOU ARE SOLDIERS. IT IS IN YOU. RIEKEN SENSED YOUR POWER. WHEN YOU FIND THAT POWER ALSO YOU WILL BE UNBEATABLE.
BUT IN THE MEANTIME, SQUIRTS LIKE YOU GET TO THROW US ACROSS THE FURNITURE
YES. I CONFESS IT HAS BEEN A PLEASURE.
HELLO, D'MER. HAVE YOU BEEN HURTING THE HUMANS, AGAIN?
ONLY WHEN THEY FORGET TO DUCK.
WHERE IS LIANA?
HOW SHOULD I KNOW? DOING LITTLE GIRL THINGS I SUPPOSE.
LADY BAST, THE LADY LIANA IS ENTRUSTED TO YOUR CARE.
YES?
YOU'VE AGREED TO TRAIN THE CHILD TO CONTROL HER POWER. WHILE I'VE NOTICED HOW APPRECIATIVE THESE GENTLEMEN ARE OF THE DECORATIVE ACCENT YOU BRING TO THESE PROCEEDINGS, SHOULDN'T YOU BE OFF TEACHING HER WHATEVER IT IS YOU'RE SUPPOSED TO BE TEACHING HER?
I SUPPOSE I SHOULD. BUT THEN, I'M NOT A BABYSITTER. THEREFORE, SERVANT, IF THE AVATAR WANTS ME TO TUTOR THE LITTLE CHERUB -
THEN THE AVATAR'S SERVANT SHOULD RUN, QUICK LIKE A LITTLE BUNNY, AND GET THE CHILD FOR ME, AT WHICH POINT I'LL BE HAPPY TO DO MY DUTY.
NOW, BE A GOOD DOG AND GO FETCH!

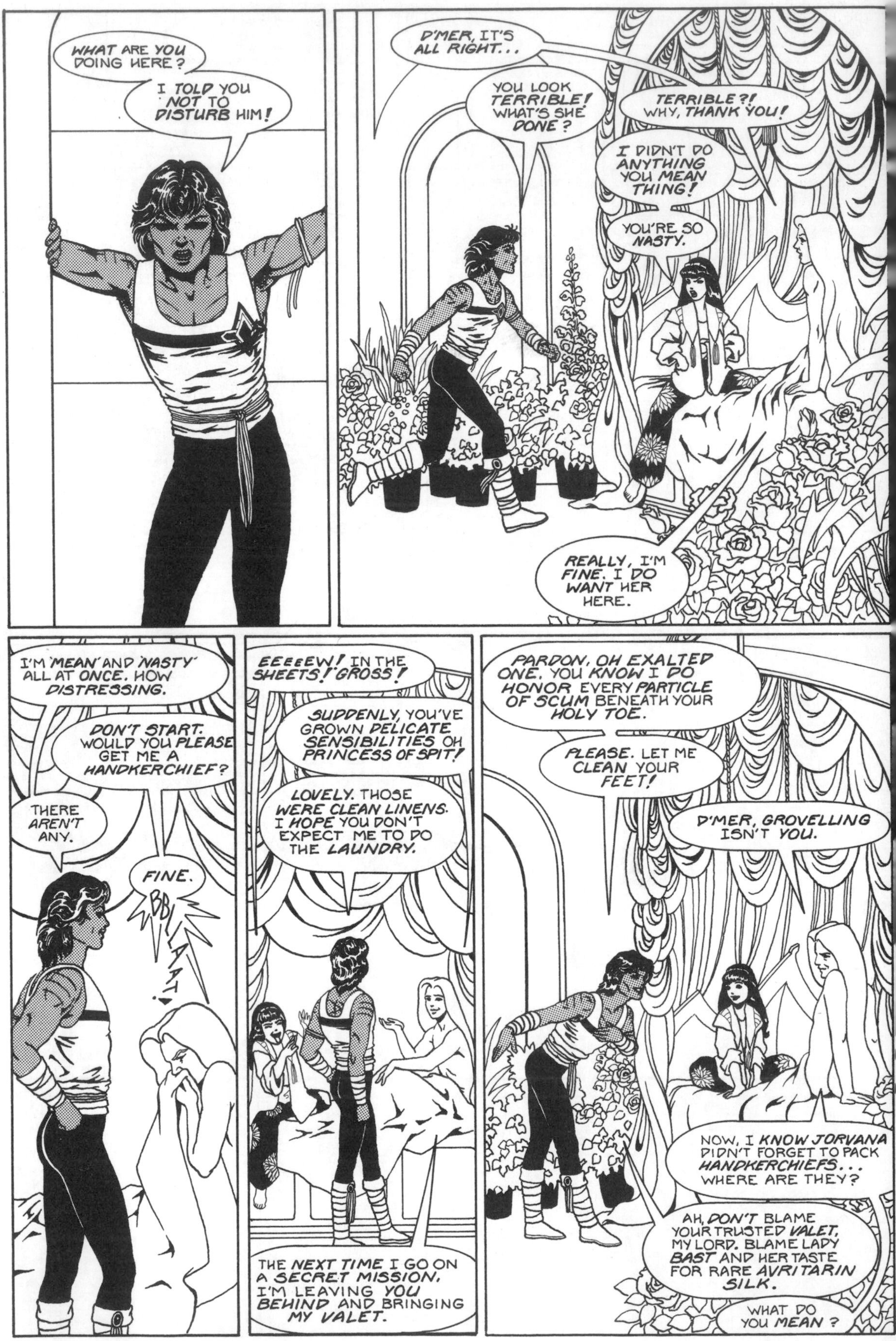
WHAT ARE YOU DOING HERE?
I TOLD YOU NOT TO DISTURB HIM!
D'MER, IT'S ALL RIGHT...
YOU LOOK TERRIBLE! WHAT'S SHE DONE?
TERRIBLE?! WHY, THANK YOU!
I DIDN'T DO ANYTHING YOU MEAN THING!
YOU'RE SO NASTY.
REALLY, I'M FINE. I DO WANT HER HERE.
I'M 'MEAN' AND 'NASTY' ALL AT ONCE. HOW DISTRESSING.
DON'T START. WOULD YOU PLEASE GET ME A HANDKERCHIEF?
THERE AREN'T ANY.
FINE.
BBLAAAT!
EEEEEW! IN THE SHEETS! GROSS!
SUDDENLY, YOU'VE GROWN DELICATE SENSIBILITIES OH PRINCESS OF SPIT!
LOVELY. THOSE WERE CLEAN LINENS. I HOPE YOU DON'T EXPECT ME TO DO THE LAUNDRY.
THE NEXT TIME I GO ON A SECRET MISSION, I'M LEAVING YOU BEHIND AND BRINGING MY VALET.
PARDON, OH EXALTED ONE. YOU KNOW I DO HONOR EVERY PARTICLE OF SCUM BENEATH YOUR HOLY TOE.
PLEASE. LET ME CLEAN YOUR FEET!
D'MER, GROVELLING ISN'T YOU.
NOW, I KNOW JORVANA DIDN'T FORGET TO PACK HANDKERCHIEFS... WHERE ARE THEY?
AH, DON'T BLAME YOUR TRUSTED VALET, MY LORD. BLAME LADY BAST AND HER TASTE FOR RARE AVRITARIN SILK.
WHAT DO YOU MEAN?

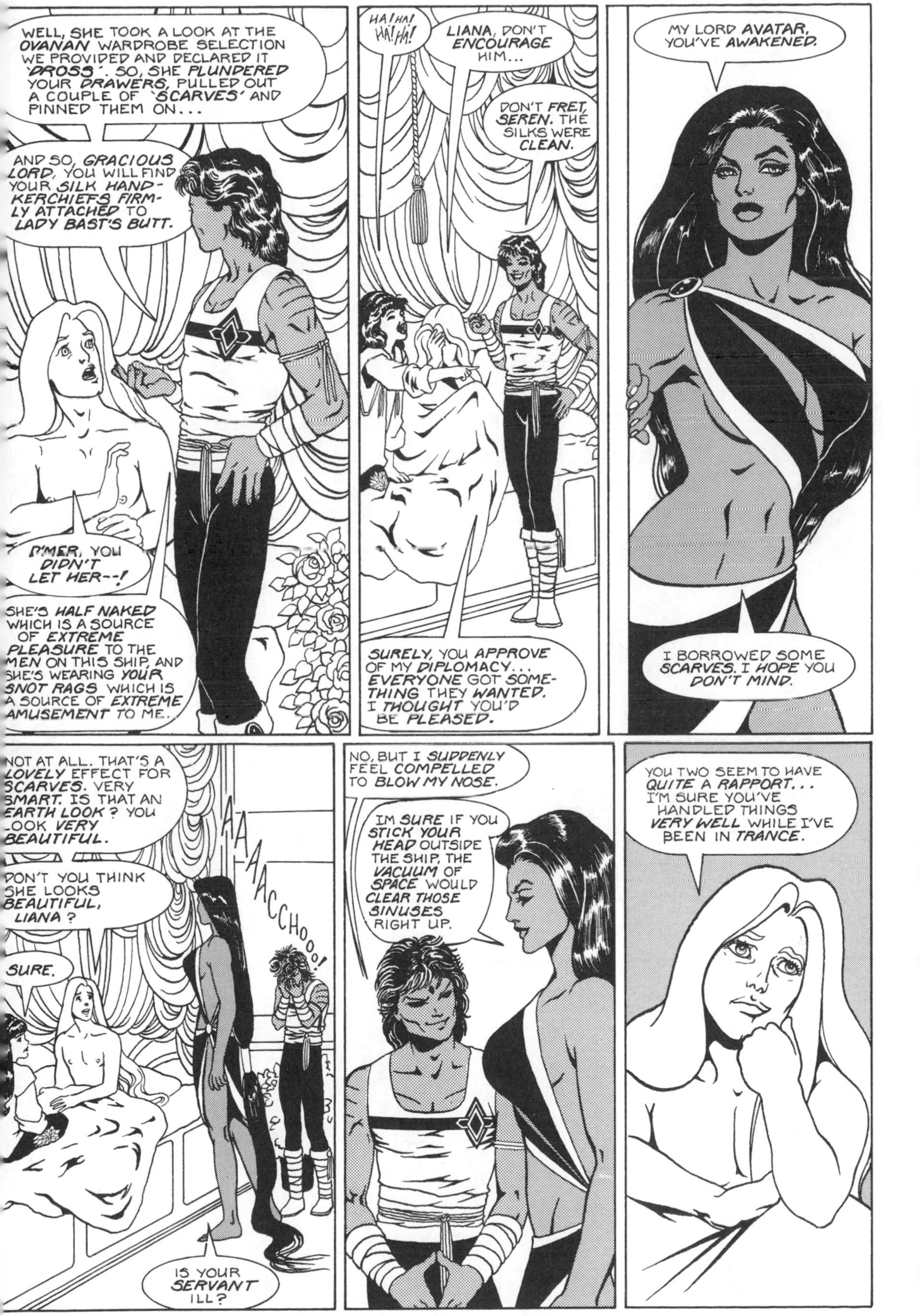
WELL, SHE TOOK A LOOK AT THE OVANAN WARDROBE SELECTION WE PROVIDED AND DECLARED IT `DROSS'. SO, SHE PLUNDERED YOUR DRAWERS, PULLED OUT A COUPLE OF `SCARVES' AND PINNED THEM ON...
AND SO, GRACIOUS LORD, YOU WILL FIND YOUR SILK HAND-KERCHIEFS FIRMLY ATTACHED TO LADY BAST'S BUTT.
RIMER, YOU DIDN'T LET HER--!
SHE'S HALF NAKED WHICH IS A SOURCE OF EXTREME PLEASURE TO THE MEN ON THIS SHIP, AND SHE'S WEARING YOUR SNOT RAGS WHICH IS A SOURCE OF EXTREME AMUSEMENT TO ME...
HA! HA! HA! HA!
LIANA, DON'T ENCOURAGE HIM...
DON'T FRET, SEREN. THE SILKS WERE CLEAN.
SURELY, YOU APPROVE OF MY DIPLOMACY... EVERYONE GOT SOMETHING THEY WANTED. I THOUGHT YOU'D BE PLEASED.
MY LORD AVATAR, YOU'VE AWAKENED.
I BORROWED SOME SCARVES. I HOPE YOU DON'T MIND.
NOT AT ALL. THAT'S A LOVELY EFFECT FOR SCARVES. VERY SMART. IS THAT AN EARTH LOOK? YOU LOOK VERY BEAUTIFUL.
DON'T YOU THINK SHE LOOKS BEAUTIFUL, LIANA?
SURE.
AAAACCHOOO!
IS YOUR SERVANT ILL?
NO, BUT I SUDDENLY FEEL COMPELLED TO BLOW MY NOSE.
IM SURE IF YOU STICK YOUR HEAD OUTSIDE THE SHIP, THE VACUUM OF SPACE WOULD CLEAR THOSE SINUSES RIGHT UP.
YOU TWO SEEM TO HAVE QUITE A RAPPORT... I'M SURE YOU'VE HANDLED THINGS VERY WELL WHILE I'VE BEEN IN TRANCE.

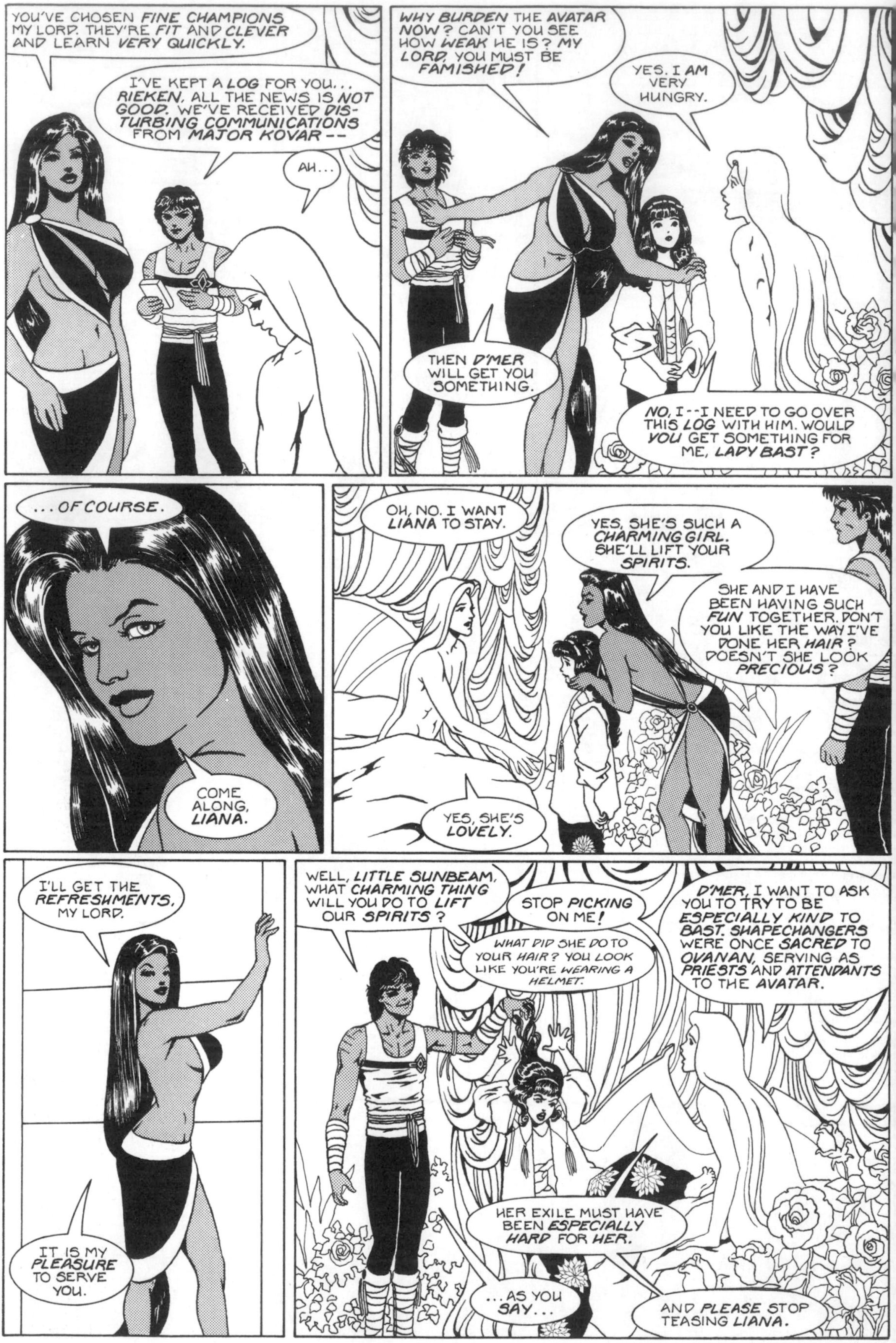
YOU'VE CHOSEN FINE CHAMPIONS MY LORD. THEY'RE FIT AND CLEVER AND LEARN VERY QUICKLY.
I'VE KEPT A LOG FOR YOU... RIEKEN, ALL THE NEWS IS NOT GOOD. WE'VE RECEIVED DISTURBING COMMUNICATIONS FROM MAJOR KOVAR --
AH...
WHY BURDEN THE AVATAR NOW? CAN'T YOU SEE HOW WEAK HE IS? MY LORD, YOU MUST BE FAMISHED!
YES. I AM VERY HUNGRY.
THEN D'MER WILL GET YOU SOMETHING.
NO, I--I NEED TO GO OVER THIS LOG WITH HIM. WOULD YOU GET SOMETHING FOR ME, LADY BAST?
... OF COURSE.
COME ALONG, LIANA.
OH, NO. I WANT LIANA TO STAY.
YES, SHE'S SUCH A CHARMING GIRL. SHE'LL LIFT YOUR SPIRITS.
SHE AND I HAVE BEEN HAVING SUCH FUN TOGETHER. DON'T YOU LIKE THE WAY I'VE DONE HER HAIR? DOESN'T SHE LOOK PRECIOUS?
YES, SHE'S LOVELY.
I'LL GET THE REFRESHMENTS, MY LORD.
IT IS MY PLEASURE TO SERVE YOU.
WELL, LITTLE SUNBEAM, WHAT CHARMING THING WILL YOU DO TO LIFT OUR SPIRITS?
STOP PICKING ON ME!
WHAT DID SHE DO TO YOUR HAIR? YOU LOOK LIKE YOU'RE WEARING A HELMET.
D'MER, I WANT TO ASK YOU TO TRY TO BE ESPECIALLY KIND TO BAST. SHAPECHANGERS WERE ONCE SACRED TO OVANAN, SERVING AS PRIESTS AND ATTENDANTS TO THE AVATAR.
HER EXILE MUST HAVE BEEN ESPECIALLY HARD FOR HER.
...AS YOU SAY...
AND PLEASE STOP TEASING LIANA.

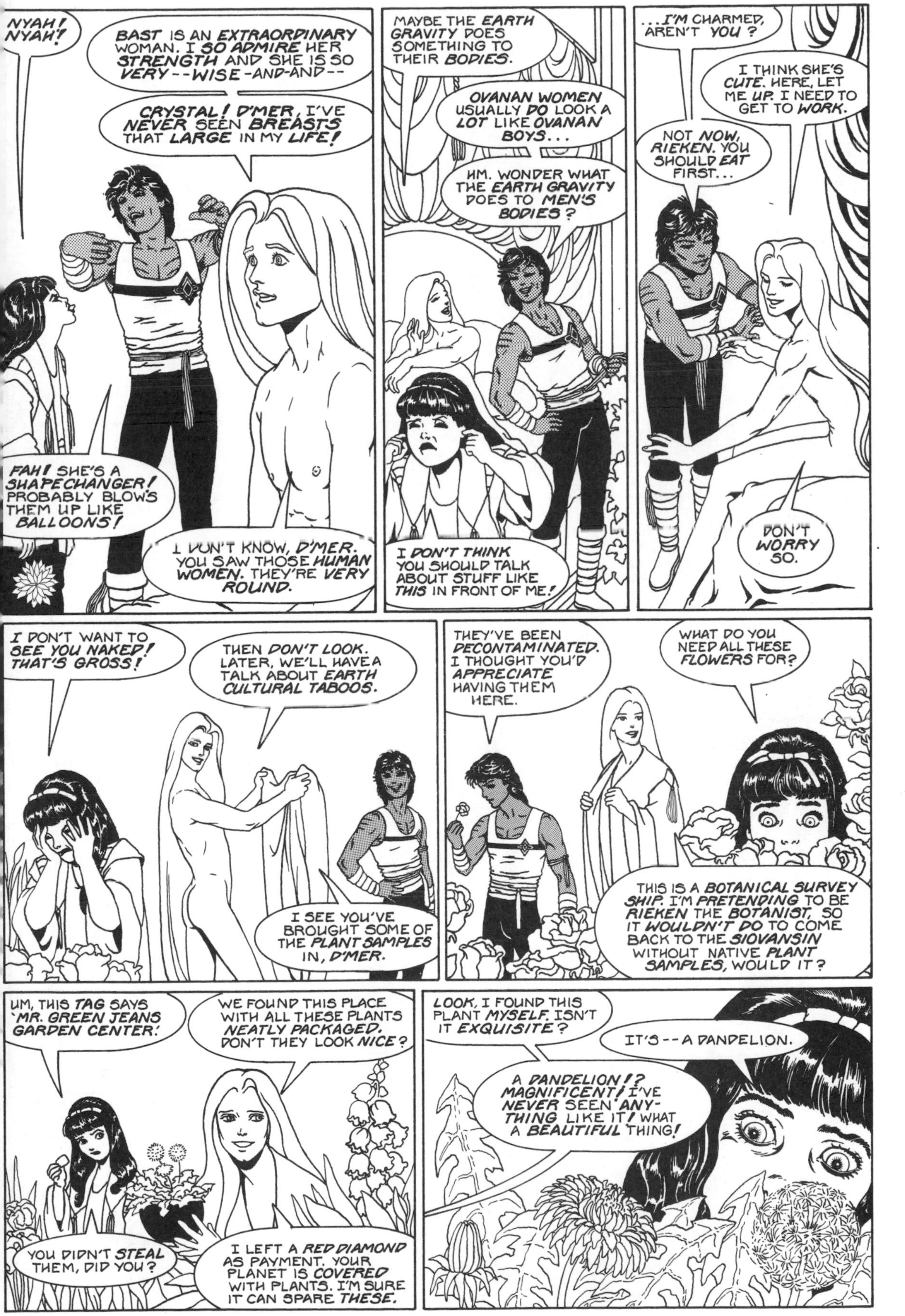
NYAH! NYAH!
BAST IS AN EXTRAORDINARY WOMAN. I SO ADMIRE HER STRENGTH AND SHE IS SO VERY--WISE-AND-AND--
CRYSTAL! D'MER, I'VE NEVER SEEN BREASTS THAT LARGE IN MY LIFE!
FAH! SHE'S A SHAPECHANGER! PROBABLY BLOWS THEM UP LIKE BALLOONS!
I DON'T KNOW, D'MER. YOU SAW THOSE HUMAN WOMEN. THEY'RE VERY ROUND.
MAYBE THE EARTH GRAVITY DOES SOMETHING TO THEIR BODIES.
OVANAN WOMEN USUALLY DO LOOK A LOT LIKE OVANAN BOYS...
HM. WONDER WHAT THE EARTH GRAVITY DOES TO MEN'S BODIES?
I DON'T THINK YOU SHOULD TALK ABOUT STUFF LIKE THIS IN FRONT OF ME!
...I'M CHARMED, AREN'T YOU?
I THINK SHE'S CUTE. HERE, LET ME UP. I NEED TO GET TO WORK.
NOT NOW, RIEKEN. YOU SHOULD EAT FIRST...
DON'T WORRY SO.
I DON'T WANT TO SEE YOU NAKED! THAT'S GROSS!
THEN DON'T LOOK. LATER, WE'LL HAVE A TALK ABOUT EARTH CULTURAL TABOOS.
I SEE YOU'VE BROUGHT SOME OF THE PLANT SAMPLES IN, D'MER.
THEY'VE BEEN DECONTAMINATED. I THOUGHT YOU'D APPRECIATE HAVING THEM HERE.
WHAT DO YOU NEED ALL THESE FLOWERS FOR?
THIS IS A BOTANICAL SURVEY SHIP. I'M PRETENDING TO BE RIEKEN THE BOTANIST, SO IT WOULDN'T DO TO COME BACK TO THE SIOVANSIN WITHOUT NATIVE PLANT SAMPLES, WOULD IT?
UM, THIS TAG SAYS 'MR. GREEN JEANS GARDEN CENTER.'
WE FOUND THIS PLACE WITH ALL THESE PLANTS NEATLY PACKAGED. DON'T THEY LOOK NICE?
YOU DIDN'T STEAL THEM, DID YOU?
I LEFT A RED DIAMOND AS PAYMENT. YOUR PLANET IS COVERED WITH PLANTS. I'M SURE IT CAN SPARE THESE.
LOOK, I FOUND THIS PLANT MYSELF. ISN'T IT EXQUISITE?
IT'S--A DANDELION.
A DANDELION!? MAGNIFICENT! I'VE NEVER SEEN ANYTHING LIKE IT! WHAT A BEAUTIFUL THING!

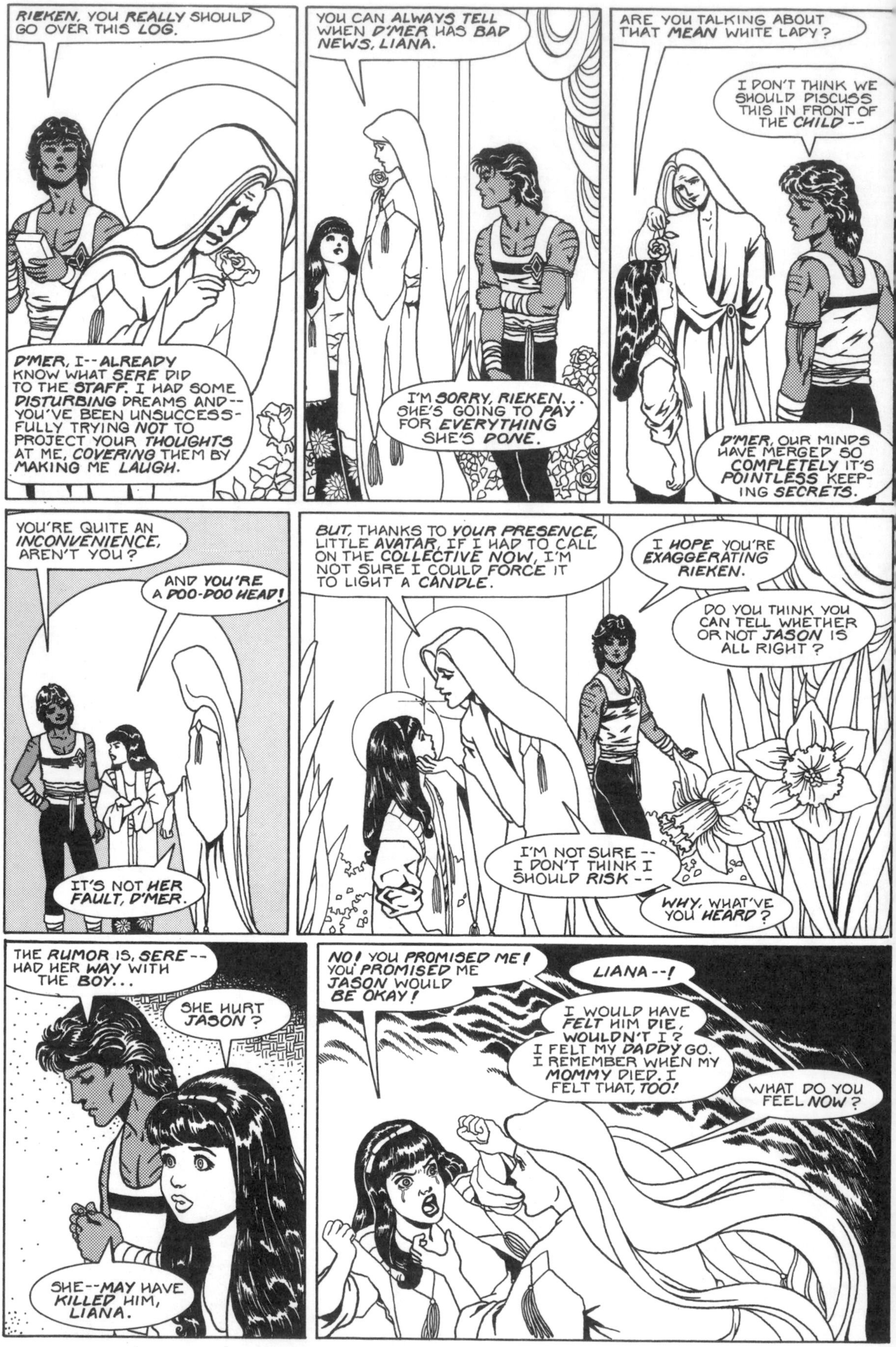
RIEKEN, YOU REALLY SHOULD GO OVER THIS LOG.
D'MER, I--ALREADY KNOW WHAT SERE DID TO THE STAFF. I HAD SOME DISTURBING DREAMS AND--YOU'VE BEEN UNSUCCESSFULLY TRYING NOT TO PROJECT YOUR THOUGHTS AT ME, COVERING THEM BY MAKING ME LAUGH.
YOU CAN ALWAYS TELL WHEN D'MER HAS BAD NEWS, LIANA.
I'M SORRY, RIEKEN... SHE'S GOING TO PAY FOR EVERYTHING SHE'S DONE.
ARE YOU TALKING ABOUT THAT MEAN WHITE LADY?
I DON'T THINK WE SHOULD DISCUSS THIS IN FRONT OF THE CHILD --
D'MER, OUR MINDS HAVE MERGED SO COMPLETELY IT'S POINTLESS KEEPING SECRETS.
YOU'RE QUITE AN INCONVENIENCE, AREN'T YOU?
AND YOU'RE A DOO-DOO HEAD!
IT'S NOT HER FAULT, D'MER.
BUT, THANKS TO YOUR PRESENCE, LITTLE AVATAR, IF I HAD TO CALL ON THE COLLECTIVE NOW, I'M NOT SURE I COULD FORCE IT TO LIGHT A CANDLE.
I HOPE YOU'RE EXAGGERATING RIEKEN.
DO YOU THINK YOU CAN TELL WHETHER OR NOT JASON IS ALL RIGHT?
I'M NOT SURE -- I DON'T THINK I SHOULD RISK --
WHY, WHAT'VE YOU HEARD?
THE RUMOR IS, SERE -- HAD HER WAY WITH THE BOY...
SHE HURT JASON?
SHE--MAY HAVE KILLED HIM, LIANA.
NO! YOU PROMISED ME! YOU PROMISED ME JASON WOULD BE OKAY!
LIANA--!
I WOULD HAVE FELT HIM DIE, WOULDN'T I? I FELT MY DADDY GO. I REMEMBER WHEN MY MOMMY DIED. I FELT THAT, TOO!
WHAT DO YOU FEEL NOW?

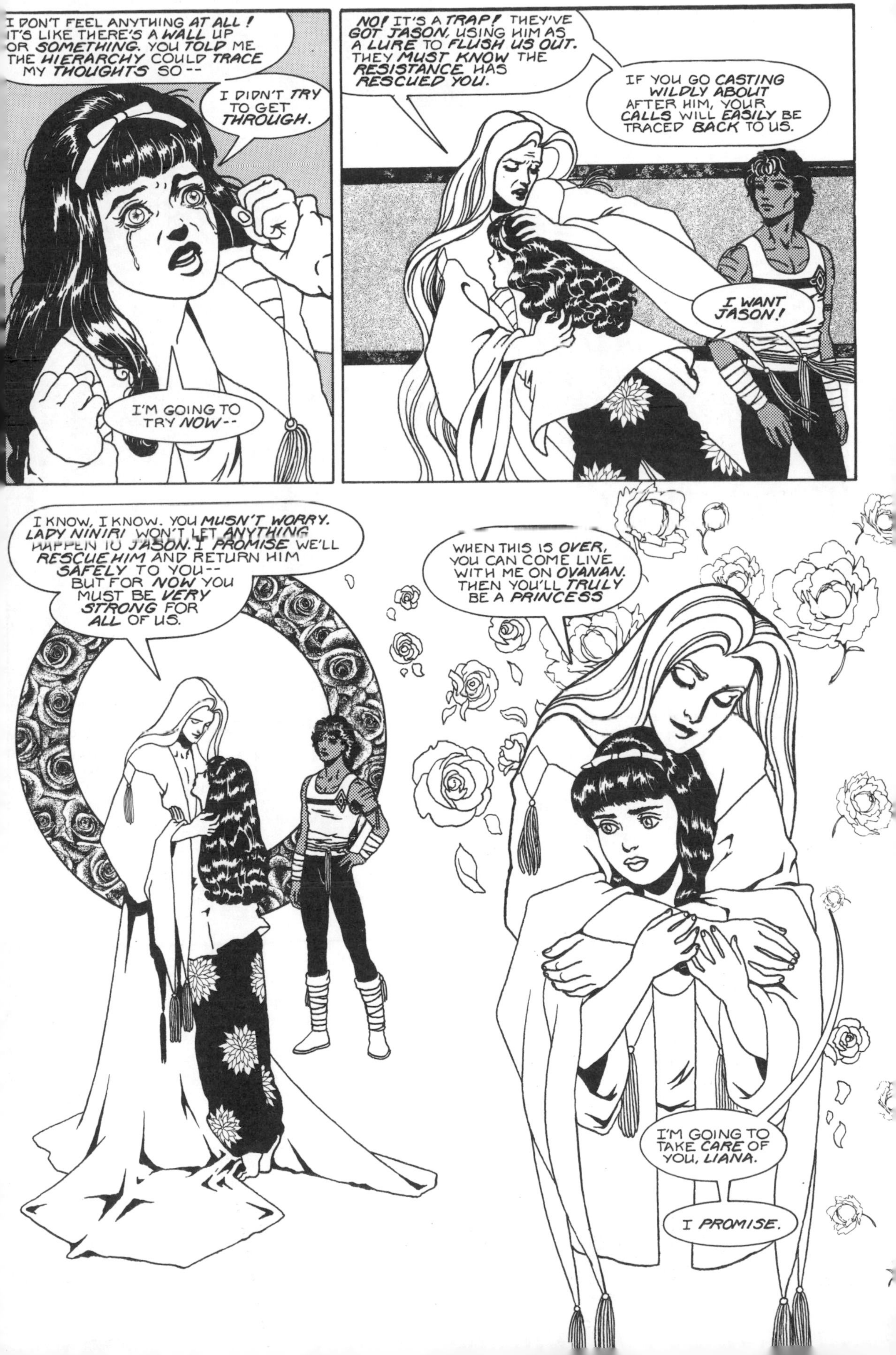
I DON'T FEEL ANYTHING AT ALL! IT'S LIKE THERE'S A WALL UP OR SOMETHING. YOU TOLD ME THE HIERARCHY COULD TRACE MY THOUGHTS SO--
I DIDN'T TRY TO GET THROUGH.
I'M GOING TO TRY NOW--
NO! IT'S A TRAP! THEY'VE GOT JASON, USING HIM AS A LURE TO FLUSH US OUT. THEY MUST KNOW THE RESISTANCE HAS RESCUED YOU.
IF YOU GO CASTING WILDLY ABOUT AFTER HIM, YOUR CALLS WILL EASILY BE TRACED BACK TO US.
I WANT JASON!
I KNOW, I KNOW. YOU MUSN'T WORRY. LADY NINIRI WON'T LET ANYTHING HAPPEN TO JASON. I PROMISE WE'LL RESCUE HIM AND RETURN HIM SAFELY TO YOU-- BUT FOR NOW YOU MUST BE VERY STRONG FOR ALL OF US.
WHEN THIS IS OVER, YOU CAN COME LIVE WITH ME ON OVANAN. THEN YOU'LL TRULY BE A PRINCESS
I'M GOING TO TAKE CARE OF YOU, LIANA.
I PROMISE.

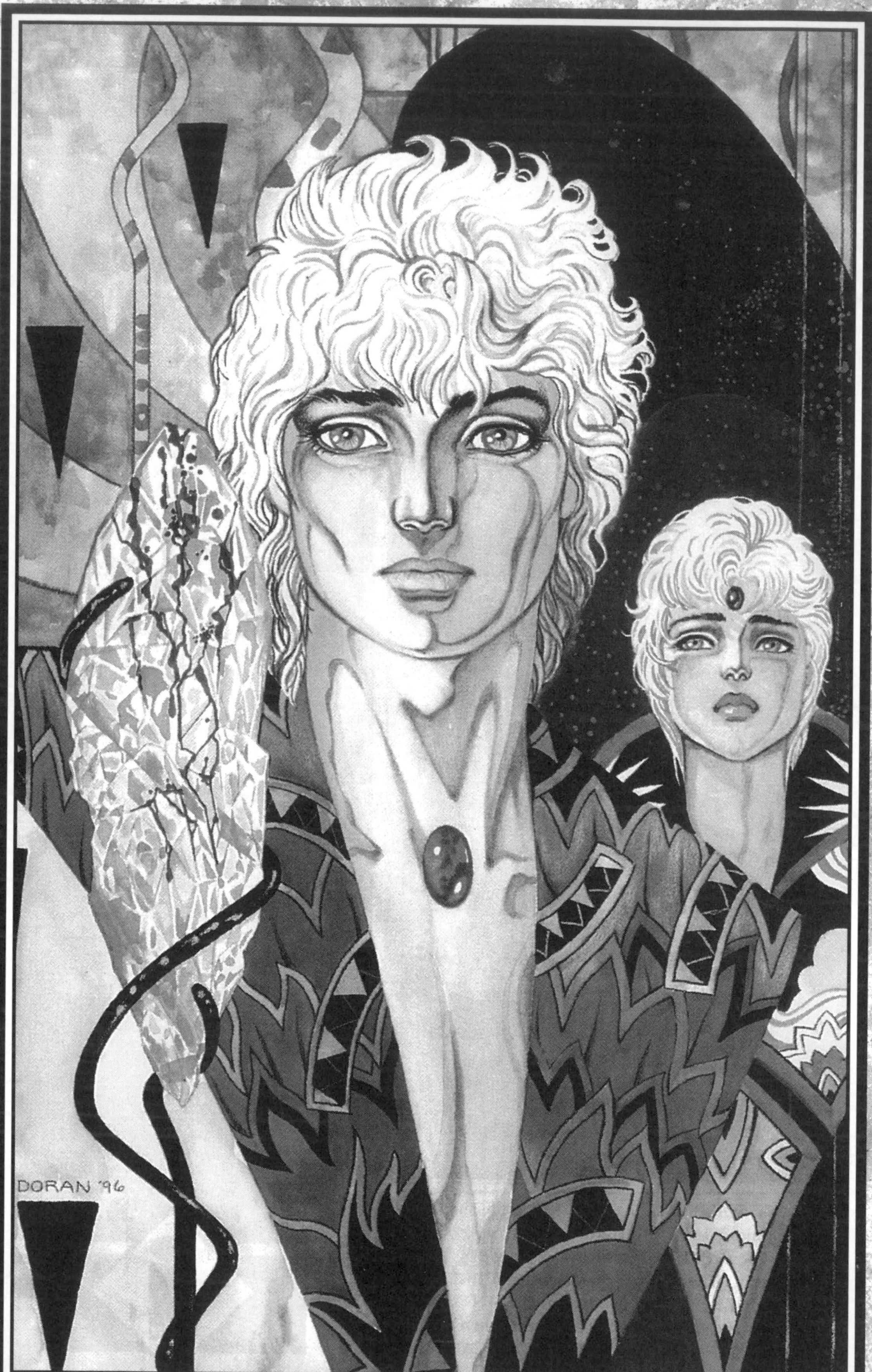
DORAN '96

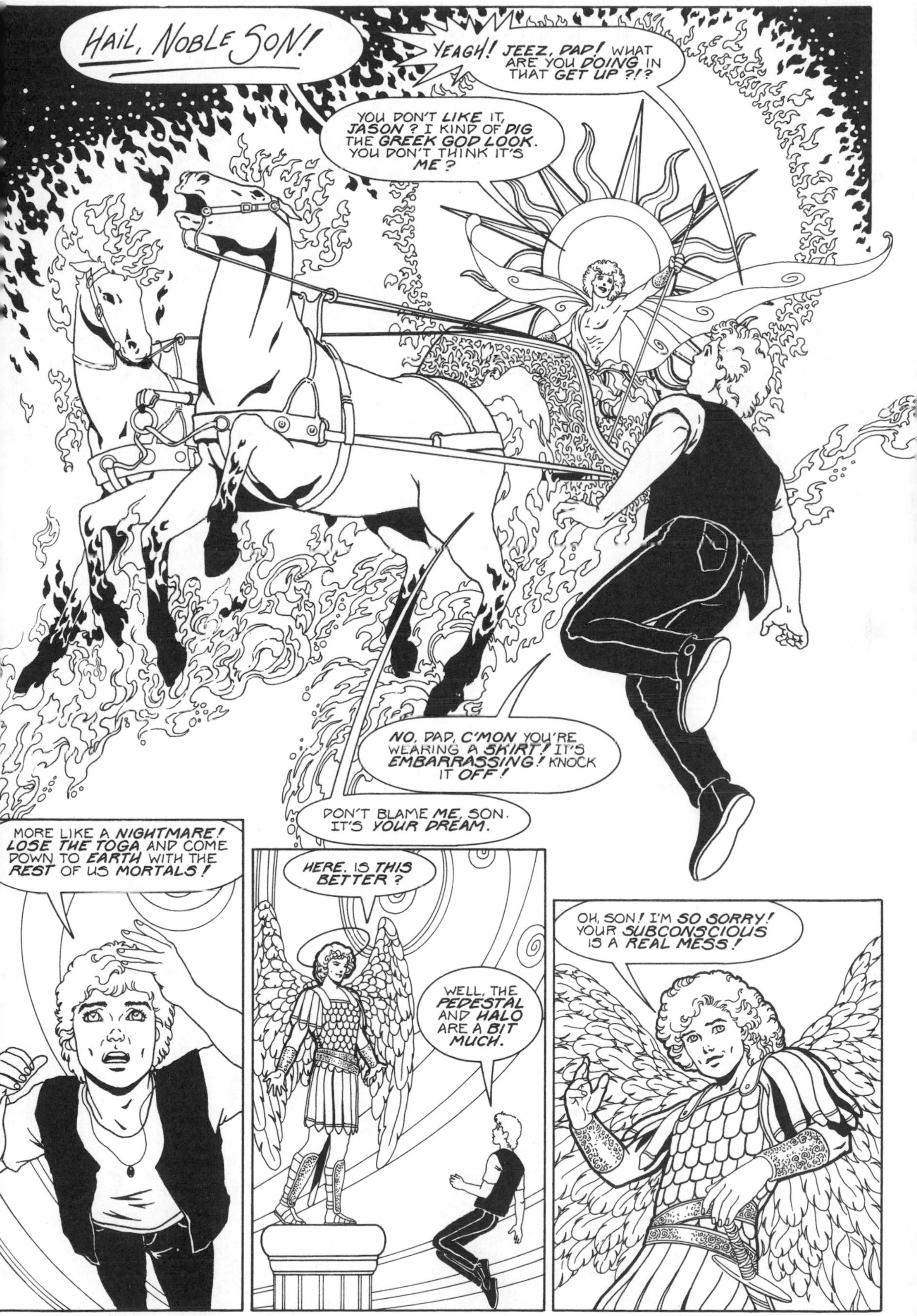
HAIL, NOBLE SON!
YEAGH! JEEZ, DAD! WHAT ARE YOU DOING IN THAT GET UP?!?
YOU DON'T LIKE IT, JASON? I KIND OF DIG THE GREEK GOD LOOK. YOU DON'T THINK IT'S ME?
NO, DAD, C'MON YOU'RE WEARING A SKIRT! IT'S EMBARRASSING! KNOCK IT OFF!
DON'T BLAME ME, SON. IT'S YOUR DREAM.
MORE LIKE A NIGHTMARE! LOSE THE TOGA AND COME DOWN TO EARTH WITH THE REST OF US MORTALS!
HERE. IS THIS BETTER?
WELL, THE PEDESTAL AND HALO ARE A BIT MUCH.
OH, SON! I'M SO SORRY! YOUR SUBCONSCIOUS IS A REAL MESS!

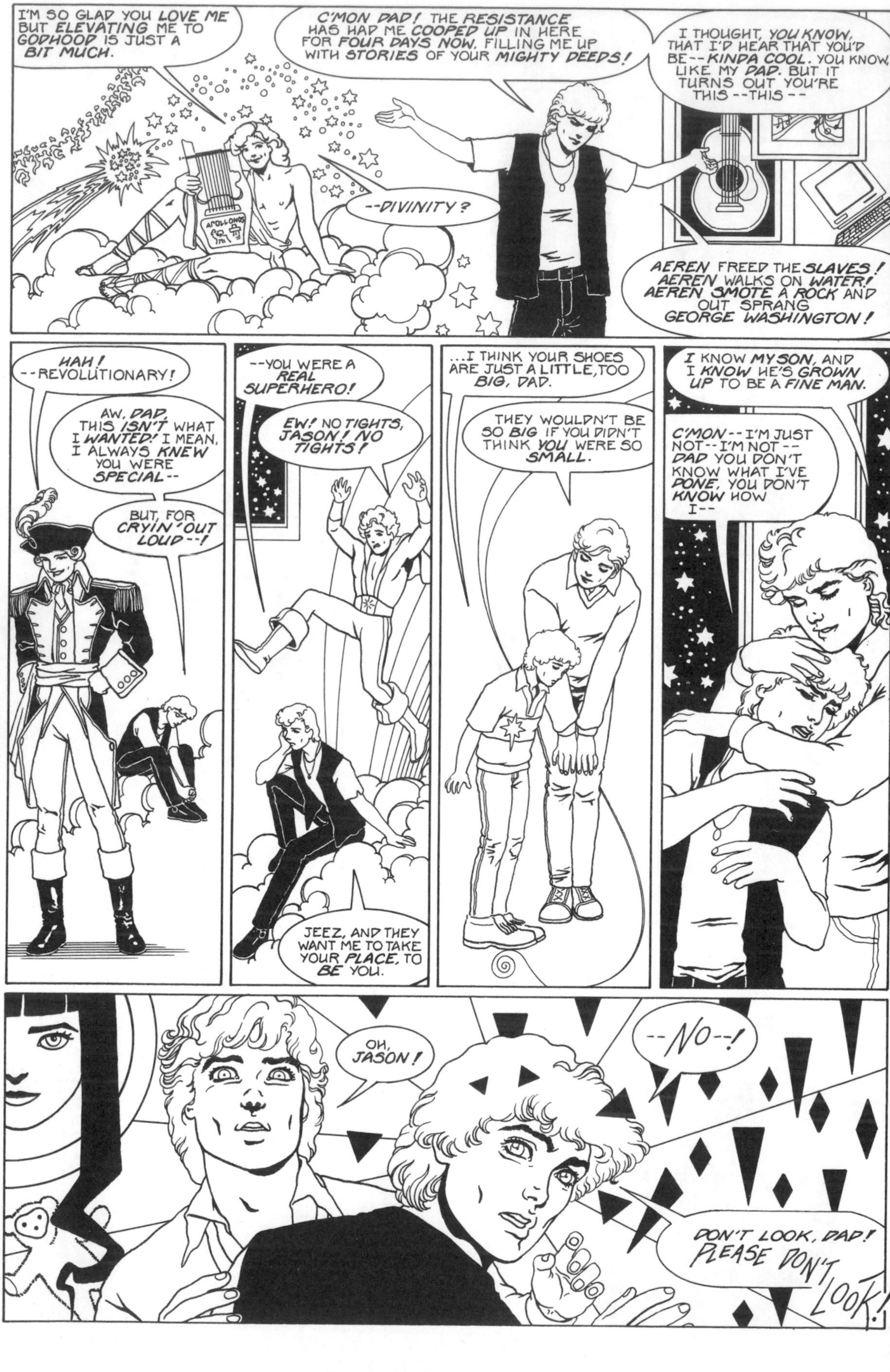
I'M SO GLAD YOU LOVE ME BUT ELEVATING ME TO GODHOOD IS JUST A BIT MUCH.
--DIVINITY?
C'MON DAD! THE RESISTANCE HAS HAD ME COOPED UP IN HERE FOR FOUR DAYS NOW, FILLING ME UP WITH STORIES OF YOUR MIGHTY DEEDS!
I THOUGHT, YOU KNOW, THAT I'D HEAR THAT YOU'D BE--KINDA COOL. YOU KNOW, LIKE MY DAD. BUT IT TURNS OUT YOU'RE THIS--THIS--
AEREN FREED THE SLAVES! AEREN WALKS ON WATER! AEREN SMOTE A ROCK AND OUT SPRANG GEORGE WASHINGTON!
APOLLONOS
HAH! --REVOLUTIONARY!
AW, DAD, THIS ISN'T WHAT I WANTED! I MEAN, I ALWAYS KNEW YOU WERE SPECIAL--
BUT, FOR CRYIN' OUT LOUD--!
--YOU WERE A REAL SUPERHERO!
EW! NO TIGHTS, JASON! NO TIGHTS!
JEEZ, AND THEY WANT ME TO TAKE YOUR PLACE, TO BE YOU.
...I THINK YOUR SHOES ARE JUST A LITTLE, TOO BIG, DAD.
THEY WOULDN'T BE SO BIG IF YOU DIDN'T THINK YOU WERE SO SMALL.
I KNOW MY SON, AND I KNOW HE'S GROWN UP TO BE A FINE MAN.
C'MON--I'M JUST NOT--I'M NOT--DAD YOU DON'T KNOW WHAT I'VE DONE, YOU DON'T KNOW HOW I--
OH, JASON!
--NO--!
DON'T LOOK, DAD! PLEASE DON'T LOOK!

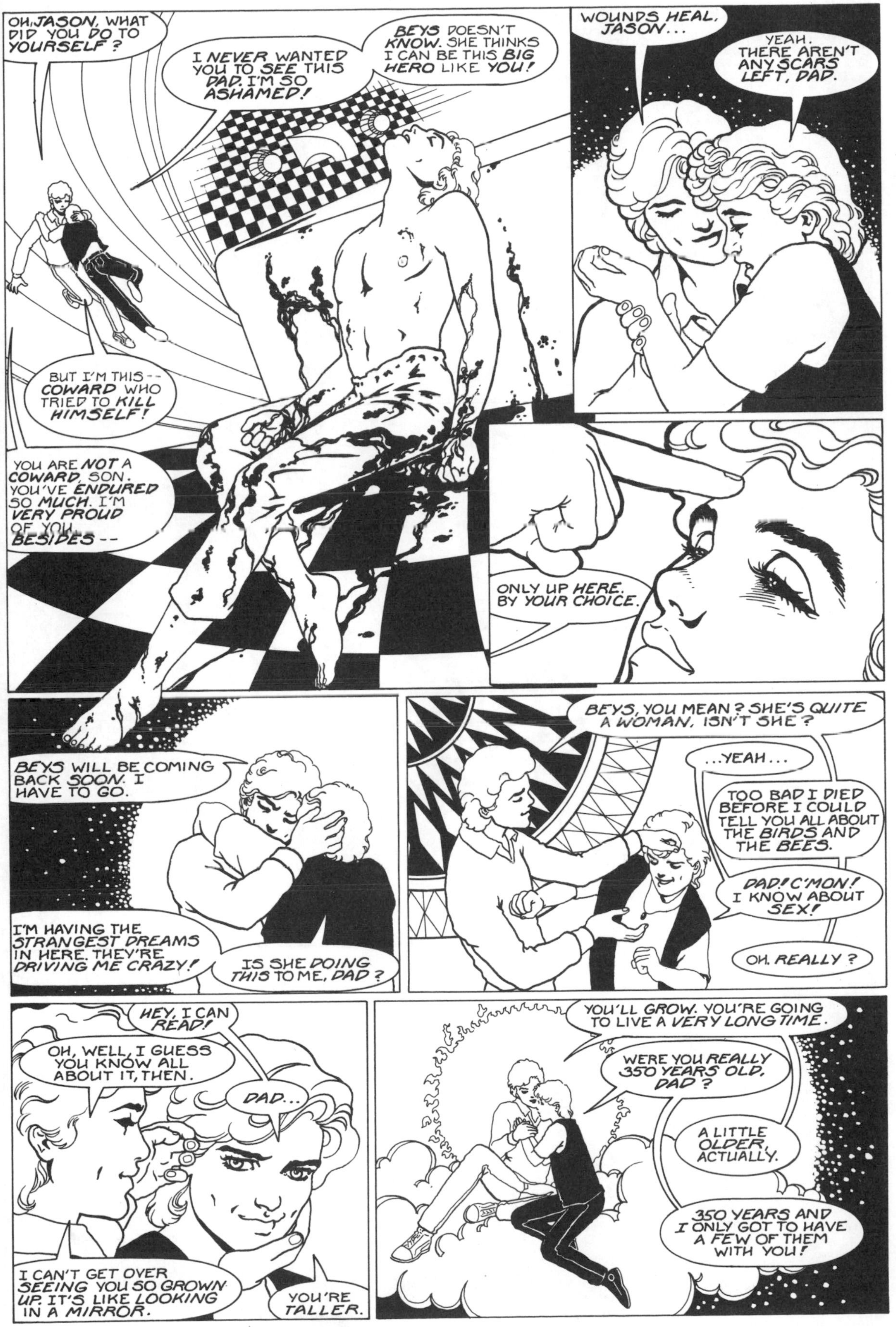
OH, JASON, WHAT DID YOU DO TO YOURSELF?
I NEVER WANTED YOU TO SEE THIS DAD. I'M SO ASHAMED!
BEYS DOESN'T KNOW. SHE THINKS I CAN BE THIS BIG HERO LIKE YOU!
BUT I'M THIS -- COWARD WHO TRIED TO KILL HIMSELF!
YOU ARE NOT A COWARD, SON. YOU'VE ENDURED SO MUCH. I'M VERY PROUD OF YOU. BESIDES --
WOUNDS HEAL, JASON...
YEAH. THERE AREN'T ANY SCARS LEFT, DAD.
ONLY UP HERE. BY YOUR CHOICE.
BEYS WILL BE COMING BACK SOON. I HAVE TO GO.
I'M HAVING THE STRANGEST DREAMS IN HERE. THEY'RE DRIVING ME CRAZY!
IS SHE DOING THIS TO ME, DAD?
BEYS, YOU MEAN? SHE'S QUITE A WOMAN, ISN'T SHE?
...YEAH...
TOO BAD I DIED BEFORE I COULD TELL YOU ALL ABOUT THE BIRDS AND THE BEES.
DAD! C'MON! I KNOW ABOUT SEX!
OH, REALLY?
OH, WELL, I GUESS YOU KNOW ALL ABOUT IT, THEN.
HEY, I CAN READ!
DAD...
I CAN'T GET OVER SEEING YOU SO GROWN-UP. IT'S LIKE LOOKING IN A MIRROR.
YOU'RE TALLER.
YOU'LL GROW. YOU'RE GOING TO LIVE A VERY LONG TIME.
WERE YOU REALLY 350 YEARS OLD, DAD?
A LITTLE OLDER, ACTUALLY.
350 YEARS AND I ONLY GOT TO HAVE A FEW OF THEM WITH YOU!

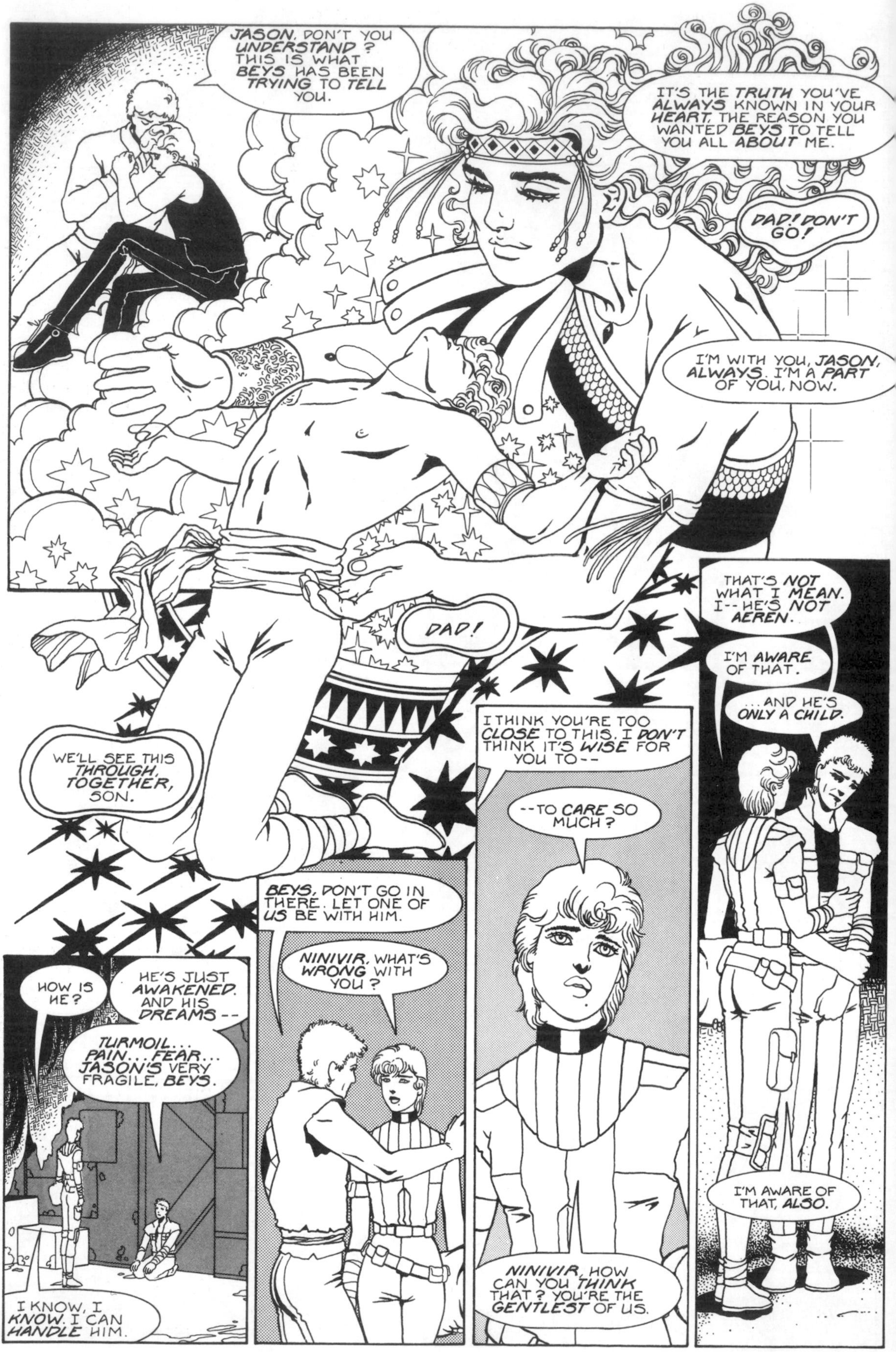
JASON, DON'T YOU UNDERSTAND? THIS IS WHAT BEYS HAS BEEN TRYING TO TELL YOU.
IT'S THE TRUTH YOU'VE ALWAYS KNOWN IN YOUR HEART, THE REASON YOU WANTED BEYS TO TELL YOU ALL ABOUT ME.
DAD! DON'T GO!
I'M WITH YOU, JASON, ALWAYS. I'M A PART OF YOU, NOW.
DAD!
WE'LL SEE THIS THROUGH, TOGETHER, SON.
HOW IS HE?
HE'S JUST AWAKENED. AND HIS DREAMS --
TURMOIL... PAIN... FEAR... JASON'S VERY FRAGILE, BEYS.
I KNOW, I KNOW. I CAN HANDLE HIM.
BEYS, DON'T GO IN THERE. LET ONE OF US BE WITH HIM.
NINIVIR, WHAT'S WRONG WITH YOU?
I THINK YOU'RE TOO CLOSE TO THIS. I DON'T THINK IT'S WISE FOR YOU TO --
--TO CARE SO MUCH?
NINIVIR, HOW CAN YOU THINK THAT? YOU'RE THE GENTLEST OF US.
THAT'S NOT WHAT I MEAN. I-- HE'S NOT AEREN.
I'M AWARE OF THAT.
...AND HE'S ONLY A CHILD.
I'M AWARE OF THAT, ALSO.

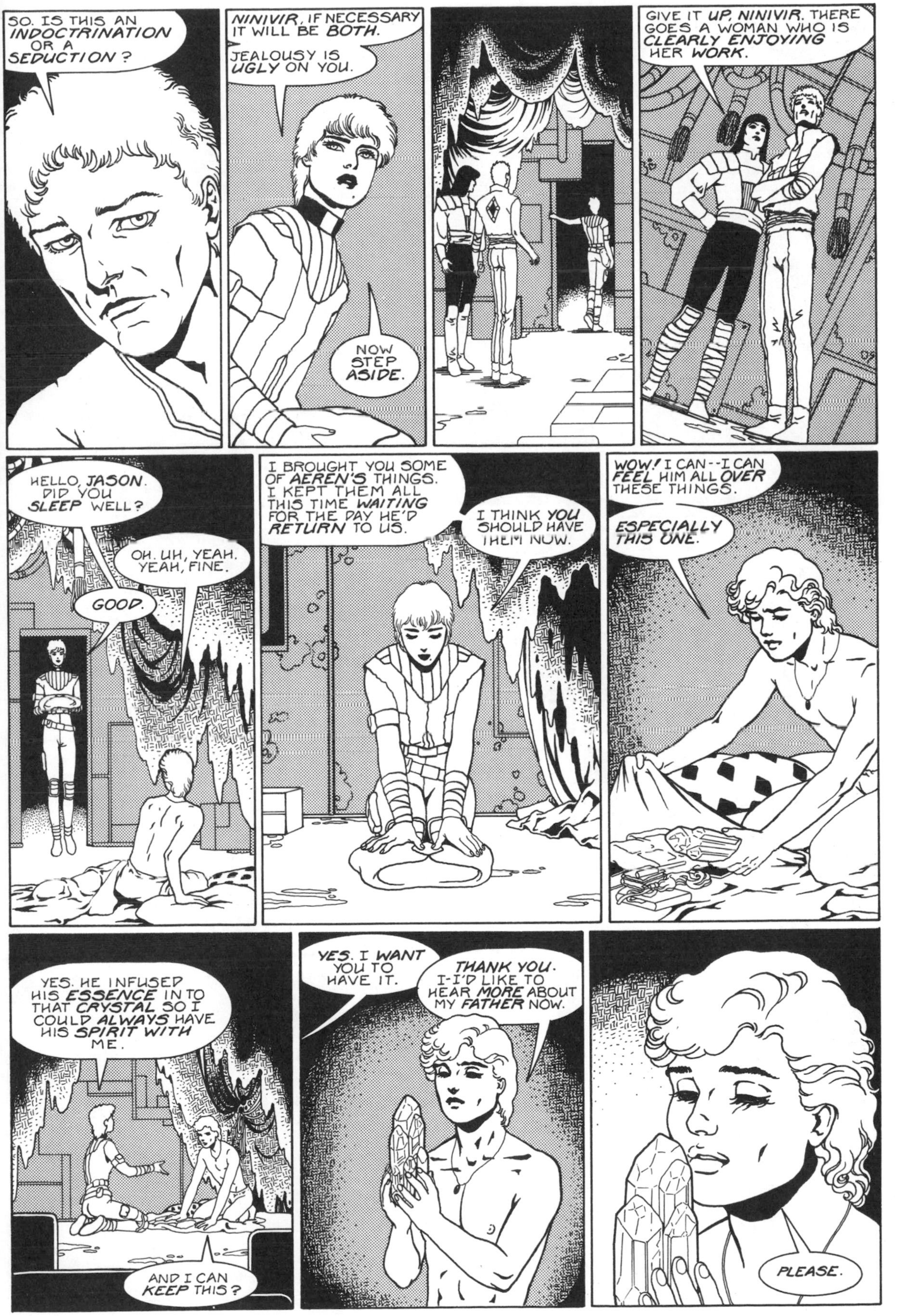
SO. IS THIS AN INDOCTRINATION OR A SEDUCTION?
NINIVIR, IF NECESSARY IT WILL BE BOTH.
JEALOUSY IS UGLY ON YOU.
NOW STEP ASIDE.
GIVE IT UP, NINIVIR. THERE GOES A WOMAN WHO IS CLEARLY ENJOYING HER WORK.
HELLO, JASON. DID YOU SLEEP WELL?
OH. UH, YEAH. YEAH, FINE.
GOOD.
I BROUGHT YOU SOME OF AEREN'S THINGS. I KEPT THEM ALL THIS TIME WAITING FOR THE DAY HE'D RETURN TO US.
I THINK YOU SHOULD HAVE THEM NOW.
WOW! I CAN--I CAN FEEL HIM ALL OVER THESE THINGS.
ESPECIALLY THIS ONE.
YES. HE INFUSED HIS ESSENCE IN TO THAT CRYSTAL SO I COULD ALWAYS HAVE HIS SPIRIT WITH ME.
AND I CAN KEEP THIS?
YES. I WANT YOU TO HAVE IT.
THANK YOU. I-I'D LIKE TO HEAR MORE ABOUT MY FATHER NOW.
PLEASE.

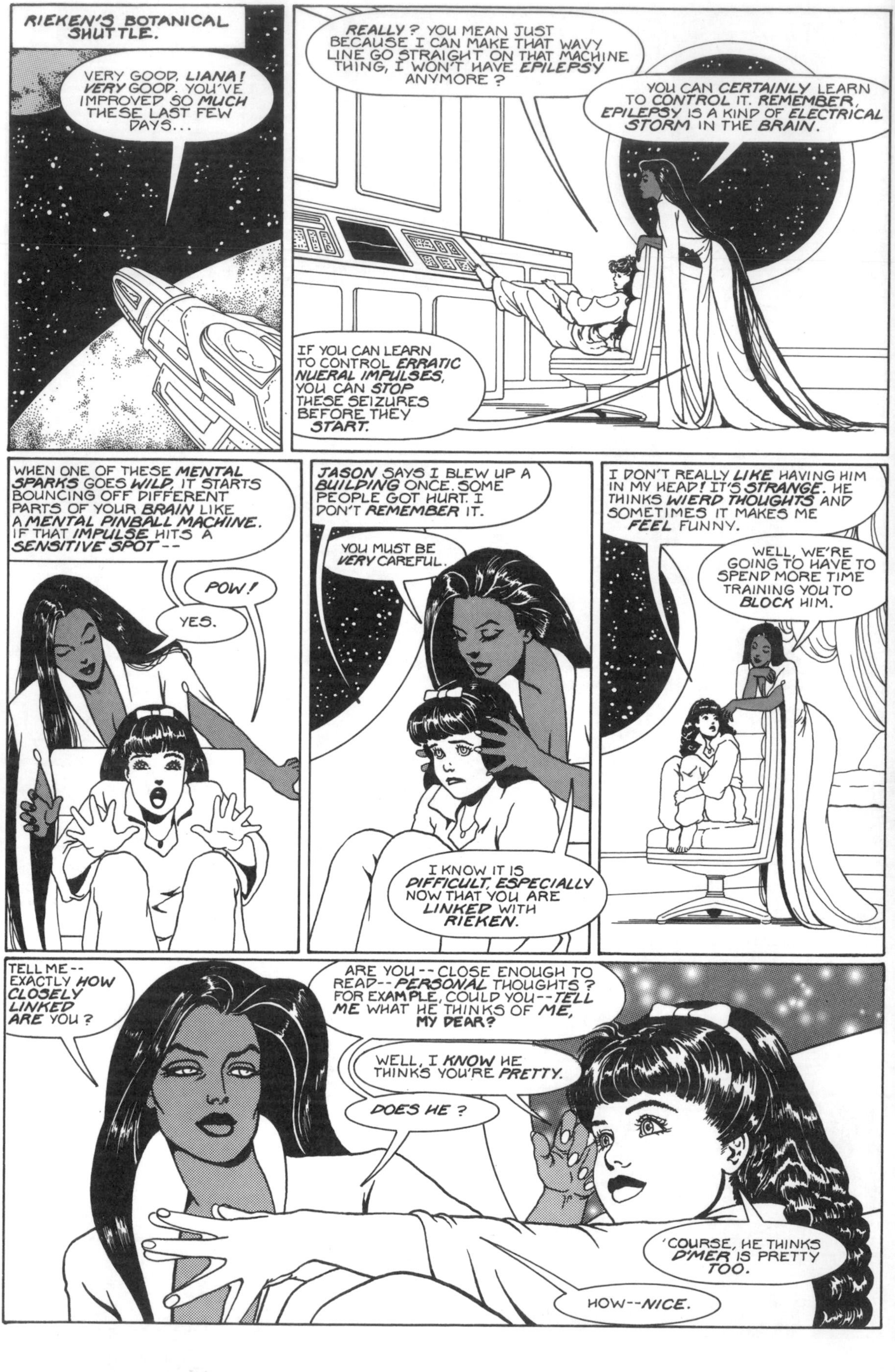

RIEKEN'S BOTANICAL SHUTTLE.
VERY GOOD, LIANA! VERY GOOD. YOU'VE IMPROVED SO MUCH THESE LAST FEW DAYS...
REALLY? YOU MEAN JUST BECAUSE I CAN MAKE THAT WAVY LINE GO STRAIGHT ON THAT MACHINE THING, I WON'T HAVE EPILEPSY ANYMORE?
YOU CAN CERTAINLY LEARN TO CONTROL IT. REMEMBER, EPILEPSY IS A KIND OF ELECTRICAL STORM IN THE BRAIN.
IF YOU CAN LEARN TO CONTROL ERRATIC NUERAL IMPULSES, YOU CAN STOP THESE SEIZURES BEFORE THEY START.
WHEN ONE OF THESE MENTAL SPARKS GOES WILD, IT STARTS BOUNCING OFF DIFFERENT PARTS OF YOUR BRAIN LIKE A MENTAL PINBALL MACHINE. IF THAT IMPULSE HITS A SENSITIVE SPOT--
POW!
YES.
JASON SAYS I BLEW UP A BUILDING ONCE. SOME PEOPLE GOT HURT. I DON'T REMEMBER IT.
YOU MUST BE VERY CAREFUL.
I KNOW IT IS DIFFICULT, ESPECIALLY NOW THAT YOU ARE LINKED WITH RIEKEN.
I DON'T REALLY LIKE HAVING HIM IN MY HEAD! IT'S STRANGE. HE THINKS WIERD THOUGHTS AND SOMETIMES IT MAKES ME FEEL FUNNY.
WELL, WE'RE GOING TO HAVE TO SPEND MORE TIME TRAINING YOU TO BLOCK HIM.
TELL ME-- EXACTLY HOW CLOSELY LINKED ARE YOU?
ARE YOU--CLOSE ENOUGH TO READ--PERSONAL THOUGHTS? FOR EXAMPLE, COULD YOU--TELL ME WHAT HE THINKS OF ME, MY DEAR?
WELL, I KNOW HE THINKS YOU'RE PRETTY.
DOES HE?
'COURSE, HE THINKS D'MER IS PRETTY TOO.
HOW--NICE.

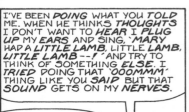

I'VE BEEN *DOING* WHAT YOU *TOLD* ME. WHEN HE THINKS *THOUGHTS* I DON'T WANT TO *HEAR* I *PLUG UP* MY *EARS* AND SING, `MARY HAD A *LITTLE LAMB,* LITTLE *LAMB, LITTLE LAMB--!*` AND TRY TO THINK OF SOMETHING *ELSE.* I *TRIED* DOING THAT `OOOMMM` THING LIKE YOU *SAID* BUT THAT *SOUND* GETS ON MY *NERVES.*

WHATEVER WORKS FOR *YOU,* LIANA.

HELLO, *LADY BAST.* HELLO, *LIANA.*

MY LORD *SEREN--* I MEAN, *RIEKEN* OF COURSE.

YES, *PLEASE* CALL ME *RIEKEN.*

HEY *YOU!* *LOOKIT!* I CAN MAKE THE *LINE* GO *FLAT.*

THAT'S *WONDERFUL!* YOU'RE *VERY* CLEVER!

THANK YOU FOR THESE *ROBES, RIEKEN.* THIS *SILK* FEELS *MARVELOUS.*

OH, UH, YOU'RE *WELCOME.* HOW *LOVELY* YOU LOOK IN THEM! THEY'RE SO MUCH MORE *FLATTERING* ON *YOU* THAN THEY *EVER* WERE ON *ME.*

BUT SUCH *BEAUTY* AS *YOURS* NEEDS NO *ADORNMENT, FAIR LORD.*

LADY, I--

MARY HAD A LITTLE LAMB! LITTLE LAMB! LITTLE LAMB!

WHAT--ARE YOU *DOING.*?

I'M *LEAVING!* AND *STOP THINKING THOSE THOUGHTS!*

WHY, I *DON'T* KNOW WHAT YOU-- I *DON'T*-- I MEAN, I *NEVER* I--I'M *SURE* I *DON'T* KNOW WHAT YOU MEAN--!

OH *NO.* OF *COURSE* NOT, MY LORD.

I-I *SUPPOSE* I SHOULD BE HELPING *D'MER* TRAIN THE *HUMANS.*

D'MER CAN *HANDLE* THEM *HIMSELF,* I'M *SURE.*

I *DO ENVY* YOUR *LOVER.*

WHAT?!? WHO DO YOU *MEAN*?

DON'T BE *COY.* YOU HAVE *NOT* BEEN *DISCREET. D'MER'S DEVOTION* TO YOU IS QUITE *PLAIN.* BUT, I *SUSPECT MISCEGENATION* IS *STILL ILLEGAL* ON *OVANAN.*

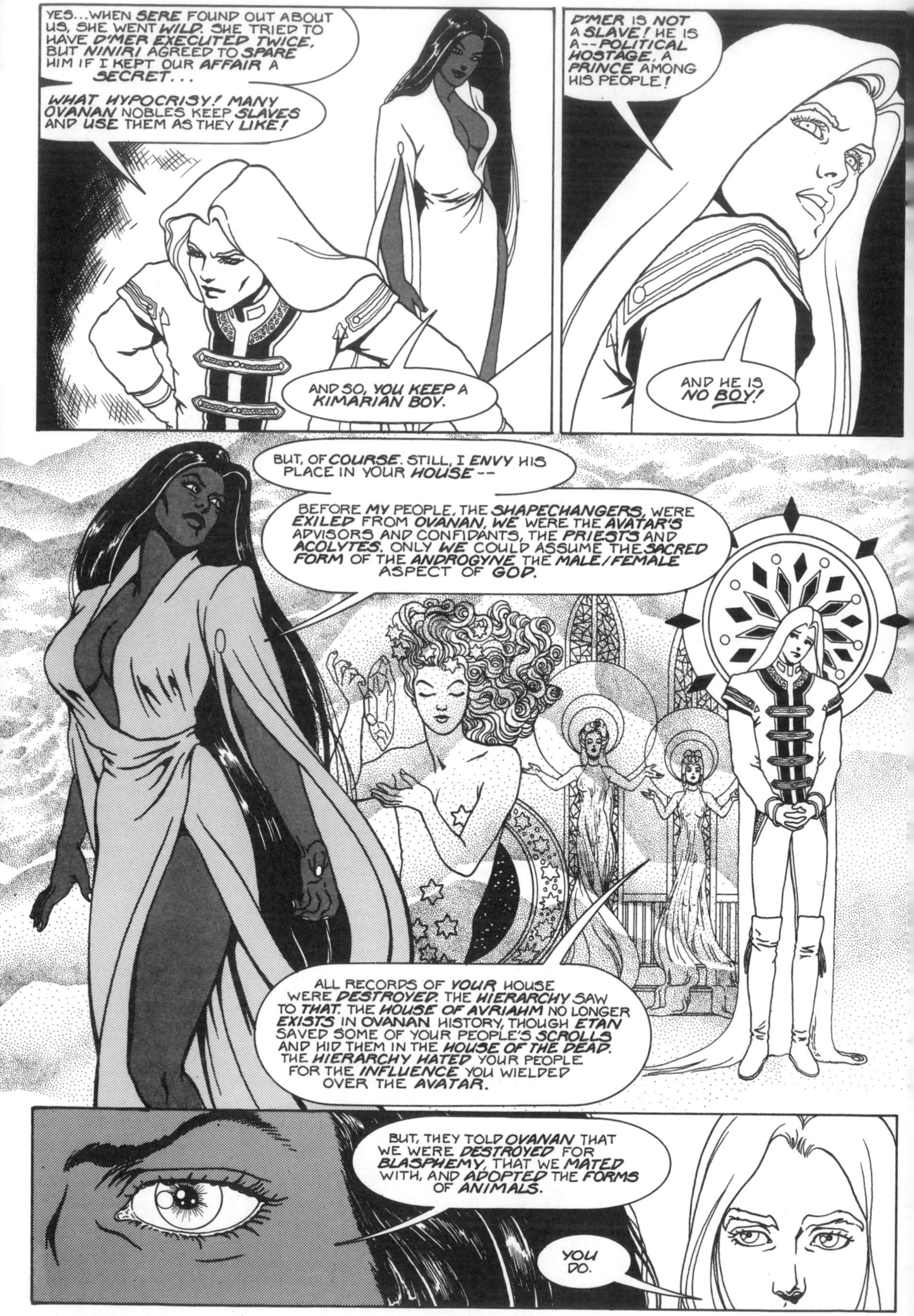

YES...WHEN SERE FOUND OUT ABOUT US, SHE WENT WILD. SHE TRIED TO HAVE D'MER EXECUTED TWICE, BUT NINIRI AGREED TO SPARE HIM IF I KEPT OUR AFFAIR A SECRET...
WHAT HYPOCRISY! MANY OVANAN NOBLES KEEP SLAVES AND USE THEM AS THEY LIKE!
AND SO, YOU KEEP A KIMARIAN BOY.
D'MER IS NOT A SLAVE! HE IS A--POLITICAL HOSTAGE, A PRINCE AMONG HIS PEOPLE!
AND HE IS NO BOY!
BUT, OF COURSE. STILL, I ENVY HIS PLACE IN YOUR HOUSE--
BEFORE MY PEOPLE, THE SHAPECHANGERS, WERE EXILED FROM OVANAN, WE WERE THE AVATAR'S ADVISORS AND CONFIDANTS, THE PRIESTS AND ACOLYTES. ONLY WE COULD ASSUME THE SACRED FORM OF THE ANDROGYNE THE MALE/FEMALE ASPECT OF GOD.
ALL RECORDS OF YOUR HOUSE WERE DESTROYED. THE HIERARCHY SAW TO THAT. THE HOUSE OF AVRIAHM NO LONGER EXISTS IN OVANAN HISTORY, THOUGH ETAN SAVED SOME OF YOUR PEOPLE'S SCROLLS AND HID THEM IN THE HOUSE OF THE DEAD. THE HIERARCHY HATED YOUR PEOPLE FOR THE INFLUENCE YOU WIELDED OVER THE AVATAR.
BUT, THEY TOLD OVANAN THAT WE WERE DESTROYED FOR BLASPHEMY, THAT WE MATED WITH, AND ADOPTED THE FORMS OF ANIMALS.
YOU DO.

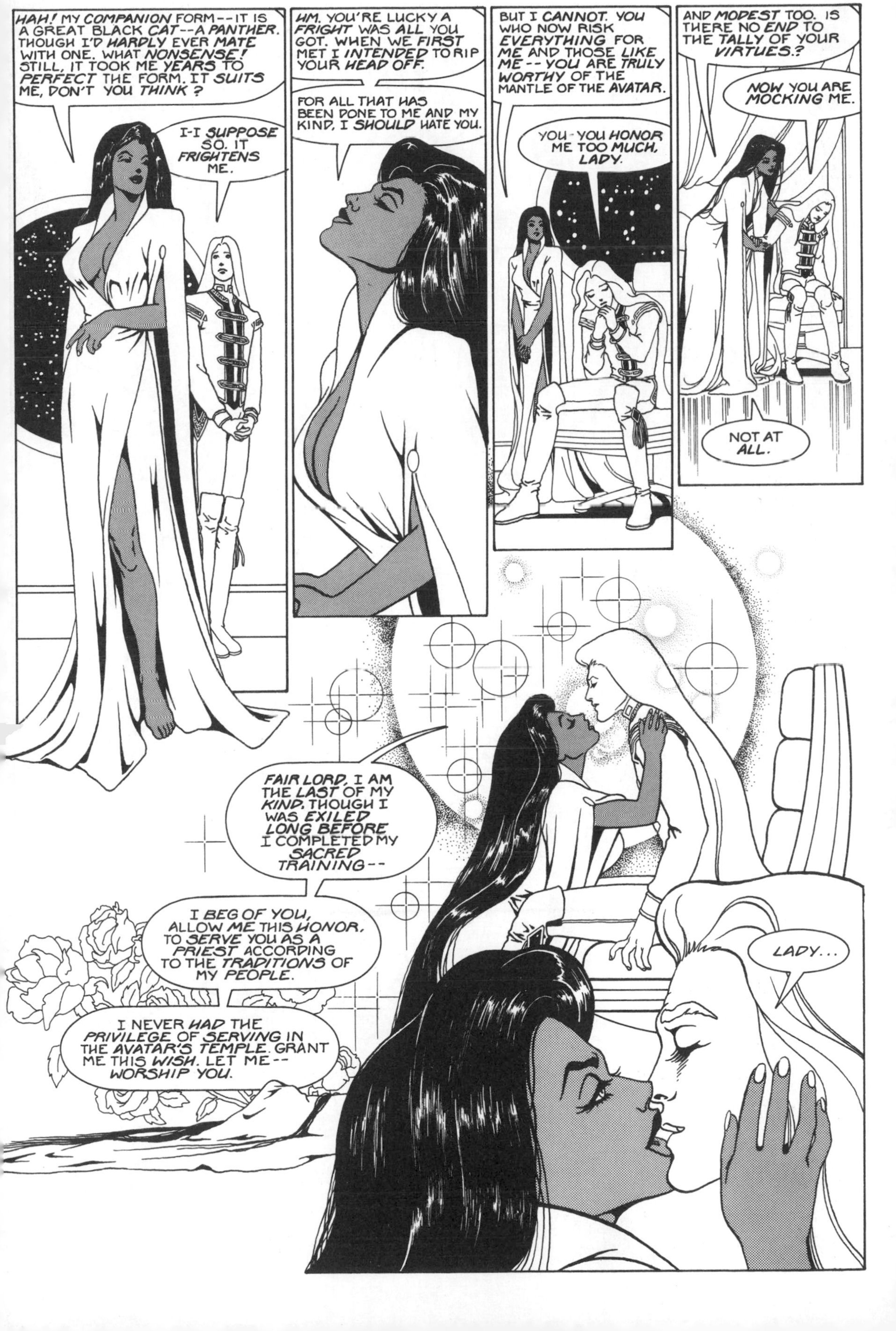
HAH! MY COMPANION FORM--IT IS A GREAT BLACK CAT--A PANTHER. THOUGH I'D HARDLY EVER MATE WITH ONE. WHAT NONSENSE! STILL, IT TOOK ME YEARS TO PERFECT THE FORM. IT SUITS ME, DON'T YOU THINK?
I-I SUPPOSE SO. IT FRIGHTENS ME.
HM. YOU'RE LUCKY A FRIGHT WAS ALL YOU GOT. WHEN WE FIRST MET I INTENDED TO RIP YOUR HEAD OFF.
FOR ALL THAT HAS BEEN DONE TO ME AND MY KIND, I SHOULD HATE YOU.
BUT I CANNOT. YOU WHO NOW RISK EVERYTHING FOR ME AND THOSE LIKE ME--YOU ARE TRULY WORTHY OF THE MANTLE OF THE AVATAR.
YOU-YOU HONOR ME TOO MUCH, LADY.
AND MODEST TOO. IS THERE NO END TO THE TALLY OF YOUR VIRTUES.?
NOW YOU ARE MOCKING ME.
NOT AT ALL.
FAIR LORD, I AM THE LAST OF MY KIND. THOUGH I WAS EXILED LONG BEFORE I COMPLETED MY SACRED TRAINING--
I BEG OF YOU, ALLOW ME THIS HONOR, TO SERVE YOU AS A PRIEST ACCORDING TO THE TRADITIONS OF MY PEOPLE.
I NEVER HAD THE PRIVILEGE OF SERVING IN THE AVATAR'S TEMPLE. GRANT ME THIS WISH. LET ME--WORSHIP YOU.
LADY...

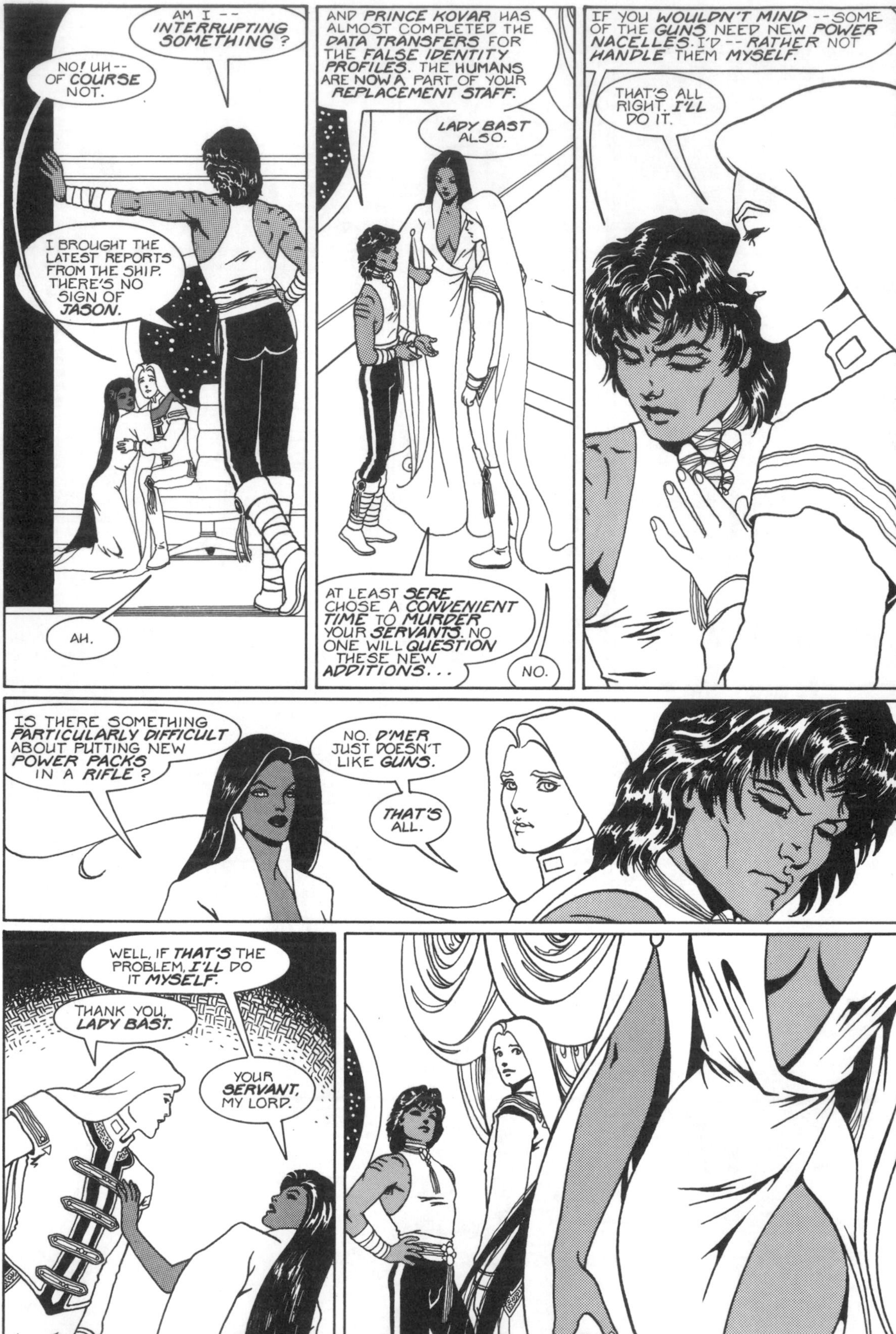

AM I -- INTERRUPTING SOMETHING?
NO! UH -- OF COURSE NOT.
I BROUGHT THE LATEST REPORTS FROM THE SHIP. THERE'S NO SIGN OF JASON.
AH.
AND PRINCE KOVAR HAS ALMOST COMPLETED THE DATA TRANSFERS FOR THE FALSE IDENTITY PROFILES. THE HUMANS ARE NOW A PART OF YOUR REPLACEMENT STAFF.
LADY BAST ALSO.
AT LEAST SERE CHOSE A CONVENIENT TIME TO MURDER YOUR SERVANTS. NO ONE WILL QUESTION THESE NEW ADDITIONS...
NO.
IF YOU WOULDN'T MIND -- SOME OF THE GUNS NEED NEW POWER NACELLES. I'D -- RATHER NOT HANDLE THEM MYSELF.
THAT'S ALL RIGHT. I'LL DO IT.
IS THERE SOMETHING PARTICULARLY DIFFICULT ABOUT PUTTING NEW POWER PACKS IN A RIFLE?
NO. D'MER JUST DOESN'T LIKE GUNS.
THAT'S ALL.
WELL, IF THAT'S THE PROBLEM, I'LL DO IT MYSELF.
THANK YOU, LADY BAST.
YOUR SERVANT, MY LORD.

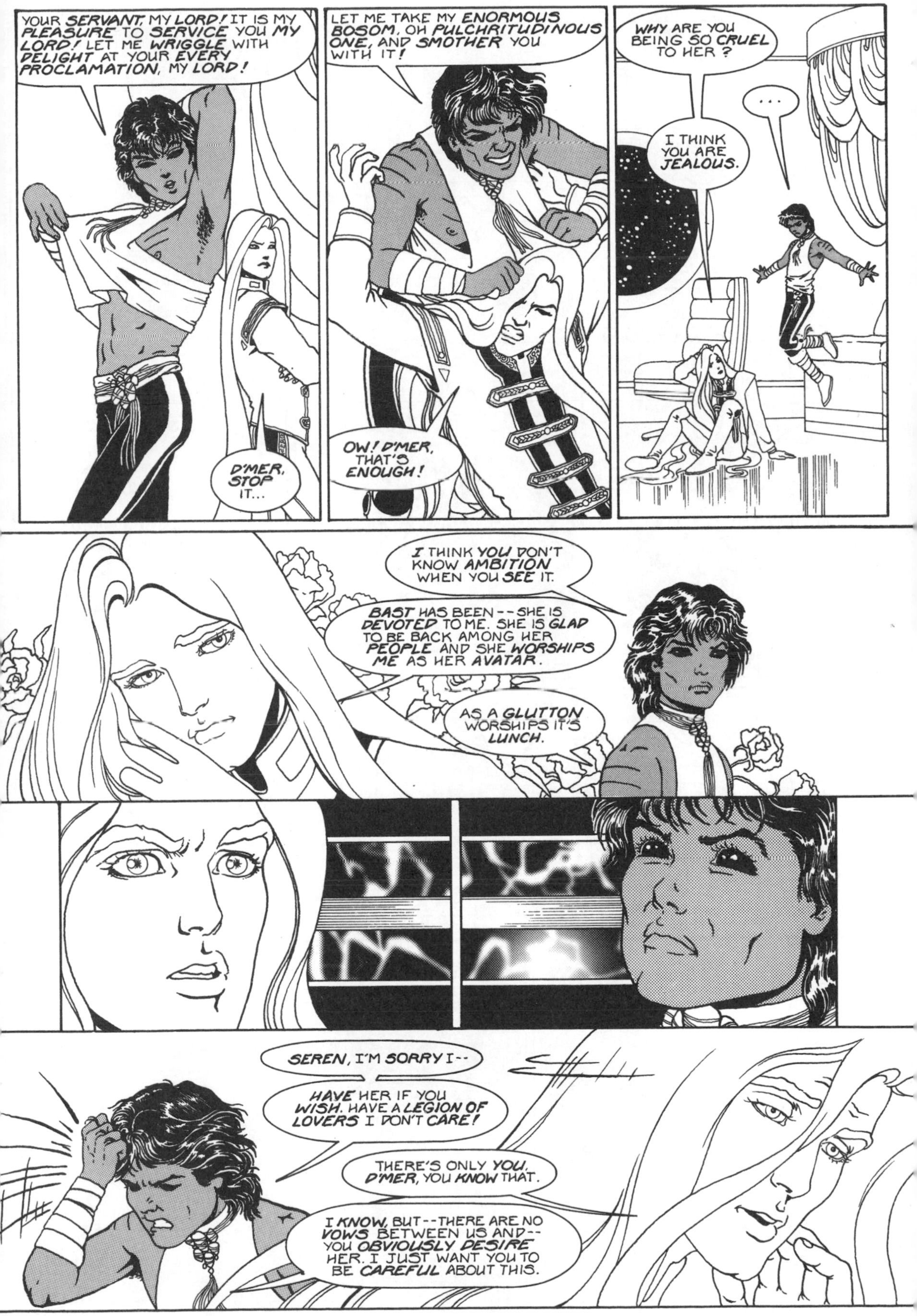
YOUR SERVANT, MY LORD! IT IS MY PLEASURE TO SERVICE YOU MY LORD! LET ME WRIGGLE WITH DELIGHT AT YOUR EVERY PROCLAMATION, MY LORD!
D'MER, STOP IT...
LET ME TAKE MY ENORMOUS BOSOM, OH PULCHRITUDINOUS ONE, AND SMOTHER YOU WITH IT!
OW! D'MER, THAT'S ENOUGH!
WHY ARE YOU BEING SO CRUEL TO HER?
...
I THINK YOU ARE JEALOUS.
I THINK YOU DON'T KNOW AMBITION WHEN YOU SEE IT.
BAST HAS BEEN--SHE IS DEVOTED TO ME. SHE IS GLAD TO BE BACK AMONG HER PEOPLE AND SHE WORSHIPS ME AS HER AVATAR.
AS A GLUTTON WORSHIPS IT'S LUNCH.
SEREN, I'M SORRY I--
HAVE HER IF YOU WISH. HAVE A LEGION OF LOVERS I DON'T CARE!
THERE'S ONLY YOU, D'MER, YOU KNOW THAT.
I KNOW, BUT--THERE ARE NO VOWS BETWEEN US AND--YOU OBVIOUSLY DESIRE HER. I JUST WANT YOU TO BE CAREFUL ABOUT THIS.

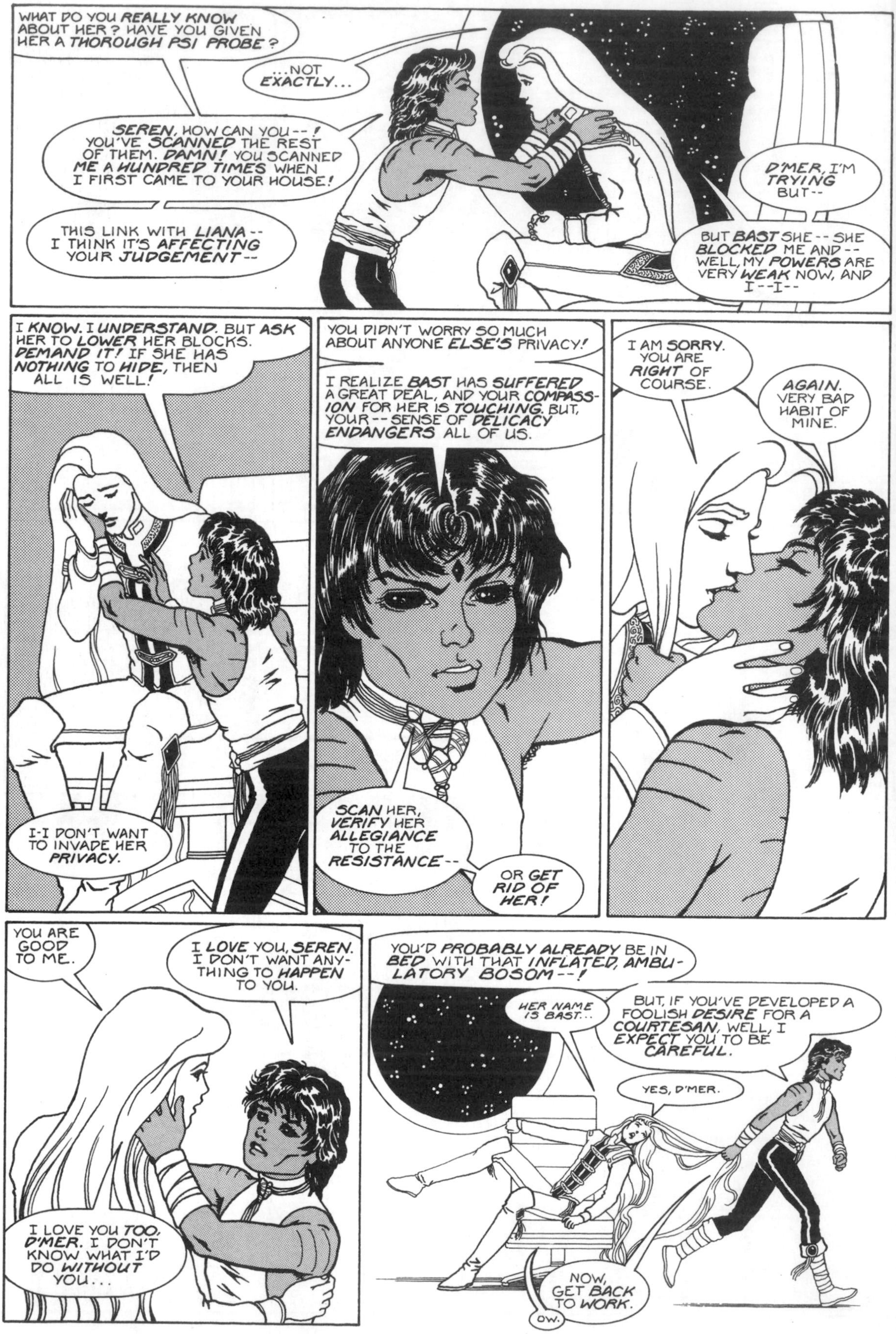
WHAT DO YOU REALLY KNOW ABOUT HER? HAVE YOU GIVEN HER A THOROUGH PSI PROBE?
...NOT EXACTLY...
SEREN, HOW CAN YOU--! YOU'VE SCANNED THE REST OF THEM. DAMN! YOU SCANNED ME A HUNDRED TIMES WHEN I FIRST CAME TO YOUR HOUSE!
THIS LINK WITH LIANA-- I THINK IT'S AFFECTING YOUR JUDGEMENT--
D'MER, I'M TRYING BUT--
BUT BAST SHE--SHE BLOCKED ME AND--WELL, MY POWERS ARE VERY WEAK NOW, AND I--I--
I KNOW. I UNDERSTAND. BUT ASK HER TO LOWER HER BLOCKS. DEMAND IT! IF SHE HAS NOTHING TO HIDE, THEN ALL IS WELL!
I-I DON'T WANT TO INVADE HER PRIVACY.
YOU DIDN'T WORRY SO MUCH ABOUT ANYONE ELSE'S PRIVACY!
I REALIZE BAST HAS SUFFERED A GREAT DEAL, AND YOUR COMPASS-ION FOR HER IS TOUCHING. BUT, YOUR--SENSE OF DELICACY ENDANGERS ALL OF US.
SCAN HER, VERIFY HER ALLEGIANCE TO THE RESISTANCE--
OR GET RID OF HER!
I AM SORRY. YOU ARE RIGHT OF COURSE.
AGAIN. VERY BAD HABIT OF MINE.
YOU ARE GOOD TO ME.
I LOVE YOU, SEREN. I DON'T WANT ANY-THING TO HAPPEN TO YOU.
I LOVE YOU TOO, D'MER. I DON'T KNOW WHAT I'D DO WITHOUT YOU...
YOU'D PROBABLY ALREADY BE IN BED WITH THAT INFLATED, AMBU-LATORY BOSOM--!
HER NAME IS BAST...
BUT, IF YOU'VE DEVELOPED A FOOLISH DESIRE FOR A COURTESAN, WELL, I EXPECT YOU TO BE CAREFUL.
YES, D'MER.
NOW, GET BACK TO WORK.
OW.

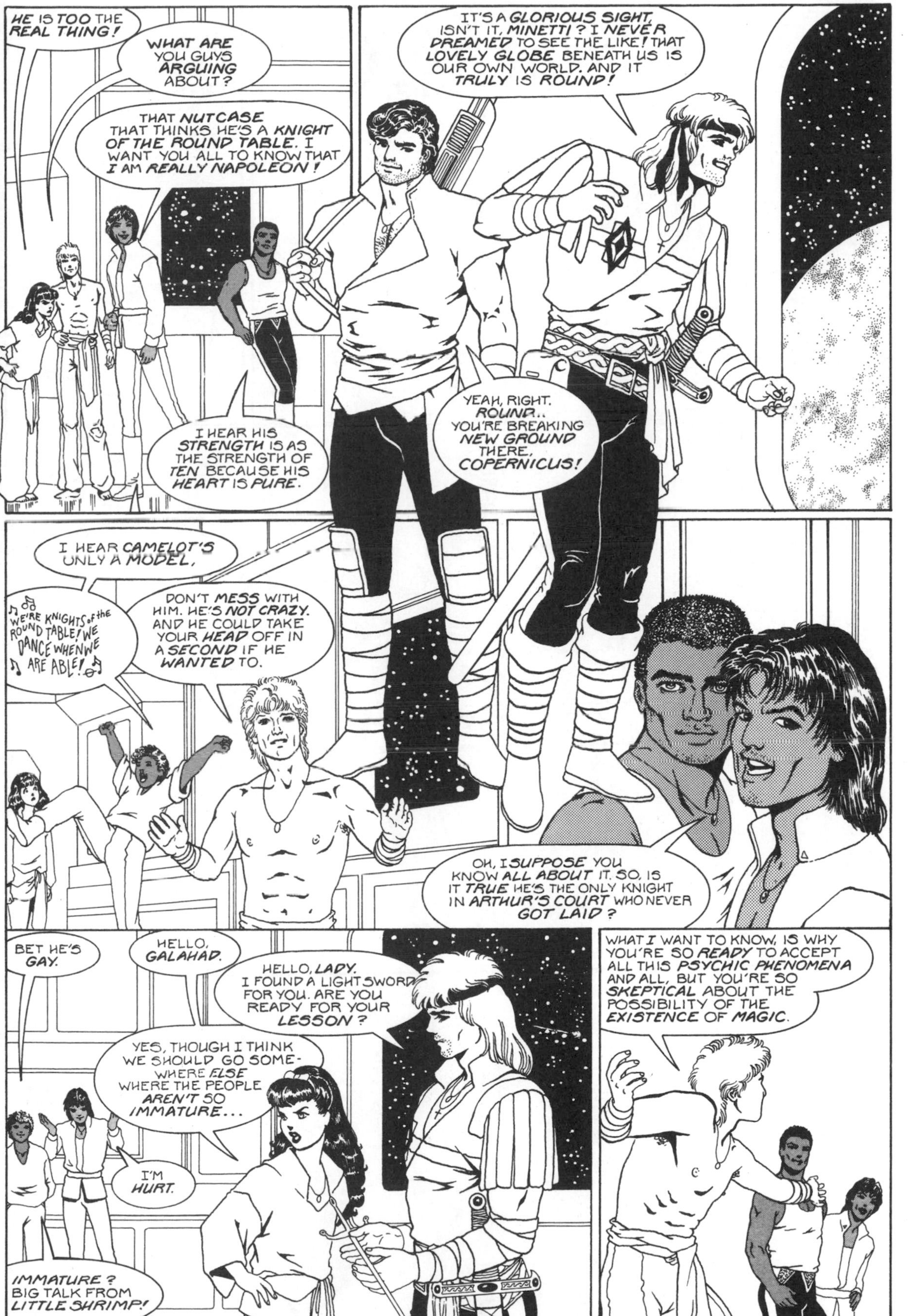
HE IS TOO THE REAL THING!
WHAT ARE YOU GUYS ARGUING ABOUT?
THAT NUTCASE THAT THINKS HE'S A KNIGHT OF THE ROUND TABLE. I WANT YOU ALL TO KNOW THAT I AM REALLY NAPOLEON!
I HEAR HIS STRENGTH IS AS THE STRENGTH OF TEN BECAUSE HIS HEART IS PURE.
IT'S A GLORIOUS SIGHT, ISN'T IT, MINETTI? I NEVER DREAMED TO SEE THE LIKE! THAT LOVELY GLOBE BENEATH US IS OUR OWN WORLD. AND IT TRULY IS ROUND!
YEAH, RIGHT. ROUND.. YOU'RE BREAKING NEW GROUND THERE, COPERNICUS!
I HEAR CAMELOT'S ONLY A MODEL,
WE'RE KNIGHTS of the ROUND TABLE! WE DANCE WHENWE ARE ABLE!
DON'T MESS WITH HIM. HE'S NOT CRAZY. AND HE COULD TAKE YOUR HEAD OFF IN A SECOND IF HE WANTED TO.
OH, I SUPPOSE YOU KNOW ALL ABOUT IT. SO, IS IT TRUE HE'S THE ONLY KNIGHT IN ARTHUR'S COURT WHO NEVER GOT LAID?
BET HE'S GAY.
HELLO, GALAHAD.
HELLO, LADY. I FOUND A LIGHT SWORD FOR YOU. ARE YOU READY FOR YOUR LESSON?
YES, THOUGH I THINK WE SHOULD GO SOMEWHERE ELSE WHERE THE PEOPLE AREN'T SO IMMATURE...
I'M HURT.
IMMATURE? BIG TALK FROM LITTLE SHRIMP!
WHAT I WANT TO KNOW, IS WHY YOU'RE SO READY TO ACCEPT ALL THIS PSYCHIC PHENOMENA AND ALL, BUT YOU'RE SO SKEPTICAL ABOUT THE POSSIBILITY OF THE EXISTENCE OF MAGIC.

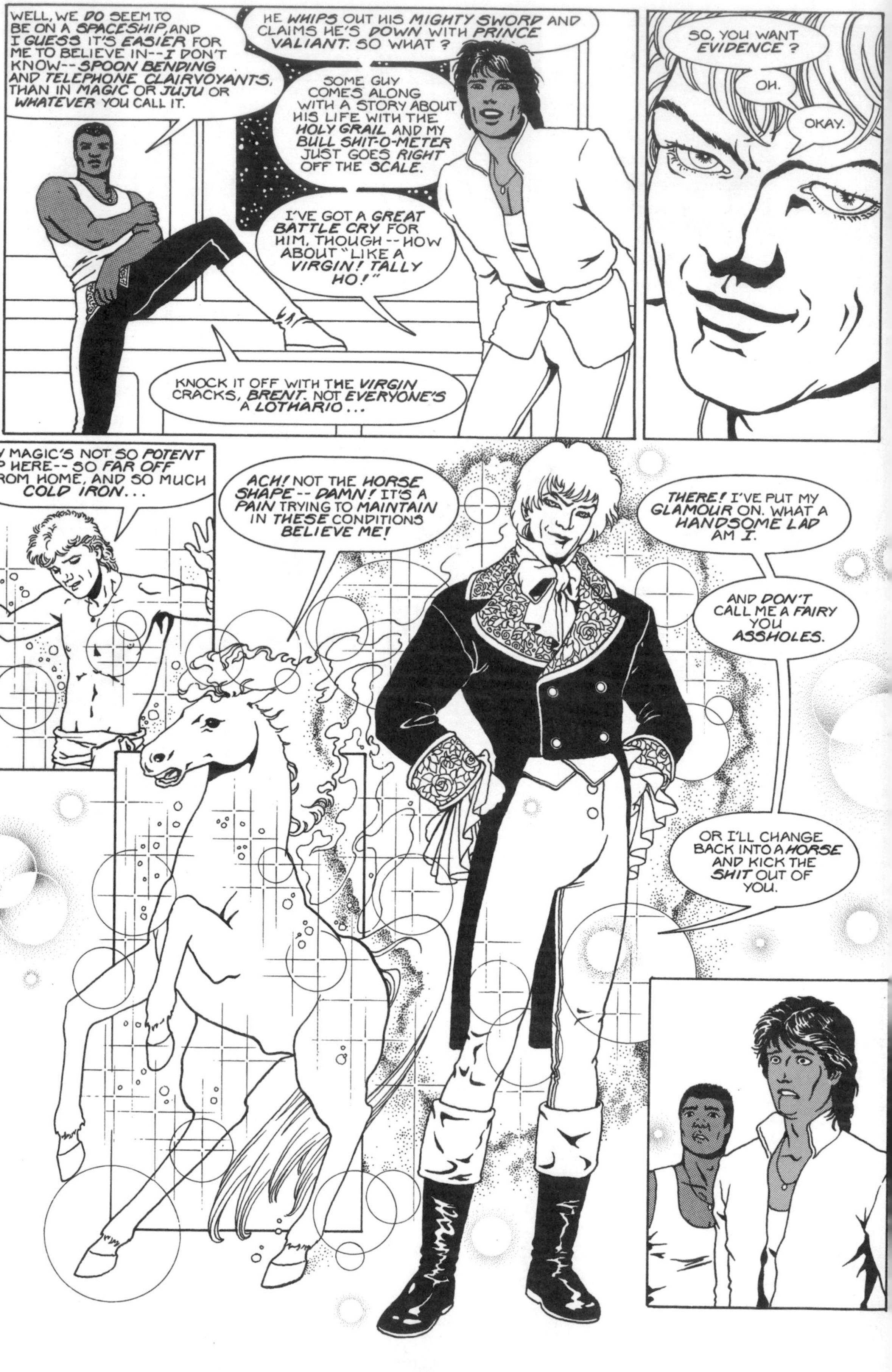
WELL, WE DO SEEM TO BE ON A SPACESHIP, AND I GUESS IT'S EASIER FOR ME TO BELIEVE IN--I DON'T KNOW--SPOON BENDING AND TELEPHONE CLAIRVOYANTS, THAN IN MAGIC OR JUJU OR WHATEVER YOU CALL IT.
HE WHIPS OUT HIS MIGHTY SWORD AND CLAIMS HE'S DOWN WITH PRINCE VALIANT. SO WHAT?
SOME GUY COMES ALONG WITH A STORY ABOUT HIS LIFE WITH THE HOLY GRAIL AND MY BULL SHIT-O-METER JUST GOES RIGHT OFF THE SCALE.
I'VE GOT A GREAT BATTLE CRY FOR HIM, THOUGH--HOW ABOUT "LIKE A VIRGIN! TALLY HO!"
KNOCK IT OFF WITH THE VIRGIN CRACKS, BRENT. NOT EVERYONE'S A LOTHARIO...
SO, YOU WANT EVIDENCE?
OH.
OKAY.
MY MAGIC'S NOT SO POTENT UP HERE--SO FAR OFF FROM HOME, AND SO MUCH COLD IRON...
ACH! NOT THE HORSE SHAPE--DAMN! IT'S A PAIN TRYING TO MAINTAIN IN THESE CONDITIONS BELIEVE ME!
THERE! I'VE PUT MY GLAMOUR ON. WHAT A HANDSOME LAD AM I.
AND DON'T CALL ME A FAIRY YOU ASSHOLES.
OR I'LL CHANGE BACK INTO A HORSE AND KICK THE SHIT OUT OF YOU.

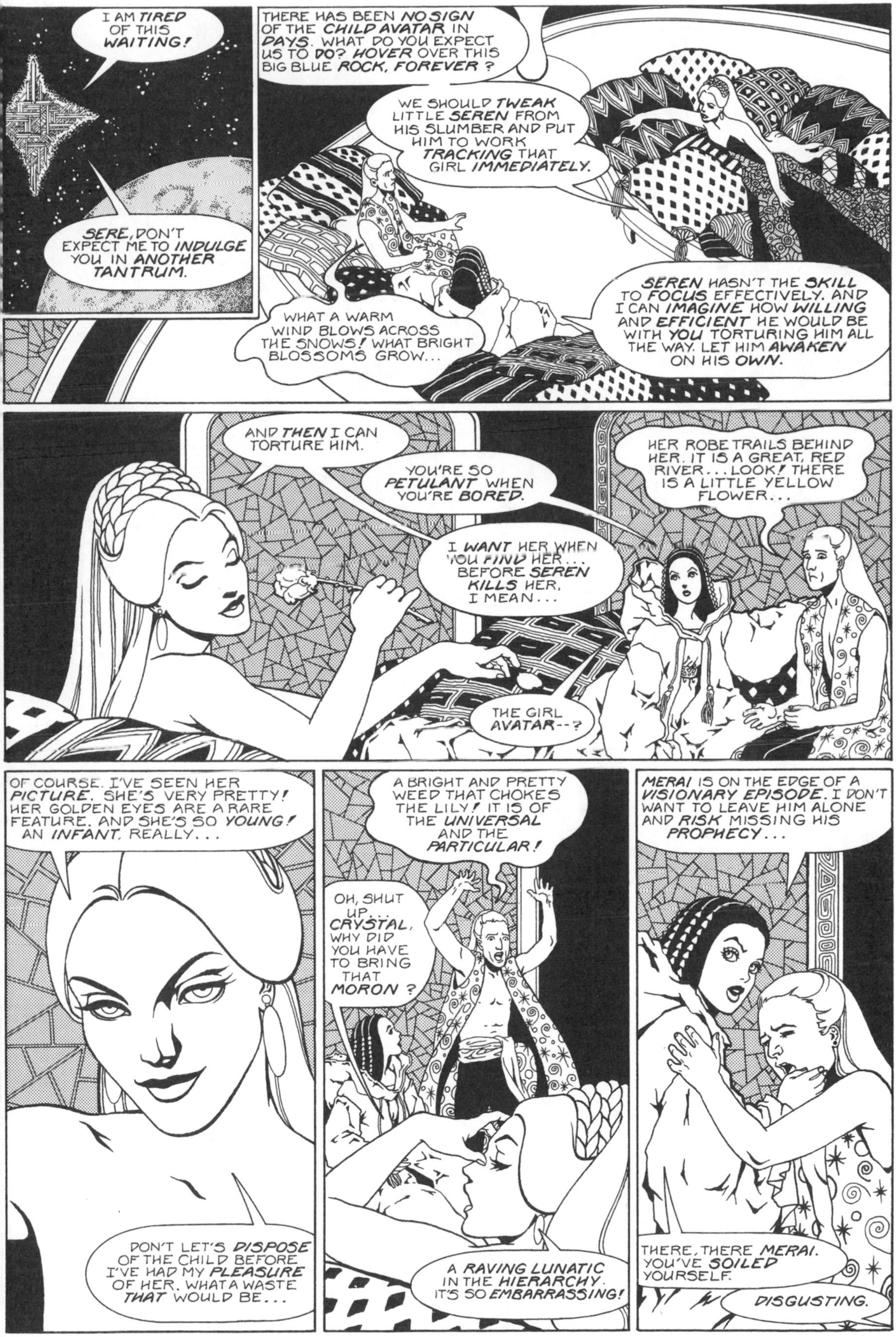
I AM TIRED OF THIS WAITING!
THERE HAS BEEN NO SIGN OF THE CHILD AVATAR IN DAYS. WHAT DO YOU EXPECT US TO DO? HOVER OVER THIS BIG BLUE ROCK, FOREVER?
WE SHOULD TWEAK LITTLE SEREN FROM HIS SLUMBER AND PUT HIM TO WORK TRACKING THAT GIRL IMMEDIATELY.
SERE, DON'T EXPECT ME TO INDULGE YOU IN ANOTHER TANTRUM.
WHAT A WARM WIND BLOWS ACROSS THE SNOWS! WHAT BRIGHT BLOSSOMS GROW...
SEREN HASN'T THE SKILL TO FOCUS EFFECTIVELY. AND I CAN IMAGINE HOW WILLING AND EFFICIENT HE WOULD BE WITH YOU TORTURING HIM ALL THE WAY. LET HIM AWAKEN ON HIS OWN.
AND THEN I CAN TORTURE HIM.
YOU'RE SO PETULANT WHEN YOU'RE BORED.
HER ROBE TRAILS BEHIND HER. IT IS A GREAT, RED RIVER... LOOK! THERE IS A LITTLE YELLOW FLOWER...
I WANT HER WHEN YOU FIND HER... BEFORE SEREN KILLS HER, I MEAN...
THE GIRL AVATAR--?
OF COURSE. I'VE SEEN HER PICTURE. SHE'S VERY PRETTY! HER GOLDEN EYES ARE A RARE FEATURE. AND SHE'S SO YOUNG! AN INFANT, REALLY...
DON'T LET'S DISPOSE OF THE CHILD BEFORE I'VE HAD MY PLEASURE OF HER. WHAT A WASTE THAT WOULD BE...
A BRIGHT AND PRETTY WEED THAT CHOKES THE LILY! IT IS OF THE UNIVERSAL AND THE PARTICULAR!
OH, SHUT UP... CRYSTAL, WHY DID YOU HAVE TO BRING THAT MORON?
A RAVING LUNATIC IN THE HIERARCHY. IT'S SO EMBARRASSING!
MERAI IS ON THE EDGE OF A VISIONARY EPISODE. I DON'T WANT TO LEAVE HIM ALONE AND RISK MISSING HIS PROPHECY...
THERE, THERE MERAI. YOU'VE SOILED YOURSELF.
DISGUSTING.

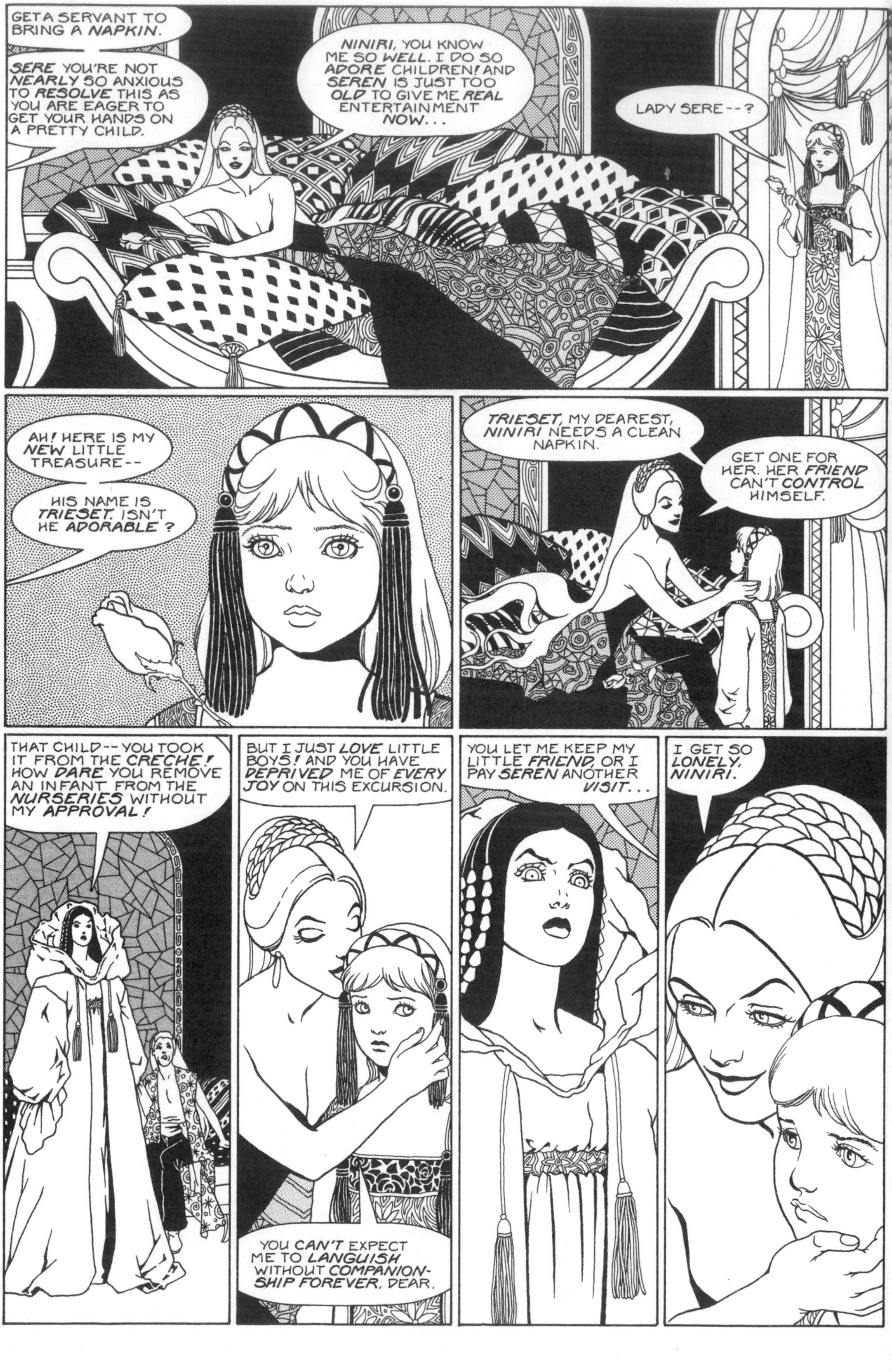
GET A SERVANT TO BRING A NAPKIN.
SERE YOU'RE NOT NEARLY SO ANXIOUS TO RESOLVE THIS AS YOU ARE EAGER TO GET YOUR HANDS ON A PRETTY CHILD.
NINIRI, YOU KNOW ME SO WELL. I DO SO ADORE CHILDREN! AND SEREN IS JUST TOO OLD TO GIVE ME REAL ENTERTAINMENT NOW...
LADY SERE--?
AH! HERE IS MY NEW LITTLE TREASURE--
HIS NAME IS TRIESET. ISN'T HE ADORABLE?
TRIESET, MY DEAREST, NINIRI NEEDS A CLEAN NAPKIN.
GET ONE FOR HER. HER FRIEND CAN'T CONTROL HIMSELF.
THAT CHILD--YOU TOOK IT FROM THE CRECHE! HOW DARE YOU REMOVE AN INFANT FROM THE NURSERIES WITHOUT MY APPROVAL!
BUT I JUST LOVE LITTLE BOYS! AND YOU HAVE DEPRIVED ME OF EVERY JOY ON THIS EXCURSION.
YOU CAN'T EXPECT ME TO LANGUISH WITHOUT COMPANIONSHIP FOREVER, DEAR.
YOU LET ME KEEP MY LITTLE FRIEND, OR I PAY SEREN ANOTHER VISIT...
I GET SO LONELY, NINIRI.

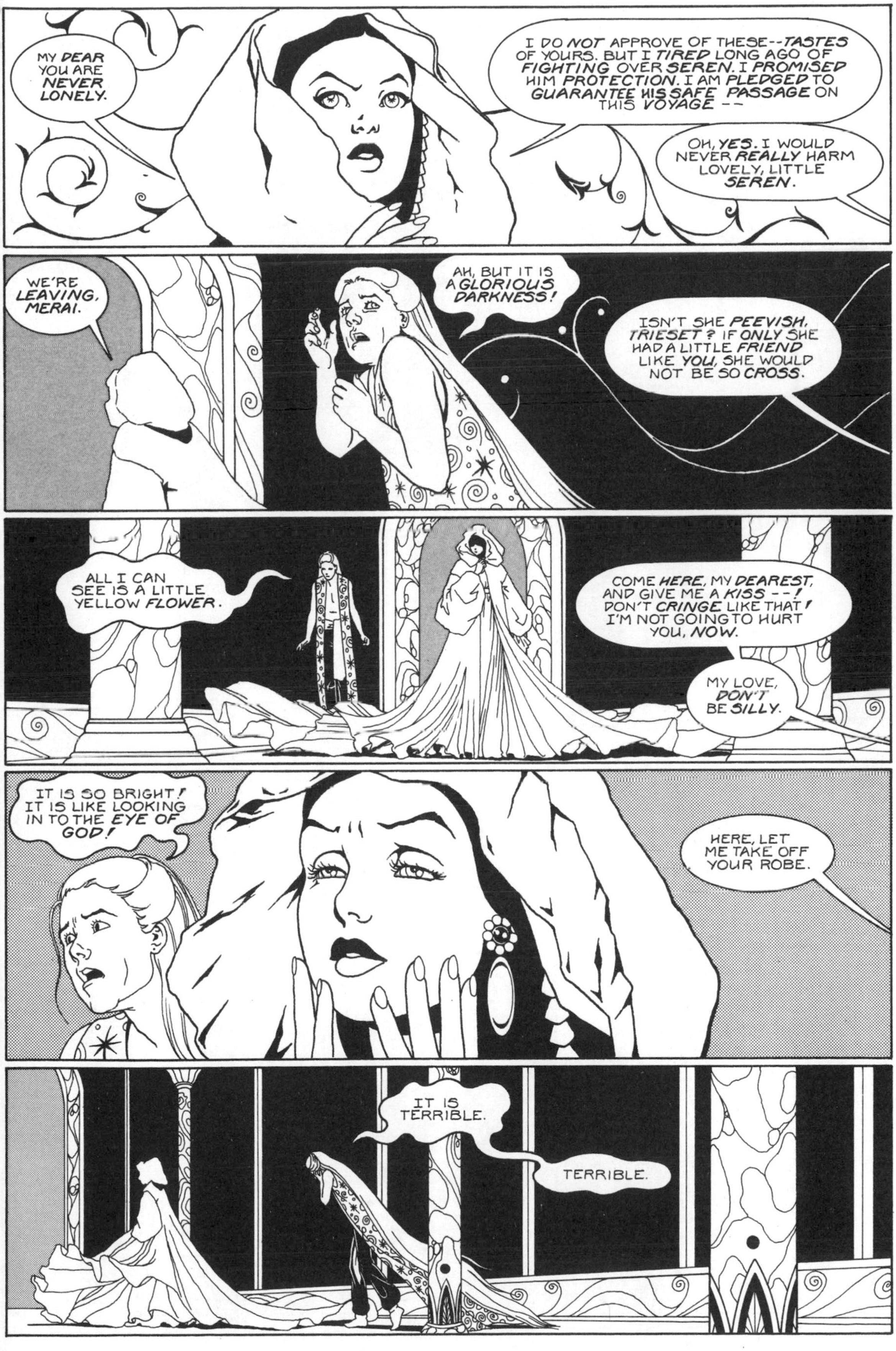
MY DEAR YOU ARE NEVER LONELY.
I DO NOT APPROVE OF THESE--TASTES OF YOURS. BUT I TIRED LONG AGO OF FIGHTING OVER SEREN. I PROMISED HIM PROTECTION. I AM PLEDGED TO GUARANTEE HIS SAFE PASSAGE ON THIS VOYAGE --
OH, YES. I WOULD NEVER REALLY HARM LOVELY, LITTLE SEREN.
WE'RE LEAVING, MERAI.
AH, BUT IT IS A GLORIOUS DARKNESS!
ISN'T SHE PEEVISH, TRIESET? IF ONLY SHE HAD A LITTLE FRIEND LIKE YOU, SHE WOULD NOT BE SO CROSS.
ALL I CAN SEE IS A LITTLE YELLOW FLOWER.
COME HERE, MY DEAREST, AND GIVE ME A KISS --! DON'T CRINGE LIKE THAT! I'M NOT GOING TO HURT YOU, NOW.
MY LOVE, DON'T BE SILLY.
IT IS SO BRIGHT! IT IS LIKE LOOKING IN TO THE EYE OF GOD!
HERE, LET ME TAKE OFF YOUR ROBE.
IT IS TERRIBLE.
TERRIBLE.

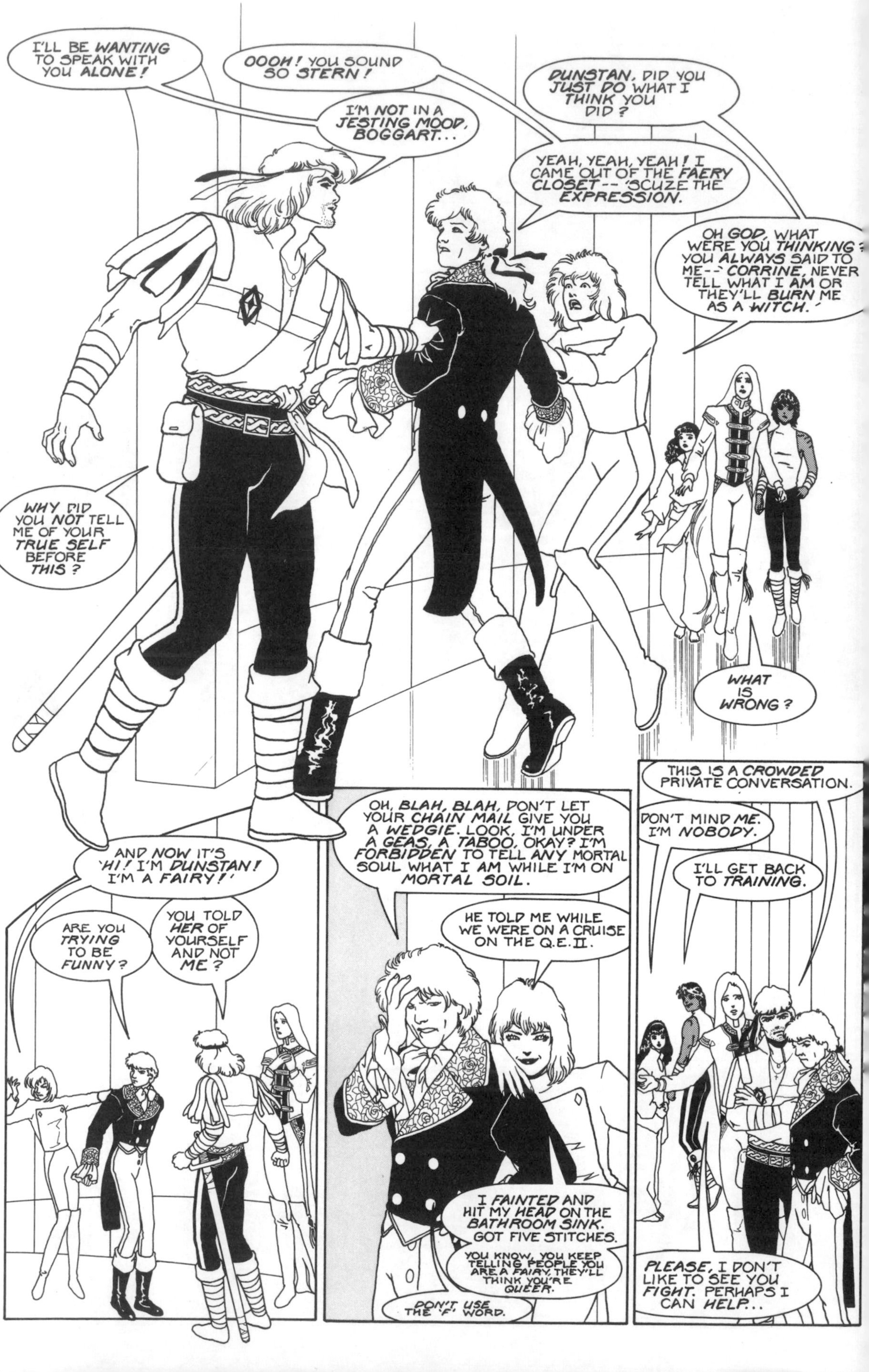
I'LL BE WANTING TO SPEAK WITH YOU ALONE!
OOOH! YOU SOUND SO STERN!
I'M NOT IN A JESTING MOOD, BOGGART...
DUNSTAN, DID YOU JUST DO WHAT I THINK YOU DID?
YEAH, YEAH, YEAH! I CAME OUT OF THE FAERY CLOSET-- 'SCUZE THE EXPRESSION.
OH GOD, WHAT WERE YOU THINKING? YOU ALWAYS SAID TO ME-- 'CORRINE, NEVER TELL WHAT I AM OR THEY'LL BURN ME AS A WITCH.'
WHY DID YOU NOT TELL ME OF YOUR TRUE SELF BEFORE THIS?
WHAT IS WRONG?
AND NOW IT'S 'HI! I'M DUNSTAN! I'M A FAIRY!'
ARE YOU TRYING TO BE FUNNY?
YOU TOLD HER OF YOURSELF AND NOT ME?
OH, BLAH, BLAH, DON'T LET YOUR CHAIN MAIL GIVE YOU A WEDGIE. LOOK, I'M UNDER A GEAS, A TABOO, OKAY? I'M FORBIDDEN TO TELL ANY MORTAL SOUL WHAT I AM WHILE I'M ON MORTAL SOIL.
HE TOLD ME WHILE WE WERE ON A CRUISE ON THE Q.E. II.
I FAINTED AND HIT MY HEAD ON THE BATHROOM SINK. GOT FIVE STITCHES.
YOU KNOW, YOU KEEP TELLING PEOPLE YOU ARE A FAIRY, THEY'LL THINK YOU'RE QUEER.
DON'T USE THE 'F' WORD.
THIS IS A CROWDED PRIVATE CONVERSATION.
DON'T MIND ME. I'M NOBODY.
I'LL GET BACK TO TRAINING.
PLEASE, I DON'T LIKE TO SEE YOU FIGHT. PERHAPS I CAN HELP...

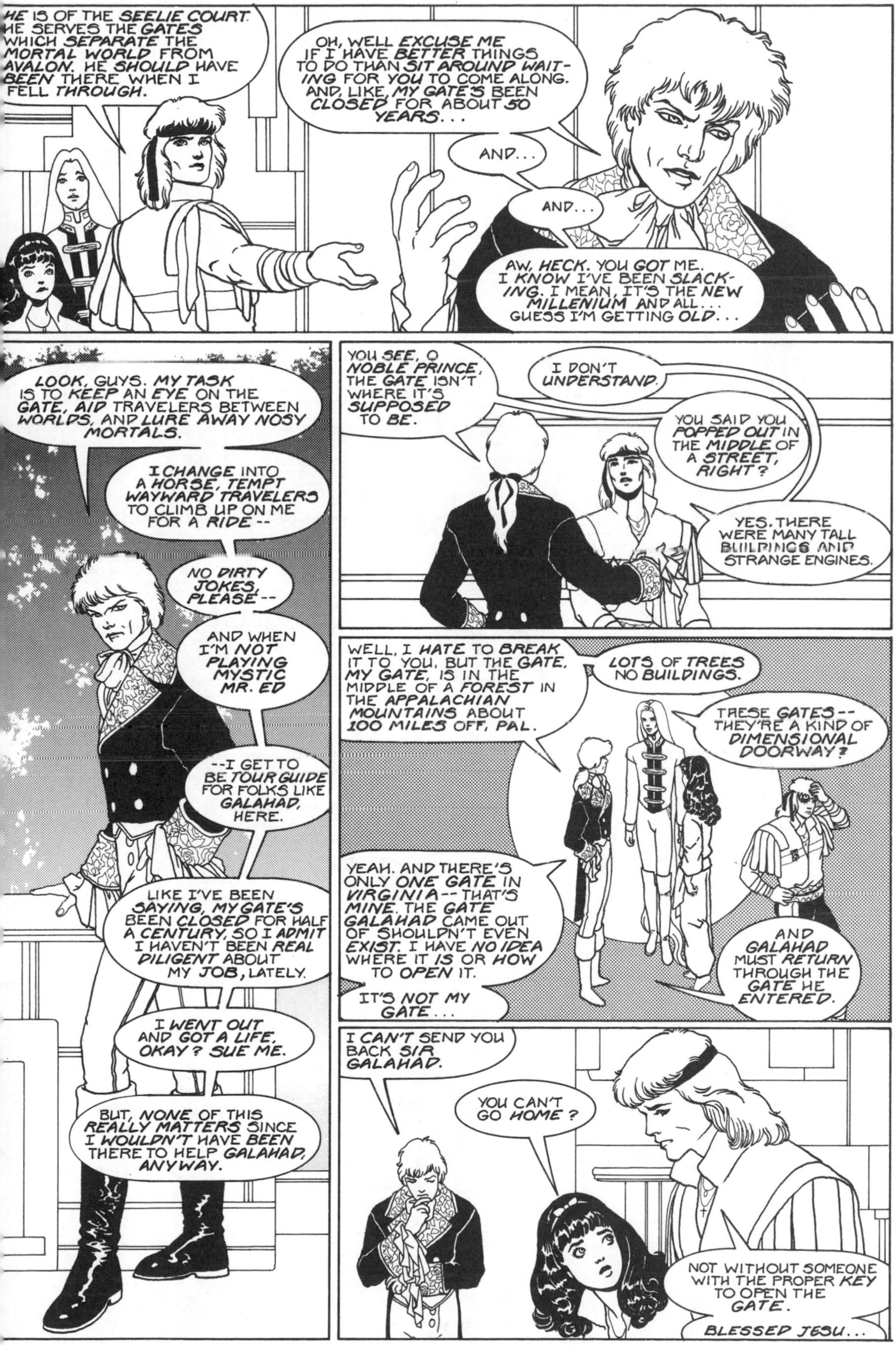
HE IS OF THE SEELIE COURT. HE SERVES THE GATES WHICH SEPARATE THE MORTAL WORLD FROM AVALON. HE SHOULD HAVE BEEN THERE WHEN I FELL THROUGH.
OH, WELL EXCUSE ME IF I HAVE BETTER THINGS TO DO THAN SIT AROUND WAITING FOR YOU TO COME ALONG. AND, LIKE, MY GATE'S BEEN CLOSED FOR ABOUT 50 YEARS...
AND...
AND...
AW, HECK. YOU GOT ME. I KNOW I'VE BEEN SLACKING. I MEAN, IT'S THE NEW MILLENIUM AND ALL... GUESS I'M GETTING OLD...
LOOK, GUYS. MY TASK IS TO KEEP AN EYE ON THE GATE, AID TRAVELERS BETWEEN WORLDS, AND LURE AWAY NOSY MORTALS.
I CHANGE INTO A HORSE, TEMPT WAYWARD TRAVELERS TO CLIMB UP ON ME FOR A RIDE--
NO DIRTY JOKES, PLEASE--
AND WHEN I'M NOT PLAYING MYSTIC MR. ED
--I GET TO BE TOUR GUIDE FOR FOLKS LIKE GALAHAD, HERE.
LIKE I'VE BEEN SAYING, MY GATE'S BEEN CLOSED FOR HALF A CENTURY, SO I ADMIT I HAVEN'T BEEN REAL DILIGENT ABOUT MY JOB, LATELY.
I WENT OUT AND GOT A LIFE, OKAY? SUE ME.
BUT, NONE OF THIS REALLY MATTERS SINCE I WOULDN'T HAVE BEEN THERE TO HELP GALAHAD, ANYWAY.
YOU SEE, O NOBLE PRINCE, THE GATE ISN'T WHERE IT'S SUPPOSED TO BE.
I DON'T UNDERSTAND.
YOU SAID YOU POPPED OUT IN THE MIDDLE OF A STREET, RIGHT?
YES. THERE WERE MANY TALL BUILDINGS AND STRANGE ENGINES.
WELL, I HATE TO BREAK IT TO YOU, BUT THE GATE, MY GATE, IS IN THE MIDDLE OF A FOREST IN THE APPALACHIAN MOUNTAINS ABOUT 100 MILES OFF, PAL.
LOTS OF TREES NO BUILDINGS.
THESE GATES--THEY'RE A KIND OF DIMENSIONAL DOORWAY?
YEAH. AND THERE'S ONLY ONE GATE IN VIRGINIA--THAT'S MINE. THE GATE GALAHAD CAME OUT OF SHOULDN'T EVEN EXIST. I HAVE NO IDEA WHERE IT IS OR HOW TO OPEN IT.
IT'S NOT MY GATE...
AND GALAHAD MUST RETURN THROUGH THE GATE HE ENTERED.
I CAN'T SEND YOU BACK SIR GALAHAD.
YOU CAN'T GO HOME?
NOT WITHOUT SOMEONE WITH THE PROPER KEY TO OPEN THE GATE.
BLESSED JESU...

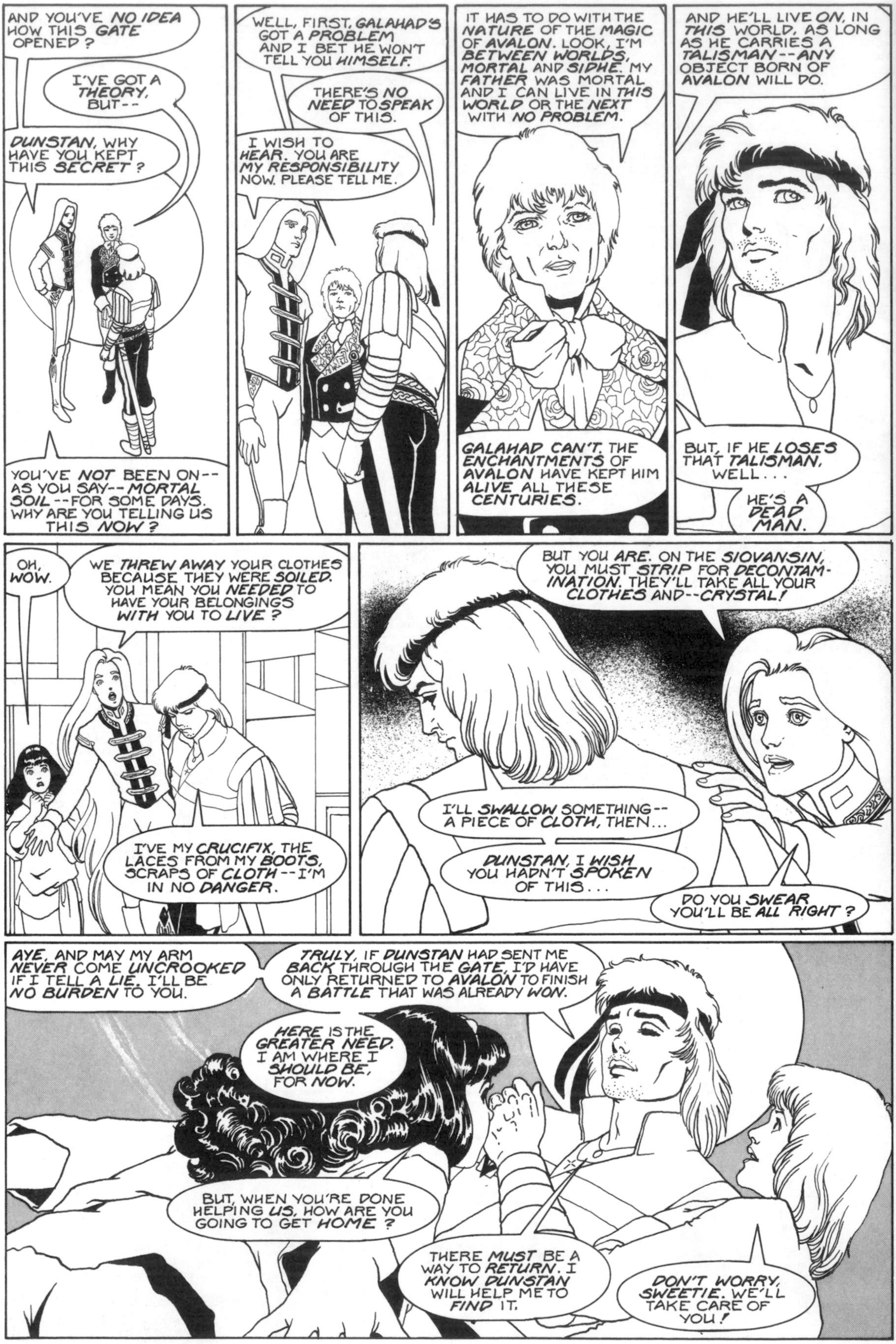
AND YOU'VE NO IDEA HOW THIS GATE OPENED?
I'VE GOT A THEORY, BUT--
DUNSTAN, WHY HAVE YOU KEPT THIS SECRET?
YOU'VE NOT BEEN ON-- AS YOU SAY-- MORTAL SOIL --FOR SOME DAYS. WHY ARE YOU TELLING US THIS NOW?
WELL, FIRST, GALAHAD'S GOT A PROBLEM AND I BET HE WON'T TELL YOU HIMSELF.
THERE'S NO NEED TO SPEAK OF THIS.
I WISH TO HEAR. YOU ARE MY RESPONSIBILITY NOW. PLEASE TELL ME.
IT HAS TO DO WITH THE NATURE OF THE MAGIC OF AVALON. LOOK, I'M BETWEEN WORLDS, MORTAL AND SIDHE. MY FATHER WAS MORTAL AND I CAN LIVE IN THIS WORLD OR THE NEXT WITH NO PROBLEM.
GALAHAD CAN'T. THE ENCHANTMENTS OF AVALON HAVE KEPT HIM ALIVE ALL THESE CENTURIES.
AND HE'LL LIVE ON, IN THIS WORLD, AS LONG AS HE CARRIES A TALISMAN--ANY OBJECT BORN OF AVALON WILL DO.
BUT, IF HE LOSES THAT TALISMAN, WELL...
HE'S A DEAD MAN.
OH, WOW.
WE THREW AWAY YOUR CLOTHES BECAUSE THEY WERE SOILED. YOU MEAN YOU NEEDED TO HAVE YOUR BELONGINGS WITH YOU TO LIVE?
I'VE MY CRUCIFIX, THE LACES FROM MY BOOTS, SCRAPS OF CLOTH --I'M IN NO DANGER.
BUT YOU ARE. ON THE SIOVANSIN, YOU MUST STRIP FOR DECONTAMINATION. THEY'LL TAKE ALL YOUR CLOTHES AND--CRYSTAL!
I'LL SWALLOW SOMETHING-- A PIECE OF CLOTH, THEN...
DUNSTAN, I WISH YOU HADN'T SPOKEN OF THIS...
DO YOU SWEAR YOU'LL BE ALL RIGHT?
AYE, AND MAY MY ARM NEVER COME UNCROOKED IF I TELL A LIE. I'LL BE NO BURDEN TO YOU.
TRULY, IF DUNSTAN HAD SENT ME BACK THROUGH THE GATE, I'D HAVE ONLY RETURNED TO AVALON TO FINISH A BATTLE THAT WAS ALREADY WON.
HERE IS THE GREATER NEED. I AM WHERE I SHOULD BE, FOR NOW.
BUT, WHEN YOU'RE DONE HELPING US, HOW ARE YOU GOING TO GET HOME?
THERE MUST BE A WAY TO RETURN. I KNOW DUNSTAN WILL HELP ME TO FIND IT.
DON'T WORRY, SWEETIE. WE'LL TAKE CARE OF YOU!

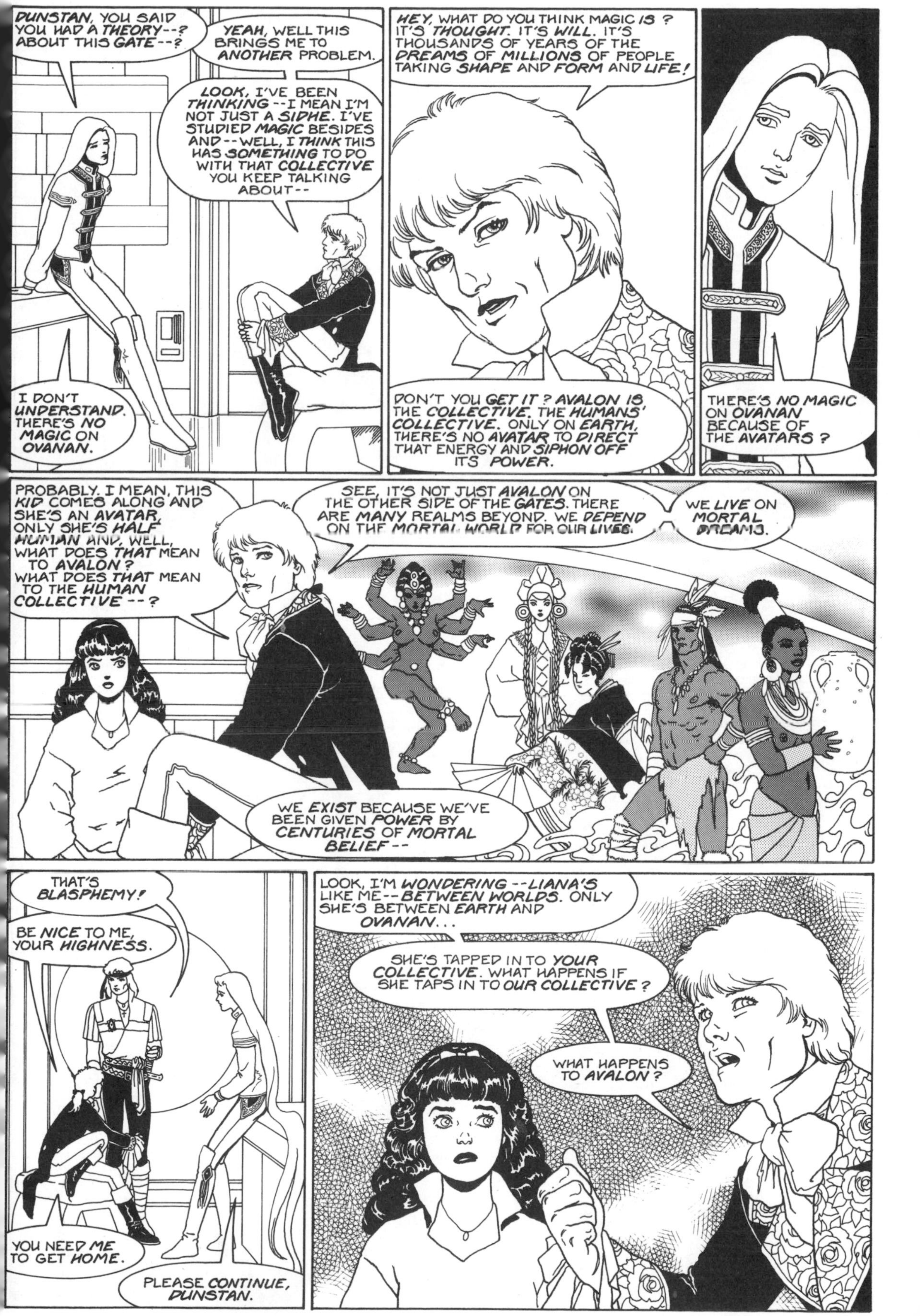
DUNSTAN, YOU SAID YOU HAD A THEORY--? ABOUT THIS GATE--?
YEAH, WELL THIS BRINGS ME TO ANOTHER PROBLEM.
LOOK, I'VE BEEN THINKING--I MEAN I'M NOT JUST A SIDHE. I'VE STUDIED MAGIC BESIDES AND--WELL, I THINK THIS HAS SOMETHING TO DO WITH THAT COLLECTIVE YOU KEEP TALKING ABOUT--
I DON'T UNDERSTAND. THERE'S NO MAGIC ON OVANAN.
HEY, WHAT DO YOU THINK MAGIC IS? IT'S THOUGHT. IT'S WILL. IT'S THOUSANDS OF YEARS OF THE DREAMS OF MILLIONS OF PEOPLE TAKING SHAPE AND FORM AND LIFE!
DON'T YOU GET IT? AVALON IS THE COLLECTIVE. THE HUMANS' COLLECTIVE. ONLY ON EARTH, THERE'S NO AVATAR TO DIRECT THAT ENERGY AND SIPHON OFF ITS POWER.
THERE'S NO MAGIC ON OVANAN BECAUSE OF THE AVATARS?
PROBABLY. I MEAN, THIS KID COMES ALONG AND SHE'S AN AVATAR, ONLY SHE'S HALF HUMAN AND, WELL, WHAT DOES THAT MEAN TO AVALON? WHAT DOES THAT MEAN TO THE HUMAN COLLECTIVE--?
SEE, IT'S NOT JUST AVALON ON THE OTHER SIDE OF THE GATES. THERE ARE MANY REALMS BEYOND. WE DEPEND ON THE MORTAL WORLD FOR OUR LIVES.
WE LIVE ON MORTAL DREAMS.
WE EXIST BECAUSE WE'VE BEEN GIVEN POWER BY CENTURIES OF MORTAL BELIEF--
THAT'S BLASPHEMY!
BE NICE TO ME, YOUR HIGHNESS.
YOU NEED ME TO GET HOME.
PLEASE CONTINUE, DUNSTAN.
LOOK, I'M WONDERING--LIANA'S LIKE ME--BETWEEN WORLDS. ONLY SHE'S BETWEEN EARTH AND OVANAN...
SHE'S TAPPED IN TO YOUR COLLECTIVE. WHAT HAPPENS IF SHE TAPS IN TO OUR COLLECTIVE?
WHAT HAPPENS TO AVALON?

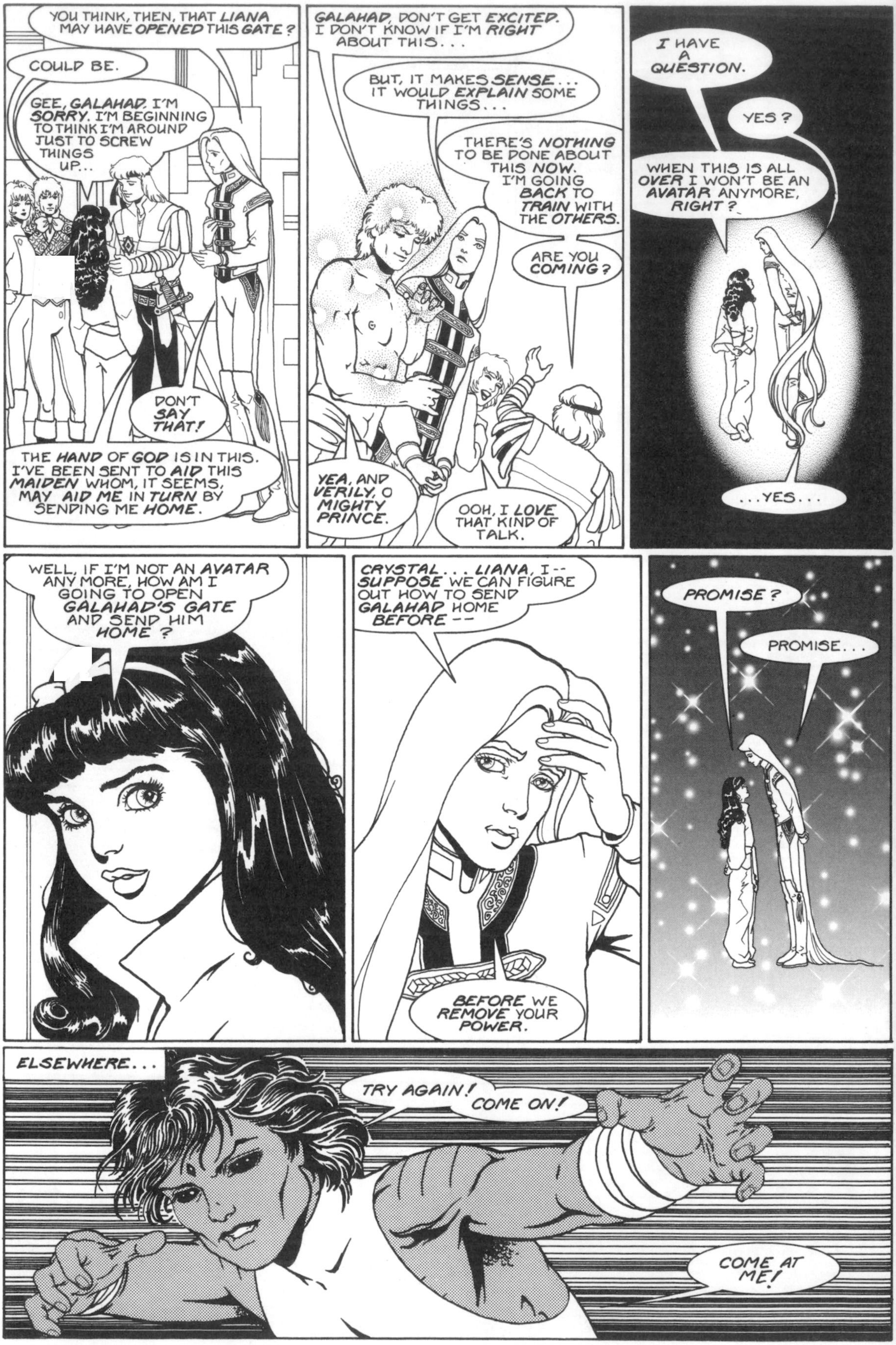
YOU THINK, THEN, THAT LIANA MAY HAVE OPENED THIS GATE?
COULD BE.
GEE, GALAHAD, I'M SORRY. I'M BEGINNING TO THINK I'M AROUND JUST TO SCREW THINGS UP...
DON'T SAY THAT!
THE HAND OF GOD IS IN THIS. I'VE BEEN SENT TO AID THIS MAIDEN WHOM, IT SEEMS, MAY AID ME IN TURN BY SENDING ME HOME.
GALAHAD, DON'T GET EXCITED. I DON'T KNOW IF I'M RIGHT ABOUT THIS...
BUT, IT MAKES SENSE... IT WOULD EXPLAIN SOME THINGS...
THERE'S NOTHING TO BE DONE ABOUT THIS NOW. I'M GOING BACK TO TRAIN WITH THE OTHERS.
ARE YOU COMING?
YEA, AND VERILY, O MIGHTY PRINCE.
OOH, I LOVE THAT KIND OF TALK.
I HAVE A QUESTION.
YES?
WHEN THIS IS ALL OVER I WON'T BE AN AVATAR ANYMORE, RIGHT?
...YES...
WELL, IF I'M NOT AN AVATAR ANY MORE, HOW AM I GOING TO OPEN GALAHAD'S GATE AND SEND HIM HOME?
CRYSTAL... LIANA, I-- SUPPOSE WE CAN FIGURE OUT HOW TO SEND GALAHAD HOME BEFORE --
BEFORE WE REMOVE YOUR POWER.
PROMISE?
PROMISE...
ELSEWHERE...
TRY AGAIN!
COME ON!
COME AT ME!

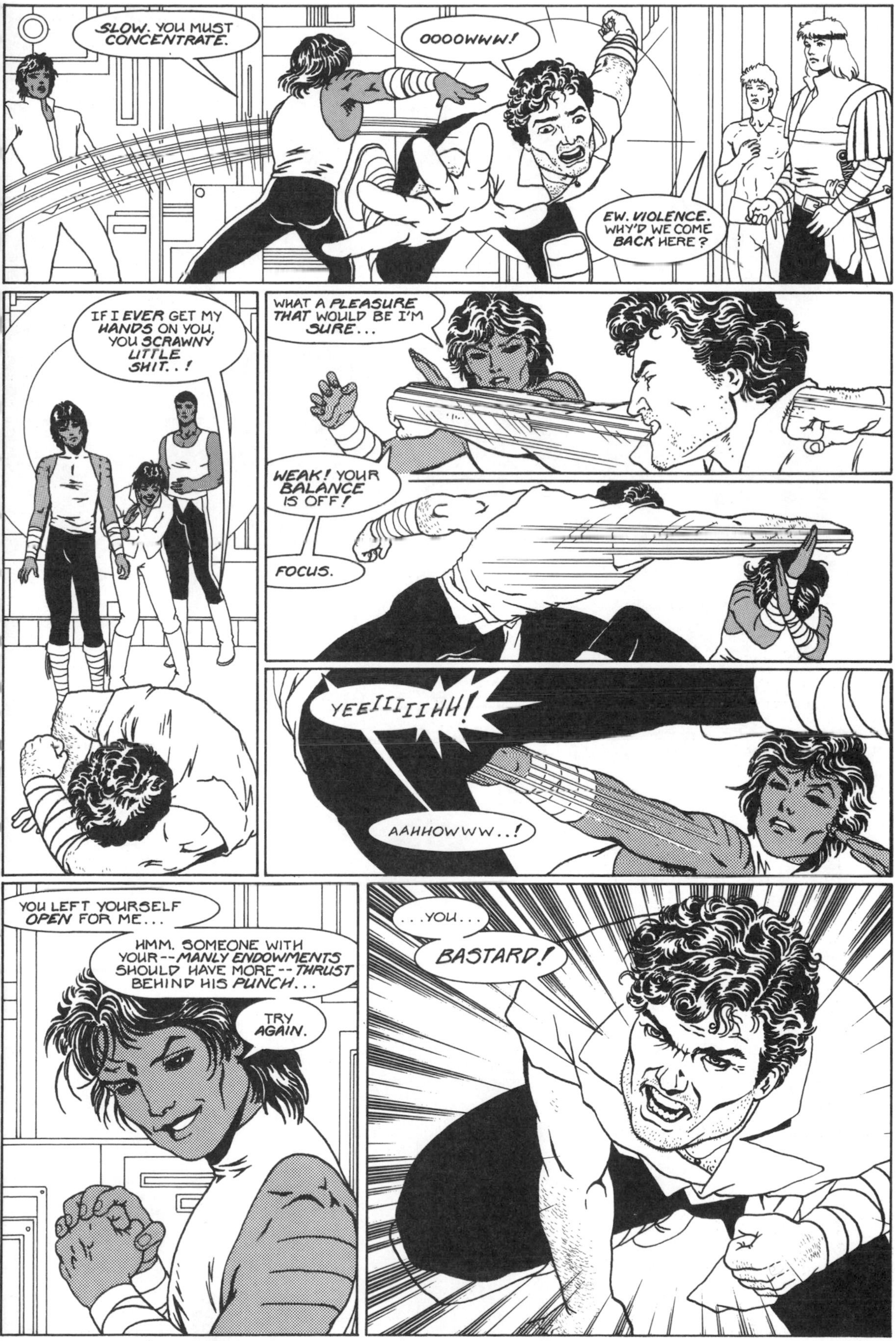
SLOW. YOU MUST CONCENTRATE.
OOOOWWW!
EW. VIOLENCE. WHY'D WE COME BACK HERE?
IF I EVER GET MY HANDS ON YOU, YOU SCRAWNY LITTLE SHIT..!
WHAT A PLEASURE THAT WOULD BE I'M SURE...
WEAK! YOUR BALANCE IS OFF!
FOCUS.
YEEIIIIIHH!
AAHHOWWW..!
YOU LEFT YOURSELF OPEN FOR ME...
HMM. SOMEONE WITH YOUR--MANLY ENDOWMENTS SHOULD HAVE MORE--THRUST BEHIND HIS PUNCH...
TRY AGAIN.
...YOU...
BASTARD!

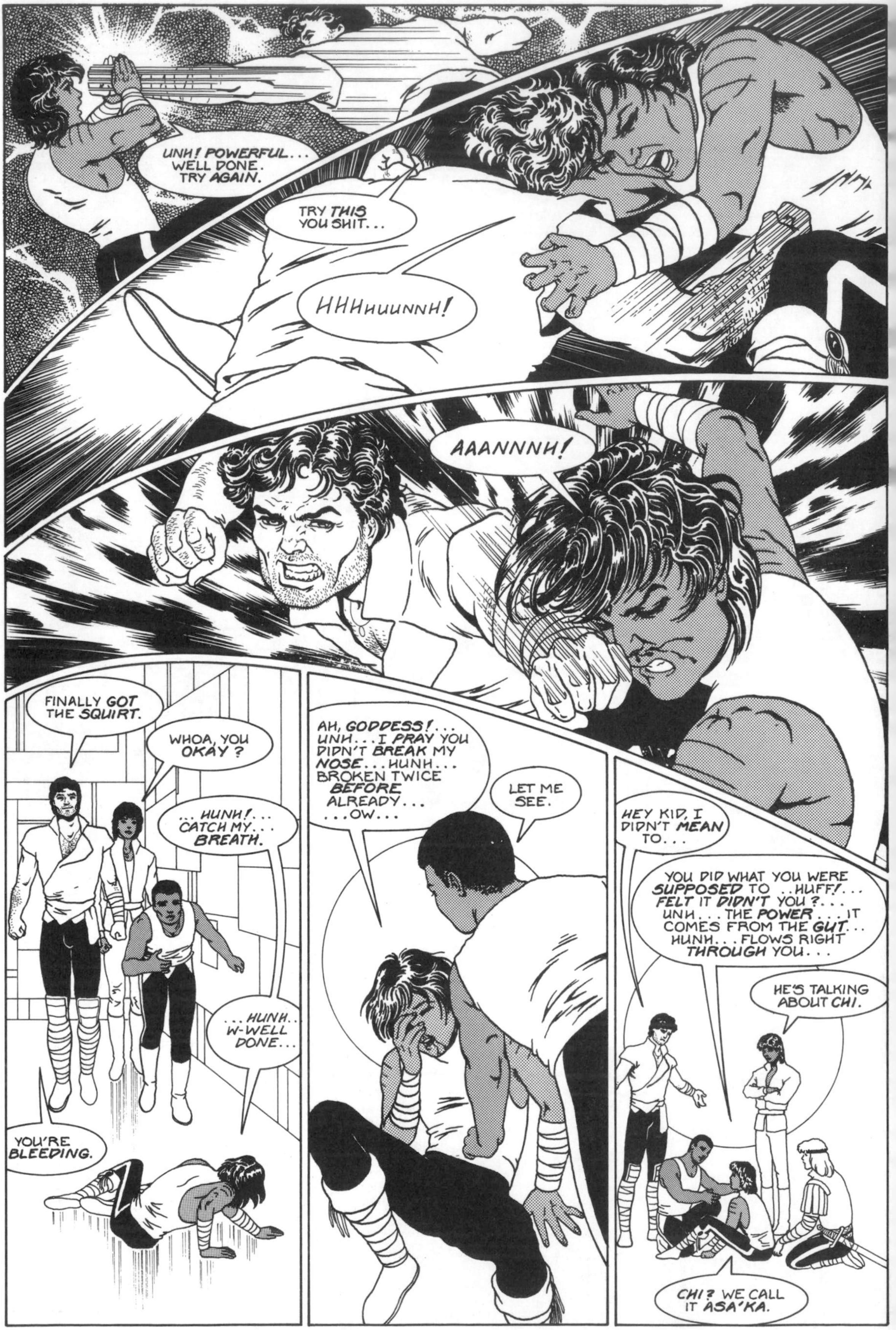
UNH! POWERFUL... WELL DONE. TRY AGAIN.
TRY THIS YOU SHIT...
HHHhuuunnh!
AAANNNH!
FINALLY GOT THE SQUIRT.
WHOA, YOU OKAY?
...HUNH!... CATCH MY... BREATH.
...HUNH... W-WELL DONE...
YOU'RE BLEEDING.
AH, GODDESS!... UNH... I PRAY YOU DIDN'T BREAK MY NOSE... HUNH... BROKEN TWICE BEFORE ALREADY... ...OW...
LET ME SEE.
HEY KID, I DIDN'T MEAN TO...
YOU DID WHAT YOU WERE SUPPOSED TO ...HUFF!... FELT IT DIDN'T YOU?... UNH... THE POWER... IT COMES FROM THE GUT... HUNH... FLOWS RIGHT THROUGH YOU...
HE'S TALKING ABOUT CHI.
CHI? WE CALL IT ASA'KA.

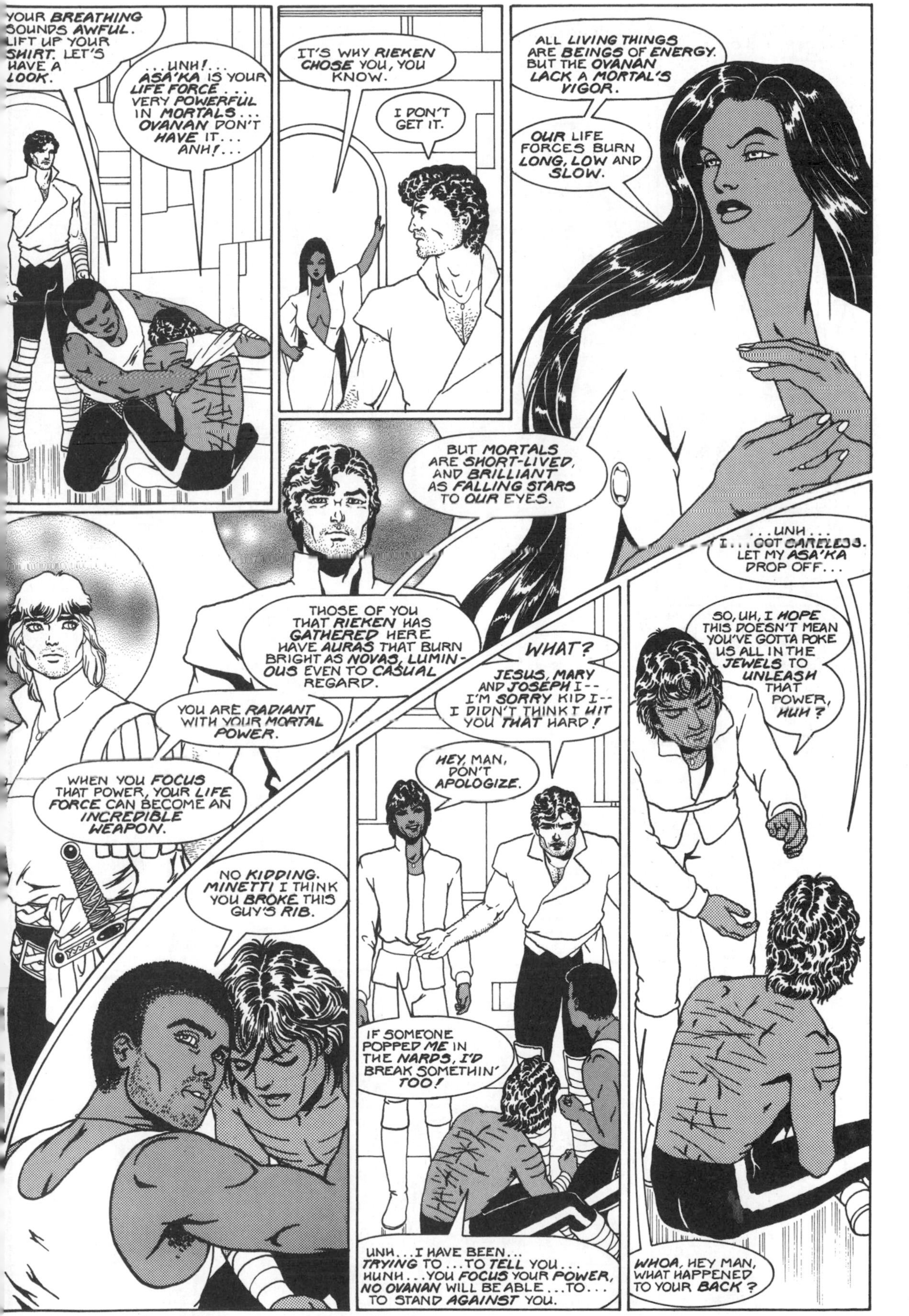
YOUR BREATHING SOUNDS AWFUL. LIFT UP YOUR SHIRT. LET'S HAVE A LOOK.
...UNH!... ASA'KA IS YOUR LIFE FORCE... VERY POWERFUL IN MORTALS... OVANAN DON'T HAVE IT... ANH!...
IT'S WHY RIEKEN CHOSE YOU, YOU KNOW.
I DON'T GET IT.
ALL LIVING THINGS ARE BEINGS OF ENERGY. BUT THE OVANAN LACK A MORTAL'S VIGOR.
OUR LIFE FORCES BURN LONG, LOW AND SLOW.
BUT MORTALS ARE SHORT-LIVED, AND BRILLIANT AS FALLING STARS TO OUR EYES.
THOSE OF YOU THAT RIEKEN HAS GATHERED HERE HAVE AURAS THAT BURN BRIGHT AS NOVAS, LUMINOUS EVEN TO CASUAL REGARD.
YOU ARE RADIANT WITH YOUR MORTAL POWER.
WHEN YOU FOCUS THAT POWER, YOUR LIFE FORCE CAN BECOME AN INCREDIBLE WEAPON.
NO KIDDING. MINETTI I THINK YOU BROKE THIS GUY'S RIB.
WHAT?
JESUS, MARY AND JOSEPH I-- I'M SORRY KID I-- I DIDN'T THINK I HIT YOU THAT HARD!
HEY, MAN, DON'T APOLOGIZE.
IF SOMEONE POPPED ME IN THE NARDS, I'D BREAK SOMETHIN' TOO!
UNH...I HAVE BEEN... TRYING TO...TO TELL YOU... HUNH...YOU FOCUS YOUR POWER, NO OVANAN WILL BE ABLE...TO... TO STAND AGAINST YOU.
...UNH... I...GOT CARELESS. LET MY ASA'KA DROP OFF...
SO, UH, I HOPE THIS DOESN'T MEAN YOU'VE GOTTA POKE US ALL IN THE JEWELS TO UNLEASH THAT POWER, HUH?
WHOA, HEY MAN, WHAT HAPPENED TO YOUR BACK?

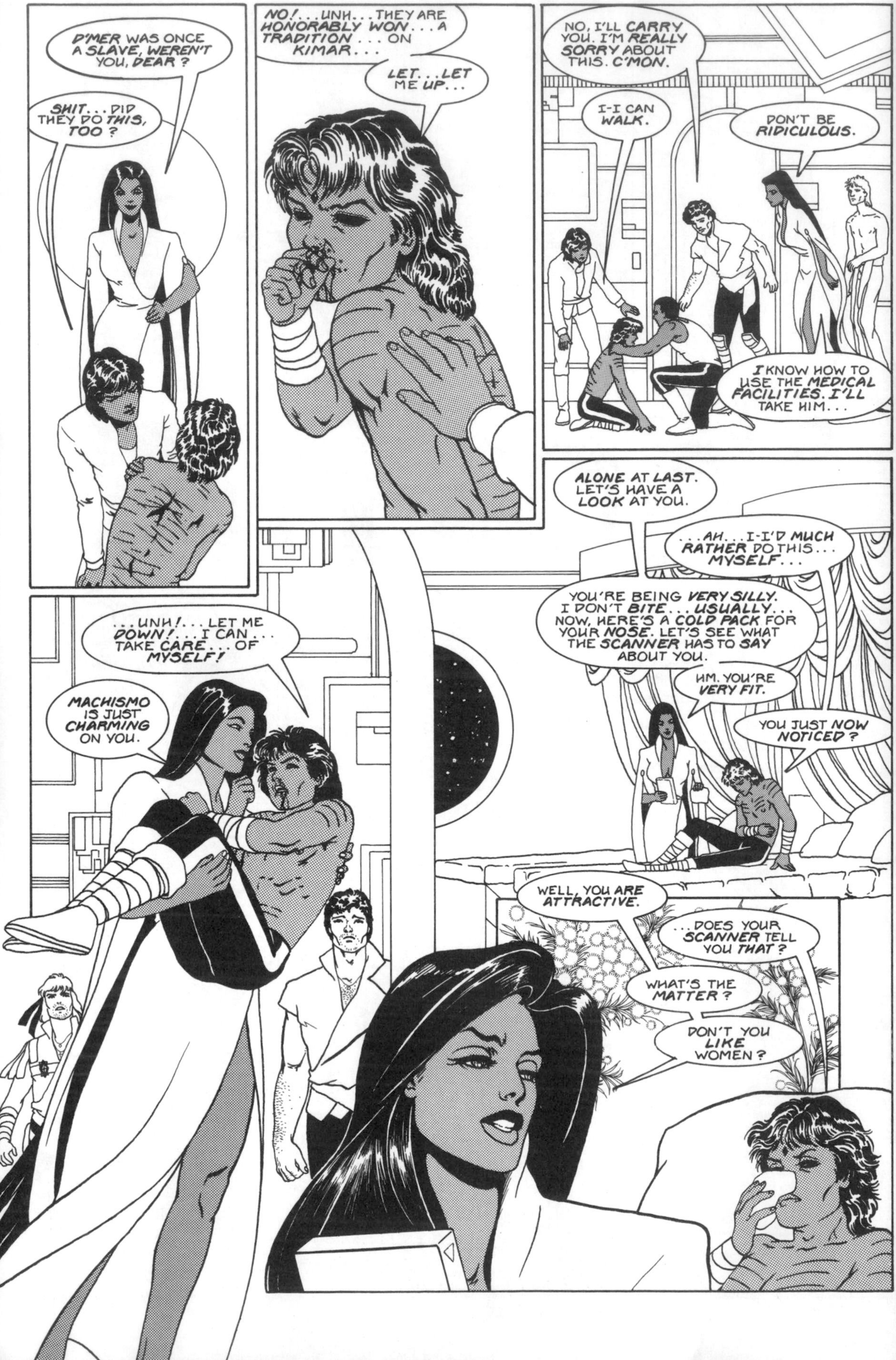
D'MER WAS ONCE A SLAVE, WEREN'T YOU, DEAR?
SHIT... DID THEY DO THIS, TOO?
NO!... UNH... THEY ARE HONORABLY WON... A TRADITION... ON KIMAR...
LET... LET ME UP...
NO, I'LL CARRY YOU. I'M REALLY SORRY ABOUT THIS. C'MON.
I-I CAN WALK.
DON'T BE RIDICULOUS.
I KNOW HOW TO USE THE MEDICAL FACILITIES. I'LL TAKE HIM...
...UNH!... LET ME DOWN!... I CAN... TAKE CARE... OF MYSELF!
MACHISMO IS JUST CHARMING ON YOU.
ALONE AT LAST. LET'S HAVE A LOOK AT YOU.
...AH... I-I'D MUCH RATHER DO THIS... MYSELF...
YOU'RE BEING VERY SILLY. I DON'T BITE... USUALLY... NOW, HERE'S A COLD PACK FOR YOUR NOSE. LET'S SEE WHAT THE SCANNER HAS TO SAY ABOUT YOU.
HM. YOU'RE VERY FIT.
YOU JUST NOW NOTICED?
WELL, YOU ARE ATTRACTIVE.
...DOES YOUR SCANNER TELL YOU THAT?
WHAT'S THE MATTER?
DON'T YOU LIKE WOMEN?

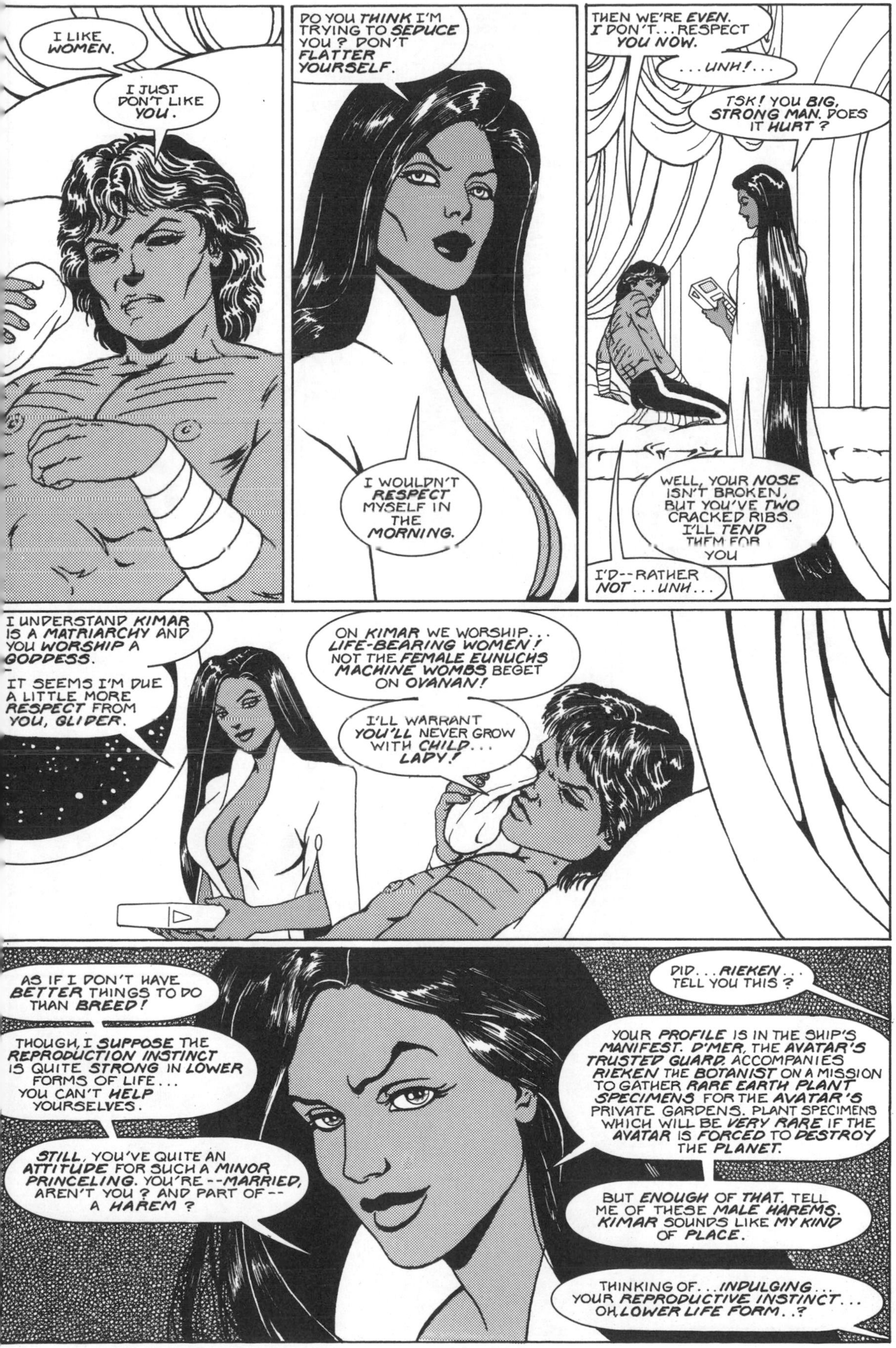
I LIKE WOMEN.
I JUST DON'T LIKE YOU.
DO YOU THINK I'M TRYING TO SEDUCE YOU? DON'T FLATTER YOURSELF.
I WOULDN'T RESPECT MYSELF IN THE MORNING.
THEN WE'RE EVEN. I DON'T... RESPECT YOU NOW.
...UNH!...
TSK! YOU BIG, STRONG MAN. DOES IT HURT?
WELL, YOUR NOSE ISN'T BROKEN, BUT YOU'VE TWO CRACKED RIBS. I'LL TEND THEM FOR YOU
I'D--RATHER NOT...UNH...
I UNDERSTAND KIMAR IS A MATRIARCHY AND YOU WORSHIP A GODDESS.
IT SEEMS I'M DUE A LITTLE MORE RESPECT FROM YOU, GLIDER.
ON KIMAR WE WORSHIP... LIFE-BEARING WOMEN! NOT THE FEMALE EUNUCHS MACHINE WOMBS BEGET ON OVANAN!
I'LL WARRANT YOU'LL NEVER GROW WITH CHILD... LADY!
AS IF I DON'T HAVE BETTER THINGS TO DO THAN BREED!
THOUGH, I SUPPOSE THE REPRODUCTION INSTINCT IS QUITE STRONG IN LOWER FORMS OF LIFE... YOU CAN'T HELP YOURSELVES.
STILL, YOU'VE QUITE AN ATTITUDE FOR SUCH A MINOR PRINCELING. YOU'RE--MARRIED, AREN'T YOU? AND PART OF-- A HAREM?
DID...RIEKEN... TELL YOU THIS?
YOUR PROFILE IS IN THE SHIP'S MANIFEST. D'MER, THE AVATAR'S TRUSTED GUARD, ACCOMPANIES RIEKEN THE BOTANIST ON A MISSION TO GATHER RARE EARTH PLANT SPECIMENS FOR THE AVATAR'S PRIVATE GARDENS. PLANT SPECIMENS WHICH WILL BE VERY RARE IF THE AVATAR IS FORCED TO DESTROY THE PLANET.
BUT ENOUGH OF THAT. TELL ME OF THESE MALE HAREMS. KIMAR SOUNDS LIKE MY KIND OF PLACE.
THINKING OF...INDULGING... YOUR REPRODUCTIVE INSTINCT... OH, LOWER LIFE FORM..?

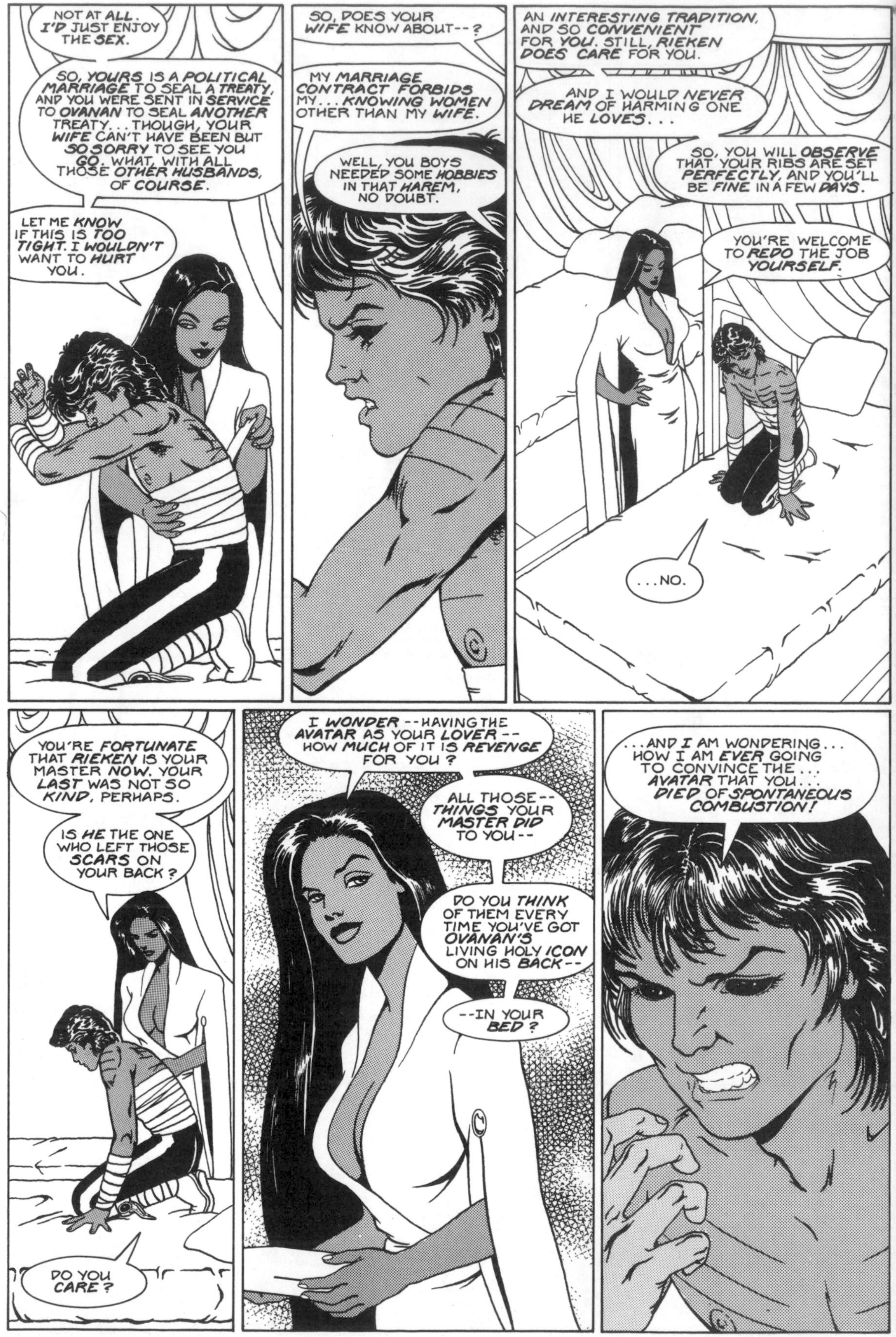
NOT AT ALL. I'D JUST ENJOY THE SEX.
SO, YOURS IS A POLITICAL MARRIAGE TO SEAL A TREATY, AND YOU WERE SENT IN SERVICE TO OVANAN TO SEAL ANOTHER TREATY... THOUGH, YOUR WIFE CAN'T HAVE BEEN BUT SO SORRY TO SEE YOU GO. WHAT, WITH ALL THOSE OTHER HUSBANDS, OF COURSE.
LET ME KNOW IF THIS IS TOO TIGHT. I WOULDN'T WANT TO HURT YOU.
SO, DOES YOUR WIFE KNOW ABOUT--?
MY MARRIAGE CONTRACT FORBIDS MY... KNOWING WOMEN OTHER THAN MY WIFE.
WELL, YOU BOYS NEEDED SOME HOBBIES IN THAT HAREM, NO DOUBT.
AN INTERESTING TRADITION, AND SO CONVENIENT FOR YOU. STILL, RIEKEN DOES CARE FOR YOU.
AND I WOULD NEVER DREAM OF HARMING ONE HE LOVES...
SO, YOU WILL OBSERVE THAT YOUR RIBS ARE SET PERFECTLY, AND YOU'LL BE FINE IN A FEW DAYS.
YOU'RE WELCOME TO REDO THE JOB YOURSELF.
...NO.
YOU'RE FORTUNATE THAT RIEKEN IS YOUR MASTER NOW. YOUR LAST WAS NOT SO KIND, PERHAPS.
IS HE THE ONE WHO LEFT THOSE SCARS ON YOUR BACK?
DO YOU CARE?
I WONDER--HAVING THE AVATAR AS YOUR LOVER--HOW MUCH OF IT IS REVENGE FOR YOU?
ALL THOSE--THINGS YOUR MASTER DID TO YOU--
DO YOU THINK OF THEM EVERY TIME YOU'VE GOT OVANAN'S LIVING HOLY ICON ON HIS BACK--
--IN YOUR BED?
...AND I AM WONDERING... HOW I AM EVER GOING TO CONVINCE THE... AVATAR THAT YOU... DIED OF SPONTANEOUS COMBUSTION!

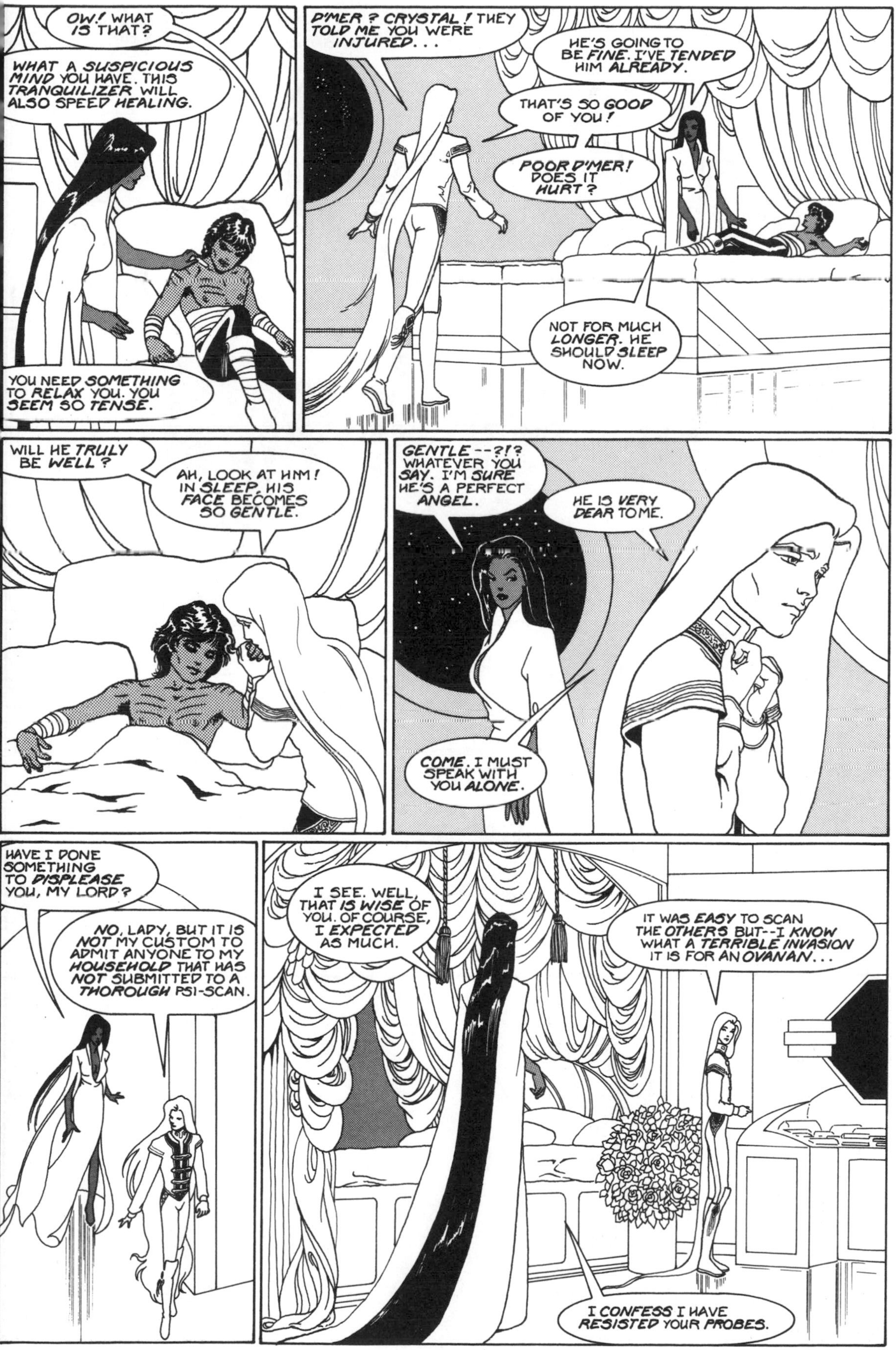
OW! WHAT IS THAT?
WHAT A SUSPICIOUS MIND YOU HAVE. THIS TRANQUILIZER WILL ALSO SPEED HEALING.
YOU NEED SOMETHING TO RELAX YOU. YOU SEEM SO TENSE.
D'MER? CRYSTAL! THEY TOLD ME YOU WERE INJURED...
HE'S GOING TO BE FINE. I'VE TENDED HIM ALREADY.
THAT'S SO GOOD OF YOU!
POOR D'MER! DOES IT HURT?
NOT FOR MUCH LONGER. HE SHOULD SLEEP NOW.
WILL HE TRULY BE WELL?
AH, LOOK AT HIM! IN SLEEP, HIS FACE BECOMES SO GENTLE.
GENTLE--?!? WHATEVER YOU SAY. I'M SURE HE'S A PERFECT ANGEL.
HE IS VERY DEAR TO ME.
COME. I MUST SPEAK WITH YOU ALONE.
HAVE I DONE SOMETHING TO DISPLEASE YOU, MY LORD?
NO, LADY, BUT IT IS NOT MY CUSTOM TO ADMIT ANYONE TO MY HOUSEHOLD THAT HAS NOT SUBMITTED TO A THOROUGH PSI-SCAN.
I SEE. WELL, THAT IS WISE OF YOU. OF COURSE, I EXPECTED AS MUCH.
IT WAS EASY TO SCAN THE OTHERS BUT--I KNOW WHAT A TERRIBLE INVASION IT IS FOR AN OVANAN...
I CONFESS I HAVE RESISTED YOUR PROBES.

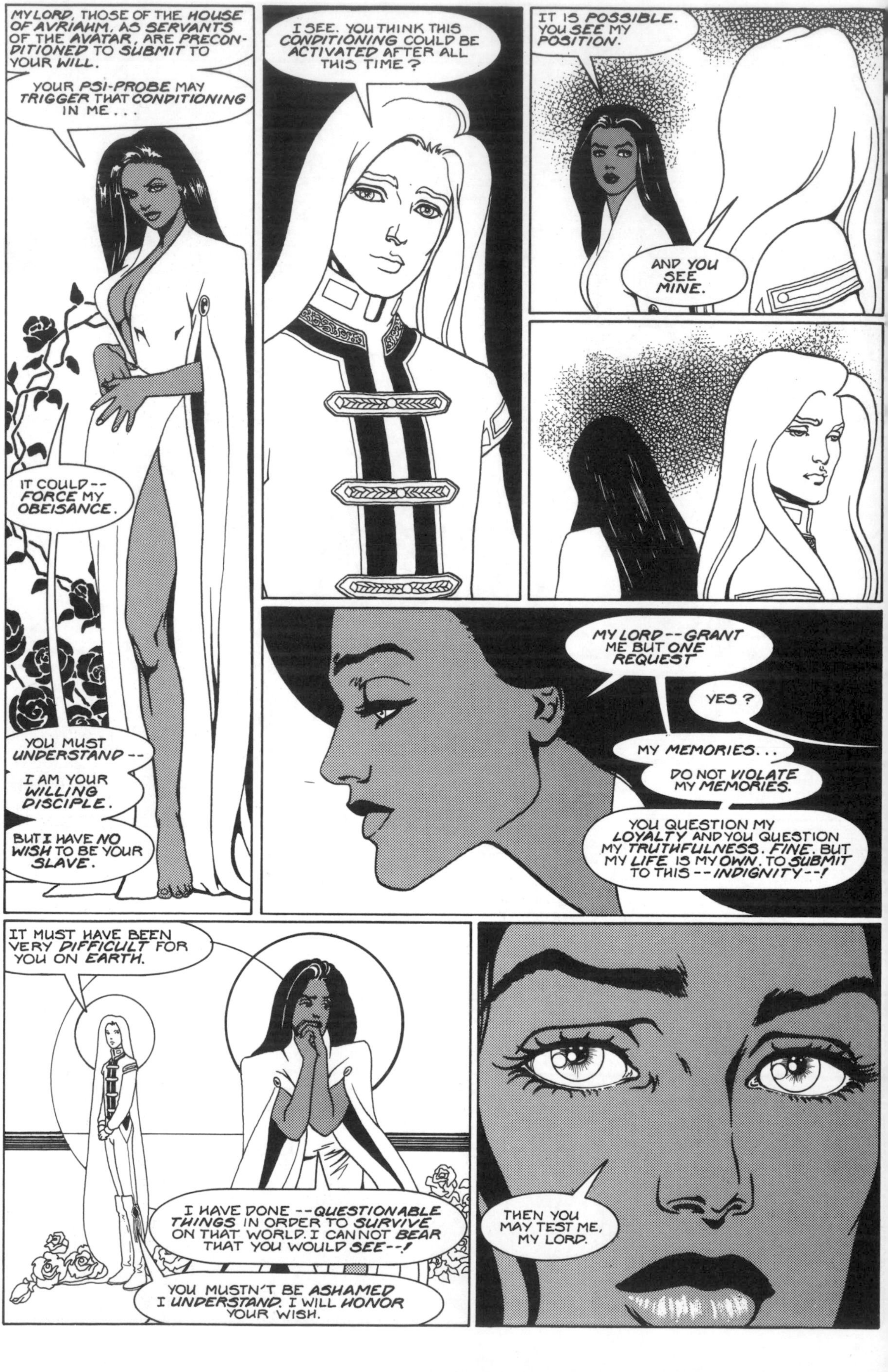
MY LORD, THOSE OF THE HOUSE OF AVRIAHM, AS SERVANTS OF THE AVATAR, ARE PRECONDITIONED TO SUBMIT TO YOUR WILL.
YOUR PSI-PROBE MAY TRIGGER THAT CONDITIONING IN ME...
IT COULD-- FORCE MY OBEISANCE.
YOU MUST UNDERSTAND--
I AM YOUR WILLING DISCIPLE.
BUT I HAVE NO WISH TO BE YOUR SLAVE.
I SEE. YOU THINK THIS CONDITIONING COULD BE ACTIVATED AFTER ALL THIS TIME?
IT IS POSSIBLE. YOU SEE MY POSITION.
AND YOU SEE MINE.
MY LORD--GRANT ME BUT ONE REQUEST
YES?
MY MEMORIES...
DO NOT VIOLATE MY MEMORIES.
YOU QUESTION MY LOYALTY AND YOU QUESTION MY TRUTHFULNESS. FINE. BUT MY LIFE IS MY OWN. TO SUBMIT TO THIS--INDIGNITY--!
IT MUST HAVE BEEN VERY DIFFICULT FOR YOU ON EARTH.
I HAVE DONE--QUESTIONABLE THINGS IN ORDER TO SURVIVE ON THAT WORLD. I CANNOT BEAR THAT YOU WOULD SEE--!
YOU MUSTN'T BE ASHAMED I UNDERSTAND. I WILL HONOR YOUR WISH.
THEN YOU MAY TEST ME, MY LORD.

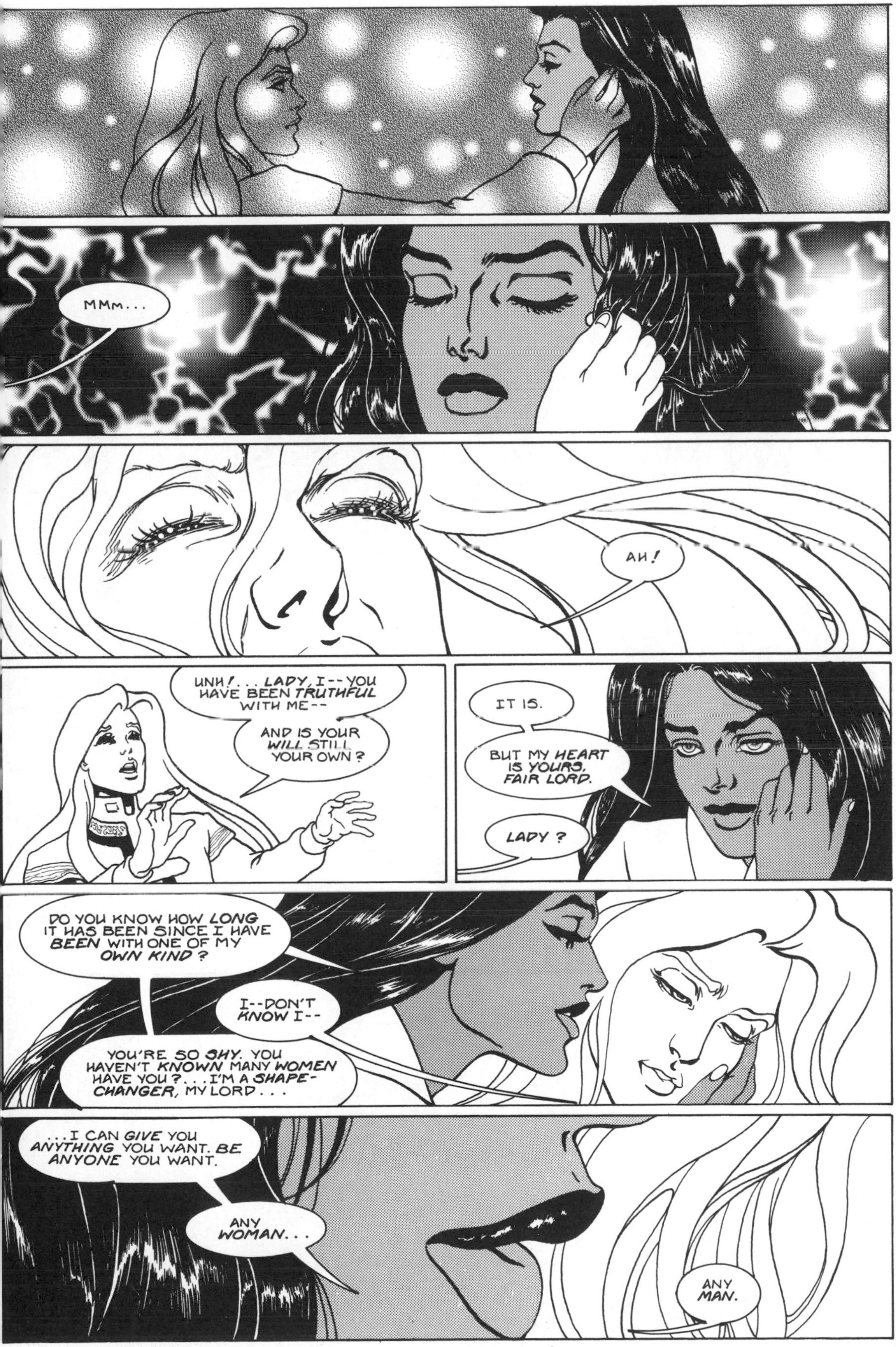
MMm...
AH!
UNH!... LADY, I--YOU HAVE BEEN TRUTHFUL WITH ME--
AND IS YOUR WILL STILL YOUR OWN?
IT IS.
BUT MY HEART IS YOURS, FAIR LORD.
LADY?
DO YOU KNOW HOW LONG IT HAS BEEN SINCE I HAVE BEEN WITH ONE OF MY OWN KIND?
I--DON'T KNOW I--
YOU'RE SO SHY. YOU HAVEN'T KNOWN MANY WOMEN HAVE YOU?... I'M A SHAPE-CHANGER, MY LORD...
...I CAN GIVE YOU ANYTHING YOU WANT. BE ANYONE YOU WANT.
ANY WOMAN...
ANY MAN.

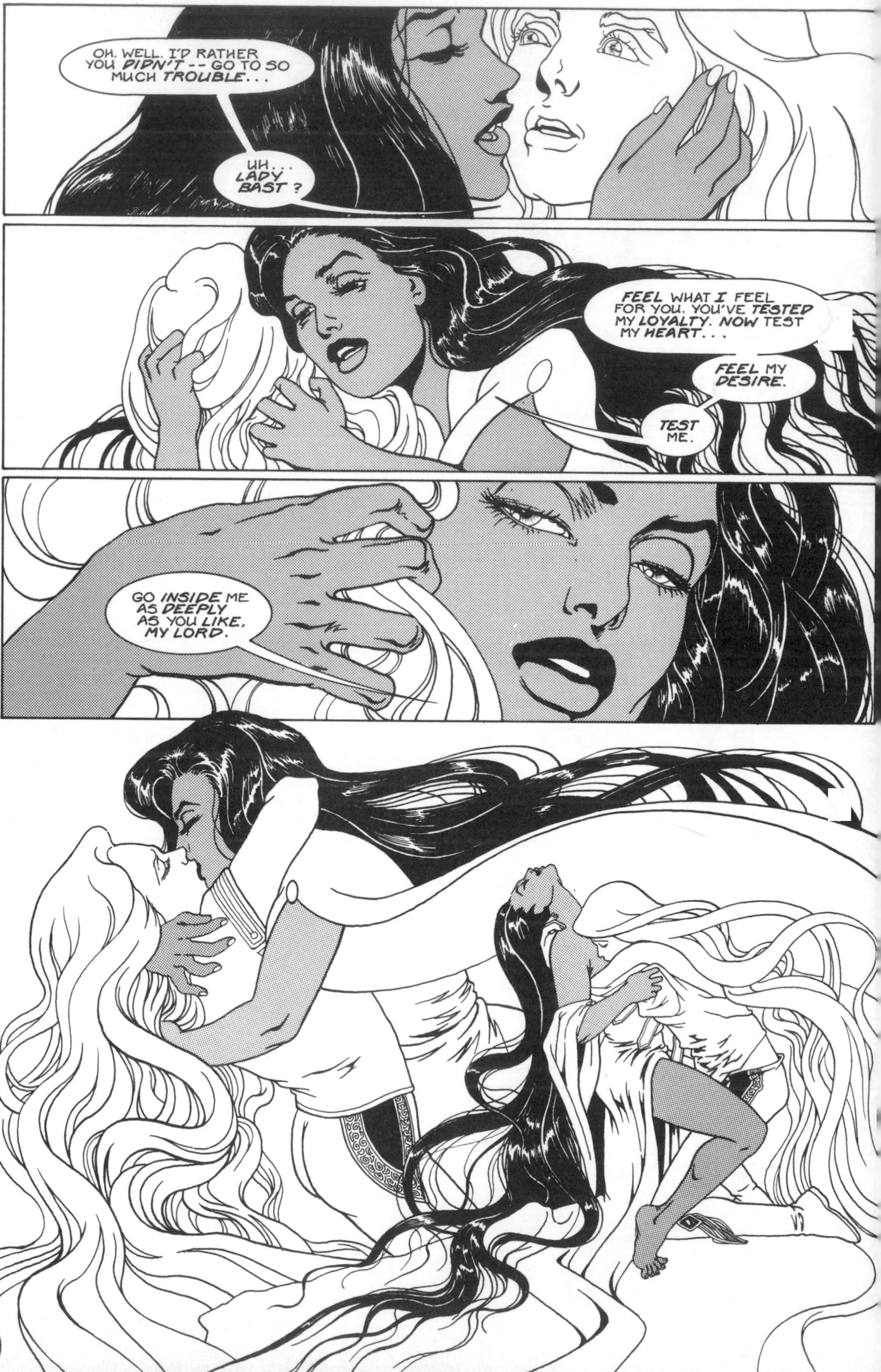
OH. WELL. I'D RATHER YOU DIDN'T -- GO TO SO MUCH TROUBLE...
UH... LADY BAST ?
FEEL WHAT I FEEL FOR YOU. YOU'VE TESTED MY LOYALTY. NOW TEST MY HEART...
FEEL MY DESIRE.
TEST ME.
GO INSIDE ME AS DEEPLY AS YOU LIKE, MY LORD.

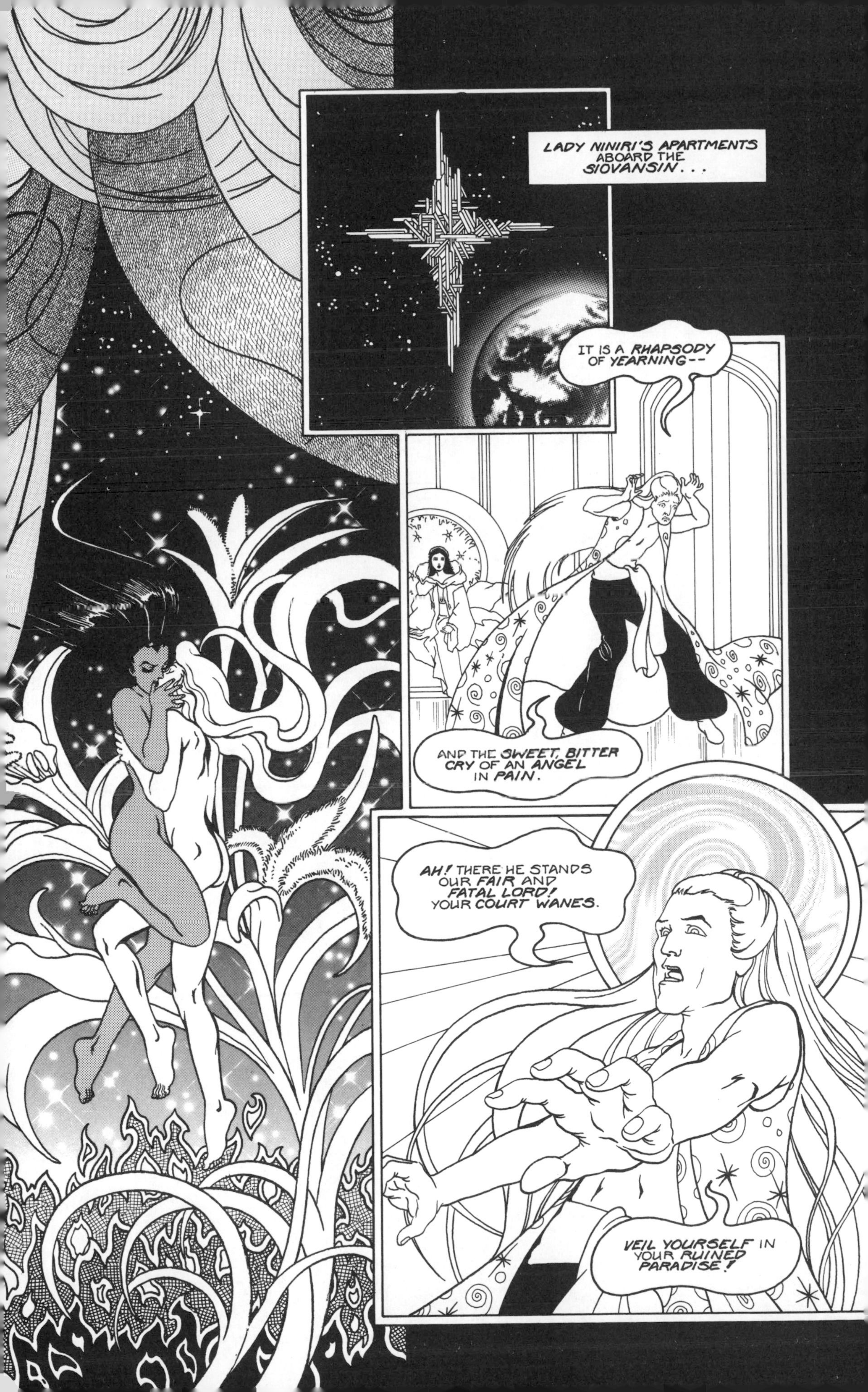

LADY NINIRI'S APARTMENTS ABOARD THE SIOVANSIN...
IT IS A RHAPSODY OF YEARNING--
AND THE SWEET, BITTER CRY OF AN ANGEL IN PAIN.
AH! THERE HE STANDS OUR FAIR AND FATAL LORD! YOUR COURT WANES.
VEIL YOURSELF IN YOUR RUINED PARADISE!

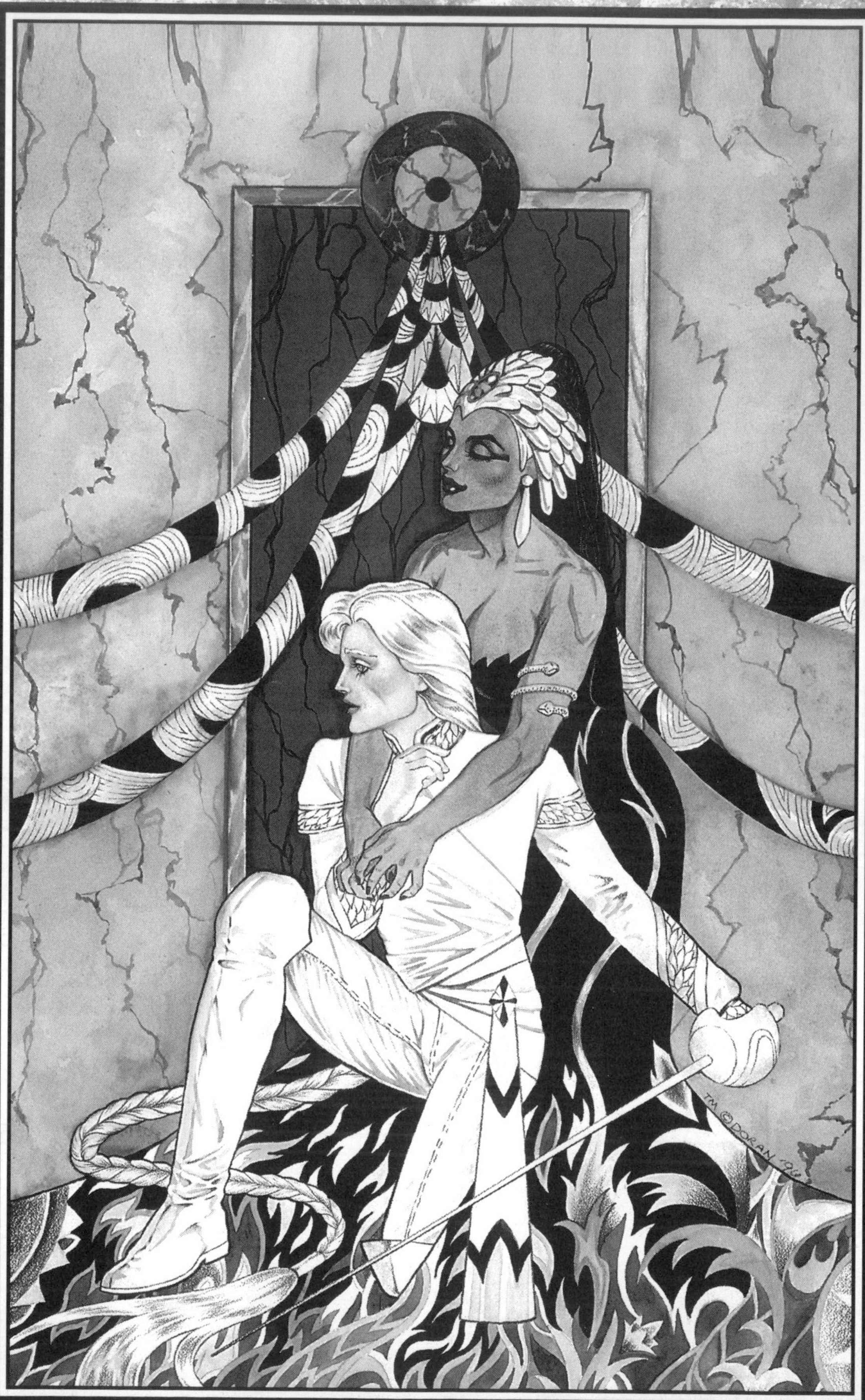

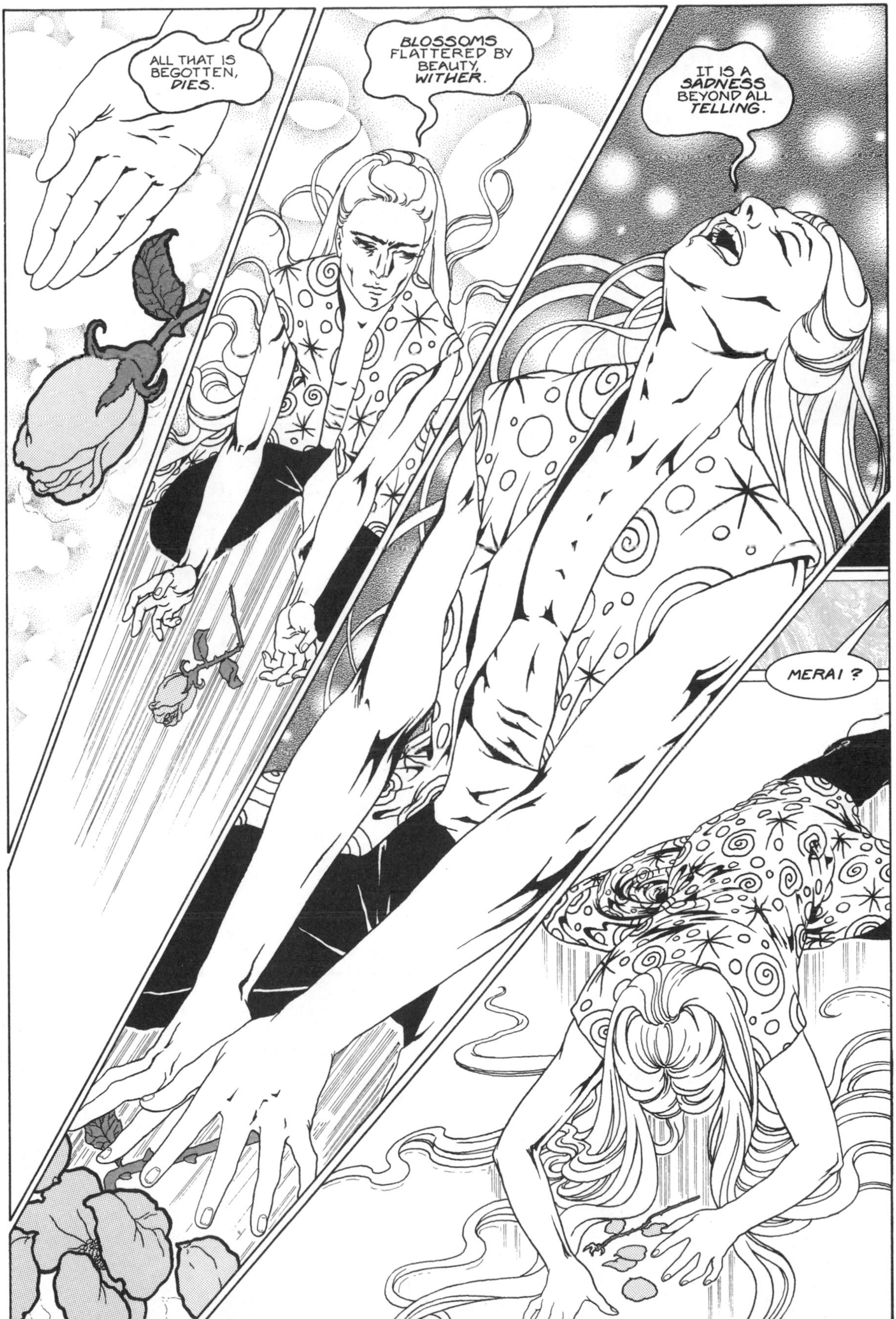
ALL THAT IS BEGOTTEN, DIES.
BLOSSOMS FLATTERED BY BEAUTY, WITHER.
IT IS A SADNESS BEYOND ALL TELLING.
MERAI ?

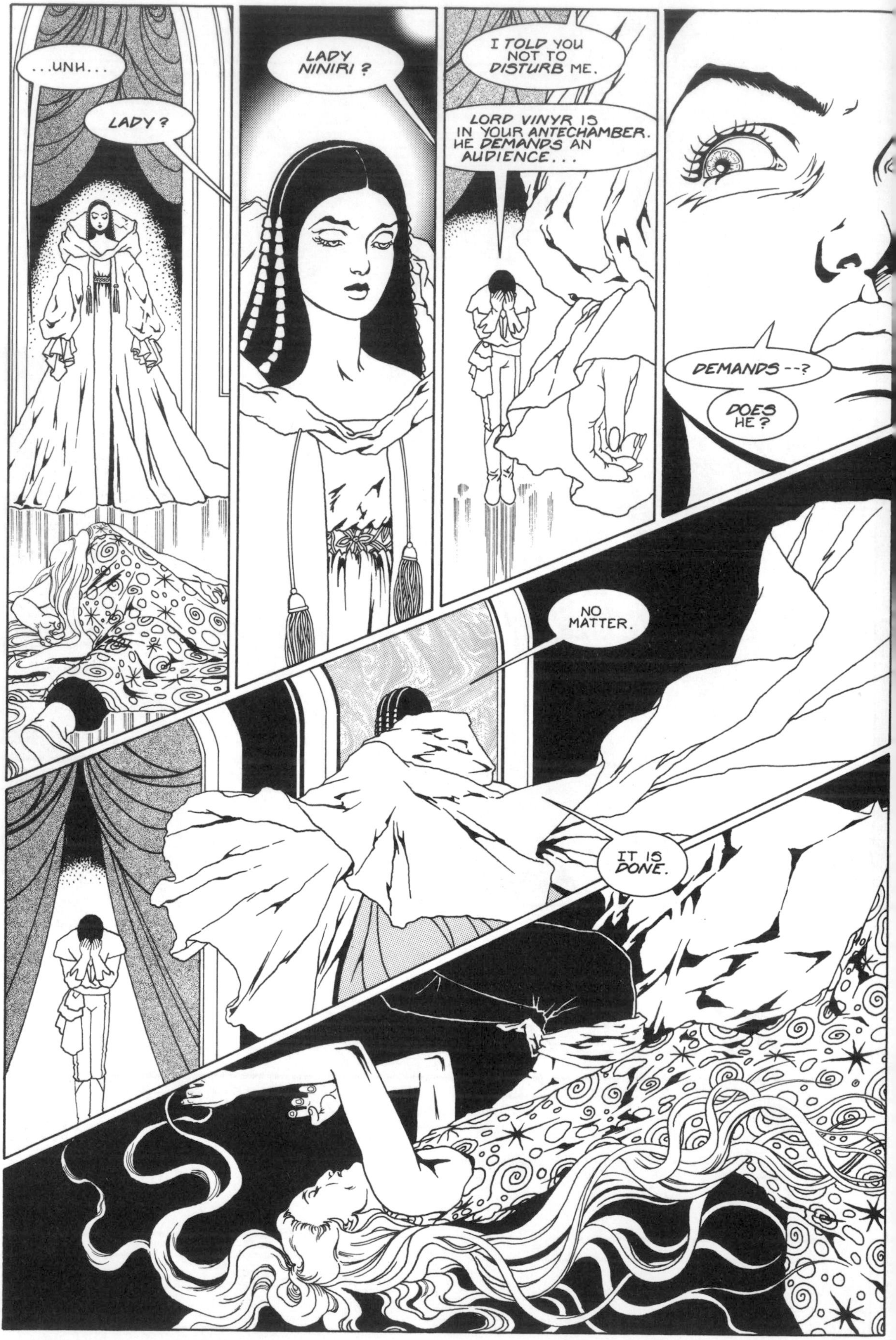
...UNH...
LADY?
LADY NINIRI?
I TOLD YOU NOT TO DISTURB ME.
LORD VINYR IS IN YOUR ANTECHAMBER. HE DEMANDS AN AUDIENCE...
DEMANDS--?
DOES HE?
NO MATTER.
IT IS DONE.

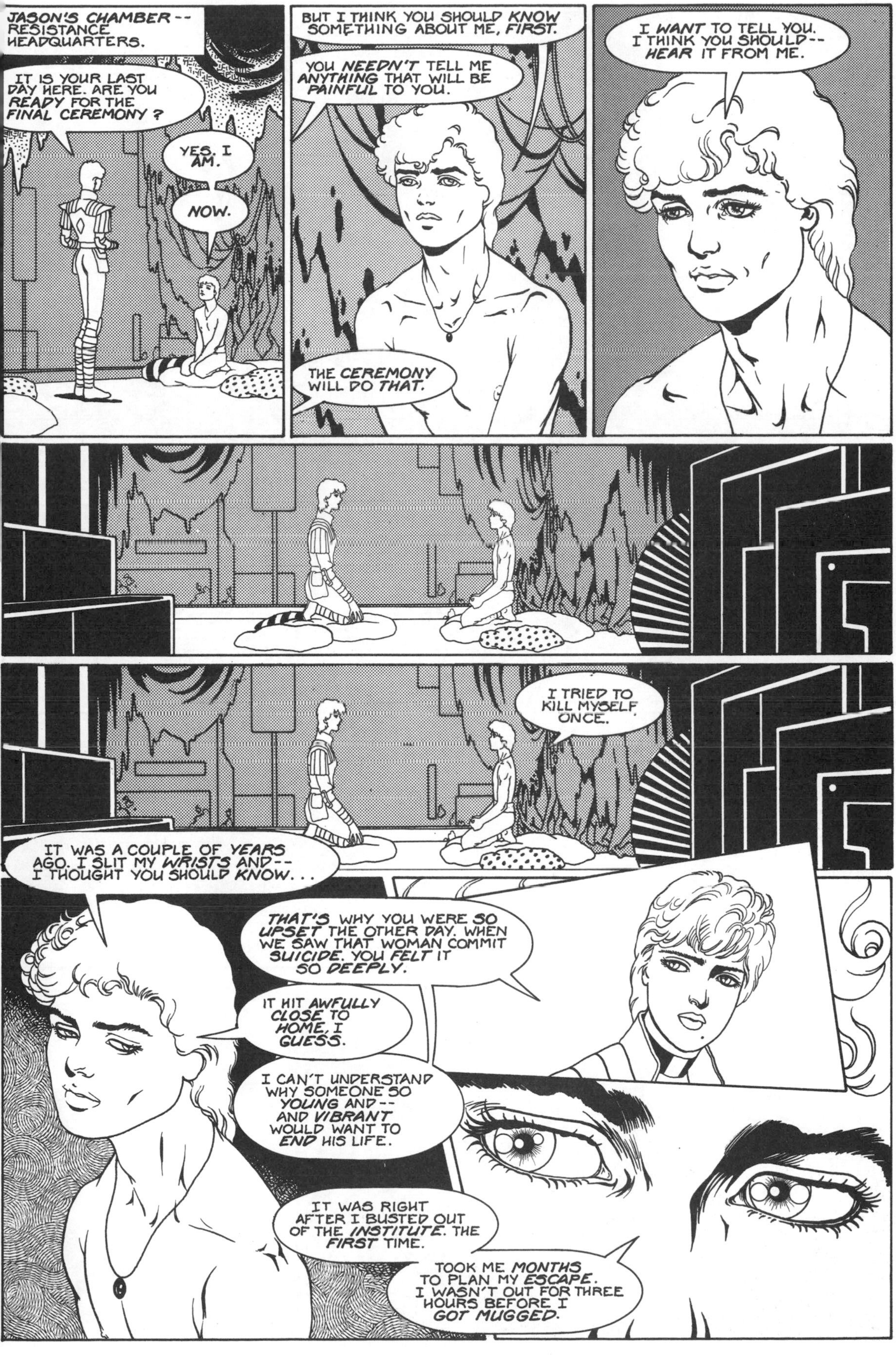
JASON'S CHAMBER -- RESISTANCE HEADQUARTERS.
IT IS YOUR LAST DAY HERE. ARE YOU READY FOR THE FINAL CEREMONY ?
YES. I AM.
NOW.
BUT I THINK YOU SHOULD KNOW SOMETHING ABOUT ME, FIRST.
YOU NEEDN'T TELL ME ANYTHING THAT WILL BE PAINFUL TO YOU.
THE CEREMONY WILL DO THAT.
I WANT TO TELL YOU. I THINK YOU SHOULD -- HEAR IT FROM ME.
I TRIED TO KILL MYSELF ONCE.
IT WAS A COUPLE OF YEARS AGO. I SLIT MY WRISTS AND -- I THOUGHT YOU SHOULD KNOW...
THAT'S WHY YOU WERE SO UPSET THE OTHER DAY. WHEN WE SAW THAT WOMAN COMMIT SUICIDE. YOU FELT IT SO DEEPLY.
IT HIT AWFULLY CLOSE TO HOME, I GUESS.
I CAN'T UNDERSTAND WHY SOMEONE SO YOUNG AND -- AND VIBRANT WOULD WANT TO END HIS LIFE.
IT WAS RIGHT AFTER I BUSTED OUT OF THE INSTITUTE. THE FIRST TIME.
TOOK ME MONTHS TO PLAN MY ESCAPE. I WASN'T OUT FOR THREE HOURS BEFORE I GOT MUGGED.

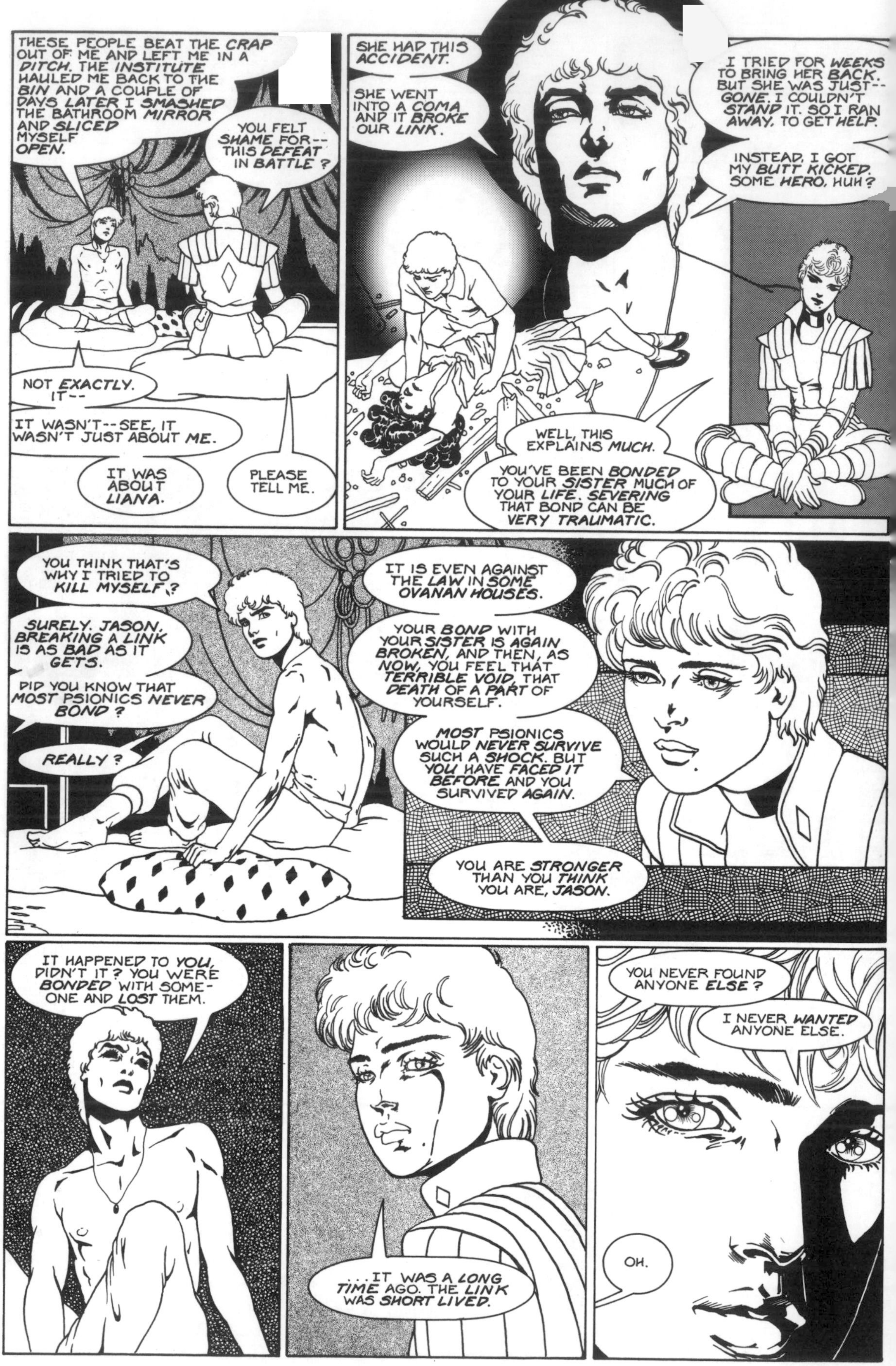
THESE PEOPLE BEAT THE CRAP OUT OF ME AND LEFT ME IN A DITCH. THE INSTITUTE HAULED ME BACK TO THE BIN AND A COUPLE OF DAYS LATER I SMASHED THE BATHROOM MIRROR AND SLICED MYSELF OPEN.
YOU FELT SHAME FOR-- THIS DEFEAT IN BATTLE ?
NOT EXACTLY. IT--
IT WASN'T--SEE, IT WASN'T JUST ABOUT ME.
IT WAS ABOUT LIANA.
PLEASE TELL ME.
SHE HAD THIS ACCIDENT.
SHE WENT INTO A COMA AND IT BROKE OUR LINK.
I TRIED FOR WEEKS TO BRING HER BACK. BUT SHE WAS JUST-- GONE. I COULDN'T STAND IT. SO I RAN AWAY, TO GET HELP.
INSTEAD, I GOT MY BUTT KICKED. SOME HERO, HUH ?
WELL, THIS EXPLAINS MUCH.
YOU'VE BEEN BONDED TO YOUR SISTER MUCH OF YOUR LIFE. SEVERING THAT BOND CAN BE VERY TRAUMATIC.
YOU THINK THAT'S WHY I TRIED TO KILL MYSELF ?
SURELY, JASON. BREAKING A LINK IS AS BAD AS IT GETS.
DID YOU KNOW THAT MOST PSIONICS NEVER BOND ?
REALLY ?
IT IS EVEN AGAINST THE LAW IN SOME OVANAN HOUSES.
YOUR BOND WITH YOUR SISTER IS AGAIN BROKEN, AND THEN, AS NOW, YOU FEEL THAT TERRIBLE VOID, THAT DEATH OF A PART OF YOURSELF.
MOST PSIONICS WOULD NEVER SURVIVE SUCH A SHOCK. BUT YOU HAVE FACED IT BEFORE AND YOU SURVIVED AGAIN.
YOU ARE STRONGER THAN YOU THINK YOU ARE, JASON.
IT HAPPENED TO YOU, DIDN'T IT ? YOU WERE BONDED WITH SOME-ONE AND LOST THEM.
...IT WAS A LONG TIME AGO. THE LINK WAS SHORT LIVED.
YOU NEVER FOUND ANYONE ELSE ?
I NEVER WANTED ANYONE ELSE.
OH.

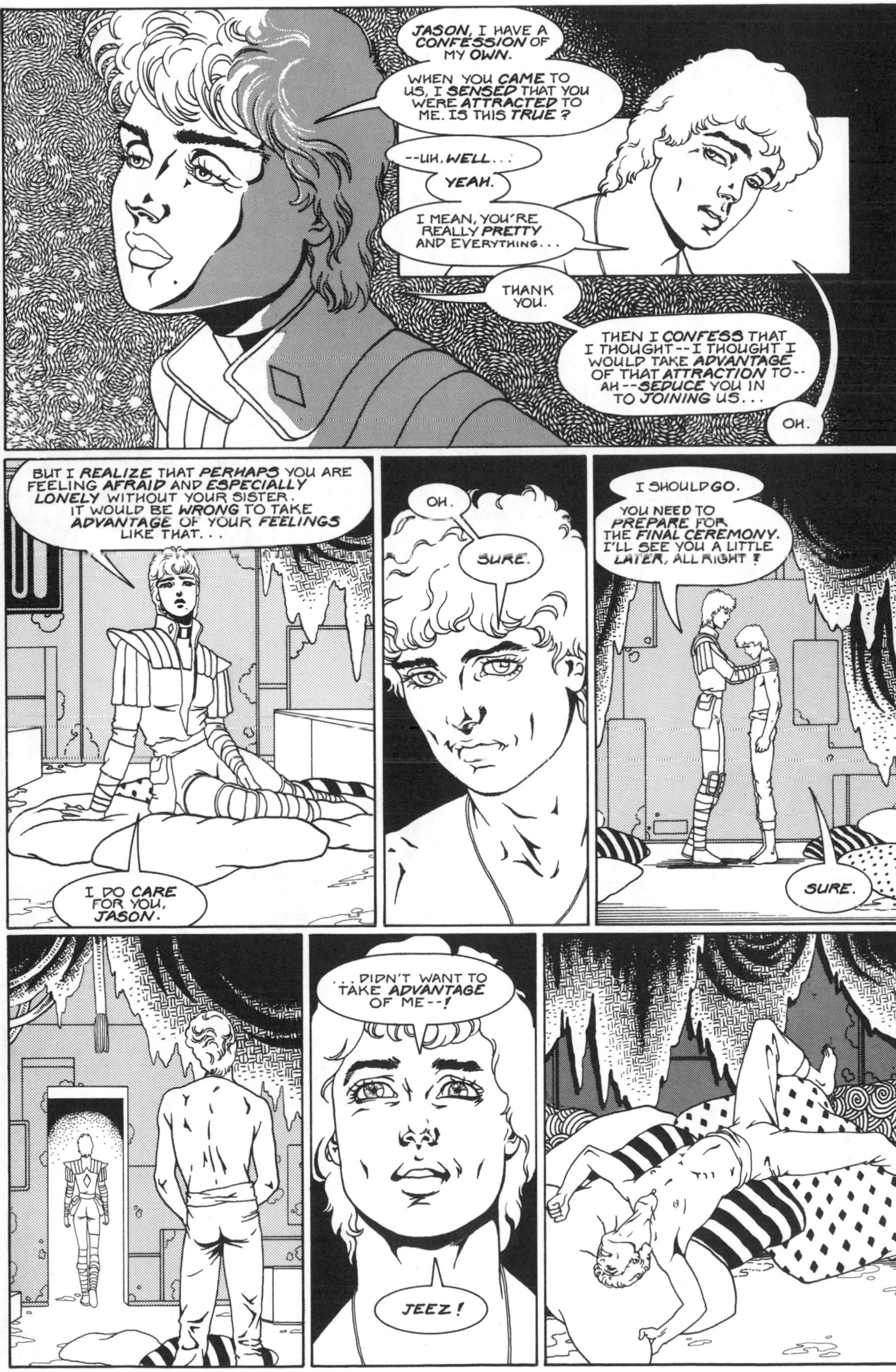
JASON, I HAVE A CONFESSION OF MY OWN.
WHEN YOU CAME TO US, I SENSED THAT YOU WERE ATTRACTED TO ME. IS THIS TRUE?
--UH, WELL...
YEAH.
I MEAN, YOU'RE REALLY PRETTY AND EVERYTHING...
THANK YOU.
THEN I CONFESS THAT I THOUGHT--I THOUGHT I WOULD TAKE ADVANTAGE OF THAT ATTRACTION TO--AH--SEDUCE YOU IN TO JOINING US...
OH.
BUT I REALIZE THAT PERHAPS YOU ARE FEELING AFRAID AND ESPECIALLY LONELY WITHOUT YOUR SISTER. IT WOULD BE WRONG TO TAKE ADVANTAGE OF YOUR FEELINGS LIKE THAT...
I DO CARE FOR YOU, JASON.
OH.
SURE.
I SHOULD GO.
YOU NEED TO PREPARE FOR THE FINAL CEREMONY. I'LL SEE YOU A LITTLE LATER, ALL RIGHT?
SURE.
...DIDN'T WANT TO TAKE ADVANTAGE OF ME--!
JEEZ!

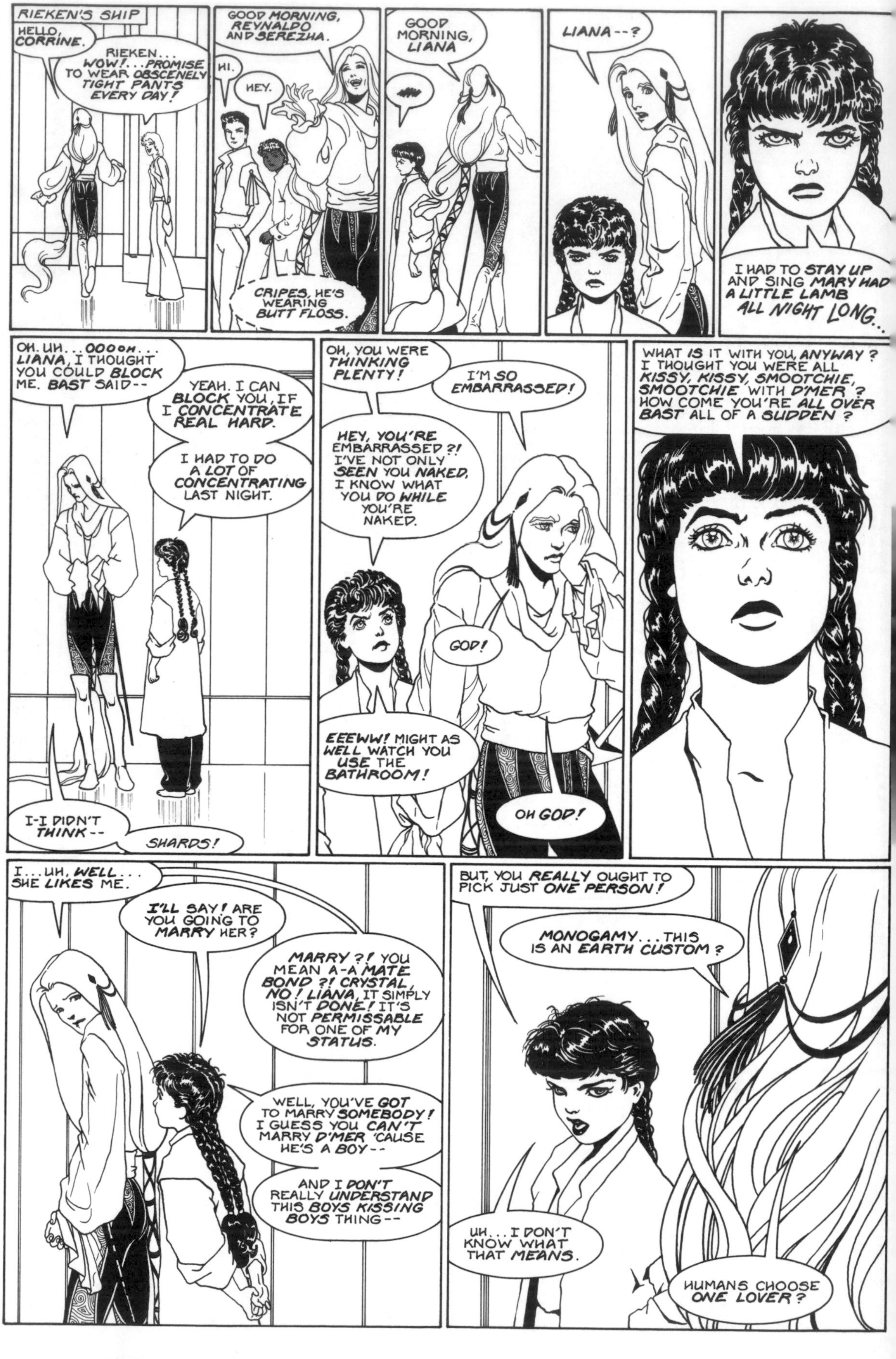
RIEKEN'S SHIP
HELLO, CORRINE.
RIEKEN... WOW!...PROMISE TO WEAR OBSCENELY TIGHT PANTS EVERY DAY!
GOOD MORNING, REYNALDO AND SEREZHA.
HI.
HEY.
CRIPES, HE'S WEARING BUTT FLOSS.
GOOD MORNING, LIANA
LIANA--?
I HAD TO STAY UP AND SING MARY HAD A LITTLE LAMB ALL NIGHT LONG...
OH. UH...OOOOH... LIANA, I THOUGHT YOU COULD BLOCK ME. BAST SAID--
YEAH. I CAN BLOCK YOU, IF I CONCENTRATE REAL HARD.
I HAD TO DO A LOT OF CONCENTRATING LAST NIGHT.
I-I DIDN'T THINK--
SHARDS!
OH, YOU WERE THINKING PLENTY!
I'M SO EMBARRASSED!
HEY, YOU'RE EMBARRASSED?! I'VE NOT ONLY SEEN YOU NAKED, I KNOW WHAT YOU DO WHILE YOU'RE NAKED.
GOD!
EEEWW! MIGHT AS WELL WATCH YOU USE THE BATHROOM!
OH GOD!
WHAT IS IT WITH YOU, ANYWAY? I THOUGHT YOU WERE ALL KISSY, KISSY, SMOOTCHIE, SMOOTCHIE WITH D'MER? HOW COME YOU'RE ALL OVER BAST ALL OF A SUDDEN?
I...UH, WELL... SHE LIKES ME.
I'LL SAY! ARE YOU GOING TO MARRY HER?
MARRY?! YOU MEAN A-A MATE BOND?! CRYSTAL, NO! LIANA, IT SIMPLY ISN'T DONE! IT'S NOT PERMISSABLE FOR ONE OF MY STATUS.
WELL, YOU'VE GOT TO MARRY SOMEBODY! I GUESS YOU CAN'T MARRY D'MER 'CAUSE HE'S A BOY--
AND I DON'T REALLY UNDERSTAND THIS BOYS KISSING BOYS THING--
BUT, YOU REALLY OUGHT TO PICK JUST ONE PERSON!
MONOGAMY...THIS IS AN EARTH CUSTOM?
UH...I DON'T KNOW WHAT THAT MEANS.
HUMANS CHOOSE ONE LOVER?

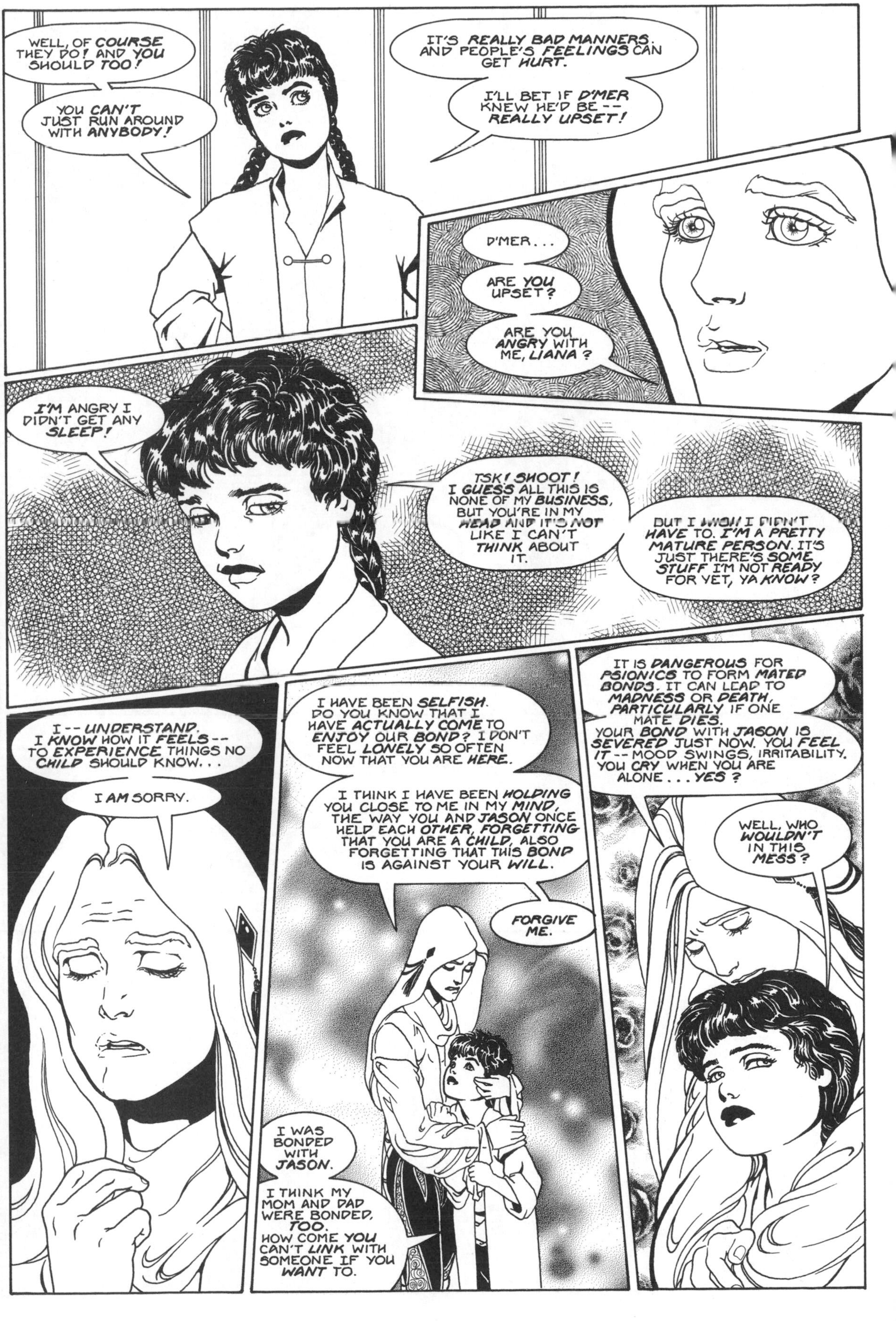
WELL, OF COURSE THEY DO! AND YOU SHOULD TOO!
YOU CAN'T JUST RUN AROUND WITH ANYBODY!
IT'S REALLY BAD MANNERS. AND PEOPLE'S FEELINGS CAN GET HURT.
I'LL BET IF D'MER KNEW HE'D BE -- REALLY UPSET!
D'MER...
ARE YOU UPSET?
ARE YOU ANGRY WITH ME, LIANA?
I'M ANGRY I DIDN'T GET ANY SLEEP!
TSK! SHOOT! I GUESS ALL THIS IS NONE OF MY BUSINESS, BUT YOU'RE IN MY HEAD AND IT'S NOT LIKE I CAN'T THINK ABOUT IT.
BUT I WISH I DIDN'T HAVE TO. I'M A PRETTY MATURE PERSON. IT'S JUST THERE'S SOME STUFF I'M NOT READY FOR YET, YA KNOW?
I -- UNDERSTAND. I KNOW HOW IT FEELS -- TO EXPERIENCE THINGS NO CHILD SHOULD KNOW...
I AM SORRY.
I HAVE BEEN SELFISH. DO YOU KNOW THAT I HAVE ACTUALLY COME TO ENJOY OUR BOND? I DON'T FEEL LONELY SO OFTEN NOW THAT YOU ARE HERE.
I THINK I HAVE BEEN HOLDING YOU CLOSE TO ME IN MY MIND, THE WAY YOU AND JASON ONCE HELD EACH OTHER, FORGETTING THAT YOU ARE A CHILD, ALSO FORGETTING THAT THIS BOND IS AGAINST YOUR WILL.
FORGIVE ME.
I WAS BONDED WITH JASON.
I THINK MY MOM AND DAD WERE BONDED, TOO. HOW COME YOU CAN'T LINK WITH SOMEONE IF YOU WANT TO.
IT IS DANGEROUS FOR PSIONICS TO FORM MATED BONDS. IT CAN LEAD TO MADNESS OR DEATH, PARTICULARLY IF ONE MATE DIES. YOUR BOND WITH JASON IS SEVERED JUST NOW. YOU FEEL IT -- MOOD SWINGS, IRRITABILITY. YOU CRY WHEN YOU ARE ALONE... YES?
WELL, WHO WOULDN'T IN THIS MESS?

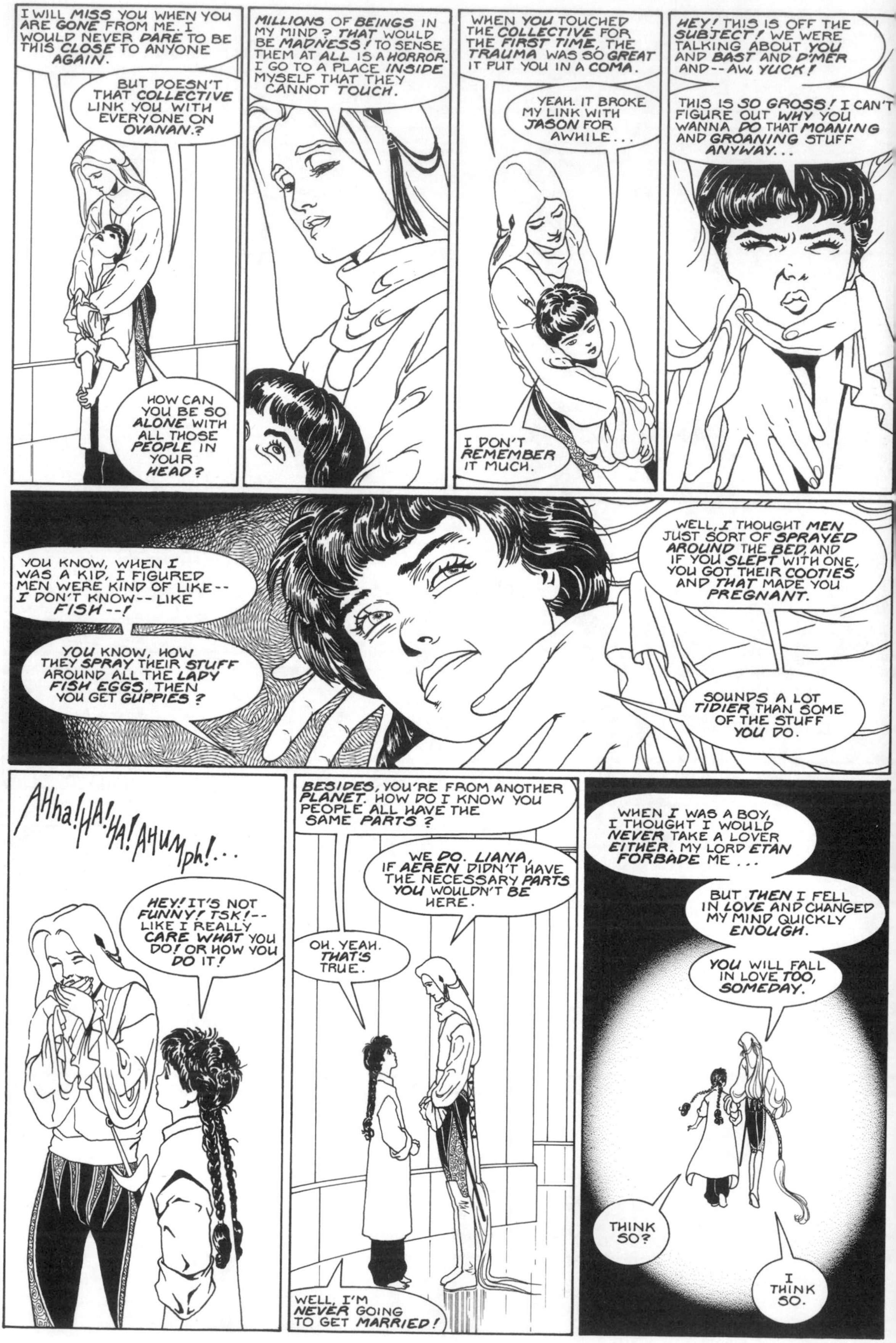
I WILL MISS YOU WHEN YOU ARE GONE FROM ME. I WOULD NEVER DARE TO BE THIS CLOSE TO ANYONE AGAIN.
BUT DOESN'T THAT COLLECTIVE LINK YOU WITH EVERYONE ON OVANAN.?
HOW CAN YOU BE SO ALONE WITH ALL THOSE PEOPLE IN YOUR HEAD?
MILLIONS OF BEINGS IN MY MIND? THAT WOULD BE MADNESS! TO SENSE THEM AT ALL IS A HORROR. I GO TO A PLACE INSIDE MYSELF THAT THEY CANNOT TOUCH.
WHEN YOU TOUCHED THE COLLECTIVE FOR THE FIRST TIME, THE TRAUMA WAS SO GREAT IT PUT YOU IN A COMA.
YEAH. IT BROKE MY LINK WITH JASON FOR AWHILE...
I DON'T REMEMBER IT MUCH.
HEY! THIS IS OFF THE SUBJECT! WE WERE TALKING ABOUT YOU AND BAST AND D'MER AND--AW, YUCK!
THIS IS SO GROSS! I CAN'T FIGURE OUT WHY YOU WANNA DO THAT MOANING AND GROANING STUFF ANYWAY...
YOU KNOW, WHEN I WAS A KID, I FIGURED MEN WERE KIND OF LIKE-- I DON'T KNOW-- LIKE FISH--!
YOU KNOW, HOW THEY SPRAY THEIR STUFF AROUND ALL THE LADY FISH EGGS, THEN YOU GET GUPPIES?
WELL, I THOUGHT MEN JUST SORT OF SPRAYED AROUND THE BED, AND IF YOU SLEPT WITH ONE, YOU GOT THEIR COOTIES AND THAT MADE YOU PREGNANT.
SOUNDS A LOT TIDIER THAN SOME OF THE STUFF YOU DO.
AHha!HA!HA!AHUMph!...
HEY! IT'S NOT FUNNY! TSK!-- LIKE I REALLY CARE WHAT YOU DO! OR HOW YOU DO IT!
BESIDES, YOU'RE FROM ANOTHER PLANET. HOW DO I KNOW YOU PEOPLE ALL HAVE THE SAME PARTS?
WE DO. LIANA, IF AEREN DIDN'T HAVE THE NECESSARY PARTS YOU WOULDN'T BE HERE.
OH. YEAH. THAT'S TRUE.
WELL, I'M NEVER GOING TO GET MARRIED!
WHEN I WAS A BOY, I THOUGHT I WOULD NEVER TAKE A LOVER EITHER. MY LORD ETAN FORBADE ME...
BUT THEN I FELL IN LOVE AND CHANGED MY MIND QUICKLY ENOUGH.
YOU WILL FALL IN LOVE TOO, SOMEDAY.
THINK SO?
I THINK SO.

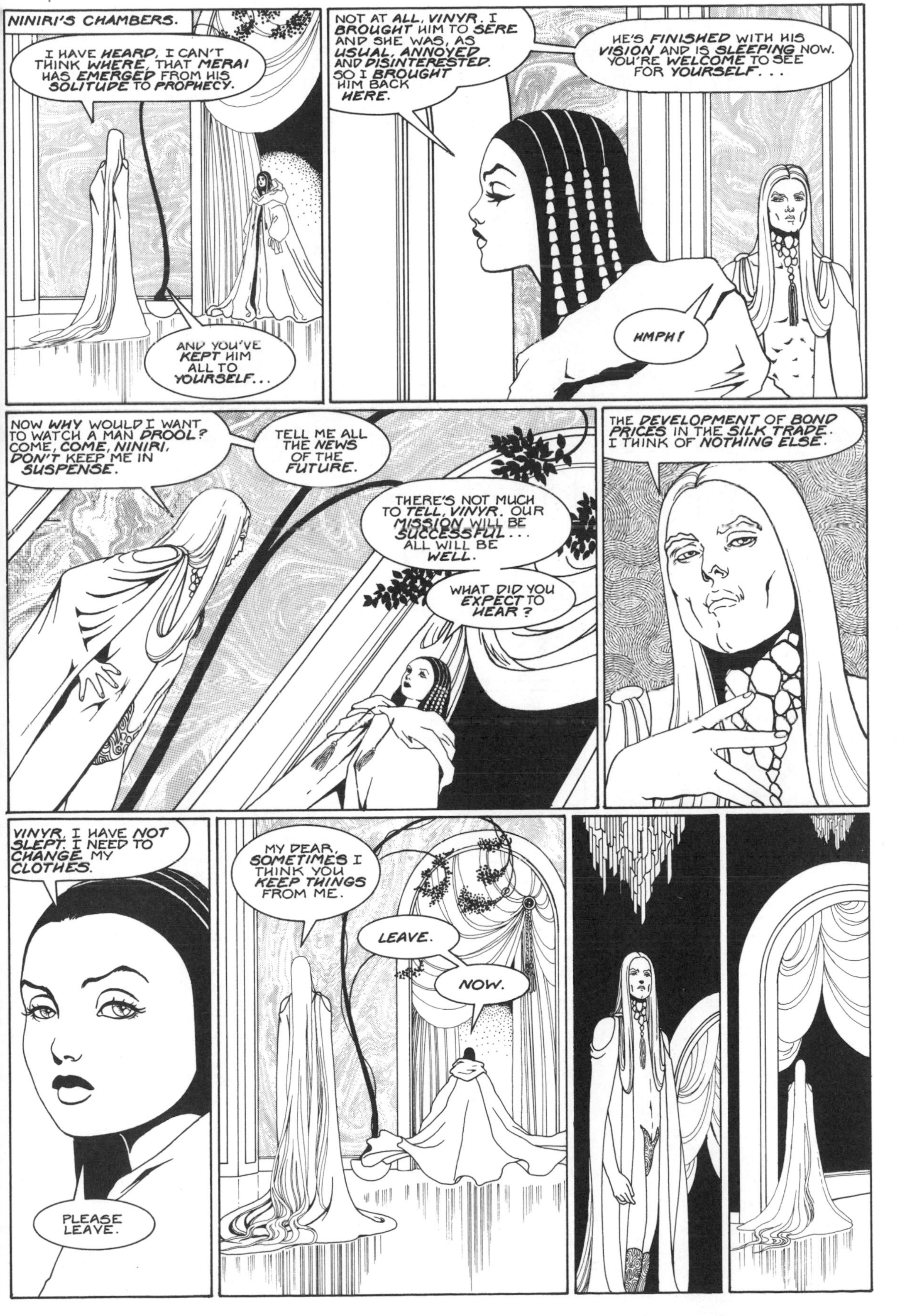
NINIRI'S CHAMBERS.
I HAVE HEARD, I CAN'T THINK WHERE, THAT MERAI HAS EMERGED FROM HIS SOLITUDE TO PROPHECY.
AND YOU'VE KEPT HIM ALL TO YOURSELF...
NOT AT ALL, VINYR. I BROUGHT HIM TO SERE AND SHE WAS, AS USUAL, ANNOYED AND DISINTERESTED. SO I BROUGHT HIM BACK HERE.
HE'S FINISHED WITH HIS VISION AND IS SLEEPING NOW. YOU'RE WELCOME TO SEE FOR YOURSELF...
HMPH!
NOW WHY WOULD I WANT TO WATCH A MAN DROOL? COME, COME, NINIRI, DON'T KEEP ME IN SUSPENSE.
TELL ME ALL THE NEWS OF THE FUTURE.
THERE'S NOT MUCH TO TELL, VINYR. OUR MISSION WILL BE SUCCESSFUL... ALL WILL BE WELL.
WHAT DID YOU EXPECT TO HEAR?
THE DEVELOPMENT OF BOND PRICES IN THE SILK TRADE. I THINK OF NOTHING ELSE.
VINYR, I HAVE NOT SLEPT. I NEED TO CHANGE MY CLOTHES.
PLEASE LEAVE.
MY DEAR, SOMETIMES I THINK YOU KEEP THINGS FROM ME.
LEAVE.
NOW.

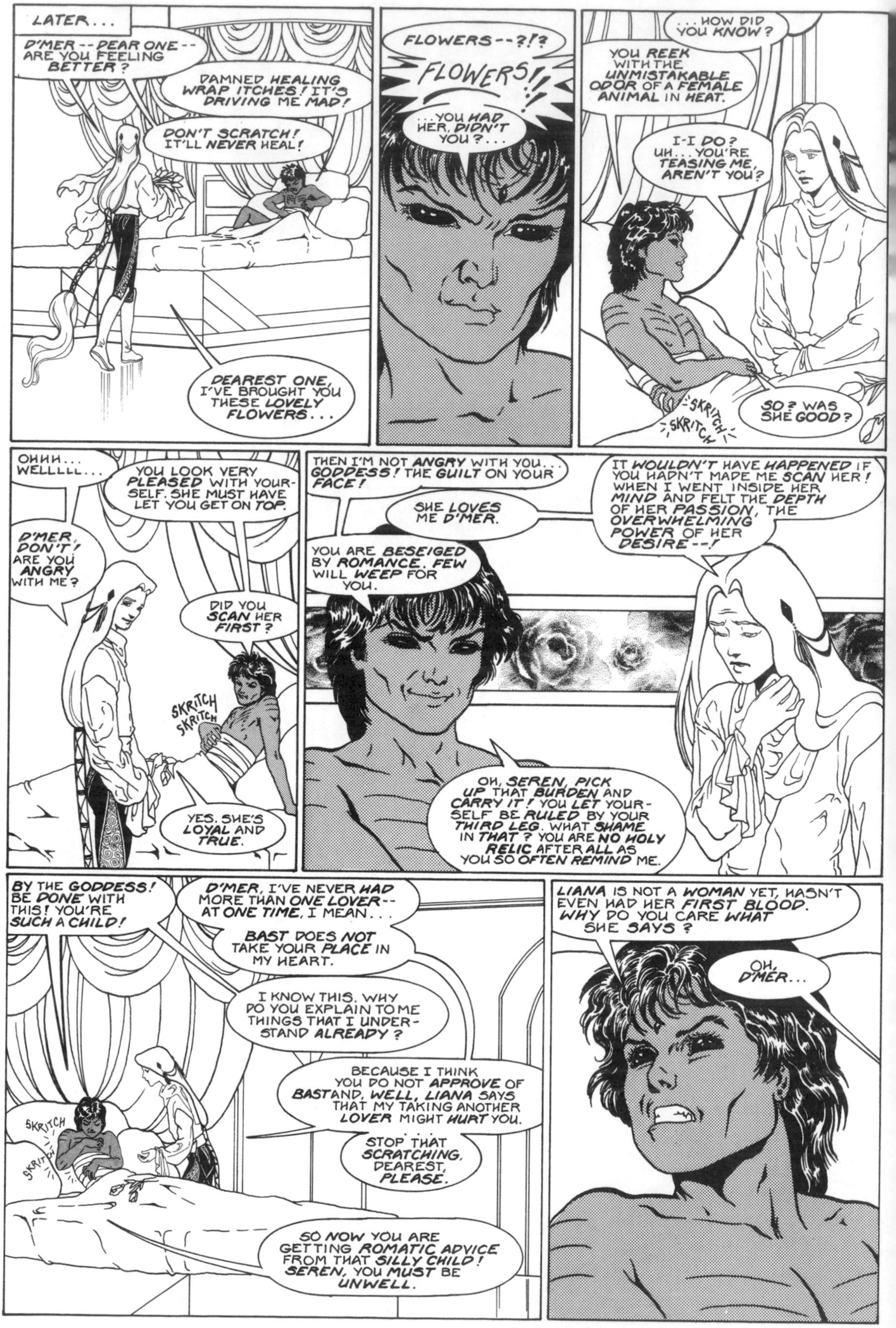

LATER...
D'MER -- DEAR ONE -- ARE YOU FEELING BETTER?
DAMNED HEALING WRAP ITCHES! IT'S DRIVING ME MAD!
DON'T SCRATCH! IT'LL NEVER HEAL!
DEAREST ONE, I'VE BROUGHT YOU THESE LOVELY FLOWERS...
FLOWERS--?!?
FLOWERS!!
...YOU HAD HER, DIDN'T YOU?...
...HOW DID YOU KNOW?
YOU REEK WITH THE UNMISTAKABLE ODOR OF A FEMALE ANIMAL IN HEAT.
I-I DO? UH... YOU'RE TEASING ME, AREN'T YOU?
SKRITCH SKRITCH
SO? WAS SHE GOOD?
OHHH... WELLLLL...
YOU LOOK VERY PLEASED WITH YOURSELF. SHE MUST HAVE LET YOU GET ON TOP.
D'MER, DON'T! ARE YOU ANGRY WITH ME?
DID YOU SCAN HER FIRST?
SKRITCH SKRITCH
YES. SHE'S LOYAL AND TRUE.
THEN I'M NOT ANGRY WITH YOU... GODDESS! THE GUILT ON YOUR FACE!
SHE LOVES ME D'MER.
IT WOULDN'T HAVE HAPPENED IF YOU HADN'T MADE ME SCAN HER! WHEN I WENT INSIDE HER MIND AND FELT THE DEPTH OF HER PASSION, THE OVERWHELMING POWER OF HER DESIRE--!
YOU ARE BESEIGED BY ROMANCE. FEW WILL WEEP FOR YOU.
OH, SEREN, PICK UP THAT BURDEN AND CARRY IT! YOU LET YOURSELF BE RULED BY YOUR THIRD LEG. WHAT SHAME IN THAT? YOU ARE NO HOLY RELIC AFTER ALL AS YOU SO OFTEN REMIND ME.
BY THE GODDESS! BE DONE WITH THIS! YOU'RE SUCH A CHILD!
D'MER, I'VE NEVER HAD MORE THAN ONE LOVER -- AT ONE TIME, I MEAN...
BAST DOES NOT TAKE YOUR PLACE IN MY HEART.
I KNOW THIS. WHY DO YOU EXPLAIN TO ME THINGS THAT I UNDERSTAND ALREADY?
BECAUSE I THINK YOU DO NOT APPROVE OF BAST AND, WELL, LIANA SAYS THAT MY TAKING ANOTHER LOVER MIGHT HURT YOU.
SKRITCH SKRITCH
STOP THAT SCRATCHING, DEAREST, PLEASE.
SO NOW YOU ARE GETTING ROMATIC ADVICE FROM THAT SILLY CHILD! SEREN, YOU MUST BE UNWELL.
LIANA IS NOT A WOMAN YET, HASN'T EVEN HAD HER FIRST BLOOD. WHY DO YOU CARE WHAT SHE SAYS?
OH, D'MER...

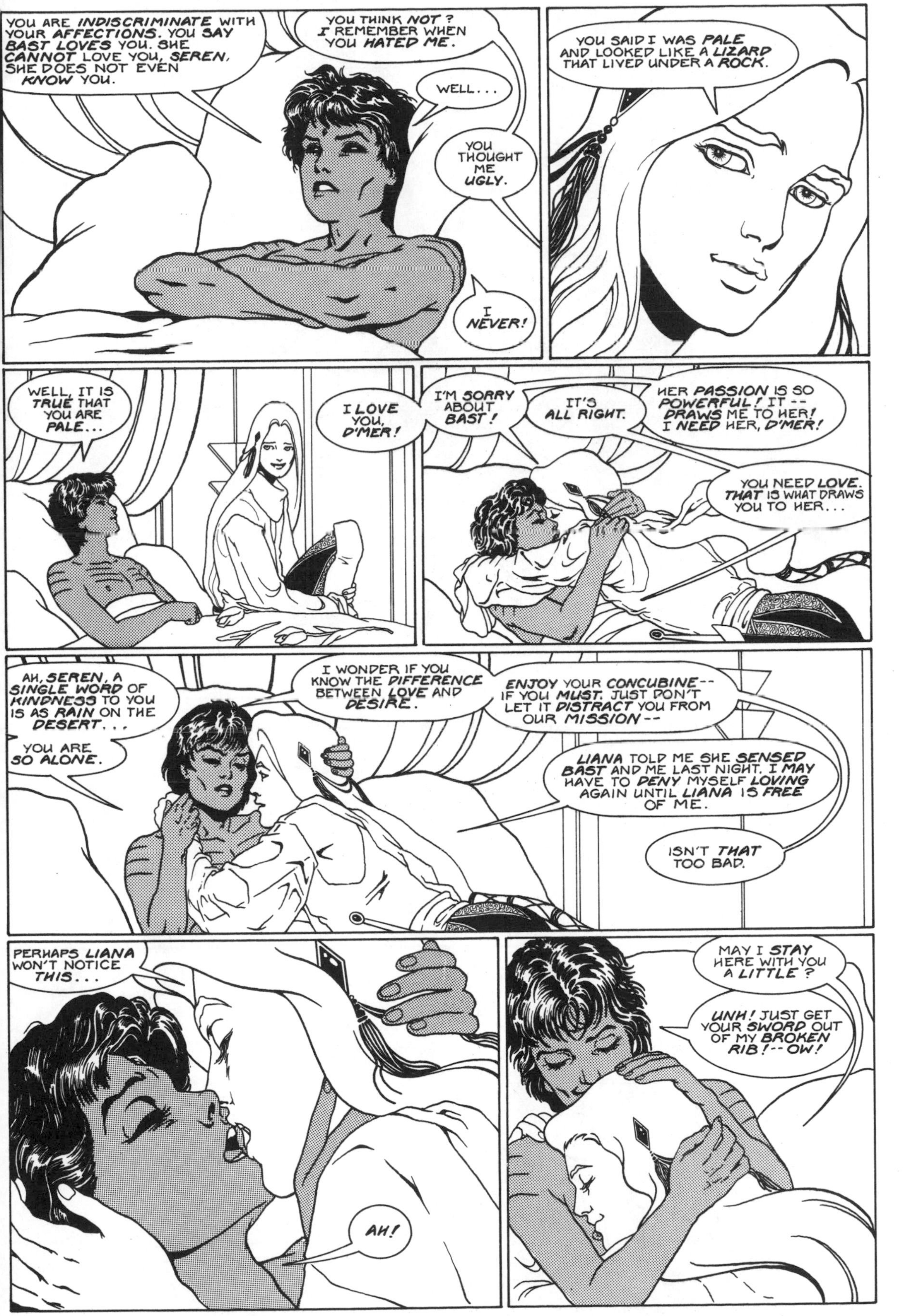
YOU ARE INDISCRIMINATE WITH YOUR AFFECTIONS. YOU SAY BAST LOVES YOU. SHE CANNOT LOVE YOU, SEREN, SHE DOES NOT EVEN KNOW YOU.
YOU THINK NOT? I REMEMBER WHEN YOU HATED ME.
WELL...
YOU THOUGHT ME UGLY.
I NEVER!
YOU SAID I WAS PALE AND LOOKED LIKE A LIZARD THAT LIVED UNDER A ROCK.
WELL, IT IS TRUE THAT YOU ARE PALE...
I LOVE YOU, D'MER!
I'M SORRY ABOUT BAST!
IT'S ALL RIGHT.
HER PASSION IS SO POWERFUL! IT -- DRAWS ME TO HER! I NEED HER, D'MER!
YOU NEED LOVE. THAT IS WHAT DRAWS YOU TO HER...
AH, SEREN, A SINGLE WORD OF KINDNESS TO YOU IS AS RAIN ON THE DESERT...
YOU ARE SO ALONE.
I WONDER IF YOU KNOW THE DIFFERENCE BETWEEN LOVE AND DESIRE.
ENJOY YOUR CONCUBINE-- IF YOU MUST. JUST DON'T LET IT DISTRACT YOU FROM OUR MISSION--
LIANA TOLD ME SHE SENSED BAST AND ME LAST NIGHT. I MAY HAVE TO DENY MYSELF LOVING AGAIN UNTIL LIANA IS FREE OF ME.
ISN'T THAT TOO BAD.
PERHAPS LIANA WON'T NOTICE THIS...
AH!
MAY I STAY HERE WITH YOU A LITTLE?
UNH! JUST GET YOUR SWORD OUT OF MY BROKEN RIB!--OW!

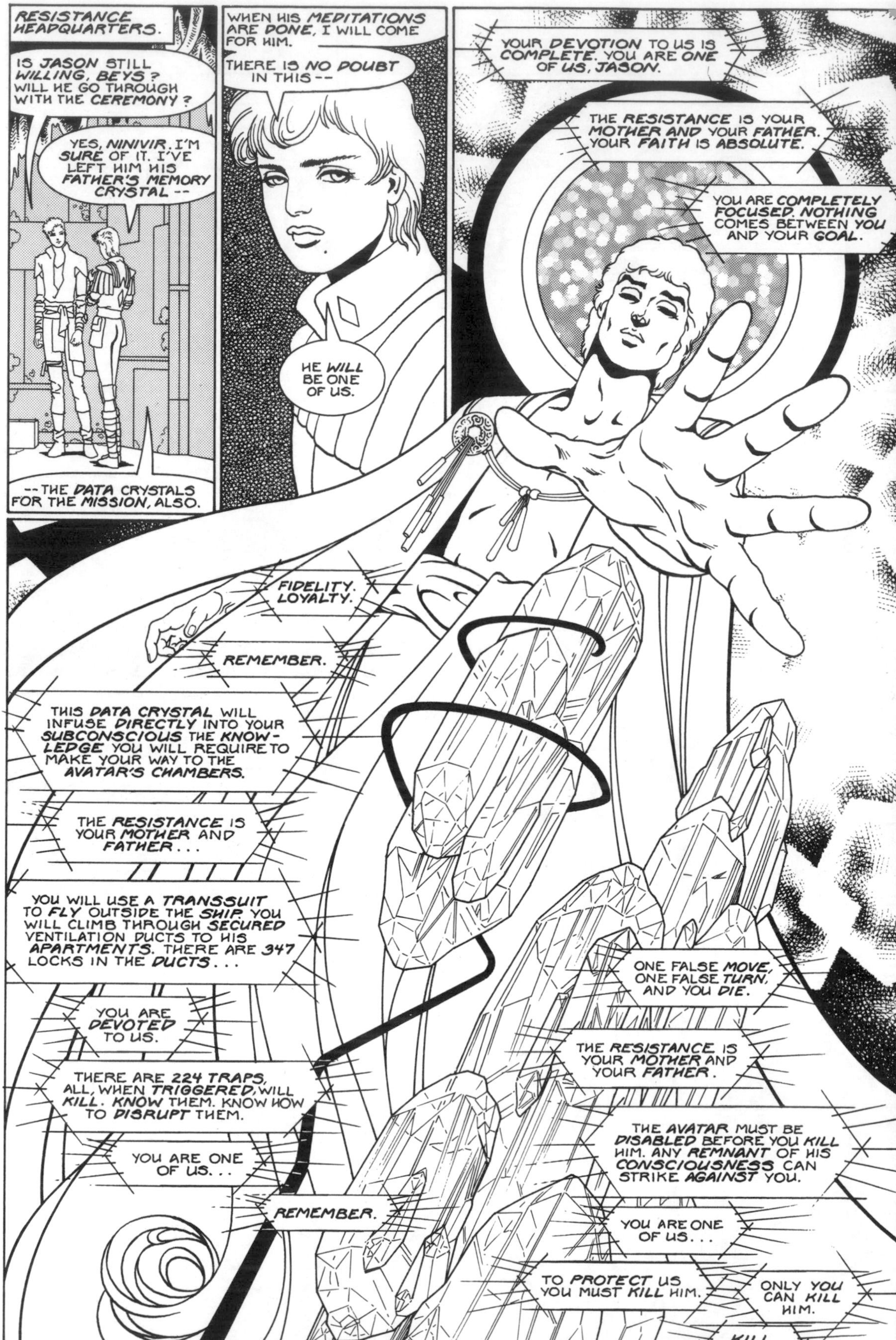
RESISTANCE HEADQUARTERS.
IS JASON STILL WILLING, BEYS? WILL HE GO THROUGH WITH THE CEREMONY?
YES, NINIVIR. I'M SURE OF IT. I'VE LEFT HIM HIS FATHER'S MEMORY CRYSTAL --
-- THE DATA CRYSTALS FOR THE MISSION, ALSO.
WHEN HIS MEDITATIONS ARE DONE, I WILL COME FOR HIM.
THERE IS NO DOUBT IN THIS --
HE WILL BE ONE OF US.
YOUR DEVOTION TO US IS COMPLETE. YOU ARE ONE OF US, JASON.
THE RESISTANCE IS YOUR MOTHER AND YOUR FATHER. YOUR FAITH IS ABSOLUTE.
YOU ARE COMPLETELY FOCUSED. NOTHING COMES BETWEEN YOU AND YOUR GOAL.
FIDELITY. LOYALTY.
REMEMBER.
THIS DATA CRYSTAL WILL INFUSE DIRECTLY INTO YOUR SUBCONSCIOUS THE KNOW-LEDGE YOU WILL REQUIRE TO MAKE YOUR WAY TO THE AVATAR'S CHAMBERS.
THE RESISTANCE IS YOUR MOTHER AND FATHER...
YOU WILL USE A TRANSSUIT TO FLY OUTSIDE THE SHIP. YOU WILL CLIMB THROUGH SECURED VENTILATION DUCTS TO HIS APARTMENTS. THERE ARE 347 LOCKS IN THE DUCTS...
YOU ARE DEVOTED TO US.
THERE ARE 224 TRAPS, ALL, WHEN TRIGGERED, WILL KILL. KNOW THEM. KNOW HOW TO DISRUPT THEM.
YOU ARE ONE OF US...
REMEMBER.
ONE FALSE MOVE, ONE FALSE TURN, AND YOU DIE.
THE RESISTANCE IS YOUR MOTHER AND YOUR FATHER.
THE AVATAR MUST BE DISABLED BEFORE YOU KILL HIM. ANY REMNANT OF HIS CONSCIOUSNESS CAN STRIKE AGAINST YOU.
YOU ARE ONE OF US...
TO PROTECT US YOU MUST KILL HIM.
ONLY YOU CAN KILL HIM.
KILL HIM!

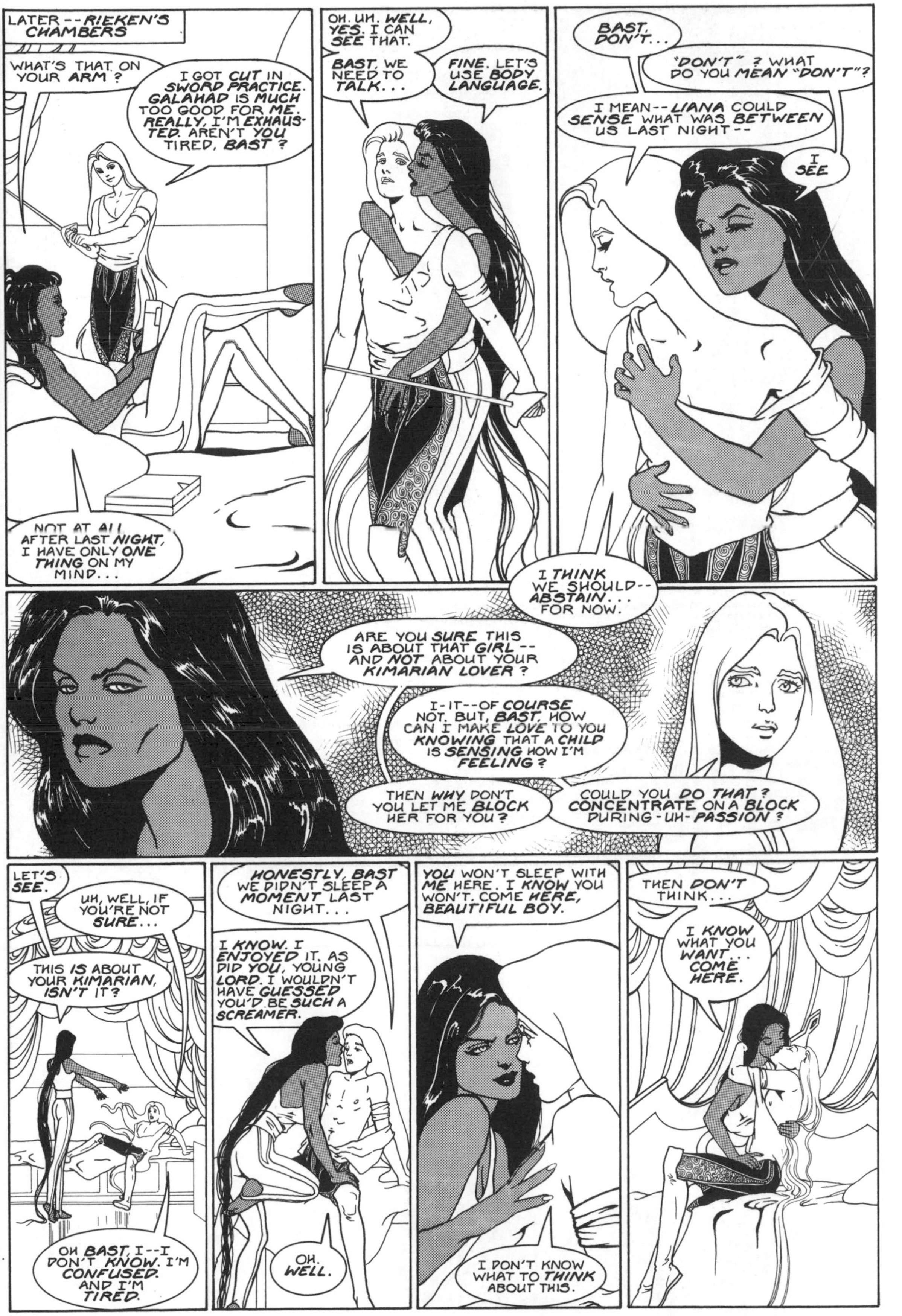
LATER--RIEKEN'S CHAMBERS
WHAT'S THAT ON YOUR ARM?
I GOT CUT IN SWORD PRACTICE. GALAHAD IS MUCH TOO GOOD FOR ME. REALLY, I'M EXHAUSTED. AREN'T YOU TIRED, BAST?
NOT AT ALL. AFTER LAST NIGHT, I HAVE ONLY ONE THING ON MY MIND...
OH. UH. WELL, YES. I CAN SEE THAT.
BAST, WE NEED TO TALK...
FINE. LET'S USE BODY LANGUAGE.
BAST. DON'T...
"DON'T"? WHAT DO YOU MEAN "DON'T"?
I MEAN--LIANA COULD SENSE WHAT WAS BETWEEN US LAST NIGHT--
I SEE
I THINK WE SHOULD--ABSTAIN... FOR NOW.
ARE YOU SURE THIS IS ABOUT THAT GIRL--AND NOT ABOUT YOUR KIMARIAN LOVER?
I-IT--OF COURSE NOT. BUT, BAST, HOW CAN I MAKE LOVE TO YOU KNOWING THAT A CHILD IS SENSING HOW I'M FEELING?
THEN WHY DON'T YOU LET ME BLOCK HER FOR YOU?
COULD YOU DO THAT? CONCENTRATE ON A BLOCK DURING-UH-PASSION?
LET'S SEE.
UH, WELL, IF YOU'RE NOT SURE...
THIS IS ABOUT YOUR KIMARIAN, ISN'T IT?
OH BAST, I--I DON'T KNOW. I'M CONFUSED. AND I'M TIRED.
HONESTLY, BAST WE DIDN'T SLEEP A MOMENT LAST NIGHT...
I KNOW. I ENJOYED IT. AS DID YOU, YOUNG LORD. I WOULDN'T HAVE GUESSED YOU'D BE SUCH A SCREAMER.
OH. WELL.
YOU WON'T SLEEP WITH ME HERE. I KNOW YOU WON'T. COME HERE, BEAUTIFUL BOY.
I DON'T KNOW WHAT TO THINK ABOUT THIS.
THEN DON'T THINK...
I KNOW WHAT YOU WANT... COME HERE.

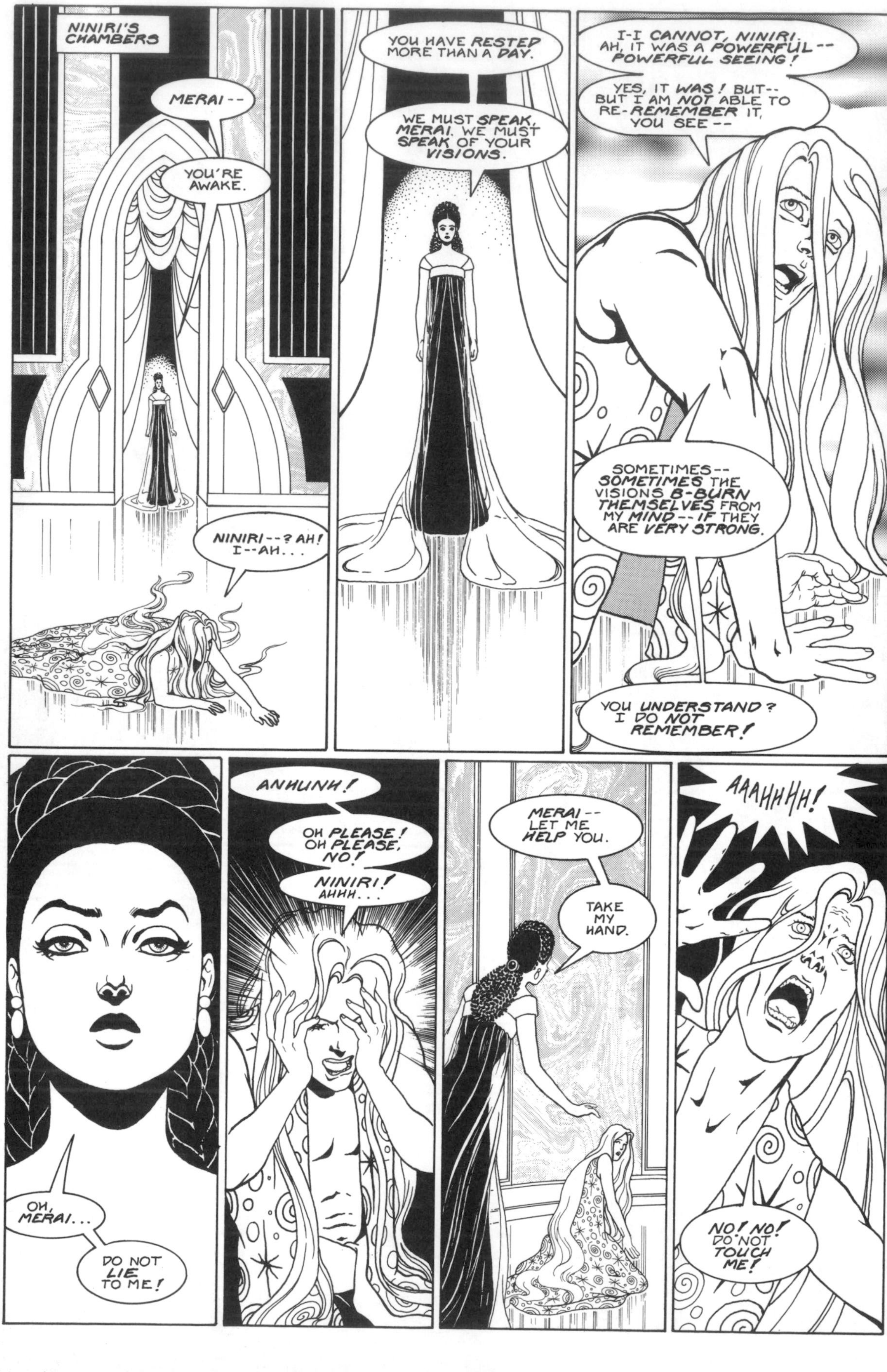
NINIRI'S CHAMBERS
MERAI--
YOU'RE AWAKE.
NINIRI--? AH! I--AH...
YOU HAVE RESTED MORE THAN A DAY.
WE MUST SPEAK, MERAI. WE MUST SPEAK OF YOUR VISIONS.
I-I CANNOT, NINIRI. AH, IT WAS A POWERFUL-- POWERFUL SEEING!
YES, IT WAS! BUT-- BUT I AM NOT ABLE TO RE-REMEMBER IT, YOU SEE--
SOMETIMES-- SOMETIMES THE VISIONS B-BURN THEMSELVES FROM MY MIND--IF THEY ARE VERY STRONG.
YOU UNDERSTAND? I DO NOT REMEMBER!
OH, MERAI...
DO NOT LIE TO ME!
ANHUNH!
OH PLEASE! OH PLEASE, NO!
NINIRI! AHHH...
MERAI-- LET ME HELP YOU.
TAKE MY HAND.
AAAHHHH!
NO! NO! DO NOT TOUCH ME!

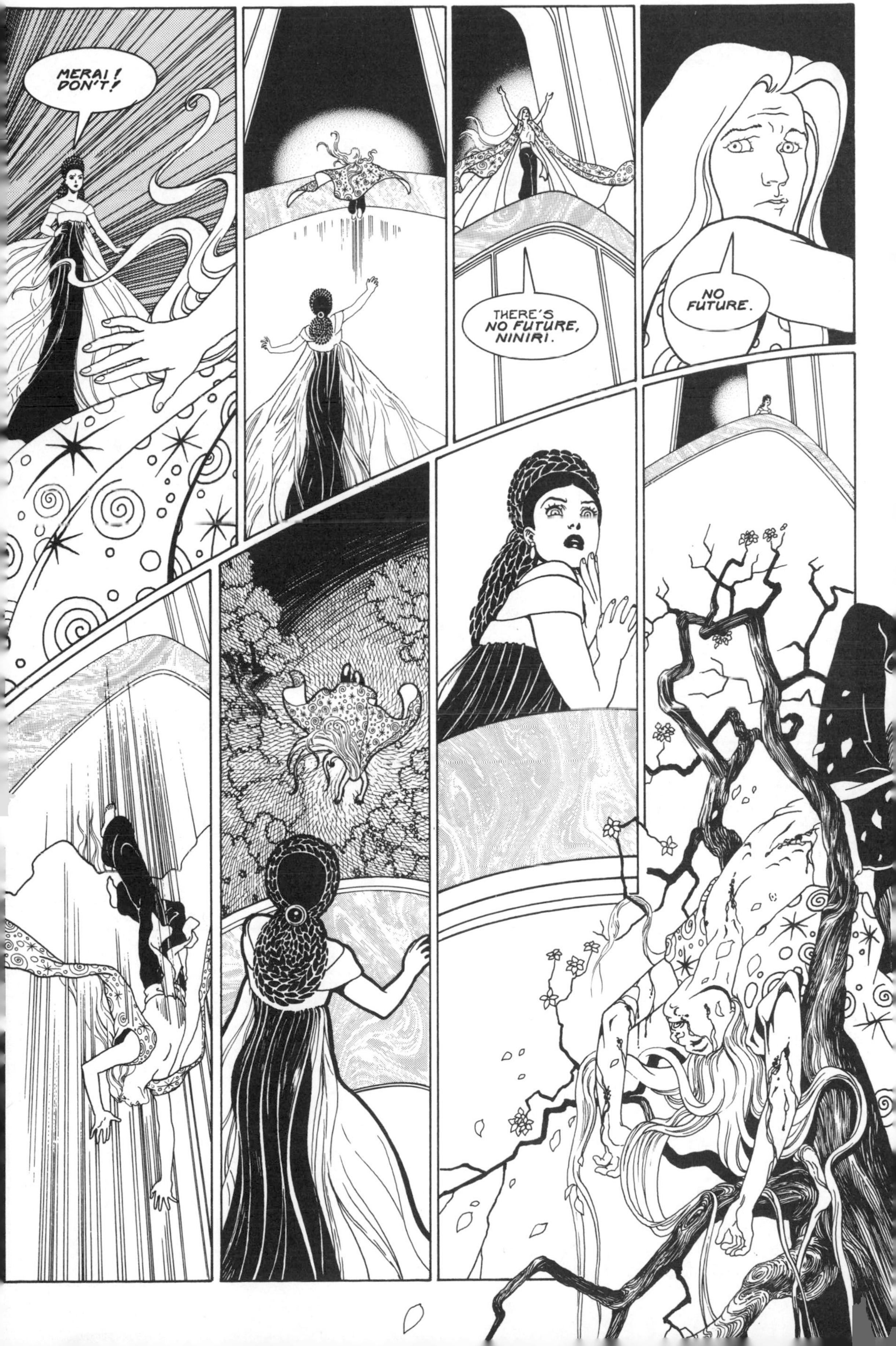
MERAI! DON'T!
THERE'S NO FUTURE, NINIRI.
NO FUTURE.

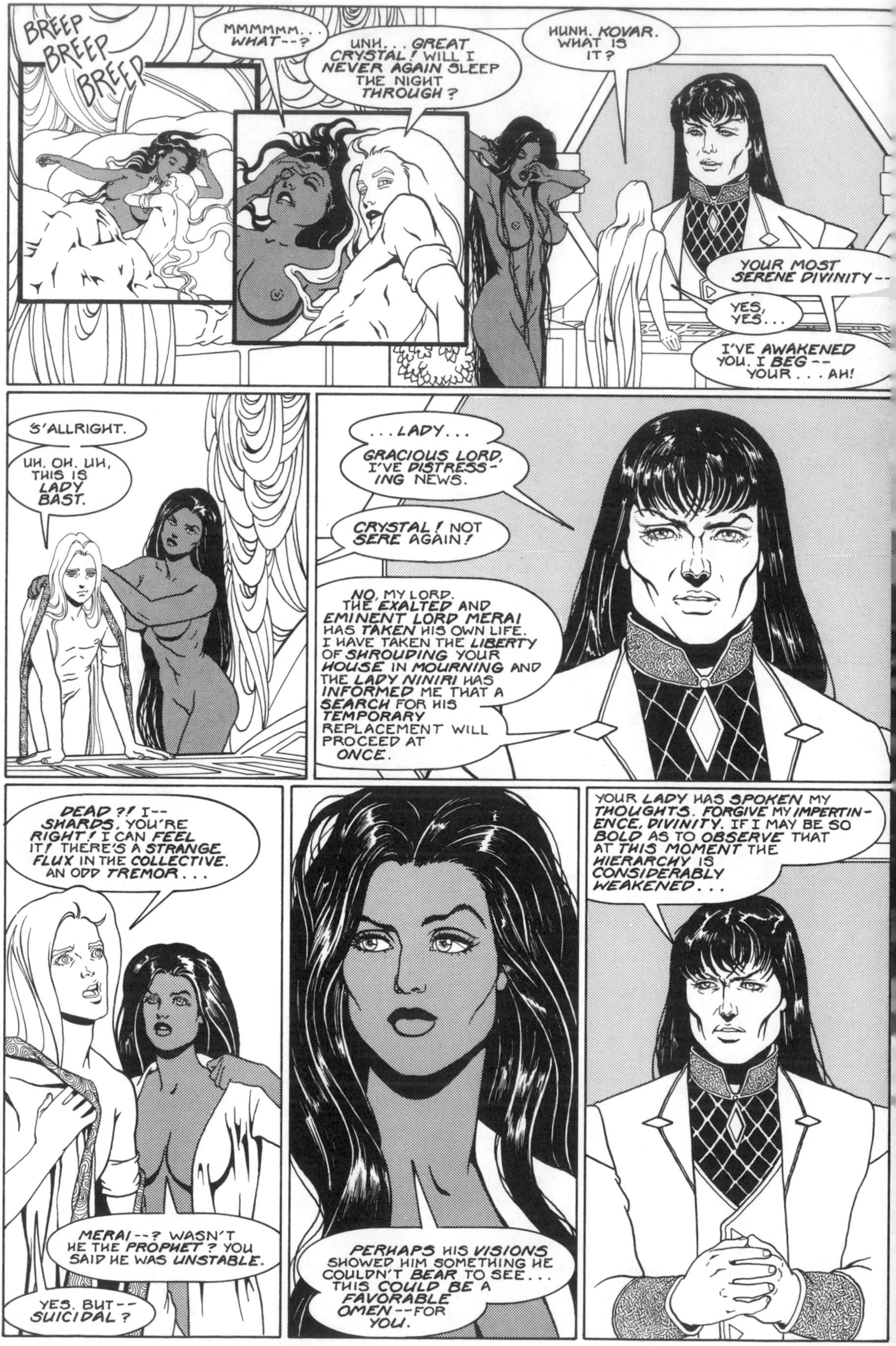
BREEP BREEP BREEP
MMMMMM... WHAT--?
UNH... GREAT CRYSTAL! WILL I NEVER AGAIN SLEEP THE NIGHT THROUGH?
HUNH. KOVAR. WHAT IS IT?
YOUR MOST SERENE DIVINITY--
YES, YES...
I'VE AWAKENED YOU. I BEG--YOUR... AH!
'S'ALLRIGHT.
UH. OH. UH, THIS IS LADY BAST.
...LADY...
GRACIOUS LORD, I'VE DISTRESSING NEWS.
CRYSTAL! NOT SERE AGAIN!
NO, MY LORD. THE EXALTED AND EMINENT LORD MERAI HAS TAKEN HIS OWN LIFE. I HAVE TAKEN THE LIBERTY OF SHROUDING YOUR HOUSE IN MOURNING AND THE LADY NINIRI HAS INFORMED ME THAT A SEARCH FOR HIS TEMPORARY REPLACEMENT WILL PROCEED AT ONCE.
DEAD?! I-- SHARDS, YOU'RE RIGHT! I CAN FEEL IT! THERE'S A STRANGE FLUX IN THE COLLECTIVE. AN ODD TREMOR...
MERAI--? WASN'T HE THE PROPHET? YOU SAID HE WAS UNSTABLE.
YES. BUT--SUICIDAL?
PERHAPS HIS VISIONS SHOWED HIM SOMETHING HE COULDN'T BEAR TO SEE... THIS COULD BE A FAVORABLE OMEN--FOR YOU.
YOUR LADY HAS SPOKEN MY THOUGHTS. FORGIVE MY IMPERTINENCE, DIVINITY. IF I MAY BE SO BOLD AS TO OBSERVE THAT AT THIS MOMENT THE HIERARCHY IS CONSIDERABLY WEAKENED...

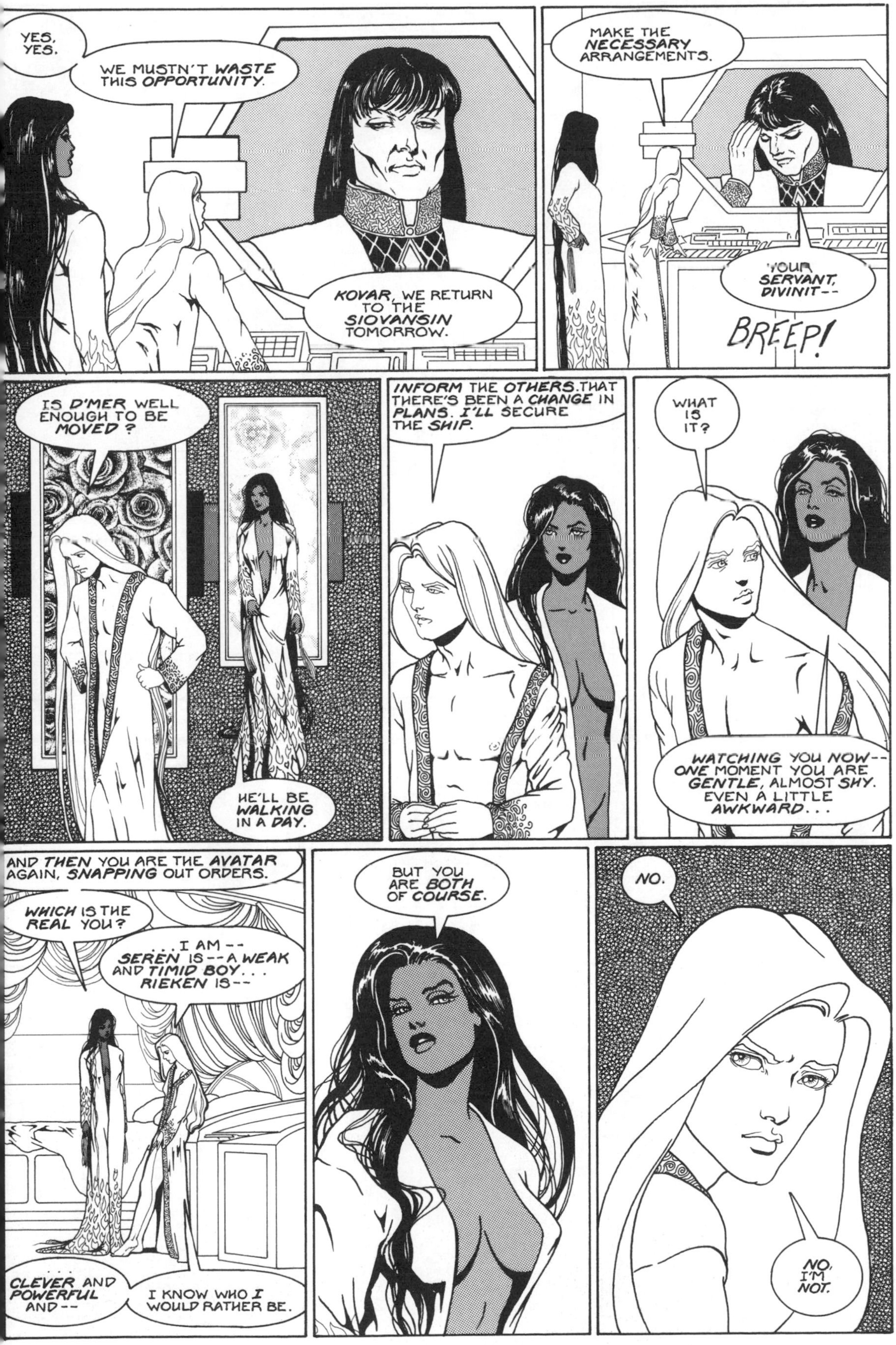
YES, YES.
WE MUSTN'T WASTE THIS OPPORTUNITY.
KOVAR, WE RETURN TO THE SIOVANSIN TOMORROW.
MAKE THE NECESSARY ARRANGEMENTS.
YOUR SERVANT, DIVINIT--
BREEP!
IS D'MER WELL ENOUGH TO BE MOVED?
HE'LL BE WALKING IN A DAY.
INFORM THE OTHERS. THAT THERE'S BEEN A CHANGE IN PLANS. I'LL SECURE THE SHIP.
WHAT IS IT?
WATCHING YOU NOW-- ONE MOMENT YOU ARE GENTLE, ALMOST SHY. EVEN A LITTLE AWKWARD...
AND THEN YOU ARE THE AVATAR AGAIN, SNAPPING OUT ORDERS.
WHICH IS THE REAL YOU?
...I AM -- SEREN IS -- A WEAK AND TIMID BOY... RIEKEN IS--
...CLEVER AND POWERFUL AND --
I KNOW WHO I WOULD RATHER BE.
BUT YOU ARE BOTH OF COURSE.
NO.
NO, I'M NOT.

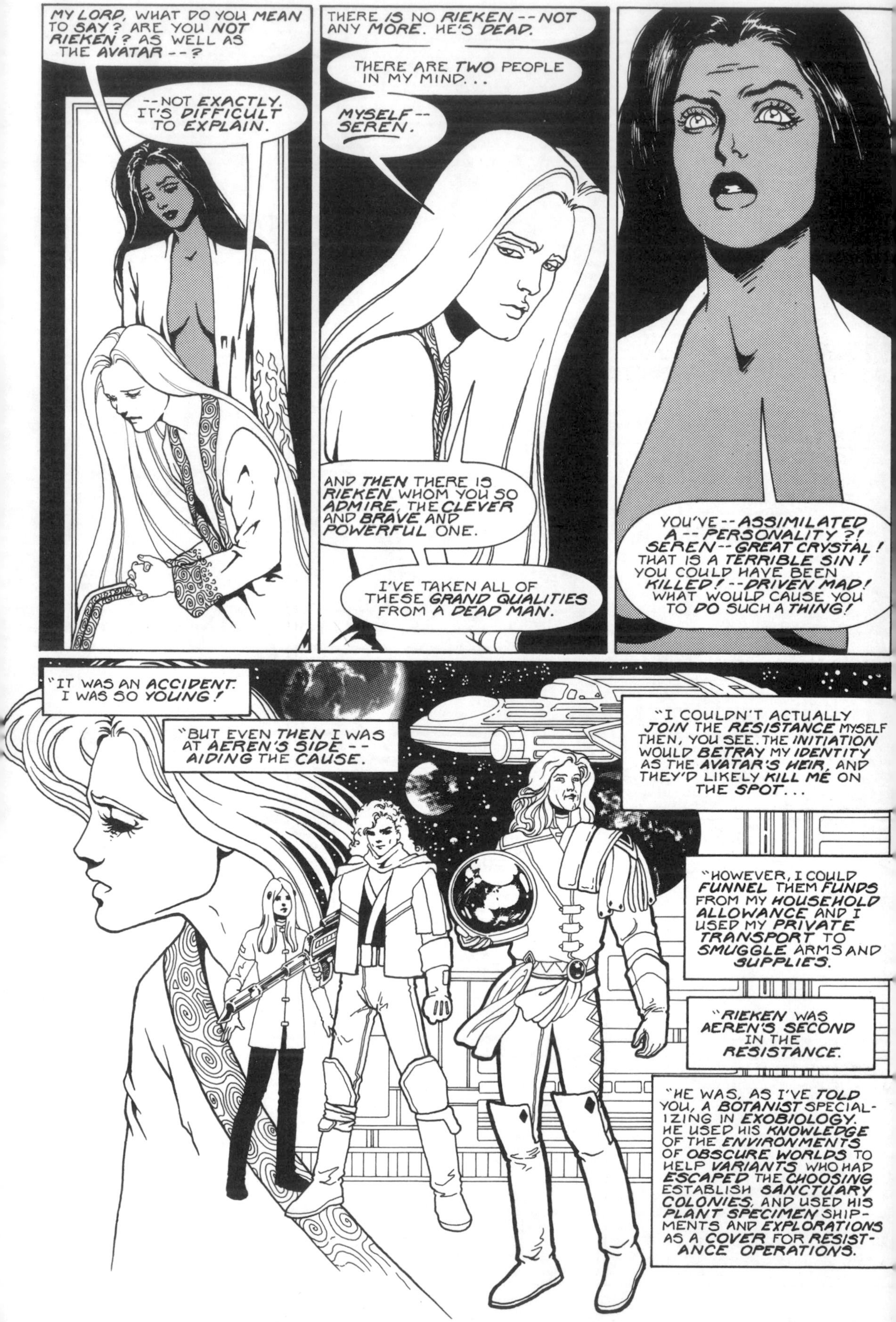

MY LORD, WHAT DO YOU MEAN TO SAY? ARE YOU NOT RIEKEN? AS WELL AS THE AVATAR --?
--NOT EXACTLY. IT'S DIFFICULT TO EXPLAIN.
THERE IS NO RIEKEN -- NOT ANY MORE. HE'S DEAD.
THERE ARE TWO PEOPLE IN MY MIND...
MYSELF -- SEREN.
AND THEN THERE IS RIEKEN WHOM YOU SO ADMIRE, THE CLEVER AND BRAVE AND POWERFUL ONE.
I'VE TAKEN ALL OF THESE GRAND QUALITIES FROM A DEAD MAN.
YOU'VE -- ASSIMILATED A -- PERSONALITY?! SEREN -- GREAT CRYSTAL! THAT IS A TERRIBLE SIN! YOU COULD HAVE BEEN KILLED! --DRIVEN MAD! WHAT WOULD CAUSE YOU TO DO SUCH A THING!
"IT WAS AN ACCIDENT. I WAS SO YOUNG!
"BUT EVEN THEN I WAS AT AEREN'S SIDE -- AIDING THE CAUSE.
"I COULDN'T ACTUALLY JOIN THE RESISTANCE MYSELF THEN, YOU SEE. THE INITIATION WOULD BETRAY MY IDENTITY AS THE AVATAR'S HEIR, AND THEY'D LIKELY KILL ME ON THE SPOT...
"HOWEVER, I COULD FUNNEL THEM FUNDS FROM MY HOUSEHOLD ALLOWANCE AND I USED MY PRIVATE TRANSPORT TO SMUGGLE ARMS AND SUPPLIES.
"RIEKEN WAS AEREN'S SECOND IN THE RESISTANCE.
"HE WAS, AS I'VE TOLD YOU, A BOTANIST SPECIALIZING IN EXOBIOLOGY. HE USED HIS KNOWLEDGE OF THE ENVIRONMENTS OF OBSCURE WORLDS TO HELP VARIANTS WHO HAD ESCAPED THE CHOOSING ESTABLISH SANCTUARY COLONIES, AND USED HIS PLANT SPECIMEN SHIPMENTS AND EXPLORATIONS AS A COVER FOR RESISTANCE OPERATIONS.

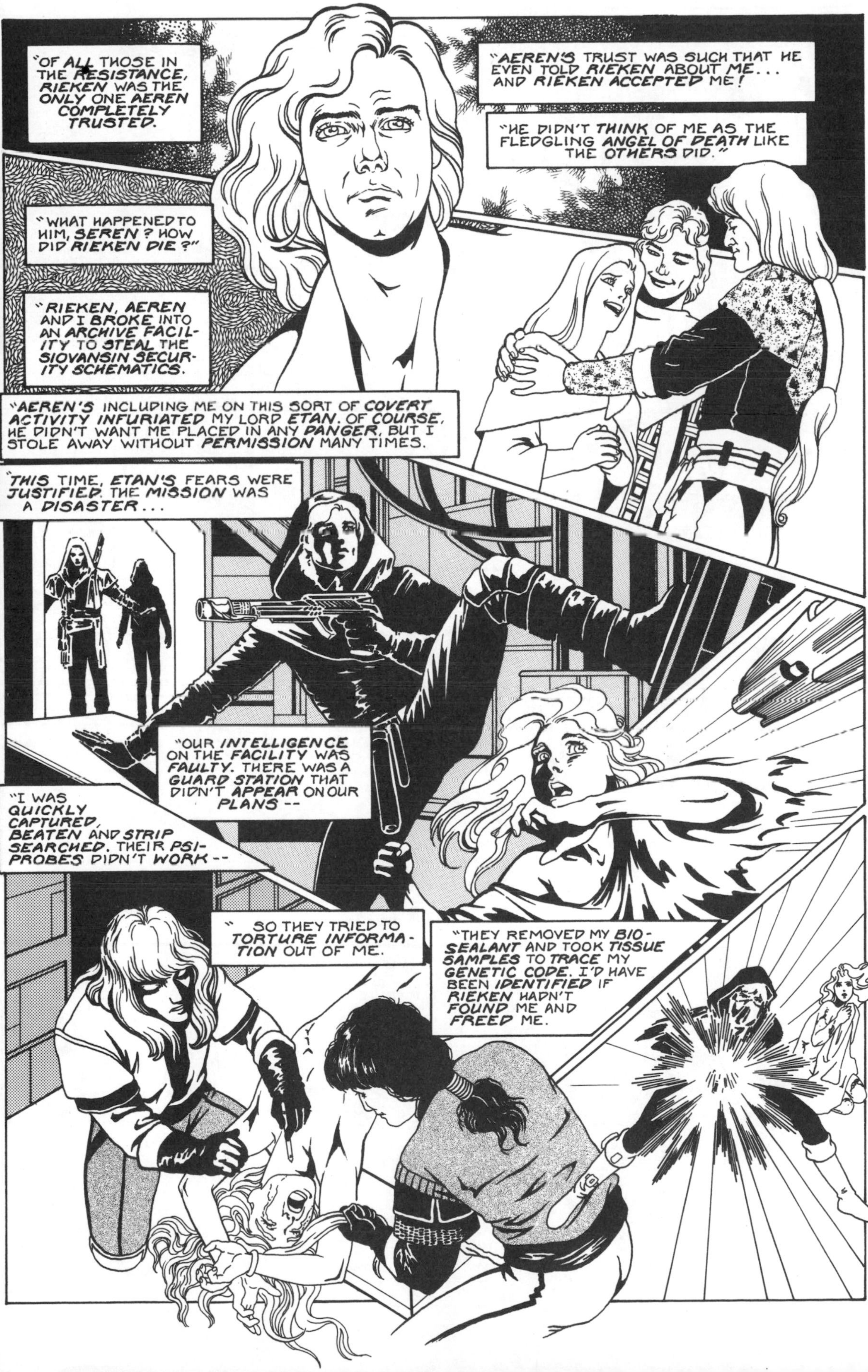
"OF ALL THOSE IN THE RESISTANCE, RIEKEN WAS THE ONLY ONE AEREN COMPLETELY TRUSTED.
"AEREN'S TRUST WAS SUCH THAT HE EVEN TOLD RIEKEN ABOUT ME... AND RIEKEN ACCEPTED ME!
"HE DIDN'T THINK OF ME AS THE FLEDGLING ANGEL OF DEATH LIKE THE OTHERS DID."
"WHAT HAPPENED TO HIM, SEREN? HOW DID RIEKEN DIE?"
"RIEKEN, AEREN AND I BROKE INTO AN ARCHIVE FACILITY TO STEAL THE SIOVANSIN SECURITY SCHEMATICS.
"AEREN'S INCLUDING ME ON THIS SORT OF COVERT ACTIVITY INFURIATED MY LORD ETAN. OF COURSE, HE DIDN'T WANT ME PLACED IN ANY DANGER, BUT I STOLE AWAY WITHOUT PERMISSION MANY TIMES.
"THIS TIME, ETAN'S FEARS WERE JUSTIFIED. THE MISSION WAS A DISASTER...
"OUR INTELLIGENCE ON THE FACILITY WAS FAULTY. THERE WAS A GUARD STATION THAT DIDN'T APPEAR ON OUR PLANS --
"I WAS QUICKLY CAPTURED, BEATEN AND STRIP SEARCHED. THEIR PSI-PROBES DIDN'T WORK --
" SO THEY TRIED TO TORTURE INFORMATION OUT OF ME.
"THEY REMOVED MY BIO-SEALANT AND TOOK TISSUE SAMPLES TO TRACE MY GENETIC CODE. I'D HAVE BEEN IDENTIFIED IF RIEKEN HADN'T FOUND ME AND FREED ME.

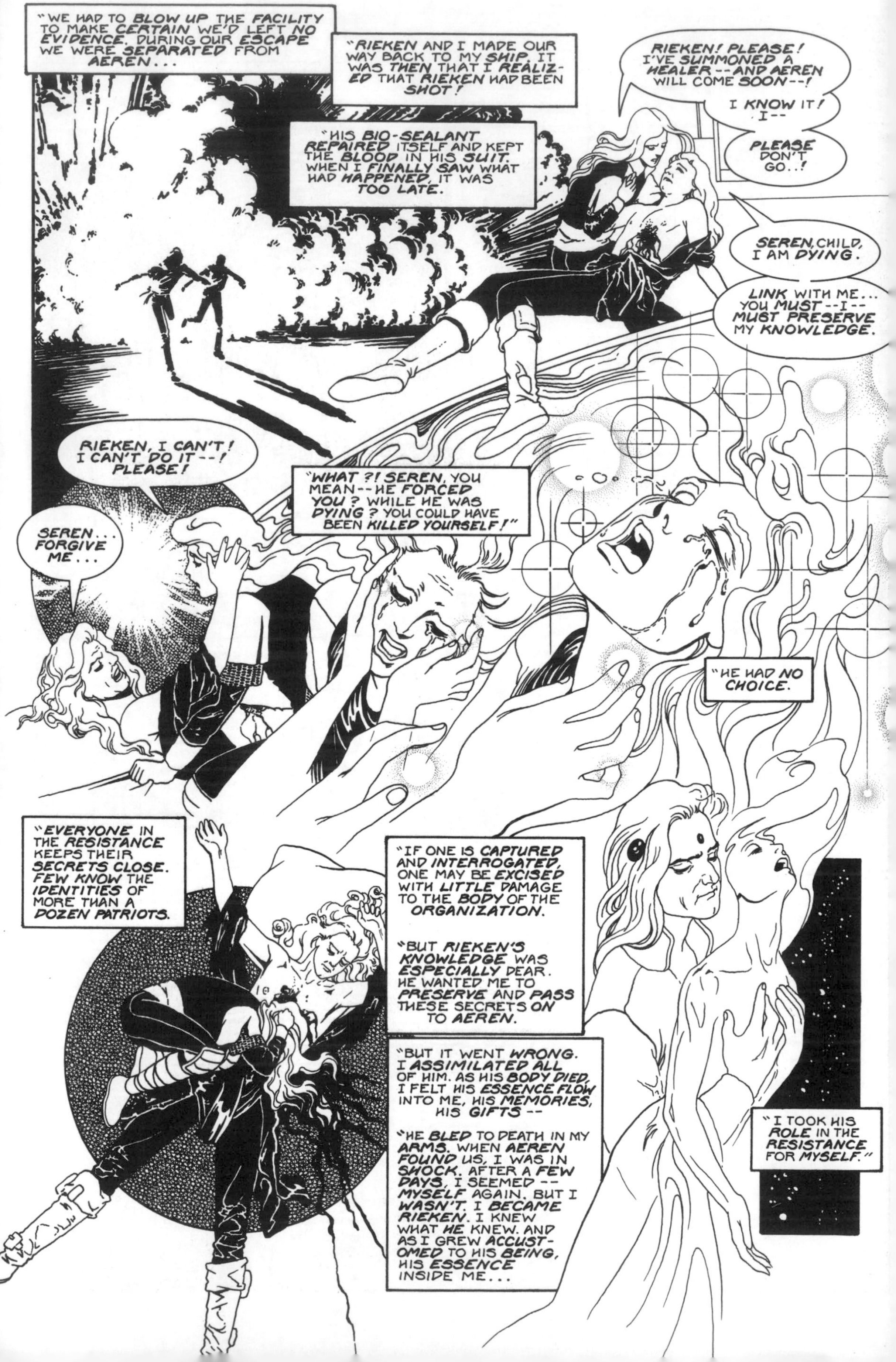
"WE HAD TO BLOW UP THE FACILITY TO MAKE CERTAIN WE'D LEFT NO EVIDENCE. DURING OUR ESCAPE WE WERE SEPARATED FROM AEREN...
"RIEKEN AND I MADE OUR WAY BACK TO MY SHIP. IT WAS THEN THAT I REALIZED THAT RIEKEN HAD BEEN SHOT!
"HIS BIO-SEALANT REPAIRED ITSELF AND KEPT THE BLOOD IN HIS SUIT. WHEN I FINALLY SAW WHAT HAD HAPPENED, IT WAS TOO LATE.
RIEKEN! PLEASE! I'VE SUMMONED A HEALER--AND AEREN WILL COME SOON--!
I KNOW IT! I--
PLEASE DON'T GO..!
SEREN, CHILD, I AM DYING.
LINK WITH ME... YOU MUST--I--MUST PRESERVE MY KNOWLEDGE.
RIEKEN, I CAN'T! I CAN'T DO IT--! PLEASE!
SEREN... FORGIVE ME...
"WHAT?! SEREN, YOU MEAN--HE FORCED YOU? WHILE HE WAS DYING? YOU COULD HAVE BEEN KILLED YOURSELF!"
"HE HAD NO CHOICE.
"EVERYONE IN THE RESISTANCE KEEPS THEIR SECRETS CLOSE. FEW KNOW THE IDENTITIES OF MORE THAN A DOZEN PATRIOTS.
"IF ONE IS CAPTURED AND INTERROGATED, ONE MAY BE EXCISED WITH LITTLE DAMAGE TO THE BODY OF THE ORGANIZATION.
"BUT RIEKEN'S KNOWLEDGE WAS ESPECIALLY DEAR. HE WANTED ME TO PRESERVE AND PASS THESE SECRETS ON TO AEREN.
"BUT IT WENT WRONG. I ASSIMILATED ALL OF HIM. AS HIS BODY DIED, I FELT HIS ESSENCE FLOW INTO ME, HIS MEMORIES, HIS GIFTS--
"HE BLED TO DEATH IN MY ARMS. WHEN AEREN FOUND US, I WAS IN SHOCK. AFTER A FEW DAYS, I SEEMED--MYSELF AGAIN. BUT I WASN'T. I BECAME RIEKEN. I KNEW WHAT HE KNEW. AND AS I GREW ACCUSTOMED TO HIS BEING, HIS ESSENCE INSIDE ME...
"I TOOK HIS ROLE IN THE RESISTANCE FOR MYSELF."

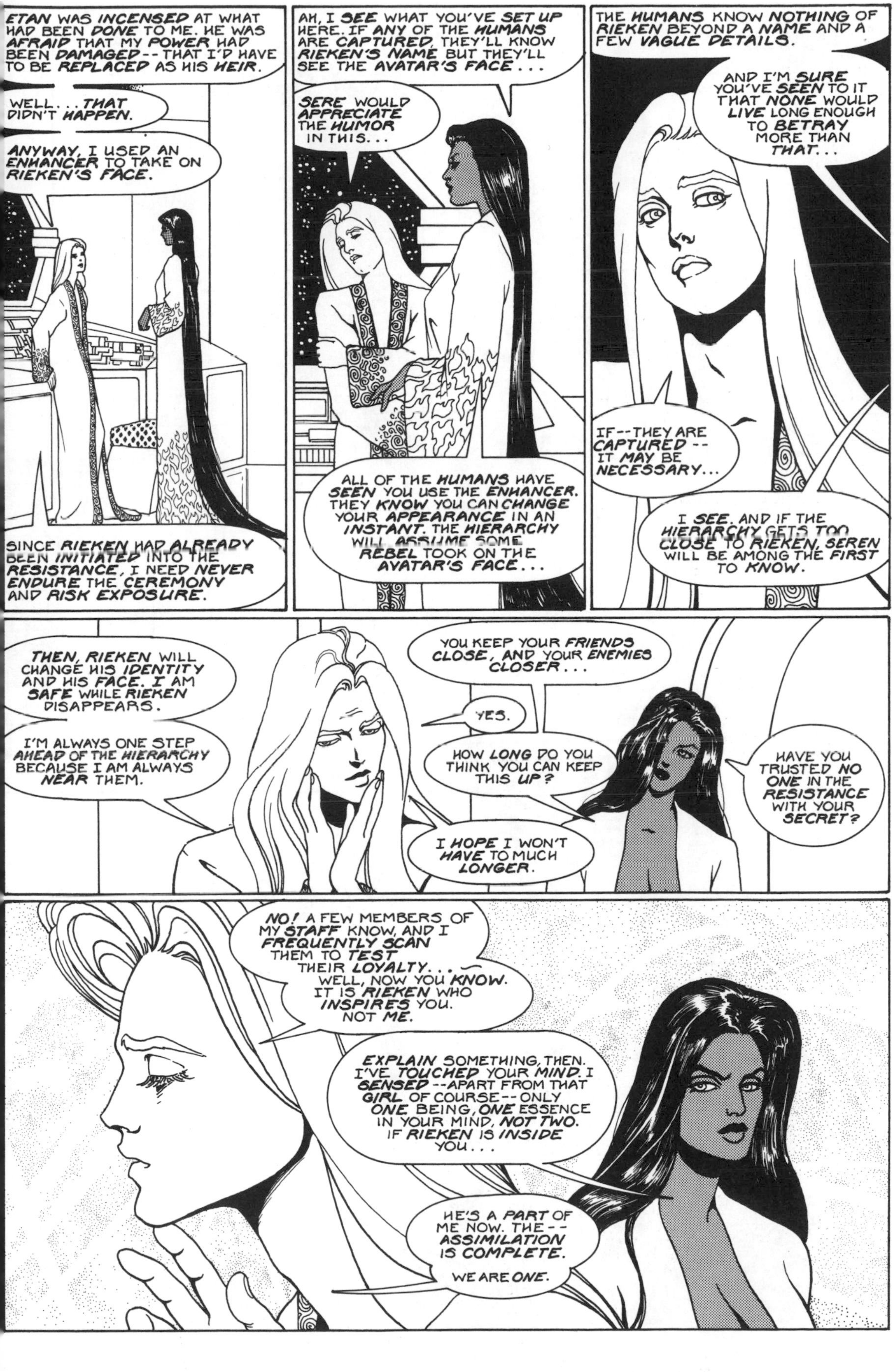
ETAN WAS INCENSED AT WHAT HAD BEEN DONE TO ME. HE WAS AFRAID THAT MY POWER HAD BEEN DAMAGED--THAT I'D HAVE TO BE REPLACED AS HIS HEIR.
WELL... THAT DIDN'T HAPPEN.
ANYWAY, I USED AN ENHANCER TO TAKE ON RIEKEN'S FACE.
SINCE RIEKEN HAD ALREADY BEEN INITIATED INTO THE RESISTANCE, I NEED NEVER ENDURE THE CEREMONY AND RISK EXPOSURE.
AH, I SEE WHAT YOU'VE SET UP HERE. IF ANY OF THE HUMANS ARE CAPTURED, THEY'LL KNOW RIEKEN'S NAME BUT THEY'LL SEE THE AVATAR'S FACE...
SERE WOULD APPRECIATE THE HUMOR IN THIS...
ALL OF THE HUMANS HAVE SEEN YOU USE THE ENHANCER. THEY KNOW YOU CAN CHANGE YOUR APPEARANCE IN AN INSTANT. THE HIERARCHY WILL ASSUME SOME REBEL TOOK ON THE AVATAR'S FACE...
THE HUMANS KNOW NOTHING OF RIEKEN BEYOND A NAME AND A FEW VAGUE DETAILS.
AND I'M SURE YOU'VE SEEN TO IT THAT NONE WOULD LIVE LONG ENOUGH TO BETRAY MORE THAN THAT...
IF--THEY ARE CAPTURED--IT MAY BE NECESSARY...
I SEE. AND IF THE HIERARCHY GETS TOO CLOSE TO RIEKEN, SEREN WILL BE AMONG THE FIRST TO KNOW.
THEN, RIEKEN WILL CHANGE HIS IDENTITY AND HIS FACE. I AM SAFE WHILE RIEKEN DISAPPEARS.
I'M ALWAYS ONE STEP AHEAD OF THE HIERARCHY BECAUSE I AM ALWAYS NEAR THEM.
YOU KEEP YOUR FRIENDS CLOSE, AND YOUR ENEMIES CLOSER...
YES.
HOW LONG DO YOU THINK YOU CAN KEEP THIS UP?
I HOPE I WON'T HAVE TO MUCH LONGER.
HAVE YOU TRUSTED NO ONE IN THE RESISTANCE WITH YOUR SECRET?
NO! A FEW MEMBERS OF MY STAFF KNOW, AND I FREQUENTLY SCAN THEM TO TEST THEIR LOYALTY...
WELL, NOW YOU KNOW. IT IS RIEKEN WHO INSPIRES YOU. NOT ME.
EXPLAIN SOMETHING, THEN. I'VE TOUCHED YOUR MIND. I SENSED--APART FROM THAT GIRL OF COURSE--ONLY ONE BEING, ONE ESSENCE IN YOUR MIND, NOT TWO. IF RIEKEN IS INSIDE YOU...
HE'S A PART OF ME NOW. THE--ASSIMILATION IS COMPLETE.
WE ARE ONE.

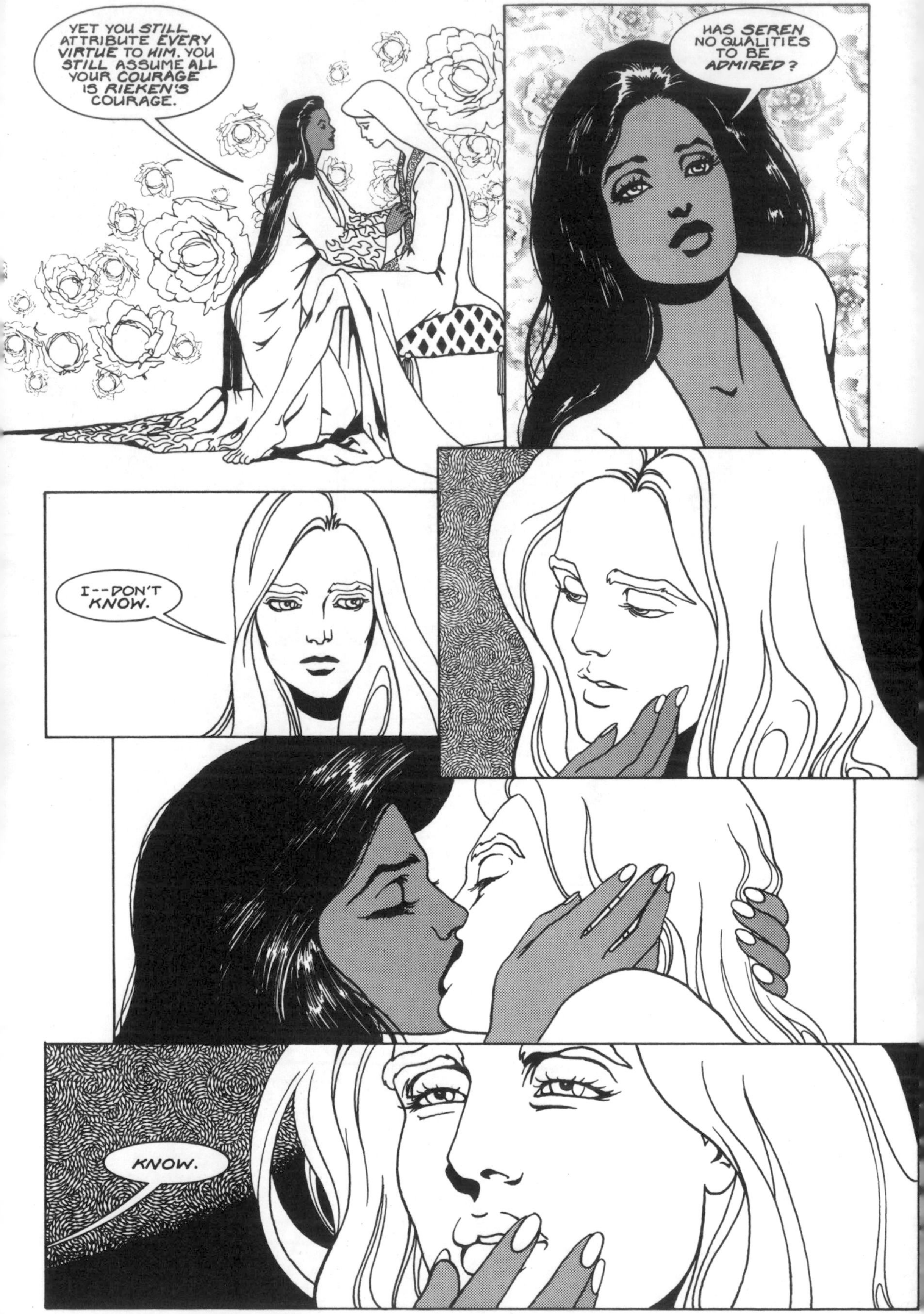
YET YOU STILL ATTRIBUTE EVERY VIRTUE TO HIM. YOU STILL ASSUME ALL YOUR COURAGE IS RIEKEN'S COURAGE.
HAS SEREN NO QUALITIES TO BE ADMIRED?
I--DON'T KNOW.
KNOW.

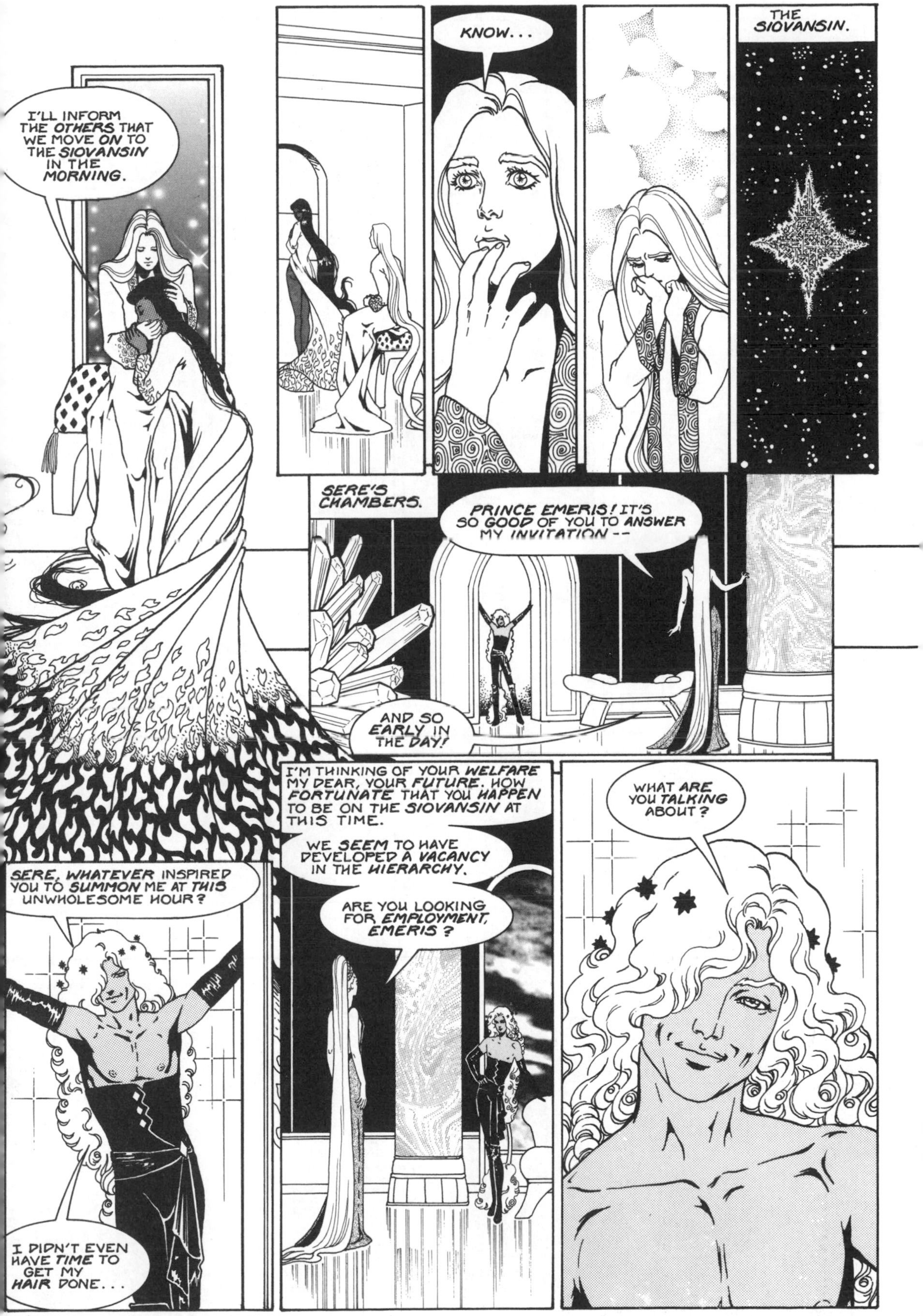
I'LL INFORM THE OTHERS THAT WE MOVE ON TO THE SIOVANSIN IN THE MORNING.
KNOW...
THE SIOVANSIN.
SERE'S CHAMBERS.
PRINCE EMERIS! IT'S SO GOOD OF YOU TO ANSWER MY INVITATION --
AND SO EARLY IN THE DAY!
SERE, WHATEVER INSPIRED YOU TO SUMMON ME AT THIS UNWHOLESOME HOUR?
I DIDN'T EVEN HAVE TIME TO GET MY HAIR DONE...
I'M THINKING OF YOUR WELFARE MY DEAR, YOUR FUTURE. HOW FORTUNATE THAT YOU HAPPEN TO BE ON THE SIOVANSIN AT THIS TIME.
WE SEEM TO HAVE DEVELOPED A VACANCY IN THE HIERARCHY.
ARE YOU LOOKING FOR EMPLOYMENT, EMERIS?
WHAT ARE YOU TALKING ABOUT?

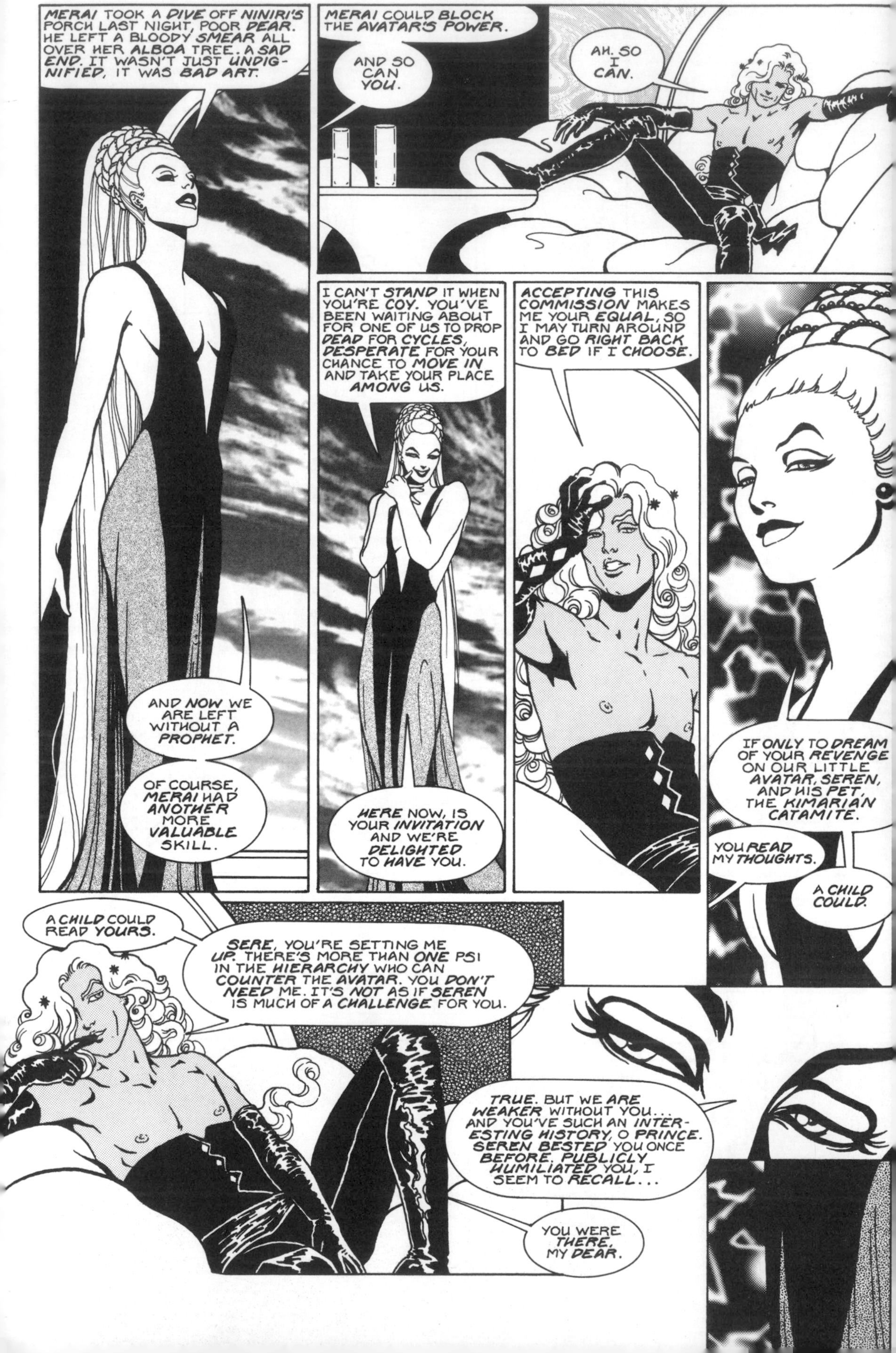
MERAI TOOK A DIVE OFF NINIRI'S PORCH LAST NIGHT, POOR DEAR. HE LEFT A BLOODY SMEAR ALL OVER HER ALBOA TREE. A SAD END. IT WASN'T JUST UNDIGNIFIED, IT WAS BAD ART.
AND NOW WE ARE LEFT WITHOUT A PROPHET.
OF COURSE, MERAI HAD ANOTHER MORE VALUABLE SKILL.
MERAI COULD BLOCK THE AVATAR'S POWER.
AND SO CAN YOU.
AH. SO I CAN.
I CAN'T STAND IT WHEN YOU'RE COY. YOU'VE BEEN WAITING ABOUT FOR ONE OF US TO DROP DEAD FOR CYCLES, DESPERATE FOR YOUR CHANCE TO MOVE IN AND TAKE YOUR PLACE AMONG US.
HERE NOW, IS YOUR INVITATION AND WE'RE DELIGHTED TO HAVE YOU.
ACCEPTING THIS COMMISSION MAKES ME YOUR EQUAL, SO I MAY TURN AROUND AND GO RIGHT BACK TO BED IF I CHOOSE.
IF ONLY TO DREAM OF YOUR REVENGE ON OUR LITTLE AVATAR, SEREN, AND HIS PET, THE KIMARIAN CATAMITE.
YOU READ MY THOUGHTS.
A CHILD COULD.
A CHILD COULD READ YOURS.
SERE, YOU'RE SETTING ME UP. THERE'S MORE THAN ONE PSI IN THE HIERARCHY WHO CAN COUNTER THE AVATAR. YOU DON'T NEED ME. IT'S NOT AS IF SEREN IS MUCH OF A CHALLENGE FOR YOU.
TRUE. BUT WE ARE WEAKER WITHOUT YOU... AND YOU'VE SUCH AN INTERESTING HISTORY, O PRINCE. SEREN BESTED YOU ONCE BEFORE. PUBLICLY HUMILIATED YOU, I SEEM TO RECALL...
YOU WERE THERE, MY DEAR.

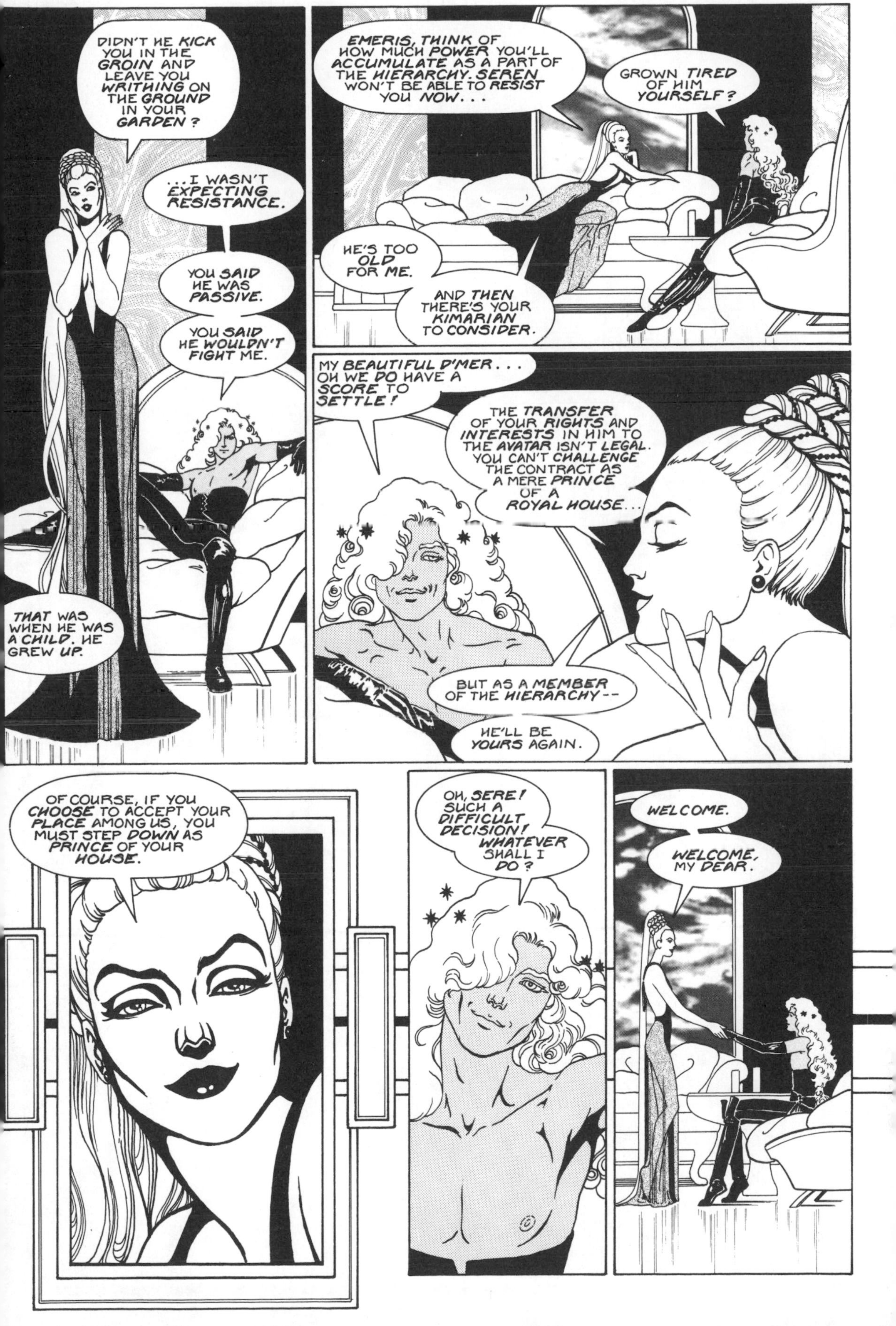
DIDN'T HE KICK YOU IN THE GROIN AND LEAVE YOU WRITHING ON THE GROUND IN YOUR GARDEN?
...I WASN'T EXPECTING RESISTANCE.
YOU SAID HE WAS PASSIVE.
YOU SAID HE WOULDN'T FIGHT ME.
THAT WAS WHEN HE WAS A CHILD. HE GREW UP.
EMERIS, THINK OF HOW MUCH POWER YOU'LL ACCUMULATE AS A PART OF THE HIERARCHY. SEREN WON'T BE ABLE TO RESIST YOU NOW...
GROWN TIRED OF HIM YOURSELF?
HE'S TOO OLD FOR ME.
AND THEN THERE'S YOUR KIMARIAN TO CONSIDER.
MY BEAUTIFUL D'MER... OH WE DO HAVE A SCORE TO SETTLE!
THE TRANSFER OF YOUR RIGHTS AND INTERESTS IN HIM TO THE AVATAR ISN'T LEGAL. YOU CAN'T CHALLENGE THE CONTRACT AS A MERE PRINCE OF A ROYAL HOUSE...
BUT AS A MEMBER OF THE HIERARCHY--
HE'LL BE YOURS AGAIN.
OF COURSE, IF YOU CHOOSE TO ACCEPT YOUR PLACE AMONG US, YOU MUST STEP DOWN AS PRINCE OF YOUR HOUSE.
OH, SERE! SUCH A DIFFICULT DECISION! WHATEVER SHALL I DO?
WELCOME.
WELCOME, MY DEAR.

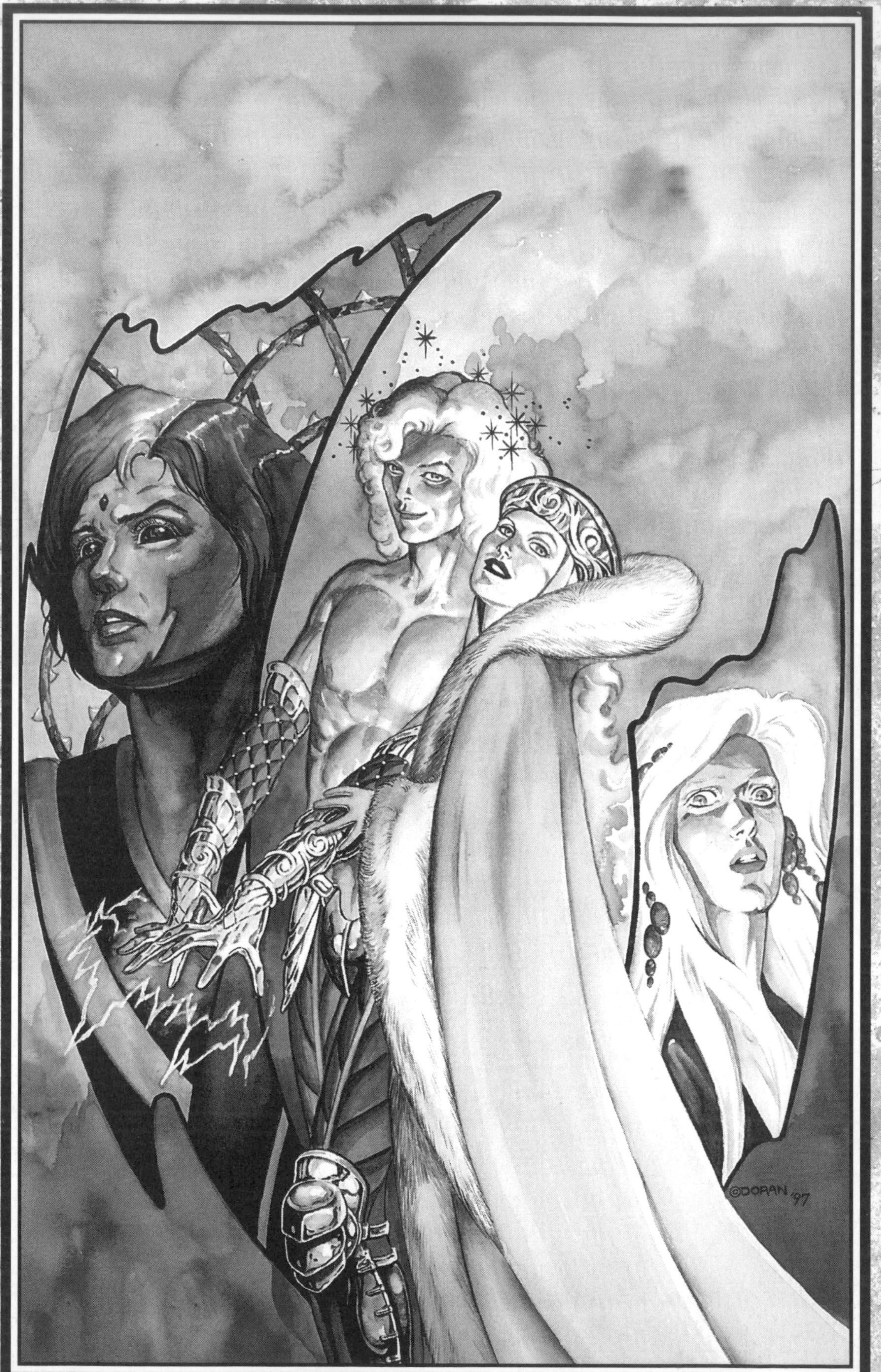
©DORAN '97

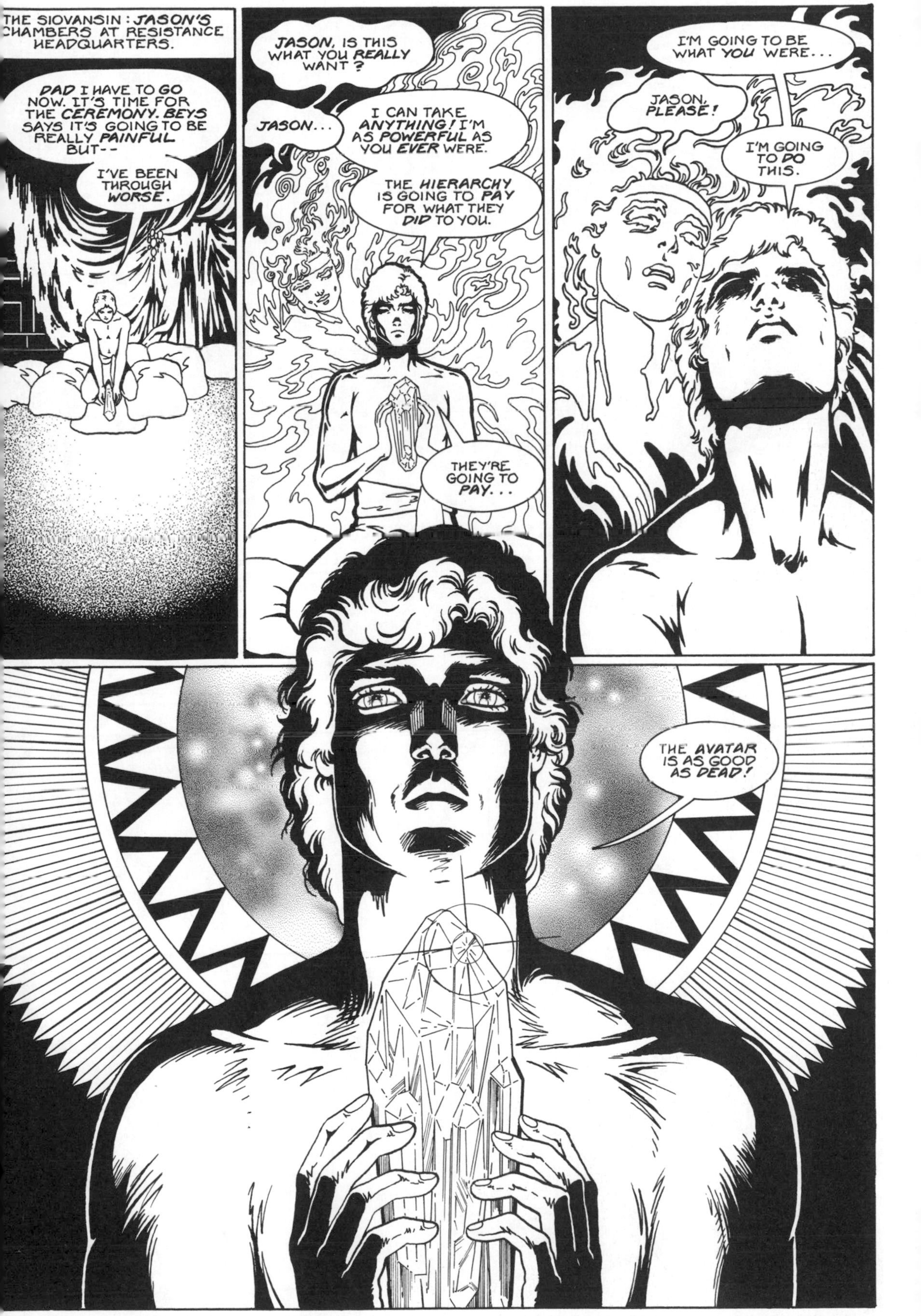
THE SIOVANSIN: JASON'S CHAMBERS AT RESISTANCE HEADQUARTERS.
DAD I HAVE TO GO NOW. IT'S TIME FOR THE CEREMONY. BEYS SAYS IT'S GOING TO BE REALLY PAINFUL BUT--
I'VE BEEN THROUGH WORSE.
JASON, IS THIS WHAT YOU REALLY WANT?
JASON...
I CAN TAKE ANYTHING! I'M AS POWERFUL AS YOU EVER WERE.
THE HIERARCHY IS GOING TO PAY FOR WHAT THEY DID TO YOU.
THEY'RE GOING TO PAY...
I'M GOING TO BE WHAT YOU WERE...
JASON, PLEASE!
I'M GOING TO DO THIS.
THE AVATAR IS AS GOOD AS DEAD!

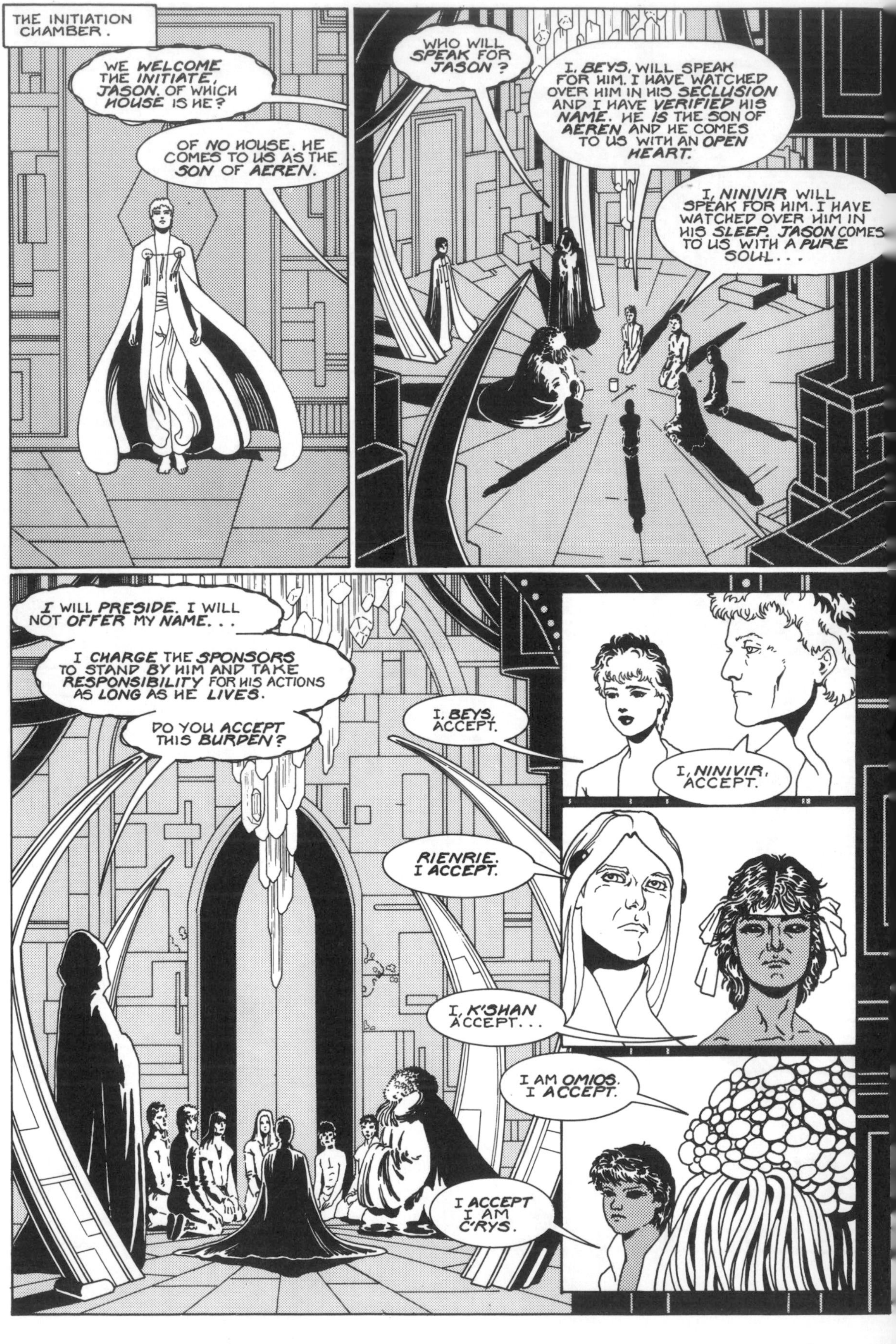
THE INITIATION CHAMBER.
WE WELCOME THE INITIATE, JASON. OF WHICH HOUSE IS HE?
OF NO HOUSE. HE COMES TO US AS THE SON OF AEREN.
WHO WILL SPEAK FOR JASON?
I, BEYS, WILL SPEAK FOR HIM. I HAVE WATCHED OVER HIM IN HIS SECLUSION AND I HAVE VERIFIED HIS NAME. HE IS THE SON OF AEREN AND HE COMES TO US WITH AN OPEN HEART.
I, NINIVIR WILL SPEAK FOR HIM. I HAVE WATCHED OVER HIM IN HIS SLEEP. JASON COMES TO US WITH A PURE SOUL...
I WILL PRESIDE. I WILL NOT OFFER MY NAME...
I CHARGE THE SPONSORS TO STAND BY HIM AND TAKE RESPONSIBILITY FOR HIS ACTIONS AS LONG AS HE LIVES.
DO YOU ACCEPT THIS BURDEN?
I, BEYS, ACCEPT.
I, NINIVIR, ACCEPT.
RIENRIE. I ACCEPT.
I, K'SHAN ACCEPT...
I AM OMIOS. I ACCEPT.
I ACCEPT I AM C'RYS.

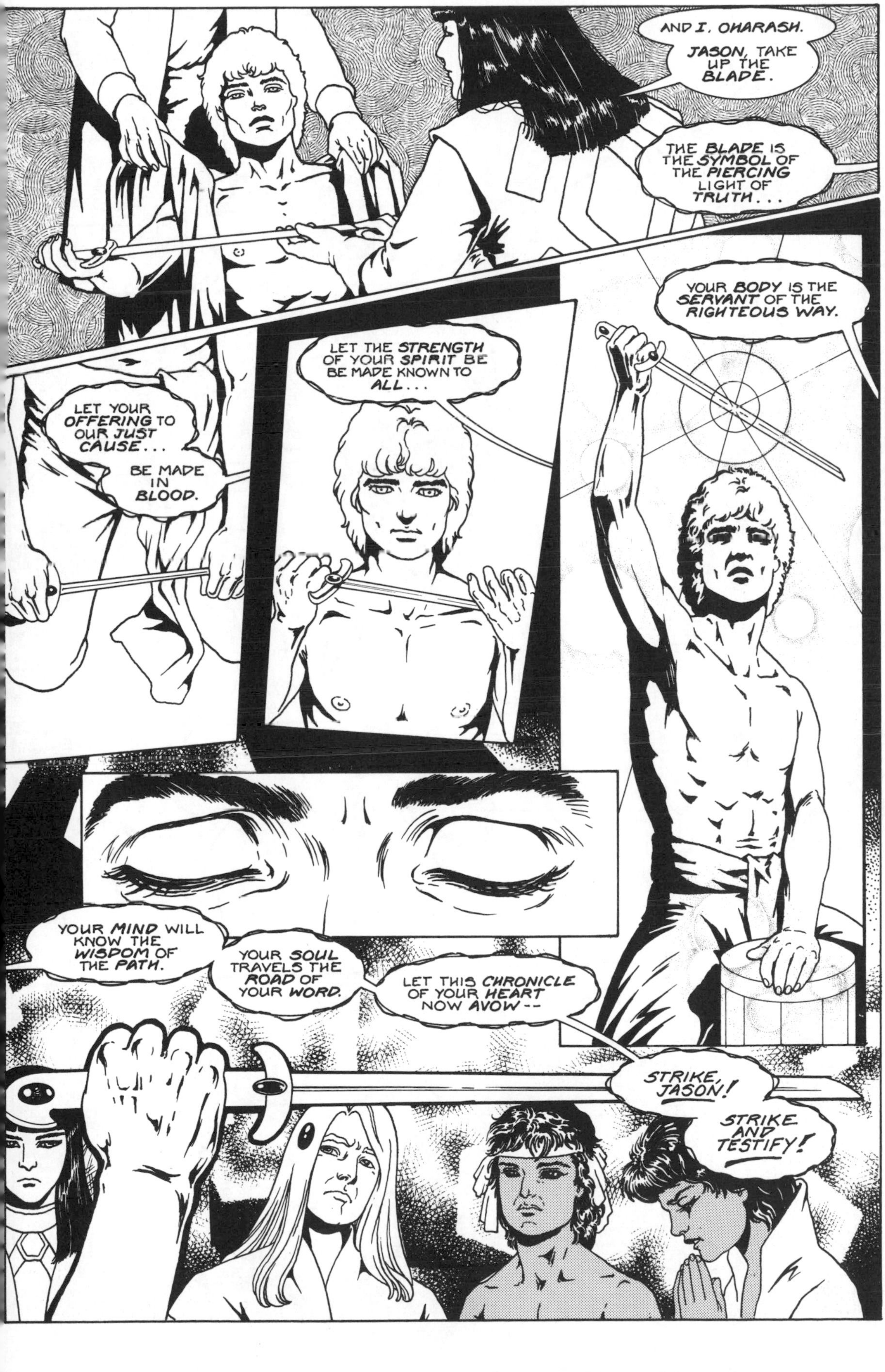
AND I, OHARASH.
JASON, TAKE UP THE BLADE.
THE BLADE IS THE SYMBOL OF THE PIERCING LIGHT OF TRUTH...
LET YOUR OFFERING TO OUR JUST CAUSE...
BE MADE IN BLOOD.
LET THE STRENGTH OF YOUR SPIRIT BE BE MADE KNOWN TO ALL...
YOUR BODY IS THE SERVANT OF THE RIGHTEOUS WAY.
YOUR MIND WILL KNOW THE WISDOM OF THE PATH.
YOUR SOUL TRAVELS THE ROAD OF YOUR WORD.
LET THIS CHRONICLE OF YOUR HEART NOW AVOW--
STRIKE, JASON!
STRIKE AND TESTIFY!

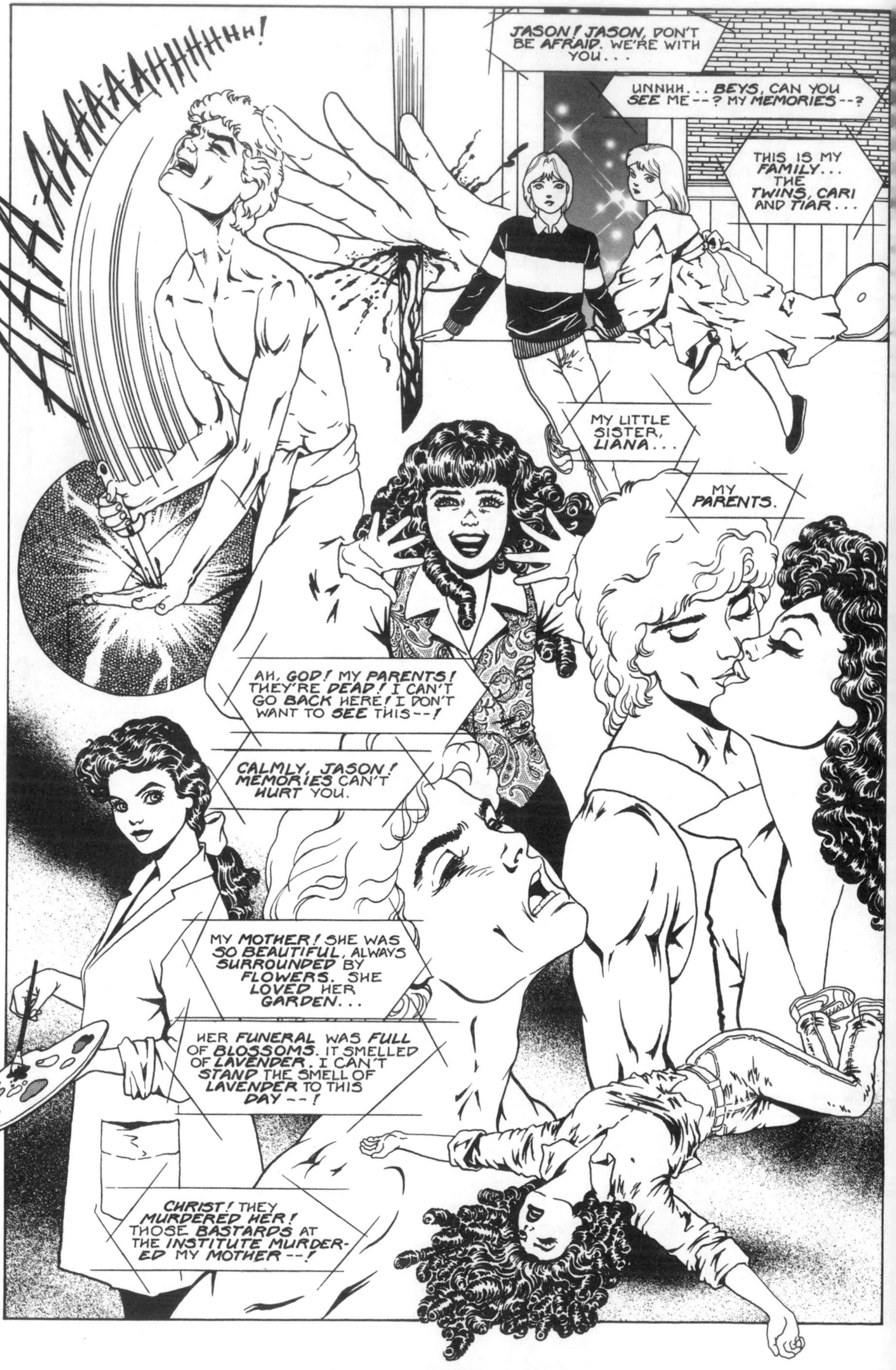
AAAA-AA-AA-AA-AAAHHHHHHhh!
JASON! JASON, DON'T BE AFRAID. WE'RE WITH YOU...
UNNHH... BEYS, CAN YOU SEE ME--? MY MEMORIES--?
THIS IS MY FAMILY... THE TWINS, CARI AND TIAR...
MY LITTLE SISTER, LIANA...
MY PARENTS.
AH, GOD! MY PARENTS! THEY'RE DEAD! I CAN'T GO BACK HERE! I DON'T WANT TO SEE THIS--!
CALMLY, JASON! MEMORIES CAN'T HURT YOU.
MY MOTHER! SHE WAS SO BEAUTIFUL, ALWAYS SURROUNDED BY FLOWERS. SHE LOVED HER GARDEN...
HER FUNERAL WAS FULL OF BLOSSOMS. IT SMELLED OF LAVENDER. I CAN'T STAND THE SMELL OF LAVENDER TO THIS DAY--!
CHRIST! THEY MURDERED HER! THOSE BASTARDS AT THE INSTITUTE MURDERED MY MOTHER--!

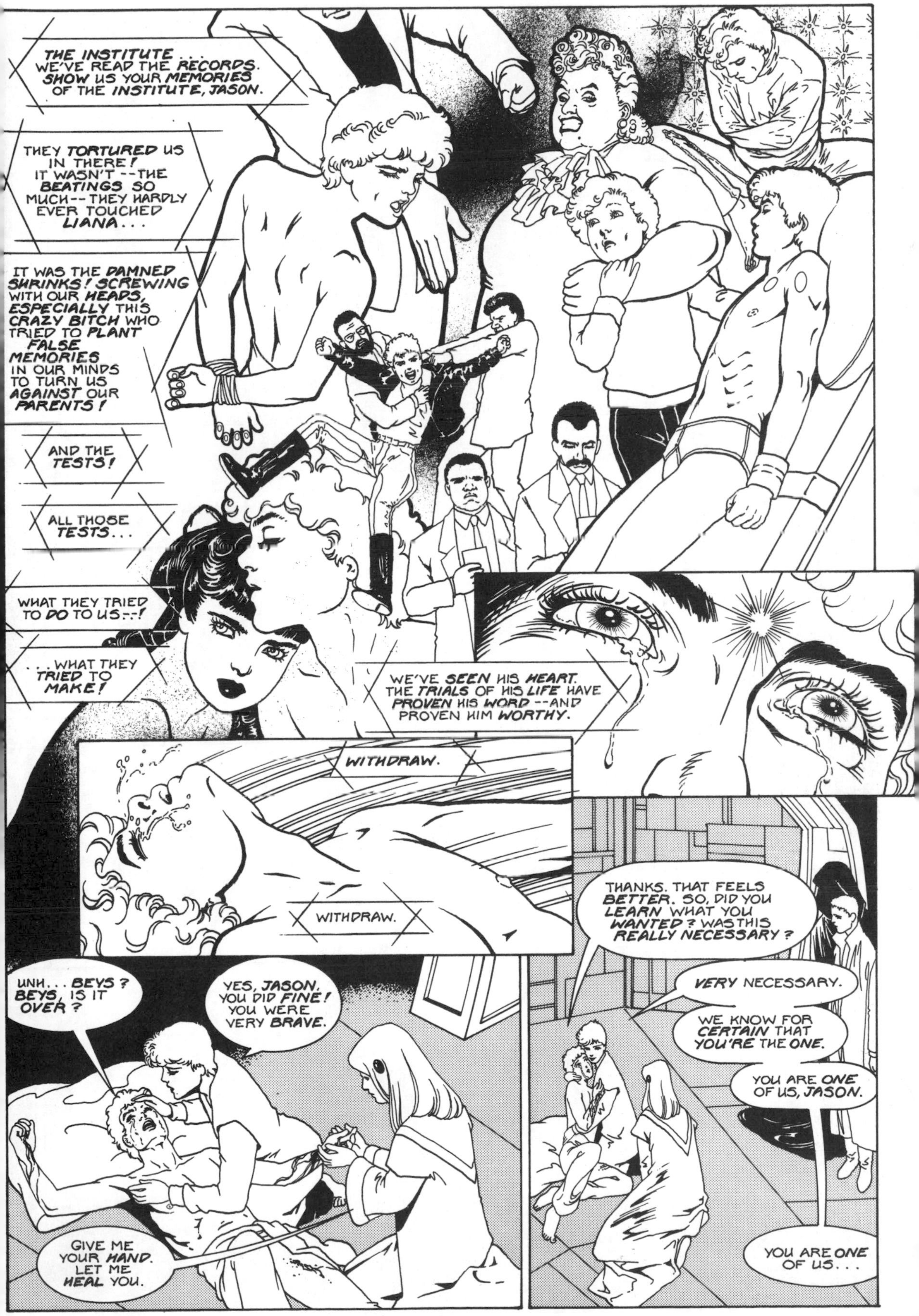
THE INSTITUTE . . . WE'VE READ THE RECORDS. SHOW US YOUR MEMORIES OF THE INSTITUTE, JASON.
THEY TORTURED US IN THERE! IT WASN'T --THE BEATINGS SO MUCH-- THEY HARDLY EVER TOUCHED LIANA . . .
IT WAS THE DAMNED SHRINKS! SCREWING WITH OUR HEADS, ESPECIALLY THIS CRAZY BITCH WHO TRIED TO PLANT FALSE MEMORIES IN OUR MINDS TO TURN US AGAINST OUR PARENTS!
AND THE TESTS!
ALL THOSE TESTS . . .
WHAT THEY TRIED TO DO TO US--!
. . . WHAT THEY TRIED TO MAKE!
WE'VE SEEN HIS HEART. THE TRIALS OF HIS LIFE HAVE PROVEN HIS WORD --AND PROVEN HIM WORTHY.
WITHDRAW.
WITHDRAW.
UNH . . . BEYS? BEYS, IS IT OVER?
YES, JASON. YOU DID FINE! YOU WERE VERY BRAVE.
GIVE ME YOUR HAND. LET ME HEAL YOU.
THANKS. THAT FEELS BETTER. SO, DID YOU LEARN WHAT YOU WANTED? WAS THIS REALLY NECESSARY?
VERY NECESSARY.
WE KNOW FOR CERTAIN THAT YOU'RE THE ONE.
YOU ARE ONE OF US, JASON.
YOU ARE ONE OF US . . .

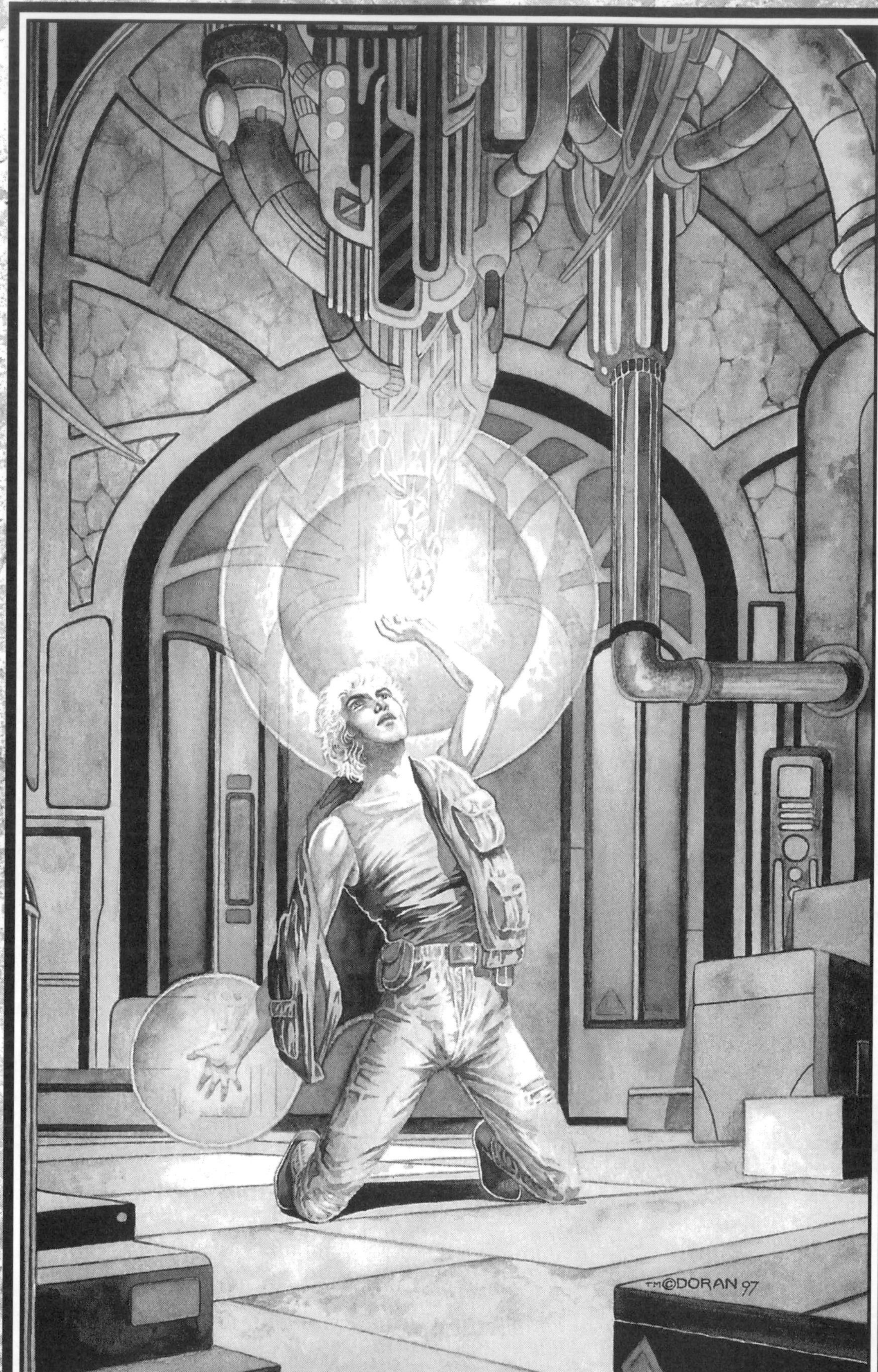
TM©DORAN 97

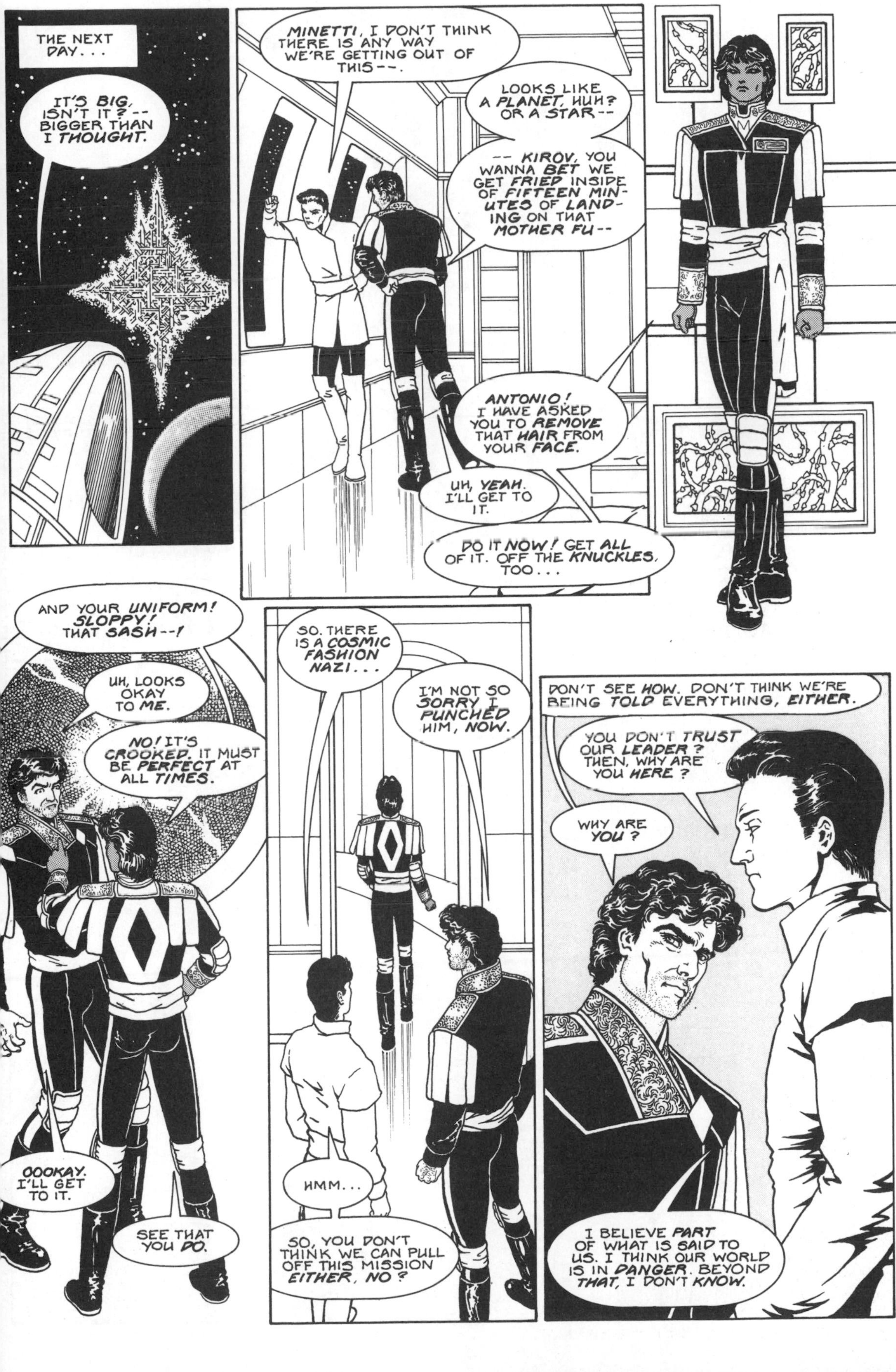
THE NEXT DAY...
IT'S BIG, ISN'T IT? -- BIGGER THAN I THOUGHT.
MINETTI, I DON'T THINK THERE IS ANY WAY WE'RE GETTING OUT OF THIS--.
LOOKS LIKE A PLANET, HUH? OR A STAR--
-- KIROV, YOU WANNA BET WE GET FRIED INSIDE OF FIFTEEN MINUTES OF LANDING ON THAT MOTHER FU--
ANTONIO! I HAVE ASKED YOU TO REMOVE THAT HAIR FROM YOUR FACE.
UH, YEAH. I'LL GET TO IT.
DO IT NOW! GET ALL OF IT. OFF THE KNUCKLES, TOO...
AND YOUR UNIFORM! SLOPPY! THAT SASH--!
UH, LOOKS OKAY TO ME.
NO! IT'S CROOKED. IT MUST BE PERFECT AT ALL TIMES.
OOOKAY. I'LL GET TO IT.
SEE THAT YOU DO.
SO. THERE IS A COSMIC FASHION NAZI...
I'M NOT SO SORRY I PUNCHED HIM, NOW.
HMM...
SO, YOU DON'T THINK WE CAN PULL OFF THIS MISSION EITHER, NO?
DON'T SEE HOW. DON'T THINK WE'RE BEING TOLD EVERYTHING, EITHER.
YOU DON'T TRUST OUR LEADER? THEN, WHY ARE YOU HERE?
WHY ARE YOU?
I BELIEVE PART OF WHAT IS SAID TO US. I THINK OUR WORLD IS IN DANGER. BEYOND THAT, I DON'T KNOW.

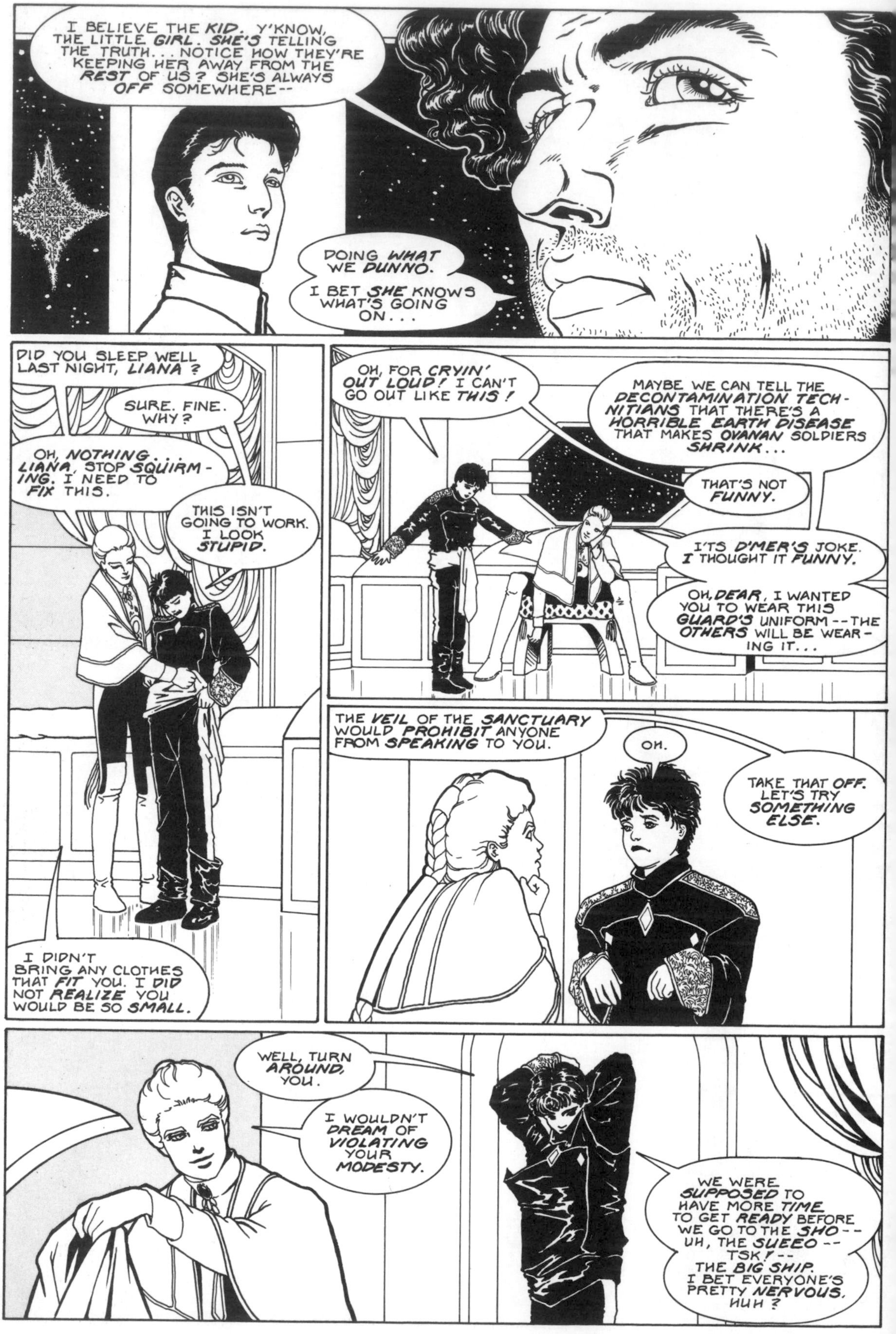

I BELIEVE THE KID. Y'KNOW, THE LITTLE GIRL. SHE'S TELLING THE TRUTH... NOTICE HOW THEY'RE KEEPING HER AWAY FROM THE REST OF US? SHE'S ALWAYS OFF SOMEWHERE--
DOING WHAT WE DUNNO.
I BET SHE KNOWS WHAT'S GOING ON...
DID YOU SLEEP WELL LAST NIGHT, LIANA?
SURE. FINE. WHY?
OH, NOTHING. LIANA, STOP SQUIRMING. I NEED TO FIX THIS.
THIS ISN'T GOING TO WORK. I LOOK STUPID.
I DIDN'T BRING ANY CLOTHES THAT FIT YOU. I DID NOT REALIZE YOU WOULD BE SO SMALL.
OH, FOR CRYIN' OUT LOUD! I CAN'T GO OUT LIKE THIS!
MAYBE WE CAN TELL THE DECONTAMINATION TECHNITIANS THAT THERE'S A HORRIBLE EARTH DISEASE THAT MAKES OVANAN SOLDIERS SHRINK...
THAT'S NOT FUNNY.
IT'S D'MER'S JOKE. I THOUGHT IT FUNNY.
OH, DEAR, I WANTED YOU TO WEAR THIS GUARD'S UNIFORM--THE OTHERS WILL BE WEARING IT...
THE VEIL OF THE SANCTUARY WOULD PROHIBIT ANYONE FROM SPEAKING TO YOU.
OH.
TAKE THAT OFF. LET'S TRY SOMETHING ELSE.
WELL, TURN AROUND, YOU.
I WOULDN'T DREAM OF VIOLATING YOUR MODESTY.
WE WERE SUPPOSED TO HAVE MORE TIME TO GET READY BEFORE WE GO TO THE SHO-- UH, THE SUEEO-- TSK!-- THE BIG SHIP. I BET EVERYONE'S PRETTY NERVOUS, HUH?

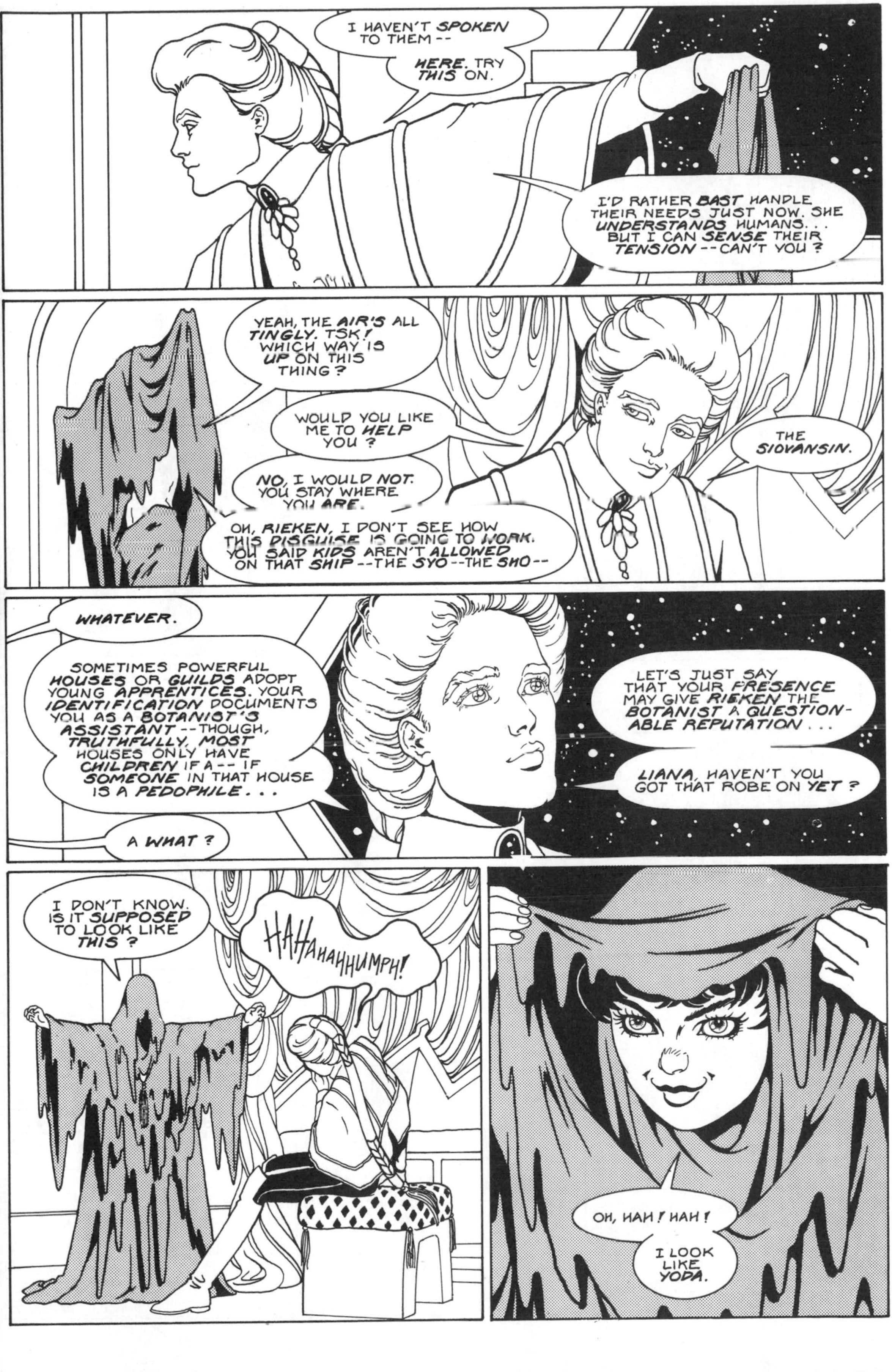
I HAVEN'T SPOKEN TO THEM --
HERE. TRY THIS ON.
I'D RATHER BAST HANDLE THEIR NEEDS JUST NOW. SHE UNDERSTANDS HUMANS. . . BUT I CAN SENSE THEIR TENSION -- CAN'T YOU ?
YEAH, THE AIR'S ALL TINGLY. TSK! WHICH WAY IS UP ON THIS THING?
WOULD YOU LIKE ME TO HELP YOU ?
NO, I WOULD NOT. YOU STAY WHERE YOU ARE.
OH, RIEKEN, I DON'T SEE HOW THIS DISGUISE IS GOING TO WORK. YOU SAID KIDS AREN'T ALLOWED ON THAT SHIP -- THE SYO -- THE SHO --
THE SIOVANSIN.
WHATEVER.
SOMETIMES POWERFUL HOUSES OR GUILDS ADOPT YOUNG APPRENTICES. YOUR IDENTIFICATION DOCUMENTS YOU AS A BOTANIST'S ASSISTANT -- THOUGH, TRUTHFULLY, MOST HOUSES ONLY HAVE CHILDREN IF A -- IF SOMEONE IN THAT HOUSE IS A PEDOPHILE . . .
A WHAT ?
LET'S JUST SAY THAT YOUR PRESENCE MAY GIVE RIEKEN THE BOTANIST A QUESTION-ABLE REPUTATION . . .
LIANA, HAVEN'T YOU GOT THAT ROBE ON YET ?
I DON'T KNOW. IS IT SUPPOSED TO LOOK LIKE THIS ?
HAHAHAHHUMPH!
OH, HAH! HAH!
I LOOK LIKE YODA.

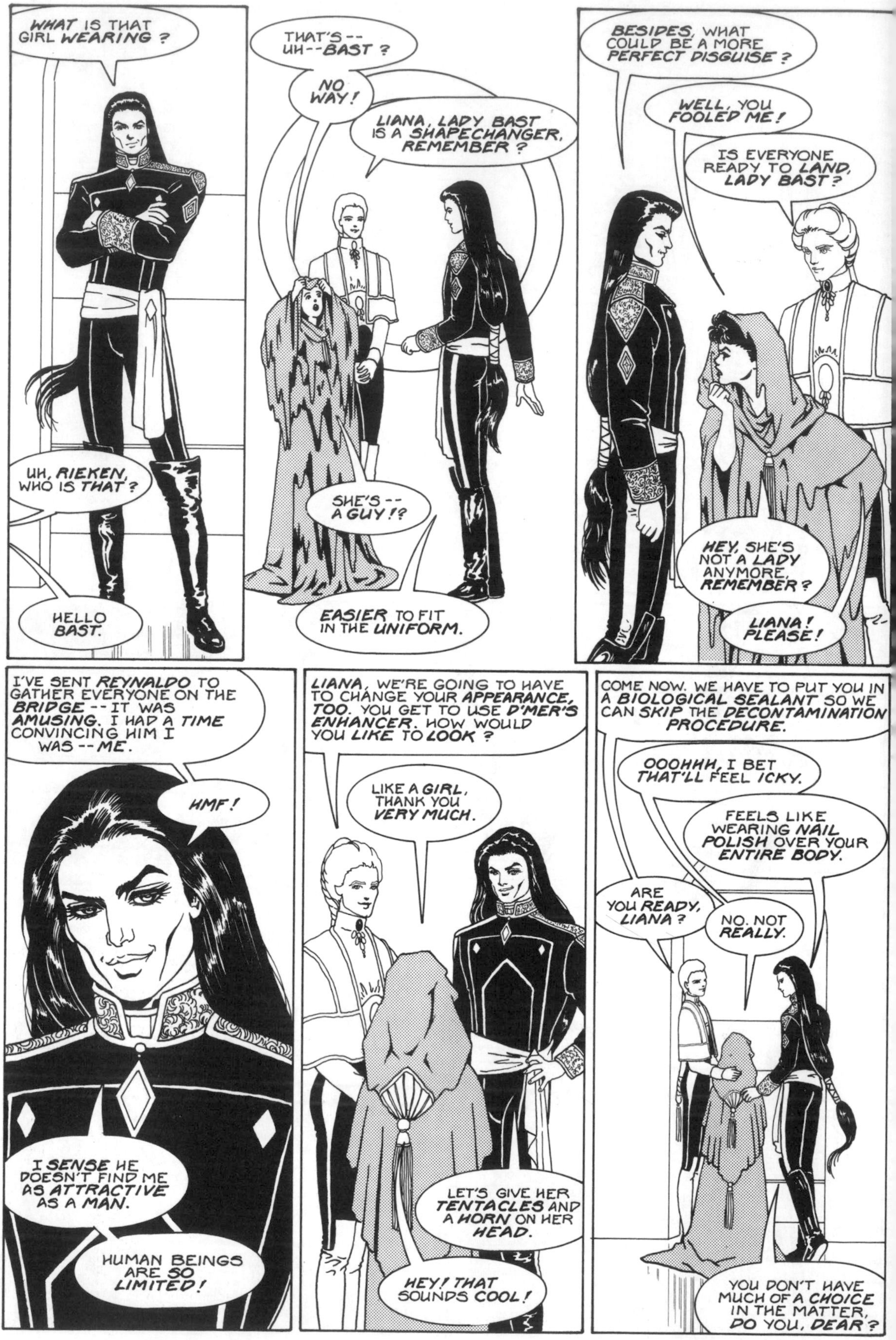
WHAT IS THAT GIRL WEARING?
UH, RIEKEN, WHO IS THAT?
HELLO BAST.
THAT'S -- UH -- BAST?
NO WAY!
LIANA, LADY BAST IS A SHAPECHANGER, REMEMBER?
SHE'S -- A GUY!?
EASIER TO FIT IN THE UNIFORM.
BESIDES, WHAT COULD BE A MORE PERFECT DISGUISE?
WELL, YOU FOOLED ME!
IS EVERYONE READY TO LAND, LADY BAST?
HEY, SHE'S NOT A LADY ANYMORE, REMEMBER?
LIANA! PLEASE!
I'VE SENT REYNALDO TO GATHER EVERYONE ON THE BRIDGE -- IT WAS AMUSING. I HAD A TIME CONVINCING HIM I WAS -- ME.
HMF!
I SENSE HE DOESN'T FIND ME AS ATTRACTIVE AS A MAN.
HUMAN BEINGS ARE SO LIMITED!
LIANA, WE'RE GOING TO HAVE TO CHANGE YOUR APPEARANCE, TOO. YOU GET TO USE D'MER'S ENHANCER. HOW WOULD YOU LIKE TO LOOK?
LIKE A GIRL, THANK YOU VERY MUCH.
LET'S GIVE HER TENTACLES AND A HORN ON HER HEAD.
HEY! THAT SOUNDS COOL!
COME NOW. WE HAVE TO PUT YOU IN A BIOLOGICAL SEALANT SO WE CAN SKIP THE DECONTAMINATION PROCEDURE.
OOOHHH, I BET THAT'LL FEEL ICKY.
FEELS LIKE WEARING NAIL POLISH OVER YOUR ENTIRE BODY.
ARE YOU READY, LIANA?
NO. NOT REALLY.
YOU DON'T HAVE MUCH OF A CHOICE IN THE MATTER, DO YOU, DEAR?

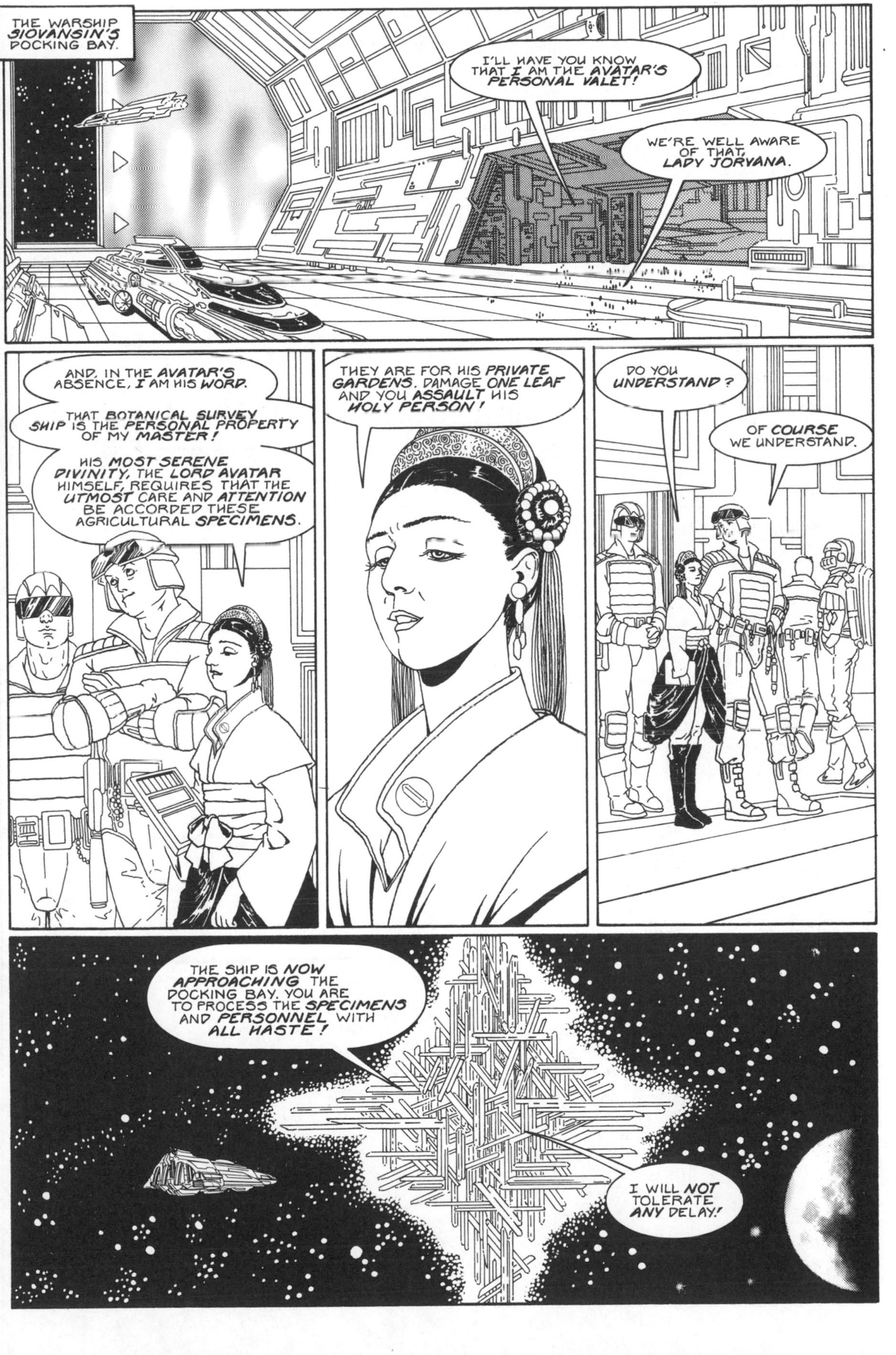
THE WARSHIP SIOVANSIN'S DOCKING BAY.
I'LL HAVE YOU KNOW THAT I AM THE AVATAR'S PERSONAL VALET!
WE'RE WELL AWARE OF THAT, LADY JORVANA.
AND, IN THE AVATAR'S ABSENCE, I AM HIS WORD.
THAT BOTANICAL SURVEY SHIP IS THE PERSONAL PROPERTY OF MY MASTER!
HIS MOST SERENE DIVINITY, THE LORD AVATAR HIMSELF, REQUIRES THAT THE UTMOST CARE AND ATTENTION BE ACCORDED THESE AGRICULTURAL SPECIMENS.
THEY ARE FOR HIS PRIVATE GARDENS. DAMAGE ONE LEAF AND YOU ASSAULT HIS HOLY PERSON!
DO YOU UNDERSTAND?
OF COURSE WE UNDERSTAND.
THE SHIP IS NOW APPROACHING THE DOCKING BAY. YOU ARE TO PROCESS THE SPECIMENS AND PERSONNEL WITH ALL HASTE!
I WILL NOT TOLERATE ANY DELAY!

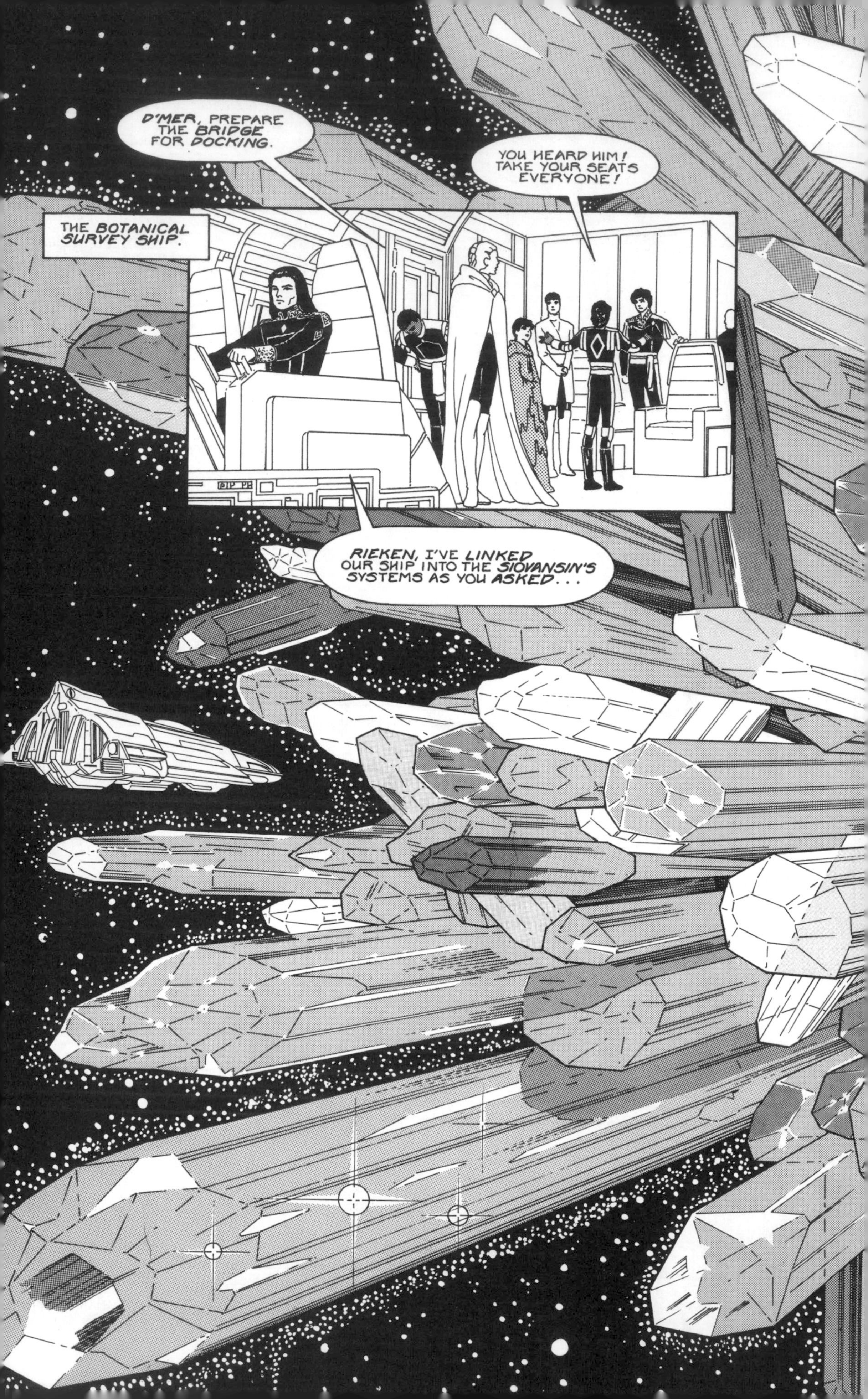
THE BOTANICAL SURVEY SHIP.
D'MER, PREPARE THE BRIDGE FOR DOCKING.
YOU HEARD HIM! TAKE YOUR SEATS EVERYONE!
RIEKEN, I'VE LINKED OUR SHIP INTO THE SIOVANSIN'S SYSTEMS AS YOU ASKED...

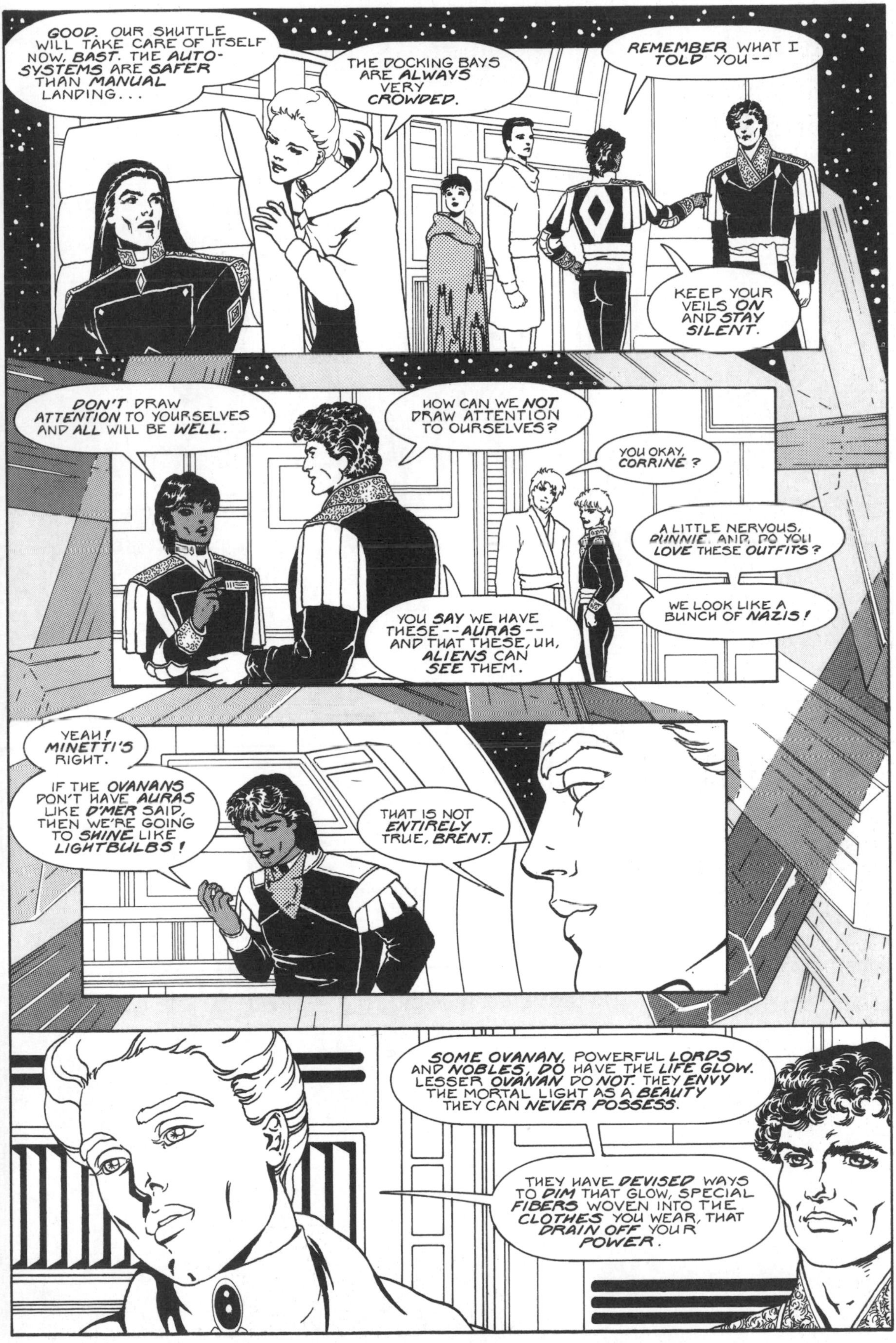
GOOD. OUR SHUTTLE WILL TAKE CARE OF ITSELF NOW, BAST. THE AUTO-SYSTEMS ARE SAFER THAN MANUAL LANDING...
THE DOCKING BAYS ARE ALWAYS VERY CROWDED.
REMEMBER WHAT I TOLD YOU--
KEEP YOUR VEILS ON AND STAY SILENT.
DON'T DRAW ATTENTION TO YOURSELVES AND ALL WILL BE WELL.
HOW CAN WE NOT DRAW ATTENTION TO OURSELVES?
YOU SAY WE HAVE THESE--AURAS--AND THAT THESE, UH, ALIENS CAN SEE THEM.
YOU OKAY, CORRINE?
A LITTLE NERVOUS, DUNNIE. AND, DO YOU LOVE THESE OUTFITS?
WE LOOK LIKE A BUNCH OF NAZIS!
YEAH! MINETTI'S RIGHT.
IF THE OVANANS DON'T HAVE AURAS LIKE D'MER SAID, THEN WE'RE GOING TO SHINE LIKE LIGHTBULBS!
THAT IS NOT ENTIRELY TRUE, BRENT.
SOME OVANAN, POWERFUL LORDS AND NOBLES, DO HAVE THE LIFE GLOW. LESSER OVANAN DO NOT. THEY ENVY THE MORTAL LIGHT AS A BEAUTY THEY CAN NEVER POSSESS.
THEY HAVE DEVISED WAYS TO DIM THAT GLOW, SPECIAL FIBERS WOVEN INTO THE CLOTHES YOU WEAR, THAT DRAIN OFF YOUR POWER.

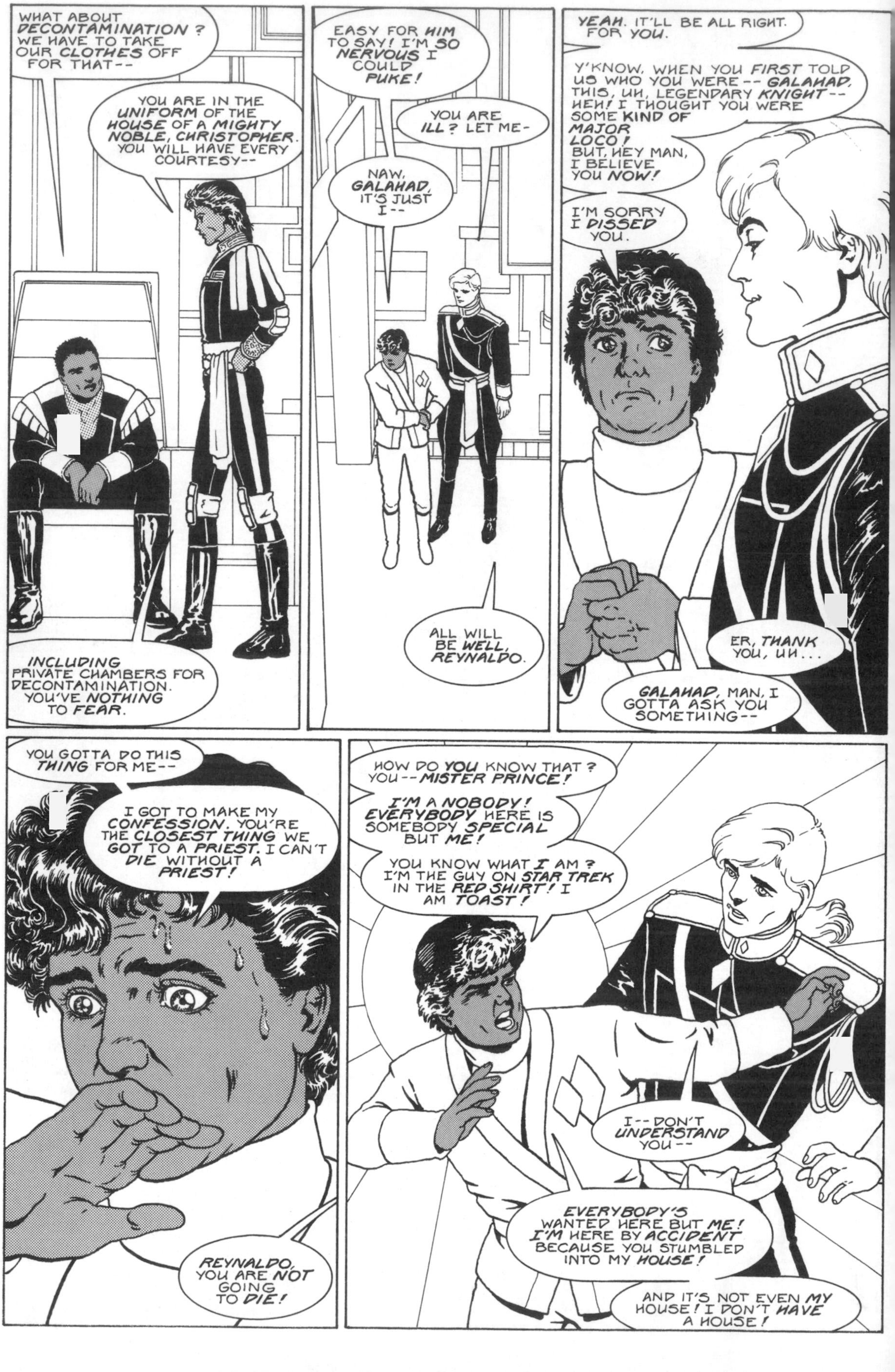
WHAT ABOUT *DECONTAMINATION* ? WE HAVE TO TAKE OUR *CLOTHES* OFF FOR THAT--
YOU ARE IN THE *UNIFORM* OF THE *HOUSE* OF A *MIGHTY NOBLE, CHRISTOPHER*. YOU WILL HAVE EVERY COURTESY--
INCLUDING PRIVATE CHAMBERS FOR DECONTAMINATION. YOU'VE *NOTHING* TO *FEAR*.
EASY FOR *HIM* TO SAY! I'M *SO NERVOUS* I COULD *PUKE!*
YOU ARE *ILL*? LET ME-
NAW, *GALAHAD*, IT'S JUST I--
ALL WILL BE *WELL*, *REYNALDO*.
YEAH. IT'LL BE ALL RIGHT. FOR *YOU*.
Y'KNOW, WHEN YOU *FIRST* TOLD US WHO YOU WERE -- *GALAHAD*, THIS, UH, LEGENDARY *KNIGHT* -- HEH! I THOUGHT YOU WERE SOME *KIND OF MAJOR LOCO!* BUT, HEY MAN, I BELIEVE YOU *NOW!*
I'M SORRY I *DISSED* YOU.
ER, *THANK* YOU, UH...
GALAHAD, MAN, I GOTTA ASK YOU SOMETHING--
YOU GOTTA DO THIS *THING* FOR ME--
I GOT TO MAKE MY *CONFESSION*. YOU'RE THE *CLOSEST THING* WE *GOT* TO A *PRIEST*. I CAN'T *DIE* WITHOUT A *PRIEST!*
REYNALDO, YOU ARE *NOT* GOING TO *DIE!*
HOW DO *YOU* KNOW THAT? YOU -- *MISTER PRINCE!*
I'M A *NOBODY! EVERYBODY* HERE IS SOMEBODY *SPECIAL* BUT *ME!*
YOU KNOW WHAT *I* AM? I'M THE GUY ON *STAR TREK* IN THE *RED SHIRT!* I AM *TOAST!*
I -- DON'T *UNDERSTAND* YOU --
EVERYBODY'S WANTED HERE BUT *ME! I'M* HERE BY *ACCIDENT* BECAUSE YOU STUMBLED INTO MY *HOUSE!*
AND IT'S NOT EVEN *MY* HOUSE! I DON'T *HAVE* A HOUSE!

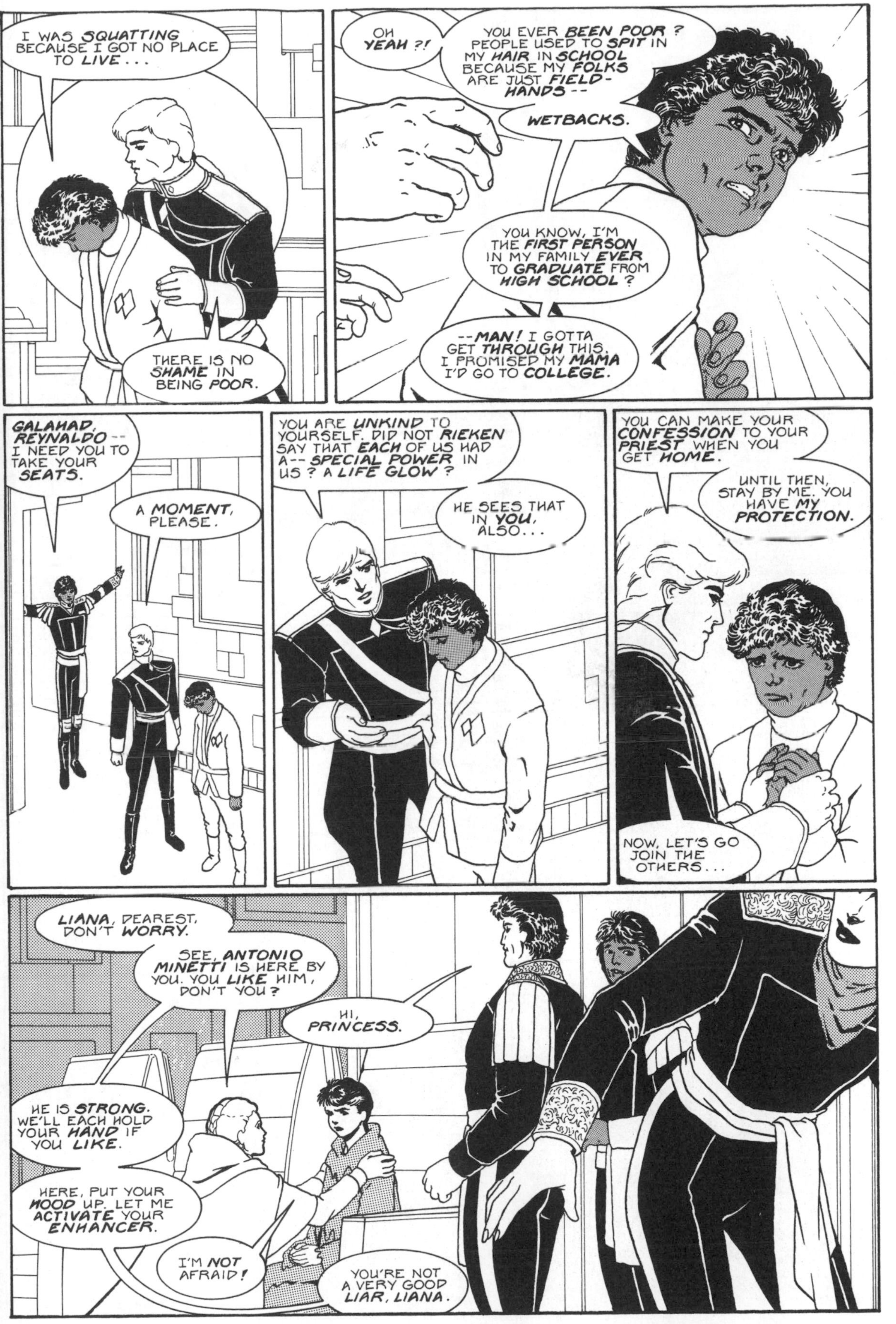
I WAS SQUATTING BECAUSE I GOT NO PLACE TO LIVE...
THERE IS NO SHAME IN BEING POOR.
OH YEAH ?!
YOU EVER BEEN POOR ? PEOPLE USED TO SPIT IN MY HAIR IN SCHOOL BECAUSE MY FOLKS ARE JUST FIELD-HANDS --
WETBACKS.
YOU KNOW, I'M THE FIRST PERSON IN MY FAMILY EVER TO GRADUATE FROM HIGH SCHOOL ?
--MAN! I GOTTA GET THROUGH THIS. I PROMISED MY MAMA I'D GO TO COLLEGE.
GALAHAD, REYNALDO -- I NEED YOU TO TAKE YOUR SEATS.
A MOMENT, PLEASE.
YOU ARE UNKIND TO YOURSELF. DID NOT RIEKEN SAY THAT EACH OF US HAD A-- SPECIAL POWER IN US ? A LIFE GLOW ?
HE SEES THAT IN YOU, ALSO...
YOU CAN MAKE YOUR CONFESSION TO YOUR PRIEST WHEN YOU GET HOME.
UNTIL THEN, STAY BY ME. YOU HAVE MY PROTECTION.
NOW, LET'S GO JOIN THE OTHERS...
LIANA, DEAREST, DON'T WORRY.
SEE, ANTONIO MINETTI IS HERE BY YOU. YOU LIKE HIM, DON'T YOU ?
HI, PRINCESS.
HE IS STRONG. WE'LL EACH HOLD YOUR HAND IF YOU LIKE.
HERE, PUT YOUR HOOD UP. LET ME ACTIVATE YOUR ENHANCER.
I'M NOT AFRAID!
YOU'RE NOT A VERY GOOD LIAR, LIANA.

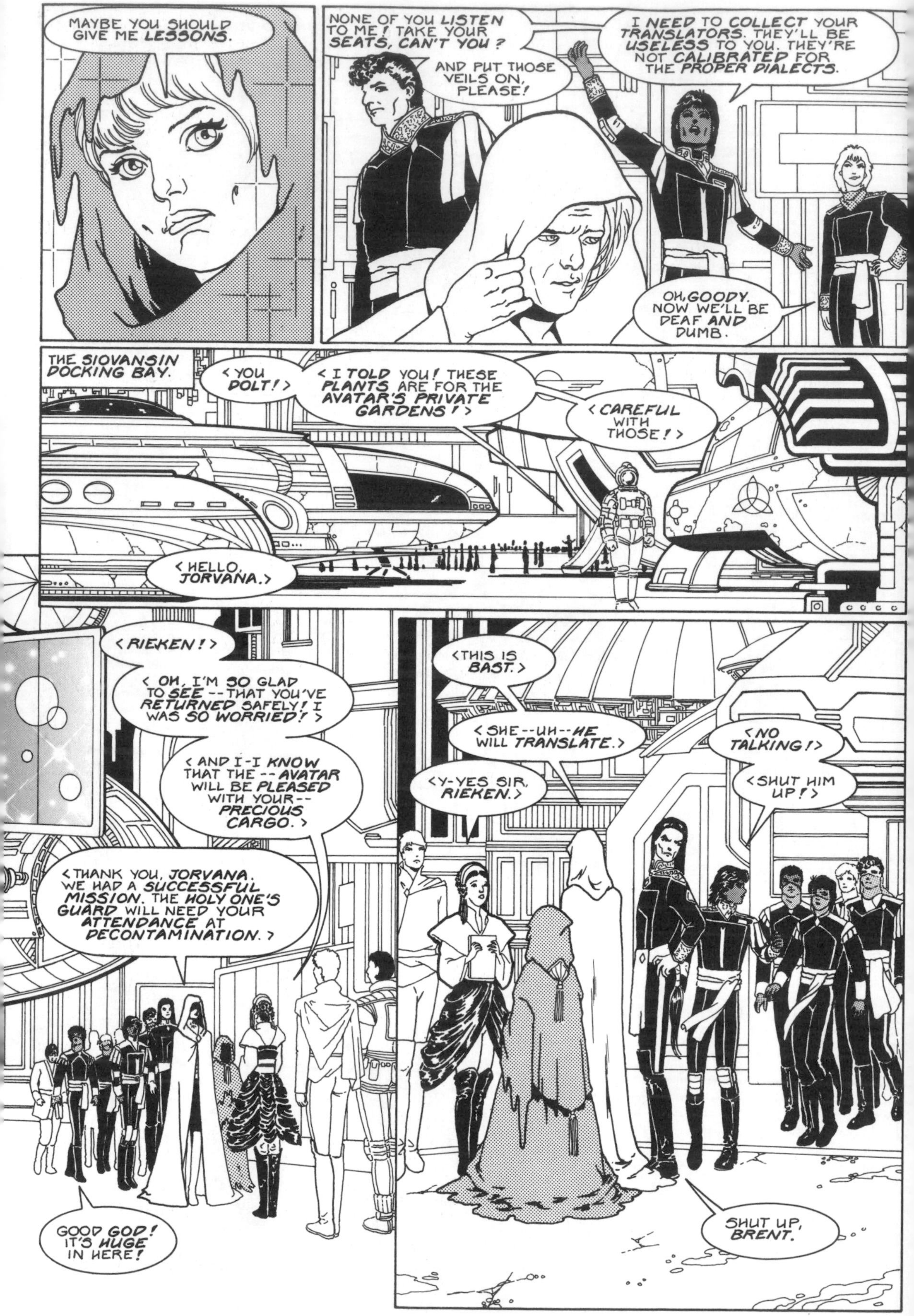
MAYBE YOU SHOULD GIVE ME LESSONS.
NONE OF YOU LISTEN TO ME! TAKE YOUR SEATS, CAN'T YOU?
AND PUT THOSE VEILS ON, PLEASE!
I NEED TO COLLECT YOUR TRANSLATORS. THEY'LL BE USELESS TO YOU. THEY'RE NOT CALIBRATED FOR THE PROPER DIALECTS.
OH, GOODY. NOW WE'LL BE DEAF AND DUMB.
THE SIOVANSIN DOCKING BAY.
<YOU DOLT!>
<I TOLD YOU! THESE PLANTS ARE FOR THE AVATAR'S PRIVATE GARDENS!>
<CAREFUL WITH THOSE!>
<HELLO, JORVANA.>
<RIEKEN!>
<OH, I'M SO GLAD TO SEE -- THAT YOU'VE RETURNED SAFELY! I WAS SO WORRIED!>
<AND I-I KNOW THAT THE -- AVATAR WILL BE PLEASED WITH YOUR -- PRECIOUS CARGO.>
<THANK YOU, JORVANA. WE HAD A SUCCESSFUL MISSION. THE HOLY ONE'S GUARD WILL NEED YOUR ATTENDANCE AT DECONTAMINATION.>
GOOD GOD! IT'S HUGE IN HERE!
<THIS IS BAST.>
<SHE--UH--HE WILL TRANSLATE.>
<Y-YES SIR, RIEKEN.>
<NO TALKING!>
<SHUT HIM UP!>
SHUT UP, BRENT.

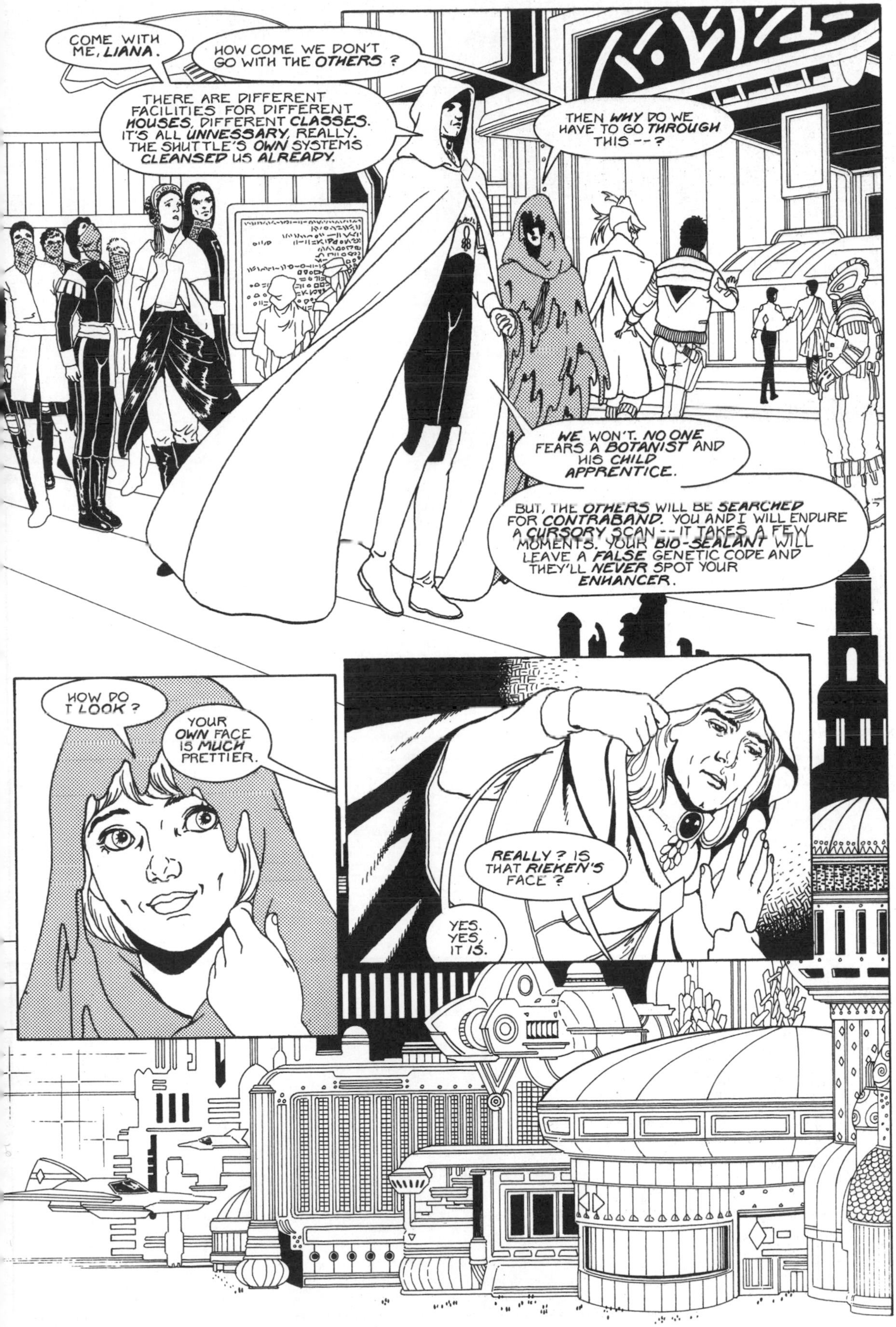

COME WITH ME, LIANA.
HOW COME WE DON'T GO WITH THE OTHERS ?
THERE ARE DIFFERENT FACILITIES FOR DIFFERENT HOUSES, DIFFERENT CLASSES. IT'S ALL UNNESSARY, REALLY. THE SHUTTLE'S OWN SYSTEMS CLEANSED US ALREADY.
THEN WHY DO WE HAVE TO GO THROUGH THIS --?
WE WON'T. NO ONE FEARS A BOTANIST AND HIS CHILD APPRENTICE.
BUT, THE OTHERS WILL BE SEARCHED FOR CONTRABAND. YOU AND I WILL ENDURE A CURSORY SCAN -- IT TAKES A FEW MOMENTS. YOUR BIO-SEALANT WILL LEAVE A FALSE GENETIC CODE AND THEY'LL NEVER SPOT YOUR ENHANCER.
HOW DO I LOOK ?
YOUR OWN FACE IS MUCH PRETTIER.
REALLY ? IS THAT RIEKEN'S FACE ?
YES. YES, IT IS.

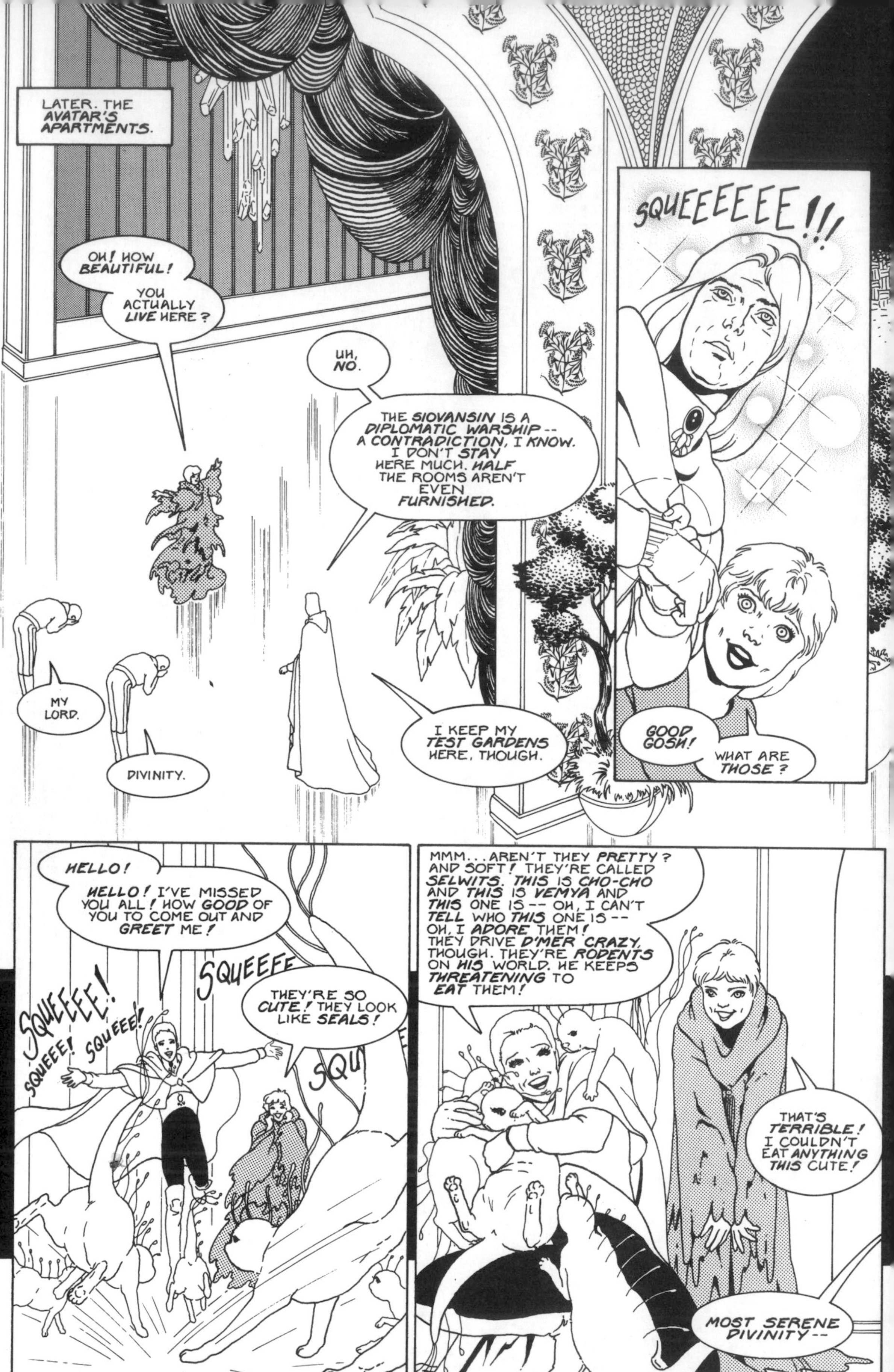
LATER. THE AVATAR'S APARTMENTS.
OH! HOW BEAUTIFUL!
YOU ACTUALLY LIVE HERE?
UH, NO.
THE SIOVANSIN IS A DIPLOMATIC WARSHIP -- A CONTRADICTION, I KNOW. I DON'T STAY HERE MUCH. HALF THE ROOMS AREN'T EVEN FURNISHED.
MY LORD.
DIVINITY.
I KEEP MY TEST GARDENS HERE, THOUGH.
SQUEEEEEE!!!
GOOD GOSH!
WHAT ARE THOSE?
HELLO!
HELLO! I'VE MISSED YOU ALL! HOW GOOD OF YOU TO COME OUT AND GREET ME!
SQUEEEE!
SQUEEEE!
SQUEEE! SQUEEE!
THEY'RE SO CUTE! THEY LOOK LIKE SEALS!
MMM... AREN'T THEY PRETTY? AND SOFT! THEY'RE CALLED SELWITS. THIS IS CHO-CHO AND THIS IS VEMYA AND THIS ONE IS -- OH, I CAN'T TELL WHO THIS ONE IS -- OH, I ADORE THEM! THEY DRIVE D'MER CRAZY, THOUGH. THEY'RE RODENTS ON HIS WORLD. HE KEEPS THREATENING TO EAT THEM!
THAT'S TERRIBLE! I COULDN'T EAT ANYTHING THIS CUTE!
MOST SERENE DIVINITY --

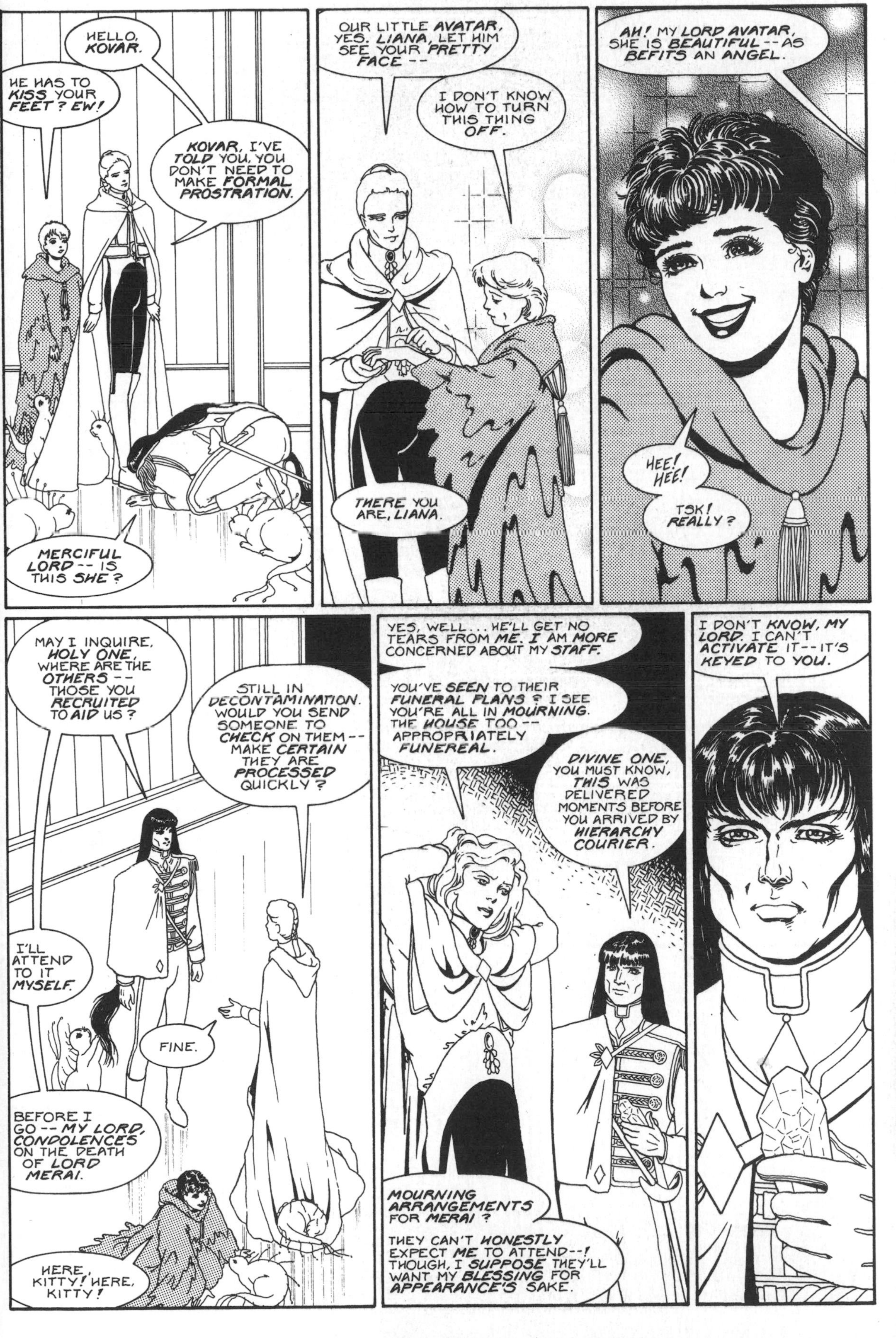
HELLO, KOVAR.
HE HAS TO KISS YOUR FEET? EW!
KOVAR, I'VE TOLD YOU, YOU DON'T NEED TO MAKE FORMAL PROSTRATION.
MERCIFUL LORD -- IS THIS SHE?
OUR LITTLE AVATAR, YES. LIANA, LET HIM SEE YOUR PRETTY FACE --
I DON'T KNOW HOW TO TURN THIS THING OFF.
THERE YOU ARE, LIANA.
AH! MY LORD AVATAR, SHE IS BEAUTIFUL -- AS BEFITS AN ANGEL.
HEE! HEE!
TSK! REALLY?
MAY I INQUIRE, HOLY ONE, WHERE ARE THE OTHERS -- THOSE YOU RECRUITED TO AID US?
STILL IN DECONTAMINATION. WOULD YOU SEND SOMEONE TO CHECK ON THEM -- MAKE CERTAIN THEY ARE PROCESSED QUICKLY?
I'LL ATTEND TO IT MYSELF.
FINE.
BEFORE I GO -- MY LORD, CONDOLENCES ON THE DEATH OF LORD MERAI.
HERE, KITTY! HERE, KITTY!
YES, WELL... HE'LL GET NO TEARS FROM ME. I AM MORE CONCERNED ABOUT MY STAFF.
YOU'VE SEEN TO THEIR FUNERAL PLANS? I SEE YOU'RE ALL IN MOURNING. THE HOUSE TOO -- APPROPRIATELY FUNEREAL.
DIVINE ONE, YOU MUST KNOW, THIS WAS DELIVERED MOMENTS BEFORE YOU ARRIVED BY HIERARCHY COURIER.
MOURNING ARRANGEMENTS FOR MERAI?
THEY CAN'T HONESTLY EXPECT ME TO ATTEND--! THOUGH, I SUPPOSE THEY'LL WANT MY BLESSING FOR APPEARANCE'S SAKE.
I DON'T KNOW, MY LORD. I CAN'T ACTIVATE IT -- IT'S KEYED TO YOU.

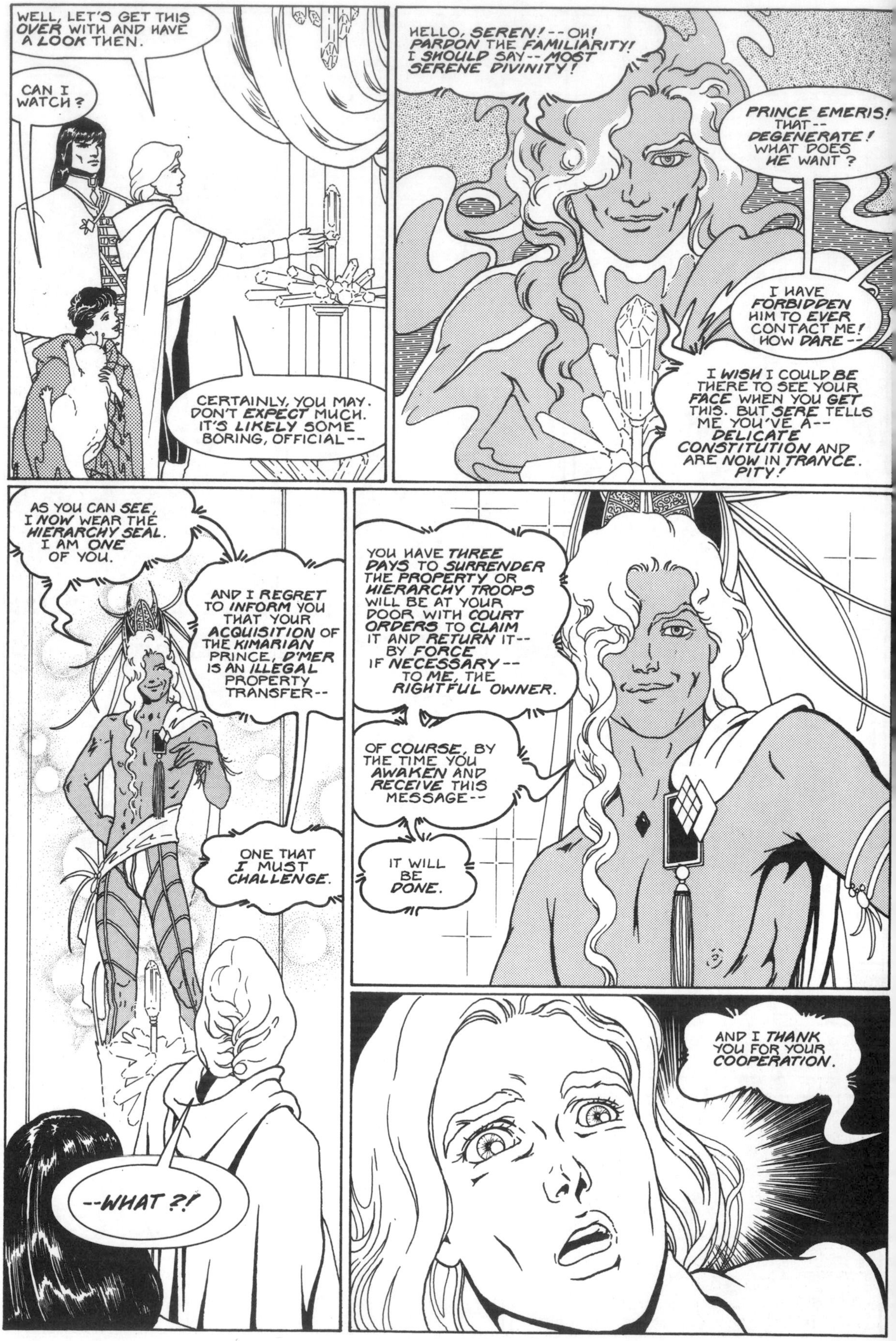
WELL, LET'S GET THIS OVER WITH AND HAVE A LOOK THEN.
CAN I WATCH?
CERTAINLY, YOU MAY. DON'T EXPECT MUCH. IT'S LIKELY SOME BORING, OFFICIAL--
HELLO, SEREN! --OH! PARDON THE FAMILIARITY! I SHOULD SAY-- MOST SERENE DIVINITY!
PRINCE EMERIS! THAT-- DEGENERATE! WHAT DOES HE WANT?
I HAVE FORBIDDEN HIM TO EVER CONTACT ME! HOW DARE--
I WISH I COULD BE THERE TO SEE YOUR FACE WHEN YOU GET THIS. BUT SERE TELLS ME YOU'VE A-- DELICATE CONSTITUTION AND ARE NOW IN TRANCE. PITY!
AS YOU CAN SEE, I NOW WEAR THE HIERARCHY SEAL. I AM ONE OF YOU.
AND I REGRET TO INFORM YOU THAT YOUR ACQUISITION OF THE KIMARIAN PRINCE, D'MER IS AN ILLEGAL PROPERTY TRANSFER--
ONE THAT I MUST CHALLENGE.
--WHAT?!
YOU HAVE THREE DAYS TO SURRENDER THE PROPERTY OR HIERARCHY TROOPS WILL BE AT YOUR DOOR WITH COURT ORDERS TO CLAIM IT AND RETURN IT-- BY FORCE IF NECESSARY-- TO ME, THE RIGHTFUL OWNER.
OF COURSE, BY THE TIME YOU AWAKEN AND RECEIVE THIS MESSAGE--
IT WILL BE DONE.
AND I THANK YOU FOR YOUR COOPERATION.

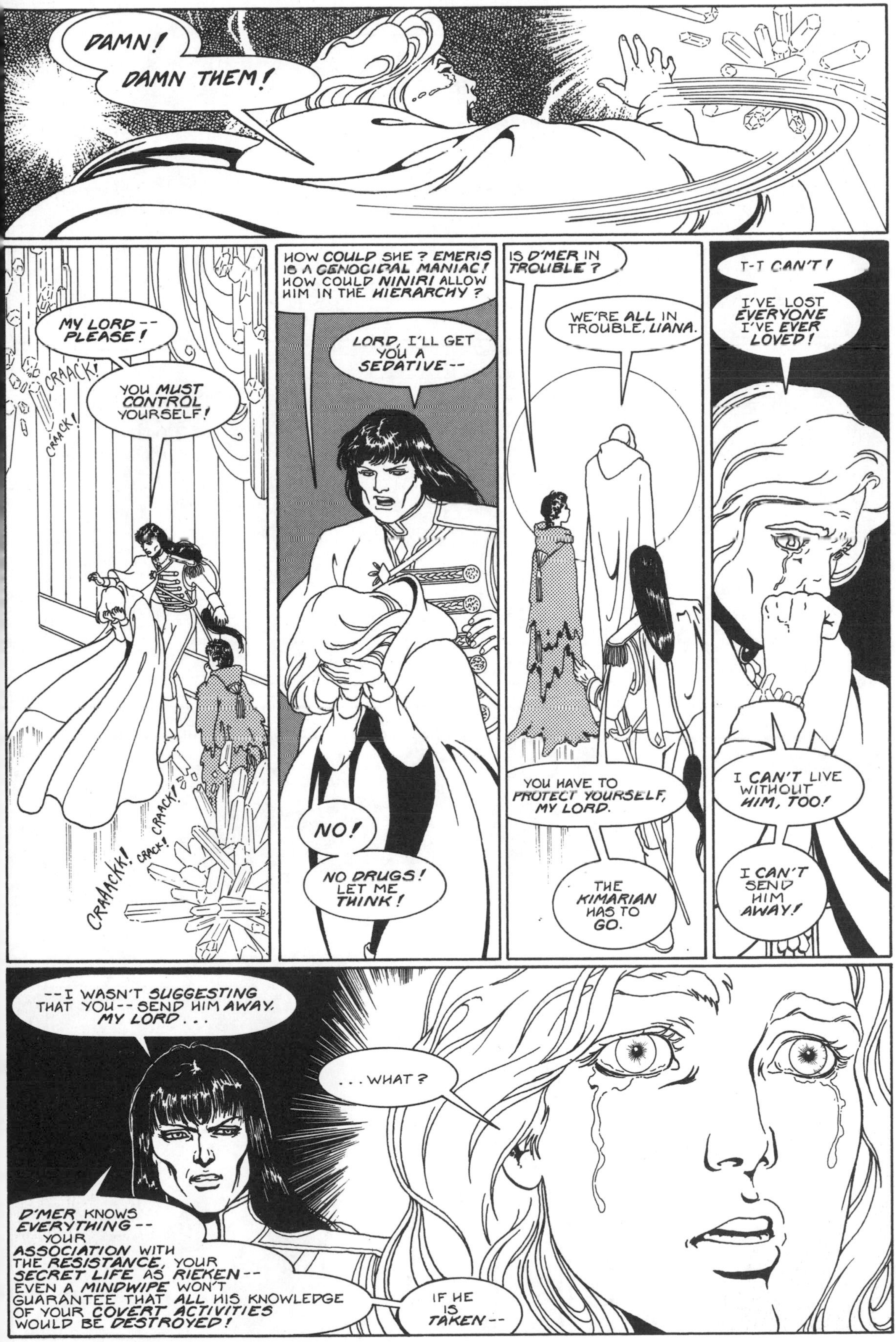

DAMN!
DAMN THEM!
MY LORD -- PLEASE!
YOU MUST CONTROL YOURSELF!
CRAACK!
CRAACK!
CRAACK!
CRACK!
CRAAACKK!
HOW COULD SHE? EMERIS IS A GENOCIDAL MANIAC! HOW COULD NINIRI ALLOW HIM IN THE HIERARCHY?
LORD, I'LL GET YOU A SEDATIVE --
NO!
NO DRUGS! LET ME THINK!
IS D'MER IN TROUBLE?
WE'RE ALL IN TROUBLE, LIANA.
YOU HAVE TO PROTECT YOURSELF, MY LORD.
THE KIMARIAN HAS TO GO.
T-I CAN'T!
I'VE LOST EVERYONE I'VE EVER LOVED!
I CAN'T LIVE WITHOUT HIM, TOO!
I CAN'T SEND HIM AWAY!
-- I WASN'T SUGGESTING THAT YOU -- SEND HIM AWAY, MY LORD...
...WHAT?
D'MER KNOWS EVERYTHING -- YOUR ASSOCIATION WITH THE RESISTANCE, YOUR SECRET LIFE AS RIEKEN -- EVEN A MINDWIPE WON'T GUARANTEE THAT ALL HIS KNOWLEDGE OF YOUR COVERT ACTIVITIES WOULD BE DESTROYED!
IF HE IS TAKEN --

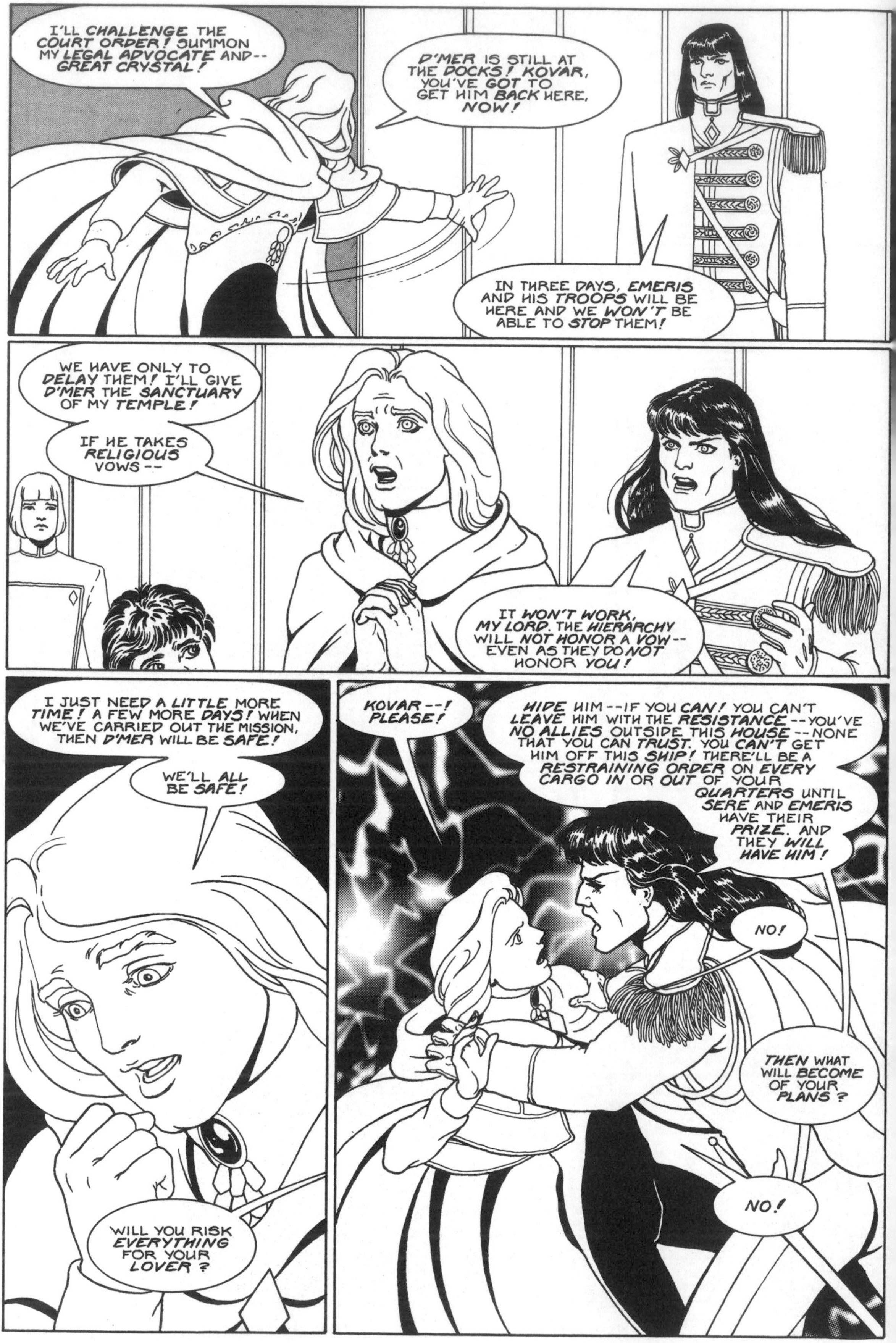
I'LL CHALLENGE THE COURT ORDER! SUMMON MY LEGAL ADVOCATE AND-- GREAT CRYSTAL!
D'MER IS STILL AT THE DOCKS! KOVAR, YOU'VE GOT TO GET HIM BACK HERE, NOW!
IN THREE DAYS, EMERIS AND HIS TROOPS WILL BE HERE AND WE WON'T BE ABLE TO STOP THEM!
WE HAVE ONLY TO DELAY THEM! I'LL GIVE D'MER THE SANCTUARY OF MY TEMPLE!
IF HE TAKES RELIGIOUS VOWS--
IT WON'T WORK, MY LORD. THE HIERARCHY WILL NOT HONOR A VOW-- EVEN AS THEY DO NOT HONOR YOU!
I JUST NEED A LITTLE MORE TIME! A FEW MORE DAYS! WHEN WE'VE CARRIED OUT THE MISSION, THEN D'MER WILL BE SAFE!
WE'LL ALL BE SAFE!
WILL YOU RISK EVERYTHING FOR YOUR LOVER?
KOVAR--! PLEASE!
HIDE HIM--IF YOU CAN! YOU CAN'T LEAVE HIM WITH THE RESISTANCE--YOU'VE NO ALLIES OUTSIDE THIS HOUSE--NONE THAT YOU CAN TRUST. YOU CAN'T GET HIM OFF THIS SHIP! THERE'LL BE A RESTRAINING ORDER ON EVERY CARGO IN OR OUT OF YOUR QUARTERS UNTIL SERE AND EMERIS HAVE THEIR PRIZE. AND THEY WILL HAVE HIM!
NO!
THEN WHAT WILL BECOME OF YOUR PLANS?
NO!

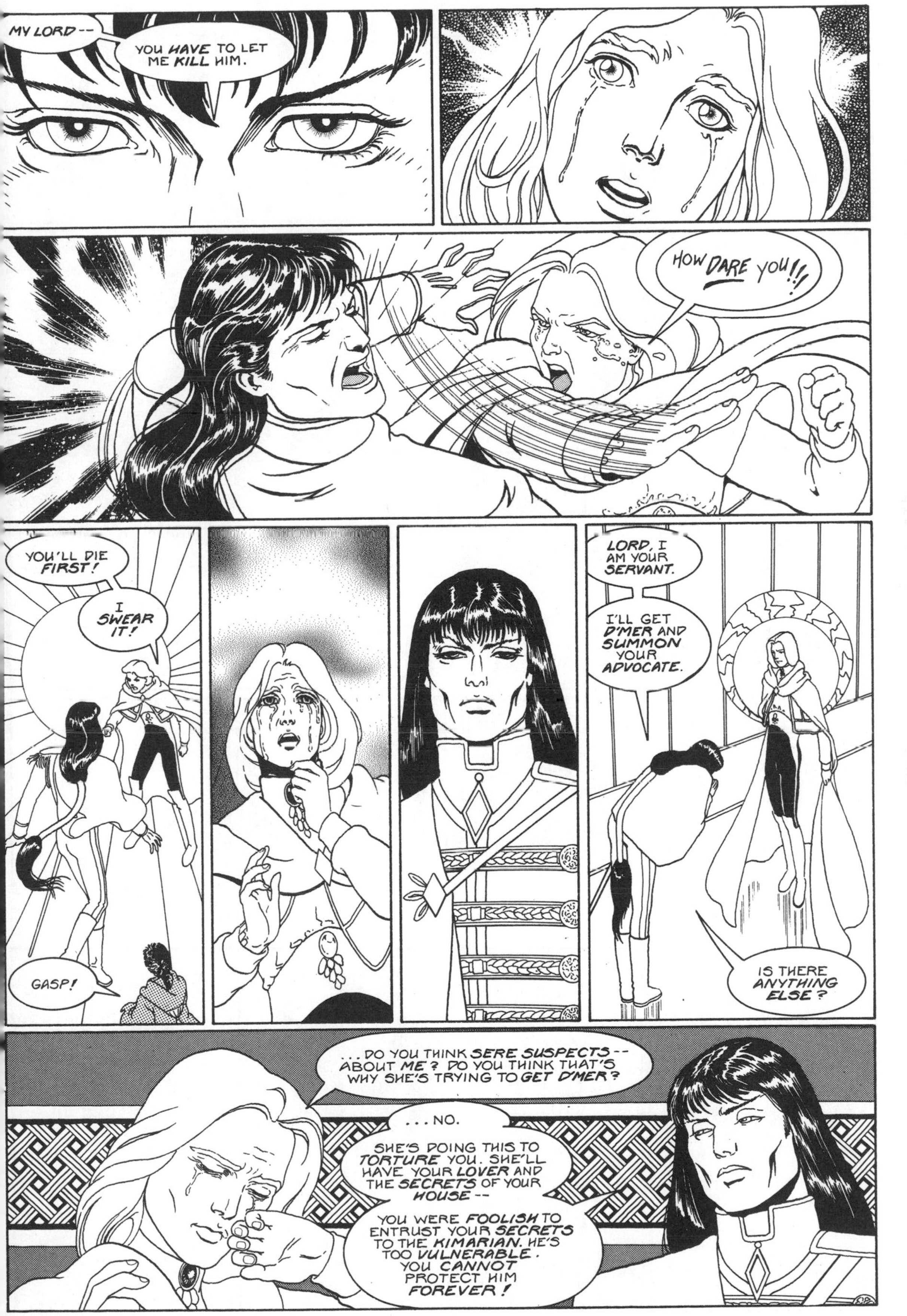
MY LORD --
YOU HAVE TO LET ME KILL HIM.
HOW DARE YOU!!!
YOU'LL DIE FIRST!
I SWEAR IT!
GASP!
LORD, I AM YOUR SERVANT.
I'LL GET D'MER AND SUMMON YOUR ADVOCATE.
IS THERE ANYTHING ELSE?
. . . DO YOU THINK SERE SUSPECTS -- ABOUT ME? DO YOU THINK THAT'S WHY SHE'S TRYING TO GET D'MER?
. . . NO.
SHE'S DOING THIS TO TORTURE YOU. SHE'LL HAVE YOUR LOVER AND THE SECRETS OF YOUR HOUSE --
YOU WERE FOOLISH TO ENTRUST YOUR SECRETS TO THE KIMARIAN. HE'S TOO VULNERABLE. YOU CANNOT PROTECT HIM FOREVER!

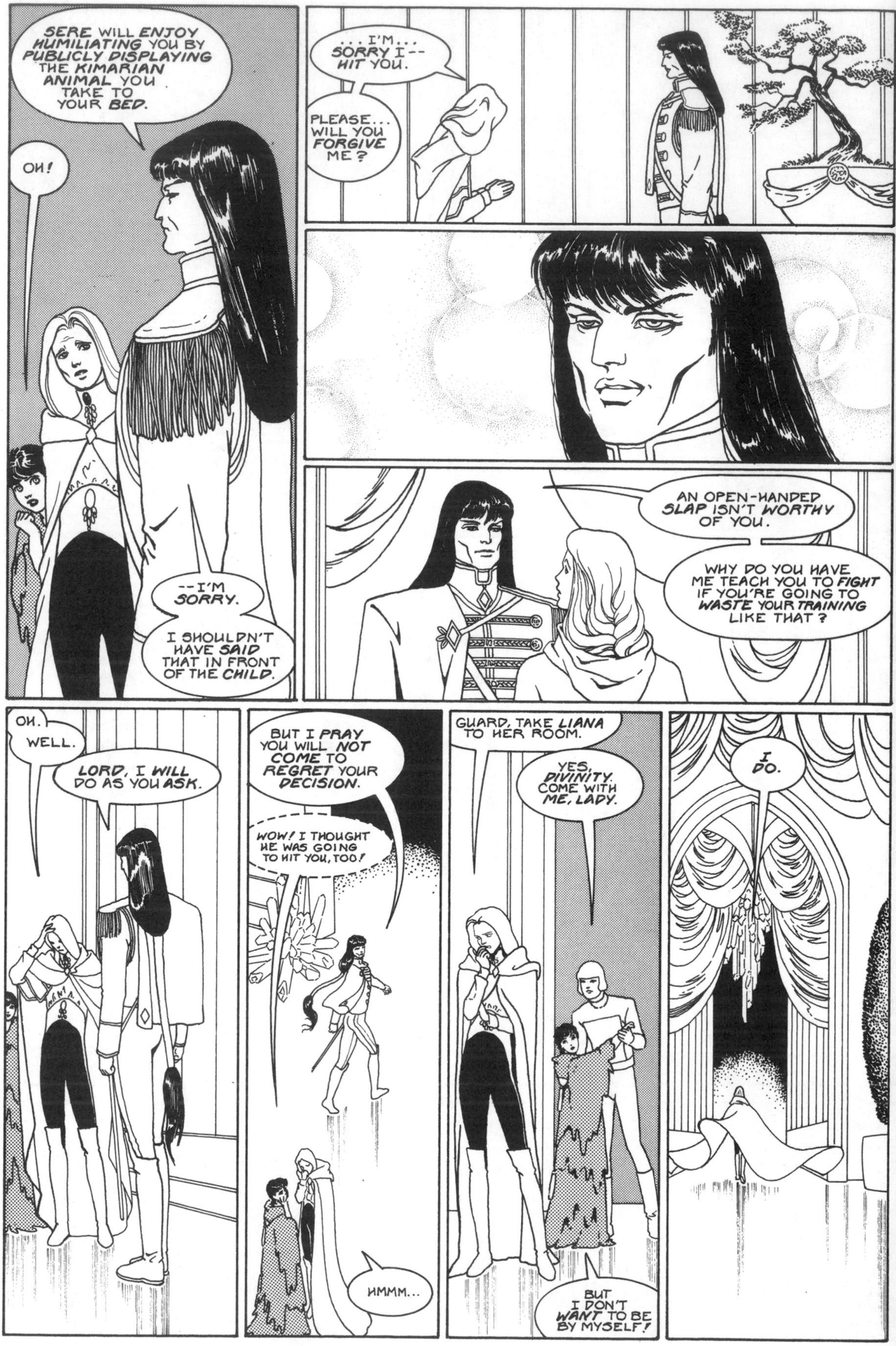
SERE WILL ENJOY HUMILIATING YOU BY PUBLICLY DISPLAYING THE KIMARIAN ANIMAL YOU TAKE TO YOUR BED.
OH!
--I'M SORRY.
I SHOULDN'T HAVE SAID THAT IN FRONT OF THE CHILD.
. . . I'M . . . SORRY I-- HIT YOU.
PLEASE . . . WILL YOU FORGIVE ME?
AN OPEN-HANDED SLAP ISN'T WORTHY OF YOU.
WHY DO YOU HAVE ME TEACH YOU TO FIGHT IF YOU'RE GOING TO WASTE YOUR TRAINING LIKE THAT?
OH.
WELL.
LORD, I WILL DO AS YOU ASK.
BUT I PRAY YOU WILL NOT COME TO REGRET YOUR DECISION.
WOW! I THOUGHT HE WAS GOING TO HIT YOU, TOO!
HMMM...
GUARD, TAKE LIANA TO HER ROOM.
YES, DIVINITY. COME WITH ME, LADY.
BUT I DON'T WANT TO BE BY MYSELF!
I DO.

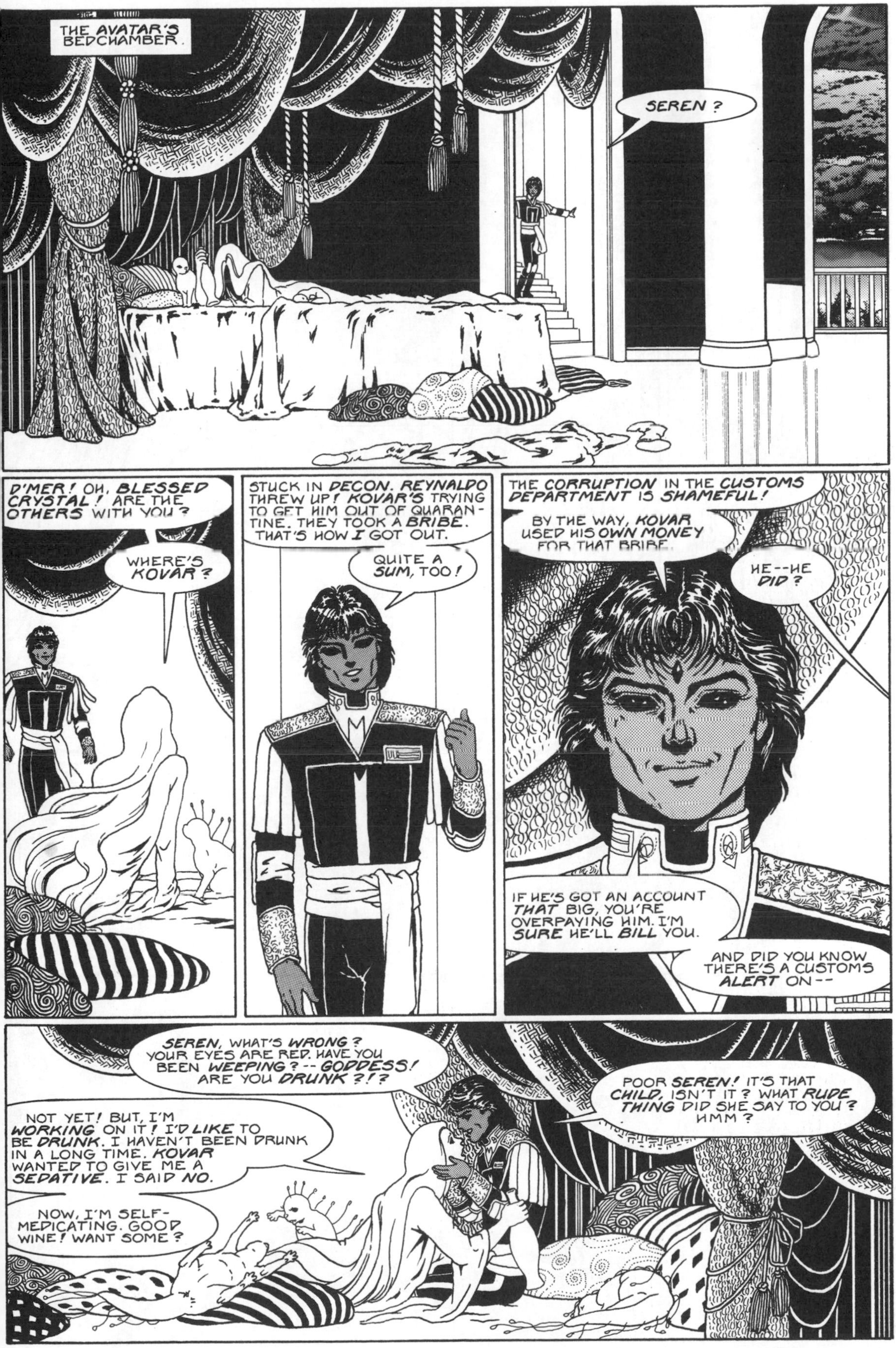
THE AVATAR'S BEDCHAMBER.
SEREN ?
D'MER! OH, BLESSED CRYSTAL! ARE THE OTHERS WITH YOU?
WHERE'S KOVAR?
STUCK IN DECON. REYNALDO THREW UP! KOVAR'S TRYING TO GET HIM OUT OF QUARANTINE. THEY TOOK A BRIBE. THAT'S HOW I GOT OUT.
QUITE A SUM, TOO!
THE CORRUPTION IN THE CUSTOMS DEPARTMENT IS SHAMEFUL!
BY THE WAY, KOVAR USED HIS OWN MONEY FOR THAT BRIBE.
HE--HE DID?
IF HE'S GOT AN ACCOUNT THAT BIG, YOU'RE OVERPAYING HIM. I'M SURE HE'LL BILL YOU.
AND DID YOU KNOW THERE'S A CUSTOMS ALERT ON--
SEREN, WHAT'S WRONG? YOUR EYES ARE RED. HAVE YOU BEEN WEEPING? -- GODDESS! ARE YOU DRUNK?!?
NOT YET! BUT, I'M WORKING ON IT! I'D LIKE TO BE DRUNK. I HAVEN'T BEEN DRUNK IN A LONG TIME. KOVAR WANTED TO GIVE ME A SEDATIVE. I SAID NO.
NOW, I'M SELF-MEDICATING. GOOD WINE! WANT SOME?
POOR SEREN! IT'S THAT CHILD, ISN'T IT? WHAT RUDE THING DID SHE SAY TO YOU? HMM?

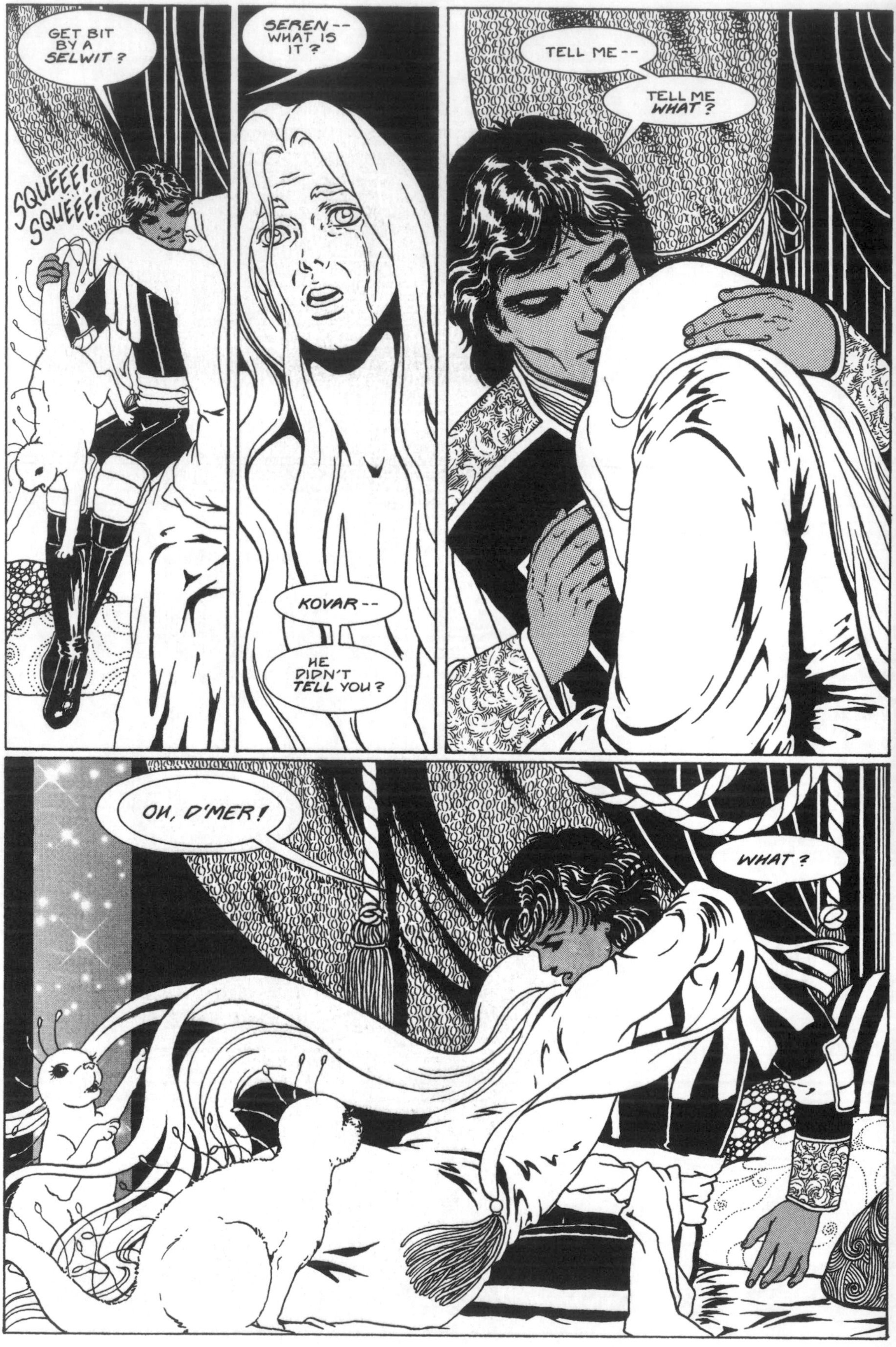
GET BIT BY A SELWIT?
SQUEEE! SQUEEE!
SEREN -- WHAT IS IT?
KOVAR --
HE DIDN'T TELL YOU?
TELL ME --
TELL ME WHAT?
OH, D'MER!
WHAT?

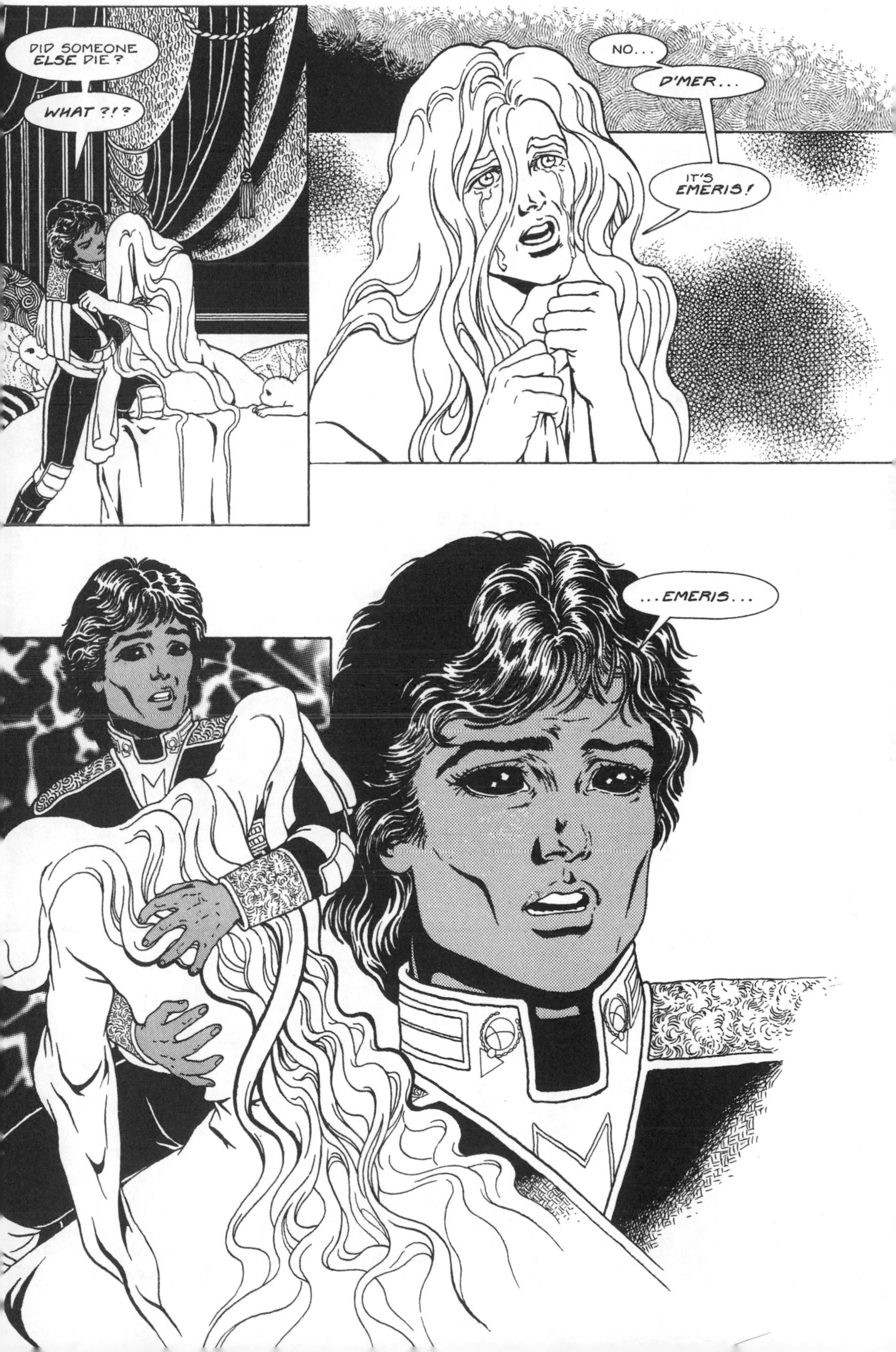
DID SOMEONE ELSE DIE?
WHAT?!?
NO...
D'MER...
IT'S EMERIS!
...EMERIS...

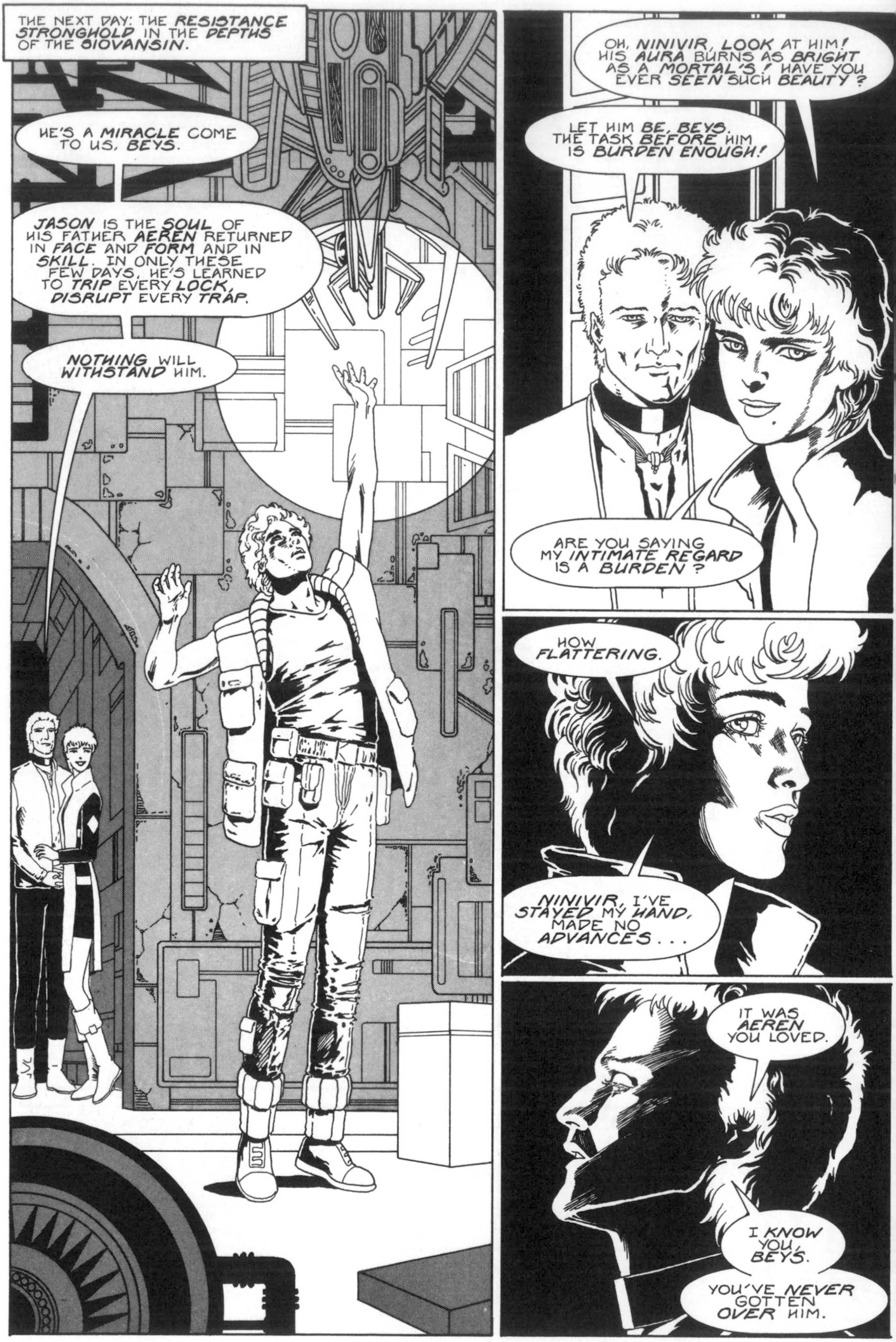
THE NEXT DAY: THE RESISTANCE STRONGHOLD IN THE DEPTHS OF THE SIOVANSIN.
HE'S A MIRACLE COME TO US, BEYS.
JASON IS THE SOUL OF HIS FATHER AEREN RETURNED IN FACE AND FORM AND IN SKILL. IN ONLY THESE FEW DAYS, HE'S LEARNED TO TRIP EVERY LOCK, DISRUPT EVERY TRAP.
NOTHING WILL WITHSTAND HIM.
OH, NINIVIR, LOOK AT HIM! HIS AURA BURNS AS BRIGHT AS A MORTAL'S! HAVE YOU EVER SEEN SUCH BEAUTY?
LET HIM BE, BEYS. THE TASK BEFORE HIM IS BURDEN ENOUGH!
ARE YOU SAYING MY INTIMATE REGARD IS A BURDEN?
HOW FLATTERING.
NINIVIR, I'VE STAYED MY HAND, MADE NO ADVANCES . . .
IT WAS AEREN YOU LOVED.
I KNOW YOU, BEYS.
YOU'VE NEVER GOTTEN OVER HIM.

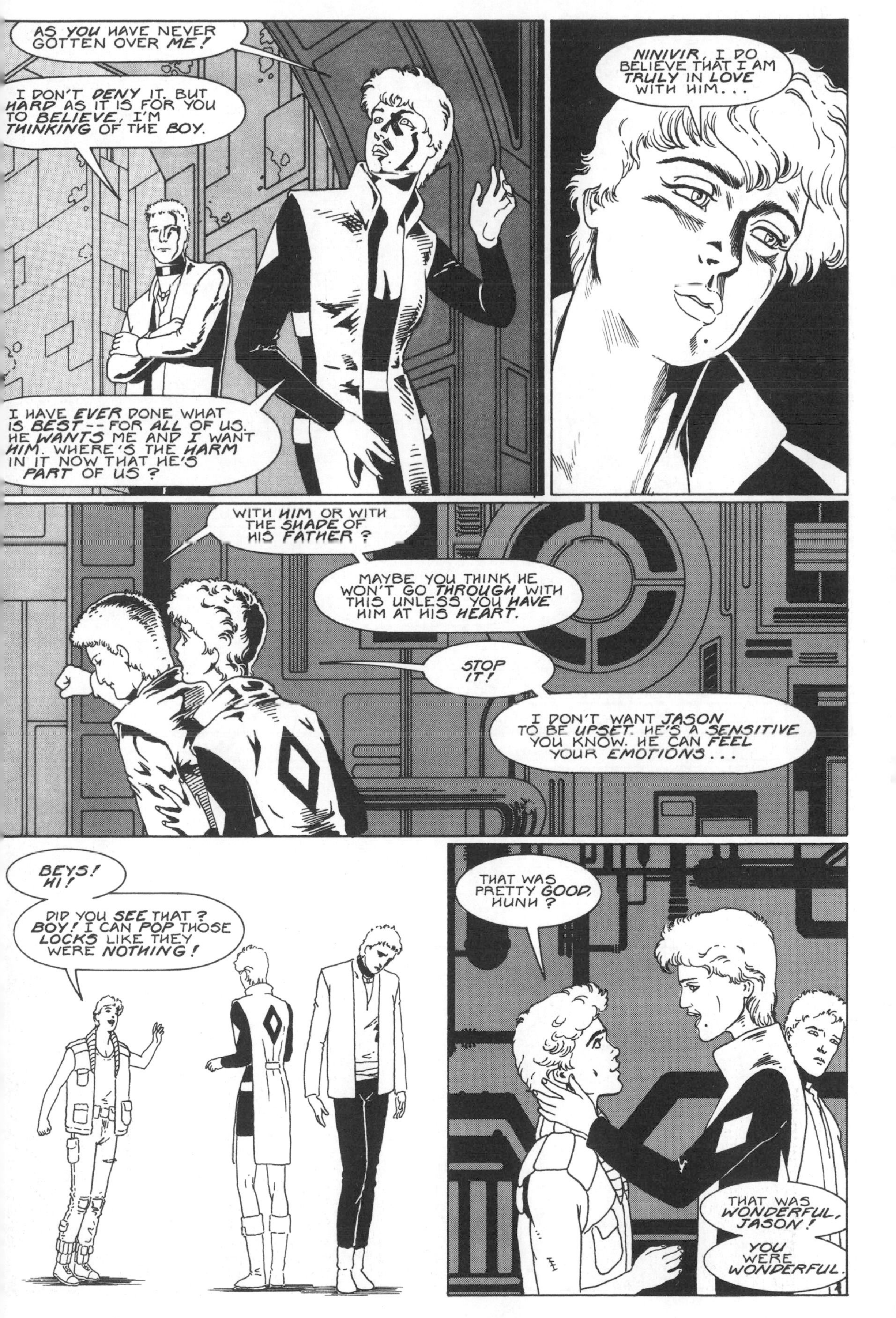
AS YOU HAVE NEVER GOTTEN OVER ME!
I DON'T DENY IT. BUT HARD AS IT IS FOR YOU TO BELIEVE, I'M THINKING OF THE BOY.
I HAVE EVER DONE WHAT IS BEST-- FOR ALL OF US. HE WANTS ME AND I WANT HIM. WHERE'S THE HARM IN IT NOW THAT HE'S PART OF US?
NINIVIR, I DO BELIEVE THAT I AM TRULY IN LOVE WITH HIM...
WITH HIM OR WITH THE SHADE OF HIS FATHER?
MAYBE YOU THINK HE WON'T GO THROUGH WITH THIS UNLESS YOU HAVE HIM AT HIS HEART.
STOP IT!
I DON'T WANT JASON TO BE UPSET. HE'S A SENSITIVE YOU KNOW. HE CAN FEEL YOUR EMOTIONS...
BEYS! HI!
DID YOU SEE THAT? BOY! I CAN POP THOSE LOCKS LIKE THEY WERE NOTHING!
THAT WAS PRETTY GOOD, HUNH?
THAT WAS WONDERFUL, JASON!
YOU WERE WONDERFUL.

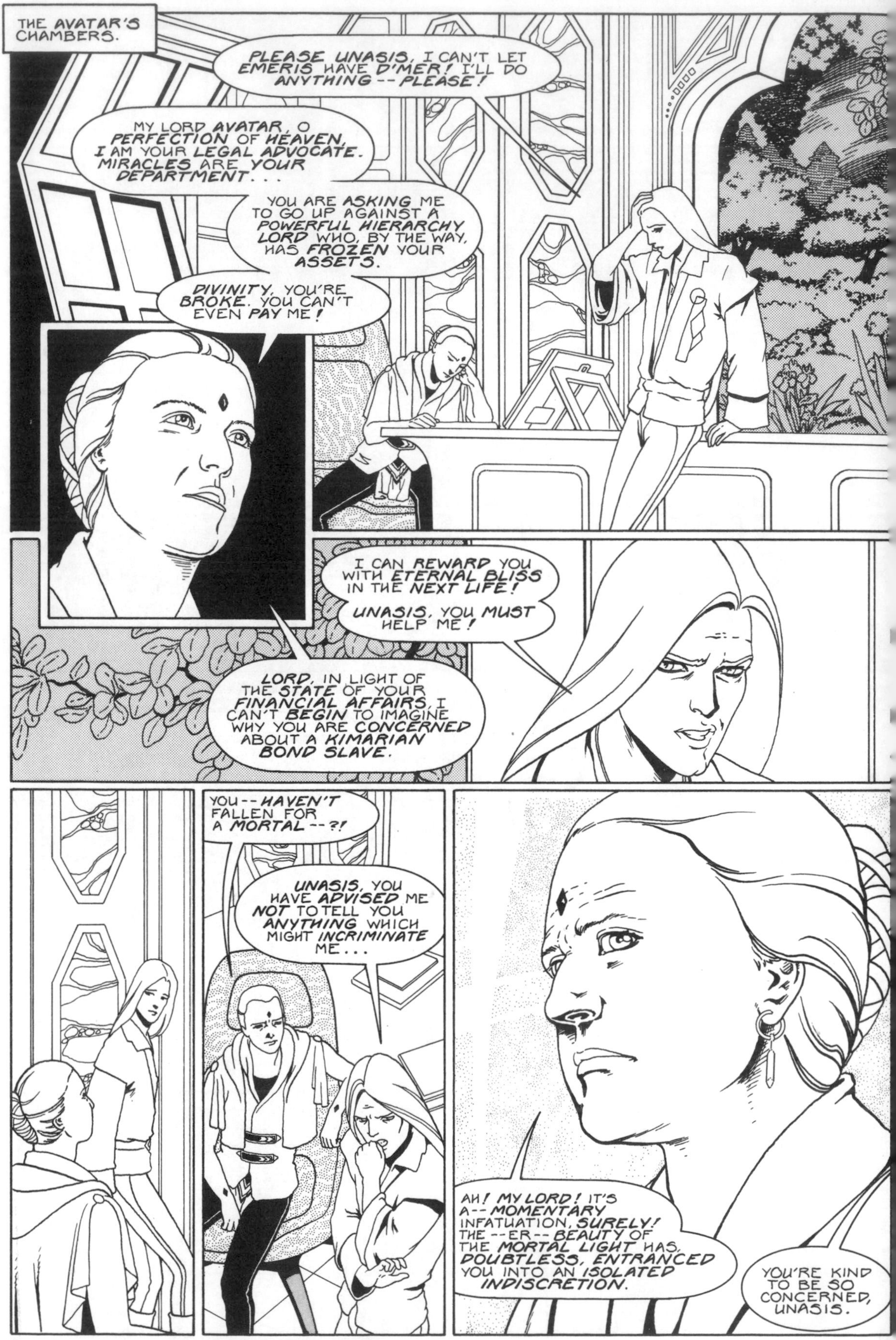
THE AVATAR'S CHAMBERS.
PLEASE UNASIS, I CAN'T LET EMERIS HAVE D'MER! I'LL DO ANYTHING -- PLEASE!
MY LORD AVATAR, O PERFECTION OF HEAVEN, I AM YOUR LEGAL ADVOCATE. MIRACLES ARE YOUR DEPARTMENT...
YOU ARE ASKING ME TO GO UP AGAINST A POWERFUL HIERARCHY LORD WHO, BY THE WAY, HAS FROZEN YOUR ASSETS.
DIVINITY, YOU'RE BROKE. YOU CAN'T EVEN PAY ME!
I CAN REWARD YOU WITH ETERNAL BLISS IN THE NEXT LIFE!
UNASIS, YOU MUST HELP ME!
LORD, IN LIGHT OF THE STATE OF YOUR FINANCIAL AFFAIRS, I CAN'T BEGIN TO IMAGINE WHY YOU ARE CONCERNED ABOUT A KIMARIAN BOND SLAVE.
YOU -- HAVEN'T FALLEN FOR A MORTAL -- ?!
UNASIS, YOU HAVE ADVISED ME NOT TO TELL YOU ANYTHING WHICH MIGHT INCRIMINATE ME...
AH! MY LORD! IT'S A -- MOMENTARY INFATUATION, SURELY! THE -- ER -- BEAUTY OF THE MORTAL LIGHT HAS, DOUBTLESS, ENTRANCED YOU INTO AN ISOLATED INDISCRETION.
YOU'RE KIND TO BE SO CONCERNED, UNASIS.

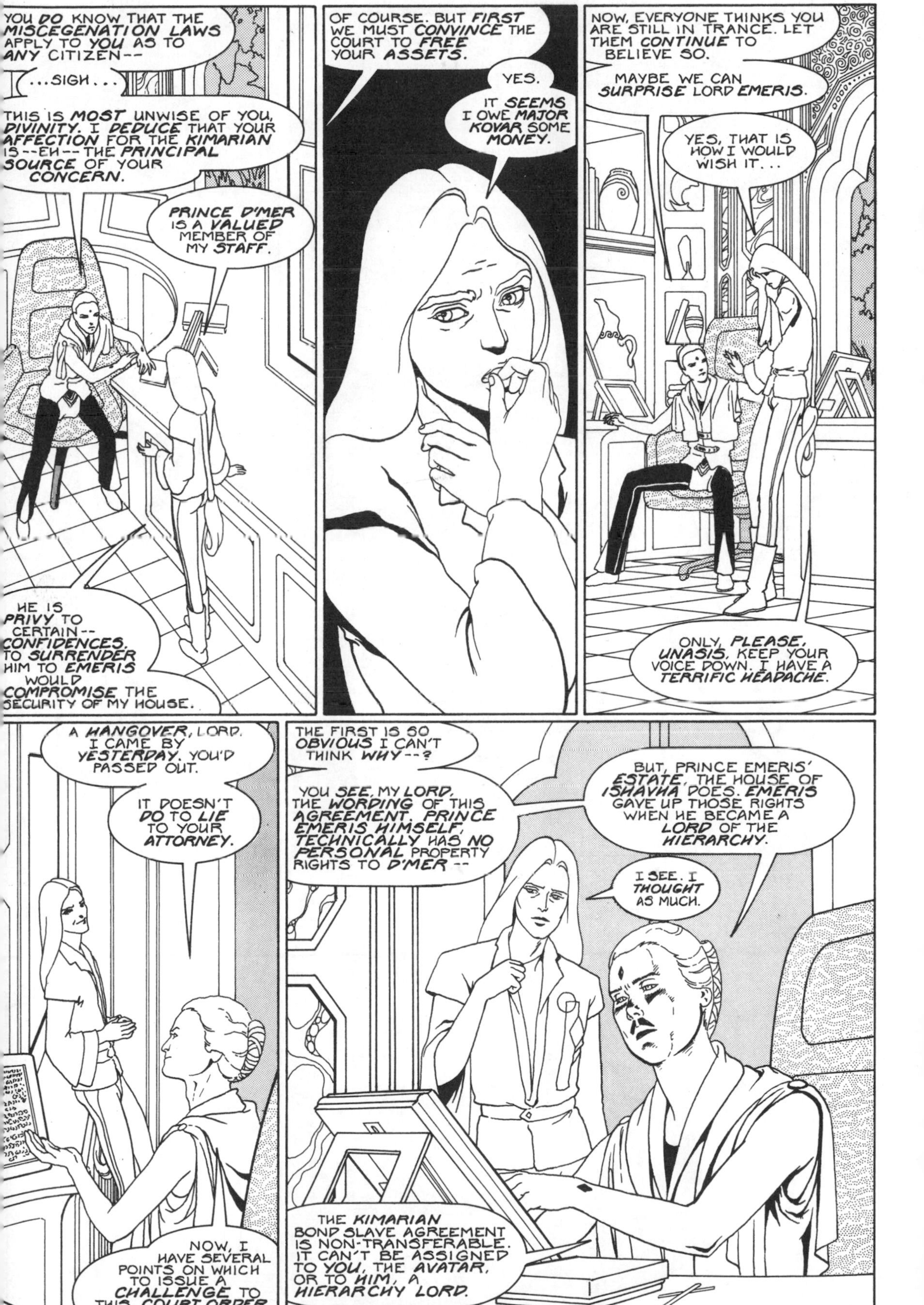
YOU DO KNOW THAT THE MISCEGENATION LAWS APPLY TO YOU AS TO ANY CITIZEN--
...SIGH...
THIS IS MOST UNWISE OF YOU, DIVINITY. I DEDUCE THAT YOUR AFFECTION FOR THE KIMARIAN IS--EH--THE PRINCIPAL SOURCE OF YOUR CONCERN.
PRINCE D'MER IS A VALUED MEMBER OF MY STAFF.
HE IS PRIVY TO CERTAIN--CONFIDENCES. TO SURRENDER HIM TO EMERIS WOULD COMPROMISE THE SECURITY OF MY HOUSE.
OF COURSE. BUT FIRST WE MUST CONVINCE THE COURT TO FREE YOUR ASSETS.
YES.
IT SEEMS I OWE MAJOR KOVAR SOME MONEY.
NOW, EVERYONE THINKS YOU ARE STILL IN TRANCE. LET THEM CONTINUE TO BELIEVE SO.
MAYBE WE CAN SURPRISE LORD EMERIS.
YES, THAT IS HOW I WOULD WISH IT...
ONLY, PLEASE, UNASIS, KEEP YOUR VOICE DOWN. I HAVE A TERRIFIC HEADACHE.
A HANGOVER, LORD. I CAME BY YESTERDAY. YOU'D PASSED OUT.
IT DOESN'T DO TO LIE TO YOUR ATTORNEY.
NOW, I HAVE SEVERAL POINTS ON WHICH TO ISSUE A CHALLENGE TO THIS COURT ORDER.
THE FIRST IS SO OBVIOUS I CAN'T THINK WHY--?
YOU SEE, MY LORD, THE WORDING OF THIS AGREEMENT, PRINCE EMERIS HIMSELF, TECHNICALLY HAS NO PERSONAL PROPERTY RIGHTS TO D'MER--
BUT, PRINCE EMERIS' ESTATE, THE HOUSE OF ISHAVHA DOES. EMERIS GAVE UP THOSE RIGHTS WHEN HE BECAME A LORD OF THE HIERARCHY.
I SEE. I THOUGHT AS MUCH.
THE KIMARIAN BOND SLAVE AGREEMENT IS NON-TRANSFERABLE. IT CAN'T BE ASSIGNED TO YOU, THE AVATAR, OR TO HIM, A HIERARCHY LORD.

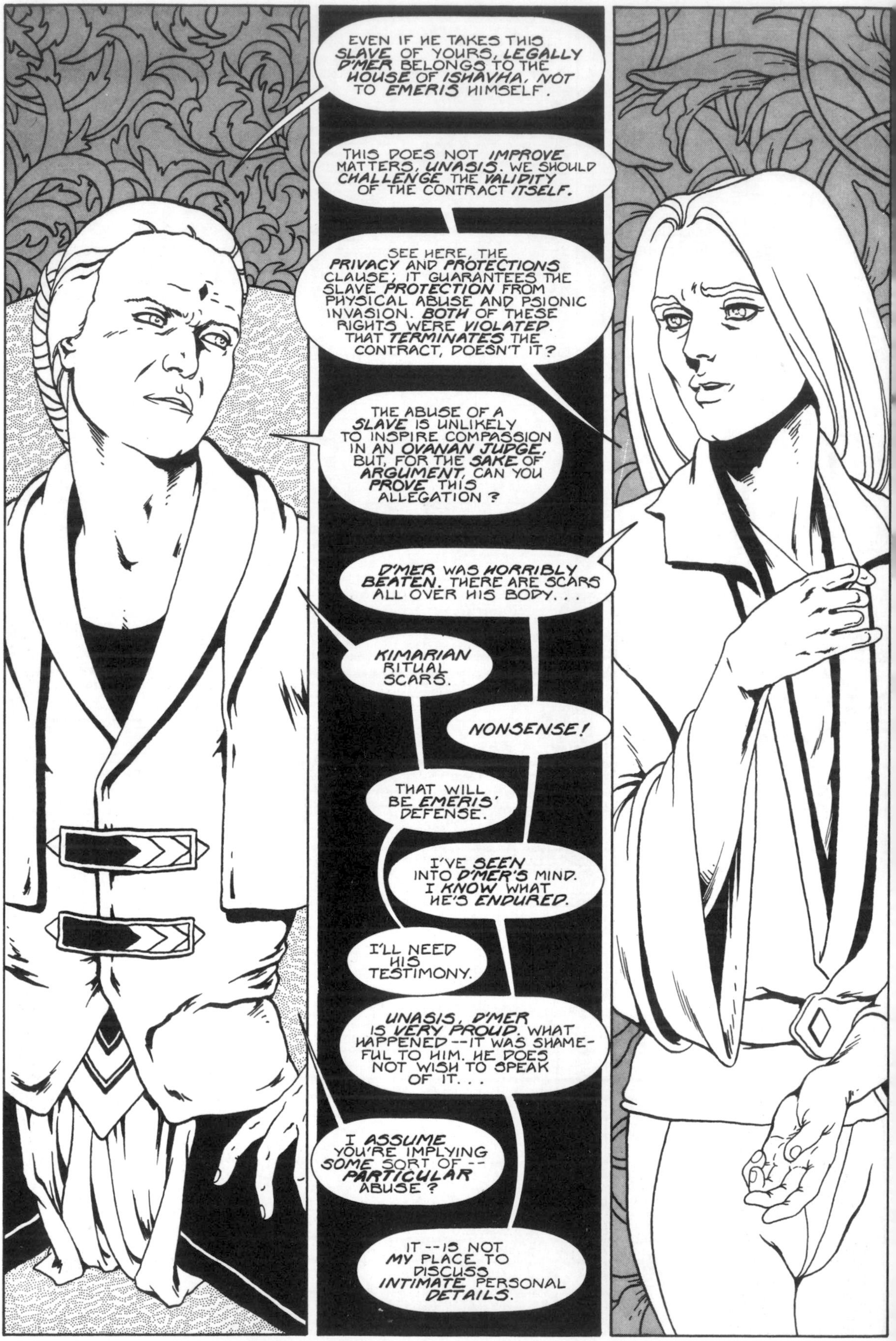
EVEN IF HE TAKES THIS SLAVE OF YOURS, LEGALLY D'MER BELONGS TO THE HOUSE OF ISHAVHA, NOT TO EMERIS HIMSELF.
THIS DOES NOT IMPROVE MATTERS, UNASIS. WE SHOULD CHALLENGE THE VALIDITY OF THE CONTRACT ITSELF.
SEE HERE, THE PRIVACY AND PROTECTIONS CLAUSE; IT GUARANTEES THE SLAVE PROTECTION FROM PHYSICAL ABUSE AND PSIONIC INVASION. BOTH OF THESE RIGHTS WERE VIOLATED. THAT TERMINATES THE CONTRACT, DOESN'T IT?
THE ABUSE OF A SLAVE IS UNLIKELY TO INSPIRE COMPASSION IN AN OVANAN JUDGE, BUT, FOR THE SAKE OF ARGUMENT, CAN YOU PROVE THIS ALLEGATION?
D'MER WAS HORRIBLY BEATEN. THERE ARE SCARS ALL OVER HIS BODY...
KIMARIAN RITUAL SCARS.
NONSENSE!
THAT WILL BE EMERIS' DEFENSE.
I'VE SEEN INTO D'MER'S MIND. I KNOW WHAT HE'S ENDURED.
I'LL NEED HIS TESTIMONY.
UNASIS, D'MER IS VERY PROUD. WHAT HAPPENED--IT WAS SHAMEFUL TO HIM. HE DOES NOT WISH TO SPEAK OF IT...
I ASSUME YOU'RE IMPLYING SOME SORT OF--PARTICULAR ABUSE?
IT--IS NOT MY PLACE TO DISCUSS INTIMATE PERSONAL DETAILS.

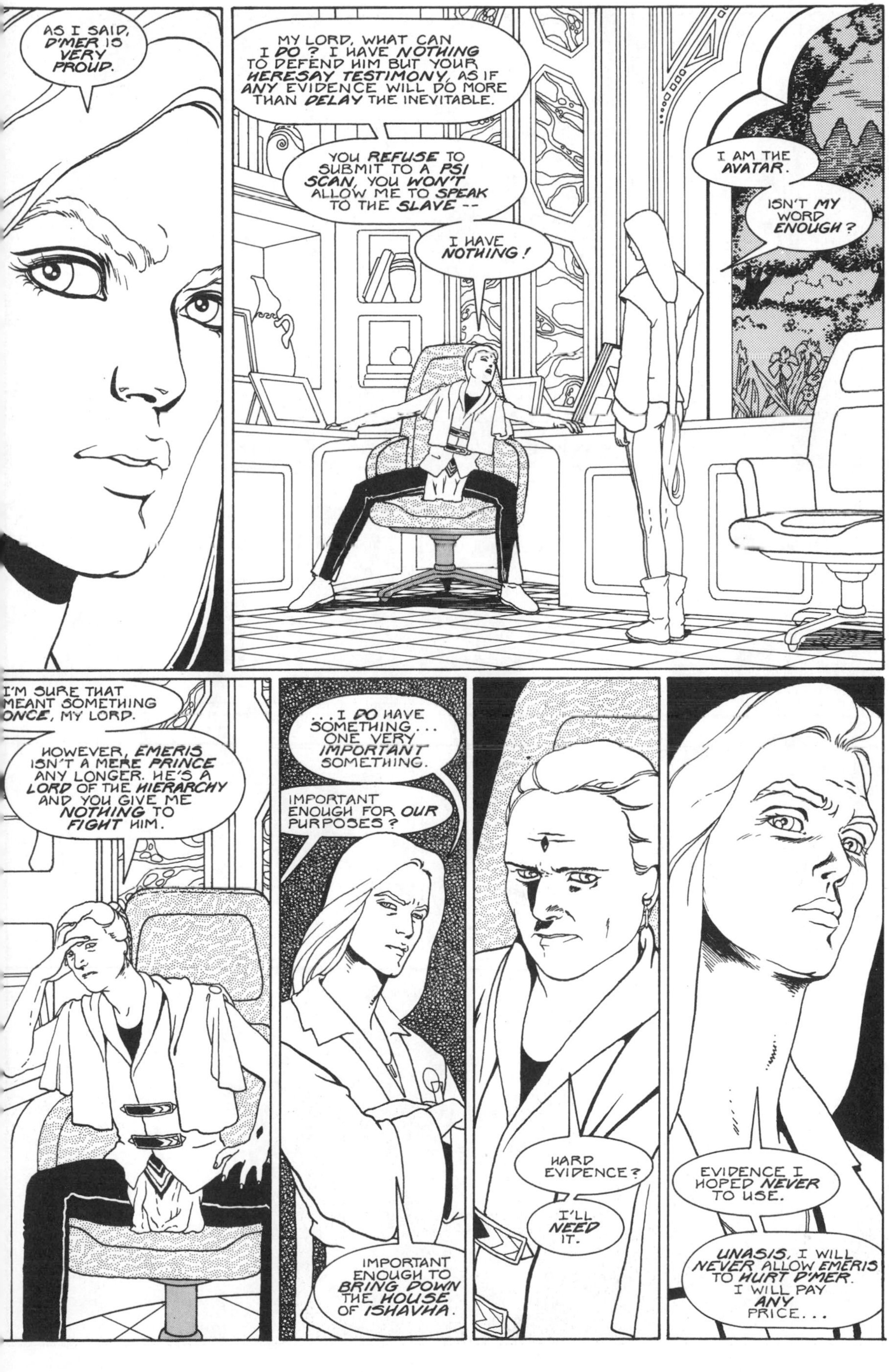
AS I SAID, D'MER IS VERY PROUD.
MY LORD, WHAT CAN I DO? I HAVE NOTHING TO DEFEND HIM BUT YOUR HERESAY TESTIMONY, AS IF ANY EVIDENCE WILL DO MORE THAN DELAY THE INEVITABLE.
YOU REFUSE TO SUBMIT TO A PSI SCAN, YOU WON'T ALLOW ME TO SPEAK TO THE SLAVE --
I HAVE NOTHING!
I AM THE AVATAR.
ISN'T MY WORD ENOUGH?
I'M SURE THAT MEANT SOMETHING ONCE, MY LORD.
HOWEVER, EMERIS ISN'T A MERE PRINCE ANY LONGER. HE'S A LORD OF THE HIERARCHY AND YOU GIVE ME NOTHING TO FIGHT HIM.
...I DO HAVE SOMETHING... ONE VERY IMPORTANT SOMETHING.
IMPORTANT ENOUGH FOR OUR PURPOSES?
IMPORTANT ENOUGH TO BRING DOWN THE HOUSE OF ISHAVHA.
HARD EVIDENCE?
I'LL NEED IT.
EVIDENCE I HOPED NEVER TO USE.
UNASIS, I WILL NEVER ALLOW EMERIS TO HURT D'MER. I WILL PAY ANY PRICE...

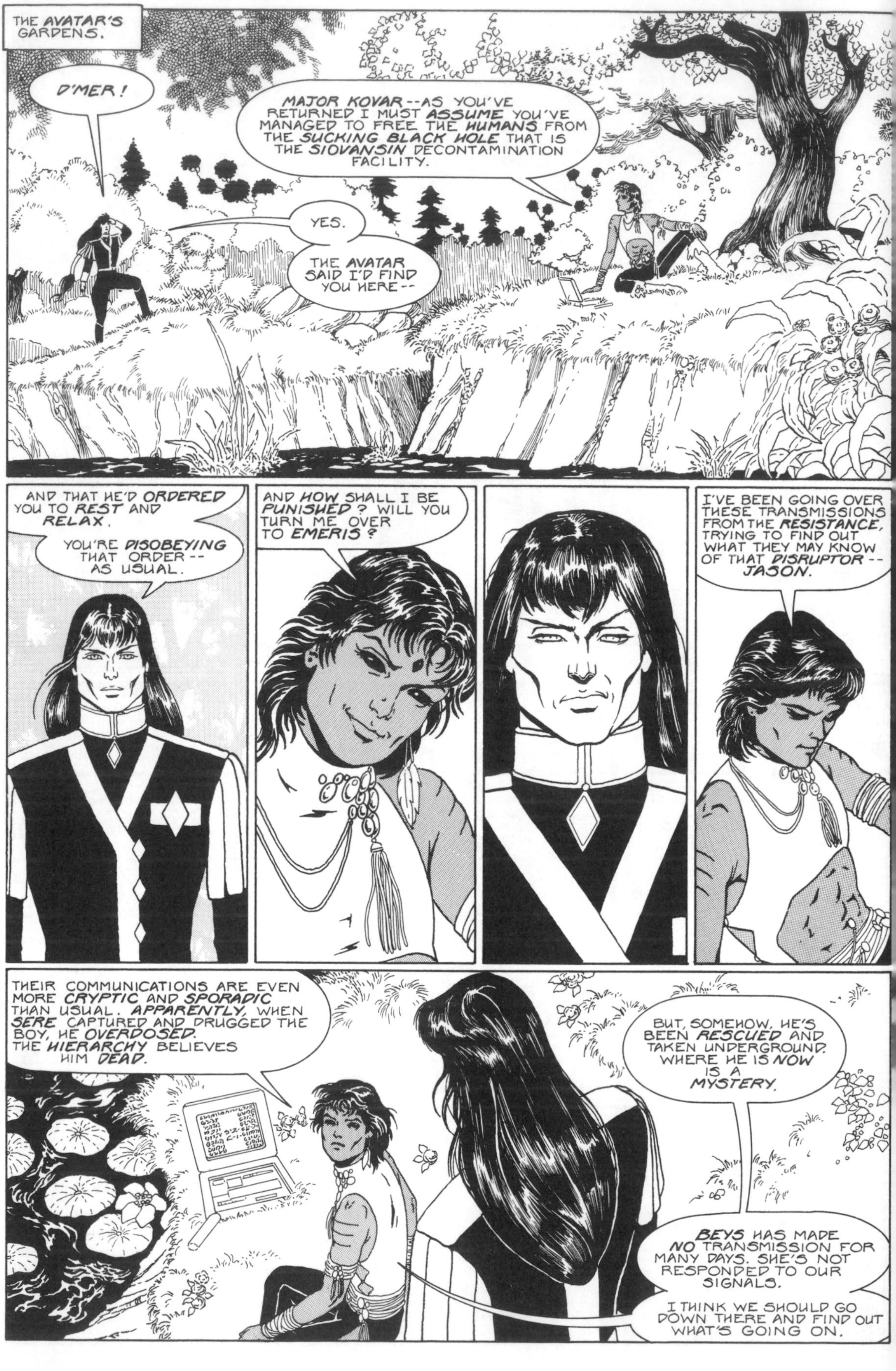
THE AVATAR'S GARDENS.
D'MER!
MAJOR KOVAR--AS YOU'VE RETURNED I MUST ASSUME YOU'VE MANAGED TO FREE THE HUMANS FROM THE SUCKING BLACK HOLE THAT IS THE SIOVANSIN DECONTAMINATION FACILITY.
YES.
THE AVATAR SAID I'D FIND YOU HERE--
AND THAT HE'D ORDERED YOU TO REST AND RELAX.
YOU'RE DISOBEYING THAT ORDER-- AS USUAL.
AND HOW SHALL I BE PUNISHED? WILL YOU TURN ME OVER TO EMERIS?
I'VE BEEN GOING OVER THESE TRANSMISSIONS FROM THE RESISTANCE, TRYING TO FIND OUT WHAT THEY MAY KNOW OF THAT DISRUPTOR-- JASON.
THEIR COMMUNICATIONS ARE EVEN MORE CRYPTIC AND SPORADIC THAN USUAL. APPARENTLY, WHEN SERE CAPTURED AND DRUGGED THE BOY, HE OVERDOSED. THE HIERARCHY BELIEVES HIM DEAD.
BUT, SOMEHOW, HE'S BEEN RESCUED AND TAKEN UNDERGROUND. WHERE HE IS NOW IS A MYSTERY.
BEYS HAS MADE NO TRANSMISSION FOR MANY DAYS. SHE'S NOT RESPONDED TO OUR SIGNALS.
I THINK WE SHOULD GO DOWN THERE AND FIND OUT WHAT'S GOING ON.

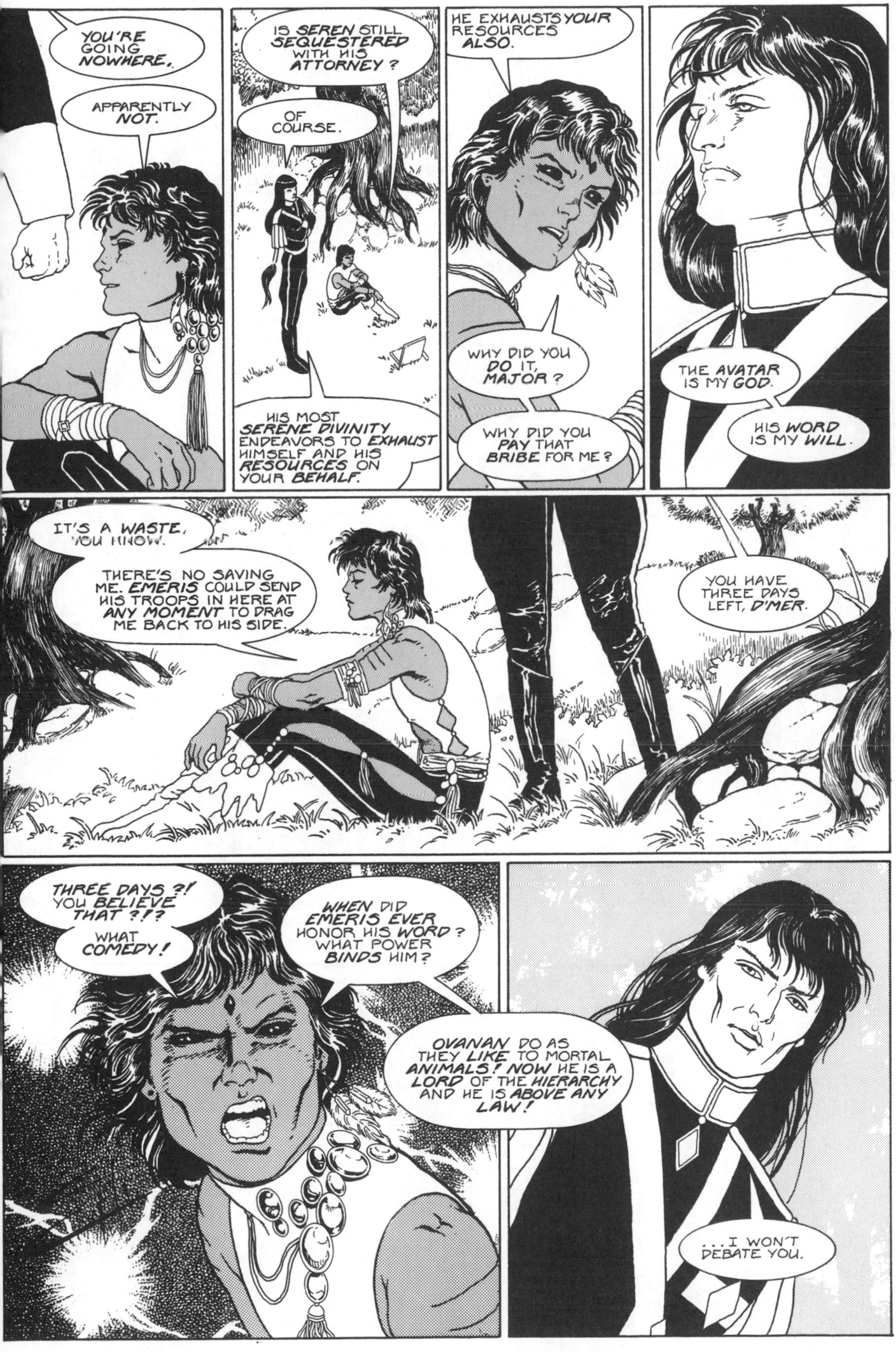
YOU'RE GOING NOWHERE.
APPARENTLY NOT.
IS SEREN STILL SEQUESTERED WITH HIS ATTORNEY?
OF COURSE.
HIS MOST SERENE DIVINITY ENDEAVORS TO EXHAUST HIMSELF AND HIS RESOURCES ON YOUR BEHALF.
HE EXHAUSTS YOUR RESOURCES ALSO.
WHY DID YOU DO IT, MAJOR?
WHY DID YOU PAY THAT BRIBE FOR ME?
THE AVATAR IS MY GOD.
HIS WORD IS MY WILL.
IT'S A WASTE, YOU KNOW.
THERE'S NO SAVING ME. EMERIS COULD SEND HIS TROOPS IN HERE AT ANY MOMENT TO DRAG ME BACK TO HIS SIDE.
YOU HAVE THREE DAYS LEFT, D'MER.
THREE DAYS?! YOU BELIEVE THAT?!?
WHAT COMEDY!
WHEN DID EMERIS EVER HONOR HIS WORD? WHAT POWER BINDS HIM?
OVANAN DO AS THEY LIKE TO MORTAL ANIMALS! NOW HE IS A LORD OF THE HIERARCHY AND HE IS ABOVE ANY LAW!
...I WON'T DEBATE YOU.

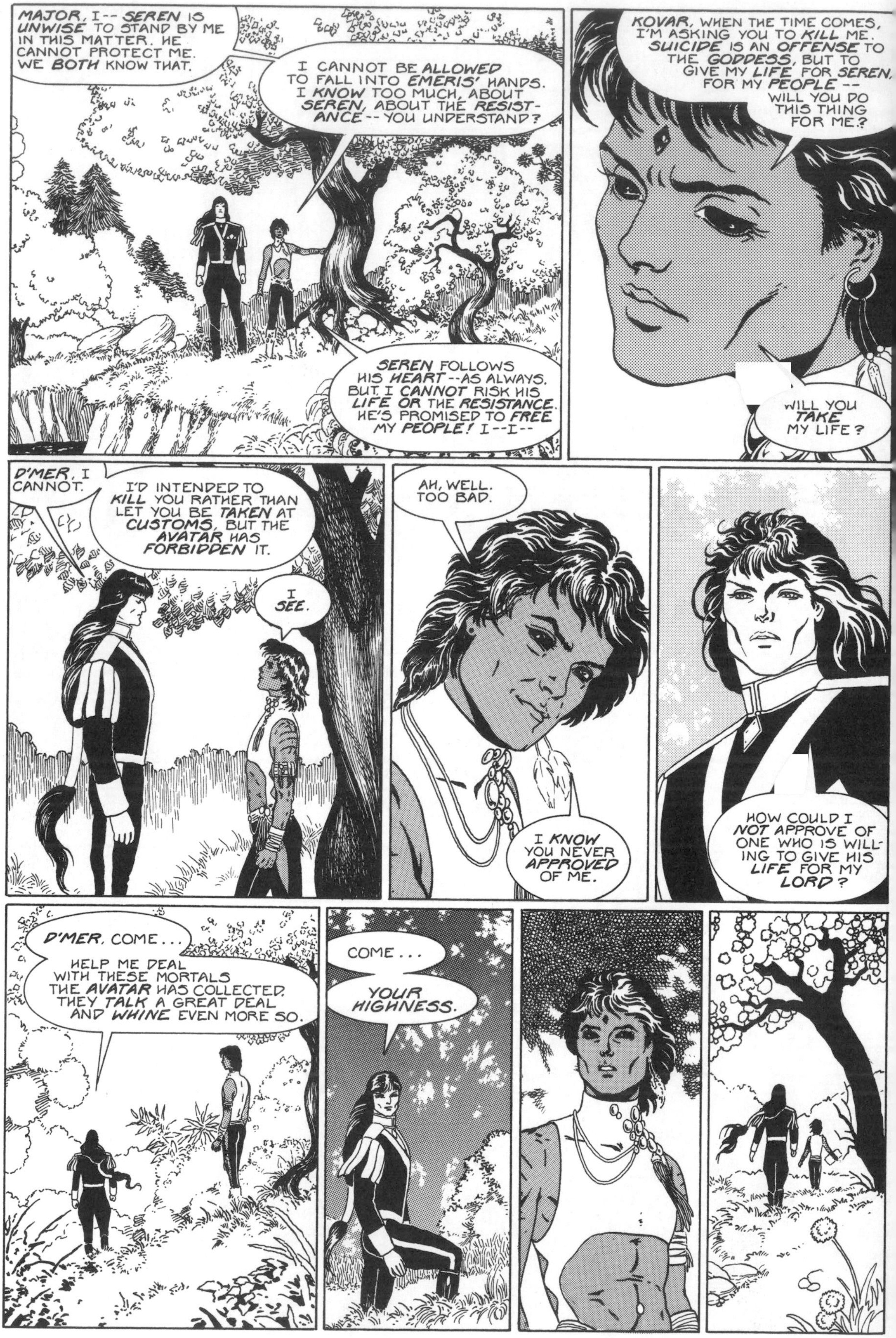
MAJOR, I-- SEREN IS UNWISE TO STAND BY ME IN THIS MATTER. HE CANNOT PROTECT ME. WE BOTH KNOW THAT.
I CANNOT BE ALLOWED TO FALL INTO EMERIS' HANDS. I KNOW TOO MUCH, ABOUT SEREN, ABOUT THE RESIST-ANCE-- YOU UNDERSTAND?
SEREN FOLLOWS HIS HEART--AS ALWAYS. BUT, I CANNOT RISK HIS LIFE OR THE RESISTANCE. HE'S PROMISED TO FREE MY PEOPLE! I--I--
KOVAR, WHEN THE TIME COMES, I'M ASKING YOU TO KILL ME. SUICIDE IS AN OFFENSE TO THE GODDESS, BUT TO GIVE MY LIFE FOR SEREN, FOR MY PEOPLE -- WILL YOU DO THIS THING FOR ME?
WILL YOU TAKE MY LIFE?
D'MER, I CANNOT.
I'D INTENDED TO KILL YOU RATHER THAN LET YOU BE TAKEN AT CUSTOMS, BUT THE AVATAR HAS FORBIDDEN IT.
I SEE.
AH, WELL. TOO BAD.
I KNOW YOU NEVER APPROVED OF ME.
HOW COULD I NOT APPROVE OF ONE WHO IS WILL-ING TO GIVE HIS LIFE FOR MY LORD?
D'MER, COME...
HELP ME DEAL WITH THESE MORTALS THE AVATAR HAS COLLECTED. THEY TALK A GREAT DEAL AND WHINE EVEN MORE SO.
COME...
YOUR HIGHNESS.

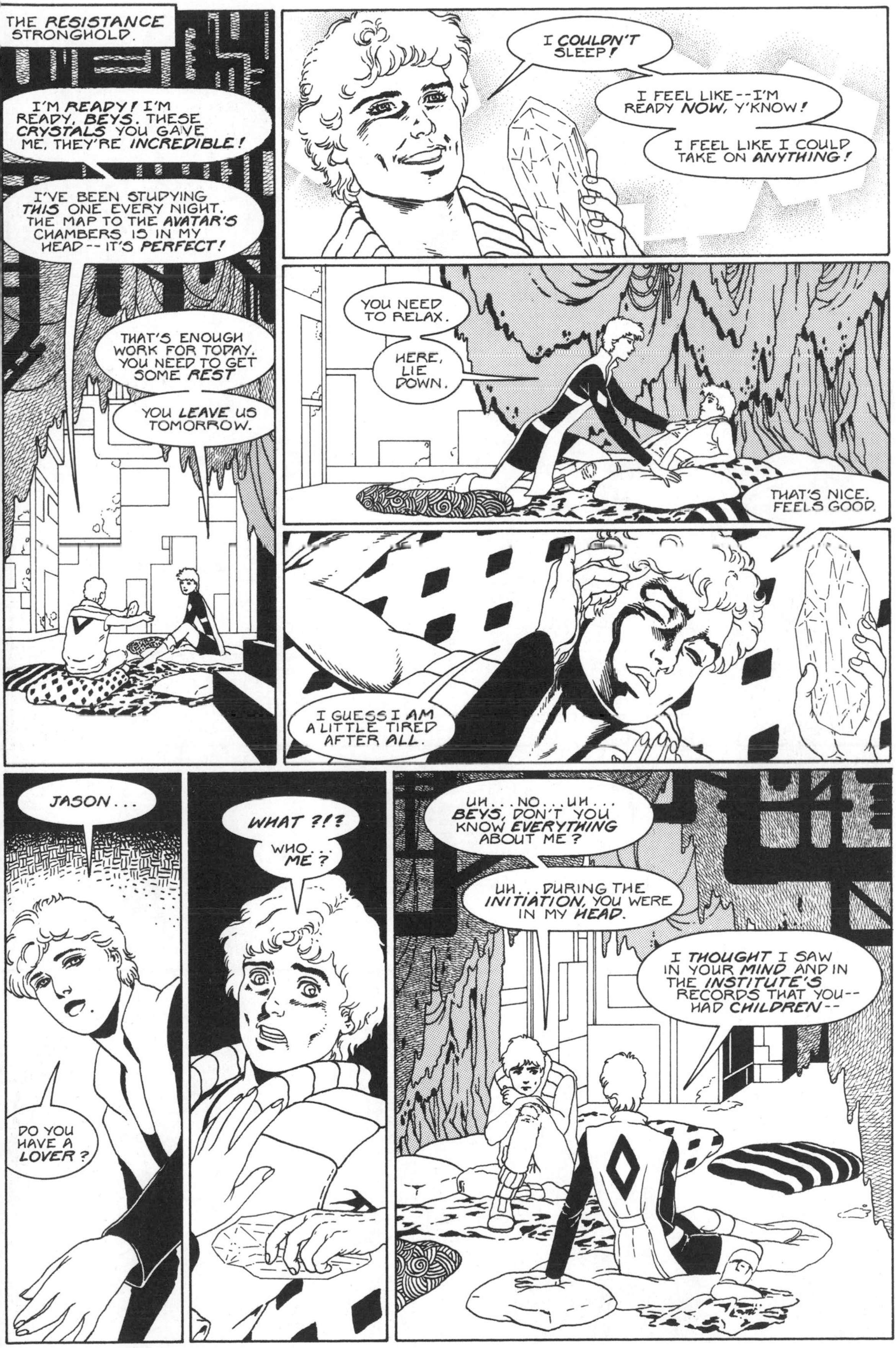
THE RESISTANCE STRONGHOLD.
I'M READY! I'M READY, BEYS. THESE CRYSTALS YOU GAVE ME, THEY'RE INCREDIBLE!
I'VE BEEN STUDYING THIS ONE EVERY NIGHT. THE MAP TO THE AVATAR'S CHAMBERS IS IN MY HEAD -- IT'S PERFECT!
THAT'S ENOUGH WORK FOR TODAY. YOU NEED TO GET SOME REST
YOU LEAVE US TOMORROW.
I COULDN'T SLEEP!
I FEEL LIKE -- I'M READY NOW, Y'KNOW!
I FEEL LIKE I COULD TAKE ON ANYTHING!
YOU NEED TO RELAX.
HERE, LIE DOWN.
THAT'S NICE. FEELS GOOD.
I GUESS I AM A LITTLE TIRED AFTER ALL.
JASON...
DO YOU HAVE A LOVER?
WHAT ?!?
WHO... ME?
UH... NO... UH... BEYS, DON'T YOU KNOW EVERYTHING ABOUT ME?
UH... DURING THE INITIATION, YOU WERE IN MY HEAD.
I THOUGHT I SAW IN YOUR MIND AND IN THE INSTITUTE'S RECORDS THAT YOU-- HAD CHILDREN--

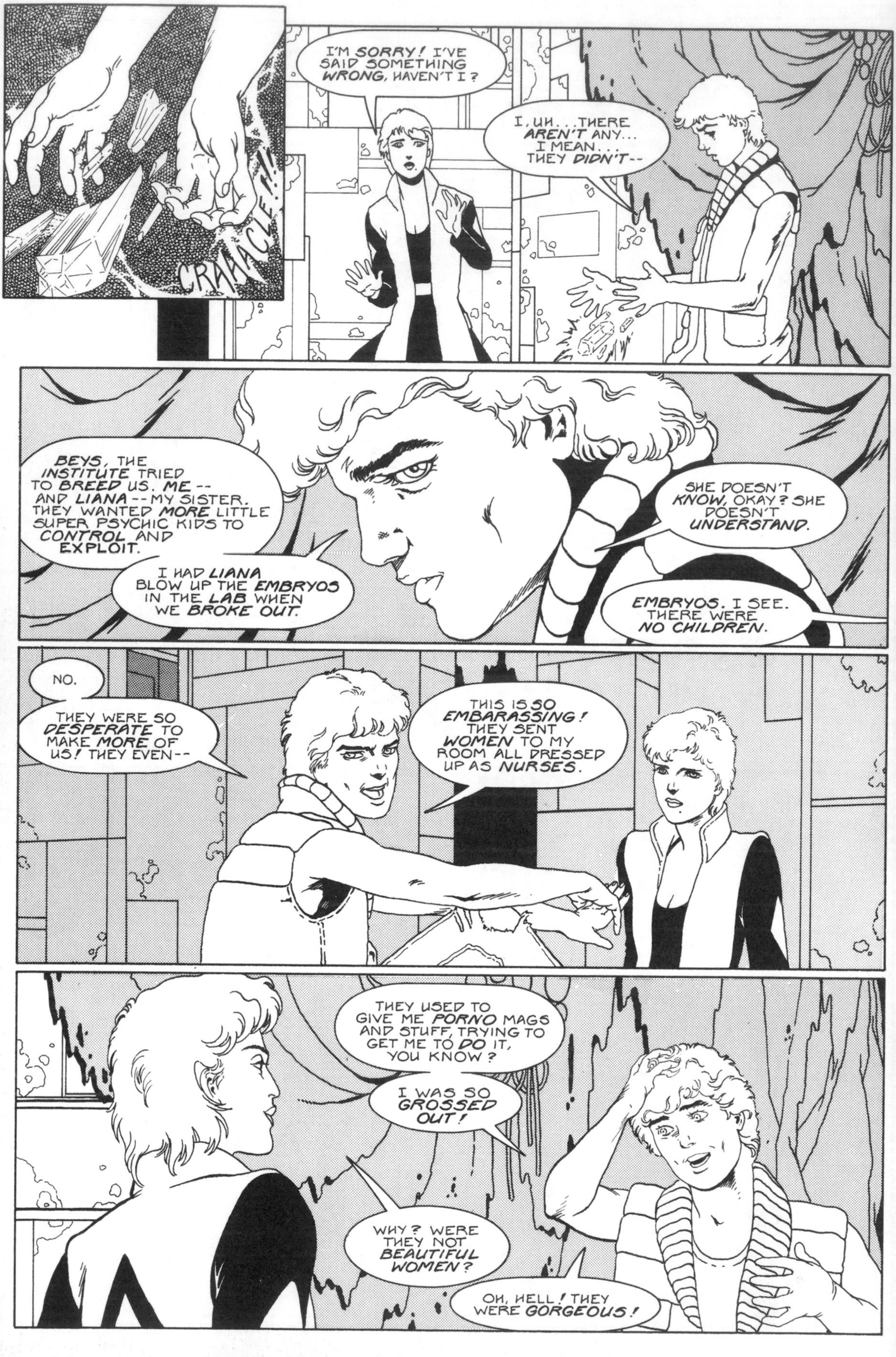
CRAAACKLE!!
I'M SORRY! I'VE SAID SOMETHING WRONG, HAVEN'T I?
I, UH... THERE AREN'T ANY... I MEAN... THEY DIDN'T--
BEYS, THE INSTITUTE TRIED TO BREED US. ME -- AND LIANA -- MY SISTER. THEY WANTED MORE LITTLE SUPER PSYCHIC KIDS TO CONTROL AND EXPLOIT.
I HAD LIANA BLOW UP THE EMBRYOS IN THE LAB WHEN WE BROKE OUT.
SHE DOESN'T KNOW, OKAY? SHE DOESN'T UNDERSTAND.
EMBRYOS. I SEE. THERE WERE NO CHILDREN.
NO.
THEY WERE SO DESPERATE TO MAKE MORE OF US! THEY EVEN--
THIS IS SO EMBARASSING! THEY SENT WOMEN TO MY ROOM ALL DRESSED UP AS NURSES.
THEY USED TO GIVE ME PORNO MAGS AND STUFF, TRYING TO GET ME TO DO IT, YOU KNOW?
I WAS SO GROSSED OUT!
WHY? WERE THEY NOT BEAUTIFUL WOMEN?
OH, HELL! THEY WERE GORGEOUS!

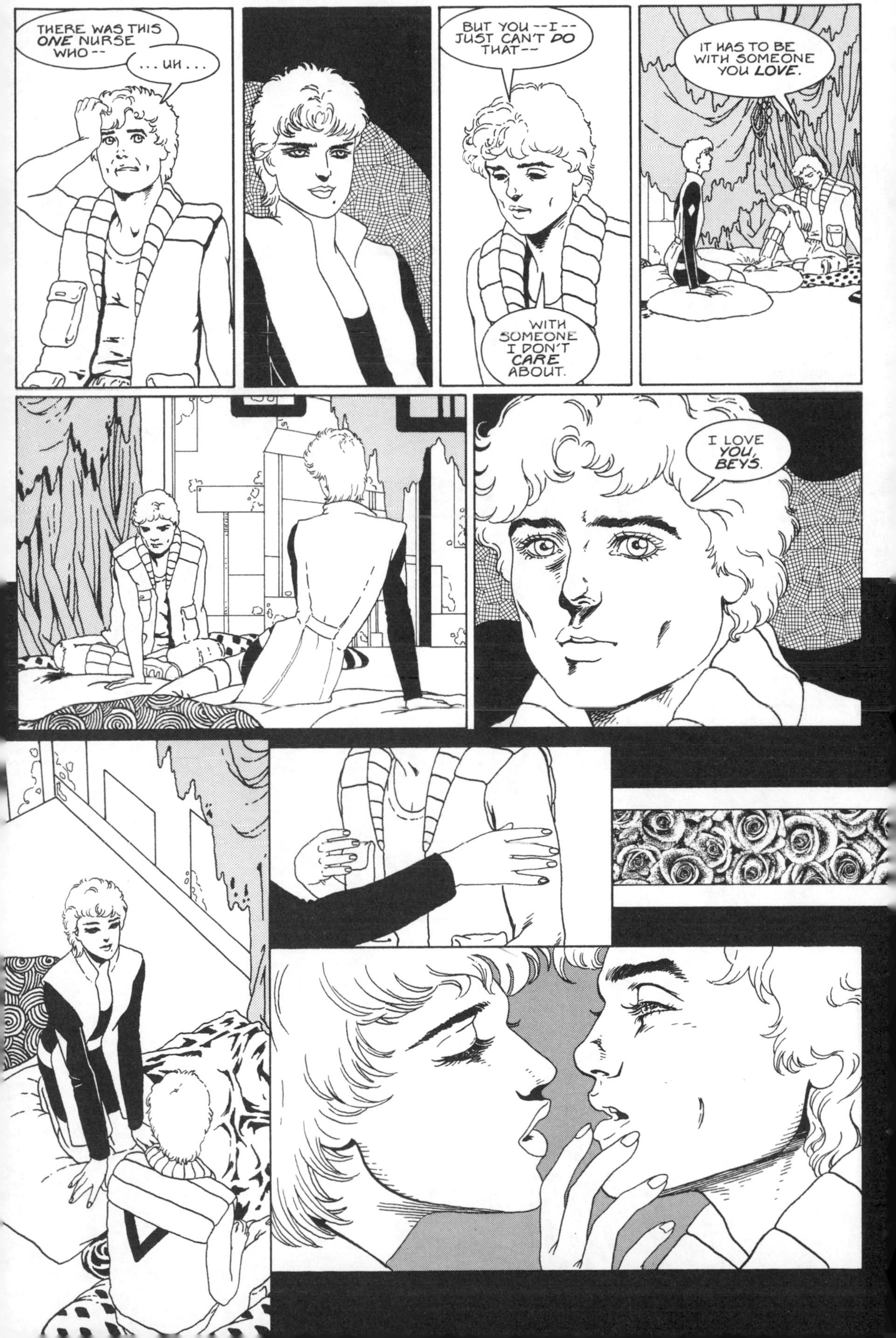
THERE WAS THIS ONE NURSE WHO--
. . . UH . . .
BUT YOU --I-- JUST CAN'T DO THAT--
WITH SOMEONE I DON'T CARE ABOUT.
IT HAS TO BE WITH SOMEONE YOU LOVE.
I LOVE YOU, BEYS.

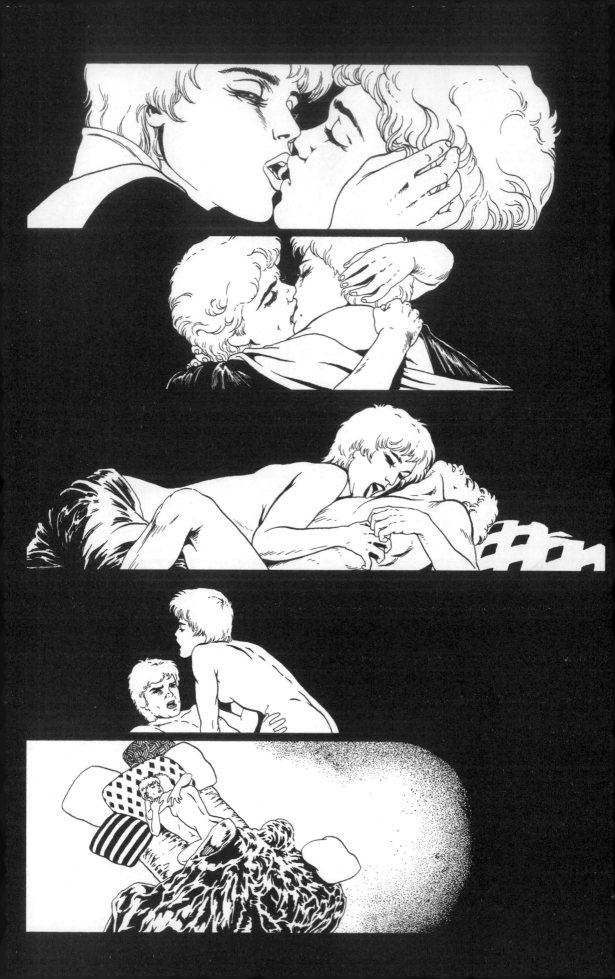

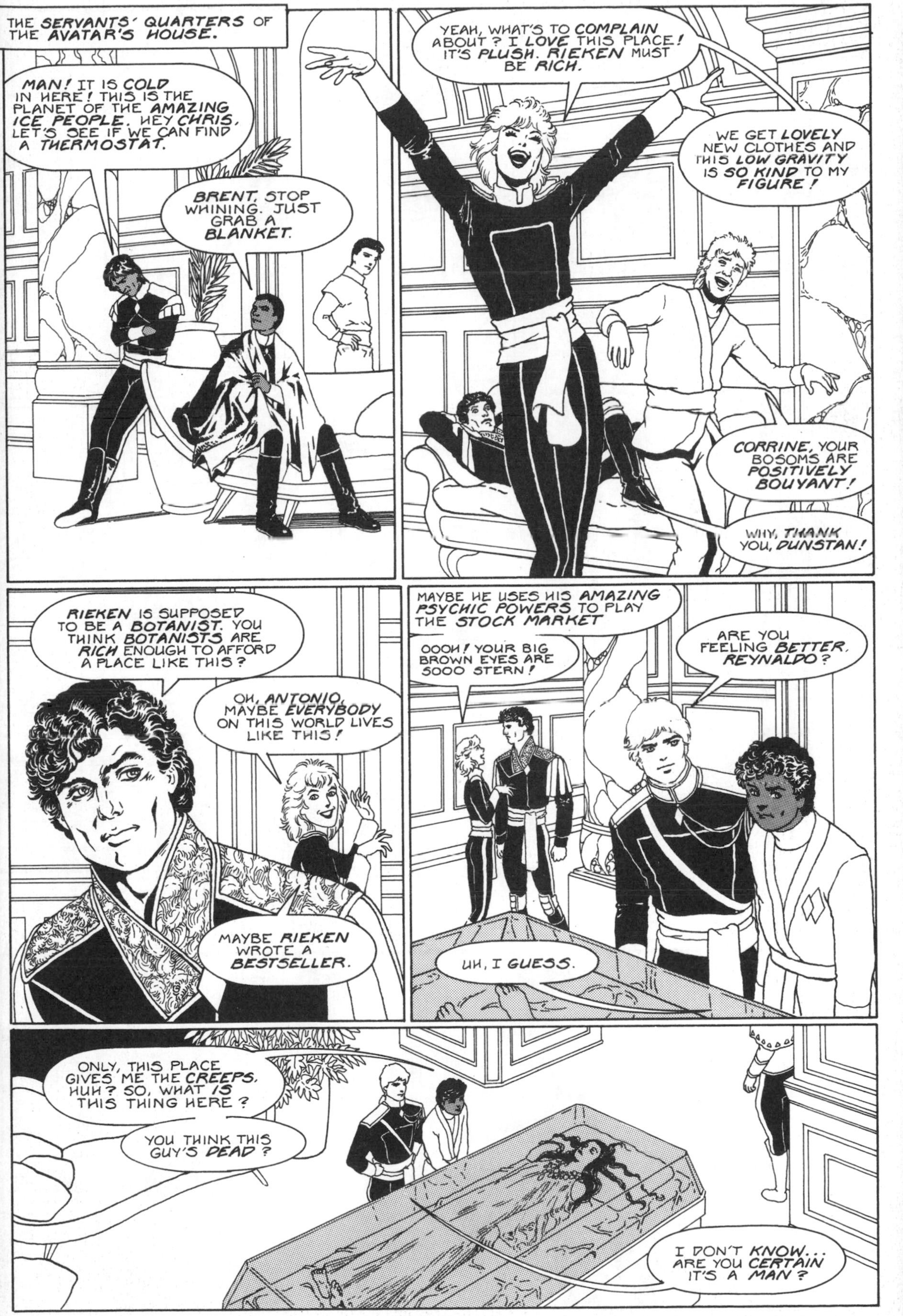
THE SERVANTS' QUARTERS OF THE AVATAR'S HOUSE.
MAN! IT IS COLD IN HERE! THIS IS THE PLANET OF THE AMAZING ICE PEOPLE. HEY CHRIS, LET'S SEE IF WE CAN FIND A THERMOSTAT.
BRENT, STOP WHINING. JUST GRAB A BLANKET.
YEAH, WHAT'S TO COMPLAIN ABOUT? I LOVE THIS PLACE! IT'S PLUSH. RIEKEN MUST BE RICH.
WE GET LOVELY NEW CLOTHES AND THIS LOW GRAVITY IS SO KIND TO MY FIGURE!
CORRINE, YOUR BOSOMS ARE POSITIVELY BOUYANT!
WHY, THANK YOU, DUNSTAN!
RIEKEN IS SUPPOSED TO BE A BOTANIST. YOU THINK BOTANISTS ARE RICH ENOUGH TO AFFORD A PLACE LIKE THIS?
OH, ANTONIO, MAYBE EVERYBODY ON THIS WORLD LIVES LIKE THIS!
MAYBE RIEKEN WROTE A BESTSELLER.
MAYBE HE USES HIS AMAZING PSYCHIC POWERS TO PLAY THE STOCK MARKET
OOOH! YOUR BIG BROWN EYES ARE SOOO STERN!
ARE YOU FEELING BETTER, REYNALDO?
UH, I GUESS.
ONLY, THIS PLACE GIVES ME THE CREEPS. HUH? SO, WHAT IS THIS THING HERE?
YOU THINK THIS GUY'S DEAD?
I DON'T KNOW... ARE YOU CERTAIN IT'S A MAN?

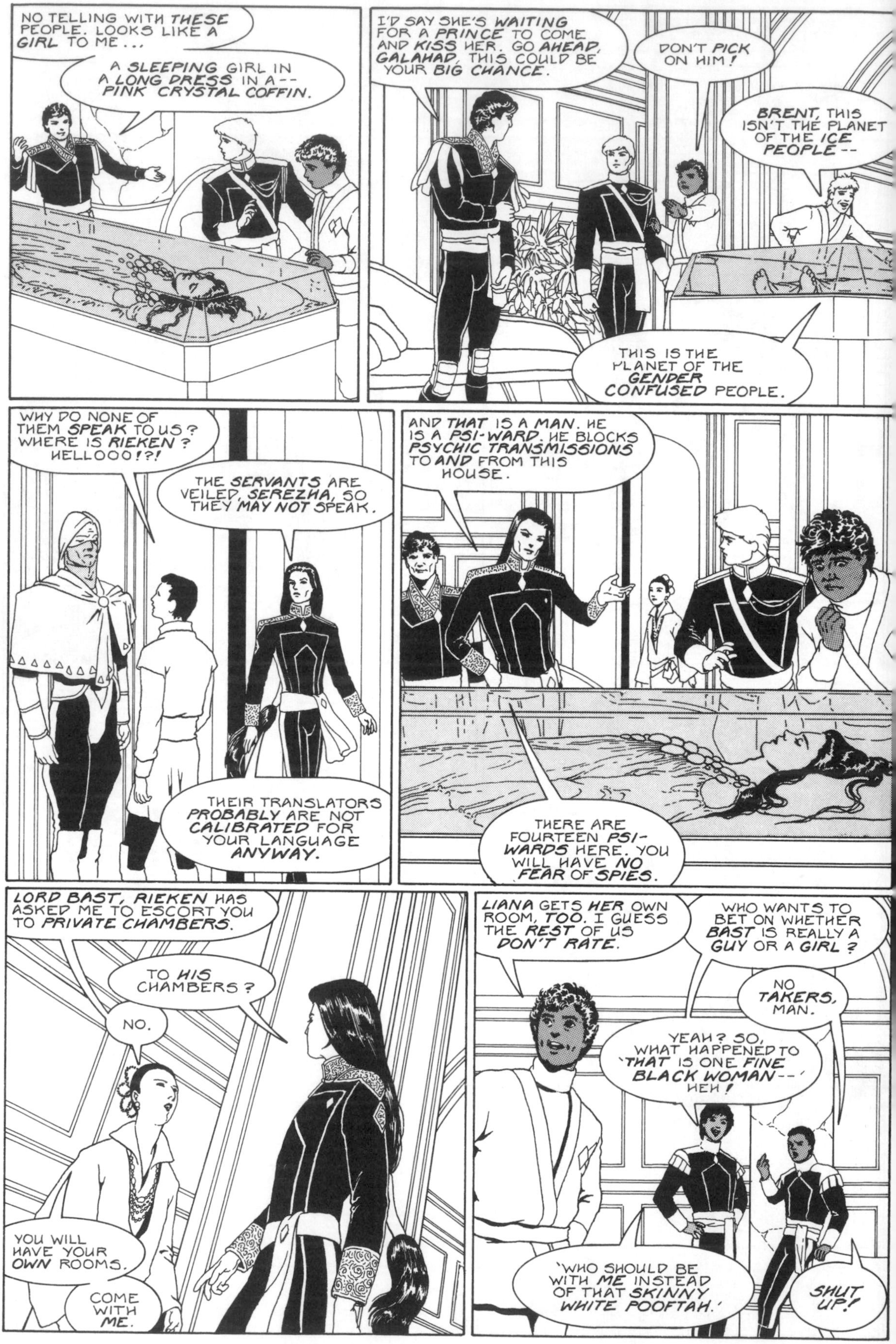
NO TELLING WITH THESE PEOPLE. LOOKS LIKE A GIRL TO ME...
A SLEEPING GIRL IN A LONG DRESS IN A-- PINK CRYSTAL COFFIN.
I'D SAY SHE'S WAITING FOR A PRINCE TO COME AND KISS HER. GO AHEAD, GALAHAD. THIS COULD BE YOUR BIG CHANCE.
DON'T PICK ON HIM!
BRENT, THIS ISN'T THE PLANET OF THE ICE PEOPLE--
THIS IS THE PLANET OF THE GENDER CONFUSED PEOPLE.
WHY DO NONE OF THEM SPEAK TO US? WHERE IS RIEKEN? HELLOOO!?!
THE SERVANTS ARE VEILED, SEREZHA, SO THEY MAY NOT SPEAK.
THEIR TRANSLATORS PROBABLY ARE NOT CALIBRATED FOR YOUR LANGUAGE ANYWAY.
AND THAT IS A MAN. HE IS A PSI-WARD. HE BLOCKS PSYCHIC TRANSMISSIONS TO AND FROM THIS HOUSE.
THERE ARE FOURTEEN PSI-WARDS HERE. YOU WILL HAVE NO FEAR OF SPIES.
LORD BAST, RIEKEN HAS ASKED ME TO ESCORT YOU TO PRIVATE CHAMBERS.
TO HIS CHAMBERS?
NO.
YOU WILL HAVE YOUR OWN ROOMS.
COME WITH ME.
LIANA GETS HER OWN ROOM, TOO. I GUESS THE REST OF US DON'T RATE.
WHO WANTS TO BET ON WHETHER BAST IS REALLY A GUY OR A GIRL?
NO TAKERS, MAN.
YEAH? SO, WHAT HAPPENED TO 'THAT IS ONE FINE BLACK WOMAN--' HEH!
'WHO SHOULD BE WITH ME INSTEAD OF THAT SKINNY WHITE POOFTAH.'
SHUT UP!

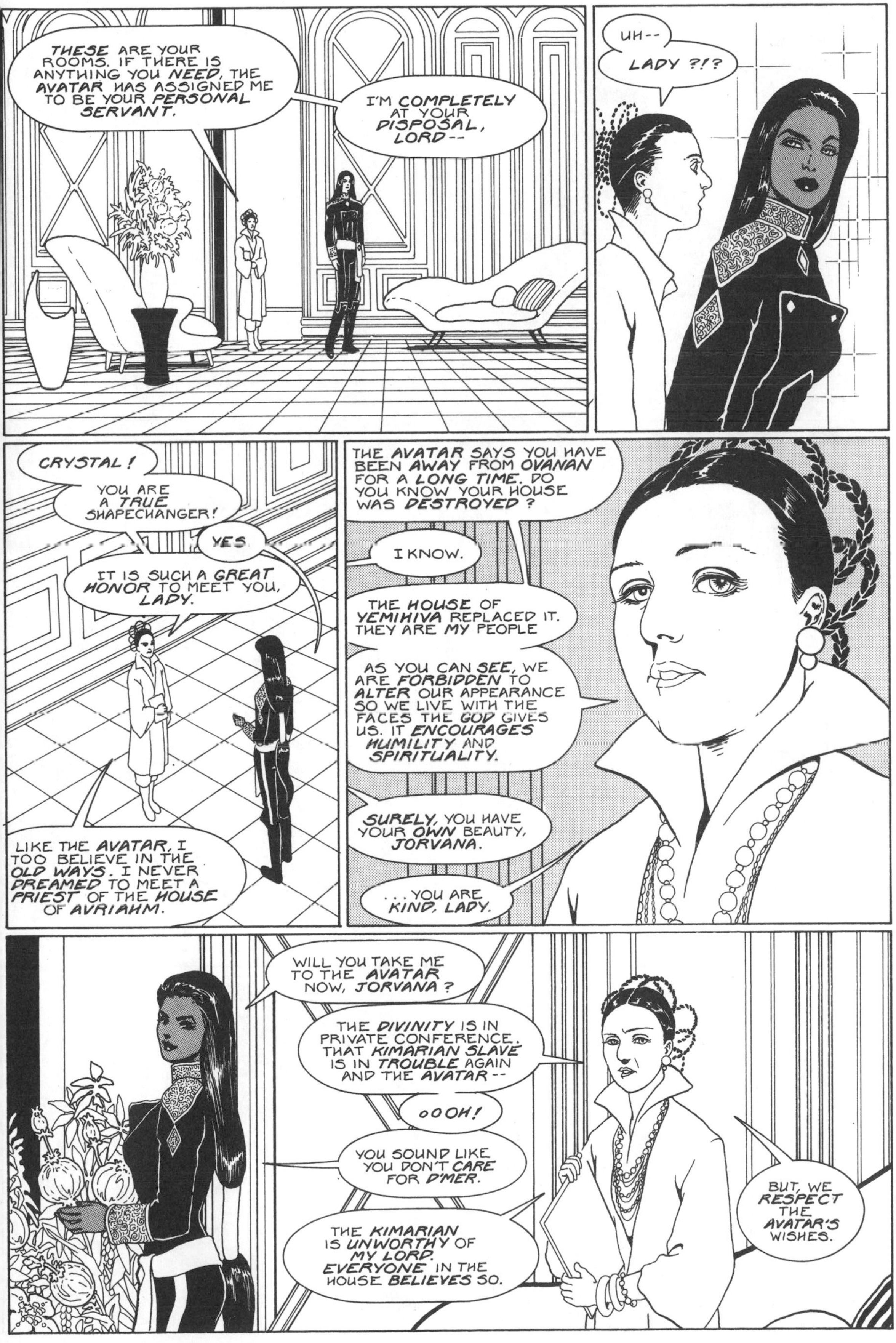
THESE ARE YOUR ROOMS. IF THERE IS ANYTHING YOU NEED, THE AVATAR HAS ASSIGNED ME TO BE YOUR PERSONAL SERVANT.
I'M COMPLETELY AT YOUR DISPOSAL, LORD--
UH--
LADY ?!?
CRYSTAL!
YOU ARE A TRUE SHAPECHANGER!
YES.
IT IS SUCH A GREAT HONOR TO MEET YOU, LADY.
LIKE THE AVATAR, I TOO BELIEVE IN THE OLD WAYS. I NEVER DREAMED TO MEET A PRIEST OF THE HOUSE OF AVRIAHM.
THE AVATAR SAYS YOU HAVE BEEN AWAY FROM OVANAN FOR A LONG TIME. DO YOU KNOW YOUR HOUSE WAS DESTROYED?
I KNOW.
THE HOUSE OF YEMIHIVA REPLACED IT. THEY ARE MY PEOPLE
AS YOU CAN SEE, WE ARE FORBIDDEN TO ALTER OUR APPEARANCE SO WE LIVE WITH THE FACES THE GOD GIVES US. IT ENCOURAGES HUMILITY AND SPIRITUALITY.
SURELY, YOU HAVE YOUR OWN BEAUTY, JORVANA.
...YOU ARE KIND, LADY.
WILL YOU TAKE ME TO THE AVATAR NOW, JORVANA?
THE DIVINITY IS IN PRIVATE CONFERENCE. THAT KIMARIAN SLAVE IS IN TROUBLE AGAIN AND THE AVATAR--
oOOH!
YOU SOUND LIKE YOU DON'T CARE FOR D'MER.
THE KIMARIAN IS UNWORTHY OF MY LORD. EVERYONE IN THE HOUSE BELIEVES SO.
BUT, WE RESPECT THE AVATAR'S WISHES.

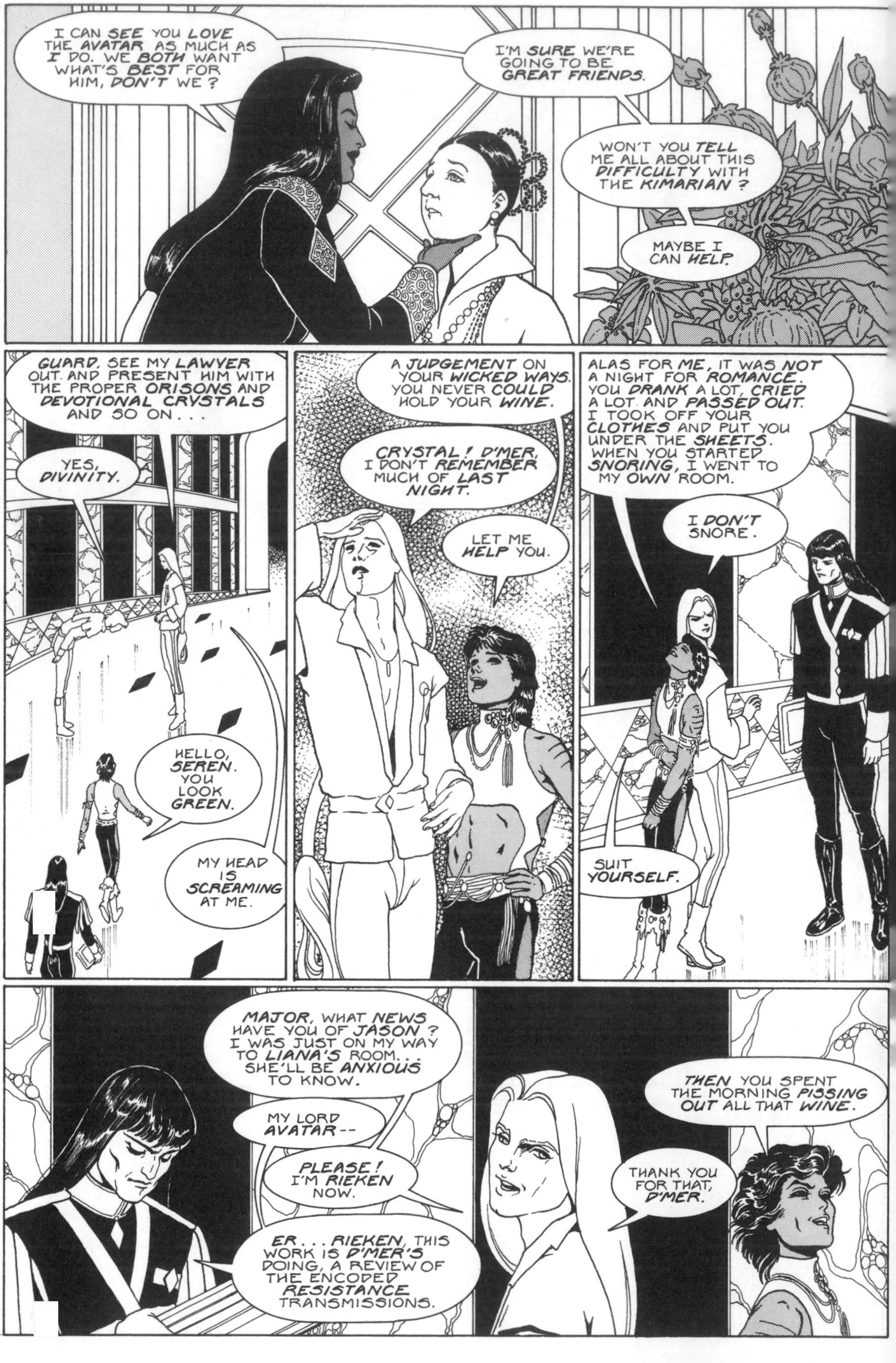
I CAN SEE YOU LOVE THE AVATAR AS MUCH AS I DO. WE BOTH WANT WHAT'S BEST FOR HIM, DON'T WE?
I'M SURE WE'RE GOING TO BE GREAT FRIENDS.
WON'T YOU TELL ME ALL ABOUT THIS DIFFICULTY WITH THE KIMARIAN?
MAYBE I CAN HELP.
GUARD, SEE MY LAWYER OUT. AND PRESENT HIM WITH THE PROPER ORISONS AND DEVOTIONAL CRYSTALS AND SO ON...
YES, DIVINITY.
HELLO, SEREN. YOU LOOK GREEN.
MY HEAD IS SCREAMING AT ME.
A JUDGEMENT ON YOUR WICKED WAYS. YOU NEVER COULD HOLD YOUR WINE.
CRYSTAL! D'MER, I DON'T REMEMBER MUCH OF LAST NIGHT.
LET ME HELP YOU.
ALAS FOR ME, IT WAS NOT A NIGHT FOR ROMANCE. YOU DRANK A LOT, CRIED A LOT, AND PASSED OUT. I TOOK OFF YOUR CLOTHES AND PUT YOU UNDER THE SHEETS. WHEN YOU STARTED SNORING, I WENT TO MY OWN ROOM.
I DON'T SNORE.
SUIT YOURSELF.
MAJOR, WHAT NEWS HAVE YOU OF JASON? I WAS JUST ON MY WAY TO LIANA'S ROOM... SHE'LL BE ANXIOUS TO KNOW.
MY LORD AVATAR--
PLEASE! I'M RIEKEN NOW.
ER... RIEKEN, THIS WORK IS D'MER'S DOING, A REVIEW OF THE ENCODED RESISTANCE TRANSMISSIONS.
THEN YOU SPENT THE MORNING PISSING OUT ALL THAT WINE.
THANK YOU FOR THAT, D'MER.

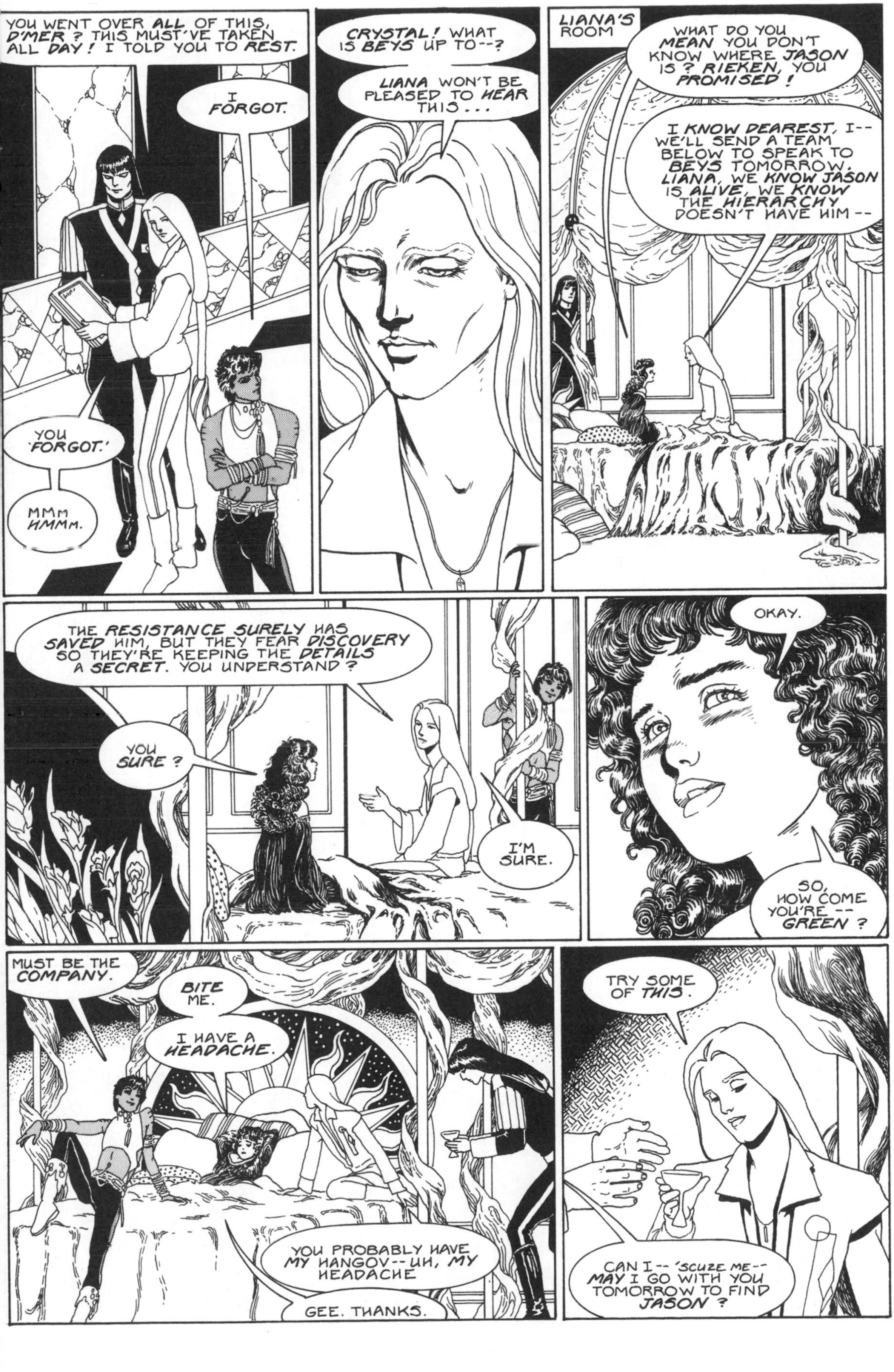
YOU WENT OVER ALL OF THIS, D'MER ? THIS MUST'VE TAKEN ALL DAY ! I TOLD YOU TO REST.
I FORGOT.
YOU 'FORGOT.'
MMM HMMM.
CRYSTAL ! WHAT IS BEYS UP TO--?
LIANA WON'T BE PLEASED TO HEAR THIS...
LIANA'S ROOM
WHAT DO YOU MEAN YOU DON'T KNOW WHERE JASON IS ? RIEKEN, YOU PROMISED !
I KNOW DEAREST, I-- WE'LL SEND A TEAM BELOW TO SPEAK TO BEYS TOMORROW. LIANA, WE KNOW JASON IS ALIVE, WE KNOW THE HIERARCHY DOESN'T HAVE HIM --
THE RESISTANCE SURELY HAS SAVED HIM, BUT THEY FEAR DISCOVERY SO THEY'RE KEEPING THE DETAILS A SECRET. YOU UNDERSTAND ?
YOU SURE ?
I'M SURE.
OKAY.
SO, HOW COME YOU'RE -- GREEN ?
MUST BE THE COMPANY.
BITE ME.
I HAVE A HEADACHE.
YOU PROBABLY HAVE MY HANGOV-- UH, MY HEADACHE
GEE. THANKS.
TRY SOME OF THIS.
CAN I -- 'SCUZE ME -- MAY I GO WITH YOU TOMORROW TO FIND JASON ?

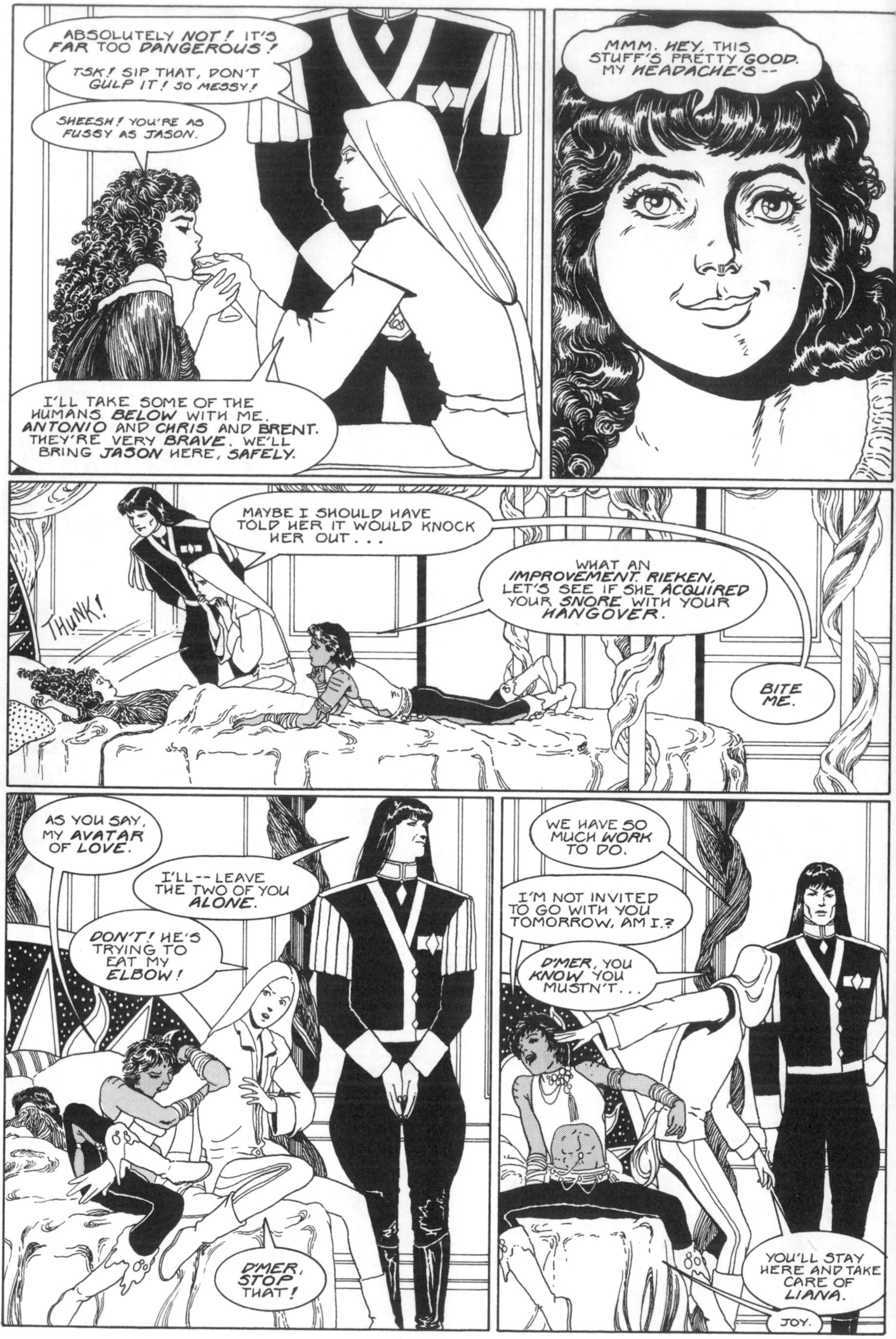

ABSOLUTELY NOT! IT'S FAR TOO DANGEROUS!
TSK! SIP THAT, DON'T GULP IT! SO MESSY!
SHEESH! YOU'RE AS FUSSY AS JASON.
I'LL TAKE SOME OF THE HUMANS BELOW WITH ME. ANTONIO AND CHRIS AND BRENT. THEY'RE VERY BRAVE. WE'LL BRING JASON HERE, SAFELY.
MMM. HEY, THIS STUFF'S PRETTY GOOD. MY HEADACHE'S --
THUNK!
MAYBE I SHOULD HAVE TOLD HER IT WOULD KNOCK HER OUT . . .
WHAT AN IMPROVEMENT. RIEKEN, LET'S SEE IF SHE ACQUIRED YOUR SNORE WITH YOUR HANGOVER.
BITE ME.
AS YOU SAY, MY AVATAR OF LOVE.
I'LL -- LEAVE THE TWO OF YOU ALONE.
DON'T! HE'S TRYING TO EAT MY ELBOW!
D'MER, STOP THAT!
WE HAVE SO MUCH WORK TO DO.
I'M NOT INVITED TO GO WITH YOU TOMORROW, AM I.?
D'MER, YOU KNOW YOU MUSTN'T. . .
YOU'LL STAY HERE AND TAKE CARE OF LIANA.
JOY.

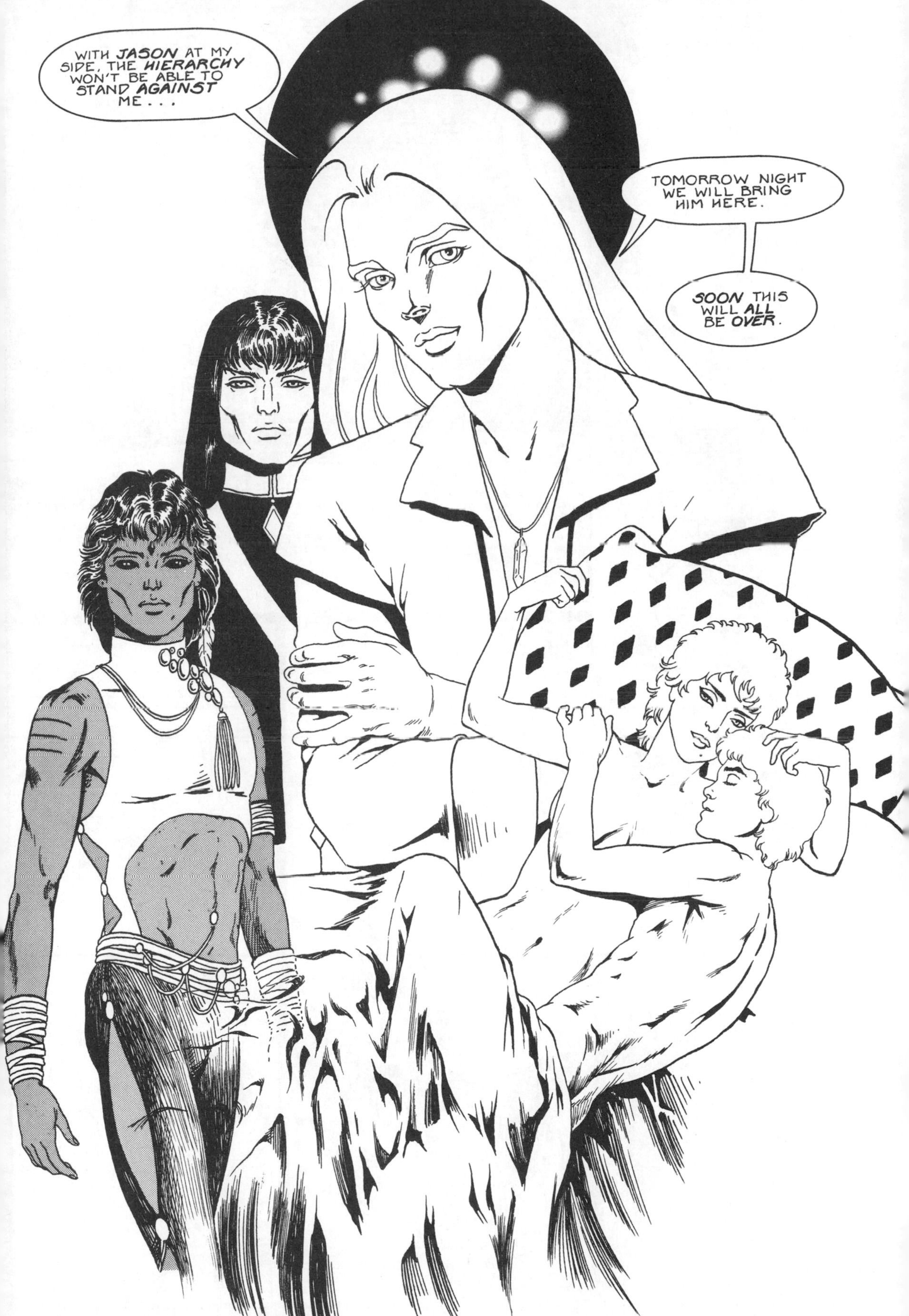
WITH JASON AT MY SIDE, THE HIERARCHY WON'T BE ABLE TO STAND AGAINST ME . . .
TOMORROW NIGHT WE WILL BRING HIM HERE.
SOON THIS WILL ALL BE OVER.

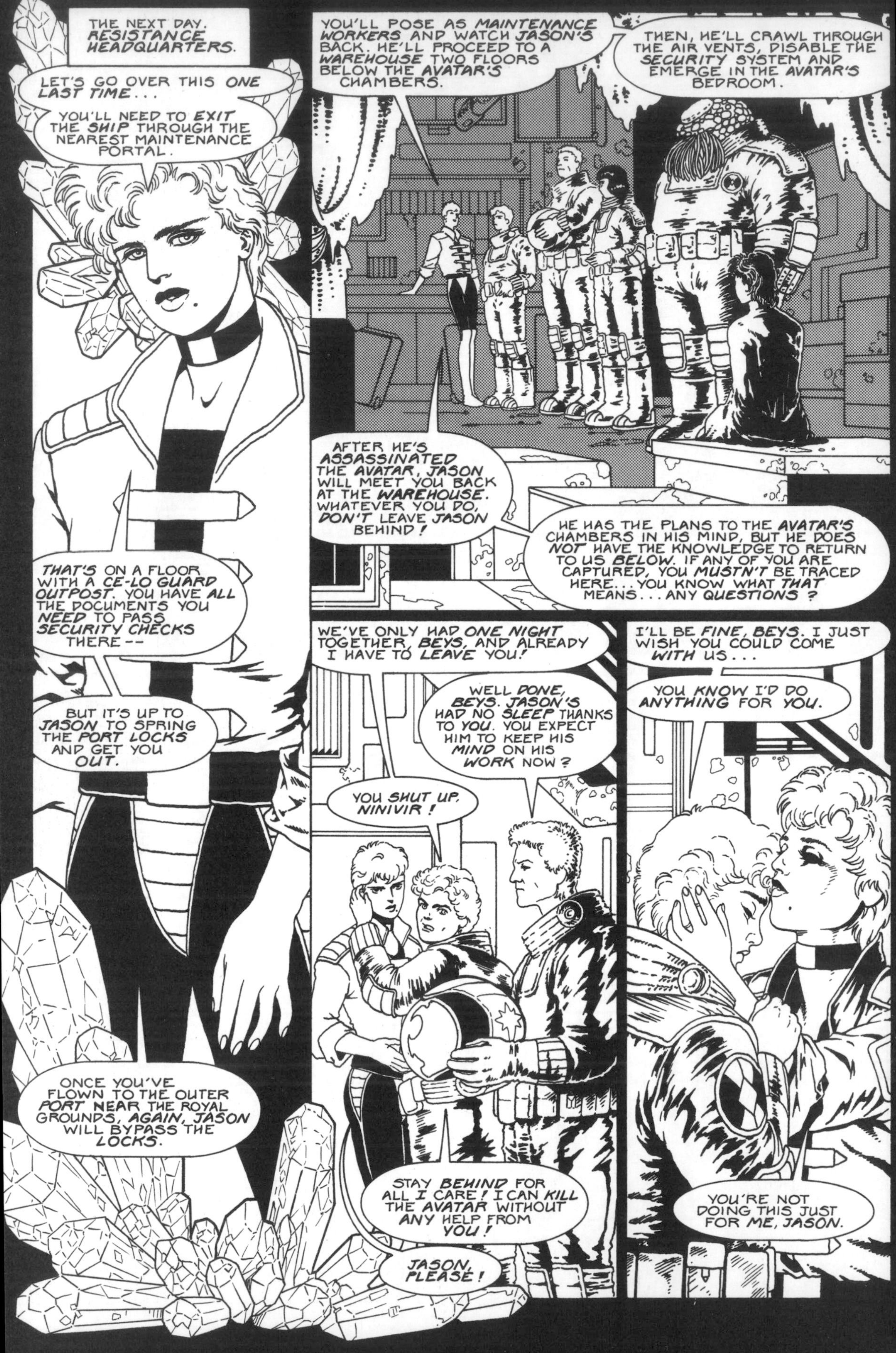
THE NEXT DAY. RESISTANCE HEADQUARTERS.
LET'S GO OVER THIS ONE LAST TIME...
YOU'LL NEED TO EXIT THE SHIP THROUGH THE NEAREST MAINTENANCE PORTAL.
THAT'S ON A FLOOR WITH A CE-LO GUARD OUTPOST. YOU HAVE ALL THE DOCUMENTS YOU NEED TO PASS SECURITY CHECKS THERE --
BUT IT'S UP TO JASON TO SPRING THE PORT LOCKS AND GET YOU OUT.
ONCE YOU'VE FLOWN TO THE OUTER PORT NEAR THE ROYAL GROUNDS, AGAIN, JASON WILL BYPASS THE LOCKS.
YOU'LL POSE AS MAINTENANCE WORKERS AND WATCH JASON'S BACK. HE'LL PROCEED TO A WAREHOUSE TWO FLOORS BELOW THE AVATAR'S CHAMBERS.
THEN, HE'LL CRAWL THROUGH THE AIR VENTS, DISABLE THE SECURITY SYSTEM AND EMERGE IN THE AVATAR'S BEDROOM.
AFTER HE'S ASSASSINATED THE AVATAR, JASON WILL MEET YOU BACK AT THE WAREHOUSE. WHATEVER YOU DO, DON'T LEAVE JASON BEHIND!
HE HAS THE PLANS TO THE AVATAR'S CHAMBERS IN HIS MIND, BUT HE DOES NOT HAVE THE KNOWLEDGE TO RETURN TO US BELOW. IF ANY OF YOU ARE CAPTURED, YOU MUSTN'T BE TRACED HERE... YOU KNOW WHAT THAT MEANS... ANY QUESTIONS?
WE'VE ONLY HAD ONE NIGHT TOGETHER, BEYS, AND ALREADY I HAVE TO LEAVE YOU!
WELL DONE, BEYS. JASON'S HAD NO SLEEP THANKS TO YOU. YOU EXPECT HIM TO KEEP HIS MIND ON HIS WORK NOW?
YOU SHUT UP, NINIVIR!
STAY BEHIND FOR ALL I CARE! I CAN KILL THE AVATAR WITHOUT ANY HELP FROM YOU!
JASON, PLEASE!
I'LL BE FINE, BEYS. I JUST WISH YOU COULD COME WITH US...
YOU KNOW I'D DO ANYTHING FOR YOU.
YOU'RE NOT DOING THIS JUST FOR ME, JASON.

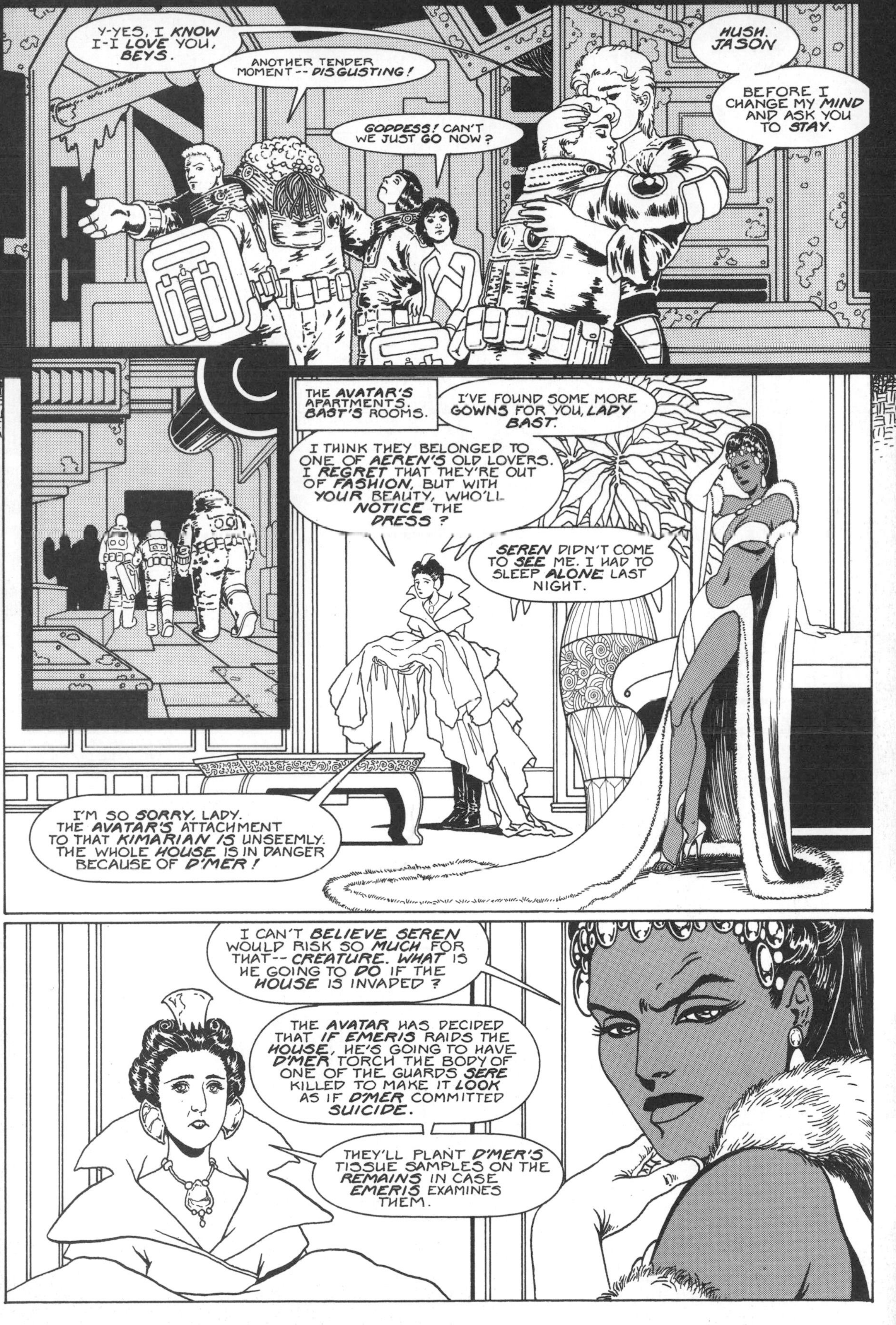
Y-YES, I KNOW I-I LOVE YOU, BEYS.
ANOTHER TENDER MOMENT -- DISGUSTING!
GODDESS! CAN'T WE JUST GO NOW?
HUSH. JASON
BEFORE I CHANGE MY MIND AND ASK YOU TO STAY.
THE AVATAR'S APARTMENTS. BAST'S ROOMS.
I'VE FOUND SOME MORE GOWNS FOR YOU, LADY BAST.
I THINK THEY BELONGED TO ONE OF AEREN'S OLD LOVERS. I REGRET THAT THEY'RE OUT OF FASHION, BUT WITH YOUR BEAUTY, WHO'LL NOTICE THE DRESS?
SEREN DIDN'T COME TO SEE ME. I HAD TO SLEEP ALONE LAST NIGHT.
I'M SO SORRY, LADY. THE AVATAR'S ATTACHMENT TO THAT KIMARIAN IS UNSEEMLY. THE WHOLE HOUSE IS IN DANGER BECAUSE OF D'MER!
I CAN'T BELIEVE SEREN WOULD RISK SO MUCH FOR THAT-- CREATURE. WHAT IS HE GOING TO DO IF THE HOUSE IS INVADED?
THE AVATAR HAS DECIDED THAT IF EMERIS RAIDS THE HOUSE, HE'S GOING TO HAVE D'MER TORCH THE BODY OF ONE OF THE GUARDS SERE KILLED TO MAKE IT LOOK AS IF D'MER COMMITTED SUICIDE.
THEY'LL PLANT D'MER'S TISSUE SAMPLES ON THE REMAINS IN CASE EMERIS EXAMINES THEM.

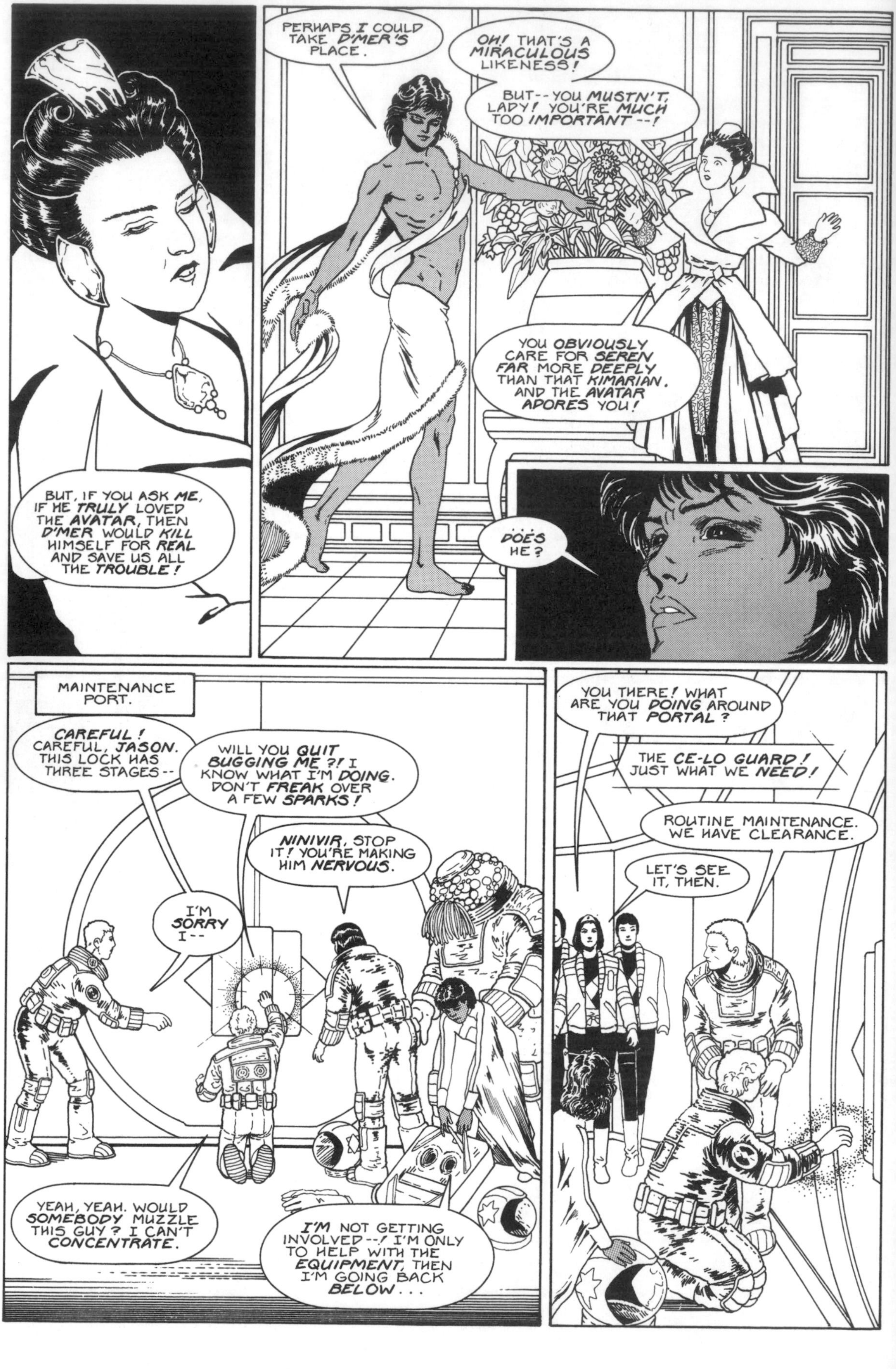
PERHAPS I COULD TAKE D'MER'S PLACE.
OH! THAT'S A MIRACULOUS LIKENESS!
BUT--YOU MUSTN'T, LADY! YOU'RE MUCH TOO IMPORTANT--!
YOU OBVIOUSLY CARE FOR SEREN FAR MORE DEEPLY THAN THAT KIMARIAN. AND THE AVATAR ADORES YOU!
BUT, IF YOU ASK ME, IF HE TRULY LOVED THE AVATAR, THEN D'MER WOULD KILL HIMSELF FOR REAL AND SAVE US ALL THE TROUBLE!
...DOES HE?
MAINTENANCE PORT.
CAREFUL! CAREFUL, JASON. THIS LOCK HAS THREE STAGES--
WILL YOU QUIT BUGGING ME?! I KNOW WHAT I'M DOING. DON'T FREAK OVER A FEW SPARKS!
NINIVIR, STOP IT! YOU'RE MAKING HIM NERVOUS.
I'M SORRY I--
YEAH, YEAH. WOULD SOMEBODY MUZZLE THIS GUY? I CAN'T CONCENTRATE.
I'M NOT GETTING INVOLVED--! I'M ONLY TO HELP WITH THE EQUIPMENT, THEN I'M GOING BACK BELOW...
YOU THERE! WHAT ARE YOU DOING AROUND THAT PORTAL?
THE CE-LO GUARD! JUST WHAT WE NEED!
ROUTINE MAINTENANCE. WE HAVE CLEARANCE.
LET'S SEE IT, THEN.

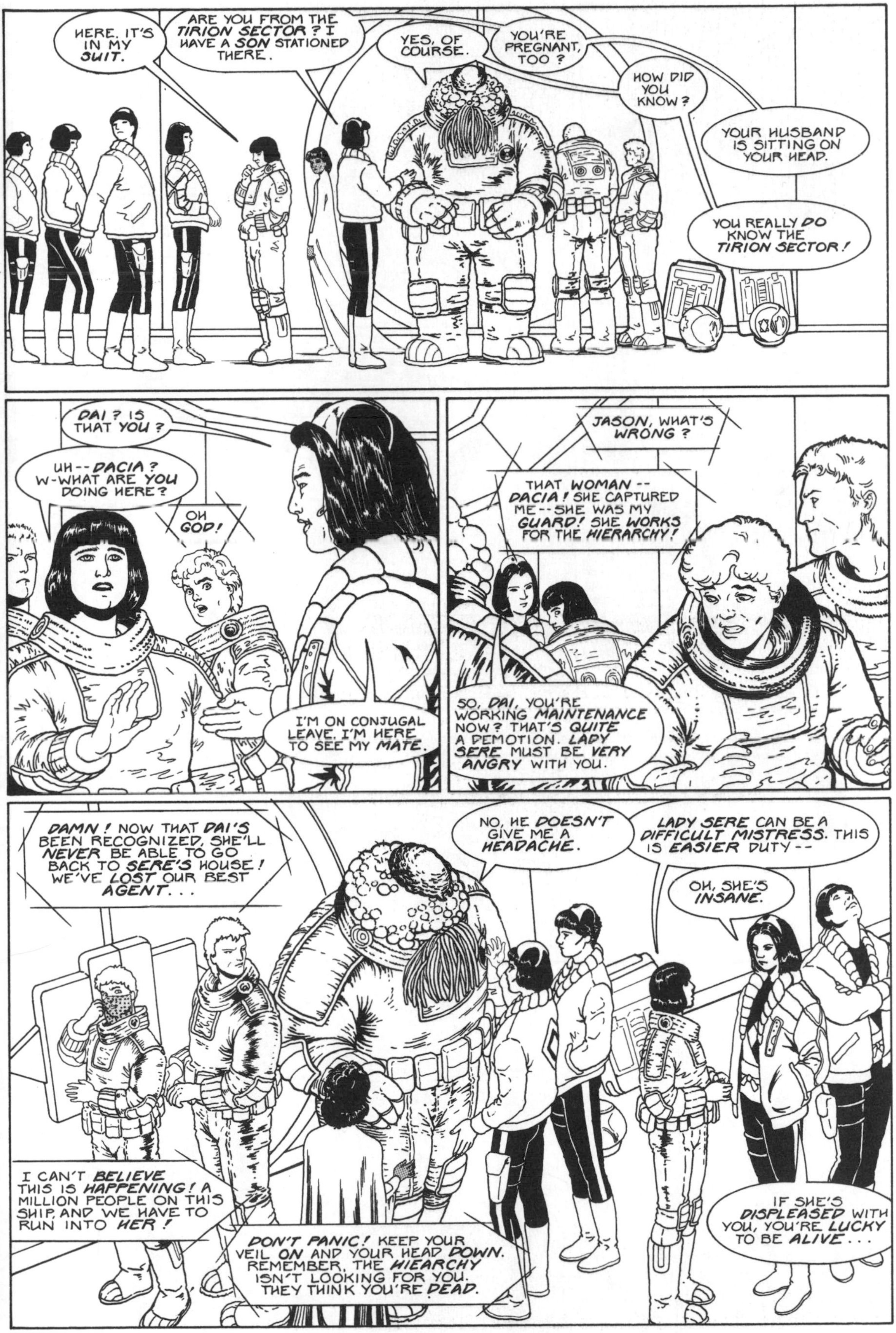
HERE, IT'S IN MY SUIT.
ARE YOU FROM THE TIRION SECTOR? I HAVE A SON STATIONED THERE.
YES, OF COURSE.
YOU'RE PREGNANT, TOO?
HOW DID YOU KNOW?
YOUR HUSBAND IS SITTING ON YOUR HEAD.
YOU REALLY DO KNOW THE TIRION SECTOR!
DAI? IS THAT YOU?
UH--DACIA? W-WHAT ARE YOU DOING HERE?
OH GOD!
I'M ON CONJUGAL LEAVE. I'M HERE TO SEE MY MATE.
JASON, WHAT'S WRONG?
THAT WOMAN--DACIA! SHE CAPTURED ME--SHE WAS MY GUARD! SHE WORKS FOR THE HIERARCHY!
SO, DAI, YOU'RE WORKING MAINTENANCE NOW? THAT'S QUITE A DEMOTION. LADY SERE MUST BE VERY ANGRY WITH YOU.
DAMN! NOW THAT DAI'S BEEN RECOGNIZED, SHE'LL NEVER BE ABLE TO GO BACK TO SERE'S HOUSE! WE'VE LOST OUR BEST AGENT...
NO, HE DOESN'T GIVE ME A HEADACHE.
LADY SERE CAN BE A DIFFICULT MISTRESS. THIS IS EASIER DUTY--
OH, SHE'S INSANE.
I CAN'T BELIEVE THIS IS HAPPENING! A MILLION PEOPLE ON THIS SHIP, AND WE HAVE TO RUN INTO HER!
DON'T PANIC! KEEP YOUR VEIL ON AND YOUR HEAD DOWN. REMEMBER, THE HIEARCHY ISN'T LOOKING FOR YOU. THEY THINK YOU'RE DEAD.
IF SHE'S DISPLEASED WITH YOU, YOU'RE LUCKY TO BE ALIVE...

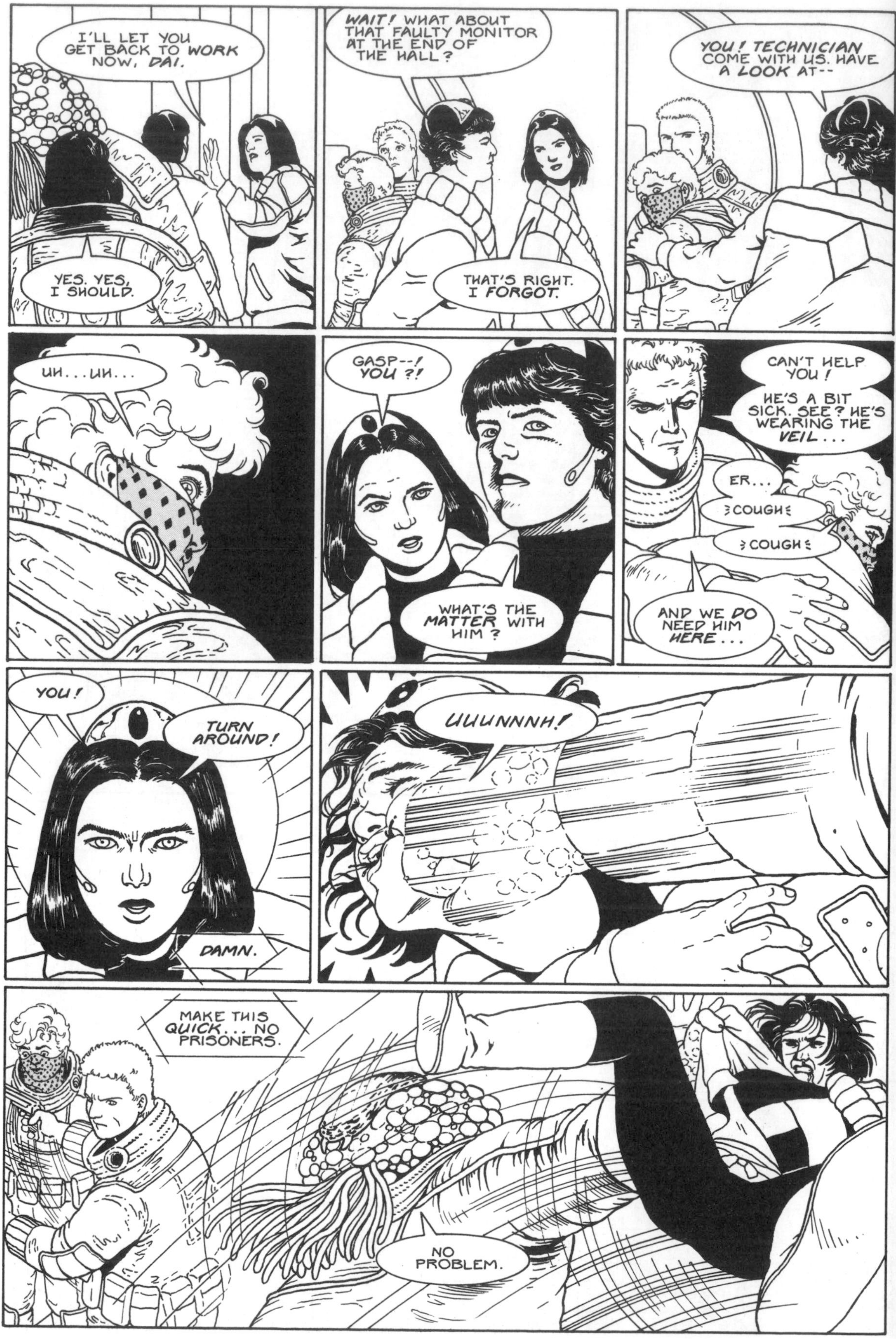
I'LL LET YOU GET BACK TO WORK NOW, DAI.
YES. YES, I SHOULD.
WAIT! WHAT ABOUT THAT FAULTY MONITOR AT THE END OF THE HALL?
THAT'S RIGHT. I FORGOT.
YOU! TECHNICIAN COME WITH US. HAVE A LOOK AT--
UH...UH...
GASP--! YOU?!
WHAT'S THE MATTER WITH HIM?
CAN'T HELP YOU!
HE'S A BIT SICK. SEE? HE'S WEARING THE VEIL...
ER...
COUGH
COUGH
AND WE DO NEED HIM HERE...
YOU!
TURN AROUND!
DAMN.
UUUNNNH!
MAKE THIS QUICK... NO PRISONERS.
NO PROBLEM.

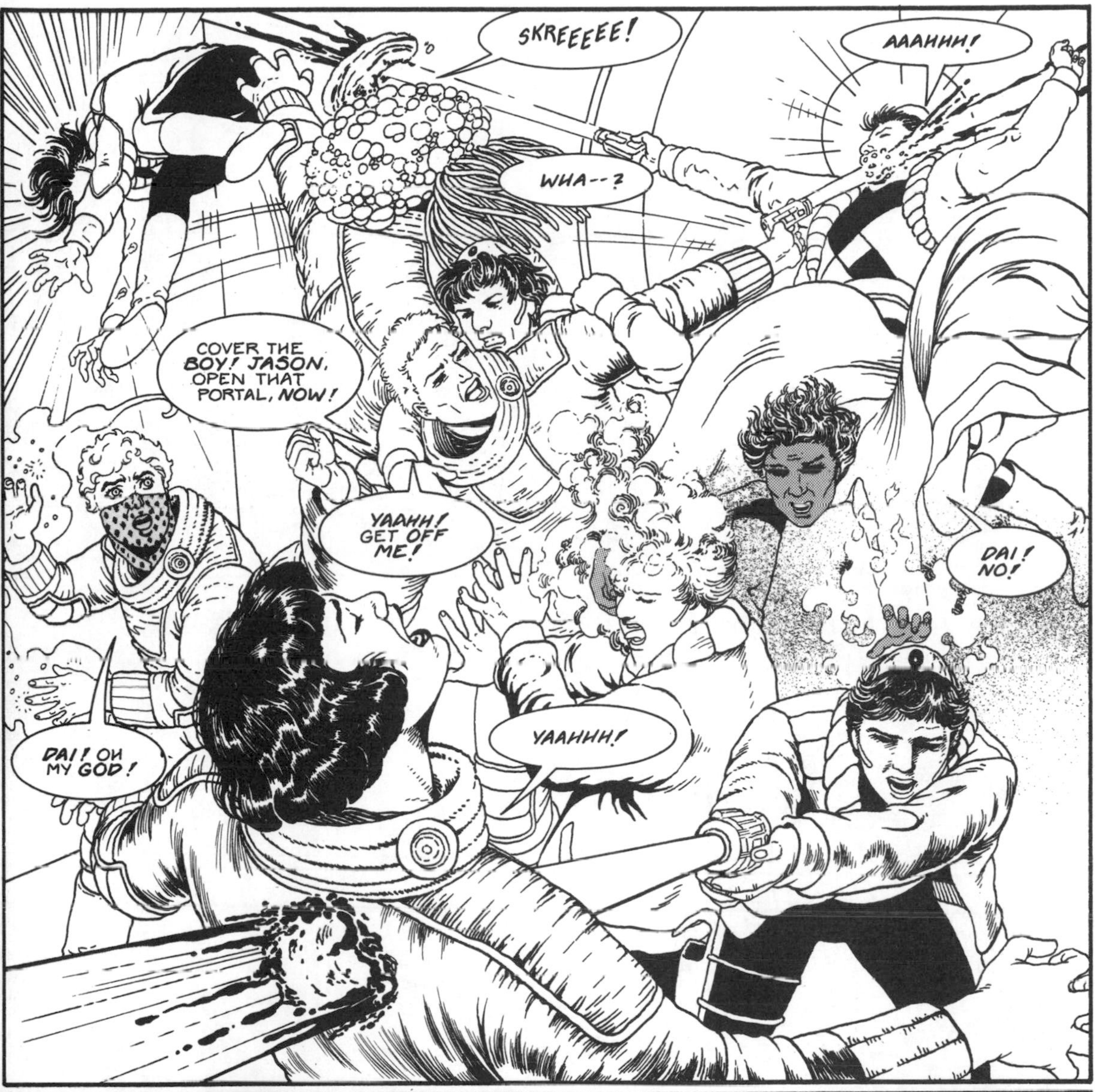
SKREEEEEE!
AAAHHH!
WHA--?
COVER THE BOY! JASON, OPEN THAT PORTAL, NOW!
YAAHH! GET OFF ME!
DAI! NO!
DAI! OH MY GOD!
YAAHHH!
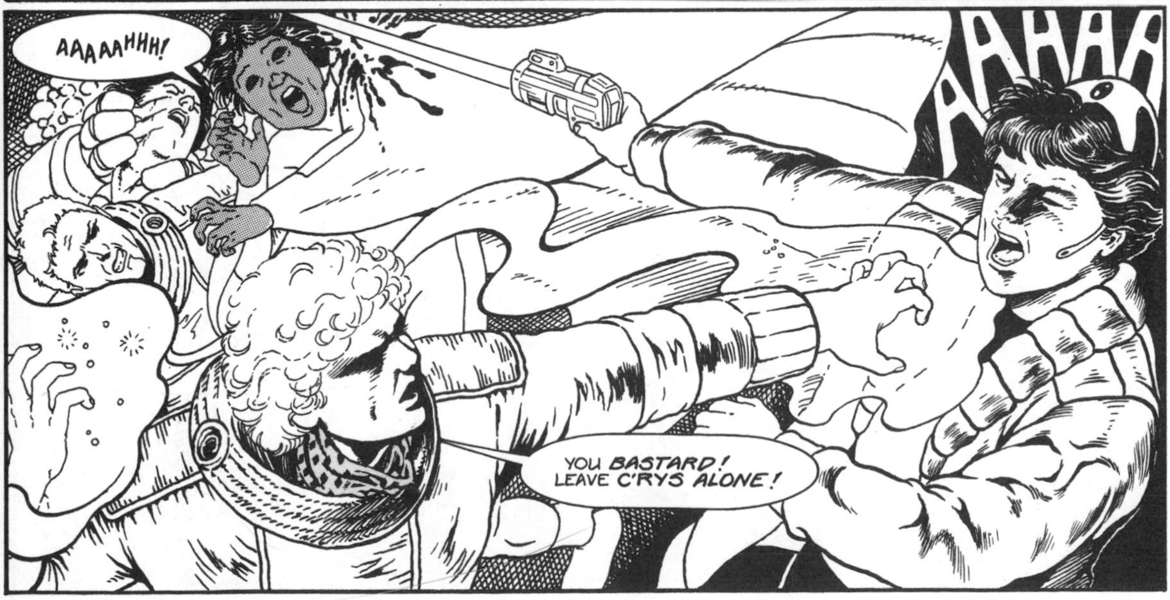
AAAAAHHH!
AAAA
YOU BASTARD! LEAVE C'RYS ALONE!

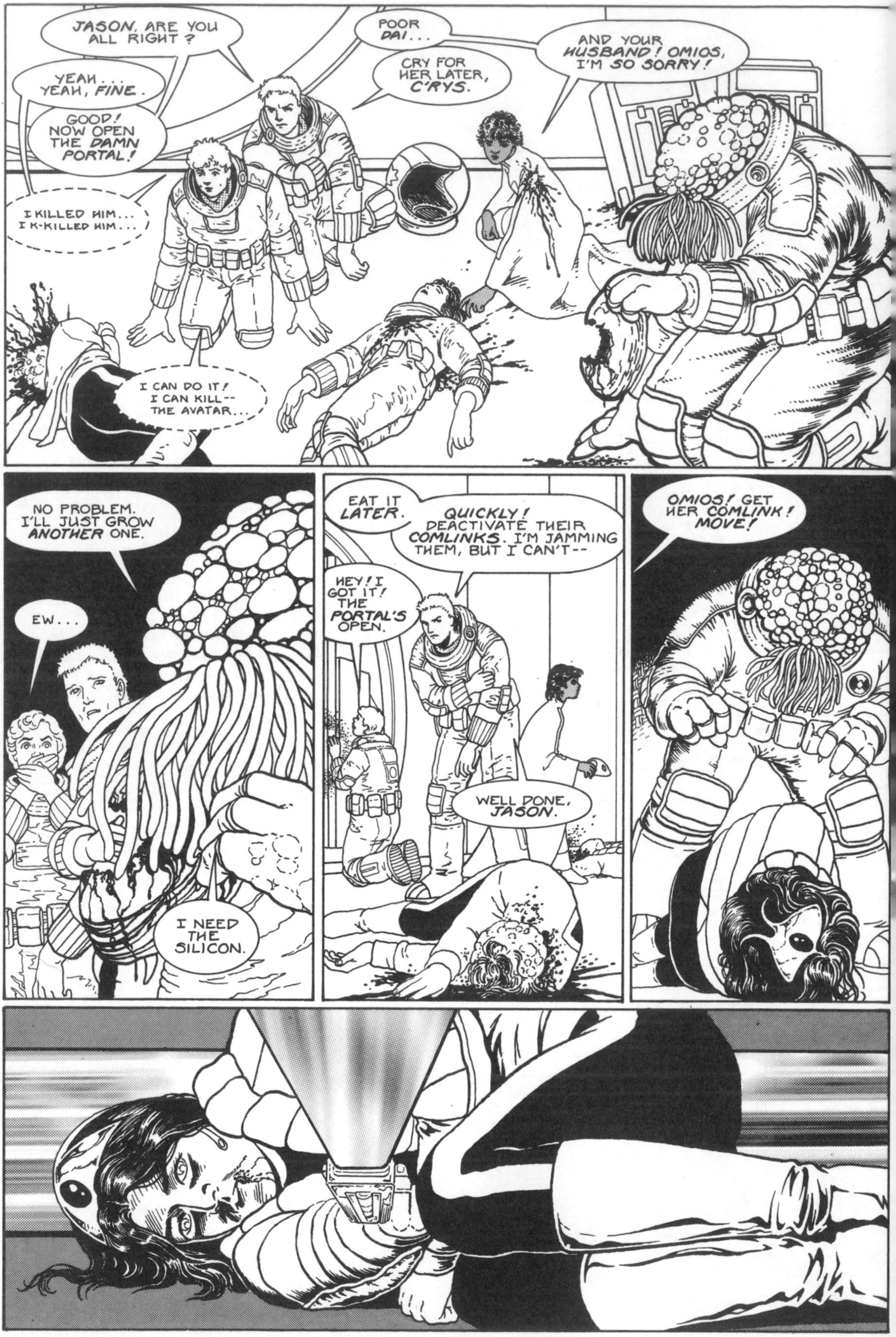
JASON, ARE YOU ALL RIGHT?
YEAH... YEAH, FINE.
GOOD! NOW OPEN THE DAMN PORTAL!
I KILLED HIM... I K-KILLED HIM...
POOR DAI...
CRY FOR HER LATER, C'RYS.
AND YOUR HUSBAND! OMIOS, I'M SO SORRY!
I CAN DO IT! I CAN KILL-- THE AVATAR...
NO PROBLEM. I'LL JUST GROW ANOTHER ONE.
EW...
I NEED THE SILICON.
EAT IT LATER.
QUICKLY! DEACTIVATE THEIR COMLINKS. I'M JAMMING THEM, BUT I CAN'T--
HEY! I GOT IT! THE PORTAL'S OPEN.
WELL DONE, JASON.
OMIOS! GET HER COMLINK! MOVE!

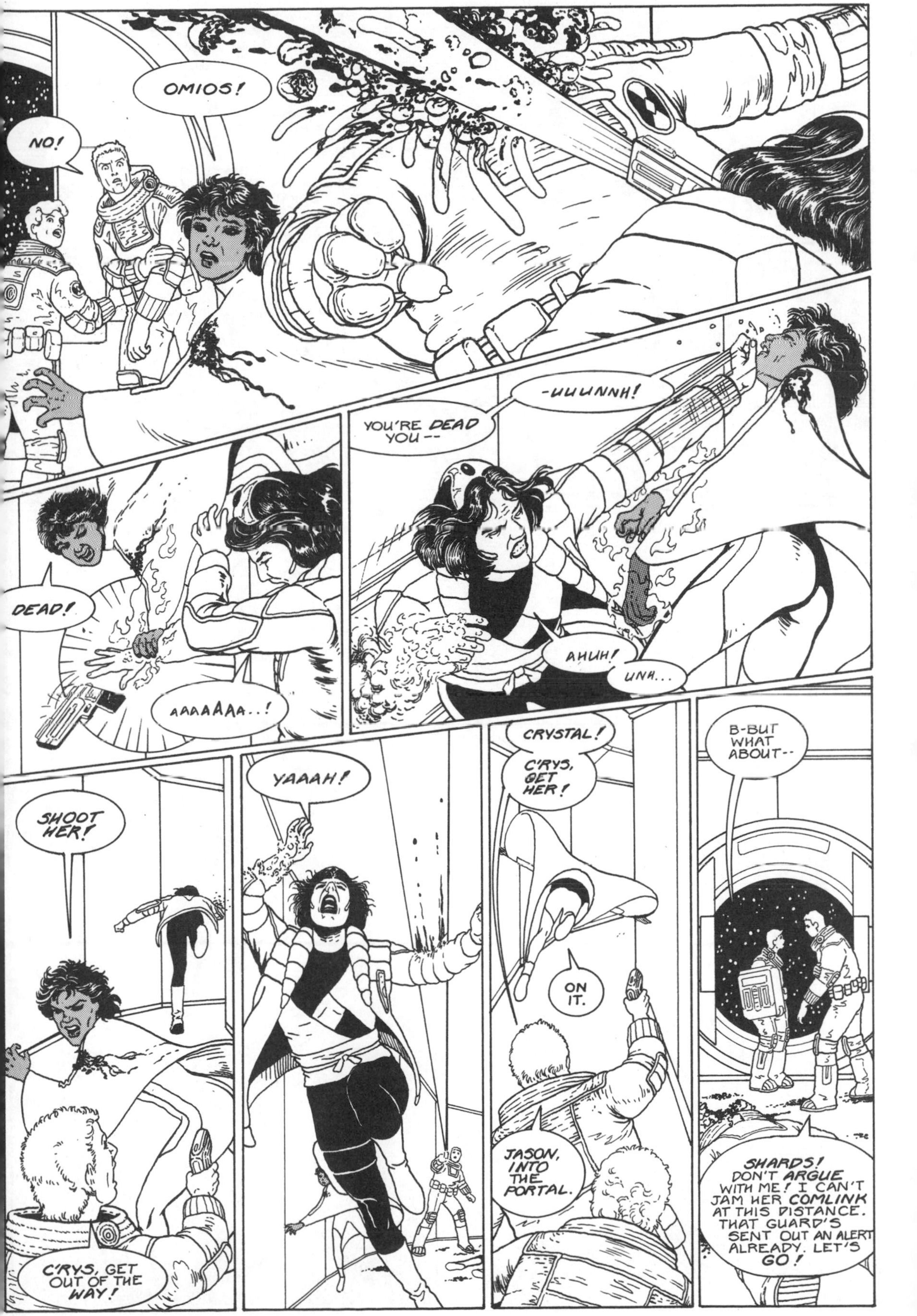

OMIOS!
NO!
-UUUNNH!
YOU'RE DEAD YOU --
DEAD!
AAAAAAA..!
AHUH!
UNH...
SHOOT HER!
C'RYS, GET OUT OF THE WAY!
YAAAH!
CRYSTAL!
C'RYS, GET HER!
ON IT.
JASON, INTO THE PORTAL.
B-BUT WHAT ABOUT--
SHARDS! DON'T ARGUE WITH ME! I CAN'T JAM HER COMLINK AT THIS DISTANCE. THAT GUARD'S SENT OUT AN ALERT ALREADY. LET'S GO!

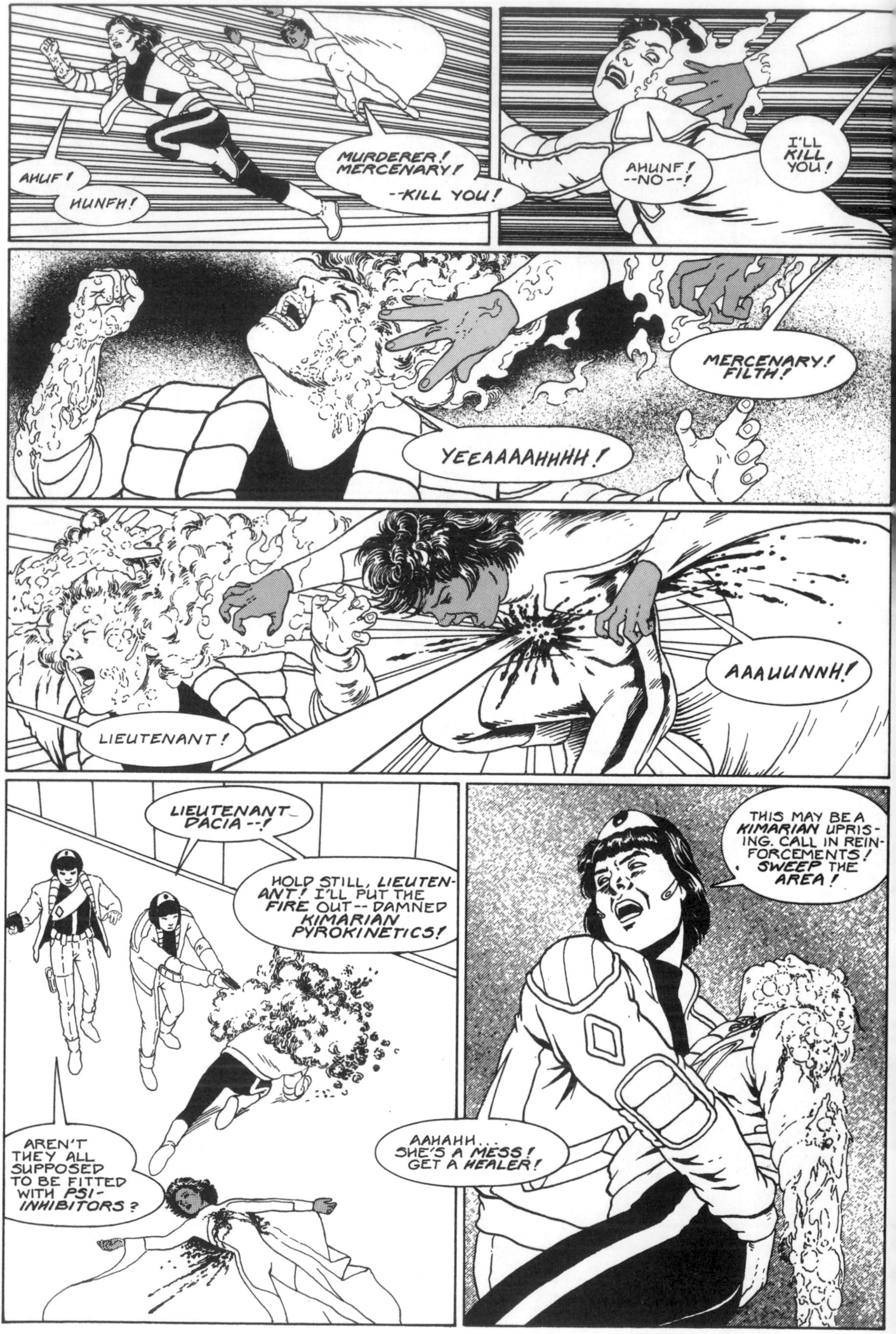
AHUF!
HUNFH!
MURDERER! MERCENARY!
--KILL YOU!
AHUNF! --NO--!
I'LL KILL YOU!
MERCENARY! FILTH!
YEEAAAAHHHH!
AAAUUNNH!
LIEUTENANT!
LIEUTENANT DACIA--!
HOLD STILL, LIEUTENANT! I'LL PUT THE FIRE OUT-- DAMNED KIMARIAN PYROKINETICS!
AREN'T THEY ALL SUPPOSED TO BE FITTED WITH PSI-INHIBITORS?
THIS MAY BE A KIMARIAN UPRISING. CALL IN REINFORCEMENTS! SWEEP THE AREA!
AAAHHH... SHE'S A MESS! GET A HEALER!

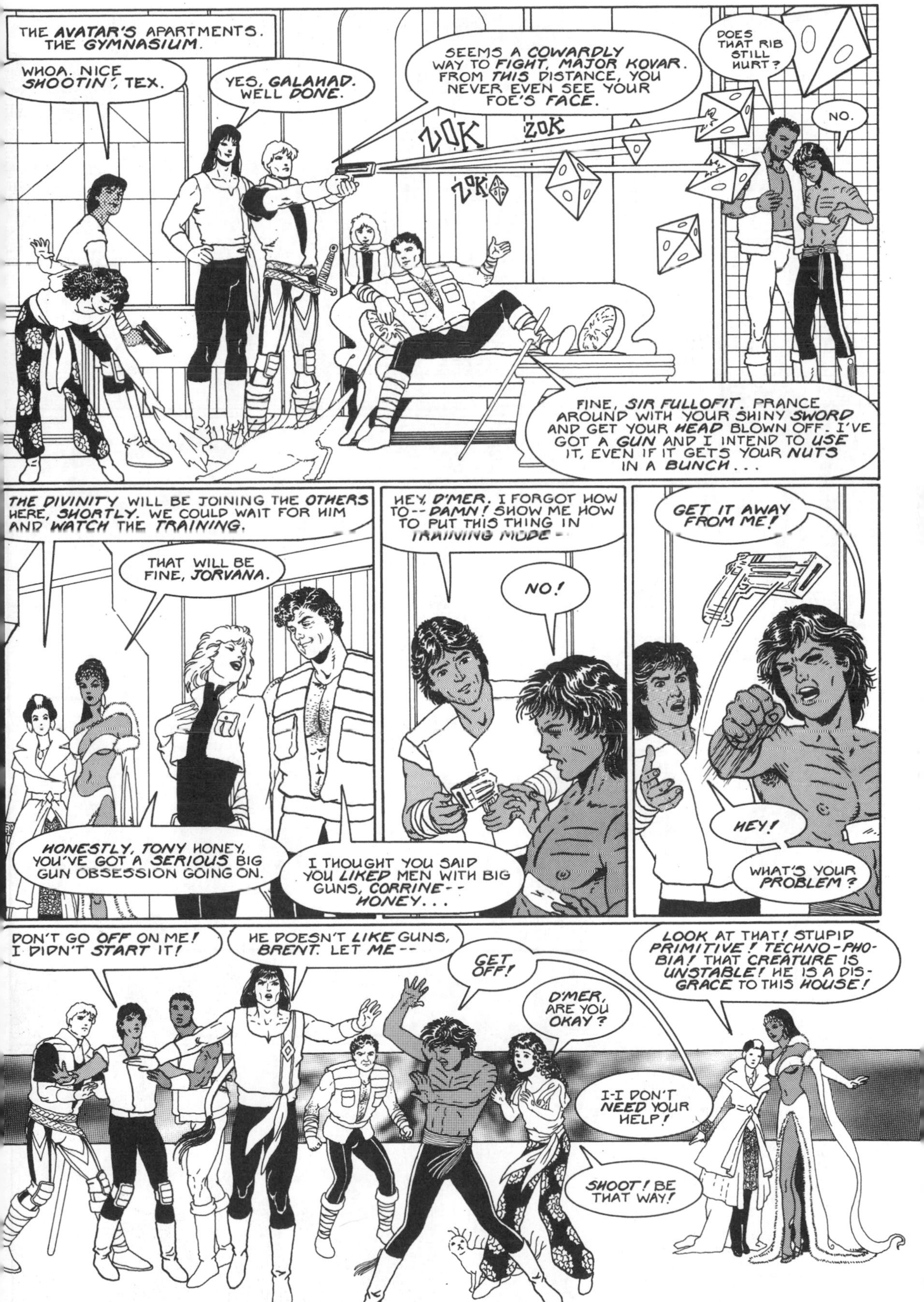
THE AVATAR'S APARTMENTS. THE GYMNASIUM.
WHOA. NICE SHOOTIN', TEX.
YES, GALAHAD. WELL DONE.
SEEMS A COWARDLY WAY TO FIGHT, MAJOR KOVAR. FROM THIS DISTANCE, YOU NEVER EVEN SEE YOUR FOE'S FACE.
ZOK
ZOK
ZOK
DOES THAT RIB STILL HURT?
NO.
FINE, SIR FULLOFIT. PRANCE AROUND WITH YOUR SHINY SWORD AND GET YOUR HEAD BLOWN OFF. I'VE GOT A GUN AND I INTEND TO USE IT, EVEN IF IT GETS YOUR NUTS IN A BUNCH...
THE DIVINITY WILL BE JOINING THE OTHERS HERE, SHORTLY. WE COULD WAIT FOR HIM AND WATCH THE TRAINING.
THAT WILL BE FINE, JORVANA.
HONESTLY, TONY HONEY, YOU'VE GOT A SERIOUS BIG GUN OBSESSION GOING ON.
I THOUGHT YOU SAID YOU LIKED MEN WITH BIG GUNS, CORRINE-- HONEY...
HEY, D'MER. I FORGOT HOW TO-- DAMN! SHOW ME HOW TO PUT THIS THING IN TRAINING MODE--
NO!
GET IT AWAY FROM ME!
HEY!
WHAT'S YOUR PROBLEM?
DON'T GO OFF ON ME! I DIDN'T START IT!
HE DOESN'T LIKE GUNS, BRENT. LET ME--
GET OFF!
D'MER, ARE YOU OKAY?
I-I DON'T NEED YOUR HELP!
SHOOT! BE THAT WAY!
LOOK AT THAT! STUPID PRIMITIVE! TECHNO-PHOBIA! THAT CREATURE IS UNSTABLE! HE IS A DISGRACE TO THIS HOUSE!

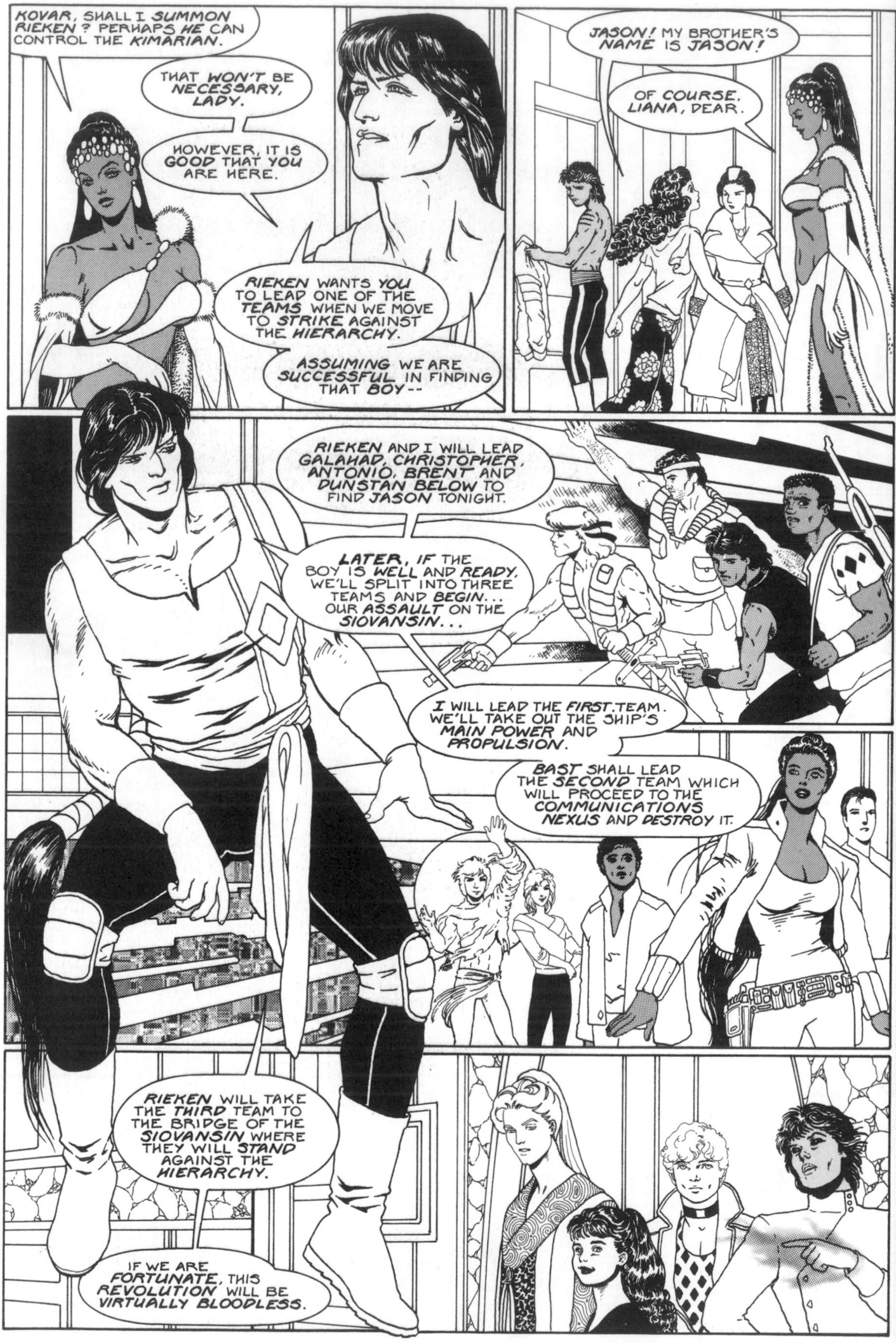

KOVAR, SHALL I SUMMON RIEKEN? PERHAPS HE CAN CONTROL THE KIMARIAN.
THAT WON'T BE NECESSARY, LADY.
HOWEVER, IT IS GOOD THAT YOU ARE HERE.
RIEKEN WANTS YOU TO LEAD ONE OF THE TEAMS WHEN WE MOVE TO STRIKE AGAINST THE HIERARCHY.
ASSUMING WE ARE SUCCESSFUL IN FINDING THAT BOY--
JASON! MY BROTHER'S NAME IS JASON!
OF COURSE. LIANA, DEAR.
RIEKEN AND I WILL LEAD GALAHAD, CHRISTOPHER, ANTONIO, BRENT AND DUNSTAN BELOW TO FIND JASON TONIGHT.
LATER, IF THE BOY IS WELL AND READY, WE'LL SPLIT INTO THREE TEAMS AND BEGIN... OUR ASSAULT ON THE SIOVANSIN...
I WILL LEAD THE FIRST TEAM. WE'LL TAKE OUT THE SHIP'S MAIN POWER AND PROPULSION.
BAST SHALL LEAD THE SECOND TEAM WHICH WILL PROCEED TO THE COMMUNICATIONS NEXUS AND DESTROY IT.
RIEKEN WILL TAKE THE THIRD TEAM TO THE BRIDGE OF THE SIOVANSIN WHERE THEY WILL STAND AGAINST THE HIERARCHY.
IF WE ARE FORTUNATE, THIS REVOLUTION WILL BE VIRTUALLY BLOODLESS.

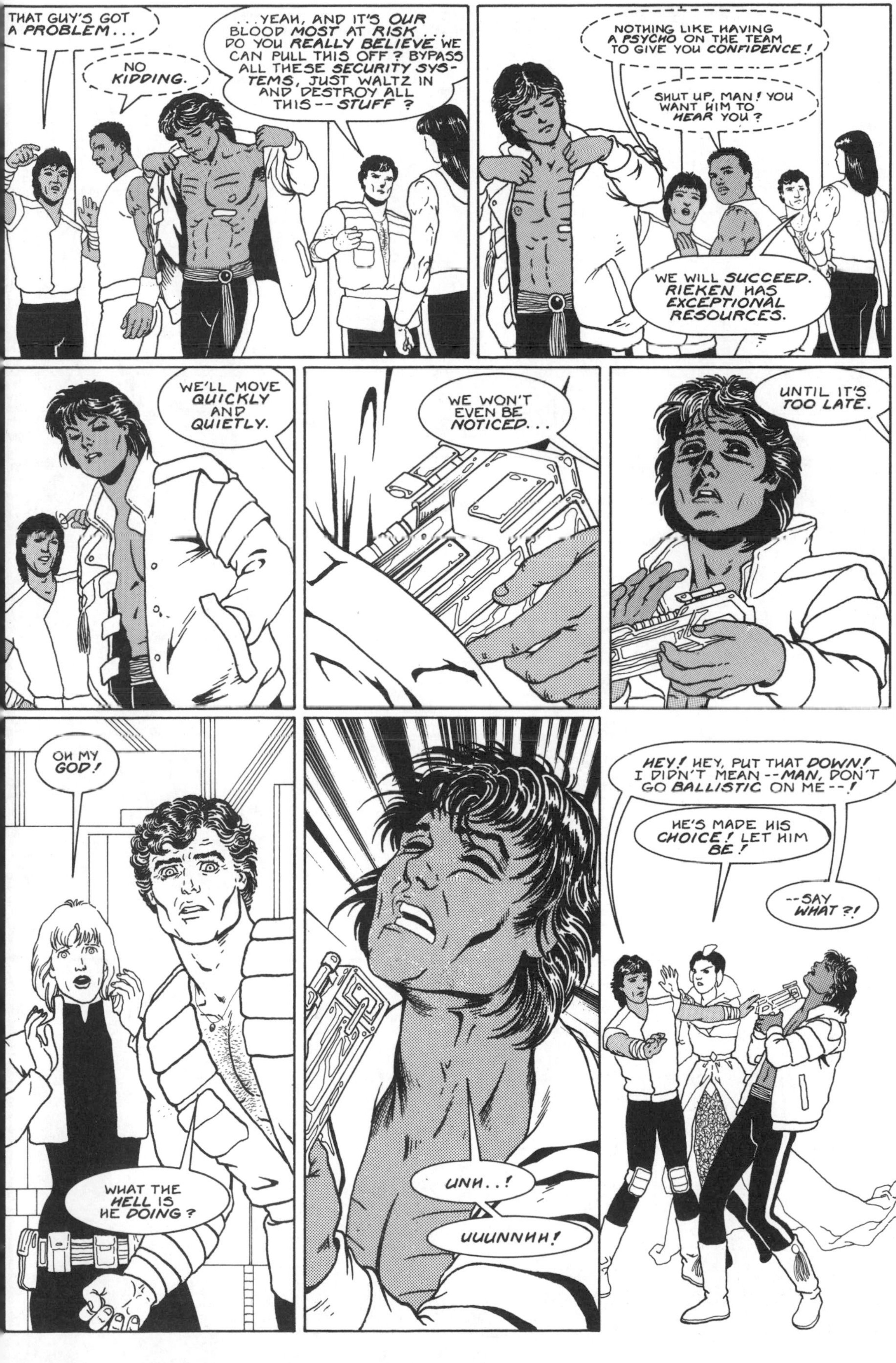
THAT GUY'S GOT A PROBLEM...
NO KIDDING.
...YEAH, AND IT'S OUR BLOOD MOST AT RISK. DO YOU REALLY BELIEVE WE CAN PULL THIS OFF? BYPASS ALL THESE SECURITY SYSTEMS, JUST WALTZ IN AND DESTROY ALL THIS--STUFF?
NOTHING LIKE HAVING A PSYCHO ON THE TEAM TO GIVE YOU CONFIDENCE!
SHUT UP, MAN! YOU WANT HIM TO HEAR YOU?
WE WILL SUCCEED. RIEKEN HAS EXCEPTIONAL RESOURCES.
WE'LL MOVE QUICKLY AND QUIETLY.
WE WON'T EVEN BE NOTICED...
UNTIL IT'S TOO LATE.
OH MY GOD!
WHAT THE HELL IS HE DOING?
UNH..!
UUUNNHH!
HEY! HEY, PUT THAT DOWN! I DIDN'T MEAN--MAN, DON'T GO BALLISTIC ON ME--!
HE'S MADE HIS CHOICE! LET HIM BE!
--SAY WHAT?!

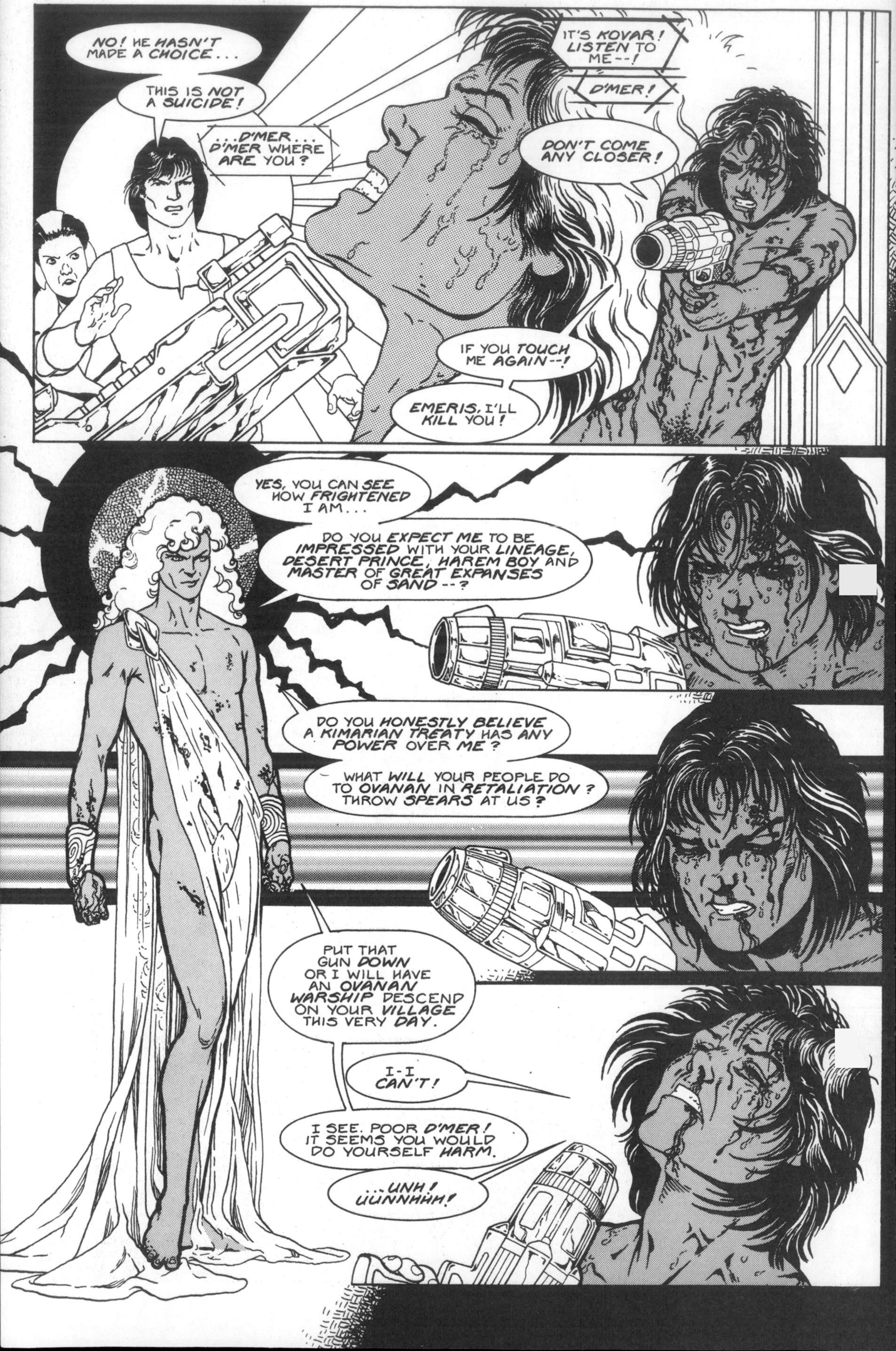
NO! HE HASN'T MADE A CHOICE...
THIS IS NOT A SUICIDE!
...D'MER... D'MER WHERE ARE YOU?
IT'S KOVAR! LISTEN TO ME--!
D'MER!
DON'T COME ANY CLOSER!
IF YOU TOUCH ME AGAIN--!
EMERIS, I'LL KILL YOU!
YES, YOU CAN SEE HOW FRIGHTENED I AM...
DO YOU EXPECT ME TO BE IMPRESSED WITH YOUR LINEAGE, DESERT PRINCE, HAREM BOY AND MASTER OF GREAT EXPANSES OF SAND--?
DO YOU HONESTLY BELIEVE A KIMARIAN TREATY HAS ANY POWER OVER ME?
WHAT WILL YOUR PEOPLE DO TO OVANAN IN RETALIATION? THROW SPEARS AT US?
PUT THAT GUN DOWN OR I WILL HAVE AN OVANAN WARSHIP DESCEND ON YOUR VILLAGE THIS VERY DAY.
I-I CAN'T!
I SEE. POOR D'MER! IT SEEMS YOU WOULD DO YOURSELF HARM.
...UNH! UUNNHHH!

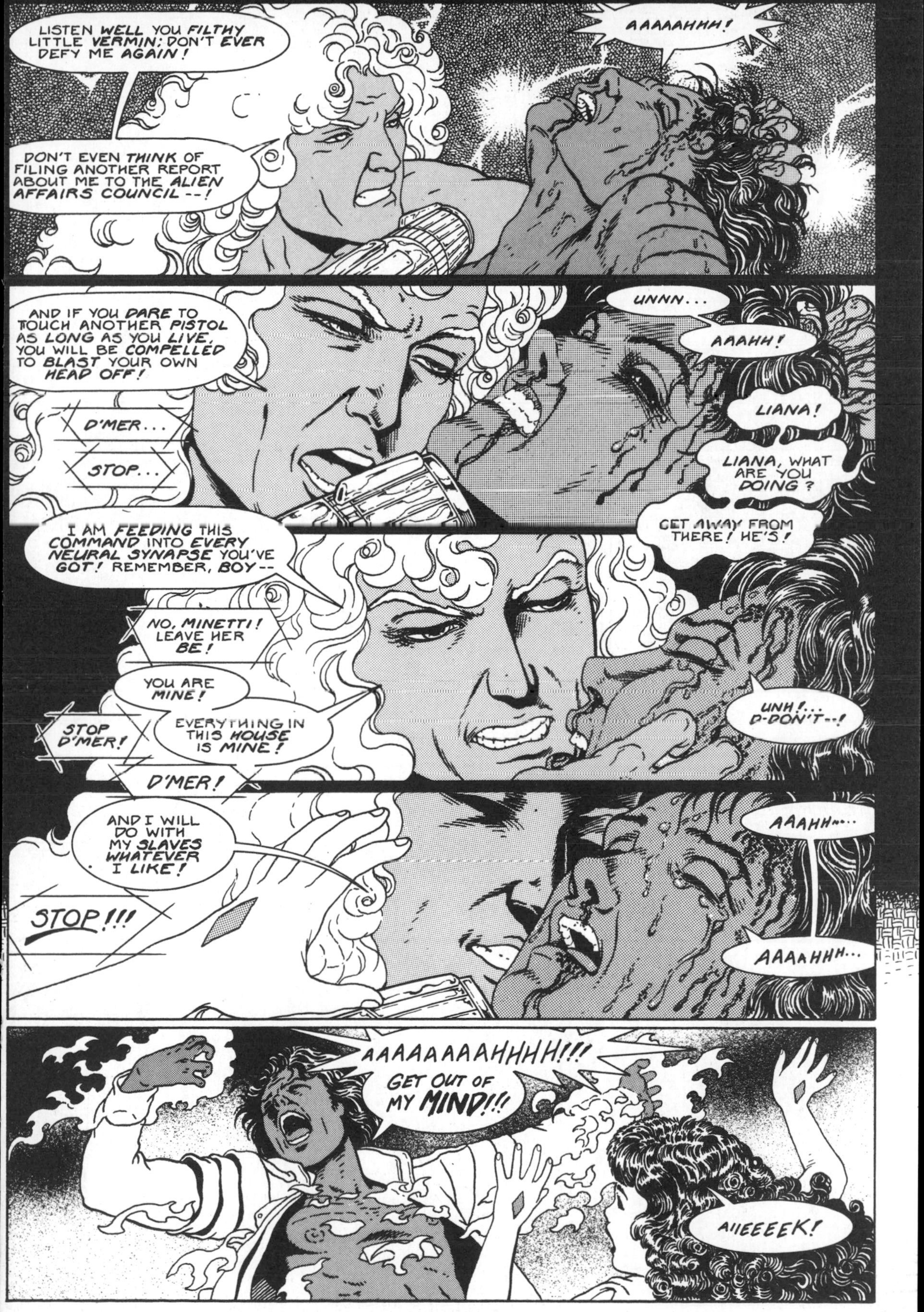

LISTEN WELL YOU FILTHY LITTLE VERMIN; DON'T EVER DEFY ME AGAIN!
AAAAAHHH!
DON'T EVEN THINK OF FILING ANOTHER REPORT ABOUT ME TO THE ALIEN AFFAIRS COUNCIL--!
AND IF YOU DARE TO TOUCH ANOTHER PISTOL AS LONG AS YOU LIVE, YOU WILL BE COMPELLED TO BLAST YOUR OWN HEAD OFF!
UNNN...
AAAHH!
D'MER...
STOP...
LIANA!
LIANA, WHAT ARE YOU DOING?
GET AWAY FROM THERE! HE'S!
I AM FEEDING THIS COMMAND INTO EVERY NEURAL SYNAPSE YOU'VE GOT! REMEMBER, BOY--
NO, MINETTI! LEAVE HER BE!
YOU ARE MINE!
EVERYTHING IN THIS HOUSE IS MINE!
STOP D'MER!
D'MER!
UNH!... D-DON'T--!
AND I WILL DO WITH MY SLAVES WHATEVER I LIKE!
AAAHH...
STOP!!!
AAAAHHH...
AAAAAAAAHHHH!!!
GET OUT OF MY MIND!!!
AIIEEEEK!

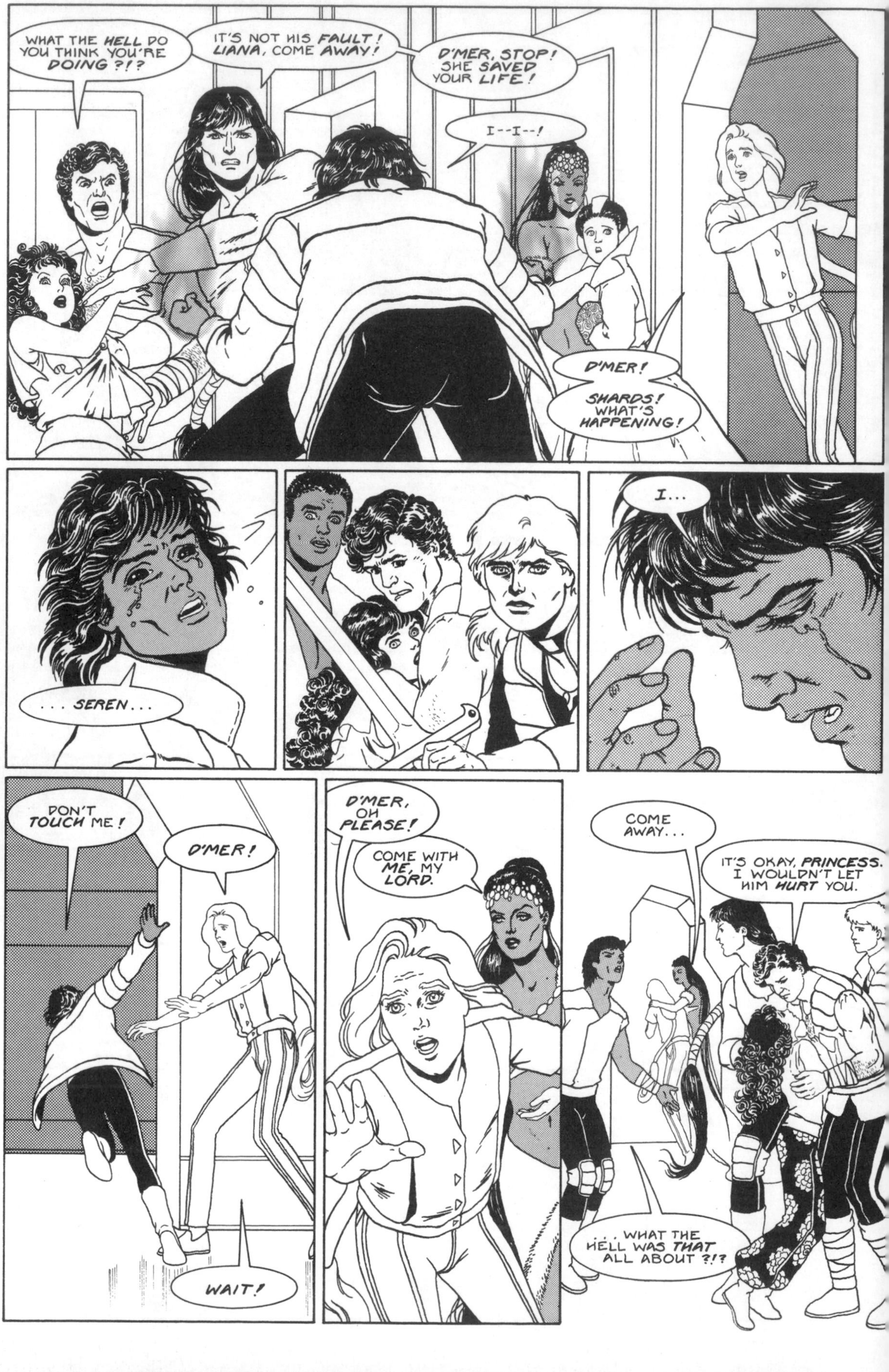
WHAT THE HELL DO YOU THINK YOU'RE DOING ?!?
IT'S NOT HIS FAULT! LIANA, COME AWAY!
D'MER, STOP! SHE SAVED YOUR LIFE!
I--I--!
D'MER!
SHARDS! WHAT'S HAPPENING!
. . . SEREN . . .
I...
DON'T TOUCH ME!
D'MER!
WAIT!
D'MER, OH PLEASE!
COME WITH ME, MY LORD.
COME AWAY...
IT'S OKAY, PRINCESS. I WOULDN'T LET HIM HURT YOU.
. . . WHAT THE HELL WAS THAT ALL ABOUT ?!?

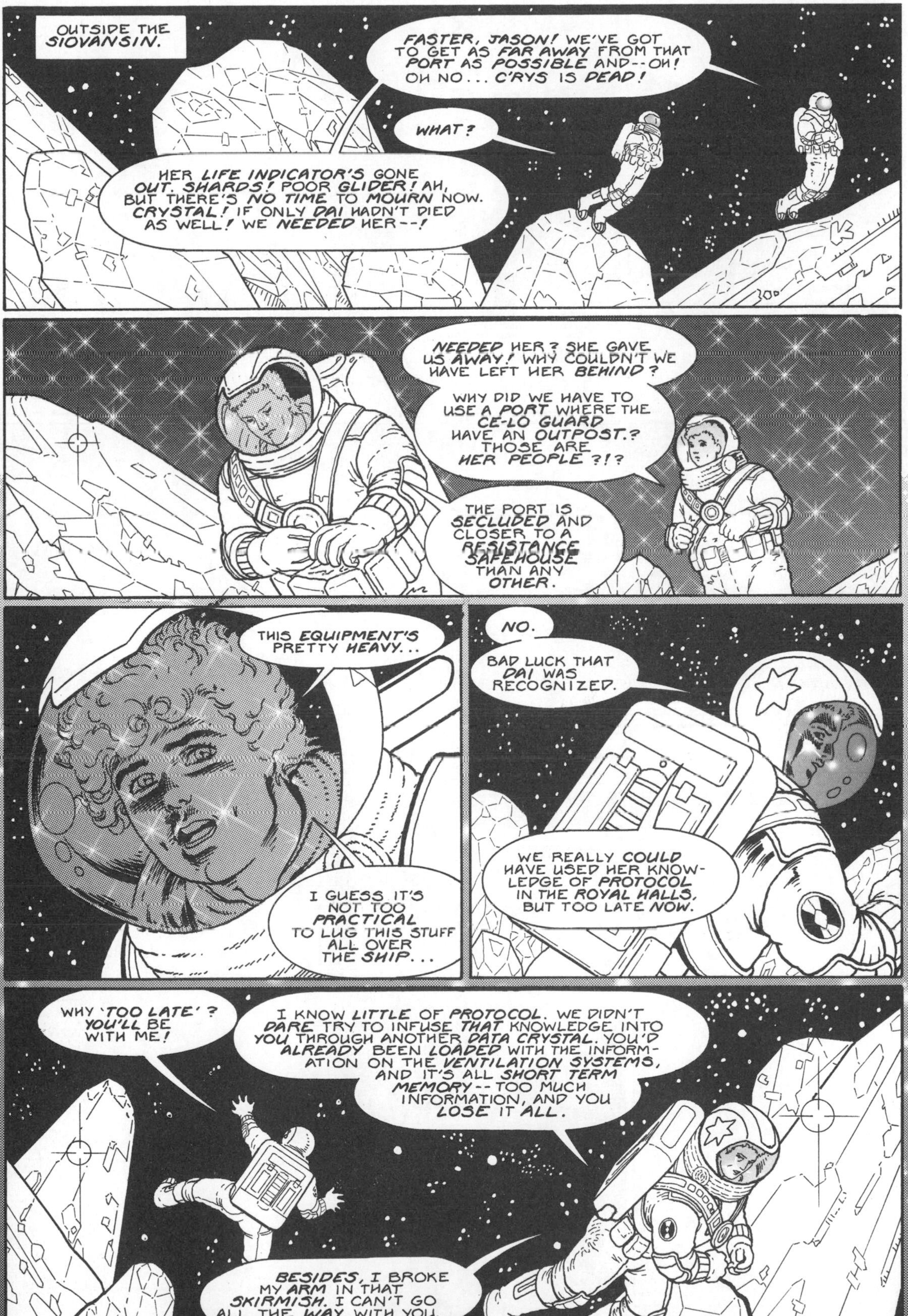
OUTSIDE THE SIOVANSIN.
FASTER, JASON! WE'VE GOT TO GET AS FAR AWAY FROM THAT PORT AS POSSIBLE AND--OH! OH NO... C'RYS IS DEAD!
WHAT?
HER LIFE INDICATOR'S GONE OUT. SHARDS! POOR GLIDER! AH, BUT THERE'S NO TIME TO MOURN NOW. CRYSTAL! IF ONLY DAI HADN'T DIED AS WELL! WE NEEDED HER--!
NEEDED HER? SHE GAVE US AWAY! WHY COULDN'T WE HAVE LEFT HER BEHIND?
WHY DID WE HAVE TO USE A PORT WHERE THE CE-LO GUARD HAVE AN OUTPOST.? THOSE ARE HER PEOPLE?!?
THE PORT IS SECLUDED AND CLOSER TO A RESISTANCE SAFEHOUSE THAN ANY OTHER.
THIS EQUIPMENT'S PRETTY HEAVY...
I GUESS IT'S NOT TOO PRACTICAL TO LUG THIS STUFF ALL OVER THE SHIP...
NO.
BAD LUCK THAT DAI WAS RECOGNIZED.
WE REALLY COULD HAVE USED HER KNOWLEDGE OF PROTOCOL IN THE ROYAL HALLS, BUT TOO LATE NOW.
WHY 'TOO LATE'? YOU'LL BE WITH ME!
I KNOW LITTLE OF PROTOCOL. WE DIDN'T DARE TRY TO INFUSE THAT KNOWLEDGE INTO YOU THROUGH ANOTHER DATA CRYSTAL. YOU'D ALREADY BEEN LOADED WITH THE INFORMATION ON THE VENTILATION SYSTEMS, AND IT'S ALL SHORT TERM MEMORY--TOO MUCH INFORMATION, AND YOU LOSE IT ALL.
BESIDES, I BROKE MY ARM IN THAT SKIRMISH. I CAN'T GO ALL THE WAY WITH YOU.

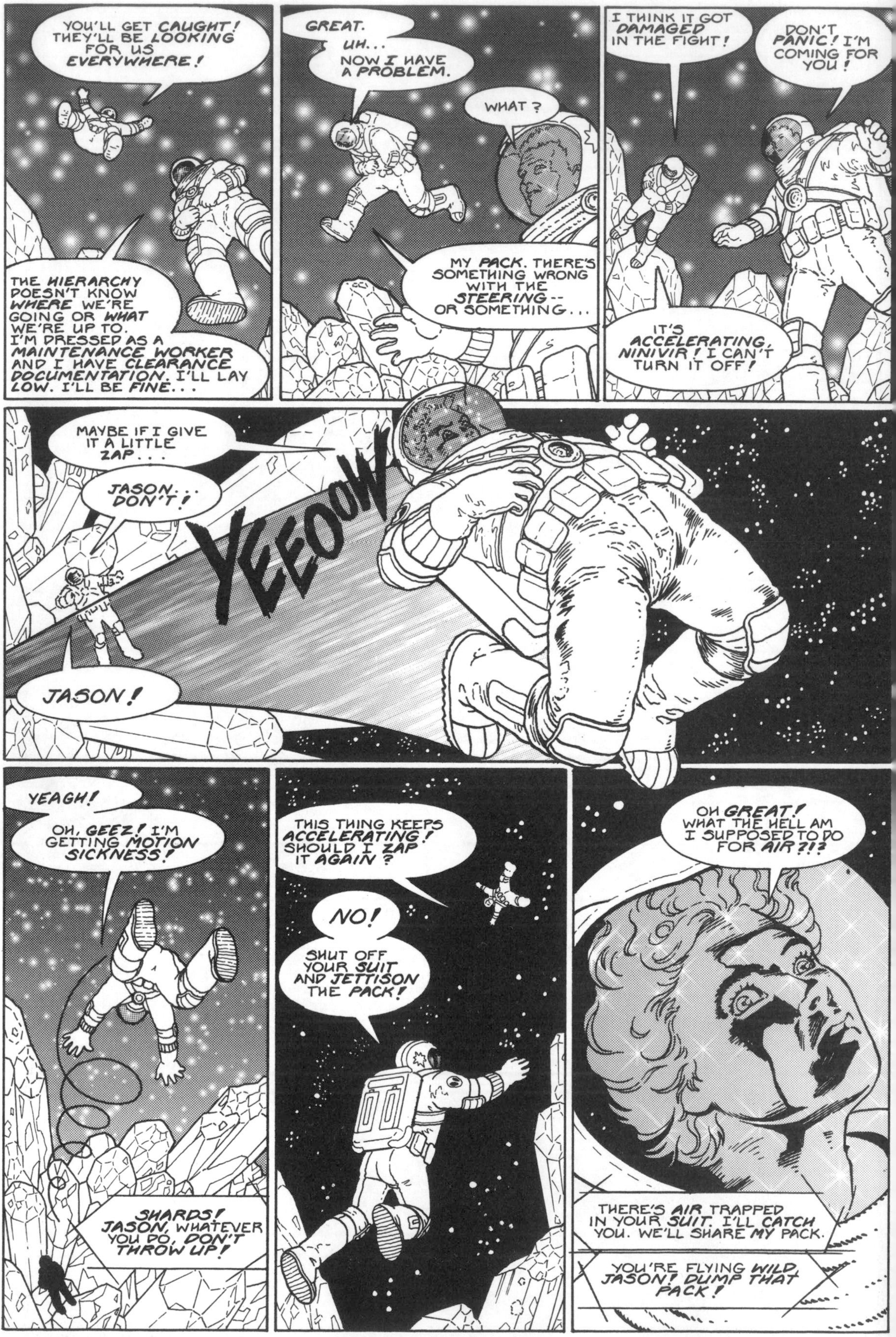
YOU'LL GET CAUGHT! THEY'LL BE LOOKING FOR US EVERYWHERE!
THE HIERARCHY DOESN'T KNOW WHERE WE'RE GOING OR WHAT WE'RE UP TO. I'M DRESSED AS A MAINTENANCE WORKER AND I HAVE CLEARANCE DOCUMENTATION. I'LL LAY LOW. I'LL BE FINE...
GREAT.
UH... NOW I HAVE A PROBLEM.
WHAT?
MY PACK. THERE'S SOMETHING WRONG WITH THE STEERING -- OR SOMETHING...
I THINK IT GOT DAMAGED IN THE FIGHT!
DON'T PANIC! I'M COMING FOR YOU!
IT'S ACCELERATING, NINIVIR! I CAN'T TURN IT OFF!
MAYBE IF I GIVE IT A LITTLE ZAP...
JASON... DON'T!
YEEOOW
JASON!
YEAGH!
OH, GEEZ! I'M GETTING MOTION SICKNESS!
SHARDS! JASON, WHATEVER YOU DO, DON'T THROW UP!
THIS THING KEEPS ACCELERATING! SHOULD I ZAP IT AGAIN?
NO!
SHUT OFF YOUR SUIT AND JETTISON THE PACK!
OH GREAT! WHAT THE HELL AM I SUPPOSED TO DO FOR AIR?!?
THERE'S AIR TRAPPED IN YOUR SUIT. I'LL CATCH YOU. WE'LL SHARE MY PACK.
YOU'RE FLYING WILD, JASON! DUMP THAT PACK!

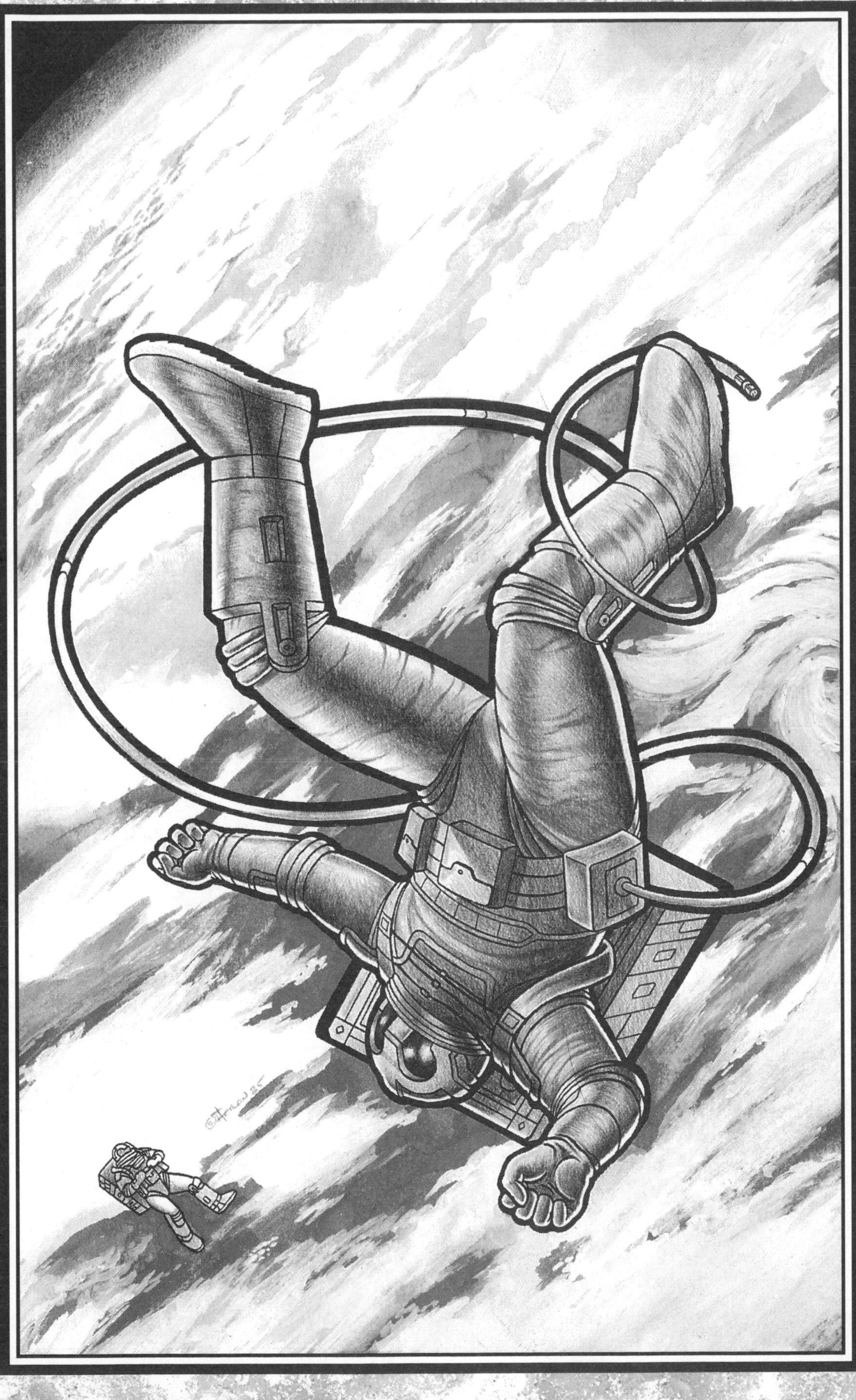

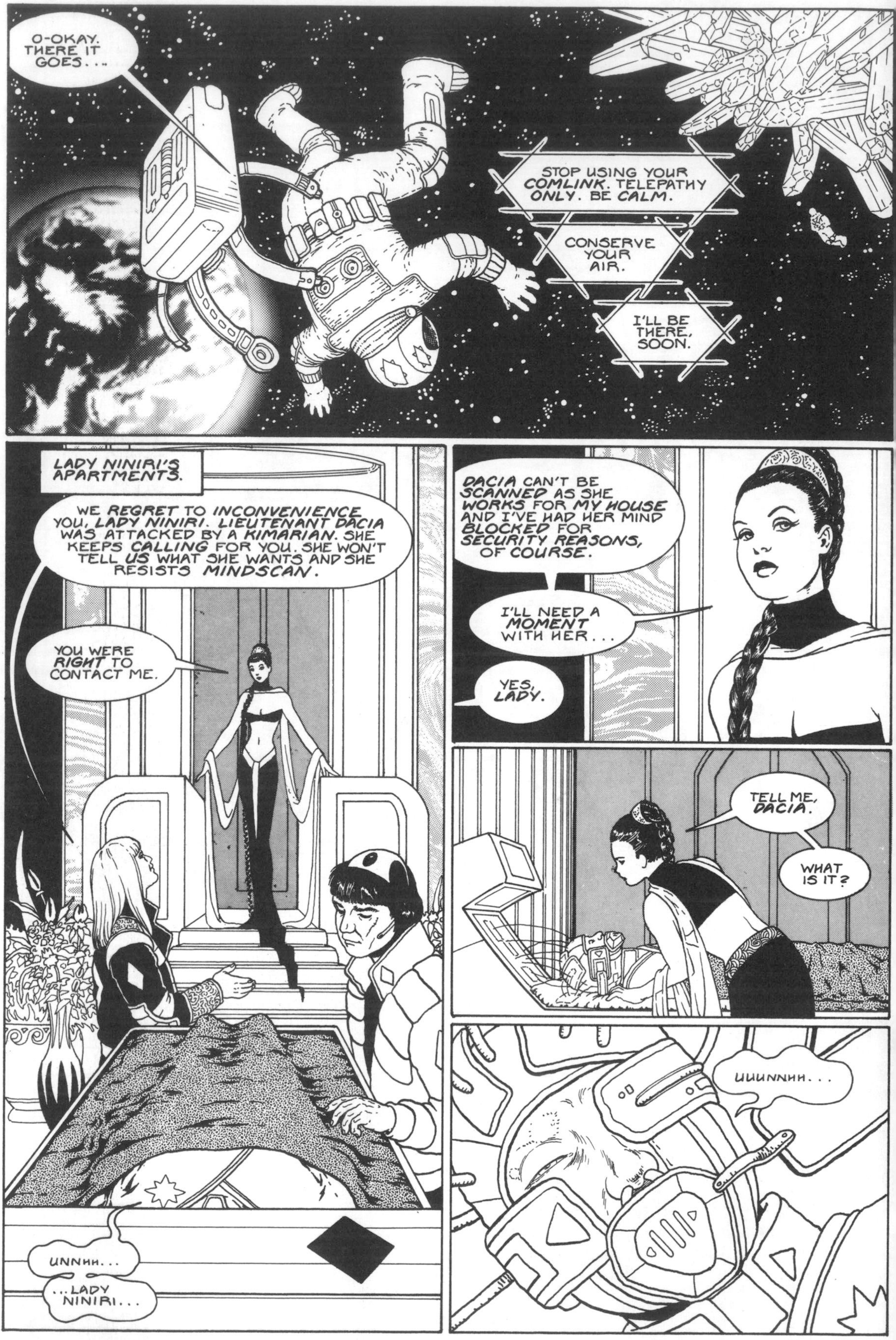

O-OKAY. THERE IT GOES...
STOP USING YOUR COMLINK. TELEPATHY ONLY. BE CALM.
CONSERVE YOUR AIR.
I'LL BE THERE, SOON.
LADY NINIRI'S APARTMENTS.
WE REGRET TO INCONVENIENCE YOU, LADY NINIRI. LIEUTENANT DACIA WAS ATTACKED BY A KIMARIAN. SHE KEEPS CALLING FOR YOU. SHE WON'T TELL US WHAT SHE WANTS AND SHE RESISTS MINDSCAN.
YOU WERE RIGHT TO CONTACT ME.
UNNHH...
...LADY NINIRI...
DACIA CAN'T BE SCANNED AS SHE WORKS FOR MY HOUSE AND I'VE HAD HER MIND BLOCKED FOR SECURITY REASONS, OF COURSE.
I'LL NEED A MOMENT WITH HER...
YES, LADY.
TELL ME, DACIA.
WHAT IS IT?
UUUNNHH...

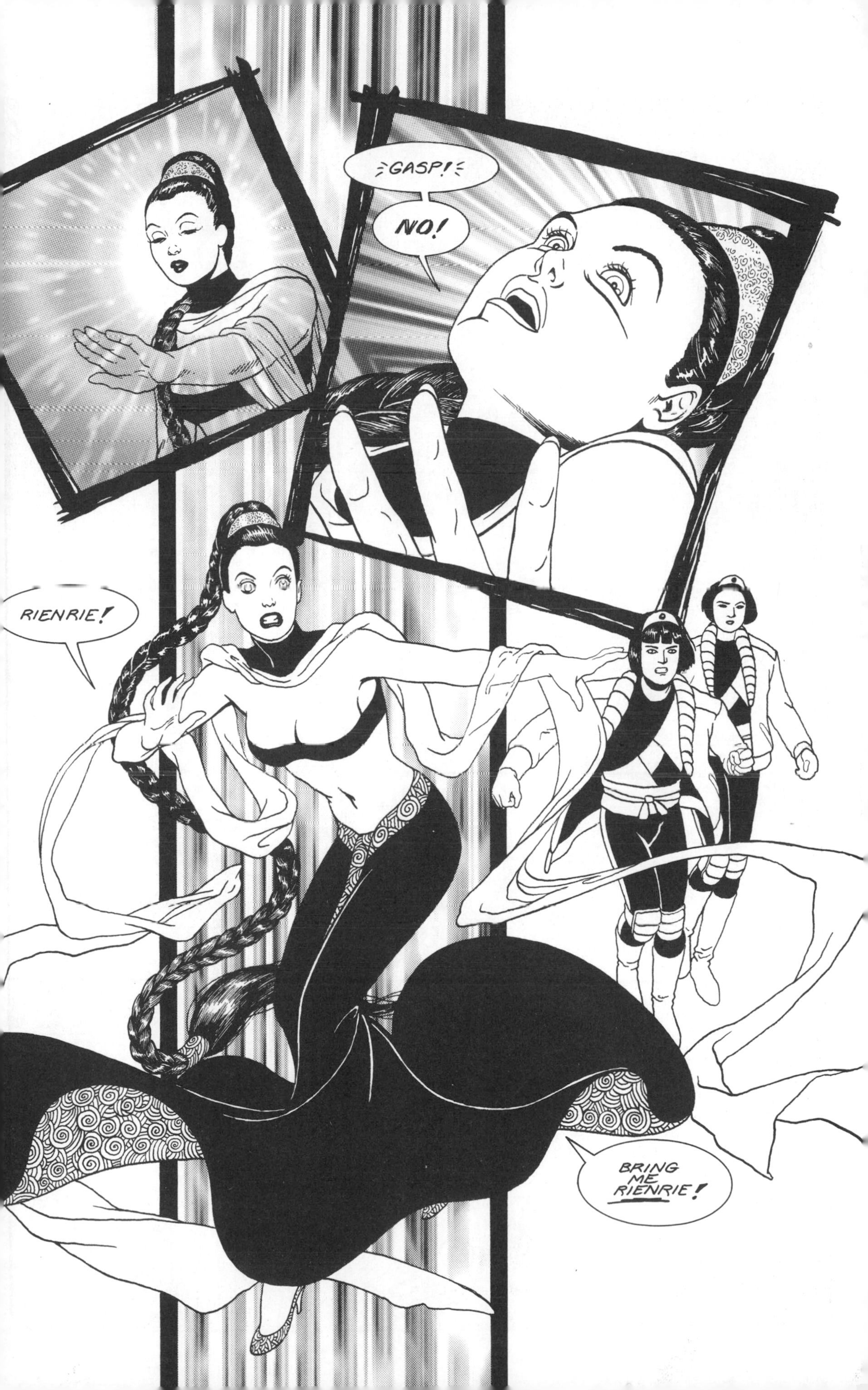
≈GASP!≈
NO!
RIENRIE!
BRING ME RIENRIE!

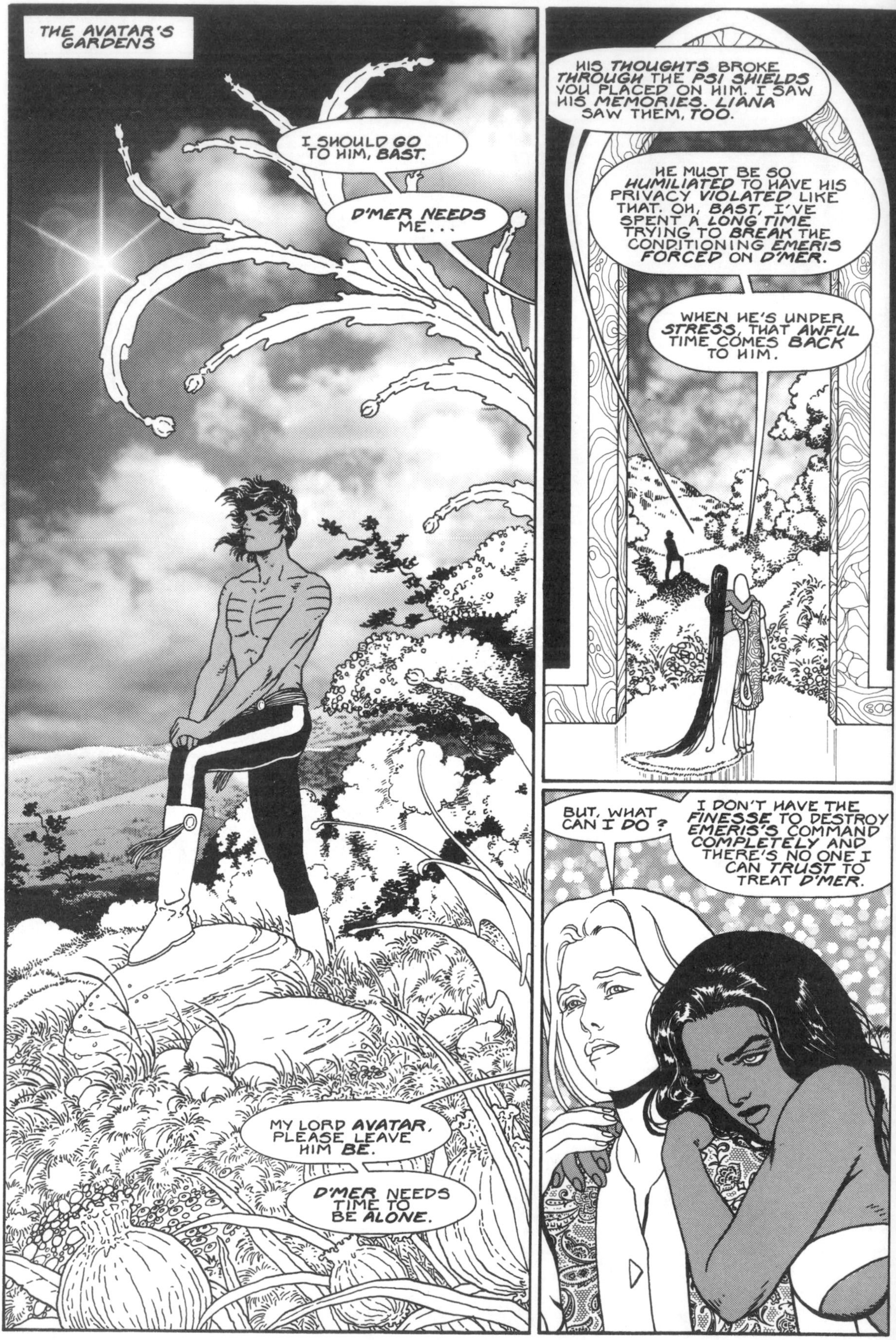
THE AVATAR'S GARDENS
I SHOULD GO TO HIM, BAST.
D'MER NEEDS ME...
MY LORD AVATAR, PLEASE LEAVE HIM BE.
D'MER NEEDS TIME TO BE ALONE.
HIS THOUGHTS BROKE THROUGH THE PSI SHIELDS YOU PLACED ON HIM. I SAW HIS MEMORIES. LIANA SAW THEM, TOO.
HE MUST BE SO HUMILIATED TO HAVE HIS PRIVACY VIOLATED LIKE THAT. OH, BAST, I'VE SPENT A LONG TIME TRYING TO BREAK THE CONDITIONING EMERIS FORCED ON D'MER.
WHEN HE'S UNDER STRESS, THAT AWFUL TIME COMES BACK TO HIM.
BUT, WHAT CAN I DO?
I DON'T HAVE THE FINESSE TO DESTROY EMERIS'S COMMAND COMPLETELY AND THERE'S NO ONE I CAN TRUST TO TREAT D'MER.

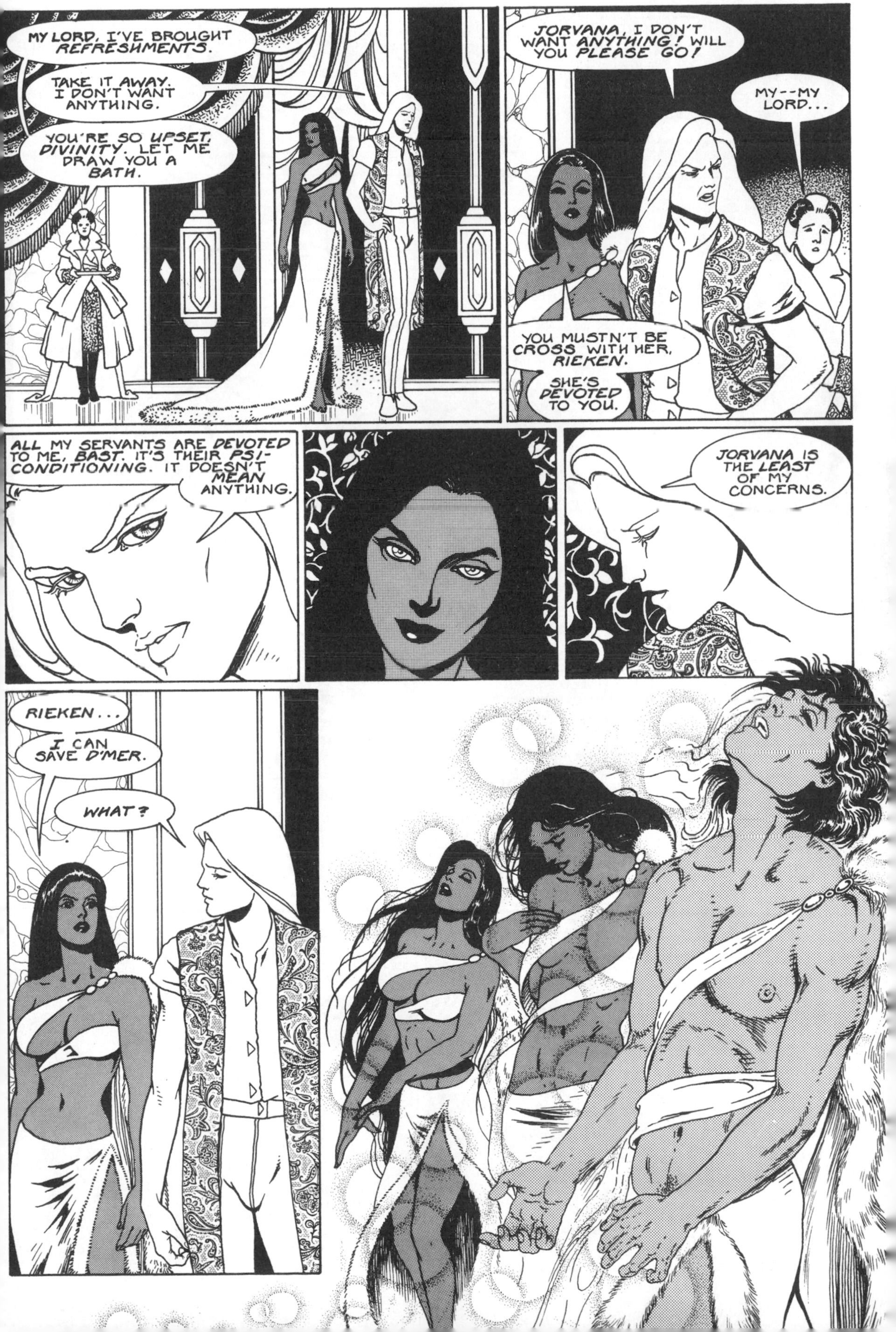
MY LORD, I'VE BROUGHT REFRESHMENTS.
TAKE IT AWAY. I DON'T WANT ANYTHING.
YOU'RE SO UPSET, DIVINITY. LET ME DRAW YOU A BATH.
JORVANA, I DON'T WANT ANYTHING! WILL YOU PLEASE GO!
MY--MY LORD...
YOU MUSTN'T BE CROSS WITH HER, RIEKEN.
SHE'S DEVOTED TO YOU.
ALL MY SERVANTS ARE DEVOTED TO ME, BAST. IT'S THEIR PSI-CONDITIONING. IT DOESN'T MEAN ANYTHING.
JORVANA IS THE LEAST OF MY CONCERNS.
RIEKEN...
I CAN SAVE D'MER.
WHAT?

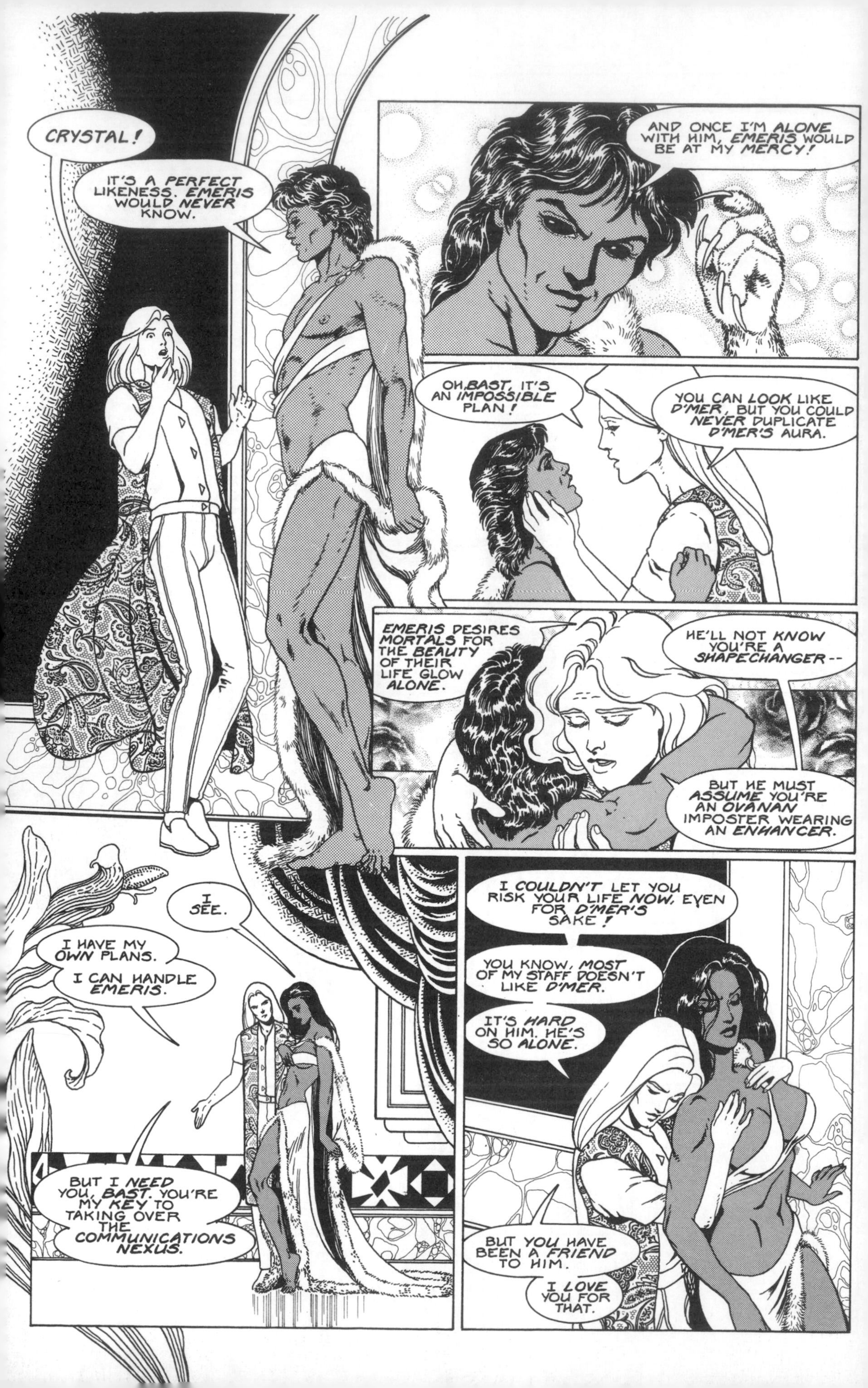
CRYSTAL!
IT'S A PERFECT LIKENESS. EMERIS WOULD NEVER KNOW.
AND ONCE I'M ALONE WITH HIM, EMERIS WOULD BE AT MY MERCY!
OH, BAST, IT'S AN IMPOSSIBLE PLAN!
YOU CAN LOOK LIKE D'MER, BUT YOU COULD NEVER DUPLICATE D'MER'S AURA.
EMERIS DESIRES MORTALS FOR THE BEAUTY OF THEIR LIFE GLOW ALONE.
HE'LL NOT KNOW YOU'RE A SHAPECHANGER--
BUT HE MUST ASSUME YOU'RE AN OVANAN IMPOSTER WEARING AN ENHANCER.
I SEE.
I HAVE MY OWN PLANS.
I CAN HANDLE EMERIS.
BUT I NEED YOU, BAST. YOU'RE MY KEY TO TAKING OVER THE COMMUNICATIONS NEXUS.
I COULDN'T LET YOU RISK YOUR LIFE NOW, EVEN FOR D'MER'S SAKE!
YOU KNOW, MOST OF MY STAFF DOESN'T LIKE D'MER.
IT'S HARD ON HIM. HE'S SO ALONE.
BUT YOU HAVE BEEN A FRIEND TO HIM.
I LOVE YOU FOR THAT.

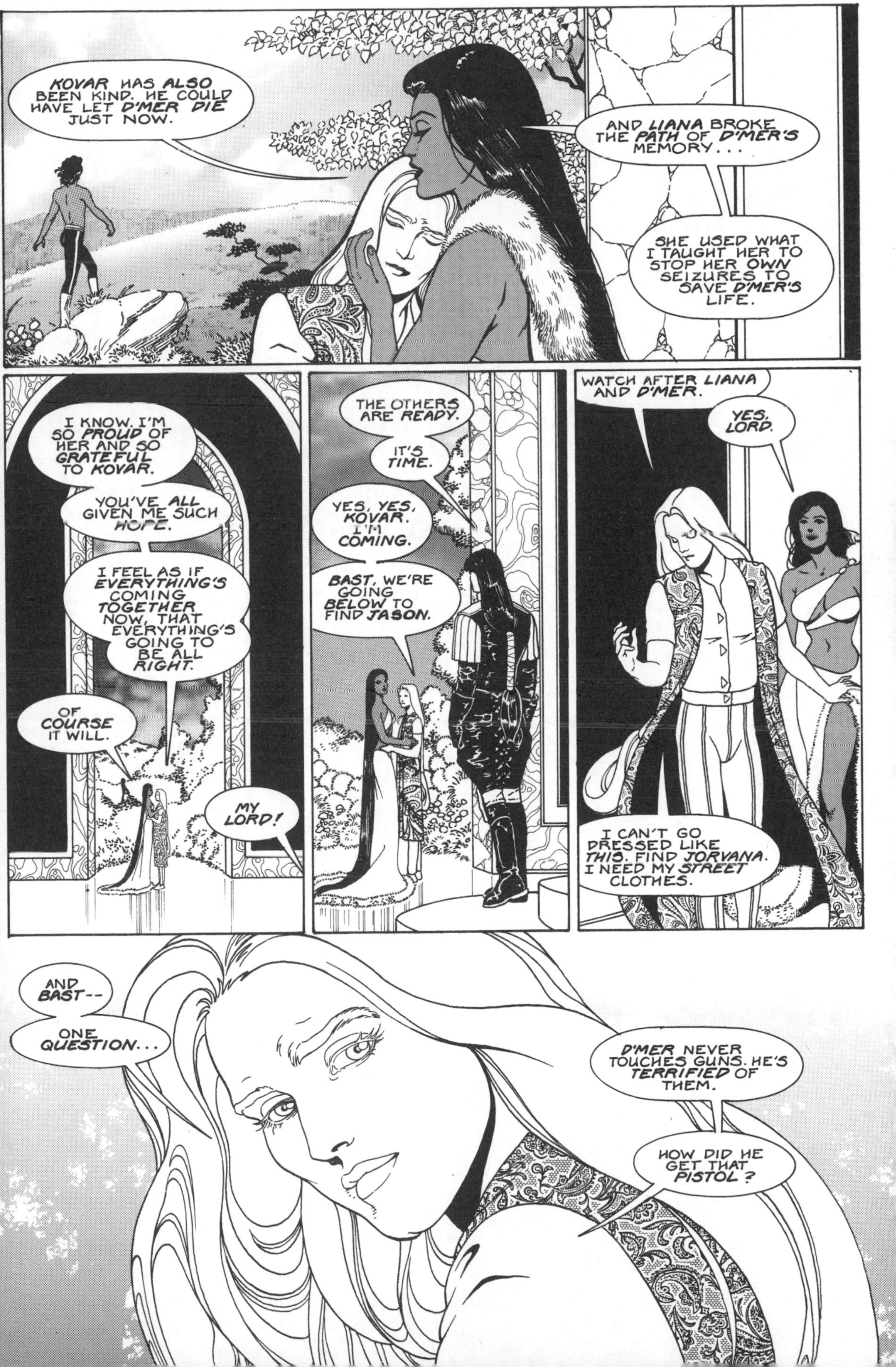
KOVAR HAS ALSO BEEN KIND. HE COULD HAVE LET D'MER DIE JUST NOW.
AND LIANA BROKE THE PATH OF D'MER'S MEMORY...
SHE USED WHAT I TAUGHT HER TO STOP HER OWN SEIZURES TO SAVE D'MER'S LIFE.
I KNOW. I'M SO PROUD OF HER AND SO GRATEFUL TO KOVAR.
YOU'VE ALL GIVEN ME SUCH HOPE.
I FEEL AS IF EVERYTHING'S COMING TOGETHER NOW, THAT EVERYTHING'S GOING TO BE ALL RIGHT.
OF COURSE IT WILL.
MY LORD!
THE OTHERS ARE READY.
IT'S TIME.
YES, YES, KOVAR. I'M COMING.
BAST, WE'RE GOING BELOW TO FIND JASON.
WATCH AFTER LIANA AND D'MER.
YES, LORD.
I CAN'T GO DRESSED LIKE THIS. FIND JORVANA. I NEED MY STREET CLOTHES.
AND BAST--
ONE QUESTION...
D'MER NEVER TOUCHES GUNS. HE'S TERRIFIED OF THEM.
HOW DID HE GET THAT PISTOL?

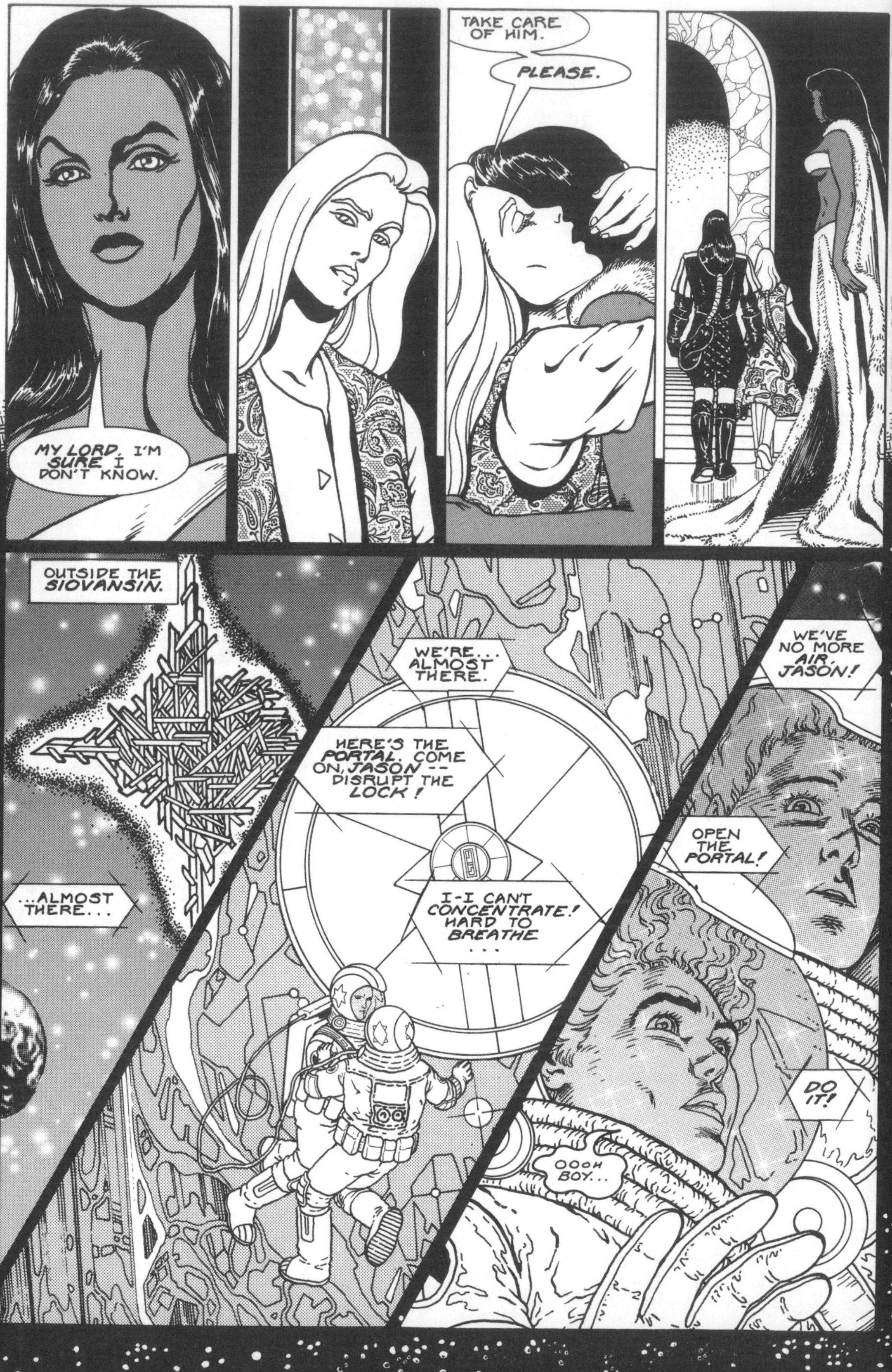
MY LORD, I'M SURE I DON'T KNOW.
TAKE CARE OF HIM.
PLEASE.
OUTSIDE THE SIOVANSIN.
...ALMOST THERE...
WE'RE... ALMOST THERE.
HERE'S THE PORTAL. COME ON, JASON -- DISRUPT THE LOCK!
I-I CAN'T CONCENTRATE! HARD TO BREATHE ...
WE'VE NO MORE AIR, JASON!
OPEN THE PORTAL!
DO IT!
OOOH BOY...

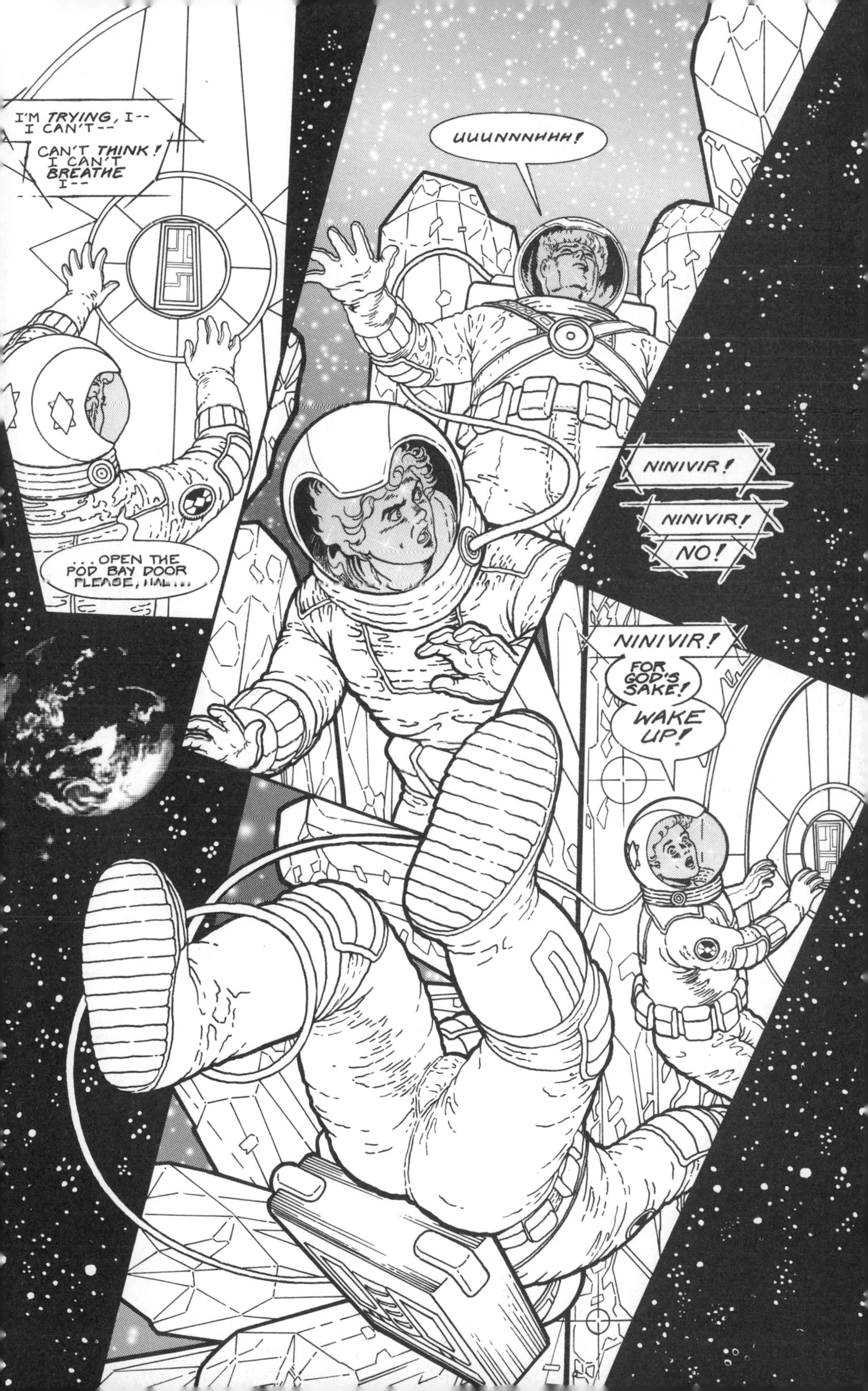
I'M TRYING, I-- I CAN'T--
CAN'T THINK! I CAN'T BREATHE I--
...OPEN THE POD BAY DOOR PLEASE, HAL...
UUUNNNHHH!
NINIVIR!
NINIVIR!
NO!
NINIVIR!
FOR GOD'S SAKE!
WAKE UP!

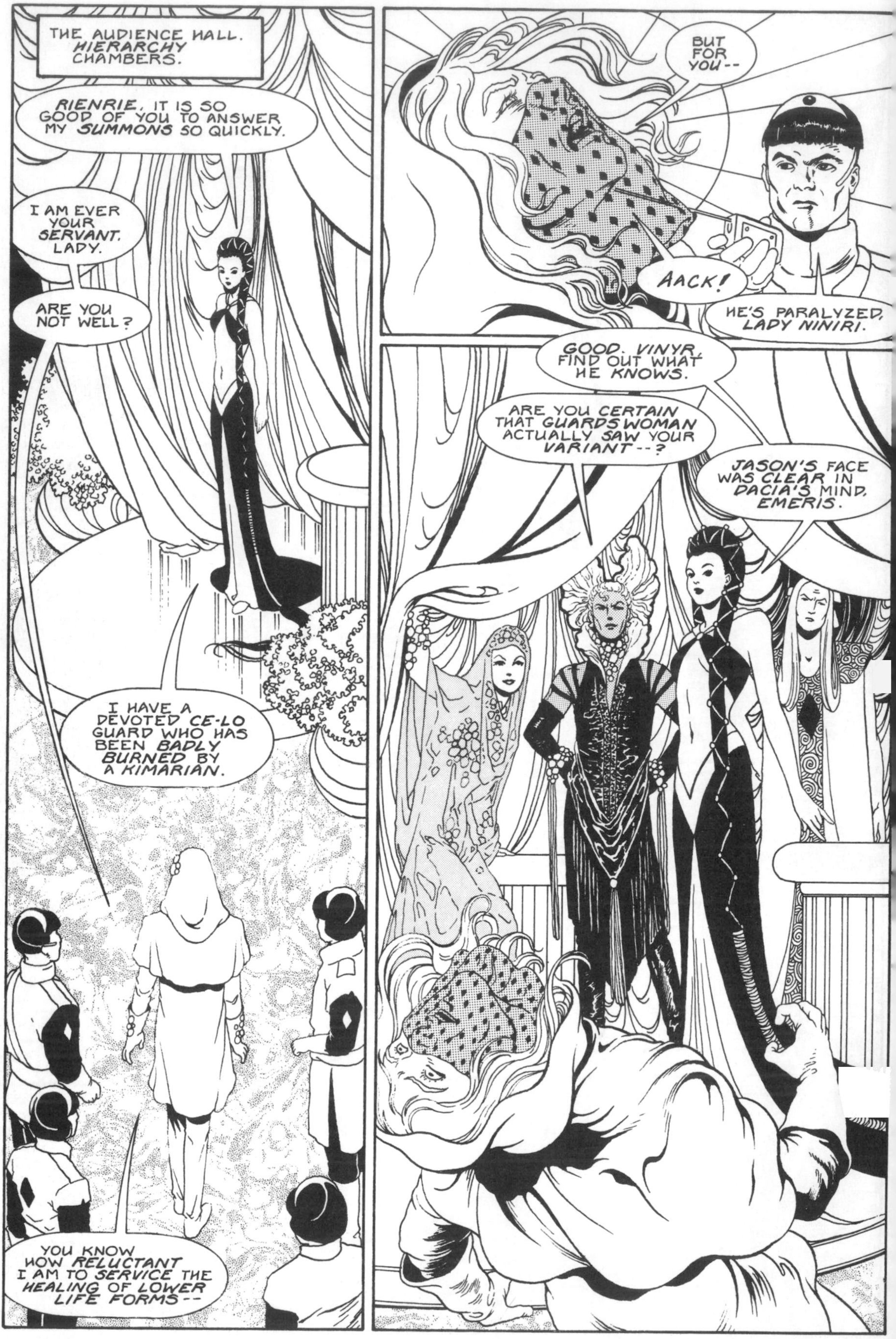
THE AUDIENCE HALL. HIERARCHY CHAMBERS.
RIENRIE, IT IS SO GOOD OF YOU TO ANSWER MY SUMMONS SO QUICKLY.
I AM EVER YOUR SERVANT, LADY.
ARE YOU NOT WELL?
I HAVE A DEVOTED CE-LO GUARD WHO HAS BEEN BADLY BURNED BY A KIMARIAN.
YOU KNOW HOW RELUCTANT I AM TO SERVICE THE HEALING OF LOWER LIFE FORMS--
BUT FOR YOU--
AACK!
HE'S PARALYZED, LADY NINIRI.
GOOD. VINYR, FIND OUT WHAT HE KNOWS.
ARE YOU CERTAIN THAT GUARDSWOMAN ACTUALLY SAW YOUR VARIANT--?
JASON'S FACE WAS CLEAR IN DACIA'S MIND, EMERIS.

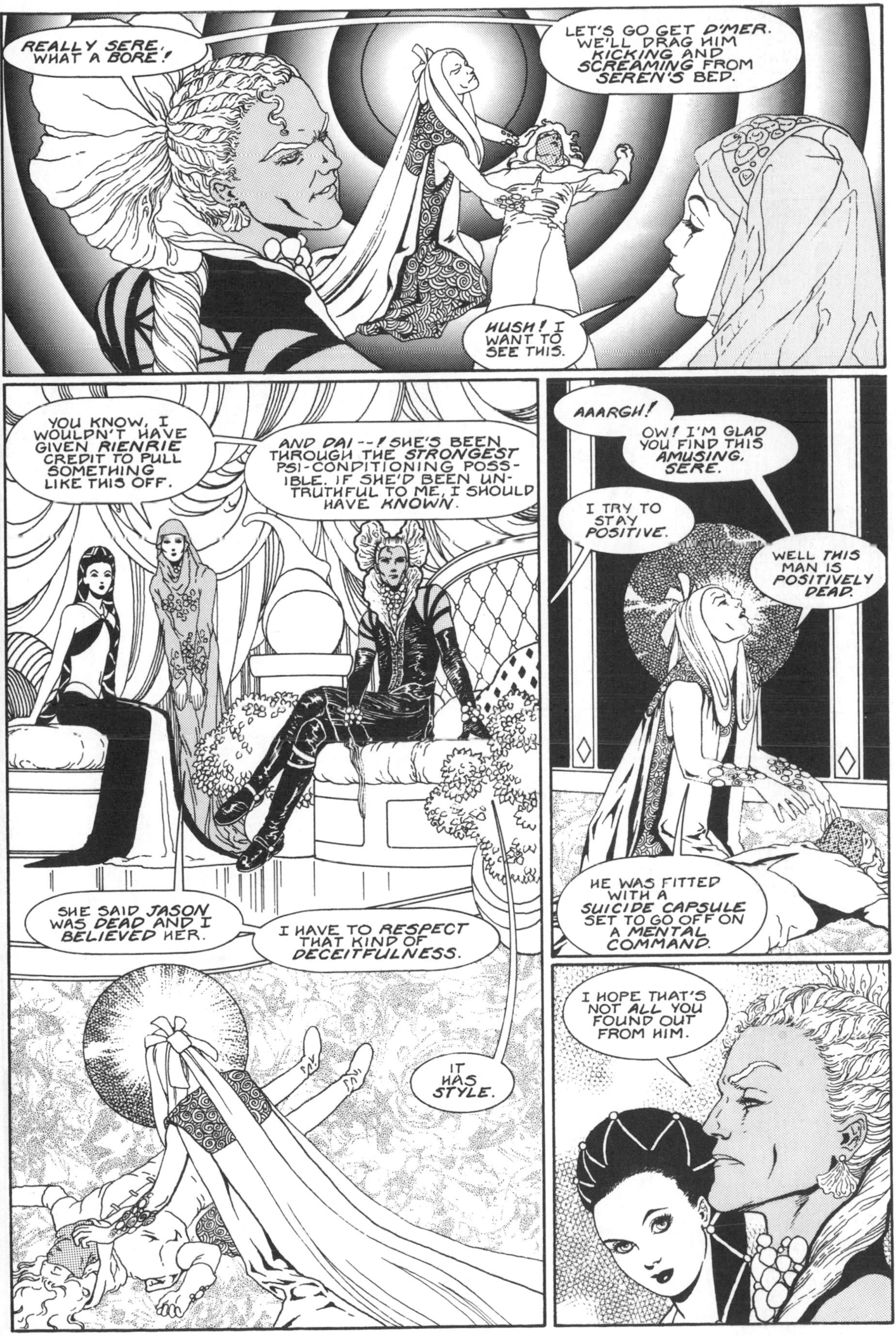
REALLY SERE, WHAT A BORE!
LET'S GO GET D'MER. WE'LL DRAG HIM KICKING AND SCREAMING FROM SEREN'S BED.
HUSH! I WANT TO SEE THIS.
YOU KNOW, I WOULDN'T HAVE GIVEN RIENRIE CREDIT TO PULL SOMETHING LIKE THIS OFF.
AND DAI--! SHE'S BEEN THROUGH THE STRONGEST PSI-CONDITIONING POSSIBLE. IF SHE'D BEEN UNTRUTHFUL TO ME, I SHOULD HAVE KNOWN.
SHE SAID JASON WAS DEAD AND I BELIEVED HER.
I HAVE TO RESPECT THAT KIND OF DECEITFULNESS.
IT HAS STYLE.
AAARGH!
OW! I'M GLAD YOU FIND THIS AMUSING, SERE.
I TRY TO STAY POSITIVE.
WELL THIS MAN IS POSITIVELY DEAD.
HE WAS FITTED WITH A SUICIDE CAPSULE SET TO GO OFF ON A MENTAL COMMAND.
I HOPE THAT'S NOT ALL YOU FOUND OUT FROM HIM.

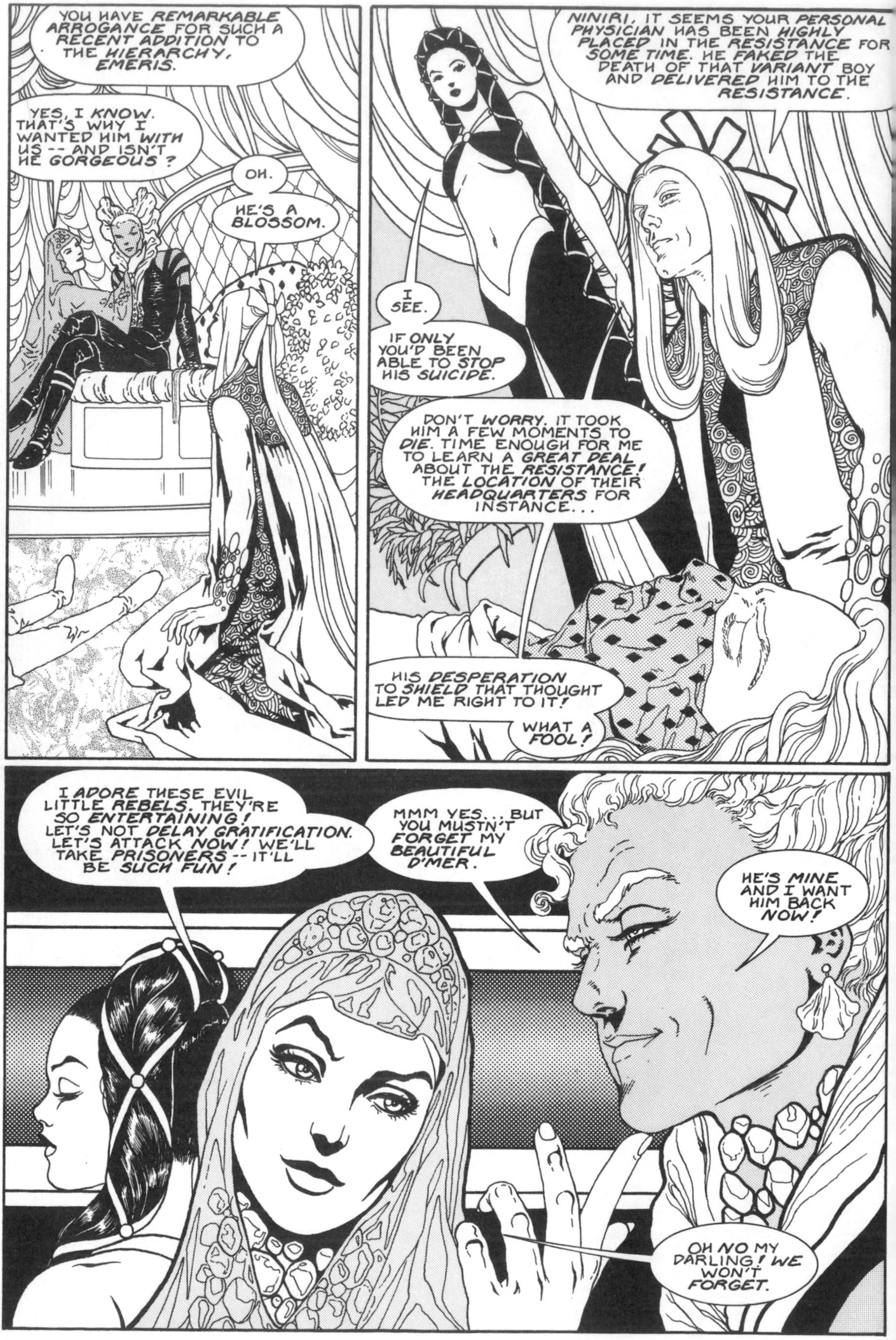
YOU HAVE REMARKABLE ARROGANCE FOR SUCH A RECENT ADDITION TO THE HIERARCHY, EMERIS.
YES, I KNOW. THAT'S WHY I WANTED HIM WITH US -- AND ISN'T HE GORGEOUS?
OH.
HE'S A BLOSSOM.
NINIRI, IT SEEMS YOUR PERSONAL PHYSICIAN HAS BEEN HIGHLY PLACED IN THE RESISTANCE FOR SOME TIME. HE FAKED THE DEATH OF THAT VARIANT BOY AND DELIVERED HIM TO THE RESISTANCE.
I SEE.
IF ONLY YOU'D BEEN ABLE TO STOP HIS SUICIDE.
DON'T WORRY. IT TOOK HIM A FEW MOMENTS TO DIE. TIME ENOUGH FOR ME TO LEARN A GREAT DEAL ABOUT THE RESISTANCE! THE LOCATION OF THEIR HEADQUARTERS FOR INSTANCE...
HIS DESPERATION TO SHIELD THAT THOUGHT LED ME RIGHT TO IT!
WHAT A FOOL!
I ADORE THESE EVIL LITTLE REBELS. THEY'RE SO ENTERTAINING! LET'S NOT DELAY GRATIFICATION. LET'S ATTACK NOW! WE'LL TAKE PRISONERS -- IT'LL BE SUCH FUN!
MMM YES... BUT YOU MUSTN'T FORGET MY BEAUTIFUL D'MER.
HE'S MINE AND I WANT HIM BACK NOW!
OH NO MY DARLING! WE WON'T FORGET.

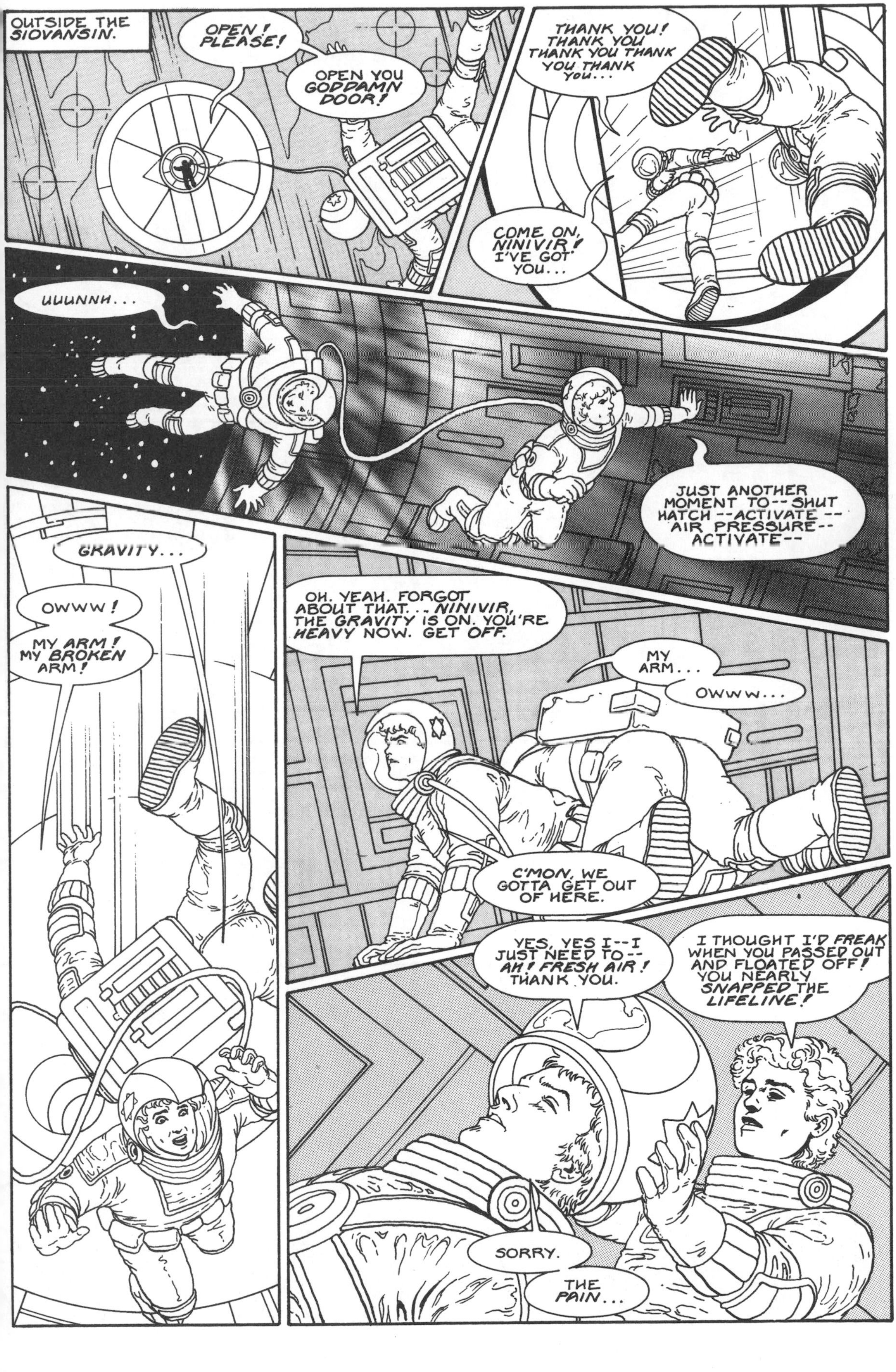
OUTSIDE THE SIOVANSIN.
OPEN! PLEASE!
OPEN YOU GODDAMN DOOR!
THANK YOU! THANK YOU THANK YOU THANK YOU THANK YOU...
COME ON, NINIVIR! I'VE GOT YOU...
UUUNNH...
JUST ANOTHER MOMENT TO--SHUT HATCH--ACTIVATE--AIR PRESSURE--ACTIVATE--
GRAVITY...
OWWW!
MY ARM! MY BROKEN ARM!
OH. YEAH. FORGOT ABOUT THAT... NINIVIR, THE GRAVITY IS ON. YOU'RE HEAVY NOW. GET OFF.
MY ARM...
OWWW...
C'MON, WE GOTTA GET OUT OF HERE.
YES, YES I--I JUST NEED TO--AH! FRESH AIR! THANK YOU.
I THOUGHT I'D FREAK WHEN YOU PASSED OUT AND FLOATED OFF! YOU NEARLY SNAPPED THE LIFELINE!
SORRY.
THE PAIN...

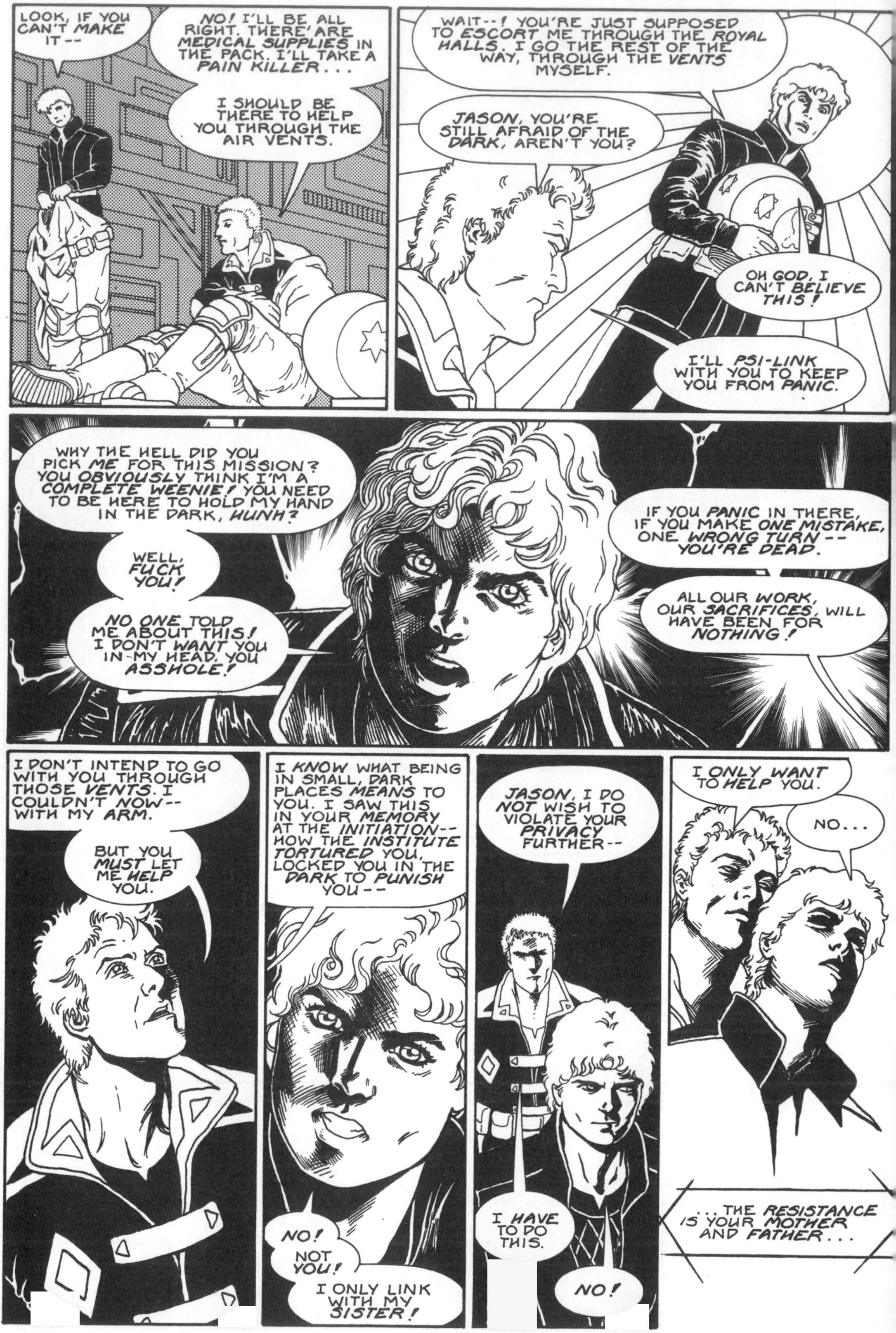
LOOK, IF YOU CAN'T MAKE IT --
NO! I'LL BE ALL RIGHT. THERE' ARE MEDICAL SUPPLIES IN THE PACK. I'LL TAKE A PAIN KILLER . . .
I SHOULD BE THERE TO HELP YOU THROUGH THE AIR VENTS.
WAIT--! YOU'RE JUST SUPPOSED TO ESCORT ME THROUGH THE ROYAL HALLS. I GO THE REST OF THE WAY, THROUGH THE VENTS MYSELF.
JASON, YOU'RE STILL AFRAID OF THE DARK, AREN'T YOU?
OH GOD, I CAN'T BELIEVE THIS!
I'LL PSI-LINK WITH YOU TO KEEP YOU FROM PANIC.
WHY THE HELL DID YOU PICK ME FOR THIS MISSION? YOU OBVIOUSLY THINK I'M A COMPLETE WEENIE! YOU NEED TO BE HERE TO HOLD MY HAND IN THE DARK, HUNH?
WELL, FUCK YOU!
NO ONE TOLD ME ABOUT THIS! I DON'T WANT YOU IN MY HEAD, YOU ASSHOLE!
IF YOU PANIC IN THERE, IF YOU MAKE ONE MISTAKE, ONE WRONG TURN -- YOU'RE DEAD.
ALL OUR WORK, OUR SACRIFICES, WILL HAVE BEEN FOR NOTHING!
I DON'T INTEND TO GO WITH YOU THROUGH THOSE VENTS. I COULDN'T NOW-- WITH MY ARM.
BUT YOU MUST LET ME HELP YOU.
I KNOW WHAT BEING IN SMALL, DARK PLACES MEANS TO YOU. I SAW THIS IN YOUR MEMORY AT THE INITIATION-- HOW THE INSTITUTE TORTURED YOU, LOCKED YOU IN THE DARK TO PUNISH YOU--
NO! NOT YOU!
I ONLY LINK WITH MY SISTER!
JASON, I DO NOT WISH TO VIOLATE YOUR PRIVACY FURTHER--
I HAVE TO DO THIS.
NO!
I ONLY WANT TO HELP YOU.
NO...
... THE RESISTANCE IS YOUR MOTHER AND FATHER...

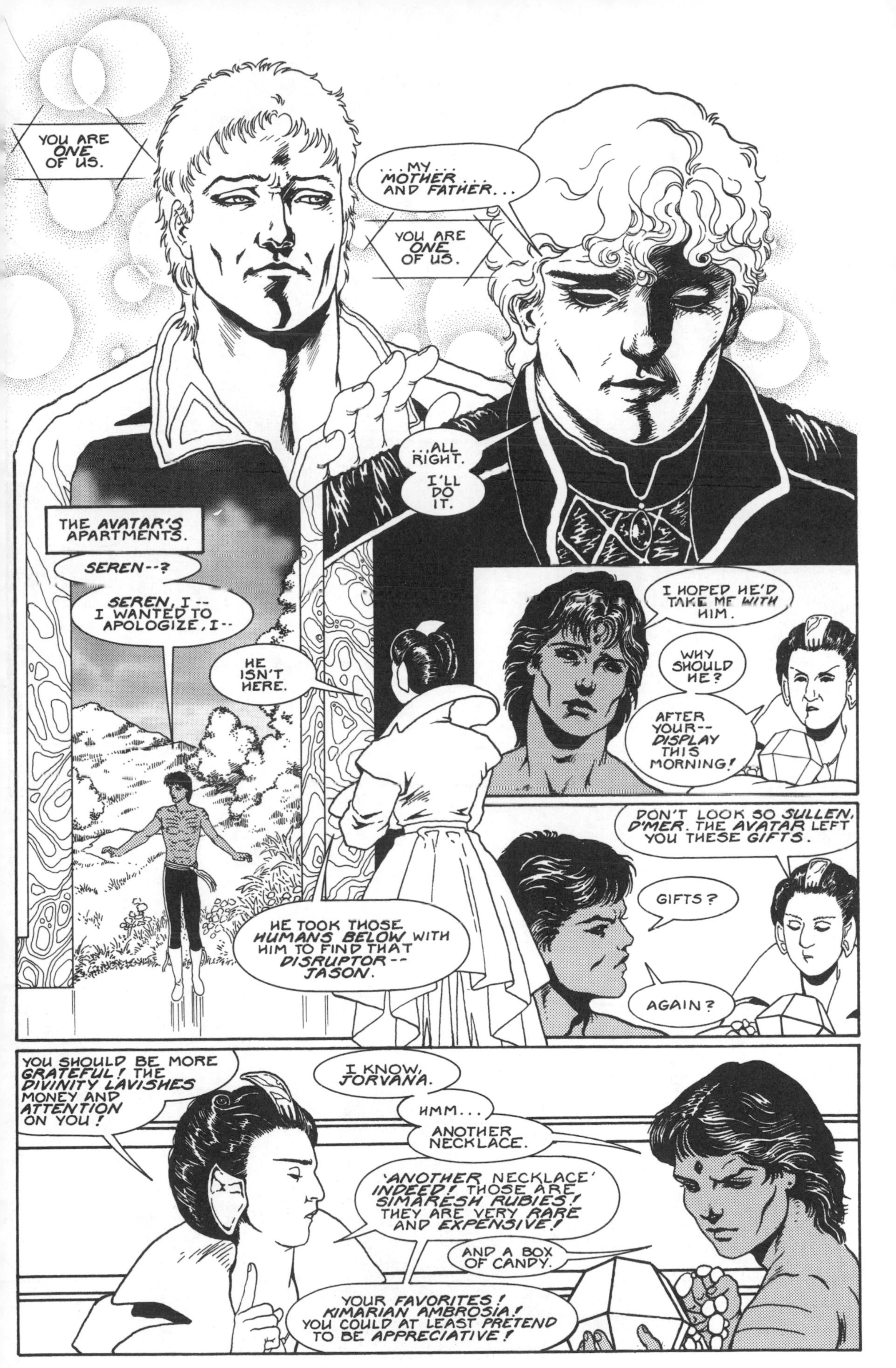
YOU ARE ONE OF US.
...MY... MOTHER... AND FATHER...
YOU ARE ONE OF US.
...ALL RIGHT.
I'LL DO IT.
THE AVATAR'S APARTMENTS.
SEREN--?
SEREN, I-- I WANTED TO APOLOGIZE, I--
HE ISN'T HERE.
HE TOOK THOSE HUMANS BELOW WITH HIM TO FIND THAT DISRUPTOR-- JASON.
I HOPED HE'D TAKE ME WITH HIM.
WHY SHOULD HE?
AFTER YOUR-- DISPLAY THIS MORNING!
DON'T LOOK SO SULLEN, D'MER. THE AVATAR LEFT YOU THESE GIFTS.
GIFTS?
AGAIN?
YOU SHOULD BE MORE GRATEFUL! THE DIVINITY LAVISHES MONEY AND ATTENTION ON YOU!
I KNOW, JORVANA.
HMM...
ANOTHER NECKLACE.
'ANOTHER NECKLACE' INDEED! THOSE ARE SIMARESH RUBIES! THEY ARE VERY RARE AND EXPENSIVE!
AND A BOX OF CANDY.
YOUR FAVORITES! KIMARIAN AMBROSIA! YOU COULD AT LEAST PRETEND TO BE APPRECIATIVE!

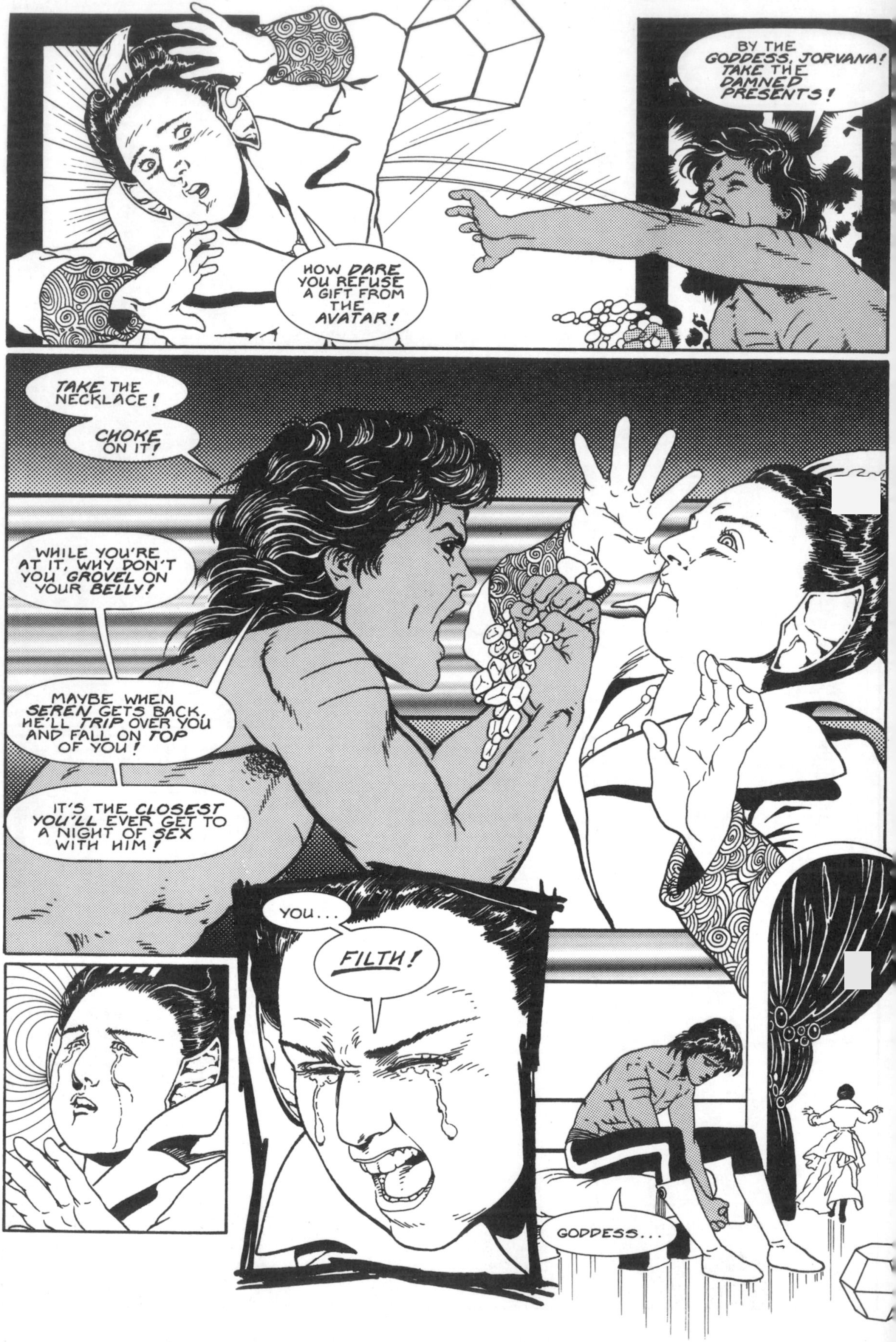
BY THE GODDESS, JORVANA! TAKE THE DAMNED PRESENTS!
HOW DARE YOU REFUSE A GIFT FROM THE AVATAR!
TAKE THE NECKLACE!
CHOKE ON IT!
WHILE YOU'RE AT IT, WHY DON'T YOU GROVEL ON YOUR BELLY!
MAYBE WHEN SEREN GETS BACK, HE'LL TRIP OVER YOU AND FALL ON TOP OF YOU!
IT'S THE CLOSEST YOU'LL EVER GET TO A NIGHT OF SEX WITH HIM!
YOU...
FILTH!
GODDESS...

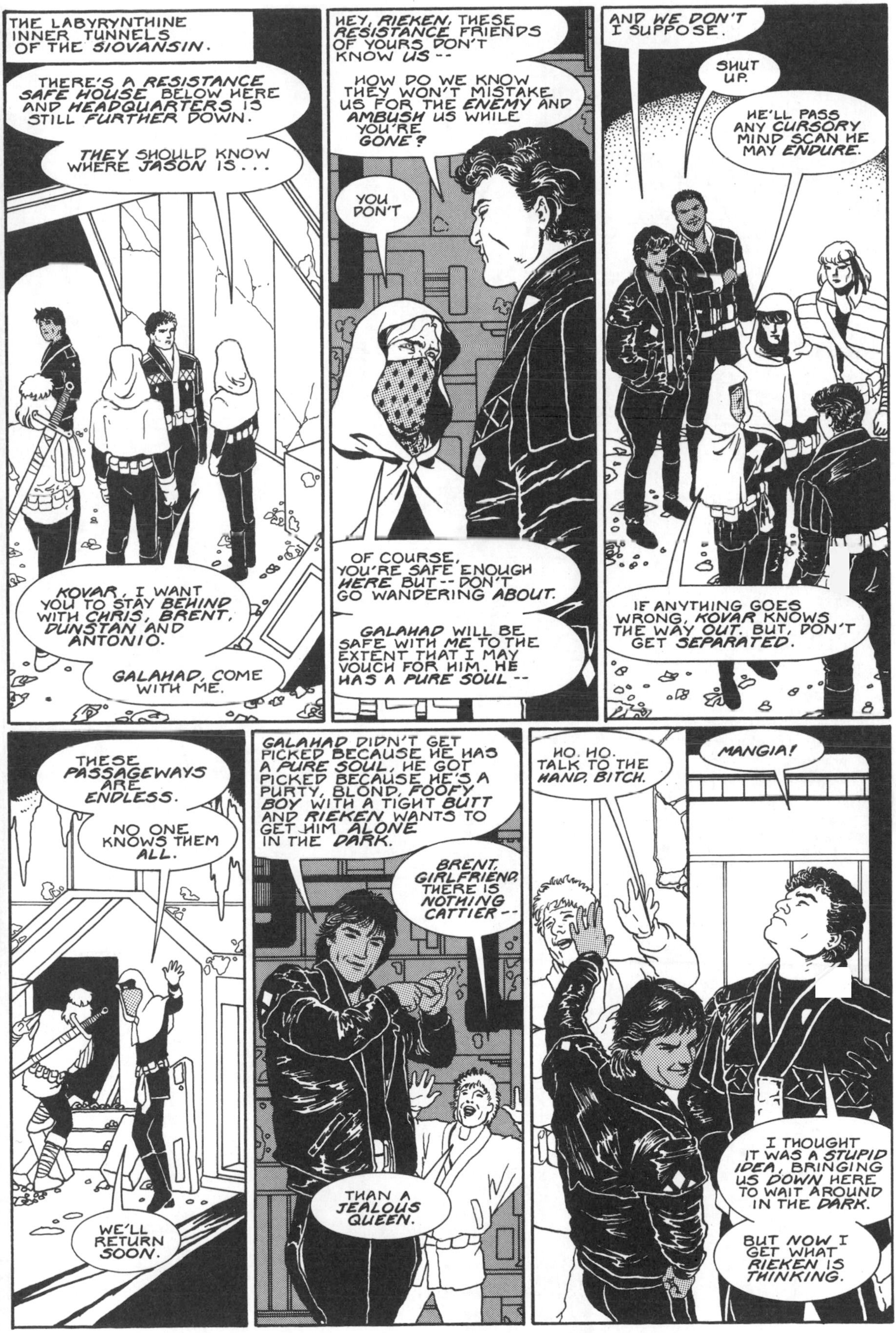
THE LABYRYNTHINE INNER TUNNELS OF THE SIOVANSIN.
THERE'S A RESISTANCE SAFE HOUSE BELOW HERE AND HEADQUARTERS IS STILL FURTHER DOWN.
THEY SHOULD KNOW WHERE JASON IS...
KOVAR, I WANT YOU TO STAY BEHIND WITH CHRIS, BRENT, DUNSTAN AND ANTONIO.
GALAHAD, COME WITH ME.
HEY, RIEKEN, THESE RESISTANCE FRIENDS OF YOURS DON'T KNOW US--
HOW DO WE KNOW THEY WON'T MISTAKE US FOR THE ENEMY AND AMBUSH US WHILE YOU'RE GONE?
YOU DON'T
OF COURSE, YOU'RE SAFE ENOUGH HERE BUT--DON'T GO WANDERING ABOUT.
GALAHAD WILL BE SAFE WITH ME TO THE EXTENT THAT I MAY VOUCH FOR HIM. HE HAS A PURE SOUL--
AND WE DON'T I SUPPOSE.
SHUT UP.
HE'LL PASS ANY CURSORY MIND SCAN HE MAY ENDURE.
IF ANYTHING GOES WRONG, KOVAR KNOWS THE WAY OUT. BUT, DON'T GET SEPARATED.
THESE PASSAGEWAYS ARE ENDLESS.
NO ONE KNOWS THEM ALL.
WE'LL RETURN SOON.
GALAHAD DIDN'T GET PICKED BECAUSE HE HAS A PURE SOUL, HE GOT PICKED BECAUSE HE'S A PURTY, BLOND, FOOFY BOY WITH A TIGHT BUTT AND RIEKEN WANTS TO GET HIM ALONE IN THE DARK.
BRENT, GIRLFRIEND, THERE IS NOTHING CATTIER--
THAN A JEALOUS QUEEN.
HO. HO. TALK TO THE HAND, BITCH.
MANGIA!
I THOUGHT IT WAS A STUPID IDEA, BRINGING US DOWN HERE TO WAIT AROUND IN THE DARK.
BUT NOW I GET WHAT RIEKEN IS THINKING.

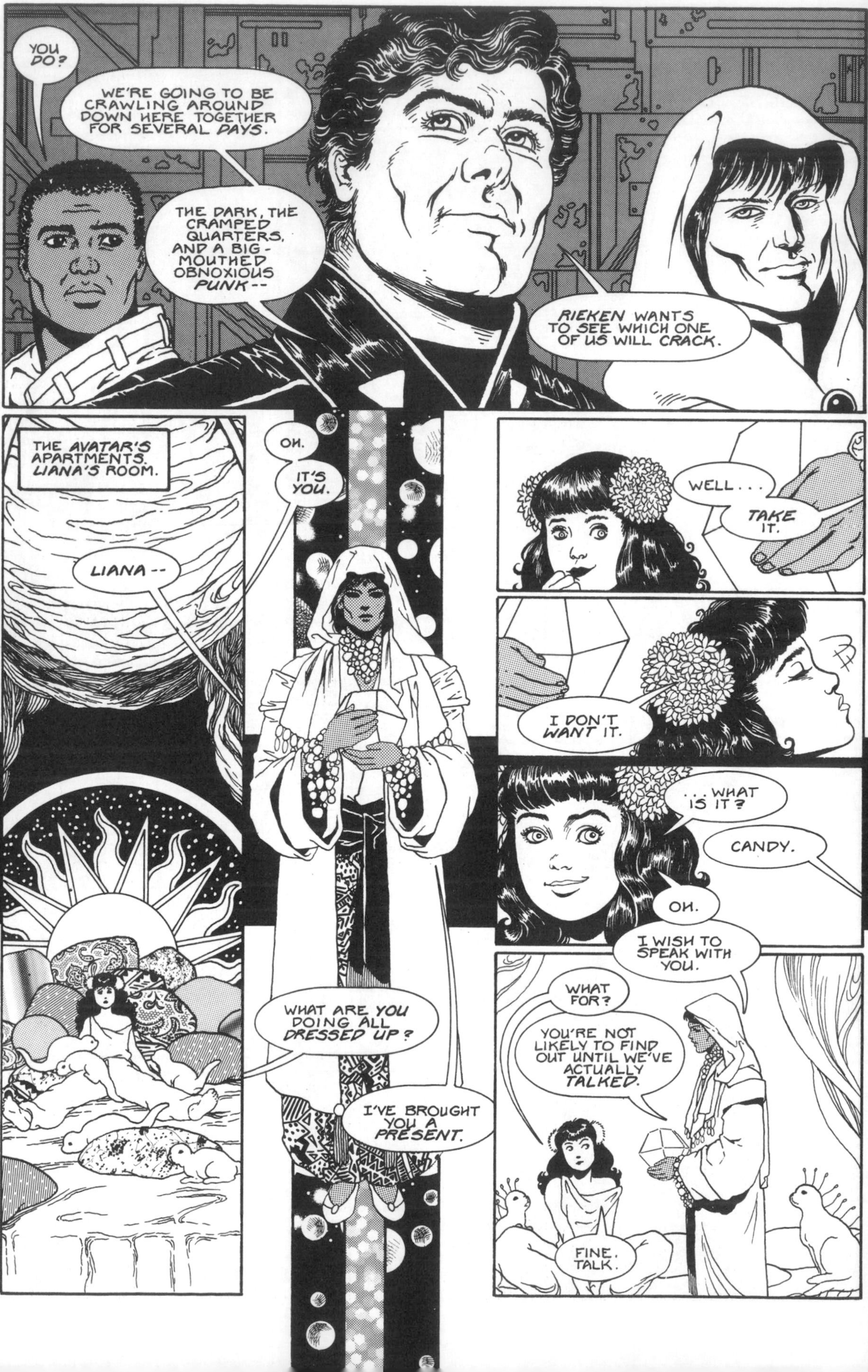
YOU DO?
WE'RE GOING TO BE CRAWLING AROUND DOWN HERE TOGETHER FOR SEVERAL DAYS.
THE DARK, THE CRAMPED QUARTERS, AND A BIG-MOUTHED OBNOXIOUS PUNK--
RIEKEN WANTS TO SEE WHICH ONE OF US WILL CRACK.
THE AVATAR'S APARTMENTS. LIANA'S ROOM.
LIANA--
OH.
IT'S YOU.
WHAT ARE YOU DOING ALL DRESSED UP?
I'VE BROUGHT YOU A PRESENT.
WELL . . .
TAKE IT.
I DON'T WANT IT.
. . . WHAT IS IT?
CANDY.
OH.
I WISH TO SPEAK WITH YOU.
WHAT FOR?
YOU'RE NOT LIKELY TO FIND OUT UNTIL WE'VE ACTUALLY TALKED.
FINE. TALK.

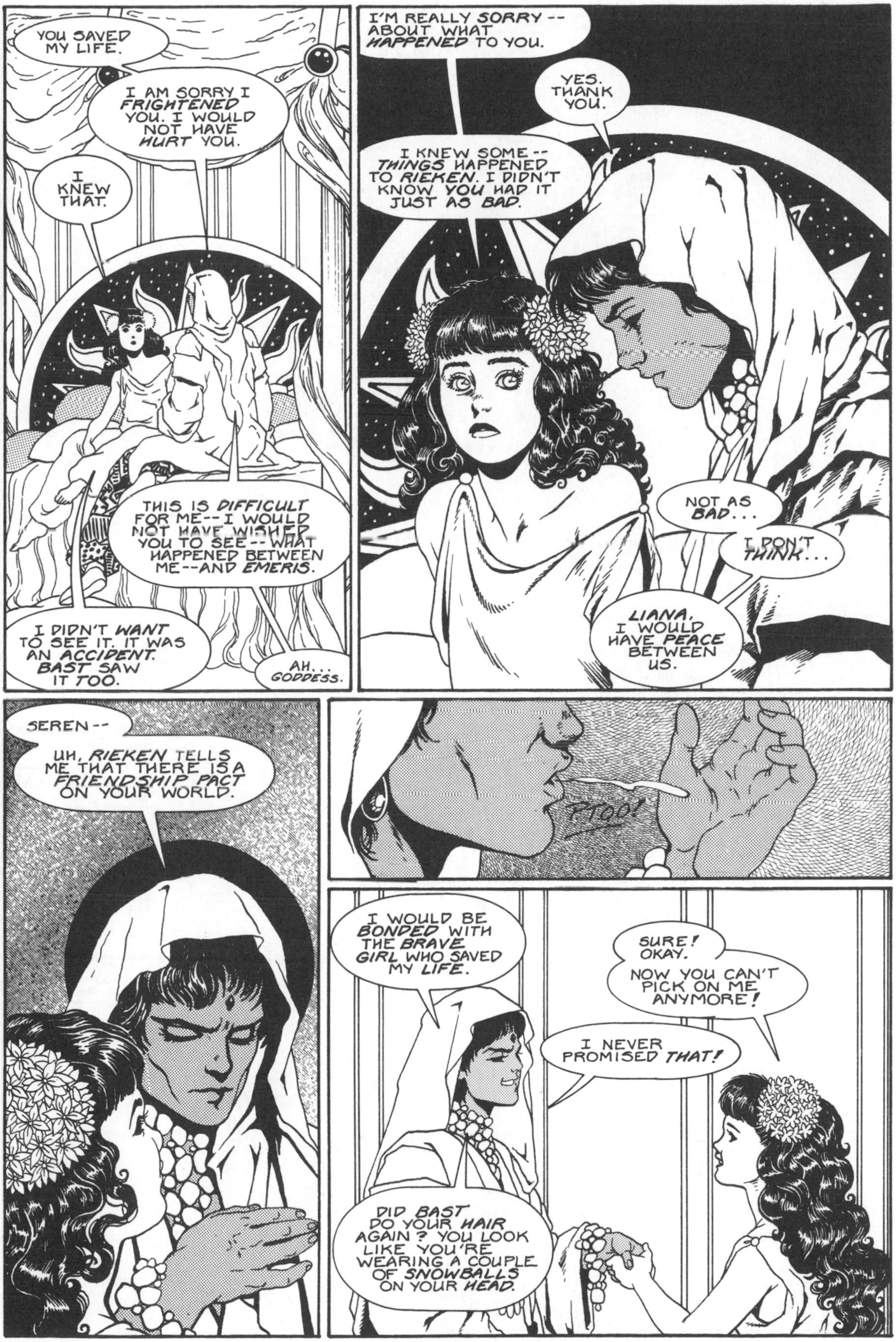
YOU SAVED MY LIFE.
I AM SORRY I FRIGHTENED YOU. I WOULD NOT HAVE HURT YOU.
I KNEW THAT.
THIS IS DIFFICULT FOR ME--I WOULD NOT HAVE WISHED YOU TO SEE--WHAT HAPPENED BETWEEN ME--AND EMERIS.
I DIDN'T WANT TO SEE IT. IT WAS AN ACCIDENT. BAST SAW IT TOO.
AH... GODDESS.
I'M REALLY SORRY--ABOUT WHAT HAPPENED TO YOU.
YES. THANK YOU.
I KNEW SOME--THINGS HAPPENED TO RIEKEN. I DIDN'T KNOW YOU HAD IT JUST AS BAD.
NOT AS BAD...
I DON'T THINK...
LIANA, I WOULD HAVE PEACE BETWEEN US.
SEREN--
UH, RIEKEN TELLS ME THAT THERE IS A FRIENDSHIP PACT ON YOUR WORLD.
PTOO!
I WOULD BE BONDED WITH THE BRAVE GIRL WHO SAVED MY LIFE.
SURE! OKAY.
NOW YOU CAN'T PICK ON ME ANYMORE!
I NEVER PROMISED THAT!
DID BAST DO YOUR HAIR AGAIN? YOU LOOK LIKE YOU'RE WEARING A COUPLE OF SNOWBALLS ON YOUR HEAD.

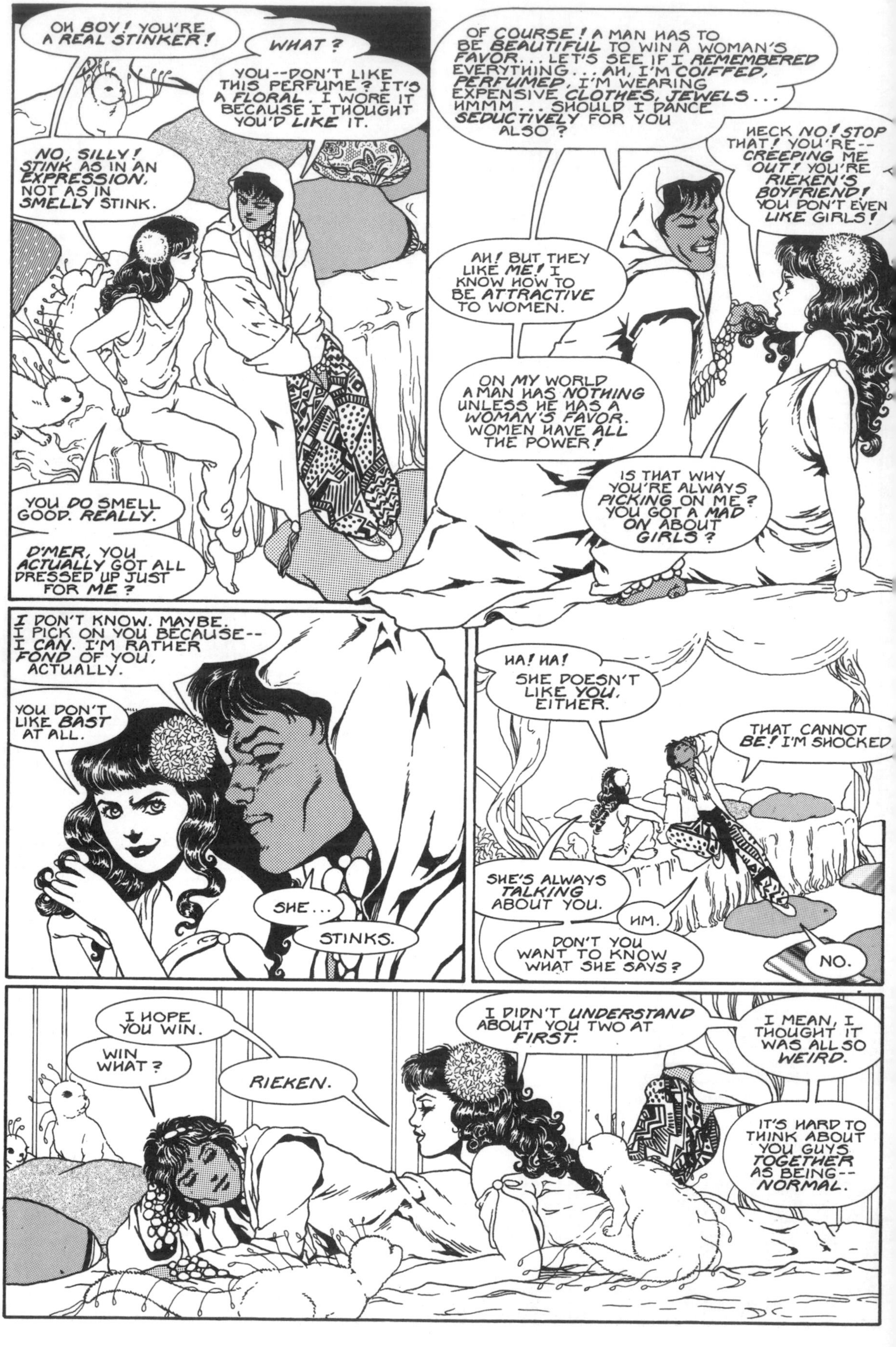
OH BOY! YOU'RE A REAL STINKER!
WHAT?
YOU--DON'T LIKE THIS PERFUME? IT'S A FLORAL. I WORE IT BECAUSE I THOUGHT YOU'D LIKE IT.
NO, SILLY! STINK AS IN AN EXPRESSION, NOT AS IN SMELLY STINK.
YOU DO SMELL GOOD. REALLY.
D'MER, YOU ACTUALLY GOT ALL DRESSED UP JUST FOR ME?
OF COURSE! A MAN HAS TO BE BEAUTIFUL TO WIN A WOMAN'S FAVOR... LET'S SEE IF I REMEMBERED EVERYTHING... AH, I'M COIFFED, PERFUMED, I'M WEARING EXPENSIVE CLOTHES, JEWELS... HMMM... SHOULD I DANCE SEDUCTIVELY FOR YOU ALSO?
HECK NO! STOP THAT! YOU'RE--CREEPING ME OUT! YOU'RE RIEKEN'S BOYFRIEND! YOU DON'T EVEN LIKE GIRLS!
AH! BUT THEY LIKE ME! I KNOW HOW TO BE ATTRACTIVE TO WOMEN.
ON MY WORLD A MAN HAS NOTHING UNLESS HE HAS A WOMAN'S FAVOR. WOMEN HAVE ALL THE POWER!
IS THAT WHY YOU'RE ALWAYS PICKING ON ME? YOU GOT A MAD ON ABOUT GIRLS?
I DON'T KNOW. MAYBE. I PICK ON YOU BECAUSE-- I CAN. I'M RATHER FOND OF YOU, ACTUALLY.
YOU DON'T LIKE BAST AT ALL.
SHE...
STINKS.
HA! HA!
SHE DOESN'T LIKE YOU, EITHER.
THAT CANNOT BE! I'M SHOCKED
SHE'S ALWAYS TALKING ABOUT YOU.
HM.
DON'T YOU WANT TO KNOW WHAT SHE SAYS?
NO.
I HOPE YOU WIN.
WIN WHAT?
RIEKEN.
I DIDN'T UNDERSTAND ABOUT YOU TWO AT FIRST.
I MEAN, I THOUGHT IT WAS ALL SO WEIRD.
IT'S HARD TO THINK ABOUT YOU GUYS TOGETHER AS BEING-- NORMAL.

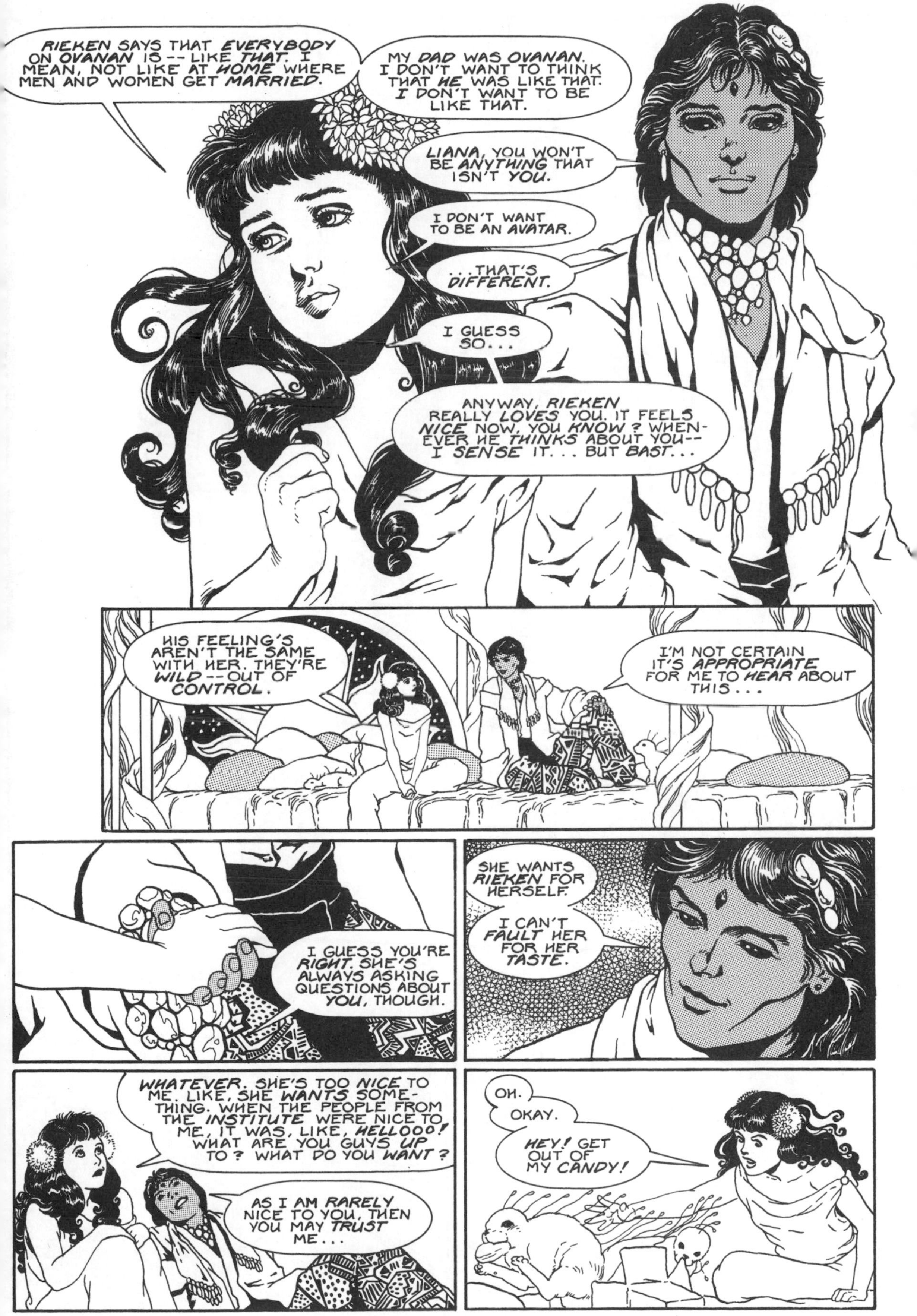
RIEKEN SAYS THAT EVERYBODY ON OVANAN IS -- LIKE THAT. I MEAN, NOT LIKE AT HOME WHERE MEN AND WOMEN GET MARRIED.
MY DAD WAS OVANAN. I DON'T WANT TO THINK THAT HE WAS LIKE THAT. I DON'T WANT TO BE LIKE THAT.
LIANA, YOU WON'T BE ANYTHING THAT ISN'T YOU.
I DON'T WANT TO BE AN AVATAR.
...THAT'S DIFFERENT.
I GUESS SO...
ANYWAY, RIEKEN REALLY LOVES YOU. IT FEELS NICE NOW, YOU KNOW? WHENEVER HE THINKS ABOUT YOU-- I SENSE IT... BUT BAST...
HIS FEELING'S AREN'T THE SAME WITH HER. THEY'RE WILD--OUT OF CONTROL.
I'M NOT CERTAIN IT'S APPROPRIATE FOR ME TO HEAR ABOUT THIS...
I GUESS YOU'RE RIGHT. SHE'S ALWAYS ASKING QUESTIONS ABOUT YOU, THOUGH.
SHE WANTS RIEKEN FOR HERSELF.
I CAN'T FAULT HER FOR HER TASTE.
WHATEVER. SHE'S TOO NICE TO ME. LIKE, SHE WANTS SOMETHING. WHEN THE PEOPLE FROM THE INSTITUTE WERE NICE TO ME, IT WAS, LIKE, HELLOOO! WHAT ARE YOU GUYS UP TO? WHAT DO YOU WANT?
AS I AM RARELY NICE TO YOU, THEN YOU MAY TRUST ME...
OH.
OKAY.
HEY! GET OUT OF MY CANDY!

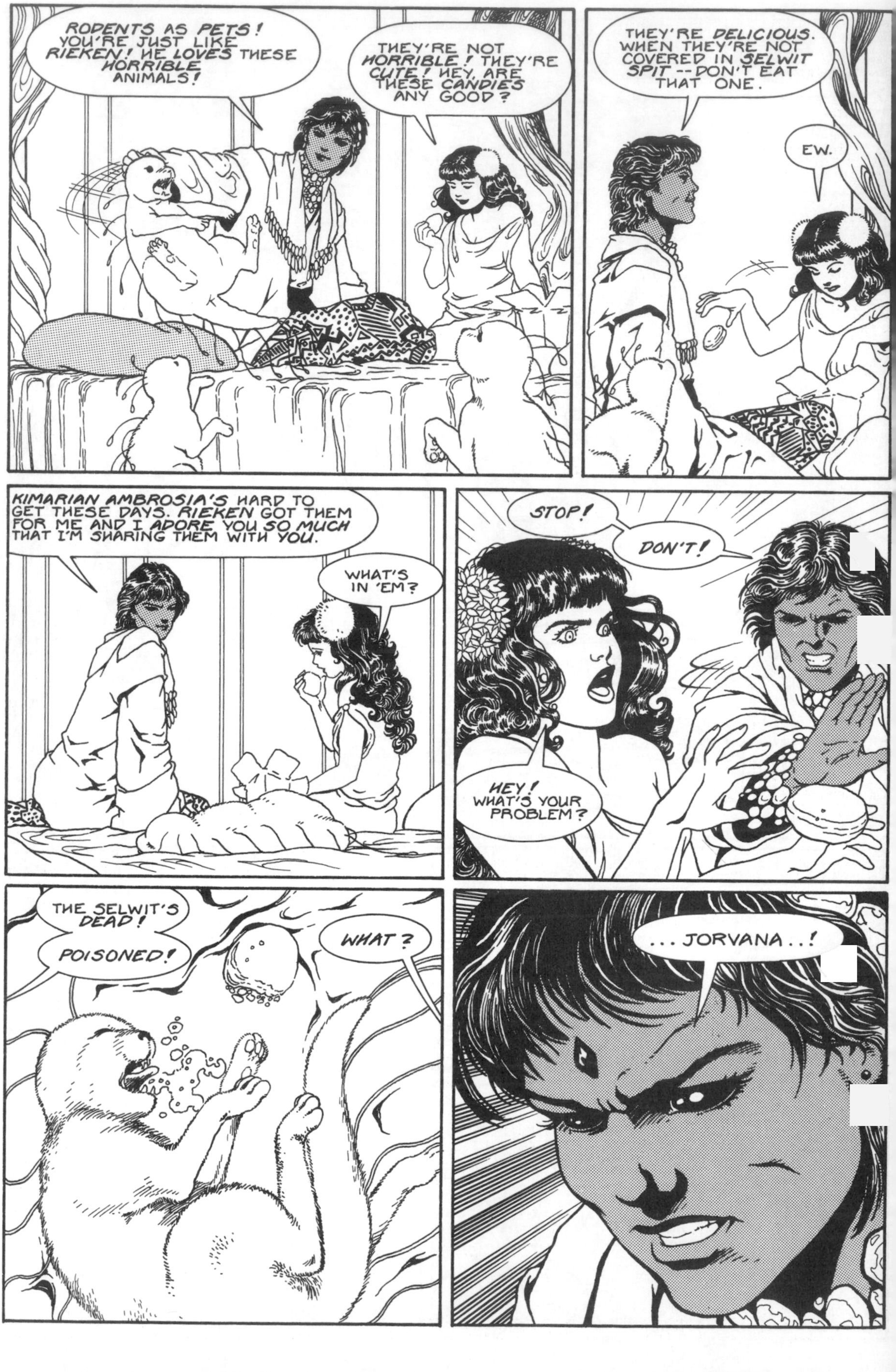
RODENTS AS PETS! YOU'RE JUST LIKE RIEKEN! HE LOVES THESE HORRIBLE ANIMALS!
THEY'RE NOT HORRIBLE! THEY'RE CUTE! HEY, ARE THESE CANDIES ANY GOOD?
THEY'RE DELICIOUS. WHEN THEY'RE NOT COVERED IN SELWIT SPIT -- DON'T EAT THAT ONE.
EW.
KIMARIAN AMBROSIA'S HARD TO GET THESE DAYS. RIEKEN GOT THEM FOR ME AND I ADORE YOU SO MUCH THAT I'M SHARING THEM WITH YOU.
WHAT'S IN 'EM?
STOP!
DON'T!
HEY! WHAT'S YOUR PROBLEM?
THE SELWIT'S DEAD!
POISONED!
WHAT?
... JORVANA ..!

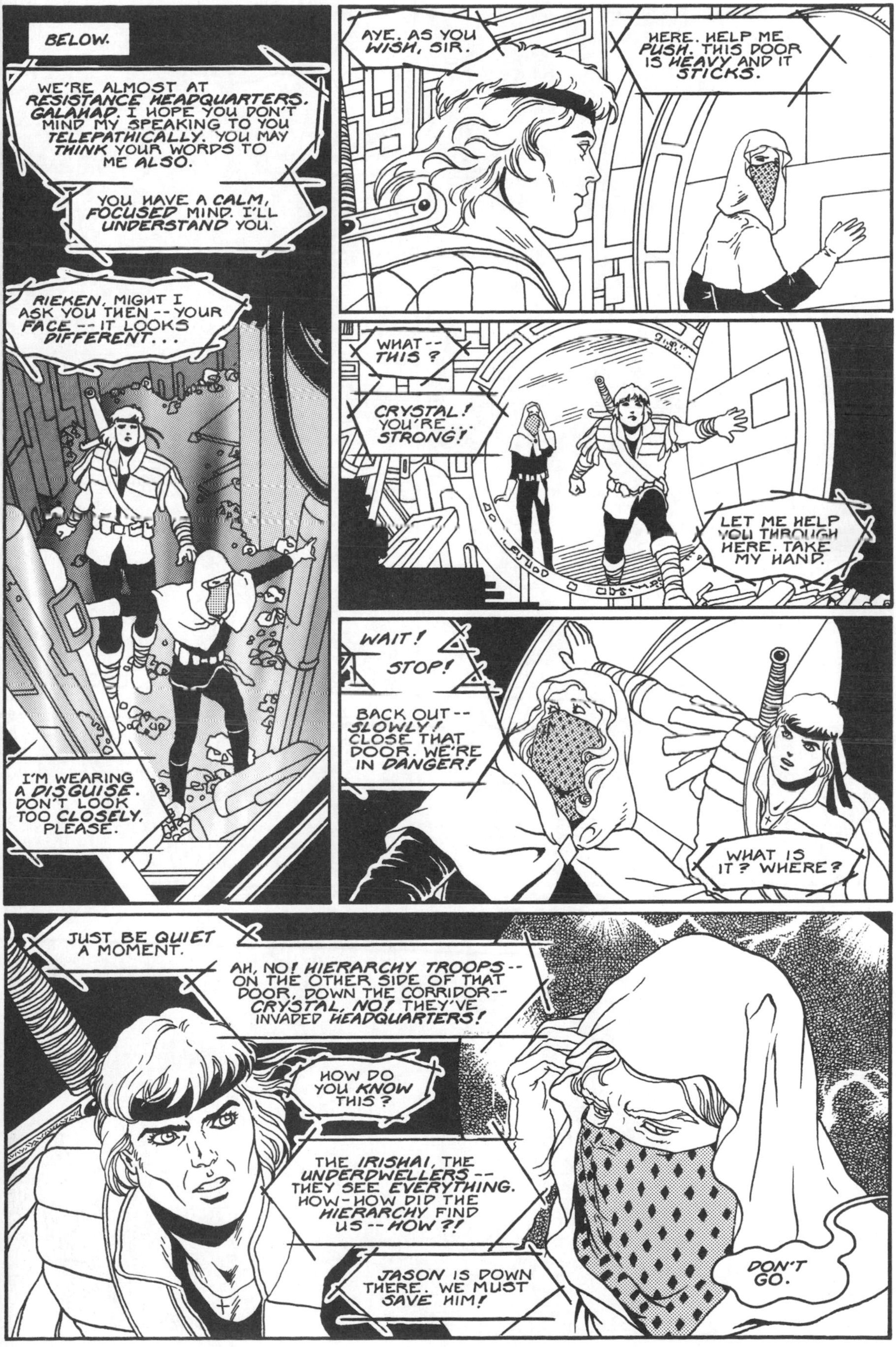
BELOW.
WE'RE ALMOST AT RESISTANCE HEADQUARTERS, GALAHAD. I HOPE YOU DON'T MIND MY SPEAKING TO YOU TELEPATHICALLY. YOU MAY THINK YOUR WORDS TO ME ALSO.
YOU HAVE A CALM, FOCUSED MIND. I'LL UNDERSTAND YOU.
RIEKEN, MIGHT I ASK YOU THEN -- YOUR FACE -- IT LOOKS DIFFERENT...
I'M WEARING A DISGUISE. DON'T LOOK TOO CLOSELY, PLEASE.
AYE. AS YOU WISH, SIR.
HERE. HELP ME PUSH. THIS DOOR IS HEAVY AND IT STICKS.
WHAT -- THIS?
CRYSTAL! YOU'RE... STRONG!
LET ME HELP YOU THROUGH HERE. TAKE MY HAND.
WAIT!
STOP!
BACK OUT -- SLOWLY! CLOSE THAT DOOR. WE'RE IN DANGER!
WHAT IS IT? WHERE?
JUST BE QUIET A MOMENT.
AH, NO! HIERARCHY TROOPS -- ON THE OTHER SIDE OF THAT DOOR, DOWN THE CORRIDOR -- CRYSTAL, NO! THEY'VE INVADED HEADQUARTERS!
HOW DO YOU KNOW THIS?
THE IRISHAI, THE UNDERDWELLERS -- THEY SEE EVERYTHING. HOW-HOW DID THE HIERARCHY FIND US -- HOW?!
JASON IS DOWN THERE. WE MUST SAVE HIM!
DON'T GO.

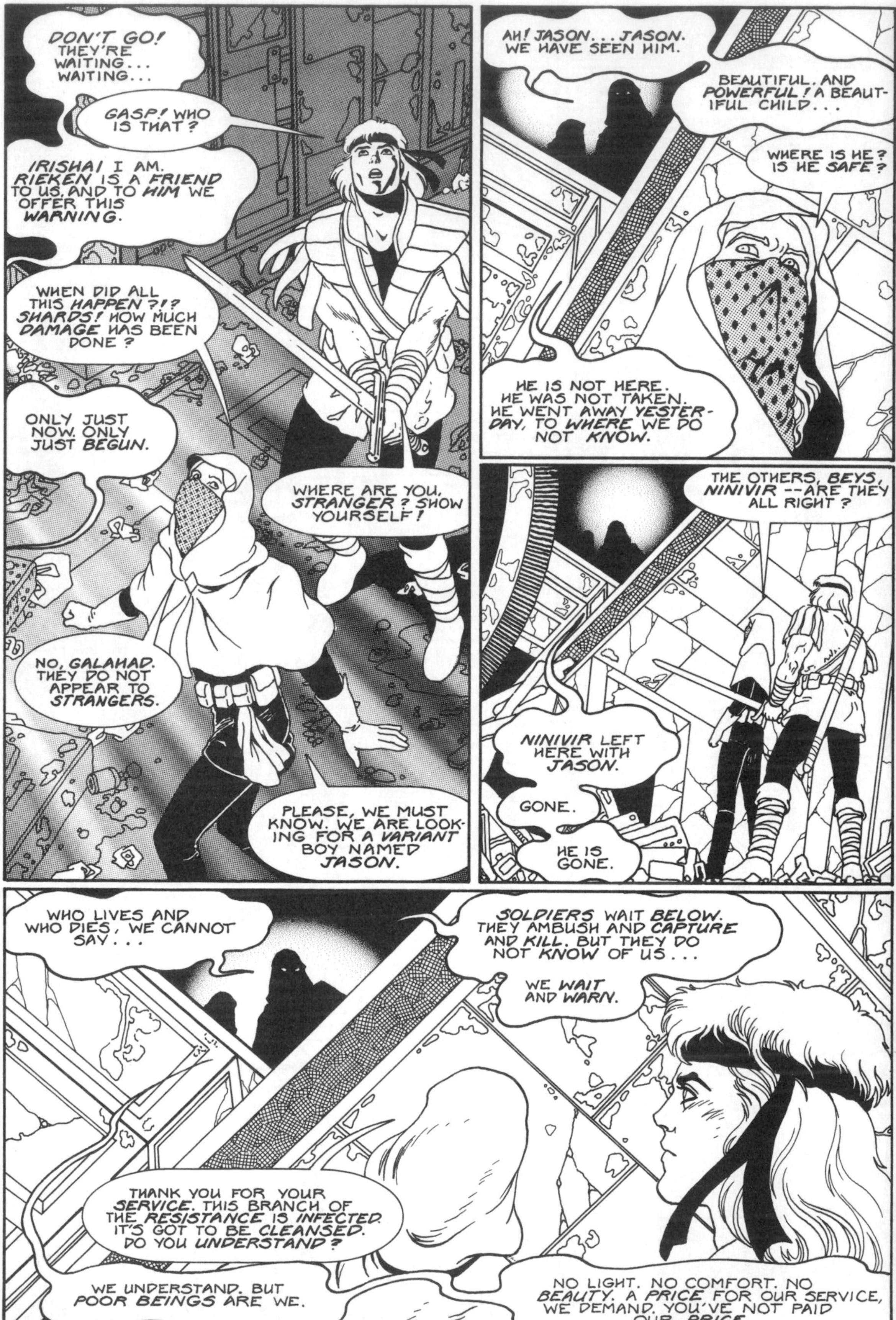
DON'T GO! THEY'RE WAITING... WAITING...
GASP! WHO IS THAT?
IRISHAI I AM. RIEKEN IS A FRIEND TO US, AND TO HIM WE OFFER THIS WARNING.
WHEN DID ALL THIS HAPPEN?!? SHARDS! HOW MUCH DAMAGE HAS BEEN DONE?
ONLY JUST NOW. ONLY JUST BEGUN.
WHERE ARE YOU, STRANGER? SHOW YOURSELF!
NO, GALAHAD. THEY DO NOT APPEAR TO STRANGERS.
PLEASE, WE MUST KNOW. WE ARE LOOKING FOR A VARIANT BOY NAMED JASON.
AH! JASON... JASON. WE HAVE SEEN HIM.
BEAUTIFUL. AND POWERFUL! A BEAUTIFUL CHILD...
WHERE IS HE? IS HE SAFE?
HE IS NOT HERE. HE WAS NOT TAKEN. HE WENT AWAY YESTERDAY, TO WHERE WE DO NOT KNOW.
THE OTHERS, BEYS, NINIVIR --ARE THEY ALL RIGHT?
NINIVIR LEFT HERE WITH JASON.
GONE.
HE IS GONE.
WHO LIVES AND WHO DIES, WE CANNOT SAY...
SOLDIERS WAIT BELOW. THEY AMBUSH AND CAPTURE AND KILL. BUT THEY DO NOT KNOW OF US...
WE WAIT AND WARN.
THANK YOU FOR YOUR SERVICE. THIS BRANCH OF THE RESISTANCE IS INFECTED. IT'S GOT TO BE CLEANSED. DO YOU UNDERSTAND?
WE UNDERSTAND. BUT POOR BEINGS ARE WE.
NO LIGHT. NO COMFORT. NO BEAUTY. A PRICE FOR OUR SERVICE, WE DEMAND. YOU'VE NOT PAID OUR PRICE.

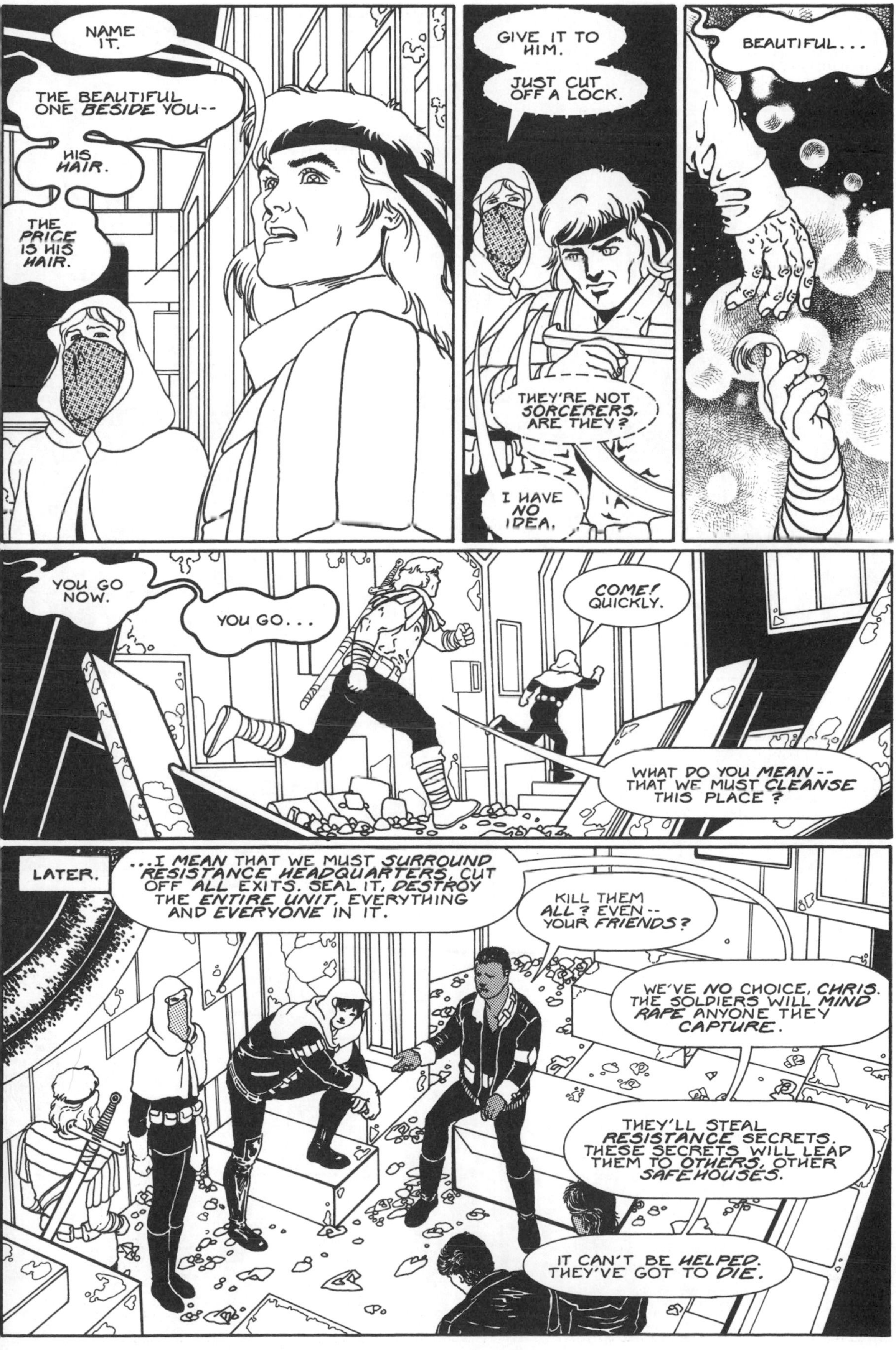
NAME IT.
THE BEAUTIFUL ONE BESIDE YOU--
HIS HAIR.
THE PRICE IS HIS HAIR.
GIVE IT TO HIM.
JUST CUT OFF A LOCK.
THEY'RE NOT SORCERERS, ARE THEY?
I HAVE NO IDEA.
BEAUTIFUL...
YOU GO NOW.
YOU GO...
COME! QUICKLY.
WHAT DO YOU MEAN-- THAT WE MUST CLEANSE THIS PLACE?
LATER.
...I MEAN THAT WE MUST SURROUND RESISTANCE HEADQUARTERS, CUT OFF ALL EXITS. SEAL IT, DESTROY THE ENTIRE UNIT, EVERYTHING AND EVERYONE IN IT.
KILL THEM ALL? EVEN-- YOUR FRIENDS?
WE'VE NO CHOICE, CHRIS. THE SOLDIERS WILL MIND RAPE ANYONE THEY CAPTURE.
THEY'LL STEAL RESISTANCE SECRETS. THESE SECRETS WILL LEAD THEM TO OTHERS, OTHER SAFEHOUSES.
IT CAN'T BE HELPED. THEY'VE GOT TO DIE.

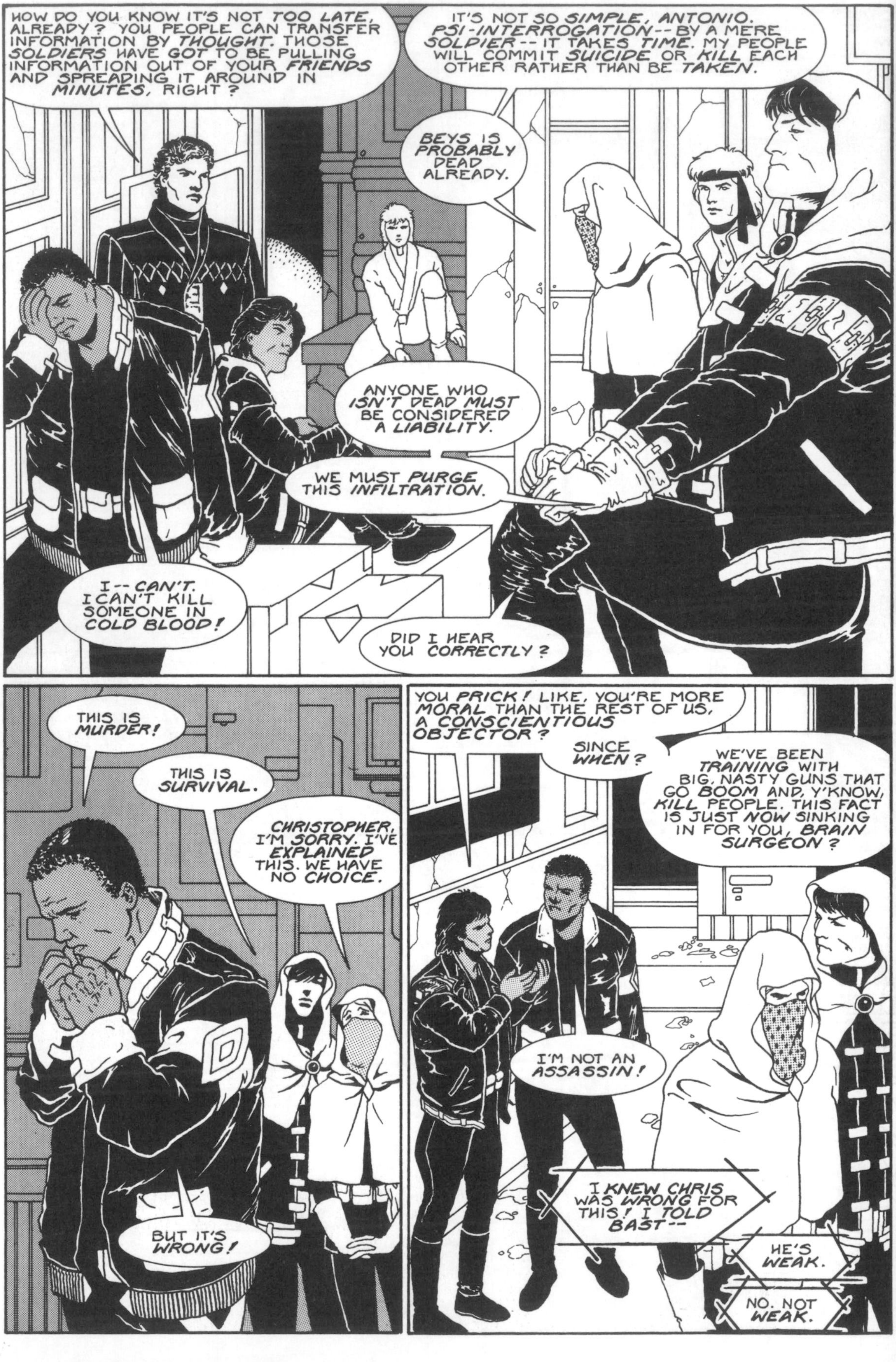
HOW DO YOU KNOW IT'S NOT TOO LATE, ALREADY? YOU PEOPLE CAN TRANSFER INFORMATION BY THOUGHT. THOSE SOLDIERS HAVE GOT TO BE PULLING INFORMATION OUT OF YOUR FRIENDS AND SPREADING IT AROUND IN MINUTES, RIGHT?
IT'S NOT SO SIMPLE, ANTONIO. PSI-INTERROGATION -- BY A MERE SOLDIER -- IT TAKES TIME. MY PEOPLE WILL COMMIT SUICIDE OR KILL EACH OTHER RATHER THAN BE TAKEN.
BEYS IS PROBABLY DEAD ALREADY.
ANYONE WHO ISN'T DEAD MUST BE CONSIDERED A LIABILITY.
WE MUST PURGE THIS INFILTRATION.
I -- CAN'T. I CAN'T KILL SOMEONE IN COLD BLOOD!
DID I HEAR YOU CORRECTLY?
THIS IS MURDER!
THIS IS SURVIVAL.
CHRISTOPHER, I'M SORRY. I'VE EXPLAINED THIS. WE HAVE NO CHOICE.
BUT IT'S WRONG!
YOU PRICK! LIKE, YOU'RE MORE MORAL THAN THE REST OF US, A CONSCIENTIOUS OBJECTOR?
SINCE WHEN?
WE'VE BEEN TRAINING WITH BIG, NASTY GUNS THAT GO BOOM AND, Y'KNOW, KILL PEOPLE. THIS FACT IS JUST NOW SINKING IN FOR YOU, BRAIN SURGEON?
I'M NOT AN ASSASSIN!
I KNEW CHRIS WAS WRONG FOR THIS! I TOLD BAST--
HE'S WEAK.
NO. NOT WEAK.

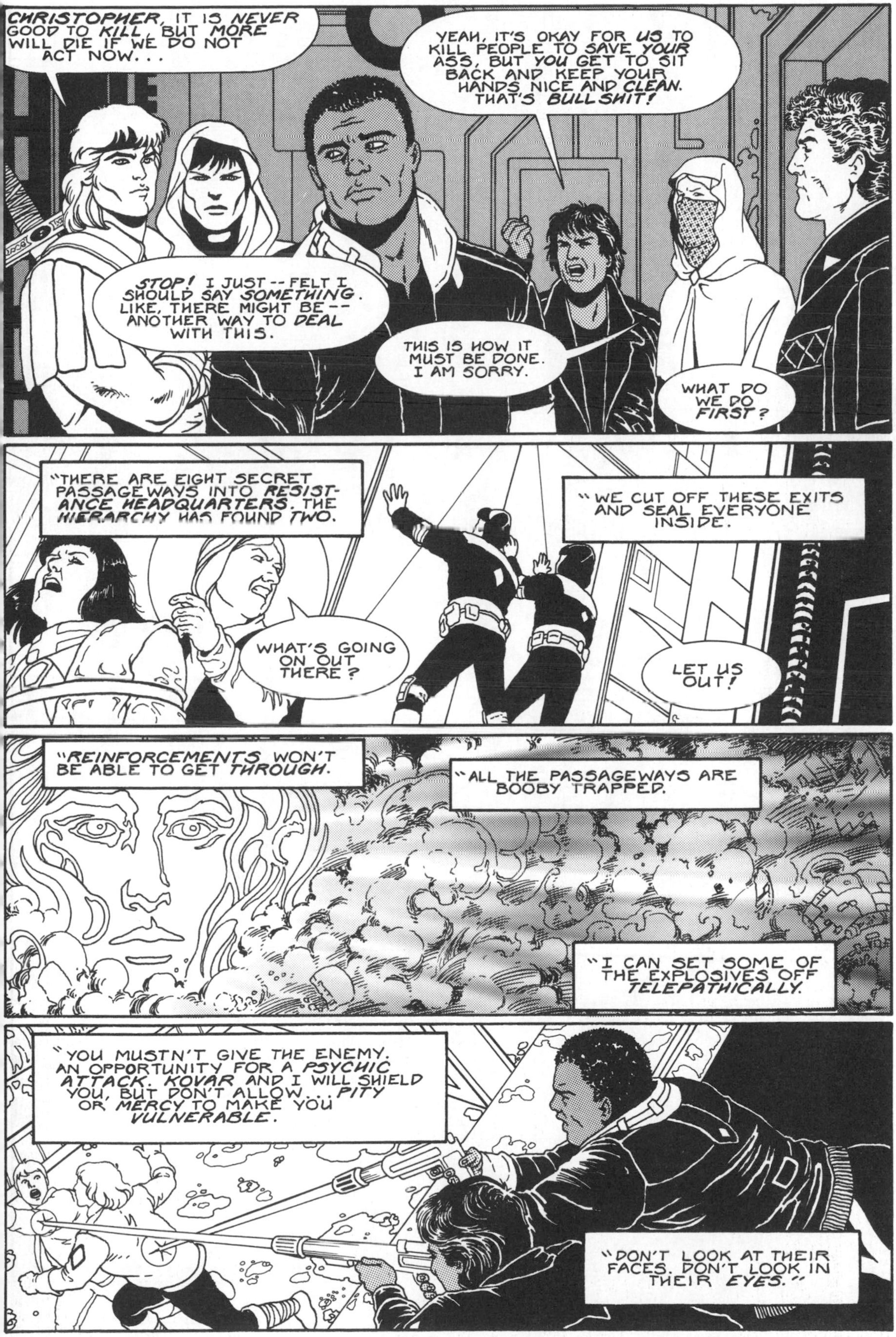
CHRISTOPHER, IT IS NEVER GOOD TO KILL, BUT MORE WILL DIE IF WE DO NOT ACT NOW...
YEAH, IT'S OKAY FOR US TO KILL PEOPLE TO SAVE YOUR ASS, BUT YOU GET TO SIT BACK AND KEEP YOUR HANDS NICE AND CLEAN. THAT'S BULLSHIT!
STOP! I JUST--FELT I SHOULD SAY SOMETHING. LIKE, THERE MIGHT BE--ANOTHER WAY TO DEAL WITH THIS.
THIS IS HOW IT MUST BE DONE. I AM SORRY.
WHAT DO WE DO FIRST?
"THERE ARE EIGHT SECRET PASSAGEWAYS INTO RESISTANCE HEADQUARTERS. THE HIERARCHY HAS FOUND TWO.
"WE CUT OFF THESE EXITS AND SEAL EVERYONE INSIDE.
WHAT'S GOING ON OUT THERE?
LET US OUT!
"REINFORCEMENTS WON'T BE ABLE TO GET THROUGH.
"ALL THE PASSAGEWAYS ARE BOOBY TRAPPED.
"I CAN SET SOME OF THE EXPLOSIVES OFF TELEPATHICALLY.
"YOU MUSTN'T GIVE THE ENEMY. AN OPPORTUNITY FOR A PSYCHIC ATTACK. KOVAR AND I WILL SHIELD YOU, BUT DON'T ALLOW... PITY OR MERCY TO MAKE YOU VULNERABLE.
"DON'T LOOK AT THEIR FACES. DON'T LOOK IN THEIR EYES."

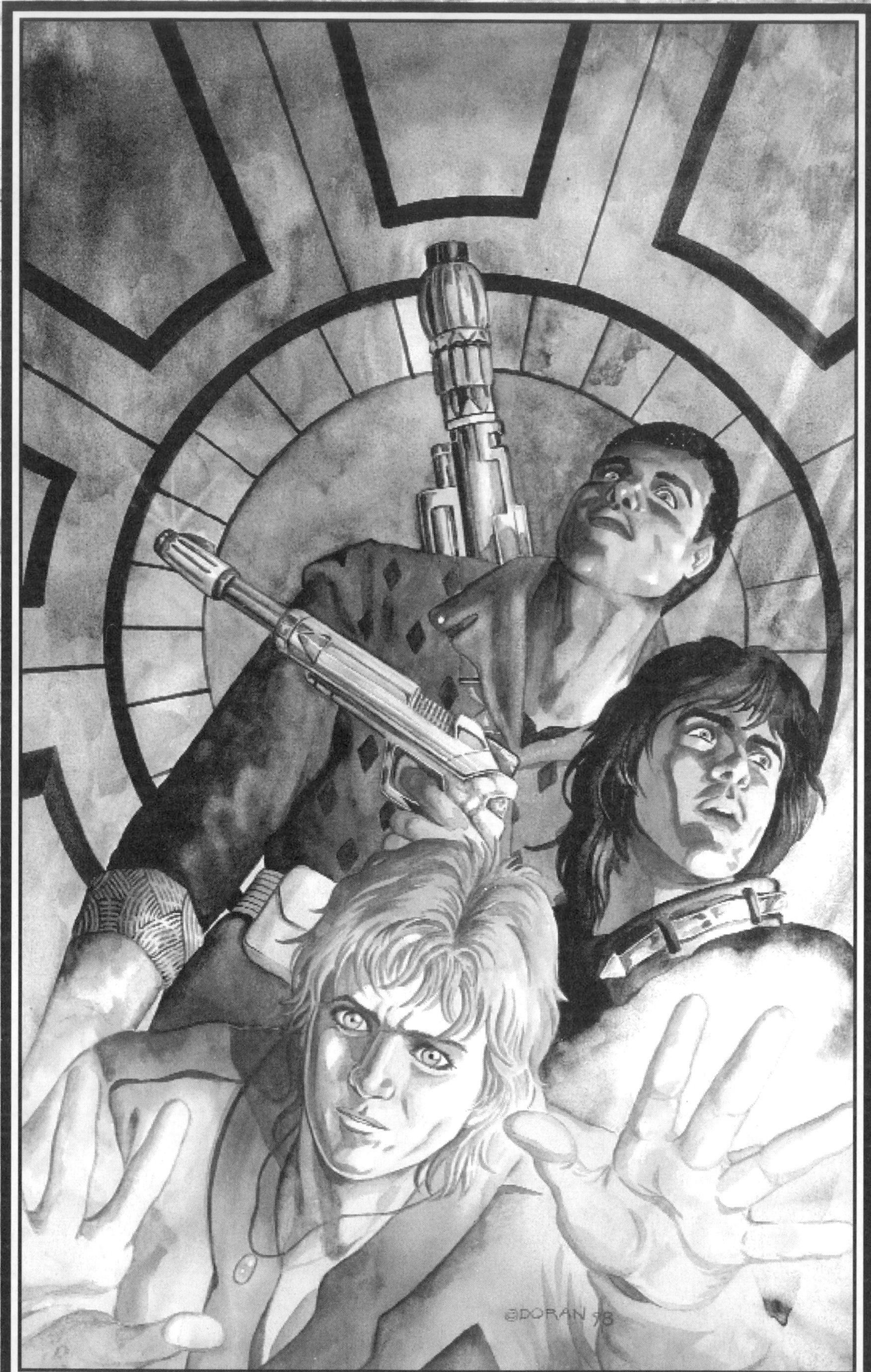
©DORAN 98

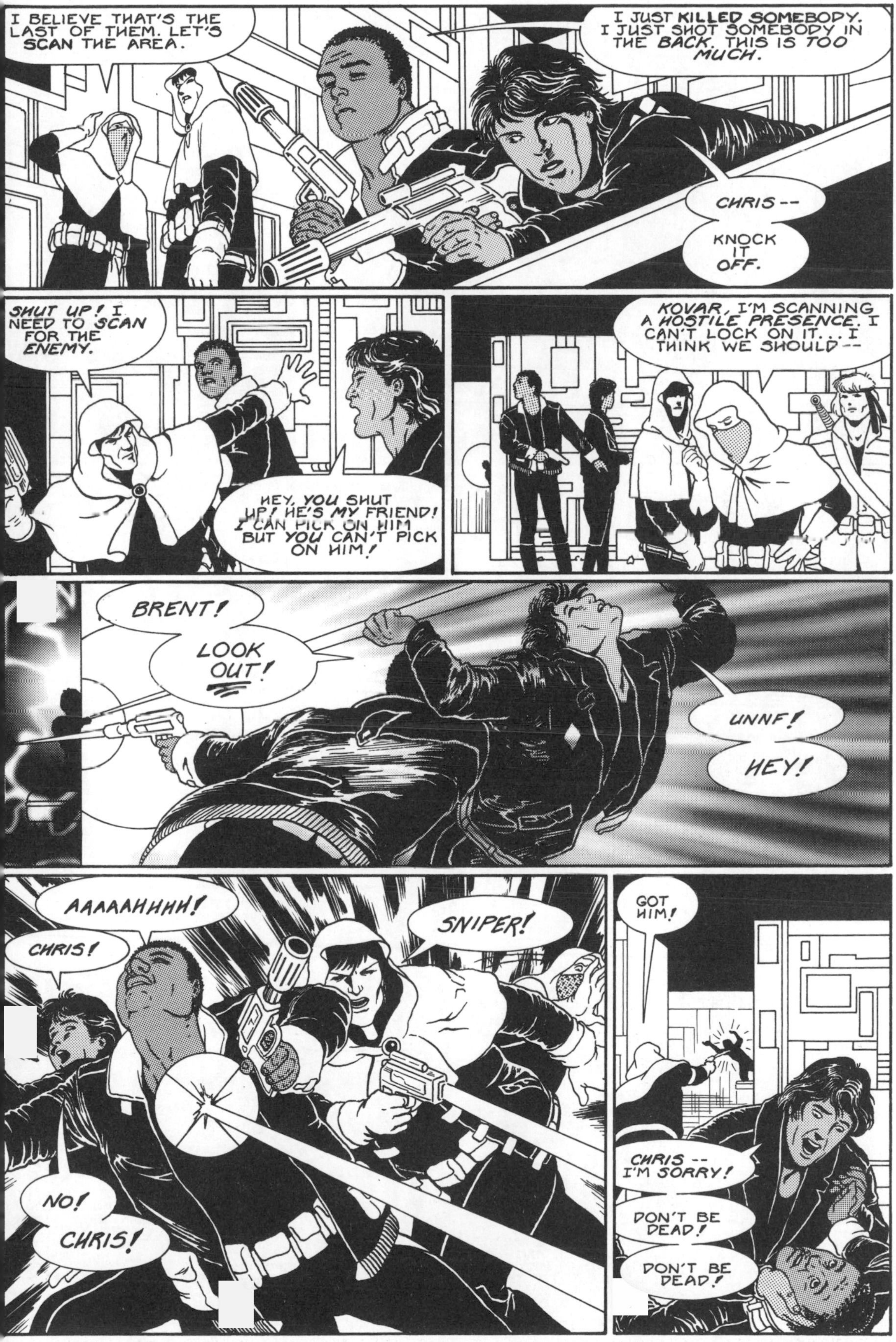

I BELIEVE THAT'S THE LAST OF THEM. LET'S SCAN THE AREA.
I JUST KILLED SOMEBODY. I JUST SHOT SOMEBODY IN THE BACK. THIS IS TOO MUCH.
CHRIS --
KNOCK IT OFF.
SHUT UP! I NEED TO SCAN FOR THE ENEMY.
HEY, YOU SHUT UP! HE'S MY FRIEND! I CAN PICK ON HIM BUT YOU CAN'T PICK ON HIM!
KOVAR, I'M SCANNING A HOSTILE PRESENCE. I CAN'T LOCK ON IT... I THINK WE SHOULD--
BRENT!
LOOK OUT!
UNNF!
HEY!
AAAAAHHHH!
CHRIS!
SNIPER!
NO!
CHRIS!
GOT HIM!
CHRIS -- I'M SORRY!
DON'T BE DEAD!
DON'T BE DEAD!

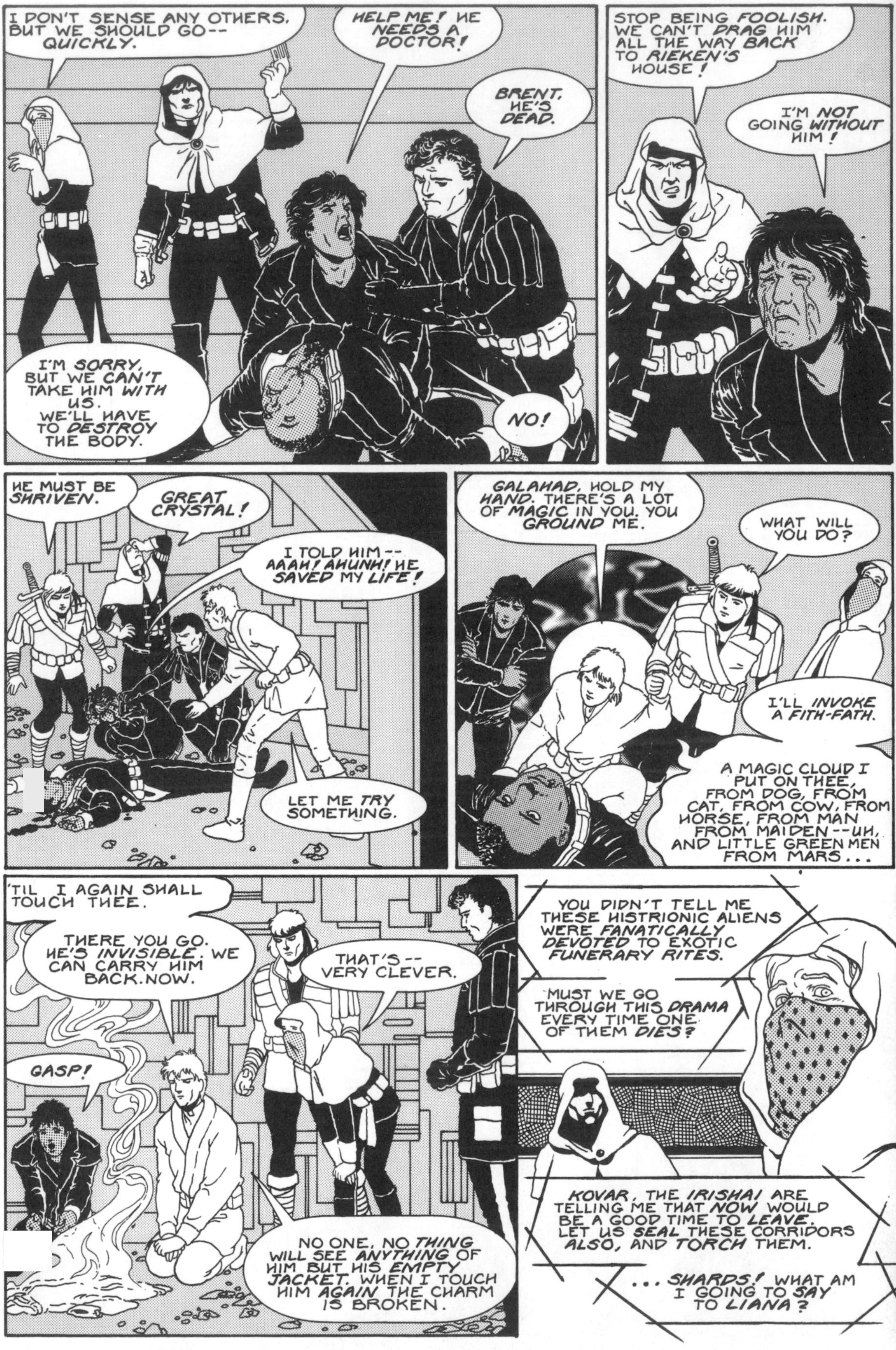
I DON'T SENSE ANY OTHERS, BUT WE SHOULD GO-- QUICKLY.
HELP ME! HE NEEDS A DOCTOR!
BRENT, HE'S DEAD.
I'M SORRY, BUT WE CAN'T TAKE HIM WITH US. WE'LL HAVE TO DESTROY THE BODY.
NO!
STOP BEING FOOLISH. WE CAN'T DRAG HIM ALL THE WAY BACK TO RIEKEN'S HOUSE!
I'M NOT GOING WITHOUT HIM!
HE MUST BE SHRIVEN.
GREAT CRYSTAL!
I TOLD HIM -- AAAH! AHUNH! HE SAVED MY LIFE!
LET ME TRY SOMETHING.
GALAHAD, HOLD MY HAND. THERE'S A LOT OF MAGIC IN YOU. YOU GROUND ME.
WHAT WILL YOU DO?
I'LL INVOKE A FITH-FATH.
A MAGIC CLOUD I PUT ON THEE, FROM DOG, FROM CAT, FROM COW, FROM HORSE, FROM MAN FROM MAIDEN--UH, AND LITTLE GREEN MEN FROM MARS...
'TIL I AGAIN SHALL TOUCH THEE.
THERE YOU GO. HE'S INVISIBLE. WE CAN CARRY HIM BACK NOW.
THAT'S -- VERY CLEVER.
GASP!
NO ONE, NO THING WILL SEE ANYTHING OF HIM BUT HIS EMPTY JACKET. WHEN I TOUCH HIM AGAIN THE CHARM IS BROKEN.
YOU DIDN'T TELL ME THESE HISTRIONIC ALIENS WERE FANATICALLY DEVOTED TO EXOTIC FUNERARY RITES.
MUST WE GO THROUGH THIS DRAMA EVERY TIME ONE OF THEM DIES?
KOVAR, THE IRISHAI ARE TELLING ME THAT NOW WOULD BE A GOOD TIME TO LEAVE. LET US SEAL THESE CORRIDORS ALSO, AND TORCH THEM.
...SHARDS! WHAT AM I GOING TO SAY TO LIANA?

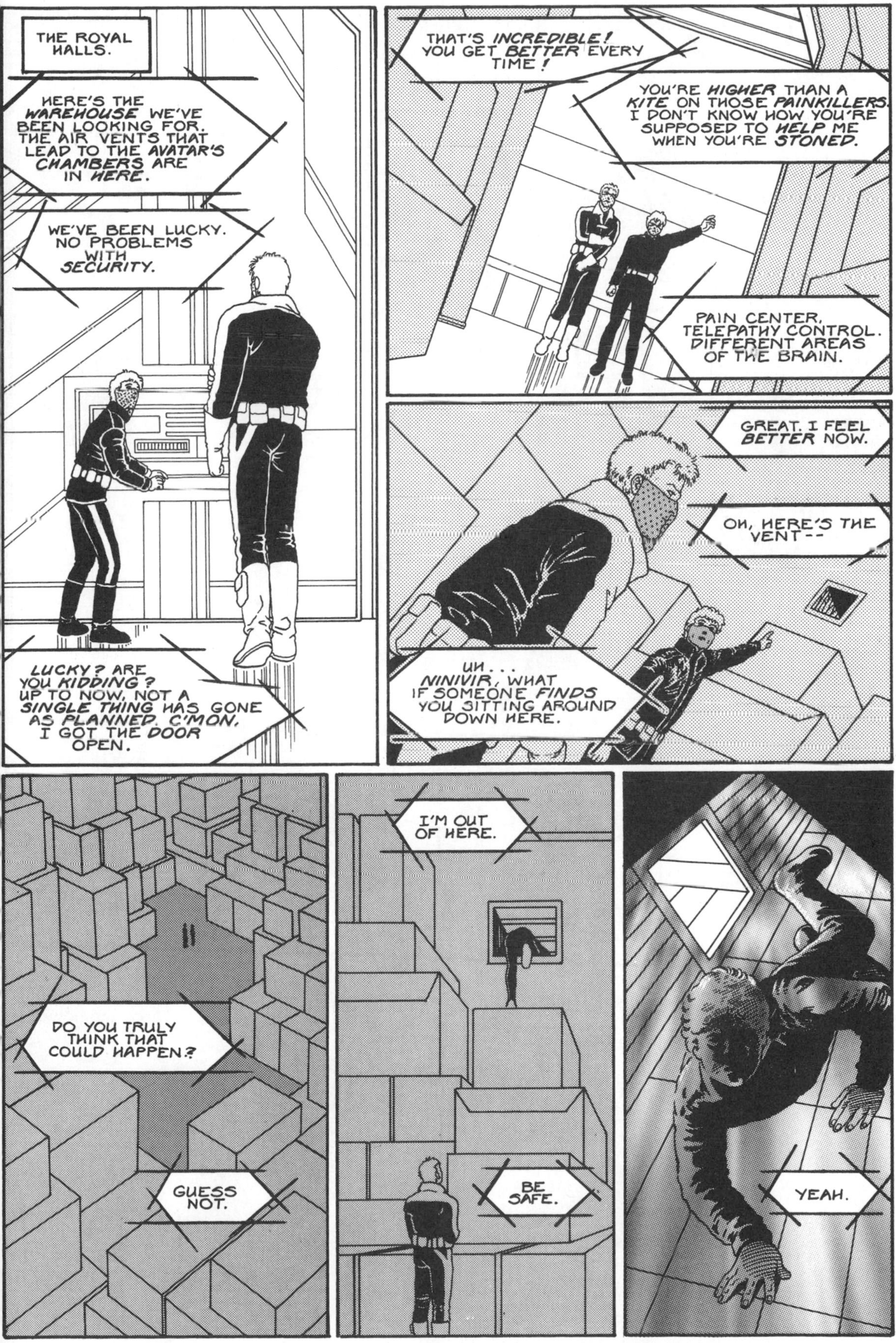
THE ROYAL HALLS.
HERE'S THE WAREHOUSE WE'VE BEEN LOOKING FOR. THE AIR VENTS THAT LEAD TO THE AVATAR'S CHAMBERS ARE IN HERE.
WE'VE BEEN LUCKY. NO PROBLEMS WITH SECURITY.
LUCKY? ARE YOU KIDDING? UP TO NOW, NOT A SINGLE THING HAS GONE AS PLANNED. C'MON, I GOT THE DOOR OPEN.
THAT'S INCREDIBLE! YOU GET BETTER EVERY TIME!
YOU'RE HIGHER THAN A KITE ON THOSE PAINKILLERS. I DON'T KNOW HOW YOU'RE SUPPOSED TO HELP ME WHEN YOU'RE STONED.
PAIN CENTER, TELEPATHY CONTROL. DIFFERENT AREAS OF THE BRAIN.
GREAT. I FEEL BETTER NOW.
OH, HERE'S THE VENT--
UH... NINIVIR, WHAT IF SOMEONE FINDS YOU SITTING AROUND DOWN HERE.
DO YOU TRULY THINK THAT COULD HAPPEN?
GUESS NOT.
I'M OUT OF HERE.
BE SAFE.
YEAH.

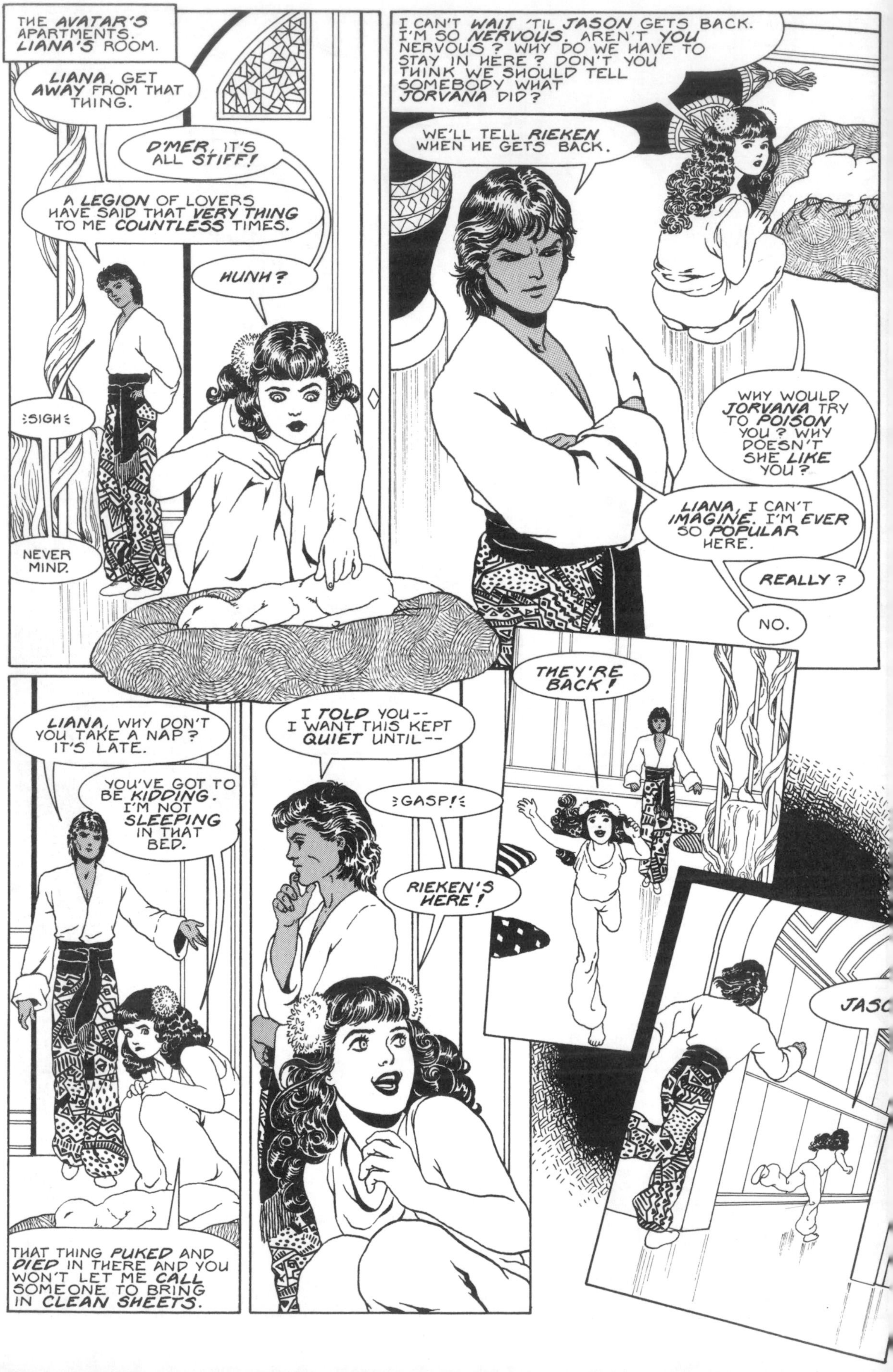
THE AVATAR'S APARTMENTS. LIANA'S ROOM.
LIANA, GET AWAY FROM THAT THING.
D'MER, IT'S ALL STIFF!
A LEGION OF LOVERS HAVE SAID THAT VERY THING TO ME COUNTLESS TIMES.
HUNH?
SIGH
NEVER MIND.
I CAN'T WAIT 'TIL JASON GETS BACK. I'M SO NERVOUS. AREN'T YOU NERVOUS? WHY DO WE HAVE TO STAY IN HERE? DON'T YOU THINK WE SHOULD TELL SOMEBODY WHAT JORVANA DID?
WE'LL TELL RIEKEN WHEN HE GETS BACK.
WHY WOULD JORVANA TRY TO POISON YOU? WHY DOESN'T SHE LIKE YOU?
LIANA, I CAN'T IMAGINE. I'M EVER SO POPULAR HERE.
REALLY?
NO.
LIANA, WHY DON'T YOU TAKE A NAP? IT'S LATE.
YOU'VE GOT TO BE KIDDING. I'M NOT SLEEPING IN THAT BED.
THAT THING PUKED AND DIED IN THERE AND YOU WON'T LET ME CALL SOMEONE TO BRING IN CLEAN SHEETS.
I TOLD YOU-- I WANT THIS KEPT QUIET UNTIL--
GASP!
RIEKEN'S HERE!
THEY'RE BACK!

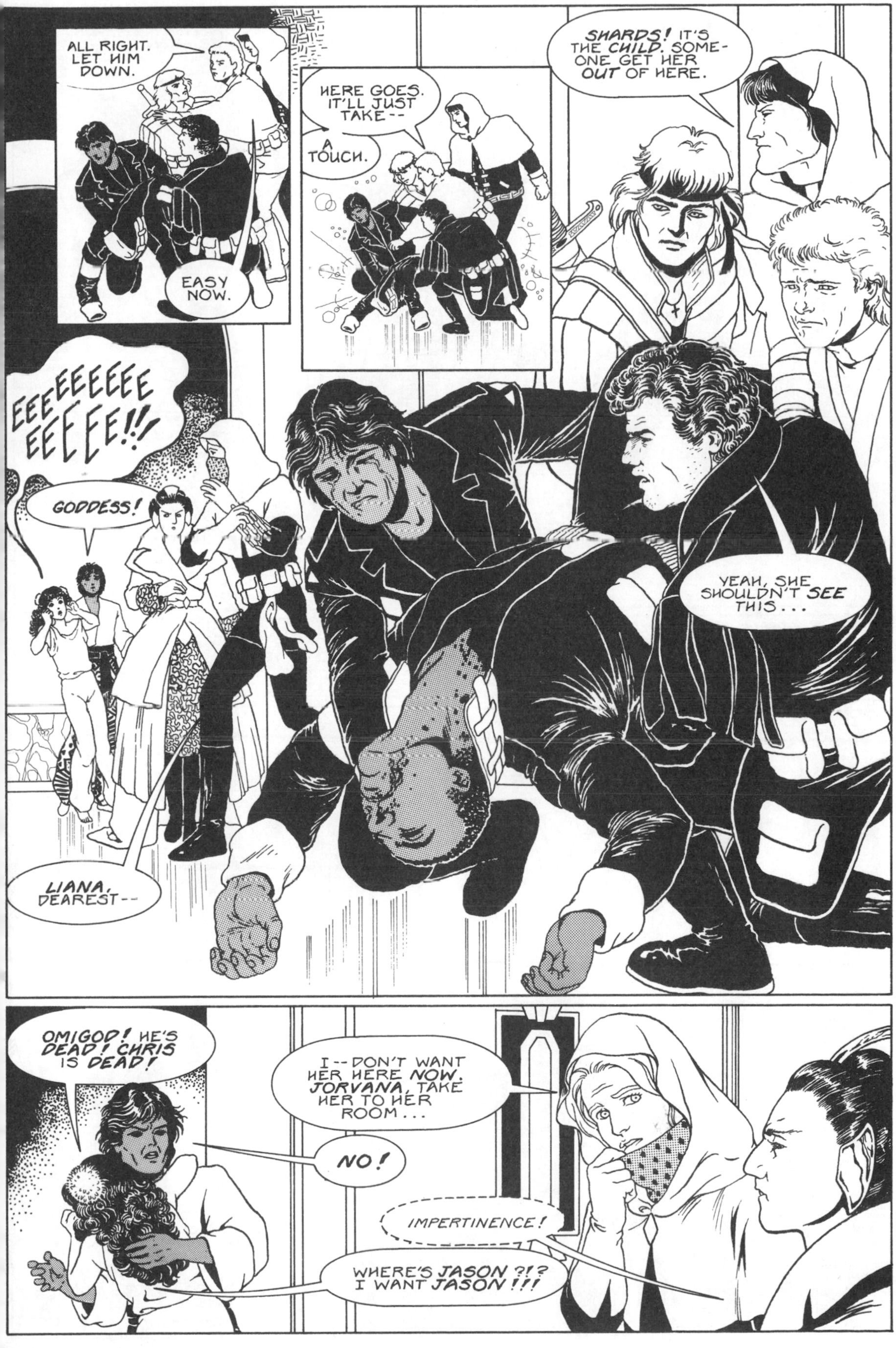
ALL RIGHT. LET HIM DOWN.
EASY NOW.
HERE GOES. IT'LL JUST TAKE--
A TOUCH.
SHARDS! IT'S THE CHILD. SOME-ONE GET HER OUT OF HERE.
EEEEEEEEE EEEEE!!!
GODDESS!
YEAH, SHE SHOULDN'T SEE THIS . . .
LIANA, DEAREST--
OMIGOD! HE'S DEAD! CHRIS IS DEAD!
I--DON'T WANT HER HERE NOW. JORVANA, TAKE HER TO HER ROOM . . .
NO!
IMPERTINENCE!
WHERE'S JASON ?!? I WANT JASON !!!

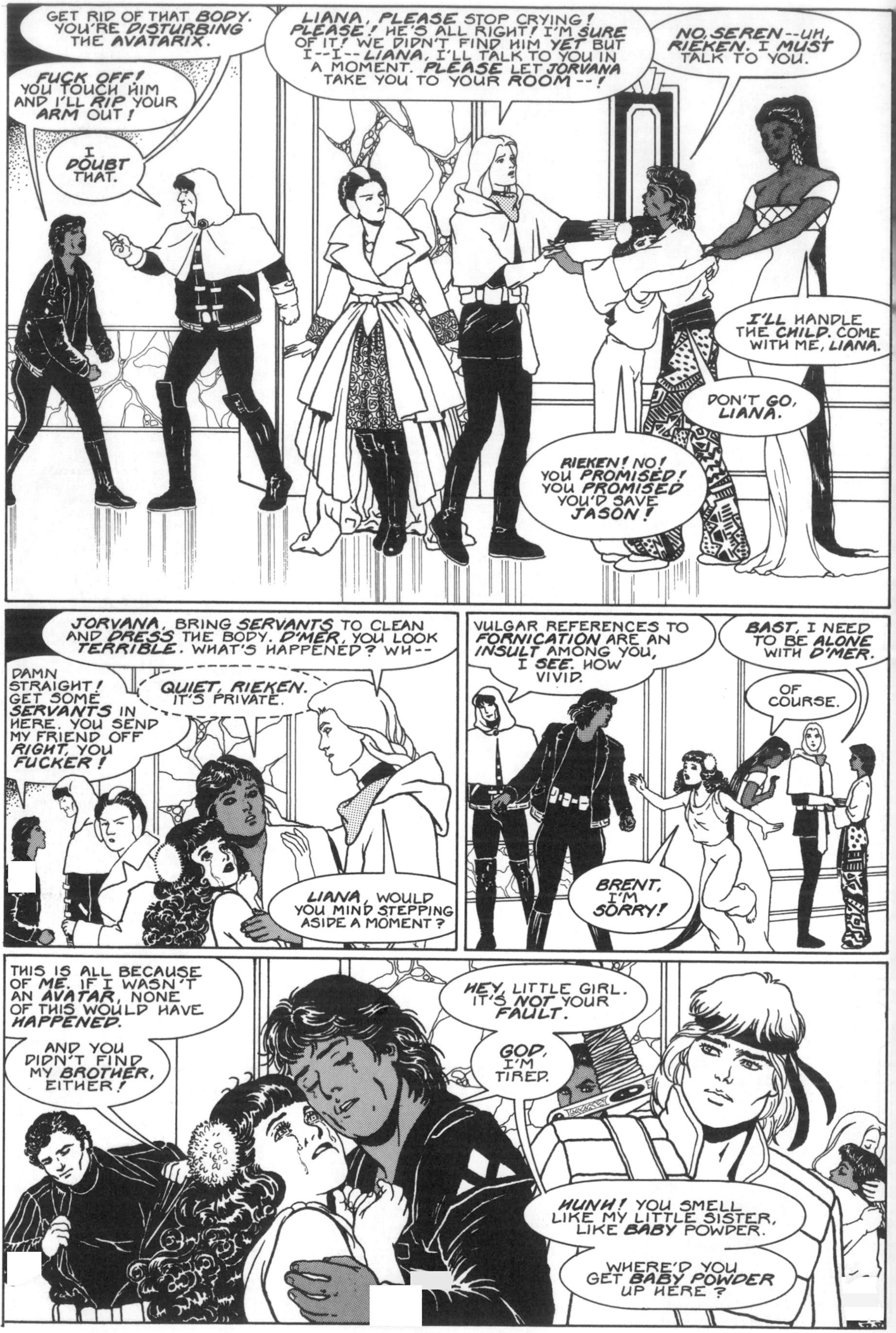
GET RID OF THAT BODY. YOU'RE DISTURBING THE AVATARIX.
FUCK OFF! YOU TOUCH HIM AND I'LL RIP YOUR ARM OUT!
I DOUBT THAT.
LIANA, PLEASE STOP CRYING! PLEASE! HE'S ALL RIGHT! I'M SURE OF IT! WE DIDN'T FIND HIM YET BUT I--I-- LIANA, I'LL TALK TO YOU IN A MOMENT. PLEASE LET JORVANA TAKE YOU TO YOUR ROOM--!
NO, SEREN--UH, RIEKEN. I MUST TALK TO YOU.
I'LL HANDLE THE CHILD. COME WITH ME, LIANA.
DON'T GO, LIANA.
RIEKEN! NO! YOU PROMISED! YOU PROMISED YOU'D SAVE JASON!
JORVANA, BRING SERVANTS TO CLEAN AND DRESS THE BODY. D'MER, YOU LOOK TERRIBLE. WHAT'S HAPPENED? WH--
DAMN STRAIGHT! GET SOME SERVANTS IN HERE. YOU SEND MY FRIEND OFF RIGHT, YOU FUCKER!
QUIET, RIEKEN. IT'S PRIVATE.
LIANA, WOULD YOU MIND STEPPING ASIDE A MOMENT?
VULGAR REFERENCES TO FORNICATION ARE AN INSULT AMONG YOU, I SEE. HOW VIVID.
BAST, I NEED TO BE ALONE WITH D'MER.
OF COURSE.
BRENT, I'M SORRY!
THIS IS ALL BECAUSE OF ME. IF I WASN'T AN AVATAR, NONE OF THIS WOULD HAVE HAPPENED.
AND YOU DIDN'T FIND MY BROTHER, EITHER!
HEY, LITTLE GIRL. IT'S NOT YOUR FAULT.
GOD, I'M TIRED.
HUNH! YOU SMELL LIKE MY LITTLE SISTER, LIKE BABY POWDER.
WHERE'D YOU GET BABY POWDER UP HERE?

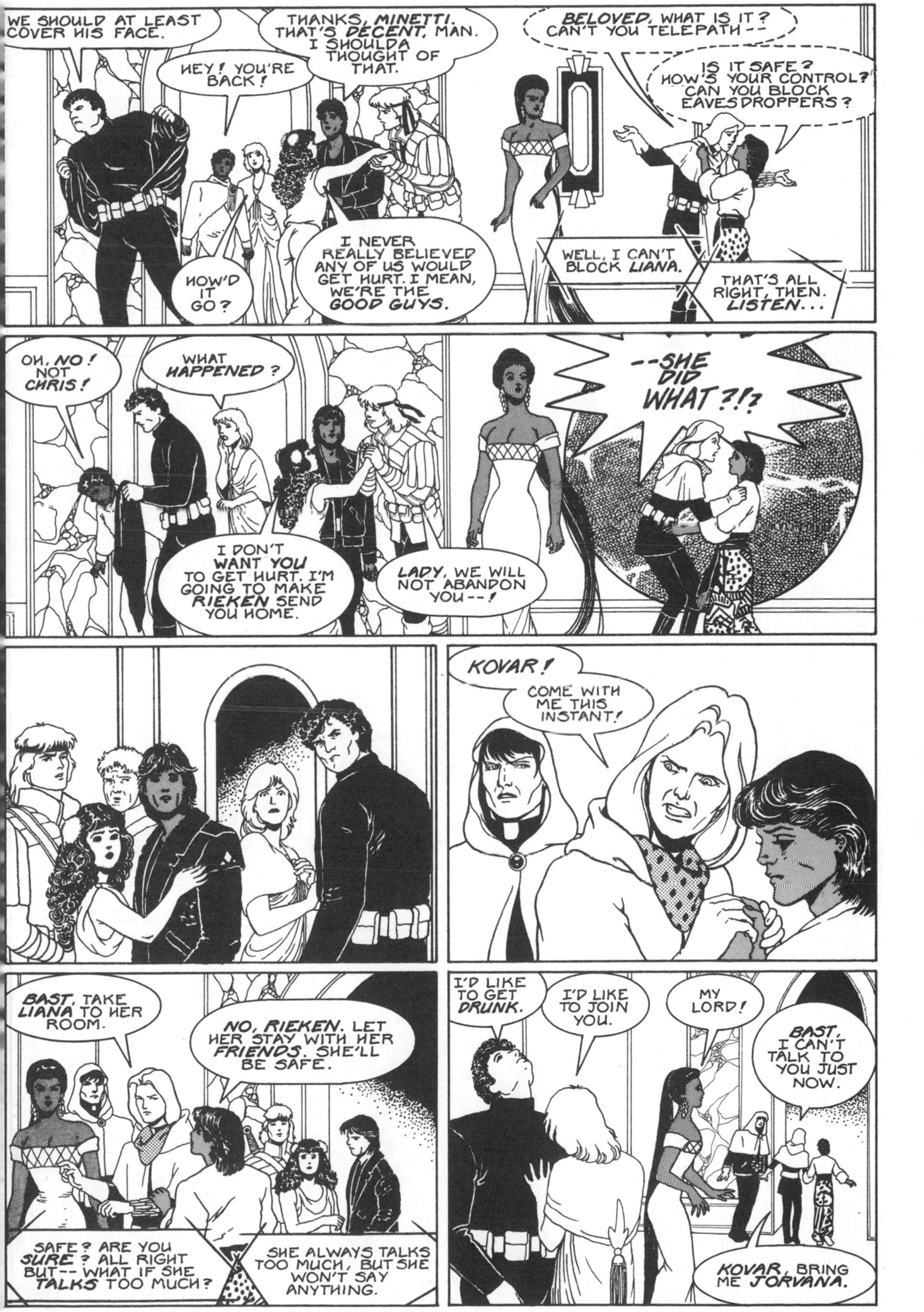
WE SHOULD AT LEAST COVER HIS FACE.
HEY! YOU'RE BACK!
THANKS, MINETTI. THAT'S DECENT, MAN. I SHOULDA THOUGHT OF THAT.
HOW'D IT GO?
I NEVER REALLY BELIEVED ANY OF US WOULD GET HURT. I MEAN, WE'RE THE GOOD GUYS.
BELOVED, WHAT IS IT? CAN'T YOU TELEPATH --
IS IT SAFE? HOW'S YOUR CONTROL? CAN YOU BLOCK EAVESDROPPERS?
WELL, I CAN'T BLOCK LIANA.
THAT'S ALL RIGHT, THEN. LISTEN...
OH, NO! NOT CHRIS!
WHAT HAPPENED?
I DON'T WANT YOU TO GET HURT. I'M GOING TO MAKE RIEKEN SEND YOU HOME.
LADY, WE WILL NOT ABANDON YOU --!
--SHE DID WHAT?!?
KOVAR!
COME WITH ME THIS INSTANT!
BAST, TAKE LIANA TO HER ROOM.
NO, RIEKEN. LET HER STAY WITH HER FRIENDS. SHE'LL BE SAFE.
SAFE? ARE YOU SURE? ALL RIGHT BUT-- WHAT IF SHE TALKS TOO MUCH?
SHE ALWAYS TALKS TOO MUCH, BUT SHE WON'T SAY ANYTHING.
I'D LIKE TO GET DRUNK.
I'D LIKE TO JOIN YOU.
MY LORD!
BAST, I CAN'T TALK TO YOU JUST NOW.
KOVAR, BRING ME JORVANA.

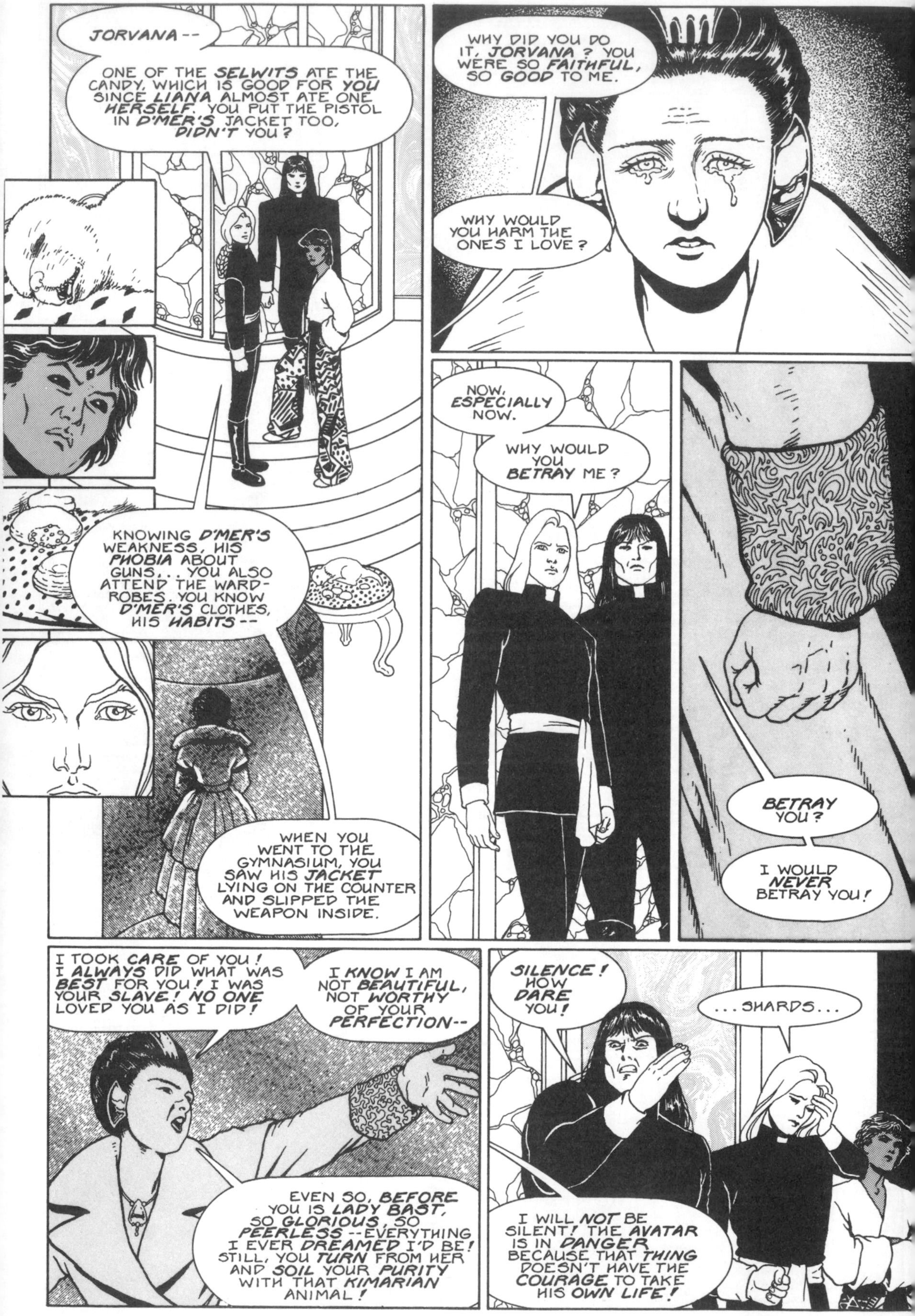
JORVANA--
ONE OF THE SELWITS ATE THE CANDY, WHICH IS GOOD FOR YOU SINCE LIANA ALMOST ATE ONE HERSELF. YOU PUT THE PISTOL IN D'MER'S JACKET TOO, DIDN'T YOU?
KNOWING D'MER'S WEAKNESS, HIS PHOBIA ABOUT GUNS... YOU ALSO ATTEND THE WARDROBES. YOU KNOW D'MER'S CLOTHES, HIS HABITS--
WHEN YOU WENT TO THE GYMNASIUM, YOU SAW HIS JACKET LYING ON THE COUNTER AND SLIPPED THE WEAPON INSIDE.
WHY DID YOU DO IT, JORVANA? YOU WERE SO FAITHFUL, SO GOOD TO ME.
WHY WOULD YOU HARM THE ONES I LOVE?
NOW, ESPECIALLY NOW.
WHY WOULD YOU BETRAY ME?
BETRAY YOU?
I WOULD NEVER BETRAY YOU!
I TOOK CARE OF YOU! I ALWAYS DID WHAT WAS BEST FOR YOU! I WAS YOUR SLAVE! NO ONE LOVED YOU AS I DID!
I KNOW I AM NOT BEAUTIFUL, NOT WORTHY OF YOUR PERFECTION--
EVEN SO, BEFORE YOU IS LADY BAST, SO GLORIOUS, SO PEERLESS--EVERYTHING I EVER DREAMED I'D BE! STILL, YOU TURN FROM HER AND SOIL YOUR PURITY WITH THAT KIMARIAN ANIMAL!
SILENCE! HOW DARE YOU!
...SHARDS...
I WILL NOT BE SILENT! THE AVATAR IS IN DANGER BECAUSE THAT THING DOESN'T HAVE THE COURAGE TO TAKE HIS OWN LIFE!

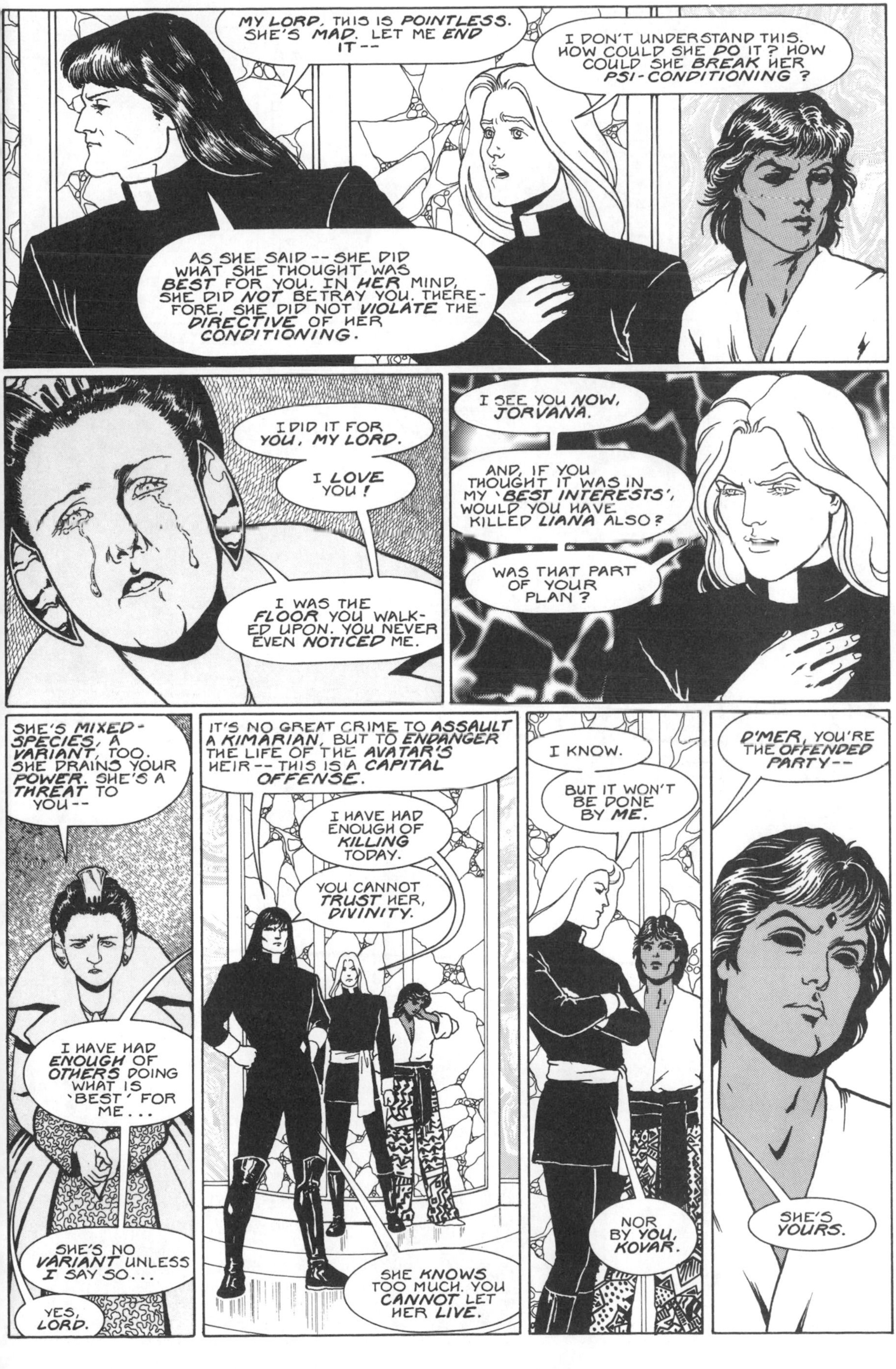
MY LORD, THIS IS POINTLESS. SHE'S MAD. LET ME END IT --
I DON'T UNDERSTAND THIS. HOW COULD SHE DO IT? HOW COULD SHE BREAK HER PSI-CONDITIONING?
AS SHE SAID -- SHE DID WHAT SHE THOUGHT WAS BEST FOR YOU. IN HER MIND, SHE DID NOT BETRAY YOU. THEREFORE, SHE DID NOT VIOLATE THE DIRECTIVE OF HER CONDITIONING.
I DID IT FOR YOU, MY LORD.
I LOVE YOU!
I WAS THE FLOOR YOU WALKED UPON. YOU NEVER EVEN NOTICED ME.
I SEE YOU NOW, JORVANA.
AND, IF YOU THOUGHT IT WAS IN MY 'BEST INTERESTS', WOULD YOU HAVE KILLED LIANA ALSO?
WAS THAT PART OF YOUR PLAN?
SHE'S MIXED-SPECIES, A VARIANT, TOO. SHE DRAINS YOUR POWER. SHE'S A THREAT TO YOU--
I HAVE HAD ENOUGH OF OTHERS DOING WHAT IS 'BEST' FOR ME...
SHE'S NO VARIANT UNLESS I SAY SO...
YES, LORD.
IT'S NO GREAT CRIME TO ASSAULT A KIMARIAN, BUT TO ENDANGER THE LIFE OF THE AVATAR'S HEIR -- THIS IS A CAPITAL OFFENSE.
I HAVE HAD ENOUGH OF KILLING TODAY.
YOU CANNOT TRUST HER, DIVINITY.
SHE KNOWS TOO MUCH. YOU CANNOT LET HER LIVE.
I KNOW.
BUT IT WON'T BE DONE BY ME.
NOR BY YOU, KOVAR.
D'MER, YOU'RE THE OFFENDED PARTY--
SHE'S YOURS.

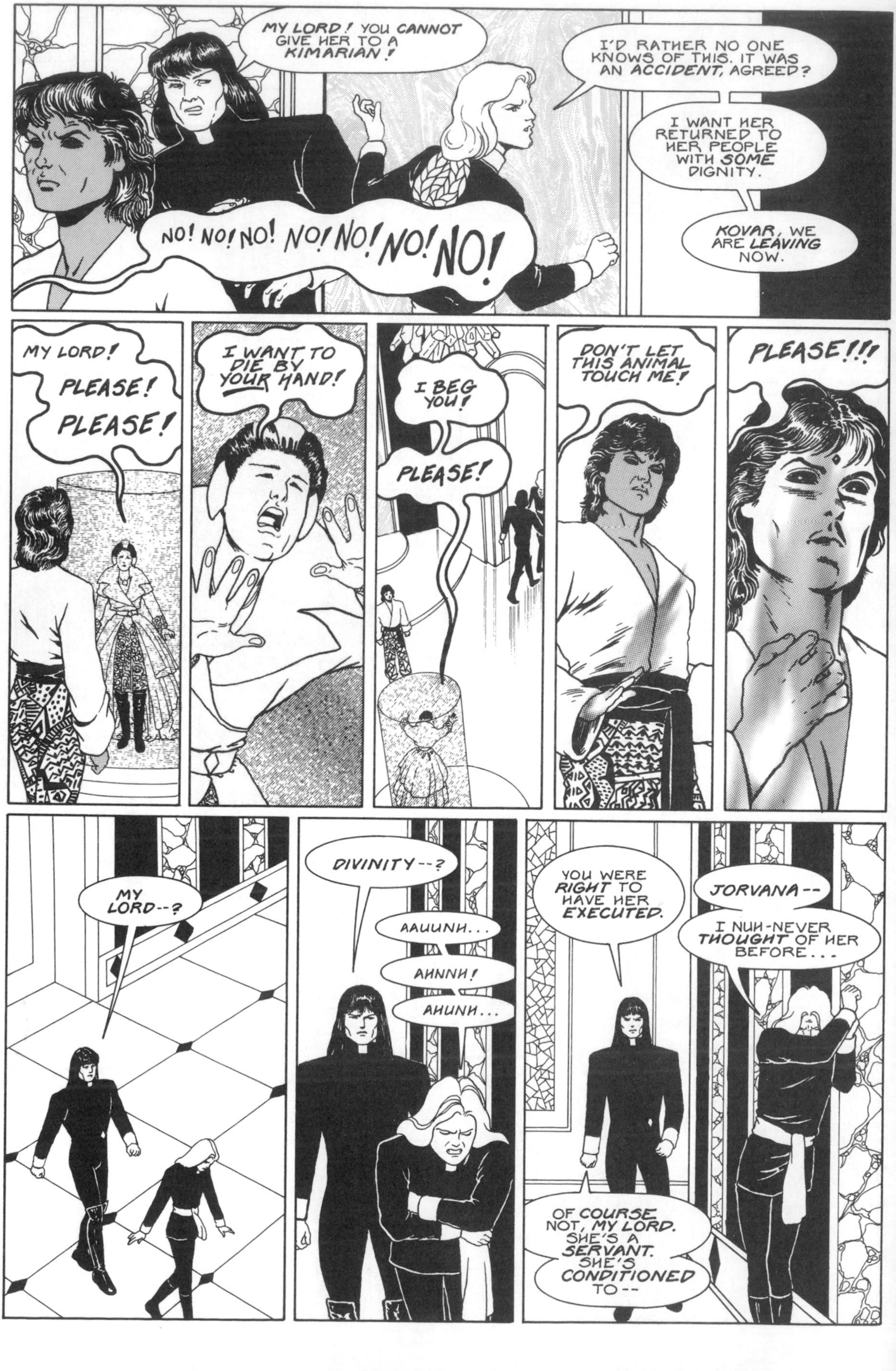
MY LORD! YOU CANNOT GIVE HER TO A KIMARIAN!
I'D RATHER NO ONE KNOWS OF THIS. IT WAS AN ACCIDENT, AGREED?
I WANT HER RETURNED TO HER PEOPLE WITH SOME DIGNITY.
NO! NO! NO! NO! NO! NO! NO!
KOVAR, WE ARE LEAVING NOW.
MY LORD! PLEASE! PLEASE!
I WANT TO DIE BY YOUR HAND!
I BEG YOU!
PLEASE!
DON'T LET THIS ANIMAL TOUCH ME!
PLEASE!!!
MY LORD--?
DIVINITY--?
AAUUNH...
AHNNH!
AHUNH...
YOU WERE RIGHT TO HAVE HER EXECUTED.
OF COURSE NOT, MY LORD. SHE'S A SERVANT. SHE'S CONDITIONED TO--
JORVANA--
I NUH-NEVER THOUGHT OF HER BEFORE...

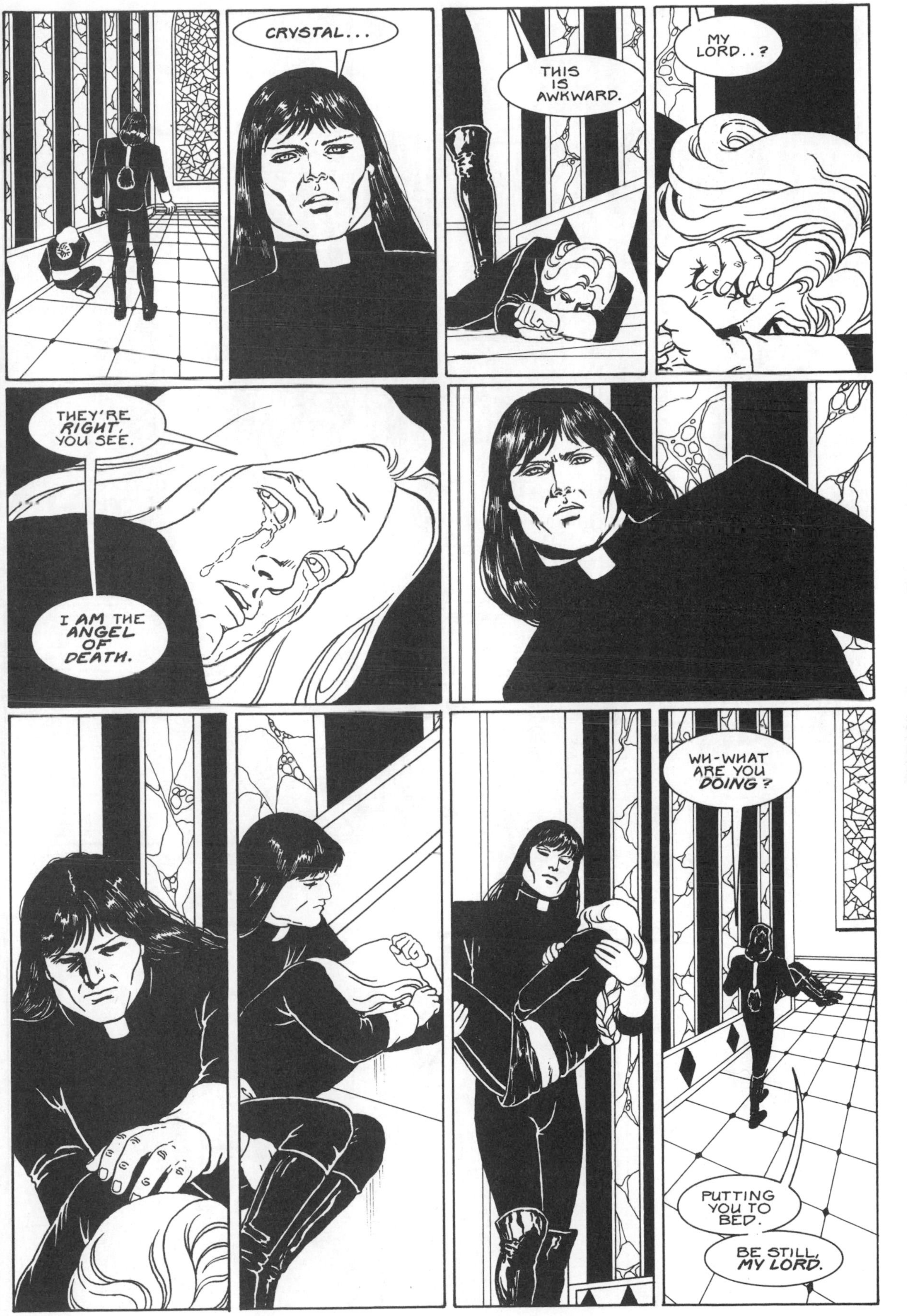
CRYSTAL...
THIS IS AWKWARD.
MY LORD..?
THEY'RE RIGHT, YOU SEE.
I AM THE ANGEL OF DEATH.
WH-WHAT ARE YOU DOING?
PUTTING YOU TO BED.
BE STILL, MY LORD.

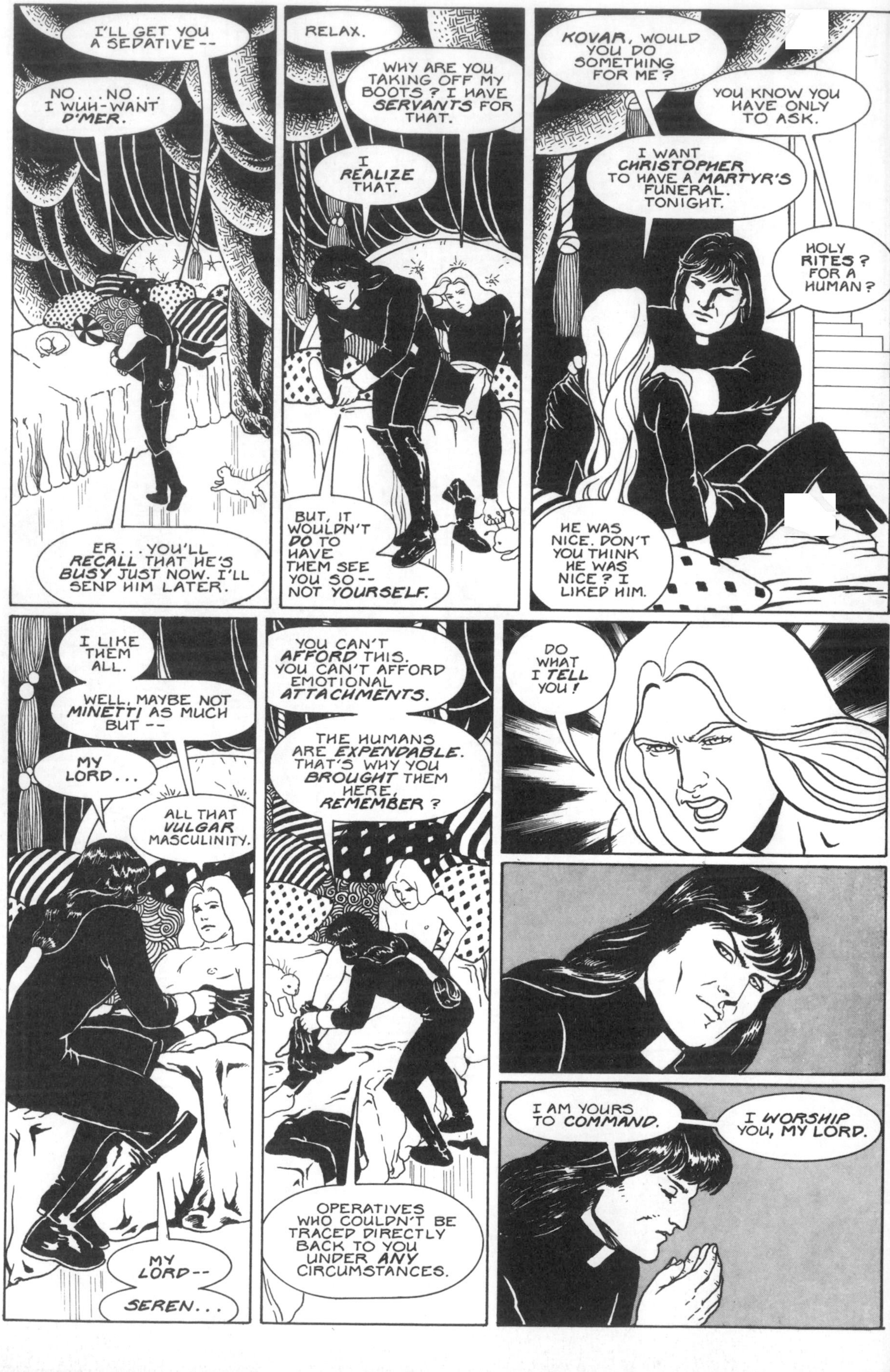
I'LL GET YOU A SEDATIVE --
NO... NO... I WUH-WANT D'MER.
ER... YOU'LL RECALL THAT HE'S BUSY JUST NOW. I'LL SEND HIM LATER.
RELAX.
WHY ARE YOU TAKING OFF MY BOOTS? I HAVE SERVANTS FOR THAT.
I REALIZE THAT.
BUT, IT WOULDN'T DO TO HAVE THEM SEE YOU SO -- NOT YOURSELF.
KOVAR, WOULD YOU DO SOMETHING FOR ME?
YOU KNOW YOU HAVE ONLY TO ASK.
I WANT CHRISTOPHER TO HAVE A MARTYR'S FUNERAL. TONIGHT.
HOLY RITES? FOR A HUMAN?
HE WAS NICE. DON'T YOU THINK HE WAS NICE? I LIKED HIM.
I LIKE THEM ALL.
WELL, MAYBE NOT MINETTI AS MUCH BUT --
MY LORD...
ALL THAT VULGAR MASCULINITY.
MY LORD --
SEREN...
YOU CAN'T AFFORD THIS. YOU CAN'T AFFORD EMOTIONAL ATTACHMENTS.
THE HUMANS ARE EXPENDABLE. THAT'S WHY YOU BROUGHT THEM HERE, REMEMBER?
OPERATIVES WHO COULDN'T BE TRACED DIRECTLY BACK TO YOU UNDER ANY CIRCUMSTANCES.
DO WHAT I TELL YOU!
I AM YOURS TO COMMAND.
I WORSHIP YOU, MY LORD.

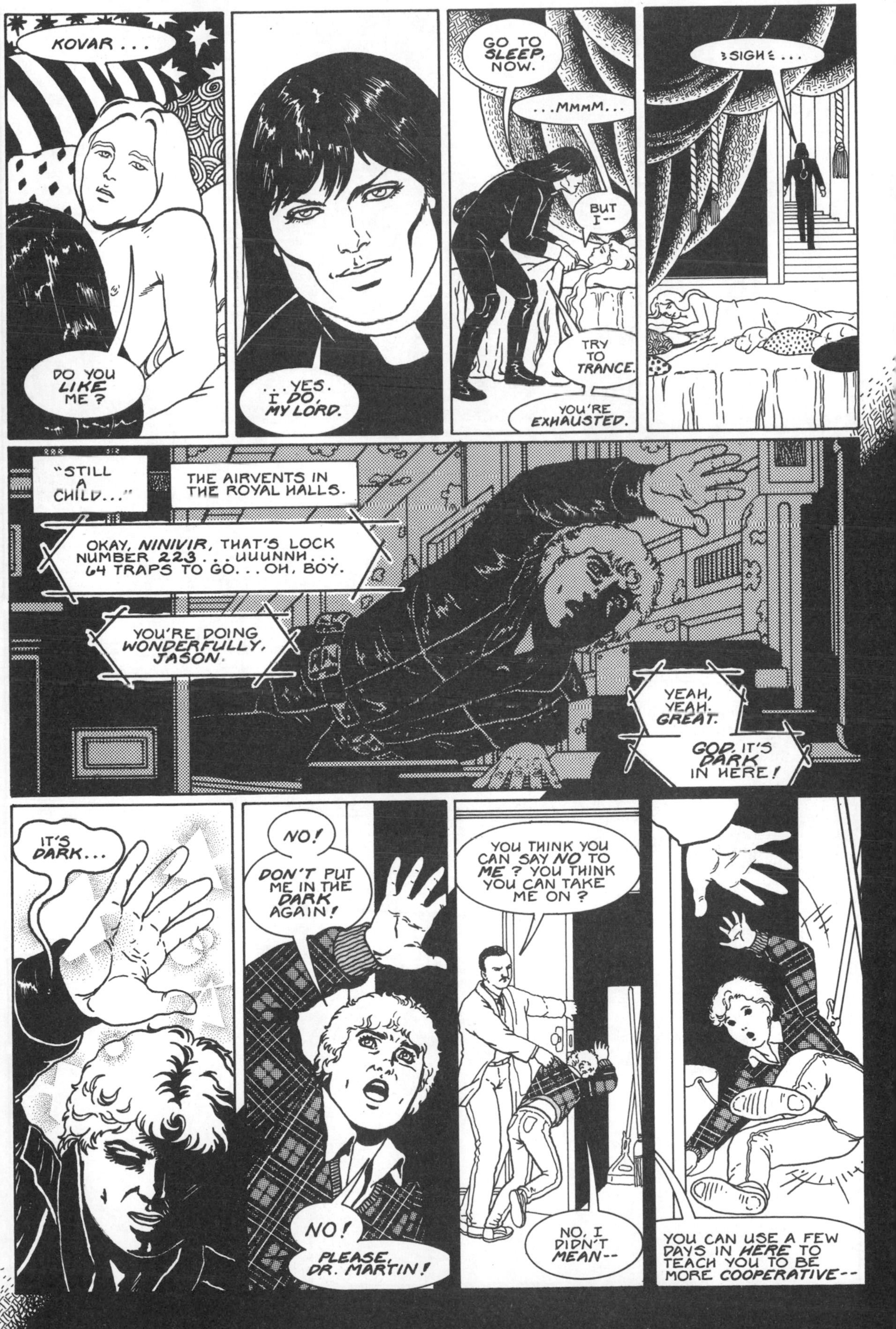
KOVAR . . .
DO YOU LIKE ME ?
. . . YES. I DO, MY LORD.
GO TO SLEEP, NOW.
. . . MMMM . . .
BUT I--
TRY TO TRANCE.
YOU'RE EXHAUSTED.
SIGH . . .
"STILL A CHILD..."
THE AIRVENTS IN THE ROYAL HALLS.
OKAY, NINIVIR, THAT'S LOCK NUMBER 223 . . . UUUNNH . . . 64 TRAPS TO GO . . . OH, BOY.
YOU'RE DOING WONDERFULLY, JASON.
YEAH, YEAH. GREAT.
GOD. IT'S DARK IN HERE!
IT'S DARK . . .
NO!
DON'T PUT ME IN THE DARK AGAIN!
NO! PLEASE, DR. MARTIN!
YOU THINK YOU CAN SAY NO TO ME ? YOU THINK YOU CAN TAKE ME ON ?
NO, I DIDN'T MEAN--
YOU CAN USE A FEW DAYS IN HERE TO TEACH YOU TO BE MORE COOPERATIVE--

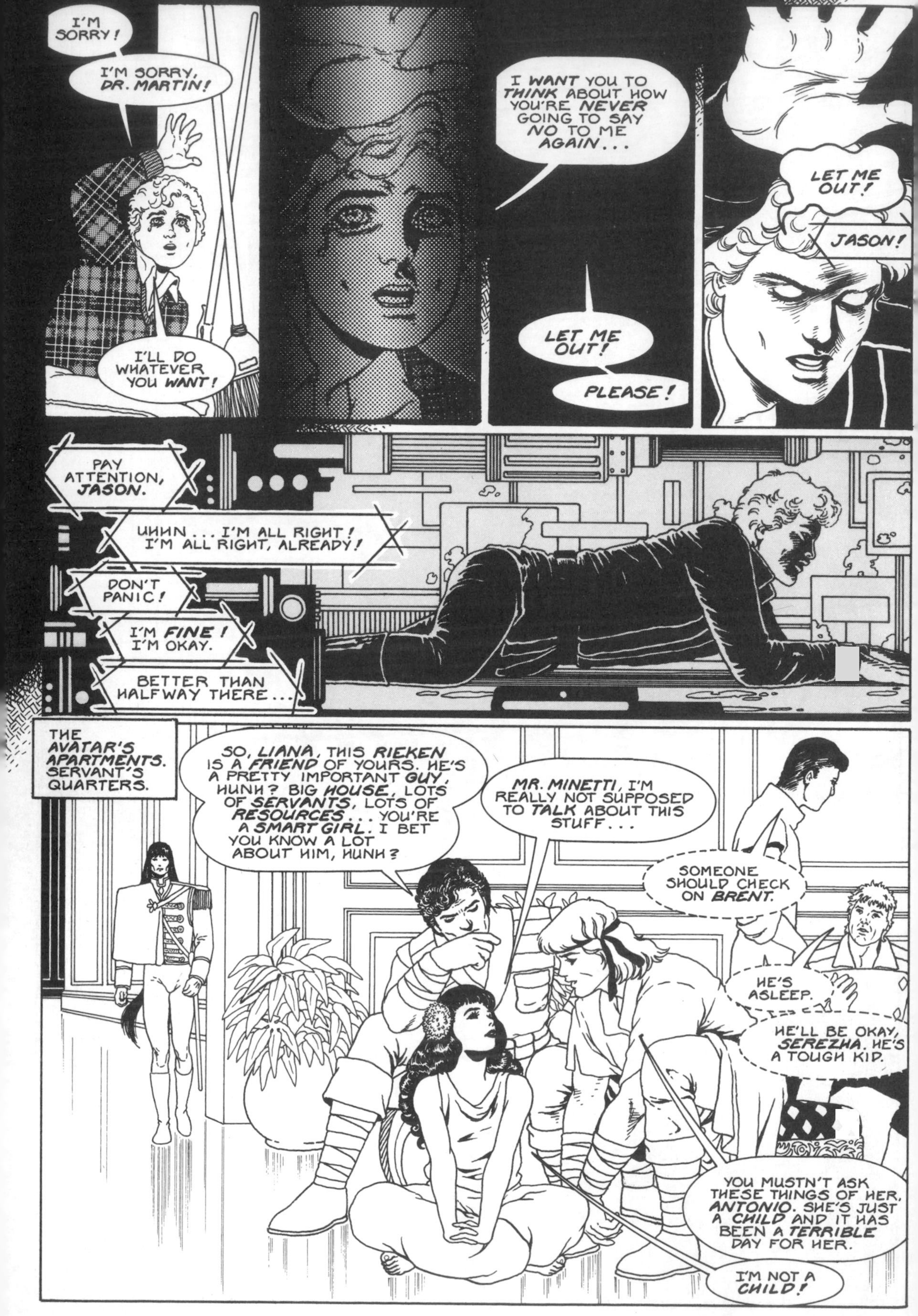
I'M SORRY!
I'M SORRY, DR. MARTIN!
I'LL DO WHATEVER YOU WANT!
I WANT YOU TO THINK ABOUT HOW YOU'RE NEVER GOING TO SAY NO TO ME AGAIN...
LET ME OUT!
PLEASE!
LET ME OUT!
JASON!
PAY ATTENTION, JASON.
UHHN... I'M ALL RIGHT! I'M ALL RIGHT, ALREADY!
DON'T PANIC!
I'M FINE! I'M OKAY.
BETTER THAN HALFWAY THERE...
THE AVATAR'S APARTMENTS. SERVANT'S QUARTERS.
SO, LIANA, THIS RIEKEN IS A FRIEND OF YOURS. HE'S A PRETTY IMPORTANT GUY, HUNH? BIG HOUSE, LOTS OF SERVANTS, LOTS OF RESOURCES... YOU'RE A SMART GIRL. I BET YOU KNOW A LOT ABOUT HIM, HUNH?
MR. MINETTI, I'M REALLY NOT SUPPOSED TO TALK ABOUT THIS STUFF...
SOMEONE SHOULD CHECK ON BRENT.
HE'S ASLEEP.
HE'LL BE OKAY, SEREZHA. HE'S A TOUGH KID.
YOU MUSTN'T ASK THESE THINGS OF HER, ANTONIO. SHE'S JUST A CHILD AND IT HAS BEEN A TERRIBLE DAY FOR HER.
I'M NOT A CHILD!

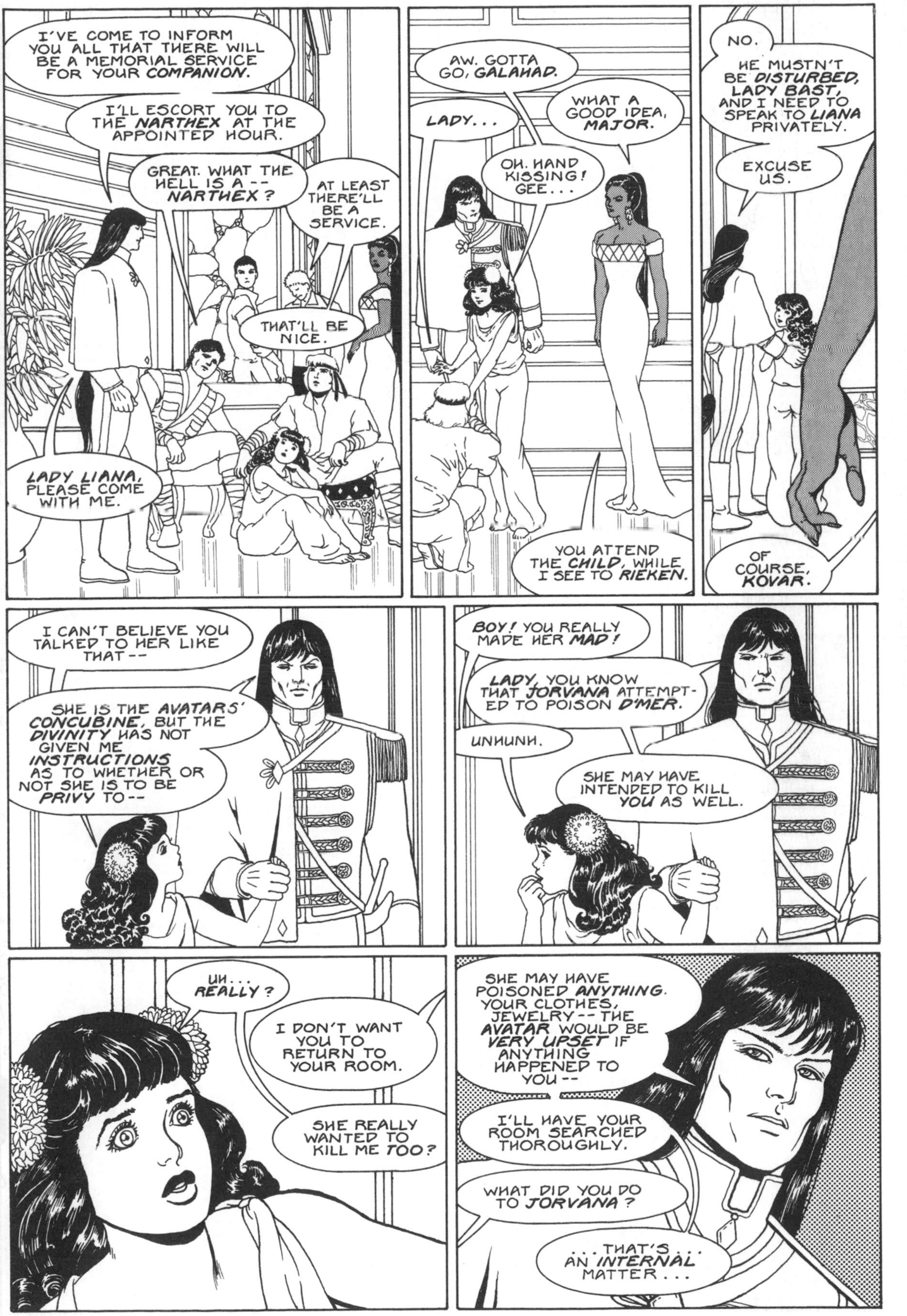
I'VE COME TO INFORM YOU ALL THAT THERE WILL BE A MEMORIAL SERVICE FOR YOUR COMPANION.
I'LL ESCORT YOU TO THE NARTHEX AT THE APPOINTED HOUR.
GREAT. WHAT THE HELL IS A -- NARTHEX?
AT LEAST THERE'LL BE A SERVICE.
THAT'LL BE NICE.
LADY LIANA, PLEASE COME WITH ME.
AW. GOTTA GO, GALAHAD.
LADY...
WHAT A GOOD IDEA, MAJOR.
OH. HAND KISSING! GEE...
YOU ATTEND THE CHILD, WHILE I SEE TO RIEKEN.
NO.
HE MUSTN'T BE DISTURBED, LADY BAST, AND I NEED TO SPEAK TO LIANA PRIVATELY.
EXCUSE US.
OF COURSE, KOVAR.
I CAN'T BELIEVE YOU TALKED TO HER LIKE THAT--
SHE IS THE AVATARS' CONCUBINE, BUT THE DIVINITY HAS NOT GIVEN ME INSTRUCTIONS AS TO WHETHER OR NOT SHE IS TO BE PRIVY TO--
BOY! YOU REALLY MADE HER MAD!
LADY, YOU KNOW THAT JORVANA ATTEMPTED TO POISON D'MER.
UNHUNH.
SHE MAY HAVE INTENDED TO KILL YOU AS WELL.
UH... REALLY?
I DON'T WANT YOU TO RETURN TO YOUR ROOM.
SHE REALLY WANTED TO KILL ME TOO?
SHE MAY HAVE POISONED ANYTHING. YOUR CLOTHES, JEWELRY -- THE AVATAR WOULD BE VERY UPSET IF ANYTHING HAPPENED TO YOU --
I'LL HAVE YOUR ROOM SEARCHED THOROUGHLY.
WHAT DID YOU DO TO JORVANA?
...THAT'S... AN INTERNAL MATTER...

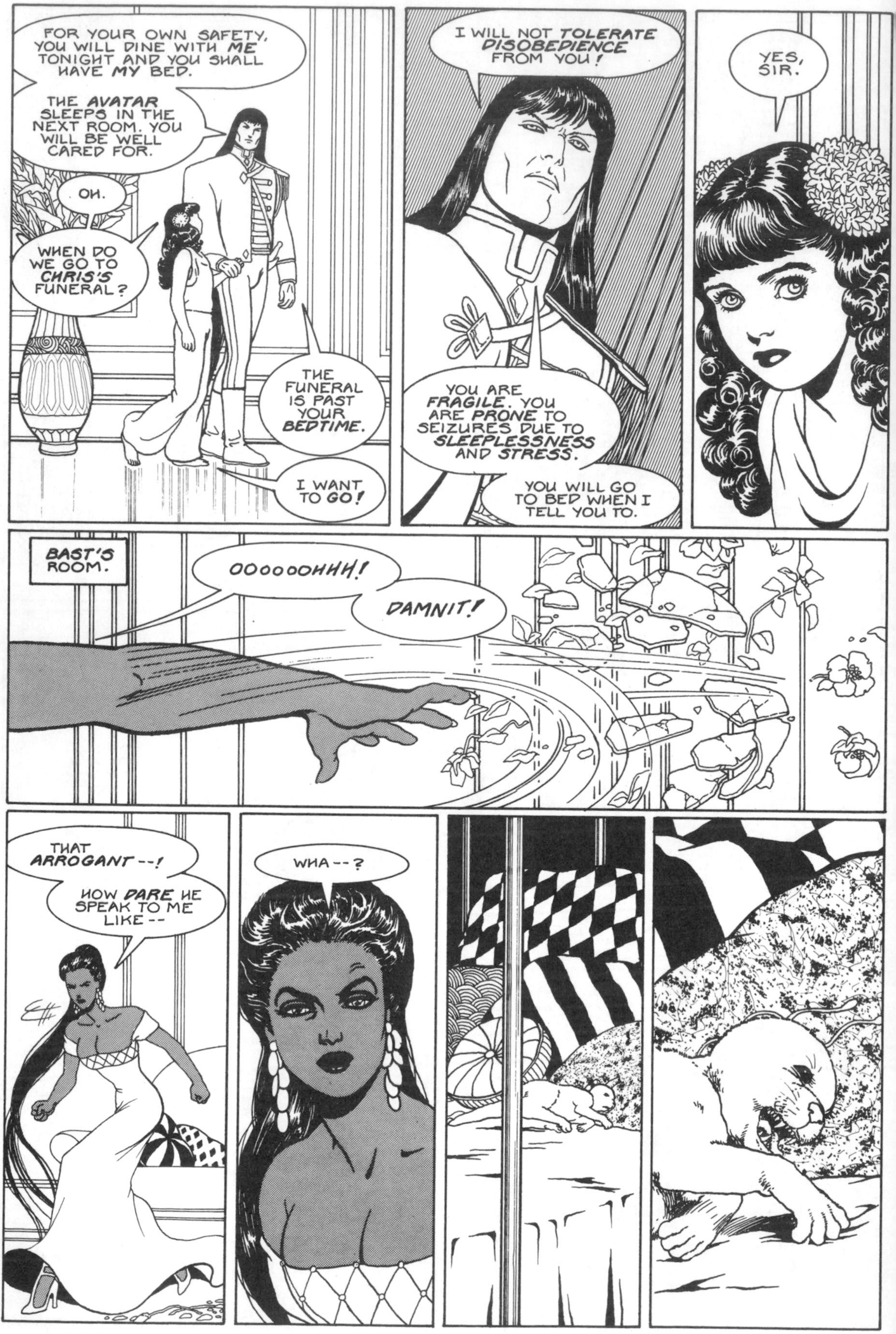

FOR YOUR OWN SAFETY, YOU WILL DINE WITH ME TONIGHT AND YOU SHALL HAVE MY BED.
THE AVATAR SLEEPS IN THE NEXT ROOM. YOU WILL BE WELL CARED FOR.
OH.
WHEN DO WE GO TO CHRIS'S FUNERAL?
THE FUNERAL IS PAST YOUR BEDTIME.
I WANT TO GO!
I WILL NOT TOLERATE DISOBEDIENCE FROM YOU!
YOU ARE FRAGILE. YOU ARE PRONE TO SEIZURES DUE TO SLEEPLESSNESS AND STRESS.
YOU WILL GO TO BED WHEN I TELL YOU TO.
YES, SIR.
BAST'S ROOM.
OOOOOOHHH!
DAMNIT!
THAT ARROGANT --!
HOW DARE HE SPEAK TO ME LIKE --
WHA --?

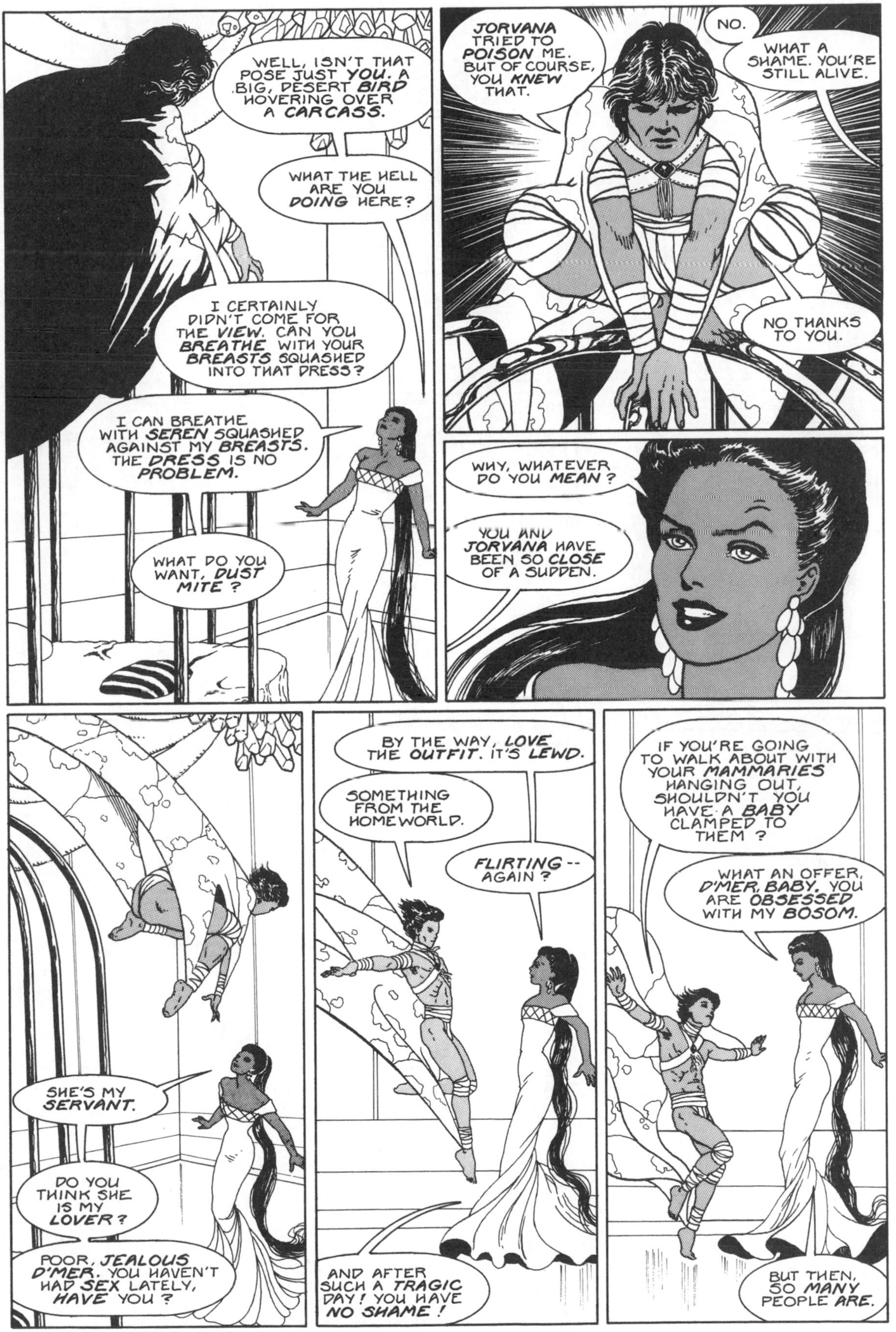
WELL, ISN'T THAT POSE JUST YOU. A BIG, DESERT BIRD HOVERING OVER A CARCASS.
WHAT THE HELL ARE YOU DOING HERE?
I CERTAINLY DIDN'T COME FOR THE VIEW. CAN YOU BREATHE WITH YOUR BREASTS SQUASHED INTO THAT DRESS?
I CAN BREATHE WITH SEREN SQUASHED AGAINST MY BREASTS. THE DRESS IS NO PROBLEM.
WHAT DO YOU WANT, DUST MITE?
JORVANA TRIED TO POISON ME. BUT OF COURSE, YOU KNEW THAT.
NO.
WHAT A SHAME. YOU'RE STILL ALIVE.
NO THANKS TO YOU.
WHY, WHATEVER DO YOU MEAN?
YOU AND JORVANA HAVE BEEN SO CLOSE OF A SUDDEN.
SHE'S MY SERVANT.
DO YOU THINK SHE IS MY LOVER?
POOR, JEALOUS D'MER. YOU HAVEN'T HAD SEX LATELY, HAVE YOU?
BY THE WAY, LOVE THE OUTFIT. IT'S LEWD.
SOMETHING FROM THE HOMEWORLD.
FLIRTING -- AGAIN?
AND AFTER SUCH A TRAGIC DAY! YOU HAVE NO SHAME!
IF YOU'RE GOING TO WALK ABOUT WITH YOUR MAMMARIES HANGING OUT, SHOULDN'T YOU HAVE A BABY CLAMPED TO THEM?
WHAT AN OFFER, D'MER, BABY. YOU ARE OBSESSED WITH MY BOSOM.
BUT THEN, SO MANY PEOPLE ARE.

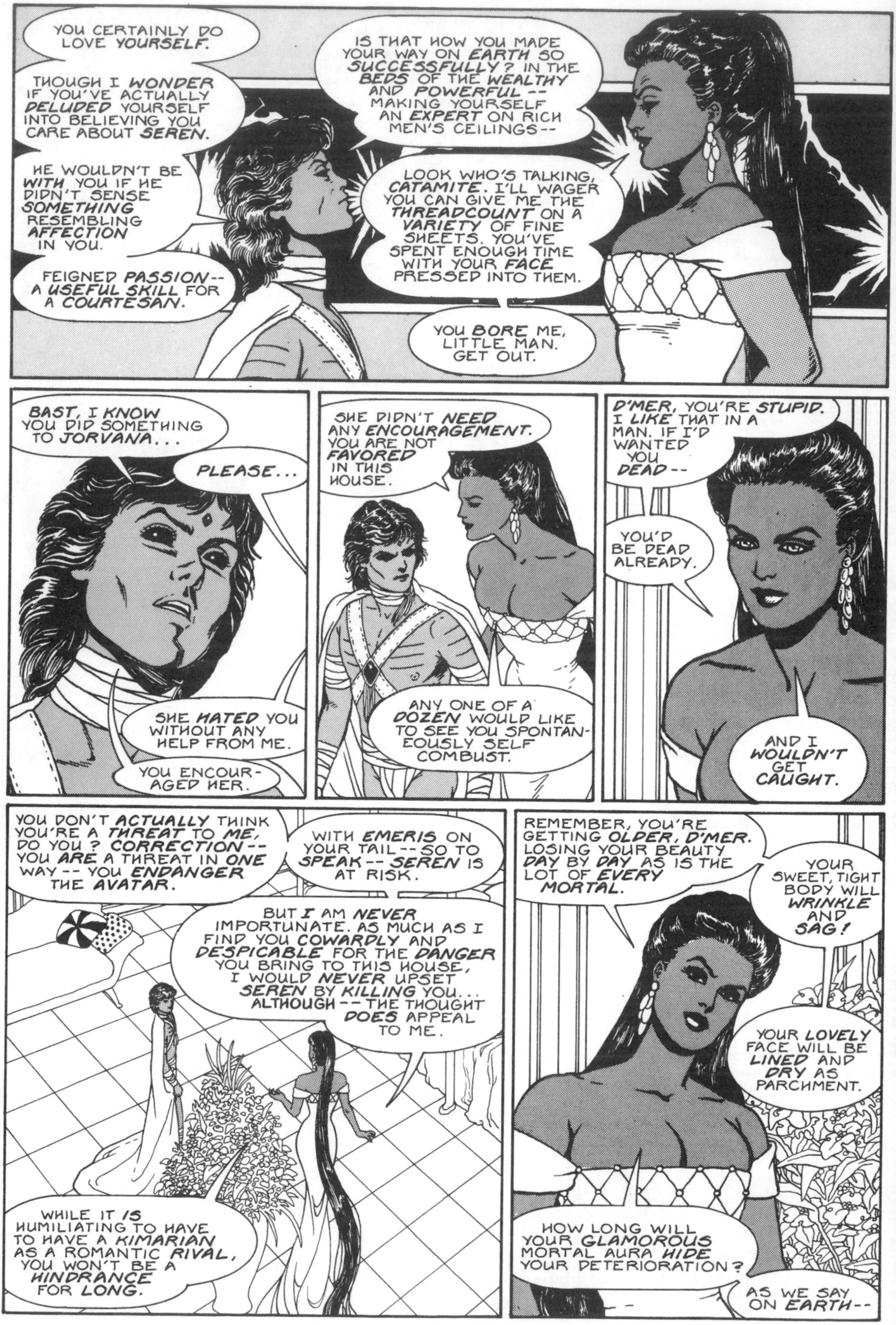
YOU CERTAINLY DO LOVE YOURSELF.
THOUGH I WONDER IF YOU'VE ACTUALLY DELUDED YOURSELF INTO BELIEVING YOU CARE ABOUT SEREN.
HE WOULDN'T BE WITH YOU IF HE DIDN'T SENSE SOMETHING RESEMBLING AFFECTION IN YOU.
FEIGNED PASSION-- A USEFUL SKILL FOR A COURTESAN.
IS THAT HOW YOU MADE YOUR WAY ON EARTH SO SUCCESSFULLY? IN THE BEDS OF THE WEALTHY AND POWERFUL-- MAKING YOURSELF AN EXPERT ON RICH MEN'S CEILINGS--
LOOK WHO'S TALKING, CATAMITE. I'LL WAGER YOU CAN GIVE ME THE THREADCOUNT ON A VARIETY OF FINE SHEETS. YOU'VE SPENT ENOUGH TIME WITH YOUR FACE PRESSED INTO THEM.
YOU BORE ME, LITTLE MAN. GET OUT.
BAST, I KNOW YOU DID SOMETHING TO JORVANA...
PLEASE...
SHE HATED YOU WITHOUT ANY HELP FROM ME.
YOU ENCOURAGED HER.
SHE DIDN'T NEED ANY ENCOURAGEMENT. YOU ARE NOT FAVORED IN THIS HOUSE.
ANY ONE OF A DOZEN WOULD LIKE TO SEE YOU SPONTANEOUSLY SELF COMBUST.
D'MER, YOU'RE STUPID. I LIKE THAT IN A MAN. IF I'D WANTED YOU DEAD--
YOU'D BE DEAD ALREADY.
AND I WOULDN'T GET CAUGHT.
YOU DON'T ACTUALLY THINK YOU'RE A THREAT TO ME, DO YOU? CORRECTION-- YOU ARE A THREAT IN ONE WAY-- YOU ENDANGER THE AVATAR.
WITH EMERIS ON YOUR TAIL--SO TO SPEAK-- SEREN IS AT RISK.
BUT I AM NEVER IMPORTUNATE. AS MUCH AS I FIND YOU COWARDLY AND DESPICABLE FOR THE DANGER YOU BRING TO THIS HOUSE, I WOULD NEVER UPSET SEREN BY KILLING YOU... ALTHOUGH-- THE THOUGHT DOES APPEAL TO ME.
WHILE IT IS HUMILIATING TO HAVE TO HAVE A KIMARIAN AS A ROMANTIC RIVAL, YOU WON'T BE A HINDRANCE FOR LONG.
REMEMBER, YOU'RE GETTING OLDER, D'MER. LOSING YOUR BEAUTY DAY BY DAY AS IS THE LOT OF EVERY MORTAL.
YOUR SWEET, TIGHT BODY WILL WRINKLE AND SAG!
YOUR LOVELY FACE WILL BE LINED AND DRY AS PARCHMENT.
HOW LONG WILL YOUR GLAMOROUS MORTAL AURA HIDE YOUR DETERIORATION?
AS WE SAY ON EARTH--

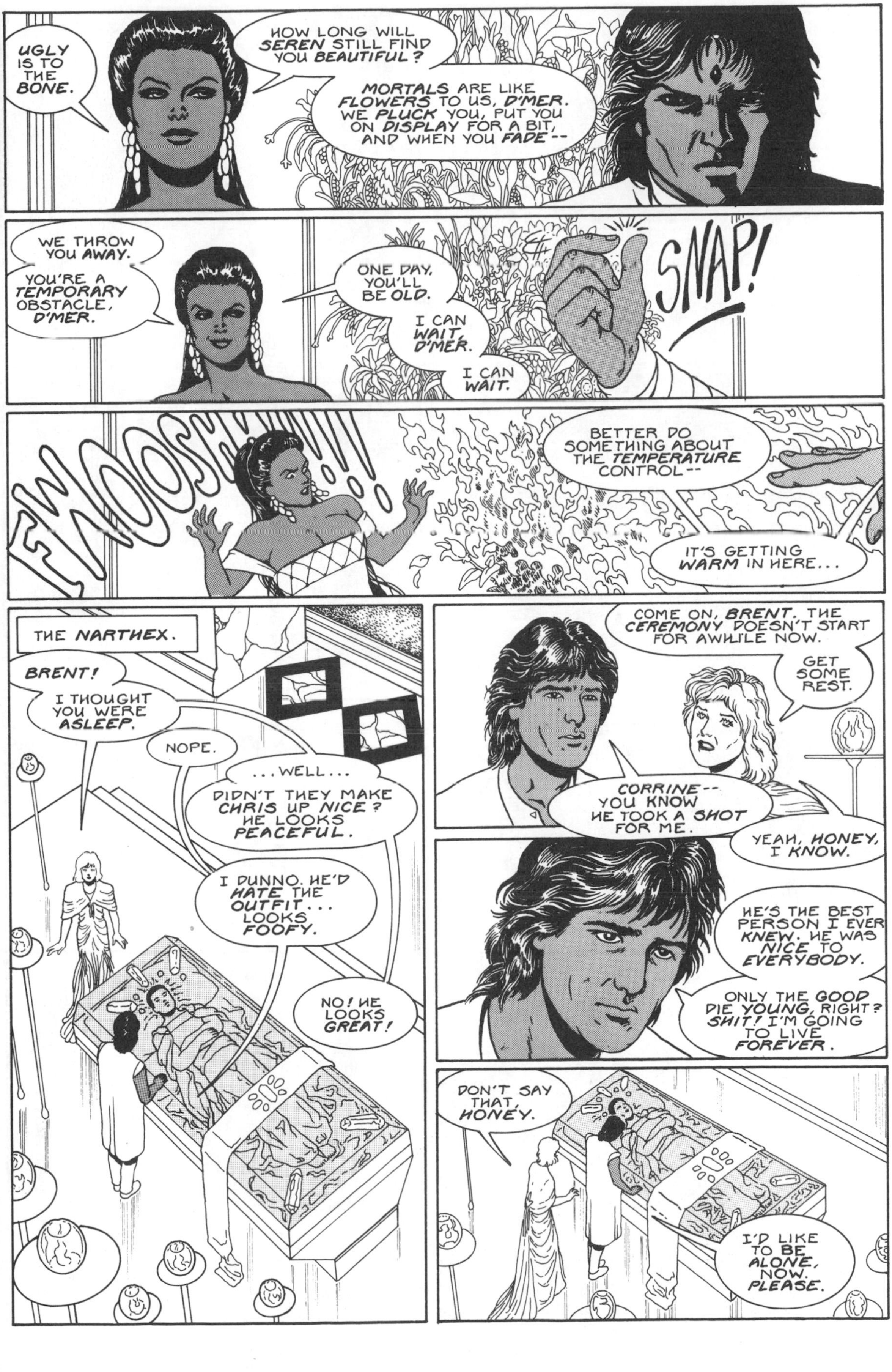
UGLY IS TO THE BONE.
HOW LONG WILL SEREN STILL FIND YOU BEAUTIFUL?
MORTALS ARE LIKE FLOWERS TO US, D'MER. WE PLUCK YOU, PUT YOU ON DISPLAY FOR A BIT, AND WHEN YOU FADE--
WE THROW YOU AWAY.
YOU'RE A TEMPORARY OBSTACLE, D'MER.
ONE DAY, YOU'LL BE OLD.
I CAN WAIT, D'MER.
I CAN WAIT.
SNAP!
FWOOSH!!
BETTER DO SOMETHING ABOUT THE TEMPERATURE CONTROL--
IT'S GETTING WARM IN HERE...
THE NARTHEX.
BRENT!
I THOUGHT YOU WERE ASLEEP.
NOPE.
...WELL...
DIDN'T THEY MAKE CHRIS UP NICE? HE LOOKS PEACEFUL.
I DUNNO. HE'D HATE THE OUTFIT... LOOKS FOOFY.
NO! HE LOOKS GREAT!
COME ON, BRENT. THE CEREMONY DOESN'T START FOR AWHILE NOW.
GET SOME REST.
CORRINE-- YOU KNOW HE TOOK A SHOT FOR ME.
YEAH, HONEY, I KNOW.
HE'S THE BEST PERSON I EVER KNEW. HE WAS NICE TO EVERYBODY.
ONLY THE GOOD DIE YOUNG, RIGHT? SHIT! I'M GOING TO LIVE FOREVER.
DON'T SAY THAT, HONEY.
I'D LIKE TO BE ALONE, NOW. PLEASE.

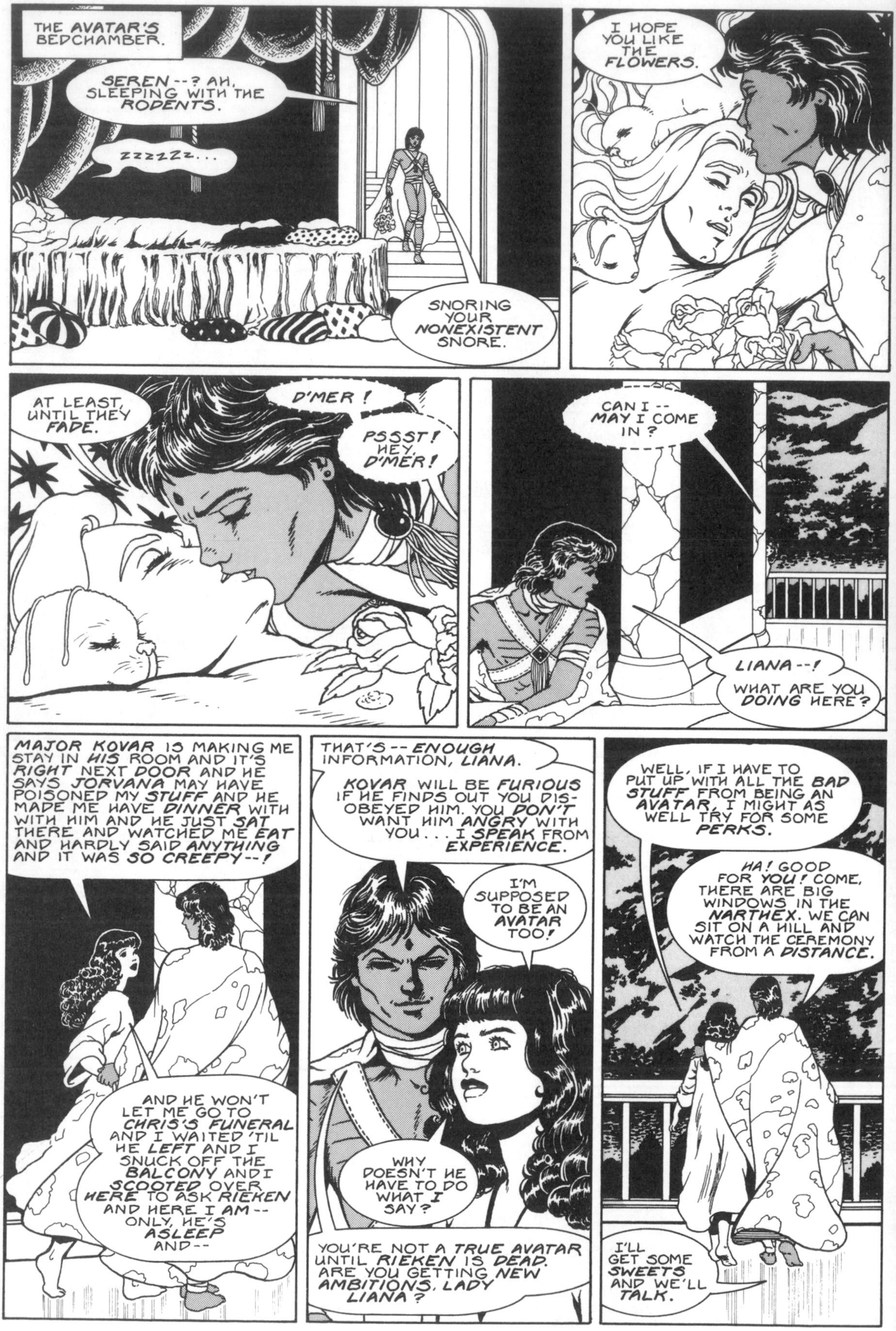
THE AVATAR'S BEDCHAMBER.
SEREN--? AH, SLEEPING WITH THE RODENTS.
ZZZZZZ...
SNORING YOUR NONEXISTENT SNORE.
I HOPE YOU LIKE THE FLOWERS.
AT LEAST, UNTIL THEY FADE.
D'MER!
PSSST! HEY, D'MER!
CAN I -- MAY I COME IN?
LIANA--!
WHAT ARE YOU DOING HERE?
MAJOR KOVAR IS MAKING ME STAY IN HIS ROOM AND IT'S RIGHT NEXT DOOR AND HE SAYS JORVANA MAY HAVE POISONED MY STUFF AND HE MADE ME HAVE DINNER WITH WITH HIM AND HE JUST SAT THERE AND WATCHED ME EAT AND HARDLY SAID ANYTHING AND IT WAS SO CREEPY--!
AND HE WON'T LET ME GO TO CHRIS'S FUNERAL AND I WAITED 'TIL HE LEFT AND I SNUCK OFF THE BALCONY AND I SCOOTED OVER HERE TO ASK RIEKEN AND HERE I AM -- ONLY, HE'S ASLEEP AND--
THAT'S -- ENOUGH INFORMATION, LIANA.
KOVAR WILL BE FURIOUS IF HE FINDS OUT YOU DIS-OBEYED HIM. YOU DON'T WANT HIM ANGRY WITH YOU . . . I SPEAK FROM EXPERIENCE.
I'M SUPPOSED TO BE AN AVATAR TOO!
WHY DOESN'T HE HAVE TO DO WHAT I SAY?
YOU'RE NOT A TRUE AVATAR UNTIL RIEKEN IS DEAD. ARE YOU GETTING NEW AMBITIONS, LADY LIANA?
WELL, IF I HAVE TO PUT UP WITH ALL THE BAD STUFF FROM BEING AN AVATAR, I MIGHT AS WELL TRY FOR SOME PERKS.
HA! GOOD FOR YOU! COME, THERE ARE BIG WINDOWS IN THE NARTHEX. WE CAN SIT ON A HILL AND WATCH THE CEREMONY FROM A DISTANCE.
I'LL GET SOME SWEETS AND WE'LL TALK.

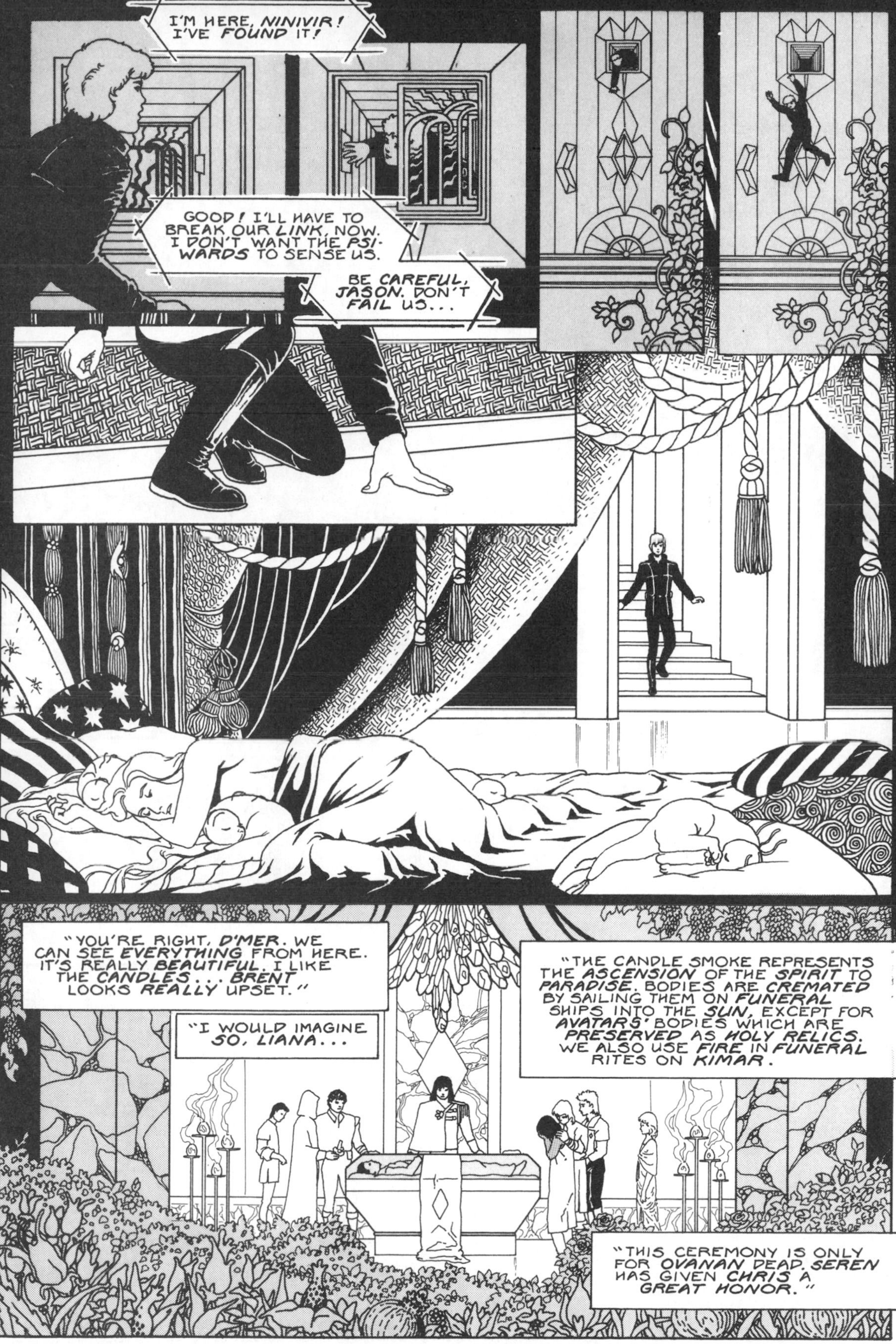
I'M HERE, NINIVIR! I'VE FOUND IT!
GOOD! I'LL HAVE TO BREAK OUR LINK, NOW. I DON'T WANT THE PSI-WARDS TO SENSE US.
BE CAREFUL, JASON. DON'T FAIL US...
"YOU'RE RIGHT, D'MER. WE CAN SEE EVERYTHING FROM HERE. IT'S REALLY BEAUTIFUL. I LIKE THE CANDLES... BRENT LOOKS REALLY UPSET."
"I WOULD IMAGINE SO, LIANA...
"THE CANDLE SMOKE REPRESENTS THE ASCENSION OF THE SPIRIT TO PARADISE. BODIES ARE CREMATED BY SAILING THEM ON FUNERAL SHIPS INTO THE SUN, EXCEPT FOR AVATARS' BODIES WHICH ARE PRESERVED AS HOLY RELICS. WE ALSO USE FIRE IN FUNERAL RITES ON KIMAR.
"THIS CEREMONY IS ONLY FOR OVANAN DEAD. SEREN HAS GIVEN CHRIS A GREAT HONOR."

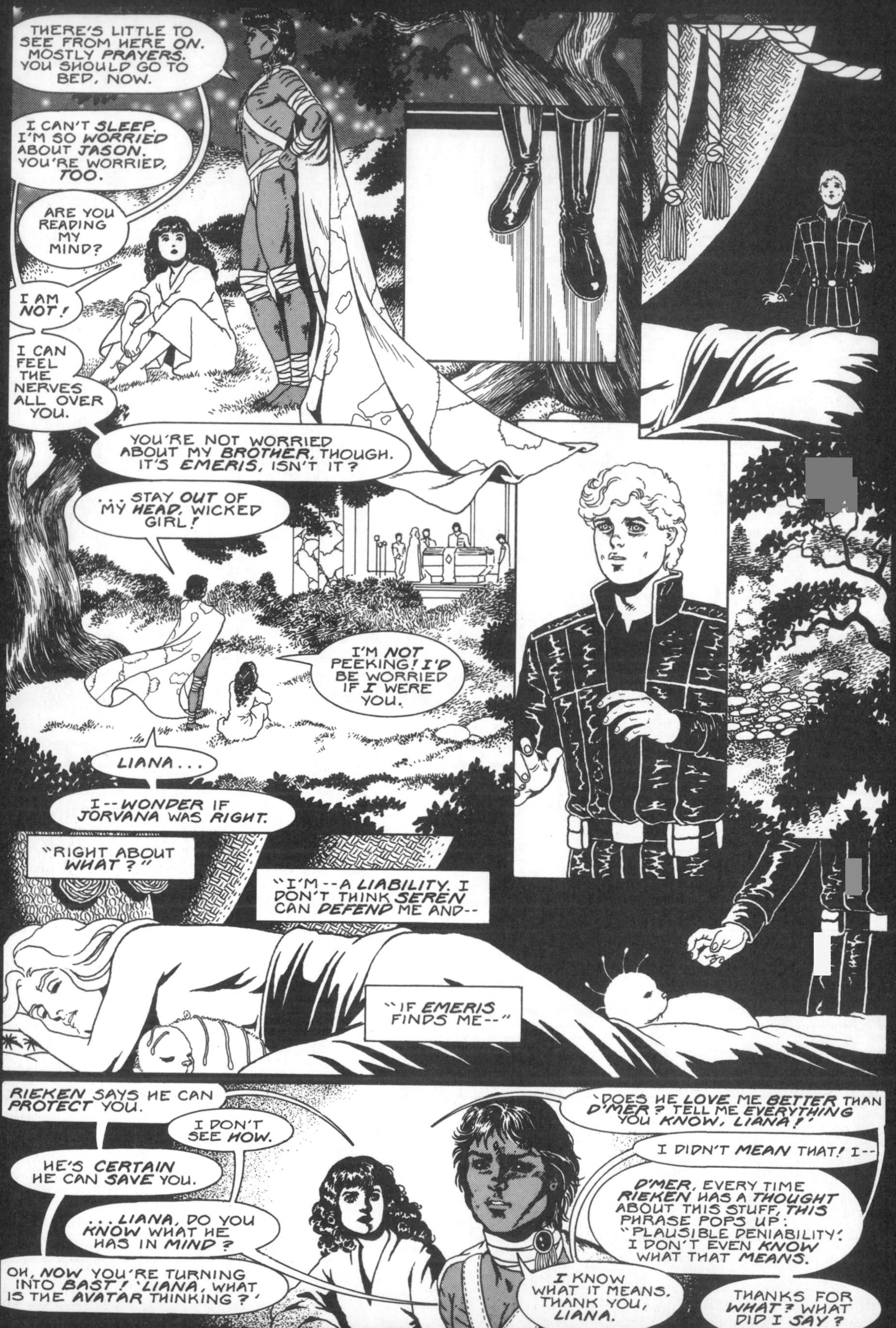
THERE'S LITTLE TO SEE FROM HERE ON. MOSTLY PRAYERS. YOU SHOULD GO TO BED, NOW.
I CAN'T SLEEP. I'M SO WORRIED ABOUT JASON. YOU'RE WORRIED, TOO.
ARE YOU READING MY MIND?
I AM NOT!
I CAN FEEL THE NERVES ALL OVER YOU.
YOU'RE NOT WORRIED ABOUT MY BROTHER, THOUGH. IT'S EMERIS, ISN'T IT?
... STAY OUT OF MY HEAD, WICKED GIRL!
I'M NOT PEEKING! I'D BE WORRIED IF I WERE YOU.
LIANA...
I--WONDER IF JORVANA WAS RIGHT.
"RIGHT ABOUT WHAT?"
"I'M--A LIABILITY. I DON'T THINK SEREN CAN DEFEND ME AND--
"IF EMERIS FINDS ME--"
RIEKEN SAYS HE CAN PROTECT YOU.
I DON'T SEE HOW.
HE'S CERTAIN HE CAN SAVE YOU.
...LIANA, DO YOU KNOW WHAT HE HAS IN MIND?
OH, NOW YOU'RE TURNING INTO BAST! 'LIANA, WHAT IS THE AVATAR THINKING?'
'DOES HE LOVE ME BETTER THAN D'MER? TELL ME EVERYTHING YOU KNOW, LIANA!'
I DIDN'T MEAN THAT! I--
D'MER, EVERY TIME RIEKEN HAS A THOUGHT ABOUT THIS STUFF, THIS PHRASE POPS UP: "PLAUSIBLE DENIABILITY." I DON'T EVEN KNOW WHAT THAT MEANS.
I KNOW WHAT IT MEANS. THANK YOU, LIANA.
THANKS FOR WHAT? WHAT DID I SAY?

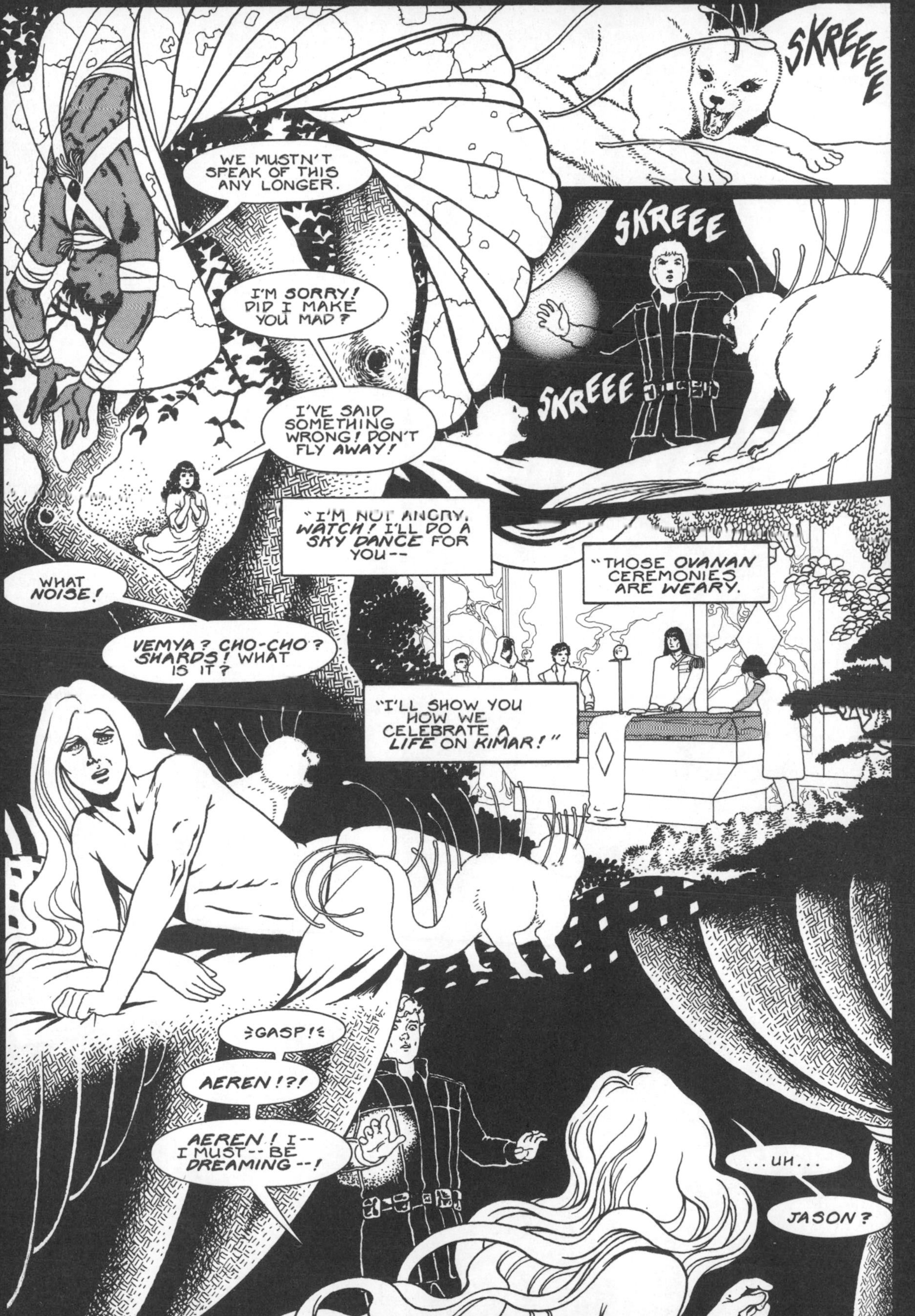

SKREEEE
WE MUSTN'T SPEAK OF THIS ANY LONGER.
I'M SORRY! DID I MAKE YOU MAD?
I'VE SAID SOMETHING WRONG! DON'T FLY AWAY!
SKREEE
SKREEE
"I'M NOT ANGRY. WATCH! I'LL DO A SKY DANCE FOR YOU--
"THOSE OVANAN CEREMONIES ARE WEARY.
"I'LL SHOW YOU HOW WE CELEBRATE A LIFE ON KIMAR!"
WHAT NOISE!
VEMYA? CHO-CHO? SHARDS! WHAT IS IT?
GASP!
AEREN!?!
AEREN! I-- I MUST-- BE DREAMING--!
...UH...
JASON?

A Distant Soil™

The story continues in

A DISTANT SOIL:
The Aria

available now from
Image Comics.

www.adistantsoil.com

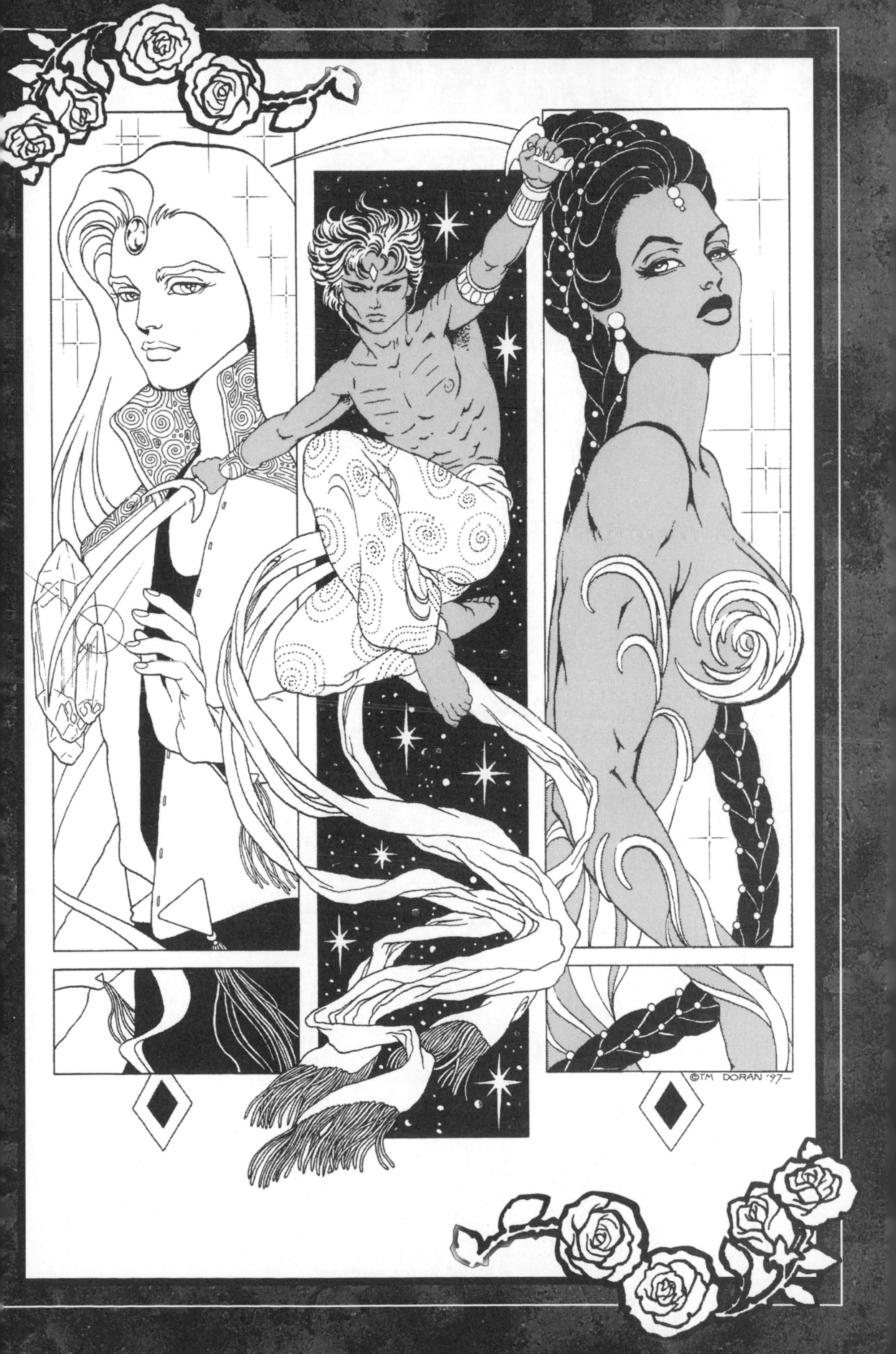
©TM DORAN '97

Character Spotlight

Antonio Minetti

Sergeant Minetti is one of my favorite character and the only character in the series to date who has ever ha his own solo stories published I'm reprinting two of them here. The second story, **D.W.** is the only tale ever to appear in *A Distant Soil* that wasn't written by me. Author Jo Duffy originally penned this for the **Punisher** comic from Marvel, but when things didn work out with her editor and, since she owed me some work she gave it to me to run as an *A Distant Soil* feature. I don't plan to have guest authors on *A Distant Soil* stories again anytime in the future, but this was a fun collaboration that turned out very well.

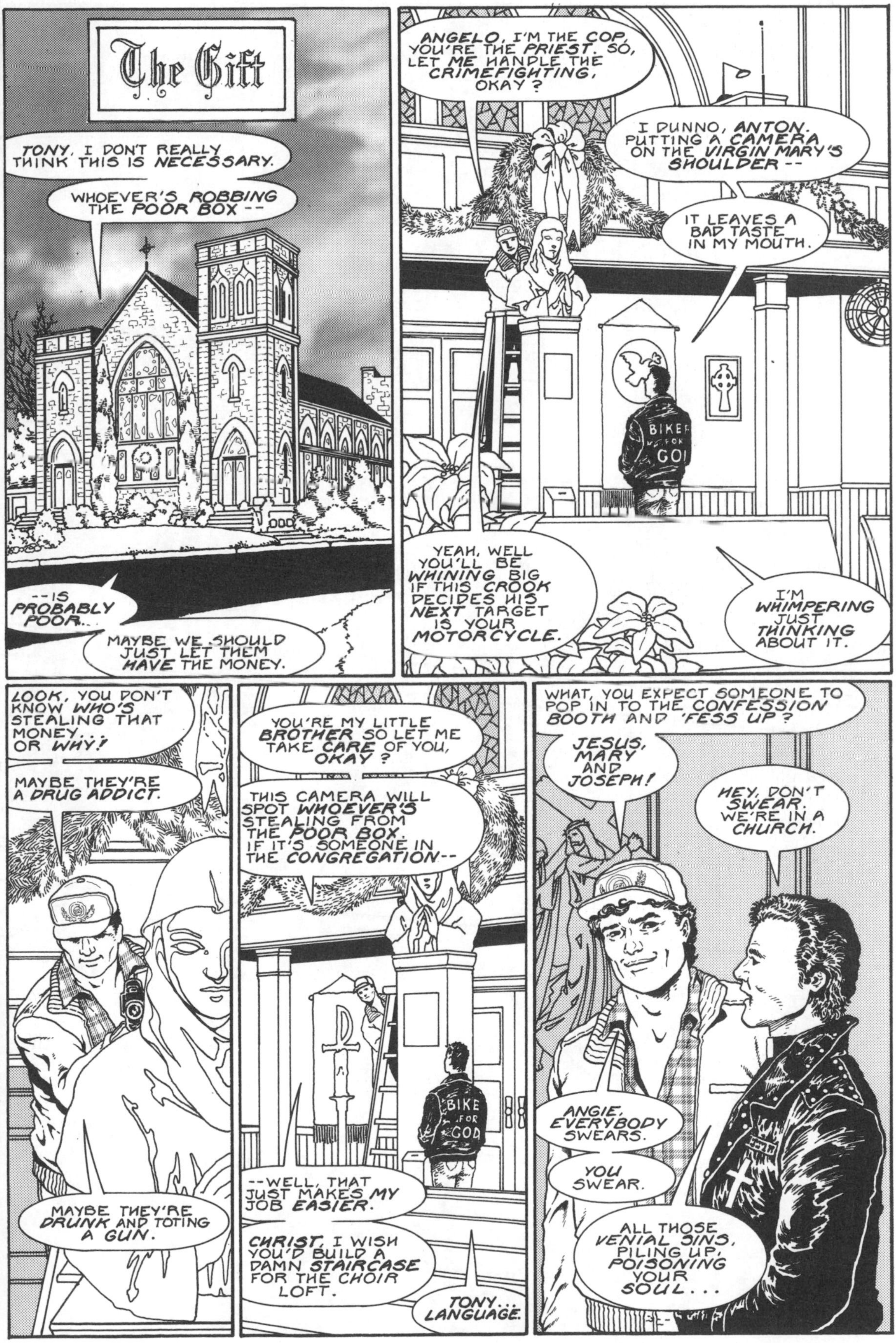
The Gift
TONY, I DON'T REALLY THINK THIS IS NECESSARY.
WHOEVER'S ROBBING THE POOR BOX --
--IS PROBABLY POOR...
MAYBE WE SHOULD JUST LET THEM HAVE THE MONEY.
ANGELO, I'M THE COP, YOU'RE THE PRIEST. SO, LET ME HANDLE THE CRIMEFIGHTING, OKAY?
I DUNNO, ANTON. PUTTING A CAMERA ON THE VIRGIN MARY'S SHOULDER --
IT LEAVES A BAD TASTE IN MY MOUTH.
BIKER FOR GOD
YEAH, WELL YOU'LL BE WHINING BIG IF THIS CROOK DECIDES HIS NEXT TARGET IS YOUR MOTORCYCLE.
I'M WHIMPERING JUST THINKING ABOUT IT.
LOOK, YOU DON'T KNOW WHO'S STEALING THAT MONEY... OR WHY!
MAYBE THEY'RE A DRUG ADDICT.
MAYBE THEY'RE DRUNK AND TOTING A GUN.
YOU'RE MY LITTLE BROTHER SO LET ME TAKE CARE OF YOU, OKAY?
THIS CAMERA WILL SPOT WHOEVER'S STEALING FROM THE POOR BOX. IF IT'S SOMEONE IN THE CONGREGATION--
BIKE FOR GOD
--WELL, THAT JUST MAKES MY JOB EASIER.
CHRIST, I WISH YOU'D BUILD A DAMN STAIRCASE FOR THE CHOIR LOFT.
TONY... LANGUAGE.
WHAT, YOU EXPECT SOMEONE TO POP IN TO THE CONFESSION BOOTH AND 'FESS UP?
JESUS, MARY AND JOSEPH!
HEY, DON'T SWEAR. WE'RE IN A CHURCH.
ANGIE, EVERYBODY SWEARS.
YOU SWEAR.
ALL THOSE VENIAL SINS, PILING UP, POISONING YOUR SOUL...

SAY A HAIL MARY.

JESUS!

YOW!

SAY IT!

OW! OW!

HALL MARY FULL OF--

CHRIST! YOU'RE BREAKING MY ARM!

BLESS YOU, MY SON.

TWO NIGHTS LATER.

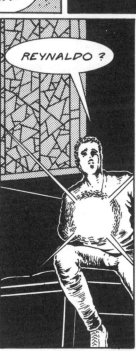

REYNALDO?

≥ GASP! ≤

REYNALDO!

DON'T GO!

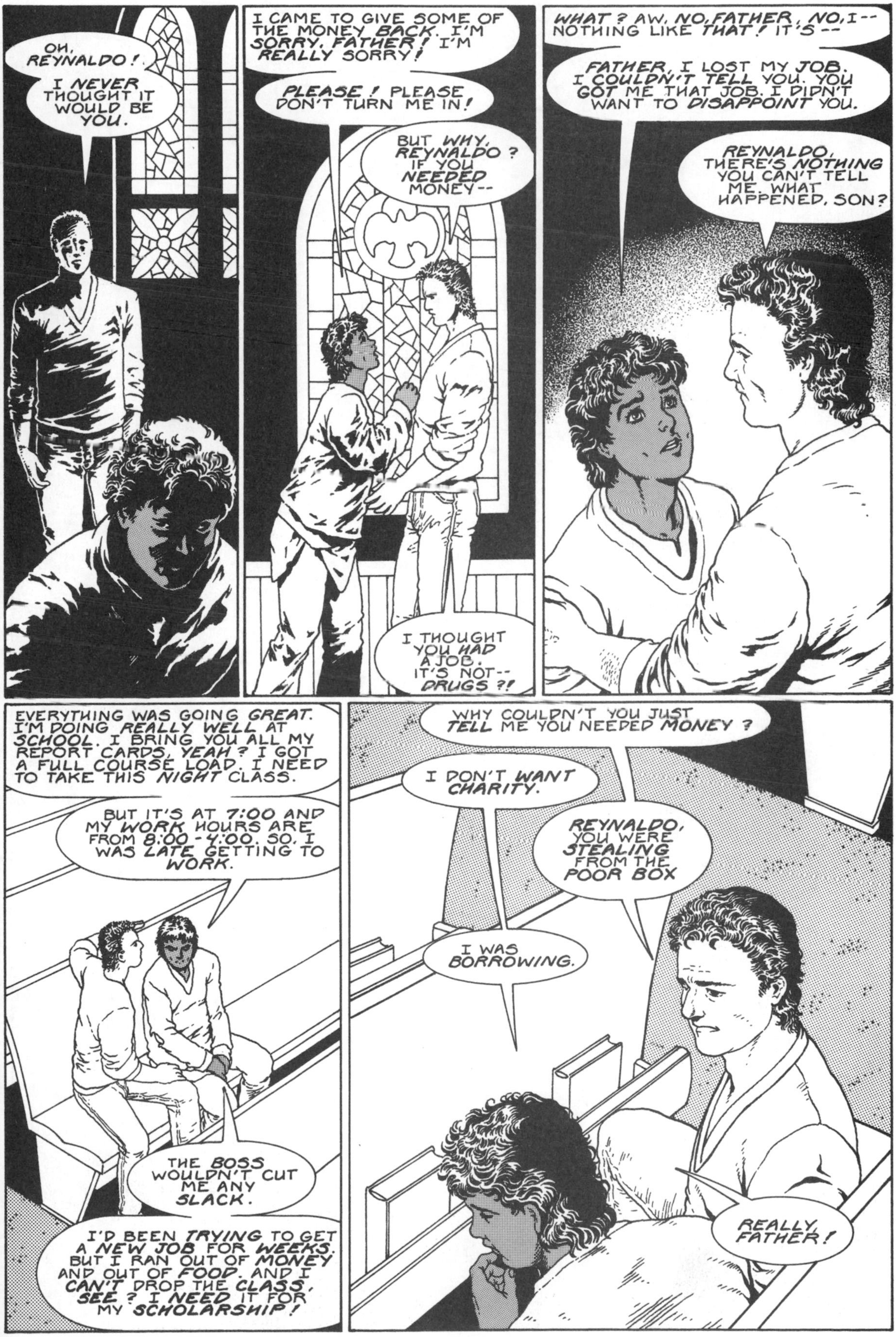
OH, REYNALDO!
I NEVER THOUGHT IT WOULD BE YOU.
I CAME TO GIVE SOME OF THE MONEY BACK. I'M SORRY, FATHER! I'M REALLY SORRY!
PLEASE! PLEASE DON'T TURN ME IN!
BUT WHY, REYNALDO? IF YOU NEEDED MONEY--
I THOUGHT YOU HAD A JOB. IT'S NOT-- DRUGS?!
WHAT? AW, NO, FATHER, NO, I-- NOTHING LIKE THAT! IT'S--
FATHER, I LOST MY JOB. I COULDN'T TELL YOU. YOU GOT ME THAT JOB. I DIDN'T WANT TO DISAPPOINT YOU.
REYNALDO, THERE'S NOTHING YOU CAN'T TELL ME. WHAT HAPPENED, SON?
EVERYTHING WAS GOING GREAT. I'M DOING REALLY WELL AT SCHOOL. I BRING YOU ALL MY REPORT CARDS, YEAH? I GOT A FULL COURSE LOAD. I NEED TO TAKE THIS NIGHT CLASS.
BUT IT'S AT 7:00 AND MY WORK HOURS ARE FROM 8:00-4:00. SO, I WAS LATE GETTING TO WORK.
THE BOSS WOULDN'T CUT ME ANY SLACK.
I'D BEEN TRYING TO GET A NEW JOB FOR WEEKS. BUT I RAN OUT OF MONEY AND OUT OF FOOD. AND I CAN'T DROP THE CLASS, SEE? I NEED IT FOR MY SCHOLARSHIP!
WHY COULDN'T YOU JUST TELL ME YOU NEEDED MONEY?
I DON'T WANT CHARITY.
REYNALDO, YOU WERE STEALING FROM THE POOR BOX
I WAS BORROWING.
REALLY, FATHER!

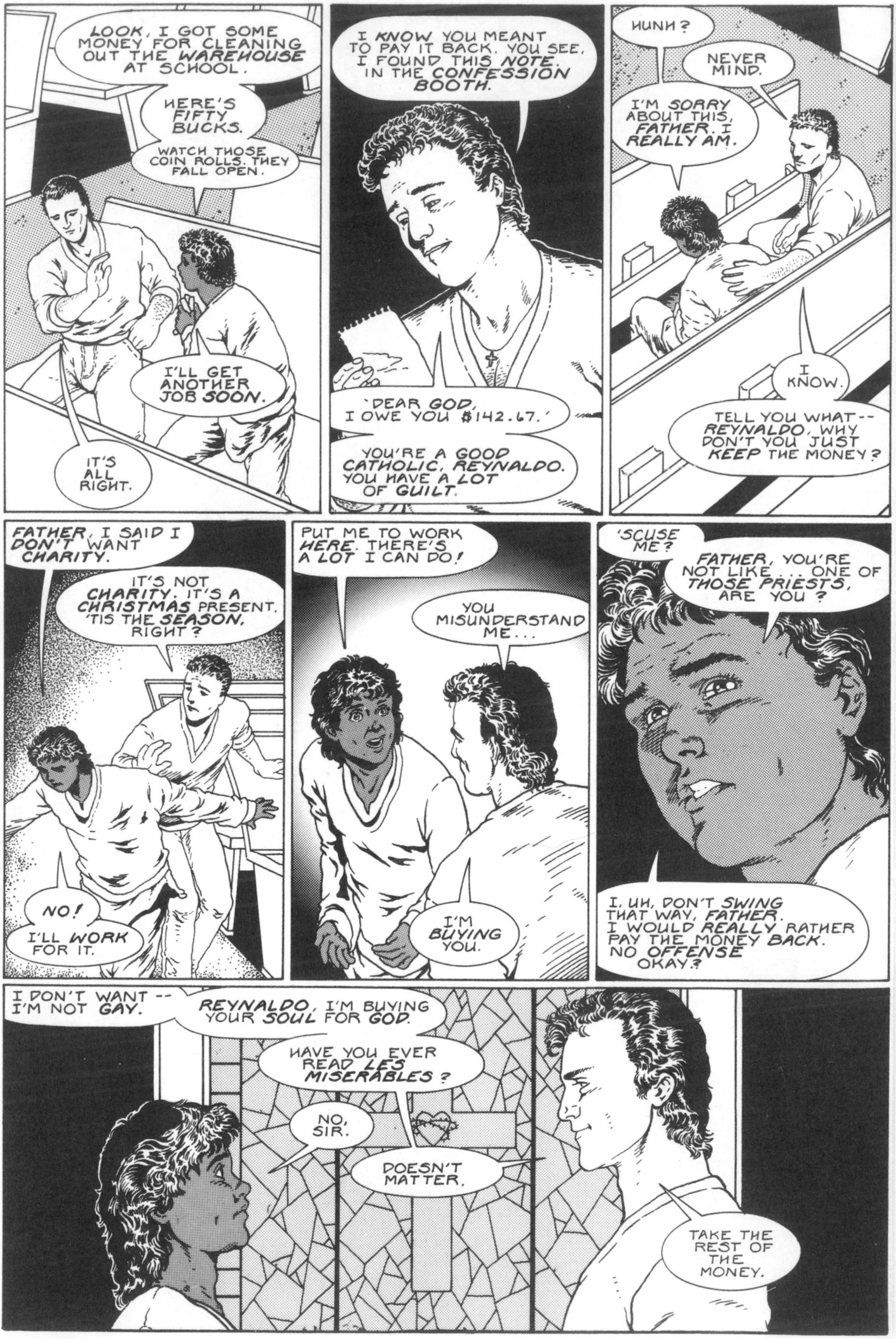
LOOK, I GOT SOME MONEY FOR CLEANING OUT THE WAREHOUSE AT SCHOOL.
HERE'S FIFTY BUCKS.
WATCH THOSE COIN ROLLS. THEY FALL OPEN.
I'LL GET ANOTHER JOB SOON.
IT'S ALL RIGHT.
I KNOW YOU MEANT TO PAY IT BACK. YOU SEE, I FOUND THIS NOTE IN THE CONFESSION BOOTH.
'DEAR GOD, I OWE YOU $142.67.'
YOU'RE A GOOD CATHOLIC, REYNALDO. YOU HAVE A LOT OF GUILT.
HUNH?
NEVER MIND.
I'M SORRY ABOUT THIS, FATHER. I REALLY AM.
I KNOW.
TELL YOU WHAT-- REYNALDO, WHY DON'T YOU JUST KEEP THE MONEY?
FATHER, I SAID I DON'T WANT CHARITY.
IT'S NOT CHARITY. IT'S A CHRISTMAS PRESENT. 'TIS THE SEASON, RIGHT?
NO! I'LL WORK FOR IT.
PUT ME TO WORK HERE. THERE'S A LOT I CAN DO!
YOU MISUNDERSTAND ME...
I'M BUYING YOU.
'SCUSE ME?
FATHER, YOU'RE NOT LIKE... ONE OF THOSE PRIESTS, ARE YOU?
I, UH, DON'T SWING THAT WAY, FATHER. I WOULD REALLY RATHER PAY THE MONEY BACK. NO OFFENSE OKAY?
I DON'T WANT -- I'M NOT GAY.
REYNALDO, I'M BUYING YOUR SOUL FOR GOD.
HAVE YOU EVER READ LES MISERABLES?
NO, SIR.
DOESN'T MATTER.
TAKE THE REST OF THE MONEY.

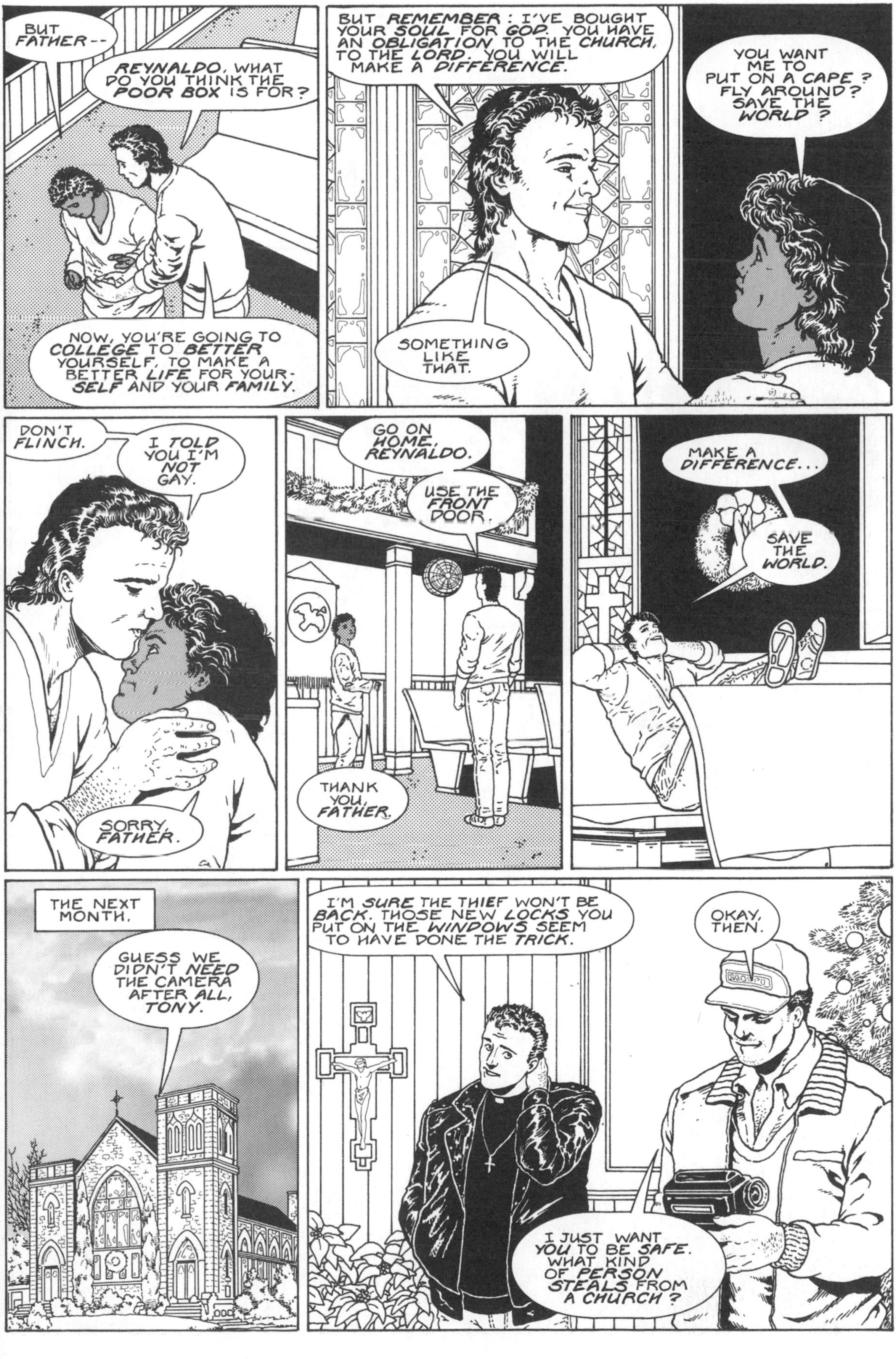

BUT FATHER--
REYNALDO, WHAT DO YOU THINK THE POOR BOX IS FOR?
NOW, YOU'RE GOING TO COLLEGE TO BETTER YOURSELF, TO MAKE A BETTER LIFE FOR YOURSELF AND YOUR FAMILY.
BUT REMEMBER: I'VE BOUGHT YOUR SOUL FOR GOD. YOU HAVE AN OBLIGATION TO THE CHURCH, TO THE LORD. YOU WILL MAKE A DIFFERENCE.
YOU WANT ME TO PUT ON A CAPE? FLY AROUND? SAVE THE WORLD?
SOMETHING LIKE THAT.
DON'T FLINCH.
I TOLD YOU I'M NOT GAY.
SORRY, FATHER.
GO ON HOME, REYNALDO.
USE THE FRONT DOOR.
THANK YOU, FATHER.
MAKE A DIFFERENCE...
SAVE THE WORLD.
THE NEXT MONTH.
GUESS WE DIDN'T NEED THE CAMERA AFTER ALL, TONY.
I'M SURE THE THIEF WON'T BE BACK. THOSE NEW LOCKS YOU PUT ON THE WINDOWS SEEM TO HAVE DONE THE TRICK.
OKAY, THEN.
I JUST WANT YOU TO BE SAFE. WHAT KIND OF PERSON STEALS FROM A CHURCH?

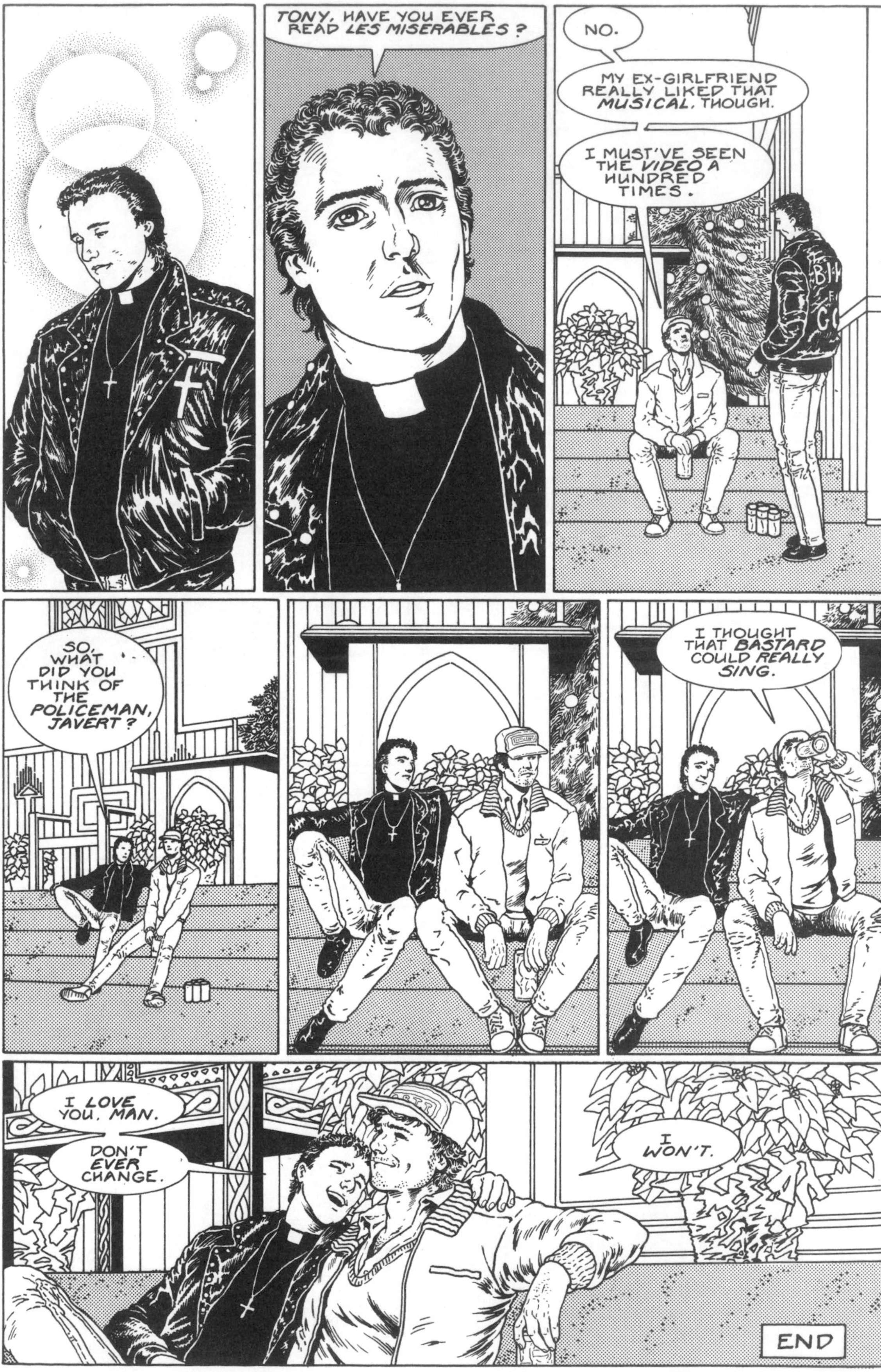
TONY, HAVE YOU EVER READ LES MISERABLES?
NO.
MY EX-GIRLFRIEND REALLY LIKED THAT MUSICAL, THOUGH.
I MUST'VE SEEN THE VIDEO A HUNDRED TIMES.
SO, WHAT DID YOU THINK OF THE POLICEMAN, JAVERT?
I THOUGHT THAT BASTARD COULD REALLY SING.
I LOVE YOU, MAN.
DON'T EVER CHANGE.
I WON'T.
END

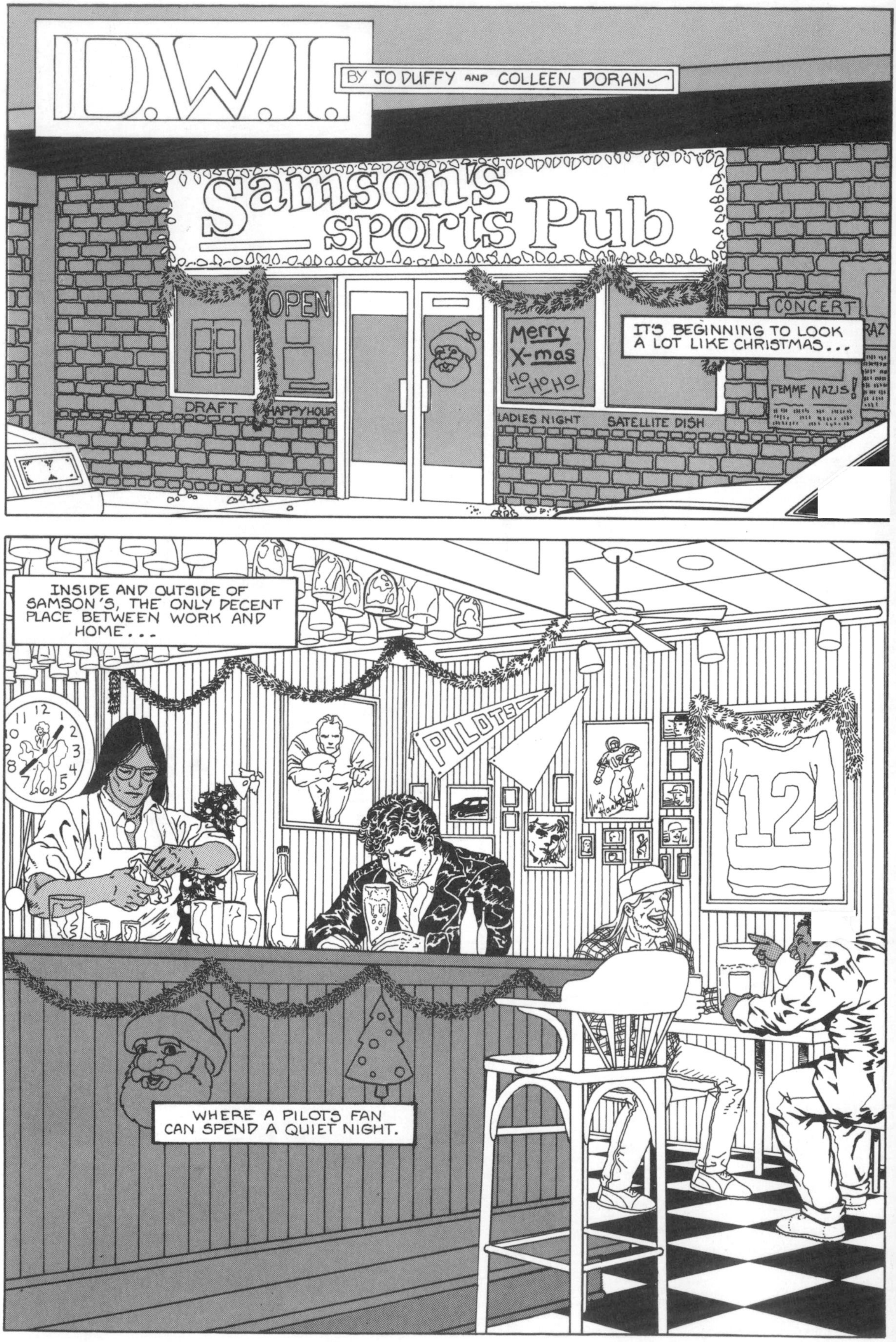
D.W.I.
BY JO DUFFY AND COLLEEN DORAN
Samson's sports Pub
OPEN
DRAFT
HAPPY HOUR
Merry X-mas
HO HO HO
LADIES NIGHT
SATELLITE DISH
CONCERT
FEMME NAZIS!
IT'S BEGINNING TO LOOK A LOT LIKE CHRISTMAS...
INSIDE AND OUTSIDE OF SAMSON'S, THE ONLY DECENT PLACE BETWEEN WORK AND HOME...
PILOTS
12
WHERE A PILOTS FAN CAN SPEND A QUIET NIGHT.

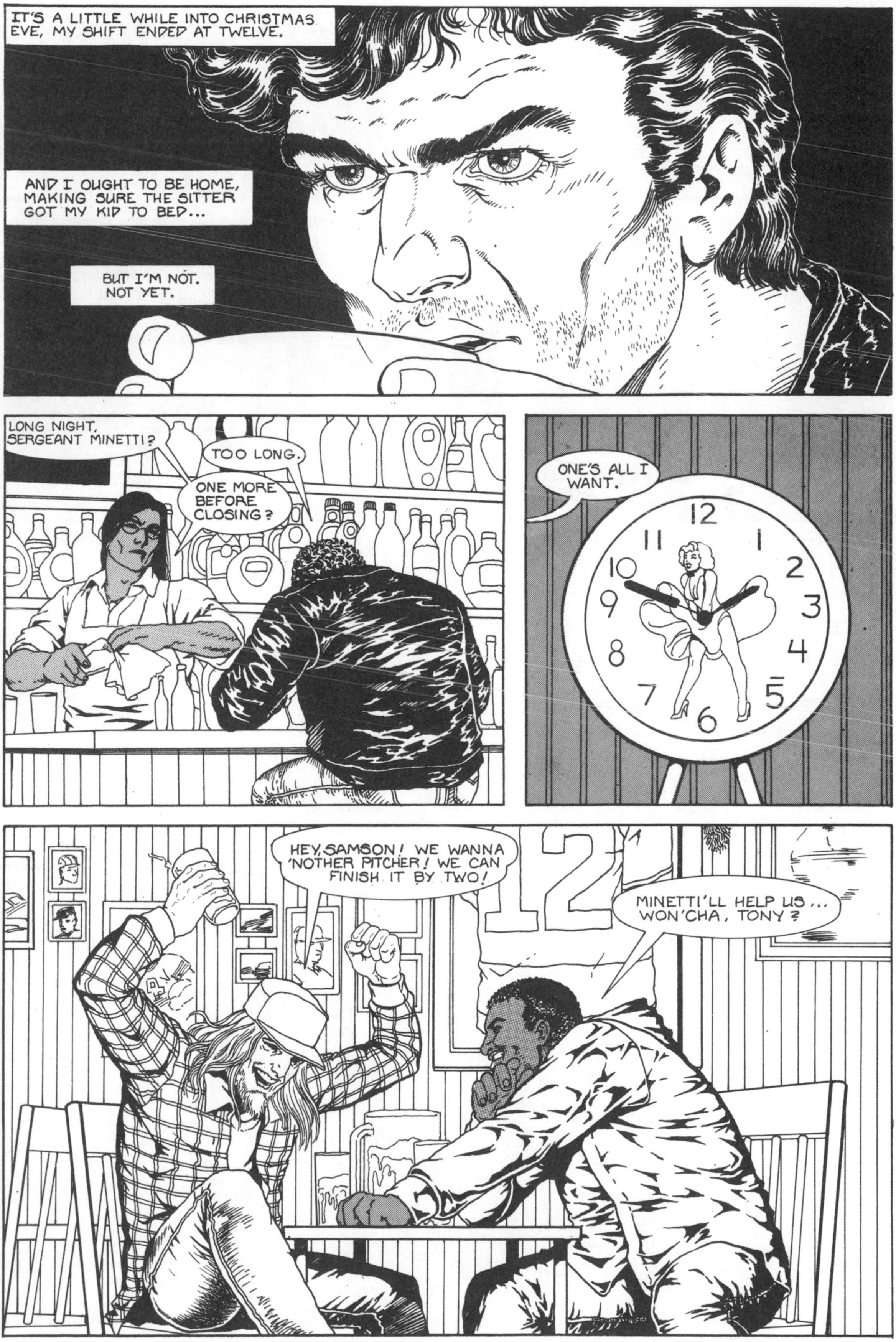
IT'S A LITTLE WHILE INTO CHRISTMAS EVE, MY SHIFT ENDED AT TWELVE.
AND I OUGHT TO BE HOME, MAKING SURE THE SITTER GOT MY KID TO BED...
BUT I'M NOT. NOT YET.
LONG NIGHT, SERGEANT MINETTI?
TOO LONG.
ONE MORE BEFORE CLOSING?
ONE'S ALL I WANT.
HEY, SAMSON! WE WANNA 'NOTHER PITCHER! WE CAN FINISH IT BY TWO!
MINETTI'LL HELP US... WON'CHA, TONY?

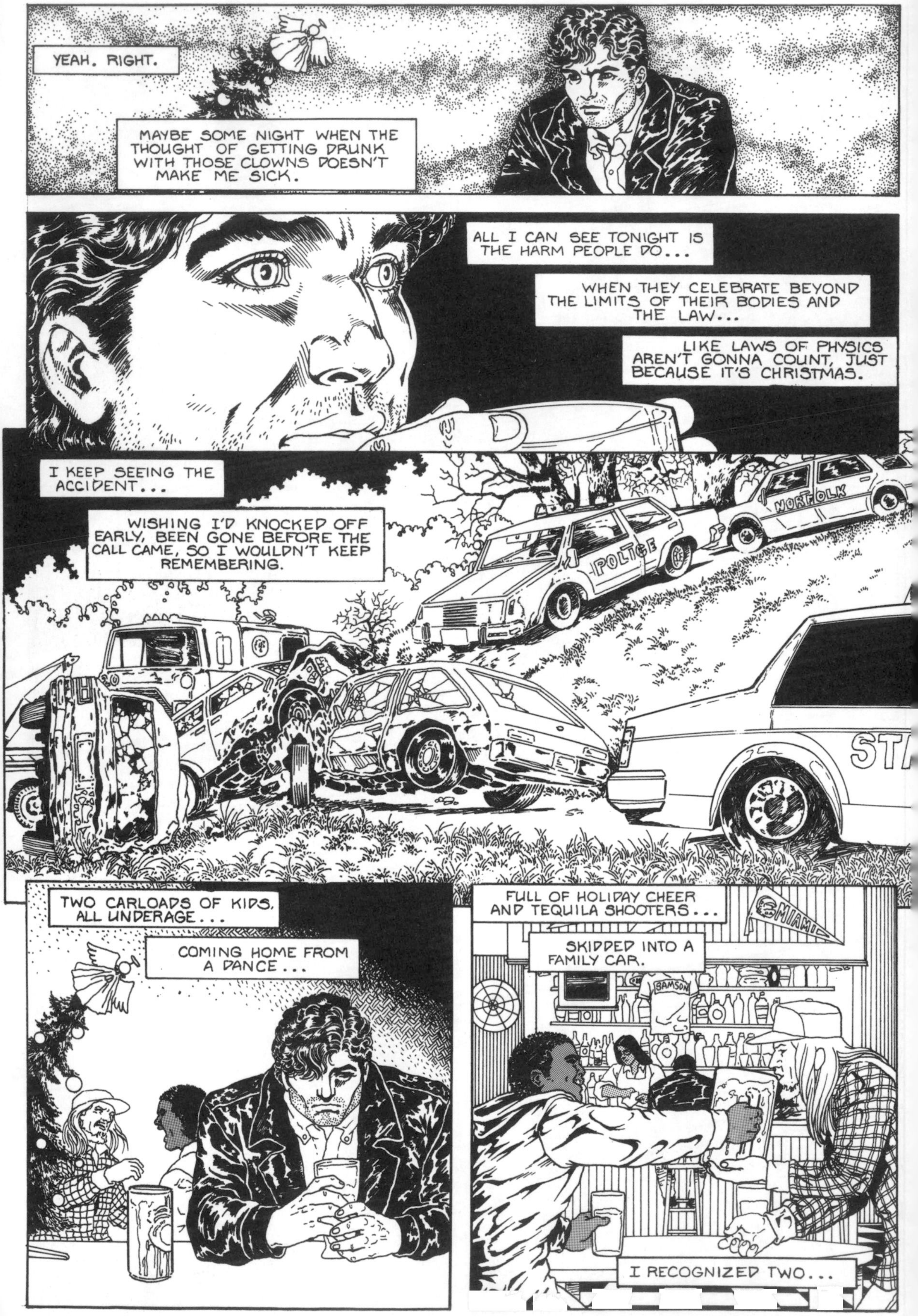
YEAH. RIGHT.
MAYBE SOME NIGHT WHEN THE THOUGHT OF GETTING DRUNK WITH THOSE CLOWNS DOESN'T MAKE ME SICK.
ALL I CAN SEE TONIGHT IS THE HARM PEOPLE DO...
WHEN THEY CELEBRATE BEYOND THE LIMITS OF THEIR BODIES AND THE LAW...
LIKE LAWS OF PHYSICS AREN'T GONNA COUNT, JUST BECAUSE IT'S CHRISTMAS.
I KEEP SEEING THE ACCIDENT...
WISHING I'D KNOCKED OFF EARLY, BEEN GONE BEFORE THE CALL CAME, SO I WOULDN'T KEEP REMEMBERING.
NORFOLK
POLICE
STA
TWO CARLOADS OF KIDS, ALL UNDERAGE...
COMING HOME FROM A DANCE...
FULL OF HOLIDAY CHEER AND TEQUILA SHOOTERS...
MIAMI
SKIDDED INTO A FAMILY CAR.
SAMSON
I RECOGNIZED TWO...

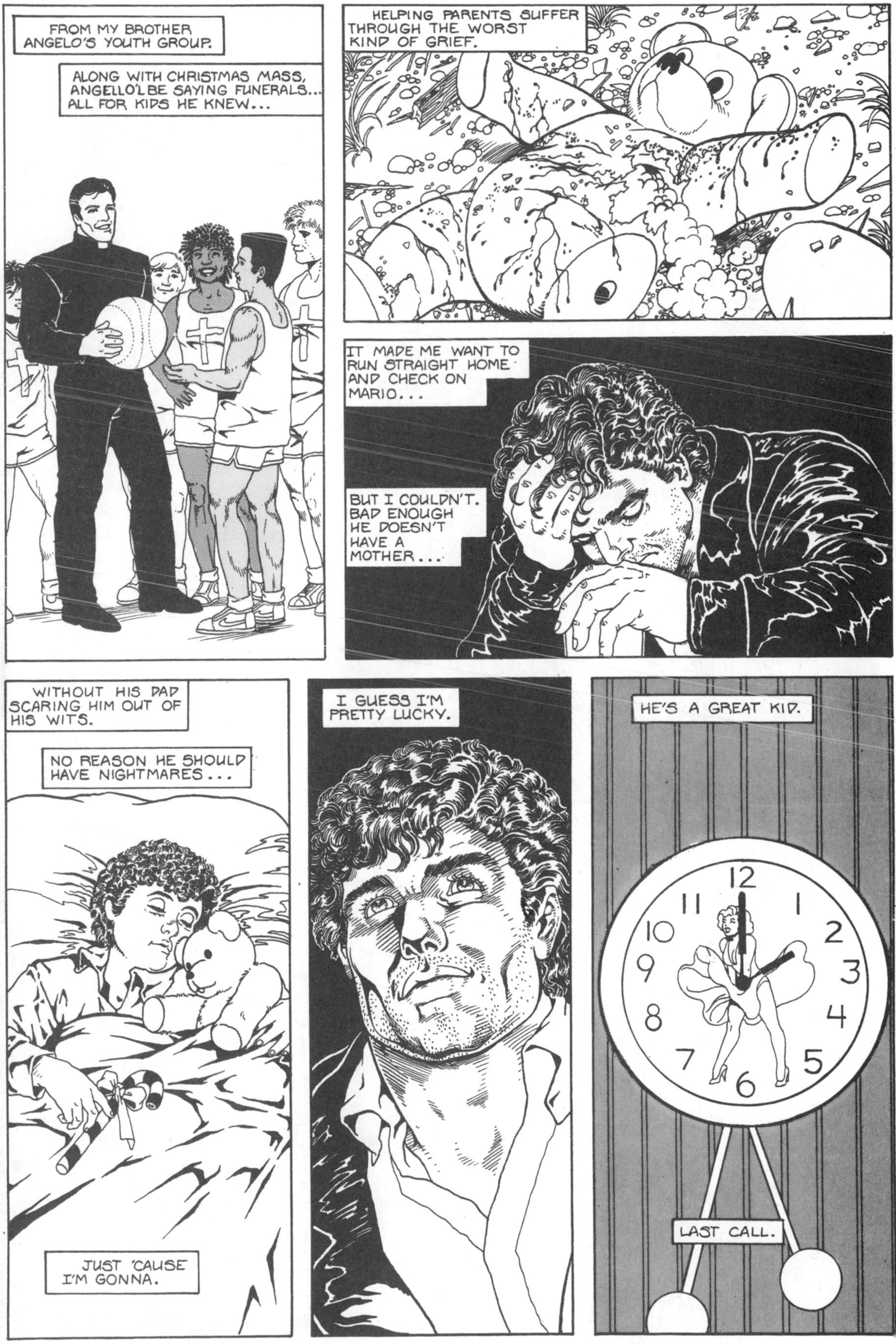
FROM MY BROTHER ANGELO'S YOUTH GROUP.
ALONG WITH CHRISTMAS MASS, ANGELLO'LBE SAYING FUNERALS... ALL FOR KIDS HE KNEW...
HELPING PARENTS SUFFER THROUGH THE WORST KIND OF GRIEF.
IT MADE ME WANT TO RUN STRAIGHT HOME AND CHECK ON MARIO...
BUT I COULDN'T. BAD ENOUGH HE DOESN'T HAVE A MOTHER...
WITHOUT HIS DAD SCARING HIM OUT OF HIS WITS.
NO REASON HE SHOULD HAVE NIGHTMARES...
JUST 'CAUSE I'M GONNA.
I GUESS I'M PRETTY LUCKY.
HE'S A GREAT KID.
12 1 2 3 4 5 6 7 8 9 10 11
LAST CALL.

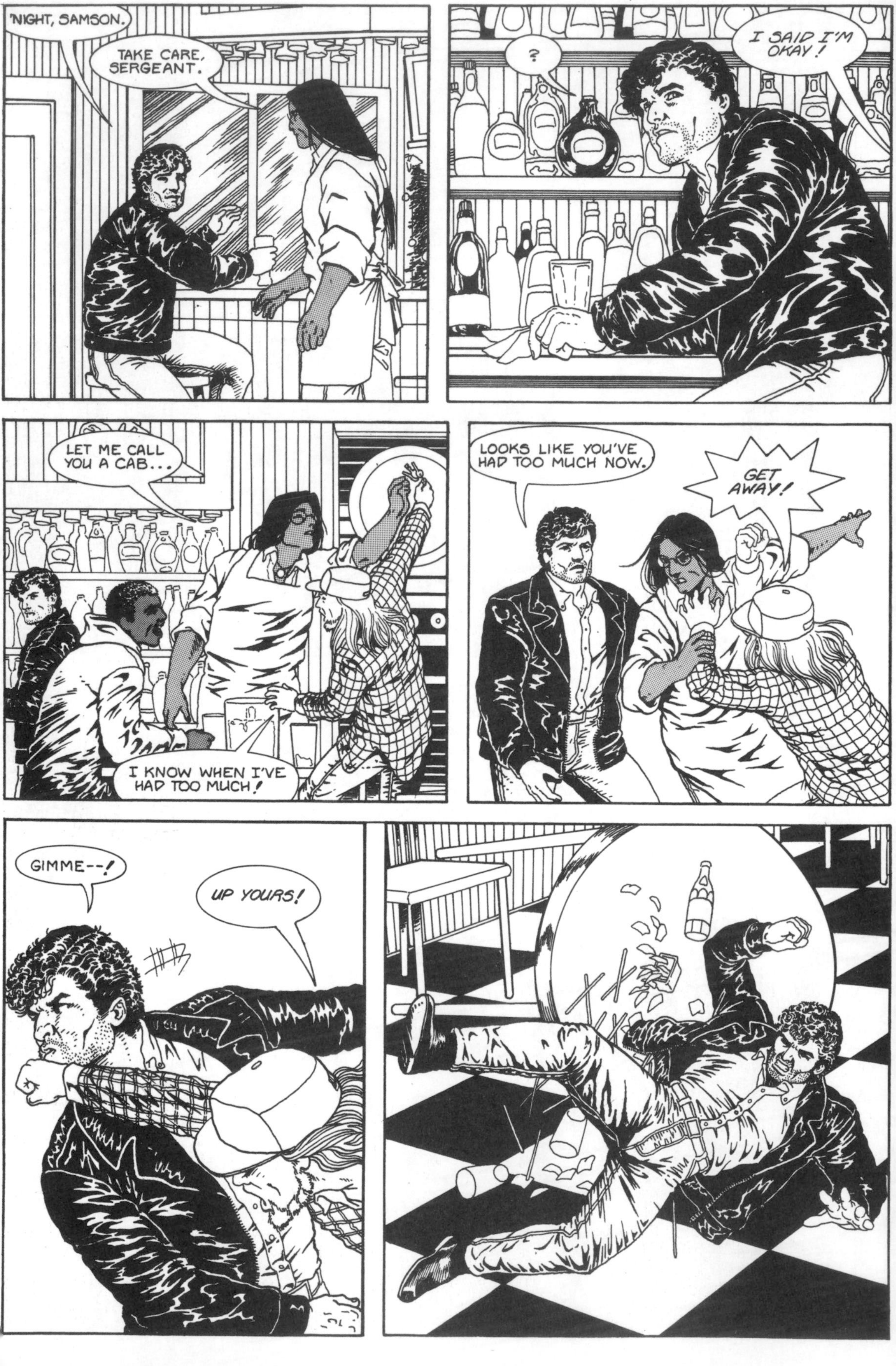

'NIGHT, SAMSON.
TAKE CARE, SERGEANT.
?
I SAID I'M OKAY!
LET ME CALL YOU A CAB...
I KNOW WHEN I'VE HAD TOO MUCH!
LOOKS LIKE YOU'VE HAD TOO MUCH NOW.
GET AWAY!
GIMME--!
UP YOURS!

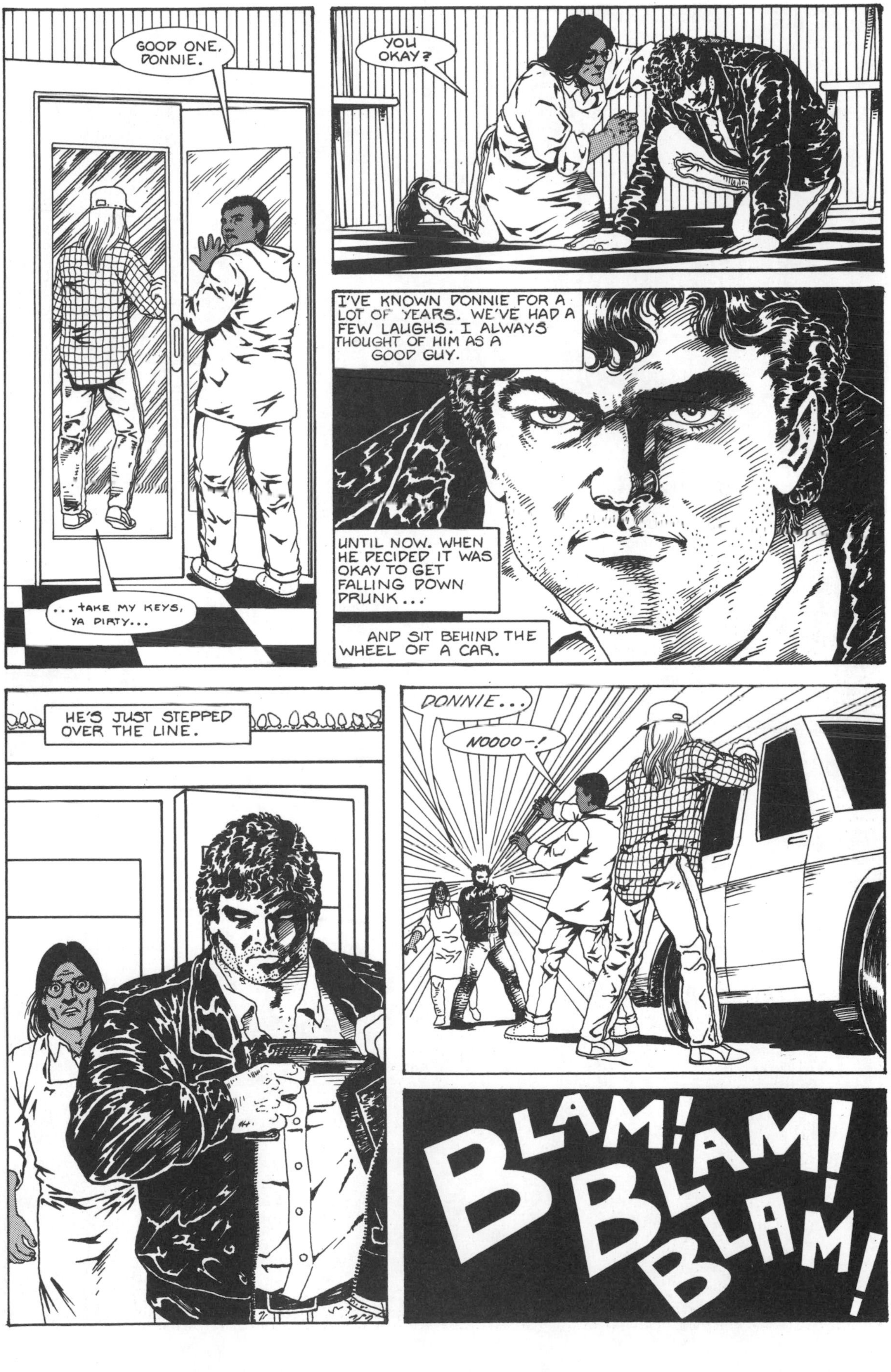
GOOD ONE, DONNIE.
...TAKE MY KEYS, YA DIRTY...
YOU OKAY?
I'VE KNOWN DONNIE FOR A LOT OF YEARS. WE'VE HAD A FEW LAUGHS. I ALWAYS THOUGHT OF HIM AS A GOOD GUY.
UNTIL NOW. WHEN HE DECIDED IT WAS OKAY TO GET FALLING DOWN DRUNK...
AND SIT BEHIND THE WHEEL OF A CAR.
HE'S JUST STEPPED OVER THE LINE.
DONNIE...
NOOOO-!
BLAM! BLAM! BLAM!

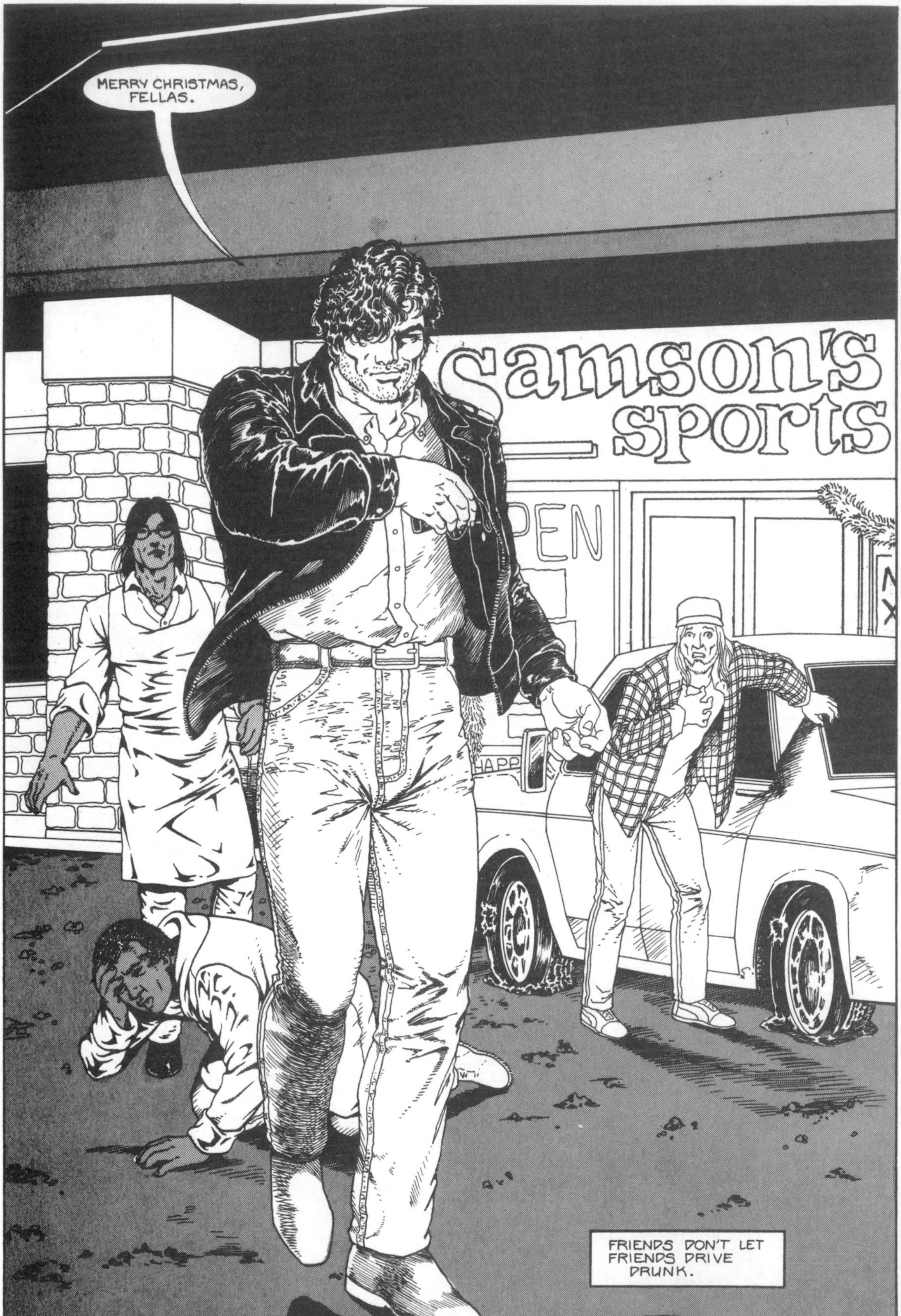
MERRY CHRISTMAS, FELLAS.
samson's sports
OPEN
HAPP
FRIENDS DON'T LET FRIENDS DRIVE DRUNK.

Portrait Gallery

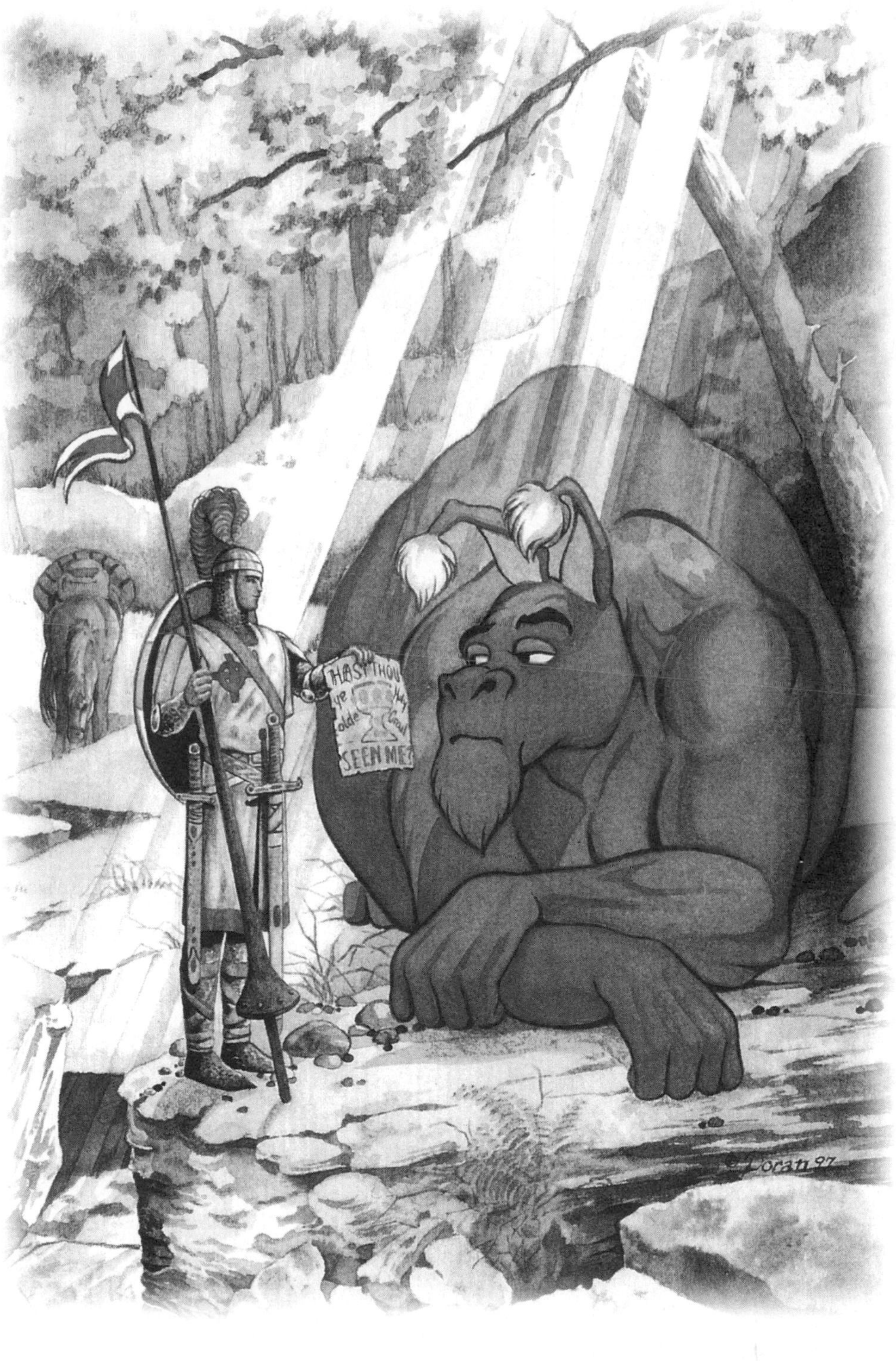
HAST THOU
ye Holy
olde Grail
SEEN ME?
© Loran 97

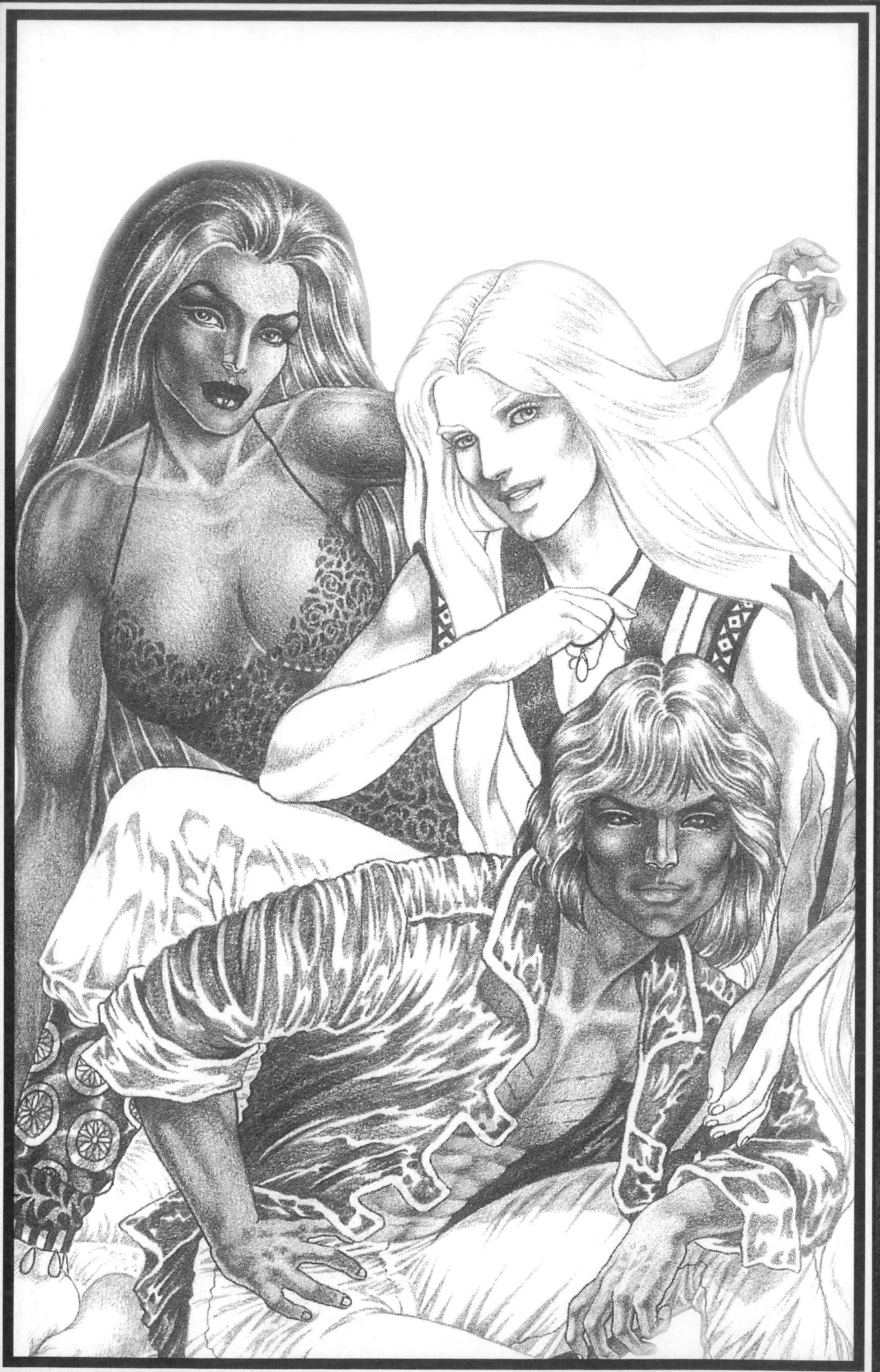

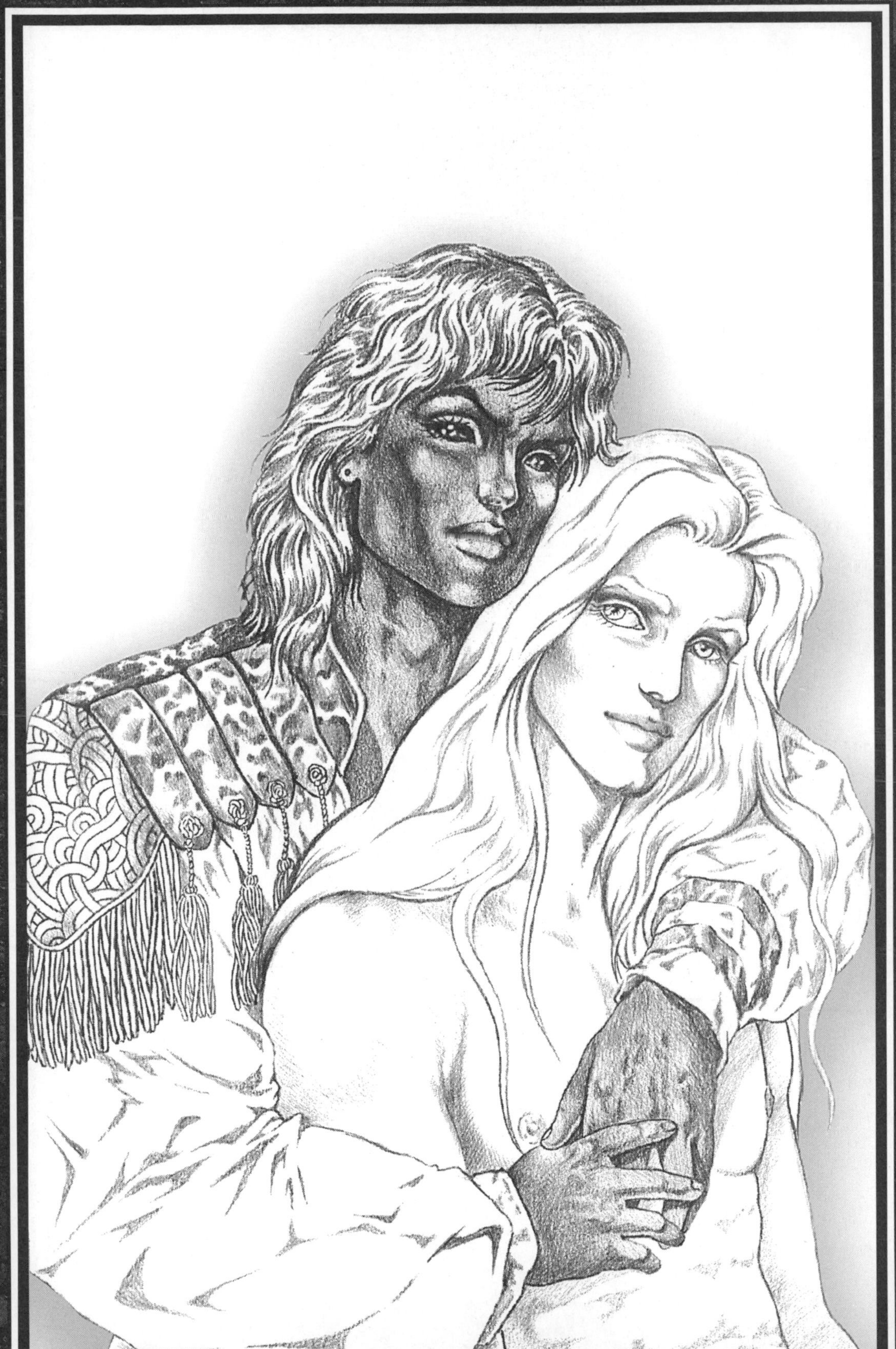

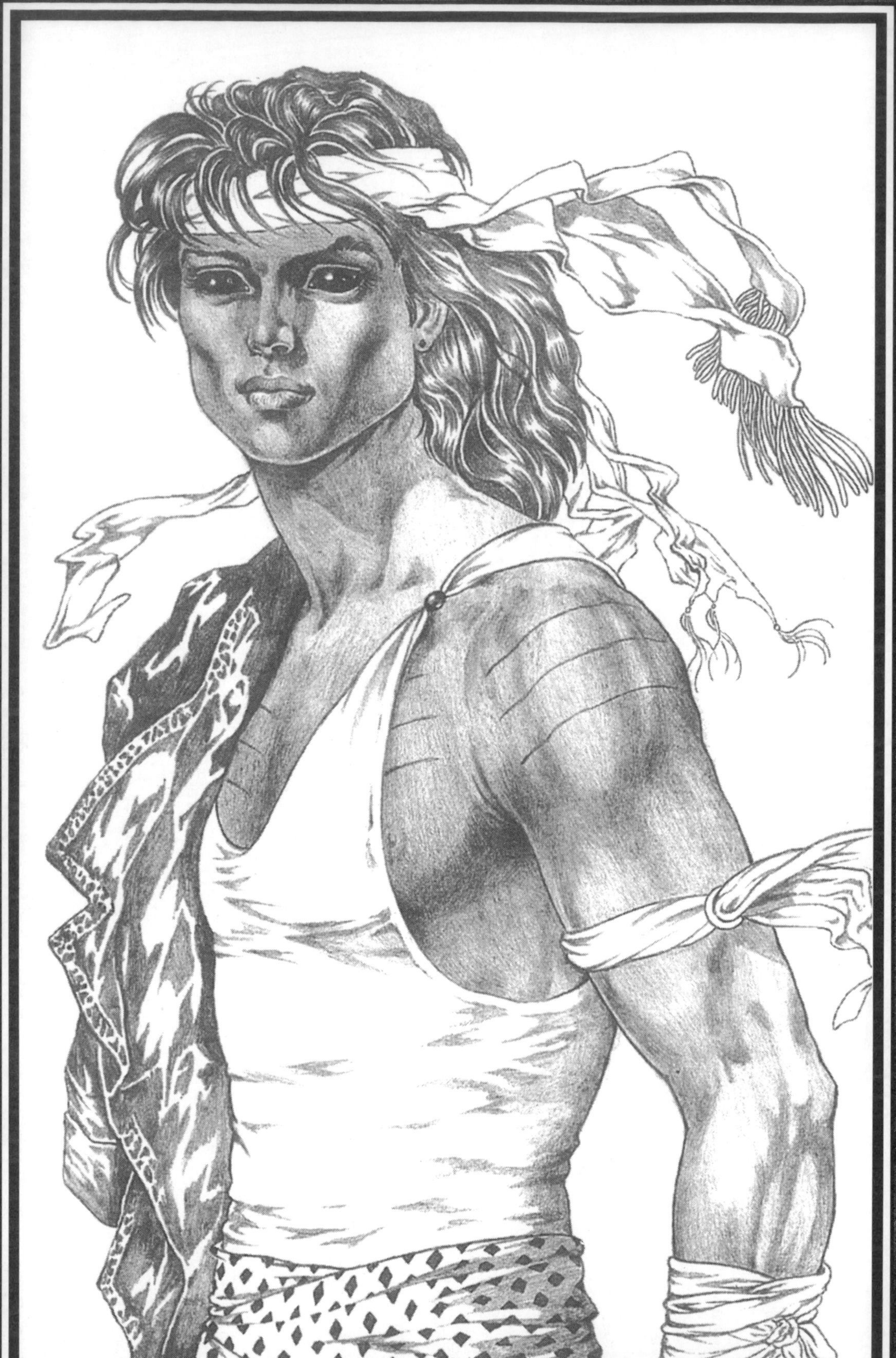

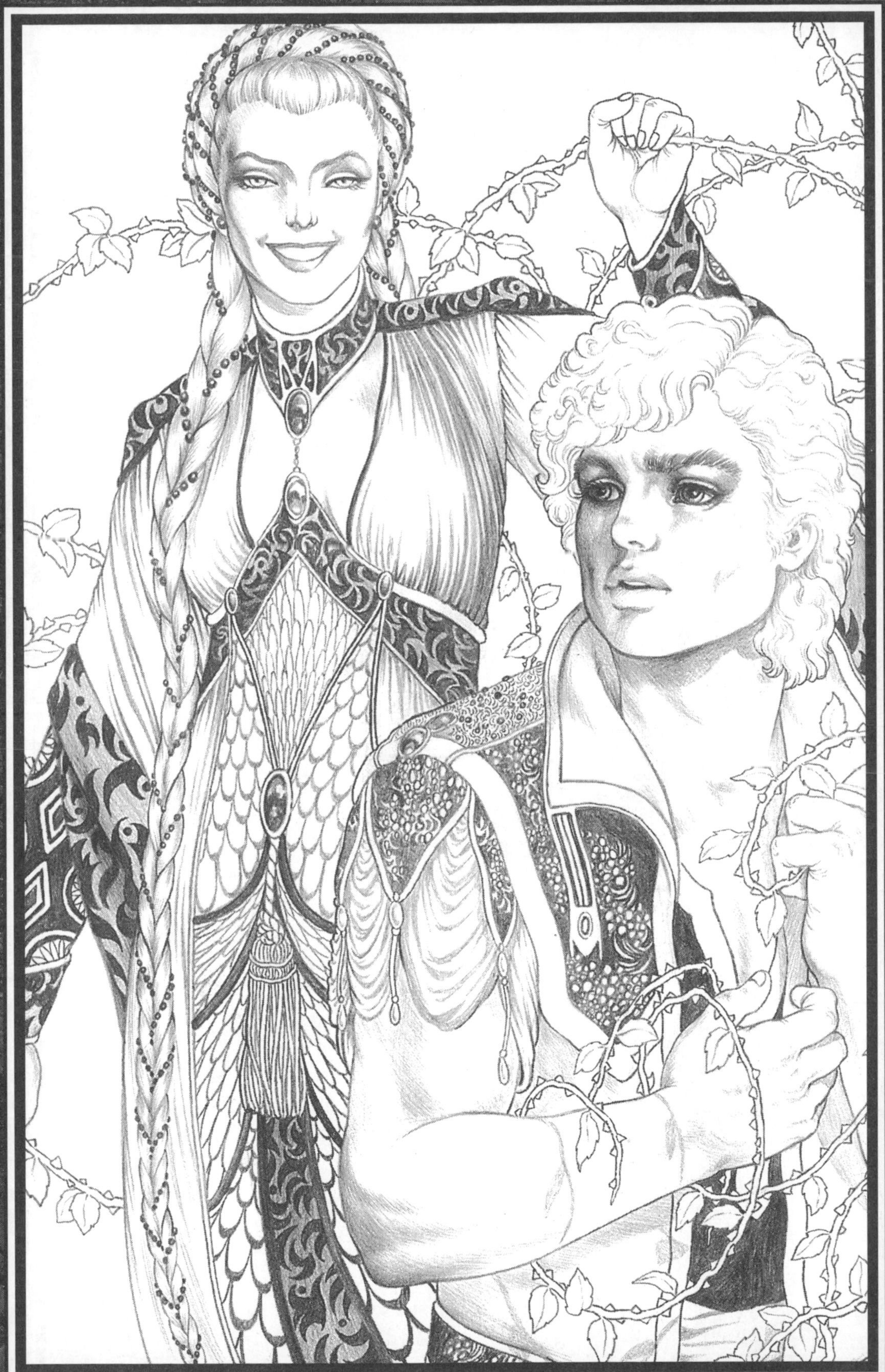

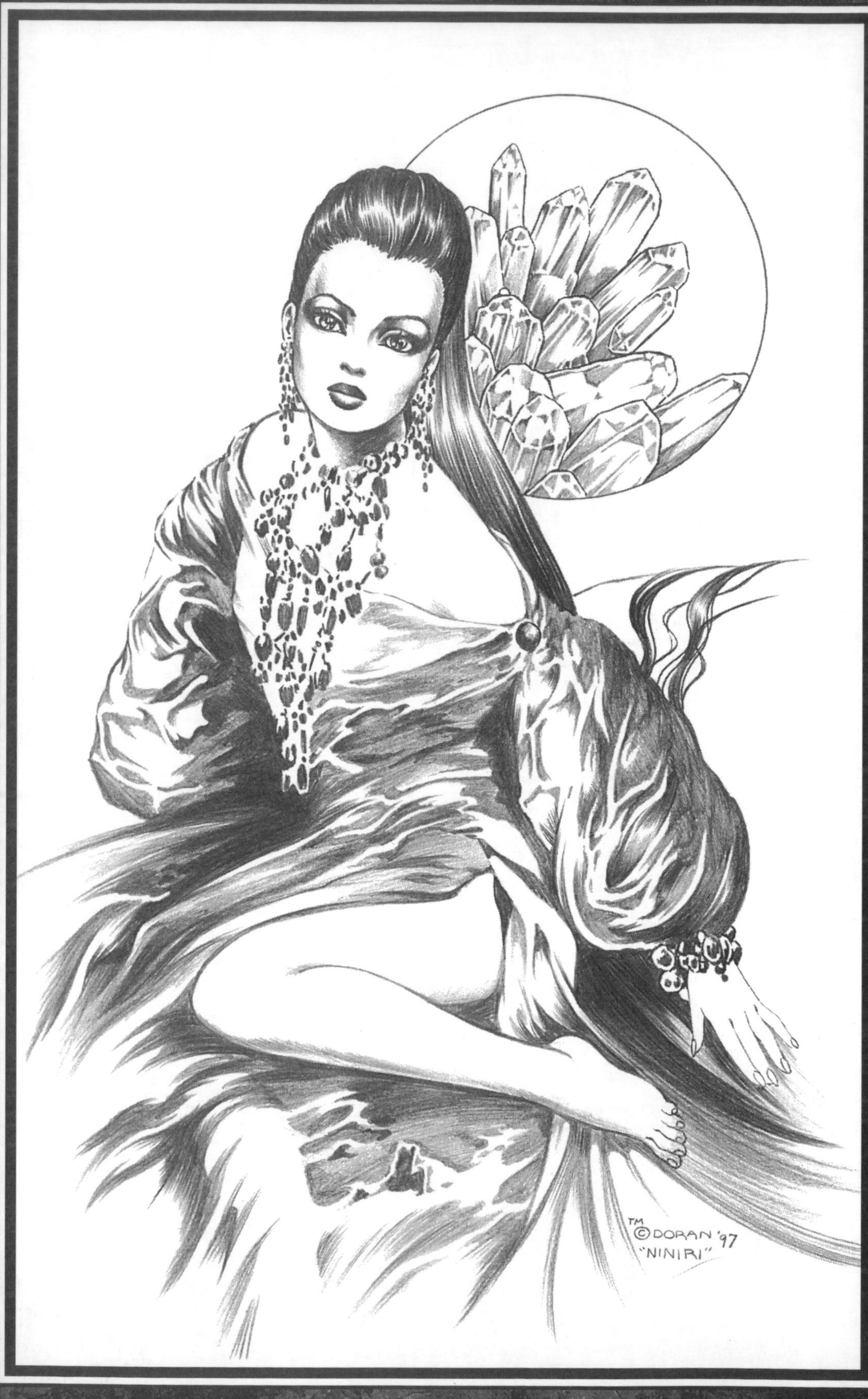
TM
©DORAN '97
"NINIRI"

Afterword

In the nearly two years it took me to complete this volume, I have traveled around the world, meeting many of my readers and fellow professionals. I thank all of you for your kind comments and your support.

I want to again thank my beloved parents, Ronald and Anita, and take a moment to emphasize the importance of my mother Anita's contribution to my work: without her, the mail doesn't get answered, the books don't get shipped, the tone sheets don't get pasted down. Every time she mentions retiring, I shudder, wondering how I am ever going to replace her!

Thanks to my Image publisher Erik Larsen, my pal Jim Valentino, and all the Image staff, especially Larry, Kenny, Lee, Ronna, Bob and Doug.

Many thanks to my pal George Beahm for help with so many things, especially teaching me about the publishing biz all these years, providing computer lessons, helping with ads, and offering much worthy advice.

Though I reserve all creative work on **A Distant Soil** for myself, occasionally, I've had folks in to pinch hit on the packing and shipping, cutting and pasting, and late night runs to Federal Express when Mom needed a break. Thanks to Ken Talton, Willow Boudell, Mike Griffith, and special thanks to Dawn Bromley who stepped in to help with the new website. Thanks also to my editor Mary Gray who catches my many goofs.

Eternal thanks to Neil Gaiman for the bridge; Takayuki Matsutani and the staff of Tezuka Productions for the very educational trip to Japan where I discovered the wonders of Japanese tone sheets; my darling agent Spencer Beck, a true friend one can call for support at any time; Caesar, Trina Robbins, Jeff Smith, Margaret Cubberly and Frank Kelly Freas, and all my friends up at DC Comics.

Thank you and farewell to Curt Swan.

Thanks for many happy memories to Alan Thorvaldson who didn't live to read the work he helped inspire.

Many, many thanks to my readers whose enthusiasm and support have enabled me to live my dreams and to the many friends and supporters I have neglected to mention here.

Colleen Doran
July 1998

A Distant Soil™ Items

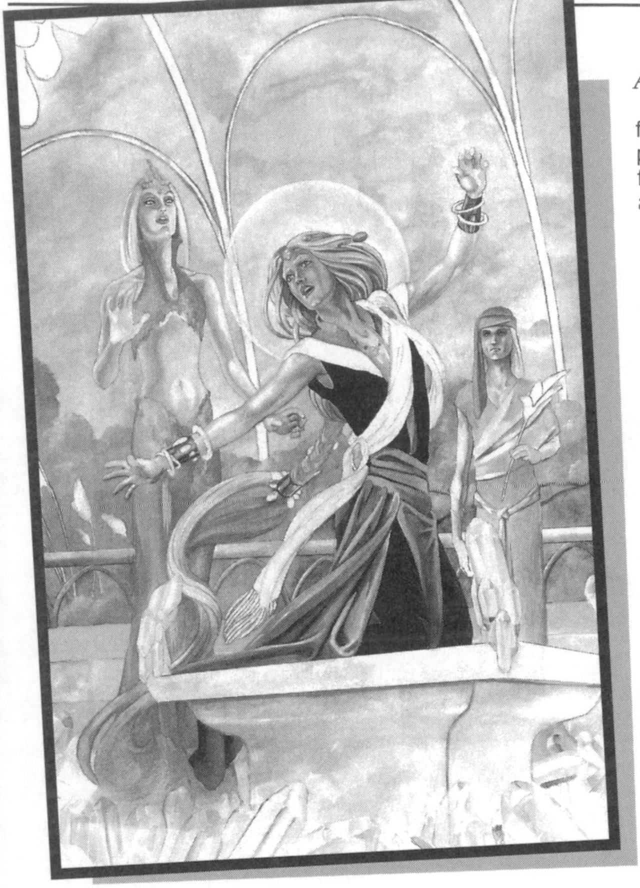

A DISTANT SOIL: THE GATHERING

Volume 1 of the acclaimed graphic novel series collects the first 13 issues of the lead story of the comic book in a big, 240 page, beautifully illustrated trade paperback! With a lovely, gold foil enhanced cover, A DISTANT SOIL: THE GATHERING is available for only $19.95!

A DISTANT SOIL II: THE ASCENDANT

240 page softcover edition for only $18.95!
Also available in a limited edition hardcover, A DISTANT SOIL: THE ASCENDANT, signed and numbered, is only $29.95 and includes a limited edition print and beautiful foil stamped cover.

The hardcover remarqued edition is all that *and* an original full page character drawing for $74.95.

A DISTANT SOIL: The Aria

Volume III in the A DISTANT SOIL saga! The story continues in this all new, beautiful collection! 164 pages of passion and intrigue, politics and betrayal! Available in a signed, numbered hardcover limited edition for $29.95 of only 150 copies. Also available in a remarqued edition of 100 copies, each featuring a hand drawn character portrait of your choice! Only $74.95 (available after July 2001.) Or get the trade paperback edition with handsome, foil enhanced cover for $16.95.

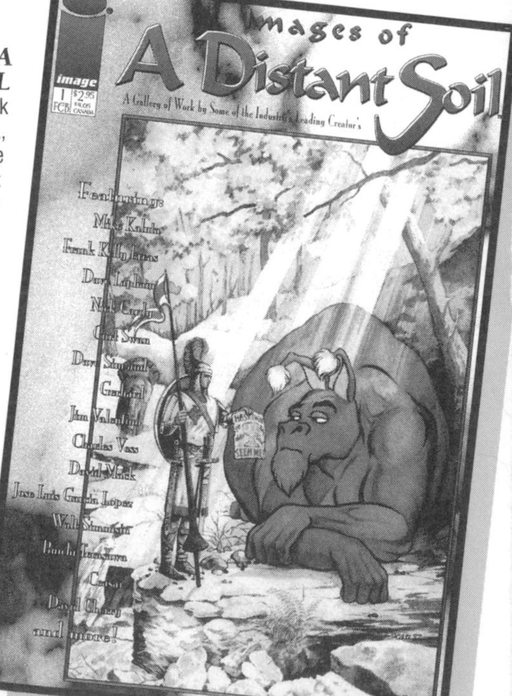
Images of
A Distant Soil
A Gallery of Work by Some of the Industry's Leading Creator's

IMAGES OF A DISTANT SOIL

A gallery of original work inspired by A DISTANT SOIL, this 32 page book from Image showcases stellar talents: Charles Vess, Frank Kelly Freas, Dave Sim and Gerhard, Jim Valentino, David Mack, Dave Lapham, Nick Cardy, Curt Swan, Joe Szekeres and others. With full color covers, character biographies and an eight page short story from A DISTANT SOIL! Only $2.95!

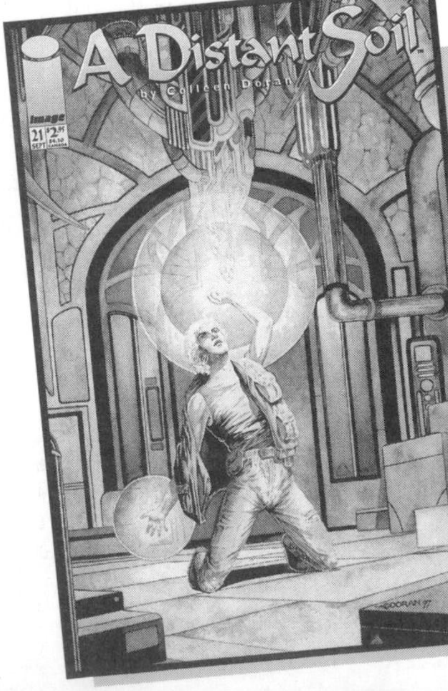
A Distant Soil
by Colleen Doran

*For more information about
A DISTANT SOIL, including never before
published art, online
interviews with
creator Colleen Doran and
other great features, visit our website!*

www.adistantsoil.com

*To find A DISTANT SOIL
comics and graphic novels,
as well as other work
by Colleen Doran and
your favorite Image artists,
call: 1-888-COMIC-BOOK*

Send to:
Colleen Doran, Colleen Doran Studios
435-2 Oriana Road PMB 610
Newport News • VA 23608 • USA

If you are paying by credit card, please fill this out:

Type of credit card: _____

Card Number: _____

Expiration Date: _____

Your name as imprinted on the card: _____

Your signature: _____

Your Name: _____

Street address: _____

City • State • Zip: _____

ITEM ORDERED	QUANTITY	PRICE EACH	TOTAL

• Important ordering information: All orders must be in U.S. funds	**subtotal**
• Shipping charges: U.S. orders under $20.00, add $3.00. Over $20.00, add $4.00 Canada, Mexico, overseas: Add $5.00 for order under $20.00. Add $10.00 for orders over $20.00	**shipping charge**
	Total enclosed:
• Virginia residents: add 4.5% sales tax	

*B*iography

*C*olleen Doran began publishing ***A Distant Soil*** while still a teenager and the series has gone on to sell some 500,000 copies. She manages her production company Colleen Doran Studios and continues to publish her ***A Distant Soil*** comic book series through Image Comics.

Her work has also appeared in Neil Gaiman's *Sandman*, Anne Rice's *The Master of Rampling Gate*, Clive Barker's *Nightbreed* and Clive Barker's *Hellraiser*, *Amazing Spiderman*, *Walt Disney's Beauty and the Beast*, *The Star Wars Galaxy*, *Excalibur*, *Captain America*, *The Legion of Superheroes*, *Wonder Woman: The Once and Future Story* , *X-Factor*, *Excalibur* and various stories for Paradox Press's *Big Books* series.

With some 400 credits, Doran has been a professional illustrator since the age of fifteen. She's also illustrated a SWAT team training manual, designed toys and games, and created corporate designs and illustrations.

Her work has been profiled in *The Anne Rice Companion*, *Comic Book Rebels*, *Censorship: War of Words* and *Women and the Comics*.

She has received a number of awards and nominations for her work. In 1989 she received a grant from the Delphi Institute to attend a multicultural, cross-country tour of the U.S. to study American pop culture with participants from diverse nations such as Zimbabwe, Nigeria, Hungary, Czechoslovakia, The Philippines and Egypt. She has also received the Amy Shultz Memorial Award for using her work to heighten awareness of Child Sexual Abuse. In 1997, she was chosen by Tezuka Productions to attend a week long comics/manga seminar in Japan with Oscar/Pulitzer Prize winning cartoonist Jules Ffeiffer, acclaimed *Bone* creator Jeff Smith, syndicated *Sylvia* cartoonist Nicole Hollander, and Dreamworks animator Denys Cowan. Colleen is just full of herself and you can tell, since she wrote this bio.

She enjoys gardening, hiking, reading and being able to afford a housekeeper. This is a picture of what Colleen Doran looks like now: